The Complete Oz

Volume 1

written by

L. Frank Baum

Royal Historian of Oz

A Classics Compilation by

TRILOGUS BOOKS
www.trilogus.com

The Complete Oz:
Volume 1
written by L.Frank Baum
Royal Historian of Oz

Copyright © 2008 by Trilogus Books

Published by Trilogus Books

ISBN-10:   1438214669
ISBN-13:   9781438214665

Trilogus Books Trade Publication / April 2008

This novel is a work of fiction. All of the events, characters, names and places depicted in this novel are entirely fictitious, or are used fictitiously. No representation that any statement made in this novel is true or that any incident depicted in this novel actually occurred is intended or should be inferred by the reader.

Table of Contents

The Wonderful Wizard Of Oz

Introduction

Folklore, legends, myths and fairy tales have followed childhood through the ages, for every healthy youngster has a wholesome and instinctive love for stories fantastic, marvelous and manifestly unreal. The winged fairies of Grimm and Andersen have brought more happiness to childish hearts than all other human creations.

Yet the old time fairy tale, having served for generations, may now be classed as "historical" in the children's library; for the time has come for a series of newer "wonder tales" in which the stereotyped genie, dwarf and fairy are eliminated, together with all the horrible and blood-curdling incidents devised by their authors to point a fearsome moral to each tale. Modern education includes morality; therefore the modern child seeks only entertainment in its wonder tales and gladly dispenses with all disagreeable incident.

Having this thought in mind, the story of "The Wonderful Wizard of Oz" was written solely to please children of today. It aspires to being a modernized fairy tale, in which the wonderment and joy are retained and the heartaches and nightmares are left out.

L. Frank Baum
Chicago, April, 1900.

LIST OF CHAPTERS

Chapter 1 - The Cyclone

Dorothy lived in the midst of the great Kansas prairies, with Uncle Henry, who was a farmer, and Aunt Em, who was the farmer's wife. Their house was small, for the lumber to build it had to be carried by wagon many miles. There were four walls, a floor and a roof, which made one room; and this room contained a rusty looking cookstove, a cupboard for the dishes, a table, three or four chairs, and the beds. Uncle Henry and Aunt Em had a big bed in one corner, and Dorothy a little bed in another corner. There was no garret at all, and no cellar—except a small hole dug in the ground, called a cyclone cellar, where the family could go in case one of those great whirlwinds arose, mighty enough to crush any building in its path. It was reached by a trap door in the middle of the floor, from which a ladder led down into the small, dark hole.

When Dorothy stood in the doorway and looked around, she could see nothing but the great gray prairie on every side. Not a tree nor a house broke the broad sweep of flat country that reached to the edge of the sky in all directions. The sun had baked the plowed land into a gray mass, with little cracks running through it. Even the grass was not green, for the sun had burned the tops of the long blades until they were the same gray color to be seen everywhere. Once the house had been painted, but the sun blistered the paint and the rains washed it away, and now the house was as dull and gray as everything else.

When Aunt Em came there to live she was a young, pretty wife. The sun and wind had changed her, too. They had taken the sparkle from her eyes and left them a sober gray; they had taken the red from her cheeks and lips, and they were gray also. She was thin and gaunt, and never smiled now. When Dorothy, who was an orphan, first came to her, Aunt Em had been so startled by the child's laughter that she would scream and press her hand upon her heart whenever Dorothy's merry voice reached her ears; and she still looked at the little girl with wonder that she could find anything to laugh at.

Uncle Henry never laughed. He worked hard from morning till night and did not know what joy was. He was gray also, from his long beard to his rough boots, and he looked stern and solemn, and rarely spoke.

It was Toto that made Dorothy laugh, and saved her from growing as gray as her other surroundings. Toto was not gray; he was a little black dog, with long silky hair and small black eyes that twinkled merrily on either side of his funny, wee nose. Toto played all day long, and Dorothy played with him, and loved him dearly.

Today, however, they were not playing. Uncle Henry sat upon the doorstep and looked anxiously at the sky, which was even grayer than usual. Dorothy stood in the door with Toto in her arms, and looked at the sky too. Aunt Em was washing the dishes.

From the far north they heard a low wail of the wind, and Uncle Henry and Dorothy could see where the long grass bowed in waves before the coming storm. There now came a sharp whistling in the air from the south, and as they turned their eyes that way they saw ripples in the grass coming from that direction also.

Suddenly Uncle Henry stood up.

"There's a cyclone coming, Em," he called to his wife. "I'll go look after the stock." Then he ran toward the sheds where the cows and horses were kept.

Aunt Em dropped her work and came to the door. One glance told her of the danger close at hand.

"Quick, Dorothy!" she screamed. "Run for the cellar!"

Toto jumped out of Dorothy's arms and hid under the bed, and the girl started to get him. Aunt Em, badly frightened, threw open the trap door in the floor and climbed down the ladder into the small, dark hole. Dorothy caught Toto at last and started to follow her aunt. When she was halfway across the room there came a great shriek from the wind, and the house shook so hard that she lost her footing and sat down suddenly upon the floor.

Then a strange thing happened.

The house whirled around two or three times and rose slowly through the air. Dorothy felt as if she were going up in a balloon.

The north and south winds met where the house stood, and made it the exact center of the cyclone. In the middle of a cyclone the air is generally still, but the great pressure of the wind on every side of the house raised it up higher and higher, until it was at the very top of the cyclone; and there it remained and was carried miles and miles away as easily as you could carry a feather.

It was very dark, and the wind howled horribly around her, but Dorothy found she was riding quite easily. After the first few whirls around, and one other time when the house tipped badly, she felt as if she were being rocked gently, like a baby in a cradle.

Toto did not like it. He ran about the room, now here, now there, barking loudly; but Dorothy sat quite still on the floor and waited to see what would happen.

Once Toto got too near the open trap door, and fell in; and at first the little girl thought she had lost him. But soon she saw one of his ears sticking up through the hole, for the strong pressure of the air was keeping him up so that he could not fall. She crept to the hole, caught Toto by the ear, and dragged him into the room again, afterward closing the trap door so that no more accidents could happen.

Hour after hour passed away, and slowly Dorothy got over her fright; but she felt quite lonely, and the wind shrieked so loudly all about her that she nearly became deaf. At first she had wondered if she would be dashed to pieces when the house fell again; but as the hours passed and nothing terrible happened, she stopped worrying and resolved to wait calmly and see what the future would bring. At last she crawled over the swaying floor to her bed, and lay down upon it; and Toto followed and lay down beside her.

In spite of the swaying of the house and the wailing of the wind, Dorothy soon closed her eyes and fell fast asleep.

Chapter 2 - The Council with the Munchkins

She was awakened by a shock, so sudden and severe that if Dorothy had not been lying on the soft bed she might have been hurt. As it was, the jar made her catch her breath and wonder what had happened; and Toto put his cold little nose into her face and whined dismally. Dorothy sat up and noticed that the house was not moving; nor was it dark, for the bright sunshine came in at the window, flooding the little room. She sprang from her bed and with Toto at her heels ran and opened the door.

The little girl gave a cry of amazement and looked about her, her eyes growing bigger and bigger at the wonderful sights she saw.

The cyclone had set the house down very gently—for a cyclone—in the midst of a country of marvelous beauty. There were lovely patches of greensward all about, with stately trees bearing rich and luscious fruits. Banks of gorgeous flowers were on every hand, and birds with rare and brilliant plumage sang and fluttered in the trees and bushes. A little way off was a small brook, rushing and sparkling along between green banks, and murmuring in a voice very grateful to a little girl who had lived so long on the dry, gray prairies.

While she stood looking eagerly at the strange and beautiful sights, she noticed coming toward her a group of the queerest people she had ever seen. They were not as big as the grown folk she had always been used to; but neither were they very small. In fact, they seemed about as tall as Dorothy, who was a well-grown child for her age, although they were, so far as looks go, many years older.

Three were men and one a woman, and all were oddly dressed. They wore round hats that rose to a small point a foot above their heads, with little bells around the brims that tinkled sweetly as they moved. The hats of the men were blue; the little woman's hat was white, and she wore a white gown that hung in pleats from her shoulders. Over it were sprinkled little stars that glistened in the sun like diamonds. The men were dressed in blue, of the same shade as their hats, and wore well-polished boots with a deep roll of blue at the tops. The men, Dorothy thought, were about as old as Uncle Henry, for two of them had beards. But the little woman was doubtless much older. Her face was covered with wrinkles, her hair was nearly white, and she walked rather stiffly.

When these people drew near the house where Dorothy was standing in the doorway, they paused and whispered among themselves, as if afraid to come farther. But the little old woman walked up to Dorothy, made a low bow and said, in a sweet voice:

"You are welcome, most noble Sorceress, to the land of the Munchkins. We are so grateful to you for having killed the Wicked Witch of the East, and for setting our people free from bondage."

Dorothy listened to this speech with wonder. What could the little woman possibly mean by calling her a sorceress, and saying she had killed the Wicked Witch of the East? Dorothy was an innocent, harmless little girl, who had been carried by a cyclone many miles from home; and she had never killed anything in all her life.

But the little woman evidently expected her to answer; so Dorothy said, with hesitation, "You are very kind, but there must be some mistake. I have not killed anything."

"Your house did, anyway," replied the little old woman, with a laugh, "and that is the same thing. See!" she continued, pointing to the corner of the house. "There are her two feet, still sticking out from under a block of wood."

Dorothy looked, and gave a little cry of fright. There, indeed, just under the corner of the great beam the house rested on, two feet were sticking out, shod in silver shoes with pointed toes.

"Oh, dear! Oh, dear!" cried Dorothy, clasping her hands together in dismay. "The house must have fallen on her. Whatever shall we do?"

"There is nothing to be done," said the little woman calmly.

"But who was she?" asked Dorothy.

"She was the Wicked Witch of the East, as I said," answered the little woman. "She has held all the Munchkins in bondage for many years, making them slave for her night and day. Now they are all set free, and are grateful to you for the favor."

"Who are the Munchkins?" inquired Dorothy.

"They are the people who live in this land of the East where the Wicked Witch ruled."

"Are you a Munchkin?" asked Dorothy.

"No, but I am their friend, although I live in the land of the North. When they saw the Witch of the East was dead the Munchkins sent a swift messenger to me, and I came at once. I am the Witch of the North."

"Oh, gracious!" cried Dorothy. "Are you a real witch?"

"Yes, indeed," answered the little woman. "But I am a good witch, and the people love me. I am not as powerful as the Wicked Witch was who ruled here, or I should have set the people free myself."

"But I thought all witches were wicked," said the girl, who was half frightened at facing a real witch. "Oh, no, that is a great mistake. There were only four witches in all the Land of Oz, and two of them, those who live in the North and the South, are good witches. I know this is true, for I am one of them myself, and cannot be mistaken. Those who dwelt in the East and the West were, indeed, wicked witches; but now that you have killed one of them, there is but one Wicked Witch in all the Land of Oz—the one who lives in the West."

"But," said Dorothy, after a moment's thought, "Aunt Em has told me that the witches were all dead—years and years ago."

"Who is Aunt Em?" inquired the little old woman.

"She is my aunt who lives in Kansas, where I came from."

The Witch of the North seemed to think for a time, with her head bowed and her eyes upon the ground. Then she looked up and said, "I do not know where Kansas is, for I have never heard that country mentioned before. But tell me, is it a civilized country?"

"Oh, yes," replied Dorothy.

"Then that accounts for it. In the civilized countries I believe there are no witches left, nor wizards, nor sorceresses, nor magicians. But, you see, the Land of Oz has never been civilized, for we are cut off from all the rest of the world. Therefore we still have witches and wizards amongst us."

"Who are the wizards?" asked Dorothy.

"Oz himself is the Great Wizard," answered the Witch, sinking her voice to a whisper. "He is more powerful than all the rest of us together. He lives in the City of Emeralds."

Dorothy was going to ask another question, but just then the Munchkins, who had been standing silently by, gave a loud shout and pointed to the corner of the house where the Wicked Witch had been lying.

"What is it?" asked the little old woman, and looked, and began to laugh. The feet of the dead Witch had disappeared entirely, and nothing was left but the silver shoes.

"She was so old," explained the Witch of the North, that she dried up quickly in the sun. That is the end of her. But the silver shoes are yours, and you shall have them to wear." She reached down and picked up the shoes, and after shaking the dust out of them handed them to Dorothy.

"The Witch of the East was proud of those silver shoes," said one of the Munchkins, "and there is some charm connected with them; but what it is we never knew."

Dorothy carried the shoes into the house and placed them on the table. Then she came out again to the Munchkins and said:

"I am anxious to get back to my aunt and uncle, for I am sure they will worry about me. Can you help me find my way?"

The Munchkins and the Witch first looked at one another, and then at Dorothy, and then shook their heads.

"At the East, not far from here," said one, "there is a great desert, and none could live to cross it."

"It is the same at the South," said another, "for I have been there and seen it. The South is the country of the Quadlings."

"I am told," said the third man, "that it is the same at the West. And that country, where the Winkies live, is ruled by the Wicked Witch of the West, who would make you her slave if you passed her way."

"The North is my home," said the old lady, "and at its edge is the same great desert that surrounds this Land of Oz. I'm afraid, my dear, you will have to live with us."

Dorothy began to sob at this, for she felt lonely among all these strange people. Her tears seemed to grieve the kind-hearted Munchkins, for they immediately took out their handkerchiefs and began to weep also. As for the little old woman, she took off her cap and balanced the point on the end of her nose, while she counted "One, two, three" in a solemn voice. At once the cap changed to a slate, on which was written in big, white chalk marks:

"LET DOROTHY GO TO THE CITY OF EMERALDS"

The little old woman took the slate from her nose, and having read the words on it, asked, "Is your name Dorothy, my dear?"

"Yes," answered the child, looking up and drying her tears.

"Then you must go to the City of Emeralds. Perhaps Oz will help you."

"Where is this city?" asked Dorothy.

"It is exactly in the center of the country, and is ruled by Oz, the Great Wizard I told you of."

"Is he a good man?" inquired the girl anxiously.

"He is a good Wizard. Whether he is a man or not I cannot tell, for I have never seen him."

"How can I get there?" asked Dorothy.

"You must walk. It is a long journey, through a country that is sometimes pleasant and sometimes dark and terrible. However, I will use all the magic arts I know of to keep you from harm."

"Won't you go with me?" pleaded the girl, who had begun to look upon the little old woman as her only friend.

"No, I cannot do that," she replied, "but I will give you my kiss, and no one will dare injure a person who has been kissed by the Witch of the North."

She came close to Dorothy and kissed her gently on the forehead. Where her lips touched the girl they left a round, shining mark, as Dorothy found out soon after.

"The road to the City of Emeralds is paved with yellow brick," said the Witch, "so you cannot miss it. When you get to Oz do not be afraid of him, but tell your story and ask him to help you. Good-bye, my dear."

The three Munchkins bowed low to her and wished her a pleasant journey, after which they walked away through the trees. The Witch gave Dorothy a friendly little nod, whirled around on her left heel three times, and straightway disappeared, much to the surprise of little Toto, who barked after her loudly enough when she had gone, because he had been afraid even to growl while she stood by.

But Dorothy, knowing her to be a witch, had expected her to disappear in just that way, and was not surprised in the least.

Chapter 3 - How Dorothy Saved the Scarecrow

When Dorothy was left alone she began to feel hungry. So she went to the cupboard and cut herself some bread, which she spread with butter. She gave some to Toto, and taking a pail from the shelf she carried it down to the little brook and filled it with clear, sparkling water. Toto ran over to the trees and began to bark at the birds sitting there. Dorothy went to get him, and saw such delicious fruit hanging from the branches that she gathered some of it, finding it just what she wanted to help out her breakfast.

Then she went back to the house, and having helped herself and Toto to a good drink of the cool, clear water, she set about making ready for the journey to the City of Emeralds.

Dorothy had only one other dress, but that happened to be clean and was hanging on a peg beside her bed. It was gingham, with checks of white and blue; and although the blue was somewhat faded with many washings, it was still a pretty frock. The girl washed herself carefully, dressed herself in the clean gingham, and tied her pink sunbonnet on her head. She took a little basket and filled it with bread from the cupboard, laying a white cloth over the top. Then she looked down at her feet and noticed how old and worn her shoes were.

"They surely will never do for a long journey, Toto," she said. And Toto looked up into her face with his little black eyes and wagged his tail to show he knew what she meant.

At that moment Dorothy saw lying on the table the silver shoes that had belonged to the Witch of the East.

"I wonder if they will fit me," she said to Toto. "They would be just the thing to take a long walk in, for they could not wear out."

She took off her old leather shoes and tried on the silver ones, which fitted her as well as if they had been made for her.

Finally she picked up her basket.

"Come along, Toto," she said. "We will go to the Emerald City and ask the Great Oz how to get back to Kansas again."

She closed the door, locked it, and put the key carefully in the pocket of her dress. And so, with Toto trotting along soberly behind her, she started on her journey.

There were several roads near by, but it did not take her long to find the one paved with yellow bricks. Within a short time she was walking briskly toward the Emerald City, her silver shoes tinkling merrily on the hard, yellow road-bed. The sun shone bright and the birds sang sweetly, and Dorothy did not feel nearly so bad as you might think a little girl would who had been suddenly whisked away from her own country and set down in the midst of a strange land.

She was surprised, as she walked along, to see how pretty the country was about her. There were neat fences at the sides of the road, painted a dainty blue color, and beyond them were fields of grain and vegetables in abundance. Evidently the Munchkins were good farmers and able to raise large crops. Once in a while she would pass a house, and the people came out to look at her and bow low as she went by; for everyone knew she had been the means of destroying the Wicked Witch and setting them free from bondage. The houses of the Munchkins were odd-looking dwellings, for each was round, with a big dome for a roof. All were painted blue, for in this country of the East blue was the favorite color.

Toward evening, when Dorothy was tired with her long walk and began to wonder where she should pass the night, she came to a house rather larger than the rest. On the green lawn before it many men and women were dancing. Five little fiddlers played as loudly as possible, and the people were laughing and singing, while a big table near by was loaded with delicious fruits and nuts, pies and cakes, and many other good things to eat.

The people greeted Dorothy kindly, and invited her to supper and to pass the night with them; for this was the home of one of the richest Munchkins in the land, and his friends were gathered with him to celebrate their freedom from bondage of the Wicked Witch.

Dorothy ate a hearty supper and was waited upon by the rich Munchkin himself, whose name was Boq. Then she sat upon a settee and watched the people dance.

When Boq saw her silver shoes he said, "You must be a great sorceress."

"Why?" asked the girl.

"Because you wear silver shoes and have killed the Wicked Witch. Besides, you have white in your frock, and only witches and sorceresses wear white."

"My dress is blue and white checked," said Dorothy, smoothing out the wrinkles in it.

"It is kind of you to wear that," said Boq. "Blue is the color of the Munchkins, and white is the witch color. So we know you are a friendly witch."

Dorothy did not know what to say to this, for all the people seemed to think her a witch, and she knew very well she was only an ordinary little girl who had come by the chance of a cyclone into a strange land.

When she had tired watching the dancing, Boq led her into the house, where he gave her a room with a pretty bed in it. The sheets were made of blue cloth, and Dorothy slept soundly in them till morning, with Toto curled up on the blue rug beside her.

She ate a hearty breakfast, and watched a wee Munchkin baby, who played with Toto and pulled his tail and crowed and laughed in a way that greatly amused Dorothy. Toto was a fine curiosity to all the people, for they had never seen a dog before.

"How far is it to the Emerald City?" the girl asked.

"I do not know," answered Boq gravely, "for I have never been there. It is better for people to keep away from Oz, unless they have business with him. But it is a long way to the Emerald City, and it will take you many days. The country here is rich and pleasant, but you must pass through rough and dangerous places before you reach the end of your journey."

This worried Dorothy a little, but she knew that only the Great Oz could help her get to Kansas again, so she bravely resolved not to turn back.

She bade her friends good-bye, and again started along the road of yellow brick. When she had gone several miles she thought she would stop to rest, and so climbed to the top of the fence beside the road and sat down. There was a great cornfield beyond the fence, and not far away she saw a Scarecrow, placed high on a pole to keep the birds from the ripe corn.

Dorothy leaned her chin upon her hand and gazed thoughtfully at the Scarecrow. Its head was a small sack stuffed with straw, with eyes, nose, and mouth painted on it to represent a face. An old, pointed blue hat, that had belonged to some Munchkin, was perched on his head, and the rest of the figure was a blue suit of clothes, worn and faded, which had also been stuffed with straw. On the feet were some old boots with blue tops, such as every man wore in this country, and the figure was raised above the stalks of corn by means of the pole stuck up its back.

While Dorothy was looking earnestly into the queer, painted face of the Scarecrow, she was surprised to see one of the eyes slowly wink at her. She thought she must have been mistaken at first, for none of the scarecrows in Kansas ever wink; but presently the figure nodded its head to her in a friendly way. Then she climbed down from the fence and walked up to it, while Toto ran around the pole and barked.

"Good day," said the Scarecrow, in a rather husky voice.

"Did you speak?" asked the girl, in wonder.

"Certainly," answered the Scarecrow. "How do you do?"

"I'm pretty well, thank you," replied Dorothy politely. "How do you do?"

"I'm not feeling well," said the Scarecrow, with a smile, "for it is very tedious being perched up here night and day to scare away crows."

"Can't you get down?" asked Dorothy.

"No, for this pole is stuck up my back. I ... ly obliged to you."

Dorothy reached up both arms and lifte ... t was quite light.

"Thank you very much," said the Scare ... l like a new man."

Dorothy was puzzled at this, for it sou ... m bow and walk along beside her.

"Who are you?" asked the Scarecrow ... re are you going?"

"My name is Dorothy," said the girl ... t Oz to send me back to Kansas."

"Where is the Emerald City?" he inc ...

"Why, don't you know?" she return ...

"No, indeed. I don't know anything ... nswered sadly.

"Oh," said Dorothy, "I'm awfully s ...

"Do you think," he asked, "if I go ... ome brains?"

"I cannot tell," she returned, "but ... e you any brains you will be no worse off than you are now."

"That is true," said the Scarecro ... d my legs and arms and body being stuffed, because I cannot get hurt. If anyo ... e, it doesn't matter, for I can't feel it. But I do not want people to call me a fool, and if my head ... stead of with brains, as yours is, how am I ever to know anything?"

"I understand how you feel," said the little girl, who was truly sorry for him. "If you will come with me I'll ask Oz to do all he can for you."

"Thank you," he answered gratefully.

They walked back to the road. Dorothy helped him over the fence, and they started along the path of yellow brick for the Emerald City.

Toto did not like this addition to the party at first. He smelled around the stuffed man as if he suspected there might be a nest of rats in the straw, and he often growled in an unfriendly way at the Scarecrow.

"Don't mind Toto," said Dorothy to her new friend. "He never bites."

"Oh, I'm not afraid," replied the Scarecrow. "He can't hurt the straw. Do let me carry that basket for you. I shall not mind it, for I can't get tired. I'll tell you a secret," he continued, as he walked along. "There is only one thing in the world I am afraid of."

"What is that?" asked Dorothy; "the Munchkin farmer who made you?"

"No," answered the Scarecrow; "it's a lighted match."

Chapter 4 - The Road Through the Forest

After a few hours the road began to be rough, and the walking grew so difficult that the Scarecrow often stumbled over the yellow bricks, which were here very uneven. Sometimes, indeed, they were broken or missing altogether, leaving holes that Toto jumped across and Dorothy walked around. As for the Scarecrow, having no brains, he walked straight ahead, and so stepped into the holes and fell at full length on the hard bricks. It never hurt him, however, and Dorothy would pick him up and set him upon his feet again, while he joined her in laughing merrily at his own mishap.

The farms were not nearly so well cared for here as they were farther back. There were fewer houses and fewer fruit trees, and the farther they went the more dismal and lonesome the country became.

At noon they sat down by the roadside, near a little brook, and Dorothy opened her basket and got out some bread. She offered a piece to the Scarecrow, but he refused.

"I am never hungry," he said, "and it is a lucky thing I am not, for my mouth is only painted, and if I should cut a hole in it so I could eat, the straw I am stuffed with would come out, and that would spoil the shape of my head."

Dorothy saw at once that this was true, so she only nodded and went on eating her bread.

"Tell me something about yourself and the country you came from," said the Scarecrow, when she had finished her dinner. So she told him all about Kansas, and how gray everything was there, and how the cyclone had carried her to this queer Land of Oz.

The Scarecrow listened carefully, and said, "I cannot understand why you should wish to leave this beautiful country and go back to the dry, gray place you call Kansas."

"That is because you have no brains" answered the girl. "No matter how dreary and gray our homes are, we people of flesh and blood would rather live there than in any other country, be it ever so beautiful. There is no place like home."

The Scarecrow sighed.

"Of course I cannot understand it," he said. "If your heads were stuffed with straw, like mine, you would probably all live in the beautiful places, and then Kansas would have no people at all. It is fortunate for Kansas that you have brains."

"Won't you tell me a story, while we are resting?" asked the child.

The Scarecrow looked at her reproachfully, and answered:

"My life has been so short that I really know nothing whatever. I was only made day before yesterday. What happened in the world before that time is all unknown to me. Luckily, when the farmer made my head, one of the first things he did was to paint my ears, so that I heard what was going on. There was another Munchkin with him, and the first thing I heard was the farmer saying, `How do you like those ears?'

"`They aren't straight,'" answered the other.

"`Never mind,'" said the farmer. "`They are ears just the same,'" which was true enough.

"`Now I'll make the eyes,'" said the farmer. So he painted my right eye, and as soon as it was finished I found myself looking at him and at everything around me with a great deal of curiosity, for this was my first glimpse of the world.

"`That's a rather pretty eye,'" remarked the Munchkin who was watching the farmer. "`Blue paint is just the color for eyes.'

"`I think I'll make the other a little bigger,'" said the farmer. And when the second eye was done I could see much better than before. Then he made my nose and my mouth. But I did not speak, because at that time I didn't know what a mouth was for. I had the fun of watching them make my body and my arms and legs; and when they fastened on my head, at last, I felt very proud, for I thought I was just as good a man as anyone.

"`This fellow will scare the crows fast enough,' said the farmer. `He looks just like a man.'

"`Why, he is a man,' said the other, and I quite agreed with him. The farmer carried me under his arm to the cornfield, and set me up on a tall stick, where you found me. He and his friend soon after walked away and left me alone.

"I did not like to be deserted this way. So I tried to walk after them. But my feet would not touch the ground, and I was forced to stay on that pole. It was a lonely life to lead, for I had nothing to think of, having been made such a little while before. Many crows and other birds flew into the cornfield, but as soon as they saw me they flew away again, thinking I was a Munchkin; and this pleased me and made me feel that I was quite an important person. By and by an old crow flew near me, and after looking at me carefully he perched upon my shoulder and said:

"`I wonder if that farmer thought to fool me in this clumsy manner. Any crow of sense could see that you are only stuffed with straw.' Then he hopped down at my feet and ate all the corn he wanted. The other birds, seeing he was not harmed by me, came to eat the corn too, so in a short time there was a great flock of them about me.

"I felt sad at this, for it showed I was not such a good Scarecrow after all; but the old crow comforted me, saying, `If you only had brains in your head you would be as good a man as any of them, and a better man than some of them. Brains are the only things worth having in this world, no matter whether one is a crow or a man.'

"After the crows had gone I thought this over, and decided I would try hard to get some brains. By good luck you came along and pulled me off the stake, and from what you say I am sure the Great Oz will give me brains as soon as we get to the Emerald City."

"I hope so," said Dorothy earnestly, "since you seem anxious to have them."

"Oh, yes; I am anxious," returned the Scarecrow. "It is such an uncomfortable feeling to know one is a fool."

"Well," said the girl, "let us go." And she handed the basket to the Scarecrow.

There were no fences at all by the roadside now, and the land was rough and untilled. Toward evening they came to a great forest, where the trees grew so big and close together that their branches met over the road of yellow brick. It was almost dark under the trees, for the branches shut out the daylight; but the travelers did not stop, and went on into the forest.

"If this road goes in, it must come out," said the Scarecrow, "and as the Emerald City is at the other end of the road, we must go wherever it leads us."

"Anyone would know that," said Dorothy.

"Certainly; that is why I know it," returned the Scarecrow. "If it required brains to figure it out, I never should have said it."

After an hour or so the light faded away, and they found themselves stumbling along in the darkness. Dorothy could not see at all, but Toto could, for some dogs see very well in the dark; and the Scarecrow declared he could see as well as by day. So she took hold of his arm and managed to get along fairly well.

"If you see any house, or any place where we can pass the night," she said, "you must tell me; for it is very uncomfortable walking in the dark."

Soon after the Scarecrow stopped.

"I see a little cottage at the right of us," he said, "built of logs and branches. Shall we go there?"

"Yes, indeed," answered the child. "I am all tired out."

So the Scarecrow led her through the trees until they reached the cottage, and Dorothy entered and found a bed of dried leaves in one corner. She lay down at once, and with Toto beside her soon fell into a sound sleep. The Scarecrow, who was never tired, stood up in another corner and waited patiently until morning came.

Chapter 5 - The Rescue of the Tin Woodman

When Dorothy awoke the sun was shining through the trees and Toto had long been out chasing birds around him and squirrels. She sat up and looked around her. Scarecrow, still standing patiently in his corner, waiting for her.

"We must go and search for water," she said to him.

"Why do you want water?" he asked.

"To wash my face clean after the dust of the road, and to drink, so the dry bread will not stick in my throat."

"It must be inconvenient to be made of flesh," said the Scarecrow thoughtfully, "for you must sleep, and eat and drink. However, you have brains, and it is worth a lot of bother to be able to think properly."

They left the cottage and walked through the trees until they found a little spring of clear water, where Dorothy drank and bathed and ate her breakfast. She saw there was not much bread left in the basket, and the girl was thankful the Scarecrow did not have to eat anything, for there was scarcely enough for herself and Toto for the day.

When she had finished her meal, and was about to go back to the road of yellow brick, she was startled to hear a deep groan near by.

"What was that?" she asked timidly.

"I cannot imagine," replied the Scarecrow; "but we can go and see."

Just then another groan reached their ears, and the sound seemed to come from behind them. They turned and walked through the forest a few steps, when Dorothy discovered something shining in a ray of sunshine that fell between the trees. She ran to the place and then stopped short, with a little cry of surprise.

One of the big trees had been partly chopped through, and standing beside it, with an uplifted axe in his hands, was a man made entirely of tin. His head and arms and legs were jointed upon his body, but he stood perfectly motionless, as if he could not stir at all.

Dorothy looked at him in amazement, and so did the Scarecrow, while Toto barked sharply and made a snap at the tin legs, which hurt his teeth.

"Did you groan?" asked Dorothy.

"Yes," answered the tin man, "I did. I've been groaning for more than a year, and no one has ever heard me before or come to help me."

"What can I do for you?" she inquired softly, for she was moved by the sad voice in which the man spoke.

"Get an oil-can and oil my joints," he answered. "They are rusted so badly that I cannot move them at all; if I am well oiled I shall soon be all right again. You will find an oil-can on a shelf in my cottage."

Dorothy at once ran back to the cottage and found the oil-can, and then she returned and asked anxiously, "Where are your joints?"

"Oil my neck, first," replied the Tin Woodman. So she oiled it, and as it was quite badly rusted the Scarecrow took hold of the tin head and moved it gently from side to side until it worked freely, and then the man could turn it himself.

"Now oil the joints in my arms," he said. And Dorothy oiled them and the Scarecrow bent them carefully until they were quite free from rust and as good as new.

The Tin Woodman gave a sigh of satisfaction and lowered his axe, which he leaned against the tree.

"This is a great comfort," he said. "I have been holding that axe in the air ever since I rusted, and I'm glad to be able to put it down at last. Now, if you will oil the joints of my legs, I shall be all right once more."

So they oiled his legs until he could move them freely; and he thanked them again and again for his release, for he seemed a very polite creature, and very grateful.

"I might have stood there always if you had not come along," he said; "so you have certainly saved my life. How did you happen to be here?"

"We are on our way to the Emerald City to see the Great Oz," she answered, "and we stopped at your cottage to pass the night."

"Why do you wish to see Oz?" he asked.

"I want him to send me back to Kansas, and the Scarecrow wants him to put a few brains into his head," she replied.

The Tin Woodman appeared to think deeply for a moment. Then he said:

"Do you suppose Oz could give me a heart?"

"Why, I guess so," Dorothy answered. "It would be as easy as to give the Scarecrow brains."

"True," the Tin Woodman returned. "So, if you will allow me to join your party, I will also go to the Emerald City and ask Oz to help me."

"Come along," said the Scarecrow heartily, and Dorothy added that she would be pleased to have his company. So the Tin Woodman shouldered his axe and they all passed through the forest until they came to the road that was paved with yellow brick.

The Tin Woodman had asked Dorothy to put the oil-can in her basket. "For," he said, "if I should get caught in the rain, and rust again, I would need the oil-can badly."

It was a bit of good luck to have their new comrade join the party, for soon after they had begun their journey again they came to a place where the trees and branches grew so thick over the road that the travelers could not pass. But the Tin Woodman set to work with his axe and chopped so well that soon he cleared a passage for the entire party.

Dorothy was thinking so earnestly as they walked along that she did not notice when the Scarecrow stumbled into a hole and rolled over to the side of the road. Indeed he was obliged to call to her to help him up again.

"Why didn't you walk around the hole?" asked the Tin Woodman.

"I don't know enough," replied the Scarecrow cheerfully. "My head is stuffed with straw, you know, and that is why I am going to Oz to ask him for some brains."

"Oh, I see," said the Tin Woodman. "But, after all, brains are not the best things in the world."

"Have you any?" inquired the Scarecrow.

14

"No, my head is quite empty," answered the Woodman. "But once I had brains, and a heart also; so, having tried them both, I should much rather have a heart."

"And why is that?" asked the Scarecrow.

"I will tell you my story, and then you will know."

So, while they were walking through the forest, the Tin Woodman told the following story:

"I was born the son of a woodman who chopped down trees in the forest and sold the wood for a living. When I grew up, I too became a woodchopper, and after my father died I took care of my old mother as long as she lived. Then I made up my mind that instead of living alone I would marry, so that I might not become lonely.

"There was one of the Munchkin girls who was so beautiful that I soon grew to love her with all my heart. She, on her part, promised to marry me as soon as I could earn enough money to build a better house for her; so I set to work harder than ever. But the girl lived with an old woman who did not want her to marry anyone, for she was so lazy she wished the girl to remain with her and do the cooking and the housework. So the old woman went to the Wicked Witch of the East, and promised her two sheep and a cow if she would prevent the marriage. Thereupon the Wicked Witch enchanted my axe, and when I was chopping away at my best one day, for I was anxious to get the new house and my wife as soon as possible, the axe slipped all at once and cut off my left leg.

"This at first seemed a great misfortune, for I knew a one-legged man could not do very well as a wood-chopper. So I went to a tinsmith and had him make me a new leg out of tin. The leg worked very well, once I was used to it. But my action angered the Wicked Witch of the East, for she had promised the old woman I should not marry the pretty Munchkin girl. When I began chopping again, my axe slipped and cut off my right leg. Again I went to the tinsmith, and again he made me a leg out of tin. After this the enchanted axe cut off my arms, one after the other; but, nothing daunted, I had them replaced with tin ones. The Wicked Witch then made the axe slip and cut off my head, and at first I thought that was the end of me. But the tinsmith happened to come along, and he made me a new head out of tin.

"I thought I had beaten the Wicked Witch then, and I worked harder than ever; but I little knew how cruel my enemy could be. She thought of a new way to kill my love for the beautiful Munchkin maiden, and made my axe slip again, so that it cut right through my body, splitting me into two halves. Once more the tinsmith came to my help and made me a body of tin, fastening my tin arms and legs and head to it, by means of joints, so that I could move around as well as ever. But, alas! I had now no heart, so that I lost all my love for the Munchkin girl, and did not care whether I married her or not. I suppose she is still living with the old woman, waiting for me to come after her.

"My body shone so brightly in the sun that I felt very proud of it and it did not matter now if my axe slipped, for it could not cut me. There was only one danger—that my joints would rust; but I kept an oil-can in my cottage and took care to oil myself whenever I needed it. However, there came a day when I forgot to do this, and, being caught in a rainstorm, before I thought of the danger my joints had rusted, and I was left to stand in the woods until you came to help me. It was a terrible thing to undergo, but during the year I stood there I had time to think that the greatest loss I had known was the loss of my heart. While I was in love I was the happiest man on earth; but no one can love who has not a heart, and so I am resolved to ask Oz to give me one. If he does, I will go back to the Munchkin maiden and marry her."

Both Dorothy and the Scarecrow had been greatly interested in the story of the Tin Woodman, and now they knew why he was so anxious to get a new heart.

"All the same," said the Scarecrow, "I shall ask for brains instead of a heart; for a fool would not know what to do with a heart if he had one."

"I shall take the heart," returned the Tin Woodman; "for brains do not make one happy, and happiness is the best thing in the world."

Dorothy did not say anything, for she was puzzled to know which of her two friends was right, and she decided if she could only get back to Kansas and Aunt Em, it did not matter so much whether the Woodman had no brains and the Scarecrow no heart, or each got what he wanted.

What worried her most was that the bread was nearly gone, and another meal for herself and Toto would empty the basket. To be sure neither the Woodman nor the Scarecrow ever ate anything, but she was not made of tin nor straw, and could not live unless she was fed.

Chapter 6 - The Cowardly Lion

All this time Dorothy and her companions had been walking through the thick woods. The road was still paved with yellow brick, but these were much covered by dried branches and dead leaves from the trees, and the walking was not at all good.

15

There were few birds in this part of the forest, for birds love the open country where there is plenty of sunshine. But now and then there came a deep growl from some wild animal hidden among the trees. These sounds made the little girl's heart beat fast, for she did not know what made them; but Toto knew, and he walked close to Dorothy's side, and did not even bark in return.

"How long will it be," the child asked of the Tin Woodman, "before we are out of the forest?"

"I cannot tell," was the answer, "for I have never been to the Emerald City. But my father went there once, when I was a boy, and he said it was a long journey through a dangerous country, although nearer to the city where Oz dwells the country is beautiful. But I am not afraid so long as I have my oil-can, and nothing can hurt the Scarecrow, while you bear upon your forehead the mark of the Good Witch's kiss, and that will protect you from harm."

"But Toto!" said the girl anxiously. "What will protect him?"

"We must protect him ourselves if he is in danger," replied the Tin Woodman.

Just as he spoke there came from the forest a terrible roar, and the next moment a great Lion bounded into the road. With one blow of his paw he sent the Scarecrow spinning over and over to the edge of the road, and then he struck at the Tin Woodman with his sharp claws. But, to the Lion's surprise, he could make no impression on the tin, although the Woodman fell over in the road and lay still.

Little Toto, now that he had an enemy to face, ran barking toward the Lion, and the great beast had opened his mouth to bite the dog, when Dorothy, fearing Toto would be killed, and heedless of danger, rushed forward and slapped the Lion upon his nose as hard as she could, while she cried out:

"Don't you dare to bite Toto! You ought to be ashamed of yourself, a big beast like you, to bite a poor little dog!"

"I didn't bite him," said the Lion, as he rubbed his nose with his paw where Dorothy had hit it.

"No, but you tried to," she retorted. "You are nothing but a big coward."

"I know it," said the Lion, hanging his head in shame. "I've always known it. But how can I help it?"

"I don't know, I'm sure. To think of your striking a stuffed man, like the poor Scarecrow!"

"Is he stuffed?" asked the Lion in surprise, as he watched her pick up the Scarecrow and set him upon his feet, while she patted him into shape again.

"Of course he's stuffed," replied Dorothy, who was still angry.

"That's why he went over so easily," remarked the Lion. "It astonished me to see him whirl around so. Is the other one stuffed also?"

"No," said Dorothy, "he's made of tin." And she helped the Woodman up again.

"That's why he nearly blunted my claws," said the Lion. "When they scratched against the tin it made a cold shiver run down my back. What is that little animal you are so tender of?"

"He is my dog, Toto," answered Dorothy.

"Is he made of tin, or stuffed?" asked the Lion.

"Neither. He's a—a—a meat dog," said the girl.

"Oh! He's a curious animal and seems remarkably small, now that I look at him. No one would think of biting such a little thing, except a coward like me," continued the Lion sadly.

"What makes you a coward?" asked Dorothy, looking at the great beast in wonder, for he was as big as a small horse.

"It's a mystery," replied the Lion. "I suppose I was born that way. All the other animals in the forest naturally expect me to be brave, for the Lion is everywhere thought to be the King of Beasts. I learned that if I roared very loudly every living thing was frightened and got out of my way. Whenever I've met a man I've been awfully scared; but I just roared at him, and he has always run away as fast as he could go. If the elephants and the tigers and the bears had ever tried to fight me, I should have run myself—I'm such a coward; but just as soon as they hear me roar they all try to get away from me, and of course I let them go."

"But that isn't right. The King of Beasts shouldn't be a coward," said the Scarecrow.

"I know it," returned the Lion, wiping a tear from his eye with the tip of his tail. "It is my great sorrow, and makes my life very unhappy. But whenever there is danger, my heart begins to beat fast."

"Perhaps you have heart disease," said the Tin Woodman.

"It may be," said the Lion.

"If you have," continued the Tin Woodman, "you ought to be glad, for it proves you have a heart. For my part, I have no heart; so I cannot have heart disease."

"Perhaps," said the Lion thoughtfully, "if I had no heart I should not be a coward."

"Have you brains?" asked the Scarecrow.

"I suppose so. I've never looked to see," replied the Lion.

"I am going to the Great Oz to ask him to give me some," remarked the Scarecrow, "for my head is stuffed with straw."

"And I am going to ask him to give me a heart," said the Woodman.

"And I am going to ask him to send Toto and me back to Kansas," added Dorothy.

"Do you think Oz could give me courage?" asked the Cowardly Lion.

"Just as easily as he could give me brains," said the Scarecrow.

"Or give me a heart," said the Tin Woodman.

"Or send me back to Kansas," said Dorothy.

"Then, if you don't mind, I'll go with you," said the Lion, "for my life is simply unbearable without a bit of courage."

"You will be very welcome," answered Dorothy, "for you will help to keep away the other wild beasts. It seems to me they must be more cowardly than you are if they allow you to scare them so easily."

"They really are," said the Lion, "but that doesn't make me any braver, and as long as I know myself to be a coward I shall be unhappy."

So once more the little company set off upon the journey, the Lion walking with stately strides at Dorothy's side. Toto did not approve this new comrade at first, for he could not forget how nearly he had been crushed between the Lion's great jaws. But after a time he became more at ease, and presently Toto and the Cowardly Lion had grown to be good friends.

During the rest of that day there was no other adventure to mar the peace of their journey. Once, indeed, the Tin Woodman stepped upon a beetle that was crawling along the road, and killed the poor little thing. This made the Tin Woodman very unhappy, for he was always careful not to hurt any living creature; and as he walked along he wept several tears of sorrow and regret. These tears ran slowly down his face and over the hinges of his jaw, and there they rusted. When Dorothy presently asked him a question the Tin Woodman could not open his mouth, for his jaws were tightly rusted together. He became greatly frightened at this and made many motions to Dorothy to relieve him, but she could not understand. The Lion was also puzzled to know what was wrong. But the Scarecrow seized the oil-can from Dorothy's basket and oiled the Woodman's jaws, so that after a few moments he could talk as well as before.

"This will serve me a lesson," said he, "to look where I step. For if I should kill another bug or beetle I should surely cry again, and crying rusts my jaws so that I cannot speak."

Thereafter he walked very carefully, with his eyes on the road, and when he saw a tiny ant toiling by he would step over it, so as not to harm it. The Tin Woodman knew very well he had no heart, and therefore he took great care never to be cruel or unkind to anything.

"You people with hearts," he said, "have something to guide you, and need never do wrong; but I have no heart, and so I must be very careful.

Chapter 7 - The Journey to the Great Oz

They were obliged to camp out that night under a large tree in the forest, for there were no houses near. The tree made a good, thick covering to protect them from the dew, and the Tin Woodman chopped a great pile of wood with his axe and Dorothy built a splendid fire that warmed her and made her feel less lonely. She and Toto ate the last of their bread, and now she did not know what they would do for breakfast.

"If you wish," said the Lion, "I will go into the forest and kill a deer for you. You can roast it by the fire, since your tastes are so peculiar that you prefer cooked food, and then you will have a very good breakfast."

"Don't! Please don't," begged the Tin Woodman. "I should certainly weep if you killed a poor deer, and then my jaws would rust again."

But the Lion went away into the forest and found his own supper, and no one ever knew what it was, for he didn't mention it. And the Scarecrow found a tree full of nuts and filled Dorothy's basket with them, so that she would not be hungry for a long time. She thought this was very kind and thoughtful of the Scarecrow, but she laughed heartily at the awkward way in which the poor creature picked up the nuts. His padded hands were so clumsy and the nuts were so small that he dropped almost as many as he put in the basket. But the Scarecrow did not mind how long it took him to fill the basket, for it enabled him to keep away from the fire, as he feared a spark might get into his straw and burn him up. So he kept a good distance away from the flames, and only came near to cover Dorothy with dry leaves when she lay down to sleep. These kept her very snug and warm, and she slept soundly until morning.

When it was daylight, the girl bathed her face in a little rippling brook, and soon after they all started toward the Emerald City.

This was to be an eventful day for the travelers. They had hardly been walking an hour when they saw before them a great ditch that crossed the road and divided the forest as far as they could see on either side. It was a very wide ditch, and when they crept up to the edge and looked into it they could see it was also very deep, and there were many big, jagged rocks at the bottom. The sides were so steep that none of them could climb down, and for a moment it seemed that their journey must end.

"What shall we do?" asked Dorothy despairingly.

"I haven't the faintest idea," said the Tin Woodman, and the Lion shook his shaggy mane and looked thoughtful.

But the Scarecrow said, "We cannot fly, that is certain. Neither can we climb down into this great ditch. Therefore, if we cannot jump over it, we must stop where we are."

"I think I could jump over it," said the Cowardly Lion, after measuring the distance carefully in his mind.

"Then we are all right," answered the Scarecrow, "for you can carry us all over on your back, one at a time."

"Well, I'll try it," said the Lion. "Who will go first?"

"I will," declared the Scarecrow, "for, if you found that you could not jump over the gulf, Dorothy would be killed, or the Tin Woodman badly dented on the rocks below. But if I am on your back it will not matter so much, for the fall would not hurt me at all."

"I am terribly afraid of falling, myself," said the Cowardly Lion, "but I suppose there is nothing to do but try it. So get on my back and we will make the attempt."

The Scarecrow sat upon the Lion's back, and the big beast walked to the edge of the gulf and crouched down.

"Why don't you run and jump?" asked the Scarecrow.

"Because that isn't the way we Lions do these things," he replied. Then giving a great spring, he shot through the air and landed safely on the other side. They were all greatly pleased to see how easily he did it, and after the Scarecrow had got down from his back the Lion sprang across the ditch again.

Dorothy thought she would go next; so she took Toto in her arms and climbed on the Lion's back, holding tightly to his mane with one hand. The next moment it seemed as if she were flying through the air; and then, before she had time to think about it, she was safe on the other side. The Lion went back a third time and got the Tin Woodman, and then they all sat down for a few moments to give the beast a chance to rest, for his great leaps had made his breath short, and he panted like a big dog that has been running too long.

They found the forest very thick on this side, and it looked dark and gloomy. After the Lion had rested they started along the road of yellow brick, silently wondering, each in his own mind, if ever they would come to the end of the woods and reach the bright sunshine again. To add to their discomfort, they soon heard strange noises in the depths of the forest, and the Lion whispered to them that it was in this part of the country that the Kalidahs lived.

"What are the Kalidahs?" asked the girl.

"They are monstrous beasts with bodies like bears and heads like tigers," replied the Lion, "and with claws so long and sharp that they could tear me in two as easily as I could kill Toto. I'm terribly afraid of the Kalidahs."

"I'm not surprised that you are," returned Dorothy. "They must be dreadful beasts."

The Lion was about to reply when suddenly they came to another gulf across the road. But this one was so broad and deep that the Lion knew at once he could not leap across it.

So they sat down to consider what they should do, and after serious thought the Scarecrow said:

"Here is a great tree, standing close to the ditch. If the Tin Woodman can chop it down, so that it will fall to the other side, we can walk across it easily."

"That is a first-rate idea," said the Lion. "One would almost suspect you had brains in your head, instead of straw."

The Woodman set to work at once, and so sharp was his axe that the tree was soon chopped nearly through. Then the Lion put his strong front legs against the tree and pushed with all his might, and slowly the big tree tipped and fell with a crash across the ditch, with its top branches on the other side.

They had just started to cross this queer bridge when a sharp growl made them all look up, and to their horror they saw running toward them two great beasts with bodies like bears and heads like tigers.

"They are the Kalidahs!" said the Cowardly Lion, beginning to tremble.

"Quick!" cried the Scarecrow. "Let us cross over."

So Dorothy went first, holding Toto in her arms, the Tin Woodman followed, and the Scarecrow came next. The Lion, although he was certainly afraid, turned to face the Kalidahs, and then he gave so loud and terrible a roar that

Dorothy screamed and the Scarecrow fell over backward, while even the fierce beasts stopped short and looked at him in surprise.

But, seeing they were bigger than the Lion, and remembering that there were two of them and only one of him, the Kalidahs again rushed forward, and the Lion crossed over the tree and turned to see what they would do next. Without stopping an instant the fierce beasts also began to cross the tree. And the Lion said to Dorothy:

"We are lost, for they will surely tear us to pieces with their sharp claws. But stand close behind me, and I will fight them as long as I am alive."

"Wait a minute!" called the Scarecrow. He had been thinking what was best to be done, and now he asked the Woodman to chop away the end of the tree that rested on their side of the ditch. The Tin Woodman began to use his axe at once, and, just as the two Kalidahs were nearly across, the tree fell with a crash into the gulf, carrying the ugly, snarling brutes with it, and both were dashed to pieces on the sharp rocks at the bottom.

"Well," said the Cowardly Lion, drawing a long breath of relief, "I see we are going to live a little while longer, and I am glad of it, for it must be a very uncomfortable thing not to be alive. Those creatures frightened me so badly that my heart is beating yet."

"Ah," said the Tin Woodman sadly, "I wish I had a heart to beat."

This adventure made the travelers more anxious than ever to get out of the forest, and they walked so fast that Dorothy became tired, and had to ride on the Lion's back. To their great joy the trees became thinner the farther they advanced, and in the afternoon they suddenly came upon a broad river, flowing swiftly just before them. On the other side of the water they could see the road of yellow brick running through a beautiful country, with green meadows dotted with bright flowers and all the road bordered with trees hanging full of delicious fruits. They were greatly pleased to see this delightful country before them.

"How shall we cross the river?" asked Dorothy.

"That is easily done," replied the Scarecrow. "The Tin Woodman must build us a raft, so we can float to the other side."

So the Woodman took his axe and began to chop down small trees to make a raft, and while he was busy at this the Scarecrow found on the riverbank a tree full of fine fruit. This pleased Dorothy, who had eaten nothing but nuts all day, and she made a hearty meal of the ripe fruit.

But it takes time to make a raft, even when one is as industrious and untiring as the Tin Woodman, and when night came the work was not done. So they found a cozy place under the trees where they slept well until the morning; and Dorothy dreamed of the Emerald City, and of the good Wizard Oz, who would soon send her back to her own home again.

Chapter 8 - The Deadly Poppy Field

Our little party of travelers awakened the next morning refreshed and full of hope, and Dorothy breakfasted like a princess off peaches and plums from the trees beside the river. Behind them was the dark forest they had passed safely through, although they had suffered many discouragements; but before them was a lovely, sunny country that seemed to beckon them on to the Emerald City.

To be sure, the broad river now cut them off from this beautiful land. But the raft was nearly done, and after the Tin Woodman had cut a few more logs and fastened them together with wooden pins, they were ready to start. Dorothy sat down in the middle of the raft and held Toto in her arms. When the Cowardly Lion stepped upon the raft it tipped badly, for he was big and heavy; but the Scarecrow and the Tin Woodman stood upon the other end to steady it, and they had long poles in their hands to push the raft through the water.

They got along quite well at first, but when they reached the middle of the river the swift current swept the raft downstream, farther and farther away from the road of yellow brick. And the water grew so deep that the long poles would not touch the bottom.

"This is bad," said the Tin Woodman, "for if we cannot get to the land we shall be carried into the country of the Wicked Witch of the West, and she will enchant us and make us her slaves."

"And then I should get no brains," said the Scarecrow.

"And I should get no courage," said the Cowardly Lion.

"And I should get no heart," said the Tin Woodman.

"And I should never get back to Kansas," said Dorothy.

"We must certainly get to the Emerald City if we can," the Scarecrow continued, and he pushed so hard on his long pole that it stuck fast in the mud at the bottom of the river. Then, before he could pull it out again—or let go—the raft was swept away, and the poor Scarecrow left clinging to the pole in the middle of the river.

"Good-bye!" he called after them, and they were very sorry to leave him. Indeed, the Tin Woodman began to cry, but fortunately remembered that he might rust, and so dried his tears on Dorothy's apron.

Of course this was a bad thing for the Scarecrow.

"I am now worse off than when I first met Dorothy," he thought. "Then, I was stuck on a pole in a cornfield, where I could make-believe scare the crows, at any rate. But surely there is no use for a Scarecrow stuck on a pole in the middle of a river. I am afraid I shall never have any brains, after all!"

Down the stream the raft floated, and the poor Scarecrow was left far behind. Then the Lion said:

"Something must be done to save us. I think I can swim to the shore and pull the raft after me, if you will only hold fast to the tip of my tail."

So he sprang into the water, and the Tin Woodman caught fast hold of his tail. Then the Lion began to swim with all his might toward the shore. It was hard work, although he was so big; but by and by they were drawn out of the current, and then Dorothy took the Tin Woodman's long pole and helped push the raft to the land.

They were all tired out when they reached the shore at last and stepped off upon the pretty green grass, and they also knew that the stream had carried them a long way past the road of yellow brick that led to the Emerald City.

"What shall we do now?" asked the Tin Woodman, as the Lion lay down on the grass to let the sun dry him.

"We must get back to the road, in some way," said Dorothy.

"The best plan will be to walk along the riverbank until we come to the road again," remarked the Lion.

So, when they were rested, Dorothy picked up her basket and they started along the grassy bank, to the road from which the river had carried them. It was a lovely country, with plenty of flowers and fruit trees and sunshine to cheer them, and had they not felt so sorry for the poor Scarecrow, they could have been very happy.

They walked along as fast as they could, Dorothy only stopping once to pick a beautiful flower; and after a time the Tin Woodman cried out: "Look!"

Then they all looked at the river and saw the Scarecrow perched upon his pole in the middle of the water, looking very lonely and sad.

"What can we do to save him?" asked Dorothy.

The Lion and the Woodman both shook their heads, for they did not know. So they sat down upon the bank and gazed wistfully at the Scarecrow until a Stork flew by, who, upon seeing them, stopped to rest at the water's edge.

"Who are you and where are you going?" asked the Stork.

"I am Dorothy," answered the girl, "and these are my friends, the Tin Woodman and the Cowardly Lion; and we are going to the Emerald City."

"This isn't the road," said the Stork, as she twisted her long neck and looked sharply at the queer party.

"I know it," returned Dorothy, "but we have lost the Scarecrow, and are wondering how we shall get him again."

"Where is he?" asked the Stork.

"Over there in the river," answered the little girl.

"If he wasn't so big and heavy I would get him for you," remarked the Stork.

"He isn't heavy a bit," said Dorothy eagerly, "for he is stuffed with straw; and if you will bring him back to us, we shall thank you ever and ever so much."

"Well, I'll try," said the Stork, "but if I find he is too heavy to carry I shall have to drop him in the river again."

So the big bird flew into the air and over the water till she came to where the Scarecrow was perched upon his pole. Then the Stork with her great claws grabbed the Scarecrow by the arm and carried him up into the air and back to the bank, where Dorothy and the Lion and the Tin Woodman and Toto were sitting.

When the Scarecrow found himself among his friends again, he was so happy that he hugged them all, even the Lion and Toto; and as they walked along he sang "Tol-de-ri-de-oh!" at every step, he felt so gay.

"I was afraid I should have to stay in the river forever," he said, "but the kind Stork saved me, and if I ever get any brains I shall find the Stork again and do her some kindness in return."

"That's all right," said the Stork, who was flying along beside them. "I always like to help anyone in trouble. But I must go now, for my babies are waiting in the nest for me. I hope you will find the Emerald City and that Oz will help you."

"Thank you," replied Dorothy, and then the kind Stork flew into the air and was soon out of sight.

They walked along listening to the singing of the brightly colored birds and looking at the lovely flowers which now became so thick that the ground was carpeted with them. There were big yellow and white and blue and purple blossoms, besides great clusters of scarlet poppies, which were so brilliant in color they almost dazzled Dorothy's eyes.

"Aren't they beautiful?" the girl asked, as she breathed in the spicy scent of the bright flowers.

"I suppose so," answered the Scarecrow. "When I have brains, I shall probably like them better."

"If I only had a heart, I should love them," added the Tin Woodman.

"I always did like flowers," said the Lion. "They of seem so helpless and frail. But there are none in the forest so bright as these."

They now came upon more and more of the big scarlet poppies, and fewer and fewer of the other flowers; and soon they found themselves in the midst of a great meadow of poppies. Now it is well known that when there are many of these flowers together their odor is so powerful that anyone who breathes it falls asleep, and if the sleeper is not carried away from the scent of the flowers, he sleeps on and on forever. But Dorothy did not know this, nor could she get away from the bright red flowers that were everywhere about; so presently her eyes grew heavy and she felt she must sit down to rest and to sleep.

But the Tin Woodman would not let her do this.

"We must hurry and get back to the road of yellow brick before dark," he said; and the Scarecrow agreed with him. So they kept walking until Dorothy could stand no longer. Her eyes closed in spite of herself and she forgot where she was and fell among the poppies, fast asleep.

"What shall we do?" asked the Tin Woodman.

"If we leave her here she will die," said the Lion. "The smell of the flowers is killing us all. I myself can scarcely keep my eyes open, and the dog is asleep already."

It was true; Toto had fallen down beside his little mistress. But the Scarecrow and the Tin Woodman, not being made of flesh, were not troubled by the scent of the flowers.

"Run fast," said the Scarecrow to the Lion, "and get out of this deadly flower bed as soon as you can. We will bring the little girl with us, but if you should fall asleep you are too big to be carried."

So the Lion aroused himself and bounded forward as fast as he could go. In a moment he was out of sight.

"Let us make a chair with our hands and carry her," said the Scarecrow. So they picked up Toto and put the dog in Dorothy's lap, and then they made a chair with their hands for the seat and their arms for the arms and carried the sleeping girl between them through the flowers.

On and on they walked, and it seemed that the great carpet of deadly flowers that surrounded them would never end. They followed the bend of the river, and at last came upon their friend the Lion, lying fast asleep among the poppies. The flowers had been too strong for the huge beast and he had given up at last, and fallen only a short distance from the end of the poppy bed, where the sweet grass spread in beautiful green fields before them.

"We can do nothing for him," said the Tin Woodman, sadly; "for he is much too heavy to lift. We must leave him here to sleep on forever, and perhaps he will dream that he has found courage at last."

"I'm sorry," said the Scarecrow. "The Lion was a very good comrade for one so cowardly. But let us go on."

They carried the sleeping girl to a pretty spot beside the river, far enough from the poppy field to prevent her breathing any more of the poison of the flowers, and here they laid her gently on the soft grass and waited for the fresh breeze to waken her.

Chapter 9 - The Queen of the Field Mice

"We cannot be far from the road of yellow brick, now," remarked the Scarecrow, as he stood beside the girl, "for we have come nearly as far as the river carried us away."

The Tin Woodman was about to reply when he heard a low growl, and turning his head (which worked beautifully on hinges) he saw a strange beast come bounding over the grass toward them. It was, indeed, a great yellow Wildcat, and the Woodman thought it must be chasing something, for its ears were lying close to its head and its mouth was wide open, showing two rows of ugly teeth, while its red eyes glowed like balls of fire. As it came nearer the Tin Woodman saw that running before the beast was a little gray field mouse, and although he had no heart he knew it was wrong for the Wildcat to try to kill such a pretty, harmless creature.

So the Woodman raised his axe, and as the Wildcat ran by he gave it a quick blow that cut the beast's head clean off from its body, and it rolled over at his feet in two pieces.

The field mouse, now that it was freed from its enemy, stopped short; and coming slowly up to the Woodman it said, in a squeaky little voice:

"Oh, thank you! Thank you ever so much for saving my life."

"Don't speak of it, I beg of you," replied the Woodman. "I have no heart, you know, so I am careful to help all those who may need a friend, even if it happens to be only a mouse."

"Only a mouse!" cried the little animal, indignantly. "Why, I am a Queen—the Queen of all the Field Mice!"

"Oh, indeed," said the Woodman, making a bow.

"Therefore you have done a great deed, as well as a brave one, in saving my life," added the Queen.

At that moment several mice were seen running up as fast as their little legs could carry them, and when they saw their Queen they exclaimed:

"Oh, your Majesty, we thought you would be killed! How did you manage to escape the great Wildcat?" They all bowed so low to the little Queen that they almost stood upon their heads.

"This funny tin man," she answered, "killed the Wildcat and saved my life. So hereafter you must all serve him, and obey his slightest wish."

"We will!" cried all the mice, in a shrill chorus. And then they scampered in all directions, for Toto had awakened from his sleep, and seeing all these mice around him he gave one bark of delight and jumped right into the middle of the group. Toto had always loved to chase mice when he lived in Kansas, and he saw no harm in it.

But the Tin Woodman caught the dog in his arms and held him tight, while he called to the mice, "Come back! Come back! Toto shall not hurt you."

At this the Queen of the Mice stuck her head out from underneath a clump of grass and asked, in a timid voice, "Are you sure he will not bite us?"

"I will not let him," said the Woodman; "so do not be afraid."

One by one the mice came creeping back, and Toto did not bark again, although he tried to get out of the Woodman's arms, and would have bitten him had he not known very well he was made of tin. Finally one of the biggest mice spoke.

"Is there anything we can do," it asked, "to repay you for saving the life of our Queen?"

"Nothing that I know of," answered the Woodman; but the Scarecrow, who had been trying to think, but could not because his head was stuffed with straw, said, quickly, "Oh, yes; you can save our friend, the Cowardly Lion, who is asleep in the poppy bed."

"A Lion!" cried the little Queen. "Why, he would eat us all up."

"Oh, no," declared the Scarecrow; "this Lion is a coward."

"Really?" asked the Mouse.

"He says so himself," answered the Scarecrow, "and he would never hurt anyone who is our friend. If you will help us to save him I promise that he shall treat you all with kindness."

"Very well," said the Queen, "we trust you. But what shall we do?"

"Are there many of these mice which call you Queen and are willing to obey you?"

"Oh, yes; there are thousands," she replied.

"Then send for them all to come here as soon as possible, and let each one bring a long piece of string."

The Queen turned to the mice that attended her and told them to go at once and get all her people. As soon as they heard her orders they ran away in every direction as fast as possible.

"Now," said the Scarecrow to the Tin Woodman, "you must go to those trees by the riverside and make a truck that will carry the Lion."

So the Woodman went at once to the trees and began to work; and he soon made a truck out of the limbs of trees, from which he chopped away all the leaves and branches. He fastened it together with wooden pegs and made the four wheels out of short pieces of a big tree trunk. So fast and so well did he work that by the time the mice began to arrive the truck was all ready for them.

They came from all directions, and there were thousands of them: big mice and little mice and middle-sized mice; and each one brought a piece of string in his mouth. It was about this time that Dorothy woke from her long sleep and opened her eyes. She was greatly astonished to find herself lying upon the grass, with thousands of mice standing around and looking at her timidly. But the Scarecrow told her about everything, and turning to the dignified little Mouse, he said:

"Permit me to introduce to you her Majesty, the Queen."

Dorothy nodded gravely and the Queen made a curtsy, after which she became quite friendly with the little girl.

22

The Scarecrow and the Woodman now began to fasten the mice to the truck, using the strings they had brought. One end of a string was tied around the neck of each mouse and the other end to the truck. Of course the truck was a thousand times bigger than any of the mice who were to draw it; but when all the mice had been harnessed, they were able to pull it quite easily. Even the Scarecrow and the Tin Woodman could sit on it, and were drawn swiftly by their queer little horses to the place where the Lion lay asleep.

After a great deal of hard work, for the Lion was heavy, they managed to get him up on the truck. Then the Queen hurriedly gave her people the order to start, for she feared if the mice stayed among the poppies too long they also would fall asleep.

At first the little creatures, many though they were, could hardly stir the heavily loaded truck; but the Woodman and the Scarecrow both pushed from behind, and they got along better. Soon they rolled the Lion out of the poppy bed to the green fields, where he could breathe the sweet, fresh air again, instead of the poisonous scent of the flowers.

Dorothy came to meet them and thanked the little mice warmly for saving her companion from death. She had grown so fond of the big Lion she was glad he had been rescued.

Then the mice were unharnessed from the truck and scampered away through the grass to their homes. The Queen of the Mice was the last to leave.

"If ever you need us again," she said, "come out into the field and call, and we shall hear you and come to your assistance. Good-bye!"

"Good-bye!" they all answered, and away the Queen ran, while Dorothy held Toto tightly lest he should run after her and frighten her.

After this they sat down beside the Lion until he should awaken; and the Scarecrow brought Dorothy some fruit from a tree near by, which she ate for her dinner.

Chapter 10 - The Guardian of the Gate

It was some time before the Cowardly Lion awakened, for he had lain among the poppies a long while, breathing in their deadly fragrance; but when he did open his eyes and roll off the truck he was very glad to find himself still alive.

"I ran as fast as I could," he said, sitting down and yawning, "but the flowers were too strong for me. How did you get me out?"

Then they told him of the field mice, and how they had generously saved him from death; and the Cowardly Lion laughed, and said:

"I have always thought myself very big and terrible; yet such little things as flowers came near to killing me, and such small animals as mice have saved my life. How strange it all is! But, comrades, what shall we do now?"

"We must journey on until we find the road of yellow brick again," said Dorothy, "and then we can keep on to the Emerald City."

So, the Lion being fully refreshed, and feeling quite himself again, they all started upon the journey, greatly enjoying the walk through the soft, fresh grass; and it was not long before they reached the road of yellow brick and turned again toward the Emerald City where the Great Oz dwelt.

The road was smooth and well paved, now, and the country about was beautiful, so that the travelers rejoiced in leaving the forest far behind, and with it the many dangers they had met in its gloomy shades. Once more they could see fences built beside the road; but these were painted green, and when they came to a small house, in which a farmer evidently lived, that also was painted green. They passed by several of these houses during the afternoon, and sometimes people came to the doors and looked at them as if they would like to ask questions; but no one came near them nor spoke to them because of the great Lion, of which they were very much afraid. The people were all dressed in clothing of a lovely emerald-green color and wore peaked hats like those of the Munchkins.

"This must be the Land of Oz," said Dorothy, "and we are surely getting near the Emerald City."

"Yes," answered the Scarecrow. "Everything is green here, while in the country of the Munchkins blue was the favorite color. But the people do not seem to be as friendly as the Munchkins, and I'm afraid we shall be unable to find a place to pass the night."

"I should like something to eat besides fruit," said the girl, "and I'm sure Toto is nearly starved. Let us stop at the next house and talk to the people."

So, when they came to a good-sized farmhouse, Dorothy walked boldly up to the door and knocked.

A woman opened it just far enough to look out, and said, "What do you want, child, and why is that great Lion with you?"

"We wish to pass the night with you, if you will allow us," answered Dorothy; "and the Lion is my friend and comrade, and would not hurt you for the world."

"Is he tame?" asked the woman, opening the door a little wider.

"Oh, yes," said the girl, "and he is a great coward, too. He will be more afraid of you than you are of him."

"Well," said the woman, after thinking it over and taking another peep at the Lion, "if that is the case you may come in, and I will give you some supper and a place to sleep."

So they all entered the house, where there were, besides the woman, two children and a man. The man had hurt his leg, and was lying on the couch in a corner. They seemed greatly surprised to see so strange a company, and while the woman was busy laying the table the man asked:

"Where are you all going?"

"To the Emerald City," said Dorothy, "to see the Great Oz."

"Oh, indeed!" exclaimed the man. "Are you sure that Oz will see you?"

"Why not?" she replied.

"Why, it is said that he never lets anyone come into his presence. I have been to the Emerald City many times, and it is a beautiful and wonderful place; but I have never been permitted to see the Great Oz, nor do I know of any living person who has seen him."

"Does he never go out?" asked the Scarecrow.

"Never. He sits day after day in the great Throne Room of his Palace, and even those who wait upon him do not see him face to face."

"What is he like?" asked the girl.

"That is hard to tell," said the man thoughtfully. "You see, Oz is a Great Wizard, and can take on any form he wishes. So that some say he looks like a bird; and some say he looks like an elephant; and some say he looks like a cat. To others he appears as a beautiful fairy, or a brownie, or in any other form that pleases him. But who the real Oz is, when he is in his own form, no living person can tell."

"That is very strange," said Dorothy, "but we must try, in some way, to see him, or we shall have made our journey for nothing."

"Why do you wish to see the terrible Oz?" asked the man.

"I want him to give me some brains," said the Scarecrow eagerly.

"Oh, Oz could do that easily enough," declared the man. "He has more brains than he needs."

"And I want him to give me a heart," said the Tin Woodman.

"That will not trouble him," continued the man, "for Oz has a large collection of hearts, of all sizes and shapes."

"And I want him to give me courage," said the Cowardly Lion.

"Oz keeps a great pot of courage in his Throne Room," said the man, "which he has covered with a golden plate, to keep it from running over. He will be glad to give you some."

"And I want him to send me back to Kansas," said Dorothy.

"Where is Kansas?" asked the man, with surprise.

"I don't know," replied Dorothy sorrowfully, "but it is my home, and I'm sure it's somewhere."

"Very likely. Well, Oz can do anything; so I suppose he will find Kansas for you. But first you must get to see him, and that will be a hard task; for the Great Wizard does not like to see anyone, and he usually has his own way. But what do YOU want?" he continued, speaking to Toto. Toto only wagged his tail; for, strange to say, he could not speak.

The woman now called to them that supper was ready, so they gathered around the table and Dorothy ate some delicious porridge and a dish of scrambled eggs and a plate of nice white bread, and enjoyed her meal. The Lion ate some of the porridge, but did not care for it, saying it was made from oats and oats were food for horses, not for lions. The Scarecrow and the Tin Woodman ate nothing at all. Toto ate a little of everything, and was glad to get a good supper again.

The woman now gave Dorothy a bed to sleep in, and Toto lay down beside her, while the Lion guarded the door of her room so she might not be disturbed. The Scarecrow and the Tin Woodman stood up in a corner and kept quiet all night, although of course they could not sleep.

The next morning, as soon as the sun was up, they started on their way, and soon saw a beautiful green glow in the sky just before them.

"That must be the Emerald City," said Dorothy.

As they walked on, the green glow became brighter and brighter, and it seemed that at last they were nearing the end of their travels. Yet it was afternoon before they came to the great wall that surrounded the City. It was high and thick and of a bright green color.

In front of them, and at the end of the road of yellow brick, was a big gate, all studded with emeralds that glittered so in the sun that even the painted eyes of the Scarecrow were dazzled by their brilliancy.

There was a bell beside the gate, and Dorothy pushed the button and heard a silvery tinkle sound within. Then the big gate swung slowly open, and they all passed through and found themselves in a high arched room, the walls of which glistened with countless emeralds.

Before them stood a little man about the same size as the Munchkins. He was clothed all in green, from his head to his feet, and even his skin was of a greenish tint. At his side was a large green box.

When he saw Dorothy and her companions the man asked, "What do you wish in the Emerald City?"

"We came here to see the Great Oz," said Dorothy.

The man was so surprised at this answer that he sat down to think it over.

"It has been many years since anyone asked me to see Oz," he said, shaking his head in perplexity. "He is powerful and terrible, and if you come on an idle or foolish errand to bother the wise reflections of the Great Wizard, he might be angry and destroy you all in an instant."

"But it is not a foolish errand, nor an idle one," replied the Scarecrow; "it is important. And we have been told that Oz is a good Wizard."

"So he is," said the green man, "and he rules the Emerald City wisely and well. But to those who are not honest, or who approach him from curiosity, he is most terrible, and few have ever dared ask to see his face. I am the Guardian of the Gates, and since you demand to see the Great Oz I must take you to his Palace. But first you must put on the spectacles."

"Why?" asked Dorothy.

"Because if you did not wear spectacles the brightness and glory of the Emerald City would blind you. Even those who live in the City must wear spectacles night and day. They are all locked on, for Oz so ordered it when the City was first built, and I have the only key that will unlock them."

He opened the big box, and Dorothy saw that it was filled with spectacles of every size and shape. All of them had green glasses in them. The Guardian of the Gates found a pair that would just fit Dorothy and put them over her eyes. There were two golden bands fastened to them that passed around the back of her head, where they were locked together by a little key that was at the end of a chain the Guardian of the Gates wore around his neck. When they were on, Dorothy could not take them off had she wished, but of course she did not wish to be blinded by the glare of the Emerald City, so she said nothing.

Then the green man fitted spectacles for the Scarecrow and the Tin Woodman and the Lion, and even on little Toto; and all were locked fast with the key.

Then the Guardian of the Gates put on his own glasses and told them he was ready to show them to the Palace. Taking a big golden key from a peg on the wall, he opened another gate, and they all followed him through the portal into the streets of the Emerald City.

Chapter 11 - The Wonderful City of Oz

Even with eyes protected by the green spectacles, Dorothy and her friends were at first dazzled by the brilliancy of the wonderful City. The streets were lined with beautiful houses all built of green marble and studded everywhere with sparkling emeralds. They walked over a pavement of the same green marble, and where the blocks were joined together were rows of emeralds, set closely, and glittering in the brightness of the sun. The window panes were of green glass; even the sky above the City had a green tint, and the rays of the sun were green.

There were many people—men, women, and children—walking about, and these were all dressed in green clothes and had greenish skins. They looked at Dorothy and her strangely assorted company with wondering eyes, and the children all ran away and hid behind their mothers when they saw the Lion; but no one spoke to them. Many shops stood in the street, and Dorothy saw that everything in them was green. Green candy and green pop corn were offered for sale, as well as green shoes, green hats, and green clothes of all sorts. At one place a man was selling green lemonade, and when the children bought it Dorothy could see that they paid for it with green pennies.

There seemed to be no horses nor animals of any kind; the men carried things around in little green carts, which they pushed before them. Everyone seemed happy and contented and prosperous.

The Guardian of the Gates led them through the streets until they came to a big building, exactly in the middle of the City, which was the Palace of Oz, the Great Wizard. There was a soldier before the door, dressed in a green uniform and wearing a long green beard.

"Here are strangers," said the Guardian of the Gates to him, "and they demand to see the Great Oz."

"Step inside," answered the soldier, "and I will carry your message to him."

So they passed through the Palace Gates and were led into a big room with a green carpet and lovely green furniture set with emeralds. The soldier made them all wipe their feet upon a green mat before entering this room, and when they were seated he said politely:

"Please make yourselves comfortable while I go to the door of the Throne Room and tell Oz you are here."

They had to wait a long time before the soldier returned. When, at last, he came back, Dorothy asked:

"Have you seen Oz?"

"Oh, no," returned the soldier; "I have never seen him. But I spoke to him as he sat behind his screen and gave him your message. He said he will grant you an audience, if you so desire; but each one of you must enter his presence alone, and he will admit but one each day. Therefore, as you must remain in the Palace for several days, I will have you shown to rooms where you may rest in comfort after your journey."

"Thank you," replied the girl; "that is very kind of Oz."

The soldier now blew upon a green whistle, and at once a young girl, dressed in a pretty green silk gown, entered the room. She had lovely green hair and green eyes, and she bowed low before Dorothy as she said, "Follow me and I will show you your room."

So Dorothy said good-bye to all her friends except Toto, and taking the dog in her arms followed the green girl through seven passages and up three flights of stairs until they came to a room at the front of the Palace. It was the sweetest little room in the world, with a soft comfortable bed that had sheets of green silk and a green velvet counterpane. There was a tiny fountain in the middle of the room, that shot a spray of green perfume into the air, to fall back into a beautifully carved green marble basin. Beautiful green flowers stood in the windows, and there was a shelf with a row of little green books. When Dorothy had time to open these books she found them full of queer green pictures that made her laugh, they were so funny.

In a wardrobe were many green dresses, made of silk and satin and velvet; and all of them fitted Dorothy exactly.

"Make yourself perfectly at home," said the green girl, "and if you wish for anything ring the bell. Oz will send for you tomorrow morning."

She left Dorothy alone and went back to the others. These she also led to rooms, and each one of them found himself lodged in a very pleasant part of the Palace. Of course this politeness was wasted on the Scarecrow; for when he found himself alone in his room he stood stupidly in one spot, just within the doorway, to wait till morning. It would not rest him to lie down, and he could not close his eyes; so he remained all night staring at a little spider which was weaving its web in a corner of the room, just as if it were not one of the most wonderful rooms in the world. The Tin Woodman lay down on his bed from force of habit, for he remembered when he was made of flesh; but not being able to sleep, he passed the night moving his joints up and down to make sure they kept in good working order. The Lion would have preferred a bed of dried leaves in the forest, and did not like being shut up in a room; but he had too much sense to let this worry him, so he sprang upon the bed and rolled himself up like a cat and purred himself asleep in a minute.

The next morning, after breakfast, the green maiden came to fetch Dorothy, and she dressed her in one of the prettiest gowns, made of green brocaded satin. Dorothy put on a green silk apron and tied a green ribbon around Toto's neck, and they started for the Throne Room of the Great Oz.

First they came to a great hall in which were many ladies and gentlemen of the court, all dressed in rich costumes. These people had nothing to do but talk to each other, but they always came to wait outside the Throne Room every morning, although they were never permitted to see Oz. As Dorothy entered they looked at her curiously, and one of them whispered:

"Are you really going to look upon the face of Oz the Terrible?"

"Of course," answered the girl, "if he will see me."

"Oh, he will see you," said the soldier who had taken her message to the Wizard, "although he does not like to have people ask to see him. Indeed, at first he was angry and said I should send you back where you came from. Then he asked me what you looked like, and when I mentioned your silver shoes he was very much interested. At last I told him about the mark upon your forehead, and he decided he would admit you to his presence."

Just then a bell rang, and the green girl said to Dorothy, "That is the signal. You must go into the Throne Room alone."

She opened a little door and Dorothy walked boldly through and found herself in a wonderful place. It was a big, round room with a high arched roof, and the walls and ceiling and floor were covered with large emeralds set closely together. In the center of the roof was a great light, as bright as the sun, which made the emeralds sparkle in a wonderful manner.

But what interested Dorothy most was the big throne of green marble that stood in the middle of the room. It was shaped like a chair and sparkled with gems, as did everything else. In the center of the chair was an enormous Head, without a body to support it or any arms or legs whatever. There was no hair upon this head, but it had eyes and a nose and mouth, and was much bigger than the head of the biggest giant.

As Dorothy gazed upon this in wonder and fear, the eyes turned slowly and looked at her sharply and steadily. Then the mouth moved, and Dorothy heard a voice say:

"I am Oz, the Great and Terrible. Who are you, and why do you seek me?"

It was not such an awful voice as she had expected to come from the big Head; so she took courage and answered:

"I am Dorothy, the Small and Meek. I have come to you for help."

The eyes looked at her thoughtfully for a full minute. Then said the voice:

"Where did you get the silver shoes?"

"I got them from the Wicked Witch of the East, when my house fell on her and killed her," she replied.

"Where did you get the mark upon your forehead?" continued the voice.

"That is where the Good Witch of the North kissed me when she bade me good-bye and sent me to you," said the girl.

Again the eyes looked at her sharply, and they saw she was telling the truth. Then Oz asked, "What do you wish me to do?"

"Send me back to Kansas, where my Aunt Em and Uncle Henry are," she answered earnestly. "I don't like your country, although it is so beautiful. And I am sure Aunt Em will be dreadfully worried over my being away so long."

The eyes winked three times, and then they turned up to the ceiling and down to the floor and rolled around so queerly that they seemed to see every part of the room. And at last they looked at Dorothy again.

"Why should I do this for you?" asked Oz.

"Because you are strong and I am weak; because you are a Great Wizard and I am only a little girl."

"But you were strong enough to kill the Wicked Witch of the East," said Oz.

"That just happened," returned Dorothy simply; "I could not help it."

"Well," said the Head, "I will give you my answer. You have no right to expect me to send you back to Kansas unless you do something for me in return. In this country everyone must pay for everything he gets. If you wish me to use my magic power to send you home again you must do something for me first. Help me and I will help you."

"What must I do?" asked the girl.

"Kill the Wicked Witch of the West," answered Oz.

"But I cannot!" exclaimed Dorothy, greatly surprised.

"You killed the Witch of the East and you wear the silver shoes, which bear a powerful charm. There is now but one Wicked Witch left in all this land, and when you can tell me she is dead I will send you back to Kansas—but not before."

The little girl began to weep, she was so much disappointed; and the eyes winked again and looked upon her anxiously, as if the Great Oz felt that she could help him if she would.

"I never killed anything, willingly," she sobbed. "Even if I wanted to, how could I kill the Wicked Witch? If you, who are Great and Terrible, cannot kill her yourself, how do you expect me to do it?"

"I do not know," said the Head; "but that is my answer, and until the Wicked Witch dies you will not see your uncle and aunt again. Remember that the Witch is Wicked—tremendously Wicked -and ought to be killed. Now go, and do not ask to see me again until you have done your task."

Sorrowfully Dorothy left the Throne Room and went back where the Lion and the Scarecrow and the Tin Woodman were waiting to hear what Oz had said to her. "There is no hope for me," she said sadly, "for Oz will not send me home until I have killed the Wicked Witch of the West; and that I can never do."

Her friends were sorry, but could do nothing to help her; so Dorothy went to her own room and lay down on the bed and cried herself to sleep.

The next morning the soldier with the green whiskers came to the Scarecrow and said:

"Come with me, for Oz has sent for you."

So the Scarecrow followed him and was admitted into the great Throne Room, where he saw, sitting in the emerald throne, a most lovely Lady. She was dressed in green silk gauze and wore upon her flowing green locks a crown of jewels. Growing from her shoulders were wings, gorgeous in color and so light that they fluttered if the slightest breath of air reached them.

When the Scarecrow had bowed, as prettily as his straw stuffing would let him, before this beautiful creature, she looked upon him sweetly, and said:

"I am Oz, the Great and Terrible. Who are you, and why do you seek me?"

Now the Scarecrow, who had expected to see the great Head Dorothy had told him of, was much astonished; but he answered her bravely.

"I am only a Scarecrow, stuffed with straw. Therefore I have no brains, and I come to you praying that you will put brains in my head instead of straw, so that I may become as much a man as any other in your dominions."

"Why should I do this for you?" asked the Lady.

"Because you are wise and powerful, and no one else can help me," answered the Scarecrow.

"I never grant favors without some return," said Oz; "but this much I will promise. If you will kill for me the Wicked Witch of the West, I will bestow upon you a great many brains, and such good brains that you will be the wisest man in all the Land of Oz."

"I thought you asked Dorothy to kill the Witch," said the Scarecrow, in surprise.

"So I did. I don't care who kills her. But until she is dead I will not grant your wish. Now go, and do not seek me again until you have earned the brains you so greatly desire."

The Scarecrow went sorrowfully back to his friends and told them what Oz had said; and Dorothy was surprised to find that the Great Wizard was not a Head, as she had seen him, but a lovely Lady.

"All the same," said the Scarecrow, "she needs a heart as much as the Tin Woodman."

On the next morning the soldier with the green whiskers came to the Tin Woodman and said:

"Oz has sent for you. Follow me."

So the Tin Woodman followed him and came to the great Throne Room. He did not know whether he would find Oz a lovely Lady or a Head, but he hoped it would be the lovely Lady. "For," he said to himself, "if it is the head, I am sure I shall not be given a heart, since a head has no heart of its own and therefore cannot feel for me. But if it is the lovely Lady I shall beg hard for a heart, for all ladies are themselves said to be kindly hearted.

But when the Woodman entered the great Throne Room he saw neither the Head nor the Lady, for Oz had taken the shape of a most terrible Beast. It was nearly as big as an elephant, and the green throne seemed hardly strong enough to hold its weight. The Beast had a head like that of a rhinoceros, only there were five eyes in its face. There were five long arms growing out of its body, and it also had five long, slim legs. Thick, woolly hair covered every part of it, and a more dreadful-looking monster could not be imagined. It was fortunate the Tin Woodman had no heart at that moment, for it would have beat loud and fast from terror. But being only tin, the Woodman was not at all afraid, although he was much disappointed.

"I am Oz, the Great and Terrible," spoke the Beast, in a voice that was one great roar. "Who are you, and why do you seek me?"

"I am a Woodman, and made of tin. Therefore I have no heart, and cannot love. I pray you to give me a heart that I may be as other men are."

"Why should I do this?" demanded the Beast.

"Because I ask it, and you alone can grant my request," answered the Woodman.

Oz gave a low growl at this, but said, gruffly: "If you indeed desire a heart, you must earn it."

"How?" asked the Woodman.

"Help Dorothy to kill the Wicked Witch of the West," replied the Beast. "When the Witch is dead, come to me, and I will then give you the biggest and kindest and most loving heart in all the Land of Oz."

So the Tin Woodman was forced to return sorrowfully to his friends and tell them of the terrible Beast he had seen. They all wondered greatly at the many forms the Great Wizard could take upon himself, and the Lion said:

"If he is a Beast when I go to see him, I shall roar my loudest, and so frighten him that he will grant all I ask. And if he is the lovely Lady, I shall pretend to spring upon her, and so compel her to do my bidding. And if he is the great Head, he will be at my mercy; for I will roll this head all about the room until he promises to give us what we desire. So be of good cheer, my friends, for all will yet be well."

The next morning the soldier with the green whiskers led the Lion to the great Throne Room and bade him enter the presence of Oz.

The Lion at once passed through the door, and glancing around saw, to his surprise, that before the throne was a Ball of Fire, so fierce and glowing he could scarcely bear to gaze upon it. His first thought was that Oz had by accident caught on fire and was burning up; but when he tried to go nearer, the heat was so intense that it singed his whiskers, and he crept back tremblingly to a spot nearer the door.

Then a low, quiet voice came from the Ball of Fire, and these were the words it spoke:

"I am Oz, the Great and Terrible. Who are you, and why do you seek me?"

And the Lion answered, "I am a Cowardly Lion, afraid of everything. I came to you to beg that you give me courage, so that in reality I may become the King of Beasts, as men call me."

"Why should I give you courage?" demanded Oz.

"Because of all Wizards you are the greatest, and alone have power to grant my request," answered the Lion.

The Ball of Fire burned fiercely for a time, and the voice said, "Bring me proof that the Wicked Witch is dead, and that moment I will give you courage. But as long as the Witch lives, you must remain a coward."

The Lion was angry at this speech, but could say nothing in reply, and while he stood silently gazing at the Ball of Fire it became so furiously hot that he turned tail and rushed from the room. He was glad to find his friends waiting for him, and told them of his terrible interview with the Wizard.

"What shall we do now?" asked Dorothy sadly.

"There is only one thing we can do," returned the Lion, "and that is to go to the land of the Winkies, seek out the Wicked Witch, and destroy her."

"But suppose we cannot?" said the girl.

"Then I shall never have courage," declared the Lion.

"And I shall never have brains," added the Scarecrow.

"And I shall never have a heart," spoke the Tin of Woodman.

"And I shall never see Aunt Em and Uncle Henry," said Dorothy, beginning to cry.

"Be careful!" cried the green girl. "The tears will fall on your green silk gown and spot it."

So Dorothy dried her eyes and said, "I suppose we must try it; but I am sure I do not want to kill anybody, even to see Aunt Em again."

"I will go with you; but I'm too much of a coward to kill the Witch," said the Lion.

"I will go too," declared the Scarecrow; "but I shall not be of much help to you, I am such a fool."

"I haven't the heart to harm even a Witch," remarked the Tin Woodman; "but if you go I certainly shall go with you."

Therefore it was decided to start upon their journey the next morning, and the Woodman sharpened his axe on a green grindstone and had all his joints properly oiled. The Scarecrow stuffed himself with fresh straw and Dorothy put new paint on his eyes that he might see better. The green girl, who was very kind to them, filled Dorothy's basket with good things to eat, and fastened a little bell around Toto's neck with a green ribbon.

They went to bed quite early and slept soundly until daylight, when they were awakened by the crowing of a green cock that lived in the back yard of the Palace, and the cackling of a hen that had laid a green egg.

Chapter 12 - The Search for the Wicked Witch

The soldier with the green whiskers led them through the streets of the Emerald City until they reached the room where the Guardian of the Gates lived. This officer unlocked their spectacles to put them back in his great box, and then he politely opened the gate for our friends.

"Which road leads to the Wicked Witch of the West?" asked Dorothy.

"There is no road," answered the Guardian of the Gates. "No one ever wishes to go that way."

"How, then, are we to find her?" inquired the girl.

"That will be easy," replied the man, "for when she knows you are in the country of the Winkies she will find you, and make you all her slaves."

"Perhaps not," said the Scarecrow, "for we mean to destroy her."

"Oh, that is different," said the Guardian of the Gates. "No one has ever destroyed her before, so I naturally thought she would make slaves of you, as she has of the rest. But take care; for she is wicked and fierce, and may not allow you to destroy her. Keep to the West, where the sun sets, and you cannot fail to find her."

They thanked him and bade him good-bye, and turned toward the West, walking over fields of soft grass dotted here and there with daisies and buttercups. Dorothy still wore the pretty silk dress she had put on in the palace, but now, to her surprise, she found it was no longer green, but pure white. The ribbon around Toto's neck had also lost its green color and was as white as Dorothy's dress.

The Emerald City was soon left far behind. As they advanced the ground became rougher and hillier, for there were no farms nor houses in this country of the West, and the ground was untilled.

In the afternoon the sun shone hot in their faces, for there were no trees to offer them shade; so that before night Dorothy and Toto and the Lion were tired, and lay down upon the grass and fell asleep, with the Woodman and the Scarecrow keeping watch.

Now the Wicked Witch of the West had but one eye, yet that was as powerful as a telescope, and could see everywhere. So, as she sat in the door of her castle, she happened to look around and saw Dorothy lying asleep, with her friends all about her. They were a long distance off, but the Wicked Witch was angry to find them in her country; so she blew upon a silver whistle that hung around her neck.

At once there came running to her from all directions a pack of great wolves. They had long legs and fierce eyes and sharp teeth.

"Go to those people," said the Witch, "and tear them to pieces."

"Are you not going to make them your slaves?" asked the leader of the wolves.

"No," she answered, "one is of tin, and one of straw; one is a girl and another a Lion. None of them is fit to work, so you may tear them into small pieces."

"Very well," said the wolf, and he dashed away at full speed, followed by the others.

It was lucky the Scarecrow and the Woodman were wide awake and heard the wolves coming.

"This is my fight," said the Woodman, "so get behind me and I will meet them as they come."

He seized his axe, which he had made very sharp, and as the leader of the wolves came on the Tin Woodman swung his arm and chopped the wolf's head from its body, so that it immediately died. As soon as he could raise his axe another wolf came up, and he also fell under the sharp edge of the Tin Woodman's weapon. There were forty wolves, and forty times a wolf was killed, so that at last they all lay dead in a heap before the Woodman.

Then he put down his axe and sat beside the Scarecrow, who said, "It was a good fight, friend."

They waited until Dorothy awoke the next morning. The little girl was quite frightened when she saw the great pile of shaggy wolves, but the Tin Woodman told her all. She thanked him for saving them and sat down to breakfast, after which they started again upon their journey.

Now this same morning the Wicked Witch came to the door of her castle and looked out with her one eye that could see far off. She saw all her wolves lying dead, and the strangers still traveling through her country. This made her angrier than before, and she blew her silver whistle twice.

Straightway a great flock of wild crows came flying toward her, enough to darken the sky.

And the Wicked Witch said to the King Crow, "Fly at once to the strangers; peck out their eyes and tear them to pieces."

The wild crows flew in one great flock toward Dorothy and her companions. When the little girl saw them coming she was afraid.

But the Scarecrow said, "This is my battle, so lie down beside me and you will not be harmed."

So they all lay upon the ground except the Scarecrow, and he stood up and stretched out his arms. And when the crows saw him they were frightened, as these birds always are by scarecrows, and did not dare to come any nearer. But the King Crow said:

"It is only a stuffed man. I will peck his eyes out."

The King Crow flew at the Scarecrow, who caught it by the head and twisted its neck until it died. And then another crow flew at him, and the Scarecrow twisted its neck also. There were forty crows, and forty times the Scarecrow twisted a neck, until at last all were lying dead beside him. Then he called to his companions to rise, and again they went upon their journey.

When the Wicked Witch looked out again and saw all her crows lying in a heap, she got into a terrible rage, and blew three times upon her silver whistle.

Forthwith there was heard a great buzzing in the air, and a swarm of black bees came flying toward her.

"Go to the strangers and sting them to death!" commanded the Witch, and the bees turned and flew rapidly until they came to where Dorothy and her friends were walking. But the Woodman had seen them coming, and the Scarecrow had decided what to do.

"Take out my straw and scatter it over the little girl and the dog and the Lion," he said to the Woodman, "and the bees cannot sting them." This the Woodman did, and as Dorothy lay close beside the Lion and held Toto in her arms, the straw covered them entirely.

The bees came and found no one but the Woodman to sting, so they flew at him and broke off all their stings against the tin, without hurting the Woodman at all. And as bees cannot live when their stings are broken that was the end of the black bees, and they lay scattered thick about the Woodman, like little heaps of fine coal.

Then Dorothy and the Lion got up, and the girl helped the Tin Woodman put the straw back into the Scarecrow again, until he was as good as ever. So they started upon their journey once more.

The Wicked Witch was so angry when she saw her black bees in little heaps like fine coal that she stamped her foot and tore her hair and gnashed her teeth. And then she called a dozen of her slaves, who were the Winkies, and gave them sharp spears, telling them to go to the strangers and destroy them.

The Winkies were not a brave people, but they had to do as they were told. So they marched away until they came near to Dorothy. Then the Lion gave a great roar and sprang towards them, and the poor Winkies were so frightened that they ran back as fast as they could.

When they returned to the castle the Wicked Witch beat them well with a strap, and sent them back to their work, after which she sat down to think what she should do next. She could not understand how all her plans to destroy these strangers had failed; but she was a powerful Witch, as well as a wicked one, and she soon made up her mind how to act.

There was, in her cupboard, a Golden Cap, with a circle of diamonds and rubies running round it. This Golden Cap had a charm. Whoever owned it could call three times upon the Winged Monkeys, who would obey any order they were given. But no person could command these strange creatures more than three times. Twice already the Wicked Witch had used the charm of the Cap. Once was when she had made the Winkies her slaves, and set herself to rule over their country. The Winged Monkeys had helped her do this. The second time was when she had fought against the Great Oz himself, and driven him out of the land of the West. The Winged Monkeys had also helped her in doing this. Only once more could she use this Golden Cap, for which reason she did not like to do so until all her other powers were exhausted. But now that her fierce wolves and her wild crows and her stinging bees were gone, and her slaves had been scared away by the Cowardly Lion, she saw there was only one way left to destroy Dorothy and her friends.

So the Wicked Witch took the Golden Cap from her cupboard and placed it upon her head. Then she stood upon her left foot and said slowly:

"Ep-pe, pep-pe, kak-ke!"

Next she stood upon her right foot and said:

"Hil-lo, hol-lo, hel-lo!"

After this she stood upon both feet and cried in a loud voice:

"Ziz-zy, zuz-zy, zik!"

Now the charm began to work. The sky was darkened, and a low rumbling sound was heard in the air. There was a rushing of many wings, a great chattering and laughing, and the sun came out of the dark sky to show the Wicked Witch surrounded by a crowd of monkeys, each with a pair of immense and powerful wings on his shoulders.

One, much bigger than the others, seemed to be their leader. He flew close to the Witch and said, "You have called us for the third and last time. What do you command?"

"Go to the strangers who are within my land and destroy them all except the Lion," said the Wicked Witch. "Bring that beast to me, for I have a mind to harness him like a horse, and make him work."

"Your commands shall be obeyed," said the leader. Then, with a great deal of chattering and noise, the Winged Monkeys flew away to the place where Dorothy and her friends were walking.

Some of the Monkeys seized the Tin Woodman and carried him through the air until they were over a country thickly covered with sharp rocks. Here they dropped the poor Woodman, who fell a great distance to the rocks, where he lay so battered and dented that he could neither move nor groan.

Others of the Monkeys caught the Scarecrow, and with their long fingers pulled all of the straw out of his clothes and head. They made his hat and boots and clothes into a small bundle and threw it into the top branches of a tall tree.

The remaining Monkeys threw pieces of stout rope around the Lion and wound many coils about his body and head and legs, until he was unable to bite or scratch or struggle in any way. Then they lifted him up and flew away with him to the Witch's castle, where he was placed in a small yard with a high iron fence around it, so that he could not escape.

But Dorothy they did not harm at all. She stood, with Toto in her arms, watching the sad fate of her comrades and thinking it would soon be her turn. The leader of the Winged Monkeys flew up to her, his long, hairy arms stretched out and his ugly face grinning terribly; but he saw the mark of the Good Witch's kiss upon her forehead and stopped short, motioning the others not to touch her.

"We dare not harm this little girl," he said to them, "for she is protected by the Power of Good, and that is greater than the Power of Evil. All we can do is to carry her to the castle of the Wicked Witch and leave her there."

So, carefully and gently, they lifted Dorothy in their arms and carried her swiftly through the air until they came to the castle, where they set her down upon the front doorstep. Then the leader said to the Witch:

"We have obeyed you as far as we were able. The Tin Woodman and the Scarecrow are destroyed, and the Lion is tied up in your yard. The little girl we dare not harm, nor the dog she carries in her arms. Your power over our band is now ended, and you will never see us again."

Then all the Winged Monkeys, with much laughing and chattering and noise, flew into the air and were soon out of sight.

The Wicked Witch was both surprised and worried when she saw the mark on Dorothy's forehead, for she knew well that neither the Winged Monkeys nor she, herself, dare hurt the girl in any way. She looked down at Dorothy's feet, and seeing the Silver Shoes, began to tremble with fear, for she knew what a powerful charm belonged to them. At first the Witch was tempted to run away from Dorothy; but she happened to look into the child's eyes and saw how simple the soul behind them was, and that the little girl did not know of the wonderful power the Silver Shoes gave her. So the Wicked Witch laughed to herself, and thought, "I can still make her my slave, for she does not know how to use her power." Then she said to Dorothy, harshly and severely:

"Come with me; and see that you mind everything I tell you, for if you do not I will make an end of you, as I did of the Tin Woodman and the Scarecrow."

Dorothy followed her through many of the beautiful rooms in her castle until they came to the kitchen, where the Witch bade her clean the pots and kettles and sweep the floor and keep the fire fed with wood.

Dorothy went to work meekly, with her mind made up to work as hard as she could; for she was glad the Wicked Witch had decided not to kill her.

With Dorothy hard at work, the Witch thought she would go into the courtyard and harness the Cowardly Lion like a horse; it would amuse her, she was sure, to make him draw her chariot whenever she wished to go to drive. But as she opened the gate the Lion gave a loud roar and bounded at her so fiercely that the Witch was afraid, and ran out and shut the gate again.

"If I cannot harness you," said the Witch to the Lion, speaking through the bars of the gate, "I can starve you. You shall have nothing to eat until you do as I wish."

So after that she took no food to the imprisoned Lion; but every day she came to the gate at noon and asked, "Are you ready to be harnessed like a horse?"

And the Lion would answer, "No. If you come in this yard, I will bite you."

The reason the Lion did not have to do as the Witch wished was that every night, while the woman was asleep, Dorothy carried him food from the cupboard. After he had eaten he would lie down on his bed of straw, and Dorothy would lie beside him and put her head on his soft, shaggy mane, while they talked of their troubles and tried to plan some way to escape. But they could find no way to get out of the castle, for it was constantly guarded by the yellow Winkies, who were the slaves of the Wicked Witch and too afraid of her not to do as she told them.

The girl had to work hard during the day, and often the Witch threatened to beat her with the same old umbrella she always carried in her hand. But, in truth, she did not dare to strike Dorothy, because of the mark upon her forehead. The child did not know this, and was full of fear for herself and Toto. Once the Witch struck Toto a blow with her umbrella and the brave little dog flew at her and bit her leg in return. The Witch did not bleed where she was bitten, for she was so wicked that the blood in her had dried up many years before.

Dorothy's life became very sad as she grew to understand that it would be harder than ever to get back to Kansas and Aunt Em again. Sometimes she would cry bitterly for hours, with Toto sitting at her feet and looking into her face, whining dismally to show how sorry he was for his little mistress. Toto did not really care whether he was in Kansas or the Land of Oz so long as Dorothy was with him; but he knew the little girl was unhappy, and that made him unhappy too.

Now the Wicked Witch had a great longing to have for her own the Silver Shoes which the girl always wore. Her bees and her crows and her wolves were lying in heaps and drying up, and she had used up all the power of the Golden Cap; but if she could only get hold of the Silver Shoes, they would give her more power than all the other things she had lost. She watched Dorothy carefully, to see if she ever took off her shoes, thinking she might steal them. But the child was so proud of her pretty shoes that she never took them off except at night and when she took her bath. The Witch was too much afraid of the dark to dare go in Dorothy's room at night to take the shoes, and her dread of water was greater than her fear of the dark, so she never came near when Dorothy was bathing. Indeed, the old Witch never touched water, nor ever let water touch her in any way.

But the wicked creature was very cunning, and she finally thought of a trick that would give her what she wanted. She placed a bar of iron in the middle of the kitchen floor, and then by her magic arts made the iron invisible to human eyes. So that when Dorothy walked across the floor she stumbled over the bar, not being able to see it, and fell at full length. She was not much hurt, but in her fall one of the Silver Shoes came off; and before she could reach it, the Witch had snatched it away and put it on her own skinny foot.

The wicked woman was greatly pleased with the success of her trick, for as long as she had one of the shoes she owned half the power of their charm, and Dorothy could not use it against her, even had she known how to do so.

The little girl, seeing she had lost one of her pretty shoes, grew angry, and said to the Witch, "Give me back my shoe!"

"I will not," retorted the Witch, "for it is now my shoe, and not yours."

"You are a wicked creature!" cried Dorothy. "You have no right to take my shoe from me."

"I shall keep it, just the same," said the Witch, laughing at her, "and someday I shall get the other one from you, too."

This made Dorothy so very angry that she picked up the bucket of water that stood near and dashed it over the Witch, wetting her from head to foot.

Instantly the wicked woman gave a loud cry of fear, and then, as Dorothy looked at her in wonder, the Witch began to shrink and fall away.

"See what you have done!" she screamed. "In a minute I shall melt away."

"I'm very sorry, indeed," said Dorothy, who was truly frightened to see the Witch actually melting away like brown sugar before her very eyes.

"Didn't you know water would be the end of me?" asked the Witch, in a wailing, despairing voice.

"Of course not," answered Dorothy. "How should I?"

"Well, in a few minutes I shall be all melted, and you will have the castle to yourself. I have been wicked in my day, but I never thought a little girl like you would ever be able to melt me and end my wicked deeds. Look out—here I go!"

With these words the Witch fell down in a brown, melted, shapeless mass and began to spread over the clean boards of the kitchen floor. Seeing that she had really melted away to nothing, Dorothy drew another bucket of water and threw it over the mess. She then swept it all out the door. After picking out the silver shoe, which was all that was left of the old woman, she cleaned and dried it with a cloth, and put it on her foot again. Then, being at last free to do as she chose, she ran out to the courtyard to tell the Lion that the Wicked Witch of the West had come to an end, and that they were no longer prisoners in a strange land.

Chapter 13 - The Rescue

The Cowardly Lion was much pleased to hear that the Wicked Witch had been melted by a bucket of water, and Dorothy at once unlocked the gate of his prison and set him free. They went in together to the castle, where Dorothy's first act was to call all the Winkies together and tell them that they were no longer slaves.

There was great rejoicing among the yellow Winkies, for they had been made to work hard during many years for the Wicked Witch, who had always treated them with great cruelty. They kept this day as a holiday, then and ever after, and spent the time in feasting and dancing.

"If our friends, the Scarecrow and the Tin Woodman, were only with us," said the Lion, "I should be quite happy."

"Don't you suppose we could rescue them?" asked the girl anxiously.

"We can try," answered the Lion.

So they called the yellow Winkies and asked them if they would help to rescue their friends, and the Winkies said that they would be delighted to do all in their power for Dorothy, who had set them free from bondage. So she chose a number of the Winkies who looked as if they knew the most, and they all started away. They traveled that day and part of the next until they came to the rocky plain where the Tin Woodman lay, all battered and bent. His axe was near him, but the blade was rusted and the handle broken off short.

The Winkies lifted him tenderly in their arms, and carried him back to the Yellow Castle again, Dorothy shedding a few tears by the way at the sad plight of her old friend, and the Lion looking sober and sorry. When they reached the castle Dorothy said to the Winkies:

"Are any of your people tinsmiths?"

"Oh, yes. Some of us are very good tinsmiths," they told her.

"Then bring them to me," she said. And when the tinsmiths came, bringing with them all their tools in baskets, she inquired, "Can you straighten out those dents in the Tin Woodman, and bend him back into shape again, and solder him together where he is broken?"

The tinsmiths looked the Woodman over carefully and then answered that they thought they could mend him so he would be as good as ever. So they set to work in one of the big yellow rooms of the castle and worked for three days and four nights, hammering and twisting and bending and soldering and polishing and pounding at the legs and body and head of the Tin Woodman, until at last he was straightened out into his old form, and his joints worked as well as ever. To be sure, there were several patches on him, but the tinsmiths did a good job, and as the Woodman was not a vain man he did not mind the patches at all.

When, at last, he walked into Dorothy's room and thanked her for rescuing him, he was so pleased that he wept tears of joy, and Dorothy had to wipe every tear carefully from his face with her apron, so his joints would not be rusted. At the same time her own tears fell thick and fast at the joy of meeting her old friend again, and these tears did not need to be wiped away. As for the Lion, he wiped his eyes so often with the tip of his tail that it became quite wet, and he was obliged to go out into the courtyard and hold it in the sun till it dried.

"If we only had the Scarecrow with us again," said the Tin Woodman, when Dorothy had finished telling him everything that had happened, "I should be quite happy."

"We must try to find him," said the girl.

So she called the Winkies to help her, and they walked all that day and part of the next until they came to the tall tree in the branches of which the Winged Monkeys had tossed the carecrow's clothes.

It was a very tall tree, and the trunk was so smooth that no one could climb it; but the Woodman said at once, "I'll chop it down, and then we can get the Scarecrow's clothes."

Now while the tinsmiths had been at work mending the Woodman himself, another of the Winkies, who was a goldsmith, had made an axe-handle of solid gold and fitted it to the Woodman's axe, instead of the old broken handle. Others polished the blade until all the rust was removed and it glistened like burnished silver.

As soon as he had spoken, the Tin Woodman began to chop, and in a short time the tree fell over with a crash, whereupon the Scarecrow's clothes fell out of the branches and rolled off on the ground.

Dorothy picked them up and had the Winkies carry them back to the castle, where they were stuffed with nice, clean straw; and behold! here was the Scarecrow, as good as ever, thanking them over and over again for saving him.

Now that they were reunited, Dorothy and her friends spent a few happy days at the Yellow Castle, where they found everything they needed to make them comfortable.

But one day the girl thought of Aunt Em, and said, "We must go back to Oz, and claim his promise."

"Yes," said the Woodman, "at last I shall get my heart."

"And I shall get my brains," added the Scarecrow joyfully.

"And I shall get my courage," said the Lion thoughtfully.

"And I shall get back to Kansas," cried Dorothy, clapping her hands. "Oh, let us start for the Emerald City tomorrow!"

This they decided to do. The next day they called the Winkies together and bade them good-bye. The Winkies were sorry to have them go, and they had grown so fond of the Tin Woodman that they begged him to stay and rule over them and the Yellow Land of the West. Finding they were determined to go, the Winkies gave Toto and the Lion each a golden collar; and to Dorothy they presented a beautiful bracelet studded with diamonds; and to the Scarecrow they gave a gold-headed walking stick, to keep   him from stumbling; and to the Tin Woodman they offered a silver oil-can, inlaid with gold and set with precious jewels.

Every one of the travelers made the Winkies a pretty speech in return, and all shook hands with them until their arms ached.

Dorothy went to the Witch's cupboard to fill her basket with food for the journey, and there she saw the Golden Cap. She tried it on her own head and found that it fitted her exactly. She did not know anything about the charm of the Golden Cap, but she saw that it was pretty, so she made up her mind to wear it and carry her sunbonnet in the basket.

Then, being prepared for the journey, they all started for the Emerald City; and the Winkies gave them three cheers and many good wishes to carry with them.

Chapter 14 - The Winged Monkeys

You will remember there was no road—not even a pathway—between the castle of the Wicked Witch and the Emerald City. When the four travelers went in search of the Witch she had seen them coming, and so sent the Winged Monkeys to bring them to her. It was much harder to find their way back through the big fields of buttercups and yellow daisies than it was being carried. They knew, of course, they must go straight east, toward the rising sun; and they started off in the right way. But at noon, when the sun was over their heads, they did not know which was east and which was west, and that was the reason they were lost in the great fields. They kept on walking, however, and at night the moon came out and shone brightly. So they lay down among the sweet smelling yellow flowers and slept soundly until morning—all but the Scarecrow and the Tin Woodman.

The next morning the sun was behind a cloud, but they started on, as if they were quite sure which way they were going.

"If we walk far enough," said Dorothy, "I am sure we shall sometime come to some place."

But day by day passed away, and they still saw nothing before them but the scarlet fields. The Scarecrow began to grumble a bit.

"We have surely lost our way," he said, "and unless we find it again in time to reach the Emerald City, I shall never get my brains."

"Nor I my heart," declared the Tin Woodman. "It seems to me I can scarcely wait till I get to Oz, and you must admit this is a very long journey."

"You see," said the Cowardly Lion, with a whimper, "I haven't the courage to keep tramping forever, without getting anywhere at all."

Then Dorothy lost heart. She sat down on the grass and looked at her companions, and they sat down and looked at her, and Toto found that for the first time in his life he was too tired to chase a butterfly that flew past his head. So he put out his tongue and panted and looked at Dorothy as if to ask what they should do next.

"Suppose we call the field mice," she suggested. "They could probably tell us the way to the Emerald City."

"To be sure they could," cried the Scarecrow. "Why didn't we think of that before?"

Dorothy blew the little whistle she had always carried about her neck since the Queen of the Mice had given it to her. In a few minutes they heard the pattering of tiny feet, and many of the small gray mice came running up to her. Among them was the Queen herself, who asked, in her squeaky little voice:

"What can I do for my friends?"

"We have lost our way," said Dorothy. "Can you tell us where the Emerald City is?"

"Certainly," answered the Queen; "but it is a great way off, for you have had it at your backs all this time." Then she noticed Dorothy's Golden Cap, and said, "Why don't you use the charm of the Cap, and call the Winged Monkeys to you? They will carry you to the City of Oz in less than an hour."

"I didn't know there was a charm," answered Dorothy, in surprise. "What is it?"

"It is written inside the Golden Cap," replied the Queen of the Mice. "But if you are going to call the Winged Monkeys we must run away, for they are full of mischief and think it great fun to plague us."

"Won't they hurt me?" asked the girl anxiously.

"Oh, no. They must obey the wearer of the Cap. Good-bye!" And she scampered out of sight, with all the mice hurrying after her.

Dorothy looked inside the Golden Cap and saw some words written upon the lining. These, she thought, must be the charm, so she read the directions carefully and put the Cap upon her head.

"Ep-pe, pep-pe, kak-ke!" she said, standing on her left foot.

"What did you say?" asked the Scarecrow, who did not know what she was doing.

"Hil-lo, hol-lo, hel-lo!" Dorothy went on, standing this time on her right foot.

"Hello!" replied the Tin Woodman calmly.

"Ziz-zy, zuz-zy, zik!" said Dorothy, who was now standing on both feet. This ended the saying of the charm, and they heard a great chattering and flapping of wings, as the band of Winged Monkeys flew up to them.

The King bowed low before Dorothy, and asked, "What is your command?"

"We wish to go to the Emerald City," said the child, "and we have lost our way."

"We will carry you," replied the King, and no sooner had he spoken than two of the Monkeys caught Dorothy in their arms and flew away with her. Others took the Scarecrow and the Woodman and the Lion, and one little Monkey seized Toto and flew after them, although the dog tried hard to bite him.

The Scarecrow and the Tin Woodman were rather frightened at first, for they remembered how badly the Winged Monkeys had treated them before; but they saw that no harm was intended, so they rode through the air quite cheerfully, and had a fine time looking at the pretty gardens and woods far below them.

Dorothy found herself riding easily between two of the biggest Monkeys, one of them the King himself. They had made a chair of their hands and were careful not to hurt her.

"Why do you have to obey the charm of the Golden Cap?" she asked.

"That is a long story," answered the King, with a Winged laugh; "but as we have a long journey before us, I will pass the time by telling you about it, if you wish."

"I shall be glad to hear it," she replied.

"Once," began the leader, "we were a free people, living happily in the great forest, flying from tree to tree, eating nuts and fruit, and doing just as we pleased without calling anybody master. Perhaps some of us were rather too full of mischief at times, flying down to pull the tails of the animals that had no wings, chasing birds, and throwing nuts at the people who walked in the forest. But we were careless and happy and full of fun, and enjoyed every minute of the day. This was many years ago, long before Oz came out of the clouds to rule over this land.

"There lived here then, away at the North, a beautiful princess, who was also a powerful sorceress. All her magic was used to help the people, and she was never known to hurt anyone who was good. Her name was Gayelette, and she lived in a handsome palace built from great blocks of ruby. Everyone loved her, but her greatest sorrow was that she could find no one to love in return, since all the men were much too stupid and ugly to mate with one so beautiful and wise. At last, however, she found a boy who was handsome and manly and wise beyond his years. Gayelette made up her mind that when he grew to be a man she would make him her husband, so she took him to her ruby palace and used all her magic powers to make him as strong and good and lovely as any woman could wish. When he grew to manhood, Quelala, as he was called, was said to be the best and wisest man in all the land, while his manly beauty was so great that Gayelette loved him dearly, and hastened to make everything ready for the wedding.

"My grandfather was at that time the King of the Winged Monkeys which lived in the forest near Gayelette's palace, and the old fellow loved a joke better than a good dinner. One day, just before the wedding, my grandfather was flying out with his band when he saw Quelala walking beside the river. He was dressed in a rich costume of pink silk and purple velvet, and my grandfather thought he would see what he could do. At his word the band flew down and seized Quelala, carried him in their arms until they were over the middle of the river, and then dropped him into the water.

"'Swim out, my fine fellow,' cried my grandfather, `and see if the water has spotted your clothes.' Quelala was much too wise not to swim, and he was not in the least spoiled by all his good fortune. He laughed, when he came to the top of the water, and swam in to shore. But when Gayelette came running out to him she found his silks and velvet all ruined by the river.

"The princess was angry, and she knew, of course, who did it. She had all the Winged Monkeys brought before her, and she said at first that their wings should be tied and they should be treated as they had treated Quelala, and dropped in the river. But my grandfather pleaded hard, for he knew the Monkeys would drown in the river with their wings tied, and Quelala said a kind word for them also; so that Gayelette finally spared them, on condition that the Winged Monkeys should ever after do three times the bidding of the owner of the Golden Cap. This Cap had been made for a wedding present to Quelala, and it is said to have cost the princess half her kingdom. Of course my grandfather and all the other Monkeys at once agreed to the condition, and that is how it happens that we are three times the slaves of the owner of the Golden Cap, whosoever he may be."

"And what became of them?" asked Dorothy, who had been greatly interested in the story.

"Quelala being the first owner of the Golden Cap," replied the Monkey, "he was the first to lay his wishes upon us. As his bride could not bear the sight of us, he called us all to him in the forest after he had married her and ordered us always to keep where she could never again set eyes on a Winged Monkey, which we were glad to do, for we were all afraid of her.

"This was all we ever had to do until the Golden Cap fell into the hands of the Wicked Witch of the West, who made us enslave the Winkies, and afterward drive Oz himself out of the Land of the West. Now the Golden Cap is yours, and three times you have the right to lay your wishes upon us."

As the Monkey King finished his story Dorothy looked down and saw the green, shining walls of the Emerald City before them. She wondered at the rapid flight of the Monkeys, but was glad the journey was over. The strange creatures set the travelers down carefully before the gate of the City, the King bowed low to Dorothy, and then flew swiftly away, followed by all his band.

"That was a good ride," said the little girl.

"Yes, and a quick way out of our troubles," replied the Lion. "How lucky it was you brought away that wonderful Cap!"

Chapter 15 - The Discovery of Oz, the Terrible

The four travelers walked up to the great gate of Emerald City and rang the bell. After ringing several times, it was opened by the same Guardian of the Gates they had met before.

"What! are you back again?" he asked, in surprise.

"Do you not see us?" answered the Scarecrow.

"But I thought you had gone to visit the Wicked Witch of the West."

"We did visit her," said the Scarecrow.

"And she let you go again?" asked the man, in wonder.

"She could not help it, for she is melted," explained the Scarecrow.

"Melted! Well, that is good news, indeed," said the man. "Who melted her?"

"It was Dorothy," said the Lion gravely.

"Good gracious!" exclaimed the man, and he bowed very low indeed before her.

Then he led them into his little room and locked the spectacles from the great box on all their eyes, just as he had done before. Afterward they passed on through the gate into the Emerald City. When the people heard from the Guardian of the Gates that Dorothy had melted the Wicked Witch of the West, they all gathered around the travelers and followed them in a great crowd to the Palace of Oz.

The soldier with the green whiskers was still on guard before the door, but he let them in at once, and they were again met by the beautiful green girl, who showed each of them to their old rooms at once, so they might rest until the Great Oz was ready to receive them.

The soldier had the news carried straight to Oz that Dorothy and the other travelers had come back again, after destroying the Wicked Witch; but Oz made no reply. They thought the Great Wizard would send for them at once, but he did not. They had no word from him the next day, nor the next, nor the next. The waiting was tiresome and wearing, and at last they grew vexed that Oz should treat them in so poor a fashion, after sending them to undergo hardships and slavery. So the Scarecrow at last asked the green girl to take another message to Oz, saying if he did not let them in to see him at once they would call the Winged Monkeys to help them, and find out whether he kept his promises or not. When the Wizard was given this message he was so frightened that he sent word for them to come to the Throne Room at four minutes after nine o'clock the next morning. He had once met the Winged Monkeys in the Land of the West, and he did not wish to meet them again.

The four travelers passed a sleepless night, each thinking of the gift Oz had promised to bestow on him. Dorothy fell asleep only once, and then she dreamed she was in Kansas, where Aunt Em was telling her how glad she was to have her little girl at home again.

Promptly at nine o'clock the next morning the green-whiskered soldier came to them, and four minutes later they all went into the Throne Room of the Great Oz.

Of course each one of them expected to see the Wizard in the shape he had taken before, and all were greatly surprised when they looked about and saw no one at all in the room. They kept close to the door and closer to one another, for the stillness of the empty room was more dreadful than any of the forms they had seen Oz take.

Presently they heard a solemn Voice, that seemed to come from somewhere near the top of the great dome, and it said:

"I am Oz, the Great and Terrible. Why do you seek me?"

They looked again in every part of the room, and then, seeing no one, Dorothy asked, "Where are you?"

"I am everywhere," answered the Voice, "but to the eyes of common mortals I am invisible. I will now seat myself upon my throne, that you may converse with me." Indeed, the Voice seemed just then to come straight from the throne itself; so they walked toward it and stood in a row while Dorothy said:

"We have come to claim our promise, O Oz."

"What promise?" asked Oz.

"You promised to send me back to Kansas when the Wicked Witch was destroyed," said the girl.

"And you promised to give me brains," said the Scarecrow.

"And you promised to give me a heart," said the Tin Woodman.

"And you promised to give me courage," said the Cowardly Lion.

"Is the Wicked Witch really destroyed?" asked the Voice, and Dorothy thought it trembled a little.

"Yes," she answered, "I melted her with a bucket of water."

"Dear me," said the Voice, "how sudden! Well, come to me tomorrow, for I must have time to think it over."

"You've had plenty of time already," said the Tin Woodman angrily.

"We shan't wait a day longer," said the Scarecrow.

"You must keep your promises to us!" exclaimed Dorothy.

The Lion thought it might be as well to frighten the Wizard, so he gave a large, loud roar, which was so fierce and dreadful that Toto jumped away from him in alarm and tipped over the screen that stood in a corner. As it fell with a crash they looked that way, and the next moment all of them were filled with wonder. For they saw, standing in just the spot the screen had hidden, a little old man, with a bald head and a wrinkled face, who seemed to be as much surprised as they were. The Tin Woodman, raising his axe, rushed toward the little man and cried out, "Who are you?"

"I am Oz, the Great and Terrible," said the little man, in a trembling voice. "But don't strike me—please don't—and I'll do anything you want me to."

Our friends looked at him in surprise and dismay.

"I thought Oz was a great Head," said Dorothy.

"And I thought Oz was a lovely Lady," said the Scarecrow.

"And I thought Oz was a terrible Beast," said the Tin Woodman.

"And I thought Oz was a Ball of Fire," exclaimed the Lion.

"No, you are all wrong," said the little man meekly. "I have been making believe."

"Making believe!" cried Dorothy. "Are you not a Great Wizard?"

"Hush, my dear," he said. "Don't speak so loud, or you will be overheard—and I should be ruined. I'm supposed to be a Great Wizard."

"And aren't you?" she asked.

"Not a bit of it, my dear; I'm just a common man."

"You're more than that," said the Scarecrow, in a grieved tone; "you're a humbug."

"Exactly so!" declared the little man, rubbing his hands together as if it pleased him. "I am a humbug."

"But this is terrible," said the Tin Woodman. "How shall I ever get my heart?"

"Or I my courage?" asked the Lion.

"Or I my brains?" wailed the Scarecrow, wiping the tears from his eyes with his coat sleeve.

"My dear friends," said Oz, "I pray you not to speak of these little things. Think of me, and the terrible trouble I'm in at being found out."

"Doesn't anyone else know you're a humbug?" asked Dorothy.

"No one knows it but you four—and myself," replied Oz. "I have fooled everyone so long that I thought I should never be found out. It was a great mistake my ever letting you into the Throne Room. Usually I will not see even my subjects, and so they believe I am something terrible."

"But, I don't understand," said Dorothy, in bewilderment. "How was it that you appeared to me as a great Head?"

"That was one of my tricks," answered Oz. "Step this way, please, and I will tell you all about it."

He led the way to a small chamber in the rear of the Throne Room, and they all followed him. He pointed to one corner, in which lay the great Head, made out of many thicknesses of paper, and with a carefully painted face.

"This I hung from the ceiling by a wire," said Oz. "I stood behind the screen and pulled a thread, to make the eyes move and the mouth open."

"But how about the voice?" she inquired.

"Oh, I am a ventriloquist," said the little man. "I can throw the sound of my voice wherever I wish, so that you thought it was coming out of the Head. Here are the other things I used to deceive you." He showed the Scarecrow the dress and the mask he had worn when he seemed to be the lovely Lady. And the Tin Woodman saw that his terrible Beast was nothing but a lot of skins, sewn together, with slats to keep their sides out. As for the Ball of Fire, the false Wizard had hung that also from the ceiling. It was really a ball of cotton, but when oil was poured upon it the ball burned fiercely.

"Really," said the Scarecrow, "you ought to be ashamed of yourself for being such a humbug."

"I am—I certainly am," answered the little man sorrowfully; "but it was the only thing I could do. Sit down, please, there are plenty of chairs; and I will tell you my story."

So they sat down and listened while he told the following tale.

"I was born in Omaha—"

"Why, that isn't very far from Kansas!" cried Dorothy.

"No, but it's farther from here," he said, shaking his head at her sadly. "When I grew up I became a ventriloquist, and at that I was very well trained by a great master. I can imitate any kind of a bird or beast." Here he mewed so like a kitten that Toto pricked up his ears and looked everywhere to see where she was. "After a time," continued Oz, "I tired of that, and became a balloonist."

"What is that?" asked Dorothy.

"A man who goes up in a balloon on circus day, so as to draw a crowd of people together and get them to pay to see the circus," he explained.

"Oh," she said, "I know."

"Well, one day I went up in a balloon and the ropes got twisted, so that I couldn't come down again. It went way up above the clouds, so far that a current of air struck it and carried it many, many miles away. For a day and a night I traveled through the air, and on the morning of the second day I awoke and found the balloon floating over a strange and beautiful country.

"It came down gradually, and I was not hurt a bit. But I found myself in the midst of a strange people, who, seeing me come from the clouds, thought I was a great Wizard. Of course I let them think so, because they were afraid of me, and promised to do anything I wished them to.

"Just to amuse myself, and keep the good people busy, I ordered them to build this City, and my Palace; and they did it all willingly and well. Then I thought, as the country was so green and beautiful, I would call it the Emerald City; and to make the name fit better I put green spectacles on all the people, so that everything they saw was green."

"But isn't everything here green?" asked Dorothy.

"No more than in any other city," replied Oz; "but when you wear green spectacles, why of course everything you see looks green to you. The Emerald City was built a great many years ago, for I was a young man when the balloon brought me here, and I am a very old man now. But my people have worn green glasses on their eyes so long that most of them think it really is an Emerald City, and it certainly is a beautiful place, abounding in jewels and precious metals, and every good thing that is needed to make one happy. I have been good to the people, and they like me; but ever since this Palace was built, I have shut myself up and would not see any of them.

"One of my greatest fears was the Witches, for while I had no magical powers at all I soon found out that the Witches were really able to do wonderful things. There were four of them in this country, and they ruled the people who live in the North and South and East and West. Fortunately, the Witches of the North and South were good, and I knew they would do me no harm; but the Witches of the East and West were terribly wicked, and had they not thought I was more powerful than they themselves, they would surely have destroyed me. As it was, I lived in deadly fear of them for many years; so you can imagine how pleased I was when I heard your house had fallen on the Wicked Witch of the East. When you came to me, I was willing to promise anything if you would only do away with the other Witch; but, now that you have melted her, I am ashamed to say that I cannot keep my promises."

"I think you are a very bad man," said Dorothy.

"Oh, no, my dear; I'm really a very good man, but I'm a very bad Wizard, I must admit."

"Can't you give me brains?" asked the Scarecrow.

"You don't need them. You are learning something every day. A baby has brains, but it doesn't know much. Experience is the only thing that brings knowledge, and the longer you are on earth the more experience you are sure to get."

"That may all be true," said the Scarecrow, "but I shall be very unhappy unless you give me brains."

The false Wizard looked at him carefully.

"Well," he said with a sigh, "I'm not much of a magician, as I said; but if you will come to me tomorrow morning, I will stuff your head with brains. I cannot tell you how to use them, however; you must find that out for yourself."

"Oh, thank you—thank you!" cried the Scarecrow. "I'll find a way to use them, never fear!"

"But how about my courage?" asked the Lion anxiously.

"You have plenty of courage, I am sure," answered Oz. "All you need is confidence in yourself. There is no living thing that is not afraid when it faces danger. The True courage is in facing danger when you are afraid, and that kind of courage you have in plenty."

"Perhaps I have, but I'm scared just the same," said the Lion. "I shall really be very unhappy unless you give me the sort of courage that makes one forget he is afraid."

"Very well, I will give you that sort of courage tomorrow," replied Oz.

"How about my heart?" asked the Tin Woodman.

"Why, as for that," answered Oz, "I think you are wrong to want a heart. It makes most people unhappy. If you only knew it, you are in luck not to have a heart."

"That must be a matter of opinion," said the Tin Woodman. "For my part, I will bear all the unhappiness without a murmur, if you will give me the heart."

"Very well," answered Oz meekly. "Come to me tomorrow and you shall have a heart. I have played Wizard for so many years that I may as well continue the part a little longer."

"And now," said Dorothy, "how am I to get back to Kansas?"

"We shall have to think about that," replied the little man. "Give me two or three days to consider the matter and I'll try to find a way to carry you over the desert. In the meantime you shall all be treated as my guests, and while you live in the Palace my people will wait upon you and obey your slightest wish. There is only one thing I ask in return for my help—such as it is. You must keep my secret and tell no one I am a humbug."

They agreed to say nothing of what they had learned, and went back to their rooms in high spirits. Even Dorothy had hope that "The Great and Terrible Humbug," as she called him, would find a way to send her back to Kansas, and if he did she was willing to forgive him everything.

Chapter 16 - The Magic Art of the Great Humbug

Next morning the Scarecrow said to his friends:

"Congratulate me. I am going to Oz to get my brains at last. When I return I shall be as other men are."

"I have always liked you as you were," said Dorothy simply.

"It is kind of you to like a Scarecrow," he replied. "But surely you will think more of me when you hear the splendid thoughts my new brain is going to turn out." Then he said good-bye to them all in a cheerful voice and went to the Throne Room, where he rapped upon the door.

"Come in," said Oz.

The Scarecrow went in and found the little man sitting down by the window, engaged in deep thought.

"I have come for my brains," remarked the Scarecrow, a little uneasily.

"Oh, yes; sit down in that chair, please," replied Oz. "You must excuse me for taking your head off, but I shall have to do it in order to put your brains in their proper place."

"That's all right," said the Scarecrow. "You are quite welcome to take my head off, as long as it will be a better one when you put it on again."

So the Wizard unfastened his head and emptied out the straw. Then he entered the back room and took up a measure of bran, which he mixed with a great many pins and needles. Having shaken them together thoroughly, he filled the top of the Scarecrow's head with the mixture and stuffed the rest of the space with straw, to hold it in place.

When he had fastened the Scarecrow's head on his body again he said to him, "Hereafter you will be a great man, for I have given you a lot of bran-new brains."

The Scarecrow was both pleased and proud at the fulfillment of his greatest wish, and having thanked Oz warmly he went back to his friends.

Dorothy looked at him curiously. His head was quite bulged out at the top with brains.

"How do you feel?" she asked.

"I feel wise indeed," he answered earnestly. "When I get used to my brains I shall know everything."

"Why are those needles and pins sticking out of your head?" asked the Tin Woodman.

"That is proof that he is sharp," remarked the Lion.

"Well, I must go to Oz and get my heart," said the Woodman. So he walked to the Throne Room and knocked at the door.

"Come in," called Oz, and the Woodman entered and said, "I have come for my heart."

"Very well," answered the little man. "But I shall have to cut a hole in your breast, so I can put your heart in the right place. I hope it won't hurt you."

"Oh, no," answered the Woodman. "I shall not feel it at all."

So Oz brought a pair of tinsmith's shears and cut a small, square hole in the left side of the Tin Woodman's breast. Then, going to a chest of drawers, he took out a pretty heart, made entirely of silk and stuffed with sawdust.

"Isn't it a beauty?" he asked.

"It is, indeed!" replied the Woodman, who was greatly pleased. "But is it a kind heart?"

"Oh, very!" answered Oz. He put the heart in the Woodman's breast and then replaced the square of tin, soldering it neatly together where it had been cut.

"There," said he; "now you have a heart that any man might be proud of. I'm sorry I had to put a patch on your breast, but it really couldn't be helped."

"Never mind the patch," exclaimed the happy Woodman. "I am very grateful to you, and shall never forget your kindness."

"Don't speak of it," replied Oz.

Then the Tin Woodman went back to his friends, who wished him every joy on account of his good fortune.

The Lion now walked to the Throne Room and knocked at the door.

"Come in," said Oz.

"I have come for my courage," announced the Lion, entering the room.

"Very well," answered the little man; "I will get it for you."

He went to a cupboard and reaching up to a high shelf took down a square green bottle, the contents of which he poured into a green-gold dish, beautifully carved. Placing this before the Cowardly Lion, who sniffed at it as if he did not like it, the Wizard said:

"Drink."

"What is it?" asked the Lion.

"Well," answered Oz, "if it were inside of you, it would be courage. You know, of course, that courage is always inside one; so that this really cannot be called courage until you have swallowed it. Therefore I advise you to drink it as soon as possible."

The Lion hesitated no longer, but drank till the dish was empty.

"How do you feel now?" asked Oz.

"Full of courage," replied the Lion, who went joyfully back to his friends to tell them of his good fortune.

Oz, left to himself, smiled to think of his success in giving the Scarecrow and the Tin Woodman and the Lion exactly what they thought they wanted. "How can I help being a humbug," he said, "when all these people make me do things that everybody knows can't be done? It was easy to make the Scarecrow and the Lion and the Woodman happy, because they imagined I could do anything. But it will take more than imagination to carry Dorothy back to Kansas, and I'm sure I don't know how it can be done."

Chapter 17 - How the Balloon Was Launched

For three days Dorothy heard nothing from Oz. These were sad days for the little girl, although her friends were all quite happy and contented. The Scarecrow told them there were wonderful thoughts in his head; but he would not say what they were because he knew no one could understand them but himself. When the Tin Woodman walked about he felt his heart rattling around in his breast; and he told Dorothy he had discovered it to be a kinder and more tender heart than the one he had owned when he was made of flesh. The Lion declared he was afraid of nothing on earth, and would gladly face an army or a dozen of the fierce Kalidahs.

Thus each of the little party was satisfied except Dorothy, who longed more than ever to get back to Kansas.

On the fourth day, to her great joy, Oz sent for her, and when she entered the Throne Room he greeted her pleasantly:

"Sit down, my dear; I think I have found the way to get you out of this country."

"And back to Kansas?" she asked eagerly.

"Well, I'm not sure about Kansas," said Oz, "for I haven't the faintest notion which way it lies. But the first thing to do is to cross the desert, and then it should be easy to find your way home."

"How can I cross the desert?" she inquired.

"Well, I'll tell you what I think," said the little man. "You see, when I came to this country it was in a balloon. You also came through the air, being carried by a cyclone. So I believe the best way to get across the desert will be through the air. Now, it is quite beyond my powers to make a cyclone; but I've been thinking the matter over, and I believe I can make a balloon."

"How?" asked Dorothy.

"A balloon," said Oz, "is made of silk, which is coated with glue to keep the gas in it. I have plenty of silk in the Palace, so it will be no trouble to make the balloon. But in all this country there is no gas to fill the balloon with, to make it float."

"If it won't float," remarked Dorothy, "it will be of no use to us."

"True," answered Oz. "But there is another way to make it float, which is to fill it with hot air. Hot air isn't as good as gas, for if the air should get cold the balloon would come down in the desert, and we should be lost."

"We!" exclaimed the girl. "Are you going with me?"

"Yes, of course," replied Oz. "I am tired of being such a humbug. If I should go out of this Palace my people would soon discover I am not a Wizard, and then they would be vexed with me for having deceived them. So I have to stay shut up in these rooms all day, and it gets tiresome. I'd much rather go back to Kansas with you and be in a circus again."

"I shall be glad to have your company," said Dorothy.

"Thank you," he answered. "Now, if you will help me sew the silk together, we will begin to work on our balloon."

So Dorothy took a needle and thread, and as fast as Oz cut the strips of silk into proper shape the girl sewed them neatly together. First there was a strip of light green silk, then a strip of dark green and then a strip of emerald green; for Oz had a fancy to make the balloon in different shades of the color about them. It took three days to sew all the strips together, but when it was finished they had a big bag of green silk more than twenty feet long.

Then Oz painted it on the inside with a coat of thin glue, to make it airtight, after which he announced that the balloon was ready.

"But we must have a basket to ride in," he said. So he sent the soldier with the green whiskers for a big clothes basket, which he fastened with many ropes to the bottom of the balloon.

When it was all ready, Oz sent word to his people that he was going to make a visit to a great brother Wizard who lived in the clouds. The news spread rapidly throughout the city and everyone came to see the wonderful sight.

Oz ordered the balloon carried out in front of the Palace, and the people gazed upon it with much curiosity. The Tin Woodman had chopped a big pile of wood, and now he made a fire of it, and Oz held the bottom of the balloon over the fire so that the hot air that arose from it would be caught in the silken bag. Gradually the balloon swelled out and rose into the air, until finally the basket just touched the ground.

Then Oz got into the basket and said to all the people in a loud voice:

"I am now going away to make a visit. While I am gone the Scarecrow will rule over you. I command you to obey him as you would me."

The balloon was by this time tugging hard at the rope that held it to the ground, for the air within it was hot, and this made it so much lighter in weight than the air without that it pulled hard to rise into the sky.

"Come, Dorothy!" cried the Wizard. "Hurry up, or the balloon will fly away."

"I can't find Toto anywhere," replied Dorothy, who did not wish to leave her little dog behind. Toto had run into the crowd to bark at a kitten, and Dorothy at last found him. She picked him up and ran towards the balloon.

She was within a few steps of it, and Oz was holding out his hands to help her into the basket, when, crack! went the ropes, and the balloon rose into the air without her.

"Come back!" she screamed. "I want to go, too!"

"I can't come back, my dear," called Oz from the basket. "Good-bye!"

"Good-bye!" shouted everyone, and all eyes were turned upward to where the Wizard was riding in the basket, rising every moment farther and farther into the sky.

And that was the last any of them ever saw of Oz, the Wonderful Wizard, though he may have reached Omaha safely, and be there now, for all we know. But the people remembered him lovingly, and said to one another:

"Oz was always our friend. When he was here he built for us this beautiful Emerald City, and now he is gone he has left the Wise Scarecrow to rule over us."

Still, for many days they grieved over the loss of the Wonderful Wizard, and would not be comforted.

Chapter 18 - Away to the South

Dorothy wept bitterly at the passing of her hope to get home to Kansas again; but when she thought it all over she was glad she had not gone up in a balloon. And she also felt sorry at losing Oz, and so did her companions.

The Tin Woodman came to her and said:

"Truly I should be ungrateful if I failed to mourn for the man who gave me my lovely heart. I should like to cry a little because Oz is gone, if you will kindly wipe away my tears, so that I shall not rust."

"With pleasure," she answered, and brought a towel at once. Then the Tin Woodman wept for several minutes, and she watched the tears carefully and wiped them away with the towel. When he had finished, he thanked her kindly and oiled himself thoroughly with his jeweled oil-can, to guard against mishap.

The Scarecrow was now the ruler of the Emerald City, and although he was not a Wizard the people were proud of him. "For," they said, "there is not another city in all the world that is ruled by a stuffed man." And, so far as they knew, they were quite right.

The morning after the balloon had gone up with Oz, the four travelers met in the Throne Room and talked matters over. The Scarecrow sat in the big throne and the others stood respectfully before him.

"We are not so unlucky," said the new ruler, "for this Palace and the Emerald City belong to us, and we can do just as we please. When I remember that a short time ago I was up on a pole in a farmer's cornfield, and that now I am the ruler of this beautiful City, I am quite satisfied with my lot."

"I also," said the Tin Woodman, "am well-pleased with my new heart; and, really, that was the only thing I wished in all the world."

"For my part, I am content in knowing I am as brave as any beast that ever lived, if not braver," said the Lion modestly.

"If Dorothy would only be contented to live in the Emerald City," continued the Scarecrow, "we might all be happy together."

"But I don't want to live here," cried Dorothy. "I want to go to Kansas, and live with Aunt Em and Uncle Henry."

"Well, then, what can be done?" inquired the Woodman.

The Scarecrow decided to think, and he thought so hard that the pins and needles began to stick out of his brains. Finally he said:

"Why not call the Winged Monkeys, and ask them to carry you over the desert?"

"I never thought of that!" said Dorothy joyfully. "It's just the thing. I'll go at once for the Golden Cap."

When she brought it into the Throne Room she spoke the magic words, and soon the band of Winged Monkeys flew in through the open window and stood beside her.

"This is the second time you have called us," said the Monkey King, bowing before the little girl. "What do you wish?"

"I want you to fly with me to Kansas," said Dorothy.

But the Monkey King shook his head.

"That cannot be done," he said. "We belong to this country alone, and cannot leave it. There has never been a Winged Monkey in Kansas yet, and I suppose there never will be, for they don't belong there. We shall be glad to serve you in any way in our power, but we cannot cross the desert. Good-bye."

And with another bow, the Monkey King spread his wings and flew away through the window, followed by all his band.

Dorothy was ready to cry with disappointment. "I have wasted the charm of the Golden Cap to no purpose," she said, "for the Winged Monkeys cannot help me."

"It is certainly too bad!" said the tender-hearted Woodman.

The Scarecrow was thinking again, and his head bulged out so horribly that Dorothy feared it would burst.

"Let us call in the soldier with the green whiskers," he said, "and ask his advice."

So the soldier was summoned and entered the Throne Room timidly, for while Oz was alive he never was allowed to come farther than the door.

"This little girl," said the Scarecrow to the soldier, "wishes to cross the desert. How can she do so?"

"I cannot tell," answered the soldier, "for nobody has ever crossed the desert, unless it is Oz himself."

"Is there no one who can help me?" asked Dorothy earnestly.

"Glinda might," he suggested.

"Who is Glinda?" inquired the Scarecrow.

"The Witch of the South. She is the most powerful of all the Witches, and rules over the Quadlings. Besides, her castle stands on the edge of the desert, so she may know a way to cross it."

"Glinda is a Good Witch, isn't she?" asked the child.

"The Quadlings think she is good," said the soldier, "and she is kind to everyone. I have heard that Glinda is a beautiful woman, who knows how to keep young in spite of the many years she has lived."

"How can I get to her castle?" asked Dorothy.

"The road is straight to the South," he answered, "but it is said to be full of dangers to travelers. There are wild beasts in the woods, and a race of queer men who do not like strangers to cross their country. For this reason none of the Quadlings ever come to the Emerald City."

The soldier then left them and the Scarecrow said:

"It seems, in spite of dangers, that the best thing Dorothy can do is to travel to the Land of the South and ask Glinda to help her. For, of course, if Dorothy stays here she will never get back to Kansas."

"You must have been thinking again," remarked the Tin Woodman.

"I have," said the Scarecrow.

"I shall go with Dorothy," declared the Lion, "for I am tired of your city and long for the woods and the country again. I am really a wild beast, you know. Besides, Dorothy will need someone to protect her."

"That is true," agreed the Woodman. "My axe may be of service to her; so I also will go with her to the Land of the South."

"When shall we start?" asked the Scarecrow.

"Are you going?" they asked, in surprise.

"Certainly. If it wasn't for Dorothy I should never have had brains. She lifted me from the pole in the cornfield and brought me to the Emerald City. So my good luck is all due to her, and I shall never leave her until she starts back to Kansas for good and all."

"Thank you," said Dorothy gratefully. "You are all very kind to me. But I should like to start as soon as possible."

"We shall go tomorrow morning," returned the Scarecrow. "So now let us all get ready, for it will be a long journey."

Chapter 19 - Attacked by the Fighting Trees

The next morning Dorothy kissed the pretty green girl good-bye, and they all shook hands with the soldier with the green whiskers, who had walked with them as far as the gate. When the Guardian of the Gate saw them again he wondered greatly that they could leave the beautiful City to get into new trouble. But he at once unlocked their spectacles, which he put back into the green box, and gave them many good wishes to carry with them.

"You are now our ruler," he said to the Scarecrow; "so you must come back to us as soon as possible."

"I certainly shall if I am able," the Scarecrow replied; "but I must help Dorothy to get home, first."

As Dorothy bade the good-natured Guardian a last farewell she said:

"I have been very kindly treated in your lovely City, and everyone has been good to me. I cannot tell you how grateful I am."

"Don't try, my dear," he answered. "We should like to keep you with us, but if it is your wish to return to Kansas, I hope you will find a way." He then opened the gate of the outer wall, and they walked forth and started upon their journey.

The sun shone brightly as our friends turned their faces toward the Land of the South. They were all in the best of spirits, and laughed and chatted together. Dorothy was once more filled with the hope of getting home, and the Scarecrow and the Tin Woodman were glad to be of use to her. As for the Lion, he sniffed the fresh air with delight and whisked his tail from side to side in pure joy at being in the country again, while Toto ran around them and chased the moths and butterflies, barking merrily all the time.

"City life does not agree with me at all," remarked the Lion, as they walked along at a brisk pace. "I have lost much flesh since I lived there, and now I am anxious for a chance to show the other beasts how courageous I have grown."

They now turned and took a last look at the Emerald City. All they could see was a mass of towers and steeples behind the green walls, and high up above everything the spires and dome of the Palace of Oz.

"Oz was not such a bad Wizard, after all," said the Tin Woodman, as he felt his heart rattling around in his breast.

"He knew how to give me brains, and very good brains, too," said the Scarecrow.

"If Oz had taken a dose of the same courage he gave me," added the Lion, "he would have been a brave man."

Dorothy said nothing. Oz had not kept the promise he made her, but he had done his best, so she forgave him. As he said, he was a good man, even if he was a bad Wizard.

The first day's journey was through the green fields and bright flowers that stretched about the Emerald City on every side. They slept that night on the grass, with nothing but the stars over them; and they rested very well indeed.

In the morning they traveled on until they came to a thick wood. There was no way of going around it, for it seemed to extend to the right and left as far as they could see; and, besides, they did not dare change the direction of their journey for fear of getting lost. So they looked for the place where it would be easiest to get into the forest.

The Scarecrow, who was in the lead, finally discovered a big tree with such wide-spreading branches that there was room for the party to pass underneath. So he walked forward to the tree, but just as he came under the first branches they bent down and twined around him, and the next minute he was raised from the ground and flung headlong among his fellow travelers.

This did not hurt the Scarecrow, but it surprised him, and he looked rather dizzy when Dorothy picked him up.

"Here is another space between the trees," called the Lion.

"Let me try it first," said the Scarecrow, "for it doesn't hurt me to get thrown about." He walked up to another tree, as he spoke, but its branches immediately seized him and tossed him back again.

"This is strange," exclaimed Dorothy. "What shall we do?"

"The trees seem to have made up their minds to fight us, and stop our journey," remarked the Lion.

"I believe I will try it myself," said the Woodman, and shouldering his axe, he marched up to the first tree that had handled the Scarecrow so roughly. When a big branch bent down to seize him the Woodman chopped at it so fiercely that he cut it in two. At once the tree began shaking all its branches as if in pain, and the Tin Woodman passed safely under it.

"Come on!" he shouted to the others. "Be quick!" They all ran forward and passed under the tree without injury, except Toto, who was caught by a small branch and shaken until he howled. But the Woodman promptly chopped off the branch and set the little dog free.

The other trees of the forest did nothing to keep them back, so they made up their minds that only the first row of trees could bend down their branches, and that probably these were the policemen of the forest, and given this wonderful power in order to keep strangers out of it.

The four travelers walked with ease through the trees until they came to the farther edge of the wood. Then, to their surprise, they found before them a high wall which seemed to be made of white china. It was smooth, like the surface of a dish, and higher than their heads.

"What shall we do now?" asked Dorothy.

"I will make a ladder," said the Tin Woodman, "for we certainly must climb over the wall."

Chapter 20 - The Dainty China Country

While the Woodman was making a ladder from wood which he found in the forest Dorothy lay down and slept, for she was tired by the long walk. The Lion also curled himself up to sleep and Toto lay beside him.

The Scarecrow watched the Woodman while he worked, and said to him:

"I cannot think why this wall is here, nor what it is made of."

"Rest your brains and do not worry about the wall," replied the Woodman. "When we have climbed over it, we shall know what is on the other side."

After a time the ladder was finished. It looked clumsy, but the Tin Woodman was sure it was strong and would answer their purpose. The Scarecrow waked Dorothy and the Lion and Toto, and told them that the ladder was ready. The Scarecrow climbed up the ladder first, but he was so awkward that Dorothy had to follow close behind and keep him from falling off. When he got his head over the top of the wall the Scarecrow said, "Oh, my!"

"Go on," exclaimed Dorothy.

So the Scarecrow climbed farther up and sat down on the top of the wall, and Dorothy put her head over and cried, "Oh, my!" just as the Scarecrow had done.

Then Toto came up, and immediately began to bark, but Dorothy made him be still.

The Lion climbed the ladder next, and the Tin Woodman came last; but both of them cried, "Oh, my!" as soon as they looked over the wall. When they were all sitting in a row on the top of the wall, they looked down and saw a strange sight.

Before them was a great stretch of country having a floor as smooth and shining and white as the bottom of a big platter. Scattered around were many houses made entirely of china and painted in the brightest colors. These houses were quite small, the biggest of them reaching only as high as Dorothy's waist. There were also pretty little barns, with china fences around them; and many cows and sheep and horses and pigs and chickens, all made of china, were standing about in groups.

But the strangest of all were the people who lived in this queer country. There were milkmaids and shepherdesses, with brightly colored bodices and golden spots all over their gowns; and princesses with most gorgeous frocks of silver and gold and purple; and shepherds dressed in knee breeches with pink and yellow and blue stripes down them, and golden buckles on their shoes; and princes with jeweled crowns upon their heads, wearing ermine robes and satin doublets; and funny clowns in ruffled gowns, with round red spots upon their cheeks and tall, pointed caps. And, strangest of all, these people were all made of china, even to their clothes, and were so small that the tallest of them was no higher than Dorothy's knee.

No one did so much as look at the travelers at first, except one little purple china dog with an extra-large head, which came to the wall and barked at them in a tiny voice, afterwards running away again.

"How shall we get down?" asked Dorothy.

They found the ladder so heavy they could not pull it up, so the Scarecrow fell off the wall and the others jumped down upon him so that the hard floor would not hurt their feet. Of course they took pains not to light on his head and get the pins in their feet. When all were safely down they picked up the Scarecrow, whose body was quite flattened out, and patted his straw into shape again.

"We must cross this strange place in order to get to the other side," said Dorothy, "for it would be unwise for us to go any other way except due South."

They began walking through the country of the china people, and the first thing they came to was a china milkmaid milking a china cow. As they drew near, the cow suddenly gave a kick and kicked over the stool, the pail, and even the milkmaid herself, and all fell on the china ground with a great clatter.

Dorothy was shocked to see that the cow had broken her leg off, and that the pail was lying in several small pieces, while the poor milkmaid had a nick in her left elbow.

"There!" cried the milkmaid angrily. "See what you have done! My cow has broken her leg, and I must take her to the mender's shop and have it glued on again. What do you mean by coming here and frightening my cow?"

"I'm very sorry," returned Dorothy. "Please forgive us."

But the pretty milkmaid was much too vexed to make any answer. She picked up the leg sulkily and led her cow away, the poor animal limping on three legs. As she left them the milkmaid cast many reproachful glances over her shoulder at the clumsy strangers, holding her nicked elbow close to her side.

Dorothy was quite grieved at this mishap.

"We must be very careful here," said the kind-hearted Woodman, "or we may hurt these pretty little people so they will never get over it."

A little farther on Dorothy met a most beautifully dressed young Princess, who stopped short as she saw the strangers and started to run away.

Dorothy wanted to see more of the Princess, so she ran after her. But the china girl cried out:

"Don't chase me! Don't chase me!"

She had such a frightened little voice that Dorothy stopped and said, "Why not?"

"Because," answered the Princess, also stopping, a safe distance away, "if I run I may fall down and break myself."

"But could you not be mended?" asked the girl.

"Oh, yes; but one is never so pretty after being mended, you know," replied the Princess.

"I suppose not," said Dorothy.

"Now there is Mr. Joker, one of our clowns," continued the china lady, "who is always trying to stand upon his head. He has broken himself so often that he is mended in a hundred places, and doesn't look at all pretty. Here he comes now, so you can see for yourself."

Indeed, a jolly little clown came walking toward them, and Dorothy could see that in spite of his pretty clothes of red and yellow and green he was completely covered with cracks, running every which way and showing plainly that he had been mended in many places.

The Clown put his hands in his pockets, and after puffing out his cheeks and nodding his head at them saucily, he said:

"My lady fair, Why do you stare At poor old Mr. Joker? You're quite as stiff And prim as if You'd eaten up a poker!"

"Be quiet, sir!" said the Princess. "Can't you see these are strangers, and should be treated with respect?"

"Well, that's respect, I expect," declared the Clown, and immediately stood upon his head.

"Don't mind Mr. Joker," said the Princess to Dorothy. "He is considerably cracked in his head, and that makes him foolish."

"Oh, I don't mind him a bit," said Dorothy. "But you are so beautiful," she continued, "that I am sure I could love you dearly. Won't you let me carry you back to Kansas, and stand you on Aunt Em's mantel? I could carry you in my basket."

"That would make me very unhappy," answered the china Princess. "You see, here in our country we live contentedly, and can talk and move around as we please. But whenever any of us are taken away our joints at once stiffen, and we can only stand straight and look pretty. Of course that is all that is expected of us when we are on mantels and cabinets and drawing-room tables, but our lives are much pleasanter here in our own country."

"I would not make you unhappy for all the world!" exclaimed Dorothy. "So I'll just say good-bye."

"Good-bye," replied the Princess.

They walked carefully through the china country. The little animals and all the people scampered out of their way, fearing the strangers would break them, and after an hour or so the travelers reached the other side of the country and came to another china wall.

It was not so high as the first, however, and by standing upon the Lion's back they all managed to scramble to the top. Then the Lion gathered his legs under him and jumped on the wall; but just as he jumped, he upset a china church with his tail and smashed it all to pieces.

"That was too bad," said Dorothy, "but really I think we were lucky in not doing these little people more harm than breaking a cow's leg and a church. They are all so brittle!"

"They are, indeed," said the Scarecrow, "and I am thankful I am made of straw and cannot be easily damaged. There are worse things in the world than being a Scarecrow."

Chapter 21 - The Lion Becomes the King of Beasts

After climbing down from the china wall the travelers found themselves in a disagreeable country, full of bogs and marshes and covered with tall, rank grass. It was difficult to walk without falling into muddy holes, for the grass was so thick that it hid them from sight. However, by carefully picking their way, they got safely along until they reached solid ground. But here the country seemed wilder than ever, and after a long and tiresome walk through the underbrush they entered another forest, where the trees were bigger and older than any they had ever seen.

"This forest is perfectly delightful," declared the Lion, looking around him with joy. "Never have I seen a more beautiful place."

"It seems gloomy," said the Scarecrow.

"Not a bit of it," answered the Lion. "I should like to live here all my life. See how soft the dried leaves are under your feet and how rich and green the moss is that clings to these old trees. Surely no wild beast could wish a pleasanter home."

"Perhaps there are wild beasts in the forest now," said Dorothy.

"I suppose there are," returned the Lion, "but I do not see any of them about."

They walked through the forest until it became too dark to go any farther. Dorothy and Toto and the Lion lay down to sleep, while the Woodman and the Scarecrow kept watch over them as usual.

When morning came, they started again. Before they had gone far they heard a low rumble, as of the growling of many wild animals. Toto whimpered a little, but none of the others was frightened, and they kept along the well-trodden path until they came to an opening in the wood, in which were gathered hundreds of beasts of every variety. There were tigers and elephants and bears and wolves and foxes and all the others in the natural history, and for a moment Dorothy was afraid. But the Lion explained that the animals were holding a meeting, and he judged by their snarling and growling that they were in great trouble.

As he spoke several of the beasts caught sight of him, and at once the great assemblage hushed as if by magic. The biggest of the tigers came up to the Lion and bowed, saying:

"Welcome, O King of Beasts! You have come in good time to fight our enemy and bring peace to all the animals of the forest once more."

"What is your trouble?" asked the Lion quietly.

"We are all threatened," answered the tiger, "by a fierce enemy which has lately come into this forest. It is a most tremendous monster, like a great spider, with a body as big as an elephant and legs as long as a tree trunk. It has eight of these long legs, and as the monster crawls through the forest he seizes an animal with a leg and drags it to his mouth, where he eats it as a spider does a fly. Not one of us is safe while this fierce creature is alive, and we had called a meeting to decide how to take care of ourselves when you came among us."

The Lion thought for a moment.

"Are there any other lions in this forest?" he asked.

"No; there were some, but the monster has eaten them all. And, besides, they were none of them nearly so large and brave as you."

"If I put an end to your enemy, will you bow down to me and obey me as King of the Forest?" inquired the Lion.

"We will do that gladly," returned the tiger; and all the other beasts roared with a mighty roar: "We will!"

"Where is this great spider of yours now?" asked the Lion.

"Yonder, among the oak trees," said the tiger, pointing with his forefoot.

"Take good care of these friends of mine," said the Lion, "and I will go at once to fight the monster."

He bade his comrades good-bye and marched proudly away to do battle with the enemy.

The great spider was lying asleep when the Lion found him, and it looked so ugly that its foe turned up his nose in disgust. Its legs were quite as long as the tiger had said, and its body covered with coarse black hair. It had a great mouth, with a row of sharp teeth a foot long; but its head was joined to the pudgy body by a neck as slender as a wasp's waist. This gave the Lion a hint of the best way to attack the creature, and as he knew it was easier to fight it asleep than awake, he gave a great spring and landed directly upon the monster's back. Then, with one blow of his heavy paw, all armed with sharp claws, he knocked the spider's head from its body. Jumping down, he watched it until the long legs stopped wiggling, when he knew it was quite dead.

The Lion went back to the opening where the beasts of the forest were waiting for him and said proudly:

"You need fear your enemy no longer."

Then the beasts bowed down to the Lion as their King, and he promised to come back and rule over them as soon as Dorothy was safely on her way to Kansas.

Chapter 22 - The Country of the Quadlings

The four travelers passed through the rest of the forest in safety, and when they came out from its gloom saw before them a steep hill, covered from top to bottom with great pieces of rock.

"That will be a hard climb," said the Scarecrow, "but we must get over the hill, nevertheless."

So he led the way and the others followed. They had nearly reached the first rock when they heard a rough voice cry out, "Keep back!"

"Who are you?" asked the Scarecrow.

Then a head showed itself over the rock and the same voice said, "This hill belongs to us, and we don't allow anyone to cross it."

"But we must cross it," said the Scarecrow. "We're going to the country of the Quadlings."

"But you shall not!" replied the voice, and there stepped from behind the rock the strangest man the travelers had ever seen.

He was quite short and stout and had a big head, which was flat at the top and supported by a thick neck full of wrinkles. But he had no arms at all, and, seeing this, the Scarecrow did not fear that so helpless a creature could prevent them from climbing the hill. So he said, "I'm sorry not to do as you wish, but we must pass over your hill whether you like it or not," and he walked boldly forward.

As quick as lightning the man's head shot forward and his neck stretched out until the top of the head, where it was flat, struck the Scarecrow in the middle and sent him tumbling, over and over, down the hill. Almost as quickly as it came the head went back to the body, and the man laughed harshly as he said, "It isn't as easy as you think!"

A chorus of boisterous laughter came from the other rocks, and Dorothy saw hundreds of the armless Hammer-Heads upon the hillside, one behind every rock.

The Lion became quite angry at the laughter caused by the Scarecrow's mishap, and giving a loud roar that echoed like thunder, he dashed up the hill.

Again a head shot swiftly out, and the great Lion went rolling down the hill as if he had been struck by a cannon ball.

Dorothy ran down and helped the Scarecrow to his feet, and the Lion came up to her, feeling rather bruised and sore, and said, "It is useless to fight people with shooting heads; no one can withstand them."

"What can we do, then?" she asked.

"Call the Winged Monkeys," suggested the Tin Woodman. "You have still the right to command them once more."

"Very well," she answered, and putting on the Golden Cap she uttered the magic words. The Monkeys were as prompt as ever, and in a few moments the entire band stood before her.

"What are your commands?" inquired the King of the Monkeys, bowing low.

"Carry us over the hill to the country of the Quadlings," answered the girl.

"It shall be done," said the King, and at once the Winged Monkeys caught the four travelers and Toto up in their arms and flew away with them. As they passed over the hill the Hammer-Heads yelled with vexation, and shot their heads high in the air, but they could not reach the Winged Monkeys, which carried Dorothy and her comrades safely over the hill and set them down in the beautiful country of the Quadlings.

"This is the last time you can summon us," said the leader to Dorothy; "so good-bye and good luck to you."

"Good-bye, and thank you very much," returned the girl; and the Monkeys rose into the air and were out of sight in a twinkling.

The country of the Quadlings seemed rich and happy. There was field upon field of ripening grain, with well-paved roads running between, and pretty rippling brooks with strong bridges across them. The fences and houses and bridges were all painted bright red, just as they had been painted yellow in the country of the Winkies and blue in the country of the Munchkins. The Quadlings themselves, who were short and fat and looked chubby and good-natured, were dressed all in red, which showed bright against the green grass and the yellowing grain.

The Monkeys had set them down near a farmhouse, and the four travelers walked up to it and knocked at the door. It was opened by the farmer's wife, and when Dorothy asked for something to eat the woman gave them all a good dinner, with three kinds of cake and four kinds of cookies, and a bowl of milk for Toto.

"How far is it to the Castle of Glinda?" asked the child.

"It is not a great way," answered the farmer's wife. "Take the road to the South and you will soon reach it."

Thanking the good woman, they started afresh and walked by the fields and across the pretty bridges until they saw before them a very beautiful Castle. Before the gates were three young girls, dressed in handsome red uniforms trimmed with gold braid; and as Dorothy approached, one of them said to her:

"Why have you come to the South Country?"

"To see the Good Witch who rules here," she answered. "Will you take me to her?"

"Let me have your name, and I will ask Glinda if she will receive you." They told who they were, and the girl soldier went into the Castle. After a few moments she came back to say that Dorothy and the others were to be admitted at once.

Chapter 23 - Glinda The Good Witch Grants Dorothy's Wish

Before they went to see Glinda, however, they were taken to a room of the Castle, where Dorothy washed her face and combed her hair, and the Lion shook the dust out of his mane, and the Scarecrow patted himself into his best shape, and the Woodman polished his tin and oiled his joints.

When they were all quite presentable they followed the soldier girl into a big room where the Witch Glinda sat upon a throne of rubies.

She was both beautiful and young to their eyes. Her hair was a rich red in color and fell in flowing ringlets over her shoulders. Her dress was pure white but her eyes were blue, and they looked kindly upon the little girl.

"What can I do for you, my child?" she asked.

Dorothy told the Witch all her story: how the cyclone had brought her to the Land of Oz, how she had found her companions, and of the wonderful adventures they had met with.

"My greatest wish now," she added, "is to get back to Kansas, for Aunt Em will surely think something dreadful has happened to me, and that will make her put on mourning; and unless the crops are better this year than they were last, I am sure Uncle Henry cannot afford it."

Glinda leaned forward and kissed the sweet, upturned face of the loving little girl.

"Bless your dear heart," she said, "I am sure I can tell you of a way to get back to Kansas." Then she added, "But, if I do, you must give me the Golden Cap."

"Willingly!" exclaimed Dorothy; "indeed, it is of no use to me now, and when you have it you can command the Winged Monkeys three times."

"And I think I shall need their service just those three times," answered Glinda, smiling.

Dorothy then gave her the Golden Cap, and the Witch said to the Scarecrow, "What will you do when Dorothy has left us?"

"I will return to the Emerald City," he replied, "for Oz has made me its ruler and the people like me. The only thing that worries me is how to cross the hill of the Hammer-Heads."

"By means of the Golden Cap I shall command the Winged Monkeys to carry you to the gates of the Emerald City," said Glinda, "for it would be a shame to deprive the people of so wonderful a ruler."

"Am I really wonderful?" asked the Scarecrow.

"You are unusual," replied Glinda.

Turning to the Tin Woodman, she asked, "What will become of you when Dorothy leaves this country?"

He leaned on his axe and thought a moment. Then he said, "The Winkies were very kind to me, and wanted me to rule over them after the Wicked Witch died. I am fond of the Winkies, and if I could get back again to the Country of the West, I should like nothing better than to rule over them forever."

"My second command to the Winged Monkeys," said Glinda "will be that they carry you safely to the land of the Winkies. Your brain may not be so large to look at as those of the Scarecrow, but you are really brighter than he is—when you are well polished—and I am sure you will rule the Winkies wisely and well."

Then the Witch looked at the big, shaggy Lion and asked, "When Dorothy has returned to her own home, what will become of you?"

"Over the hill of the Hammer-Heads," he answered, "lies a grand old forest, and all the beasts that live there have made me their King. If I could only get back to this forest, I would pass my life very happily there."

"My third command to the Winged Monkeys," said Glinda, "shall be to carry you to your forest. Then, having used up the powers of the Golden Cap, I shall give it to the King of the Monkeys, that he and his band may thereafter be free for evermore."

The Scarecrow and the Tin Woodman and the Lion now thanked the Good Witch earnestly for her kindness; and Dorothy exclaimed:

"You are certainly as good as you are beautiful! But you have not yet told me how to get back to Kansas."

"Your Silver Shoes will carry you over the desert," replied Glinda. "If you had known their power you could have gone back to your Aunt Em the very first day you came to this country."

"But then I should not have had my wonderful brains!" cried the Scarecrow. "I might have passed my whole life in the farmer's cornfield."

"And I should not have had my lovely heart," said the Tin Woodman. "I might have stood and rusted in the forest till the end of the world."

"And I should have lived a coward forever," declared the Lion, "and no beast in all the forest would have had a good word to say to me."

"This is all true," said Dorothy, "and I am glad I was of use to these good friends. But now that each of them has had what he most desired, and each is happy in having a kingdom to rule besides, I think I should like to go back to Kansas."

"The Silver Shoes," said the Good Witch, "have wonderful powers. And one of the most curious things about them is that they can carry you to any place in the world in three steps, and each step will be made in the wink of an eye. All you have to do is to knock the heels together three times and command the shoes to carry you wherever you wish to go."

"If that is so," said the child joyfully, "I will ask them to carry me back to Kansas at once."

She threw her arms around the Lion's neck and kissed him, patting his big head tenderly. Then she kissed the Tin Woodman, who was weeping in a way most dangerous to his joints. But she hugged the soft, stuffed body of the Scarecrow in her arms instead of kissing his painted face, and found she was crying herself at this sorrowful parting from her loving comrades.

Glinda the Good stepped down from her ruby throne to give the little girl a good-bye kiss, and Dorothy thanked her for all the kindness she had shown to her friends and herself.

Dorothy now took Toto up solemnly in her arms, and having said one last good-bye she clapped the heels of her shoes together three times, saying:

"Take me home to Aunt Em!"

Instantly she was whirling through the air, so swiftly that all she could see or feel was the wind whistling past her ears.

The Silver Shoes took but three steps, and then she stopped so suddenly that she rolled over upon the grass several times before she knew where she was.

At length, however, she sat up and looked about her.

"Good gracious!" she cried.

For she was sitting on the broad Kansas prairie, and just before her was the new farmhouse Uncle Henry built after the cyclone had carried away the old one. Uncle Henry was milking the cows in the barnyard, and Toto had jumped out of her arms and was running toward the barn, barking furiously.

Dorothy stood up and found she was in her stocking-feet. For the Silver Shoes had fallen off in her flight through the air, and were lost forever in the desert.

Chapter 24 - Home Again

Aunt Em had just come out of the house to water the cabbages when she looked up and saw Dorothy running toward her.

"My darling child!" she cried, folding the little girl in her arms and covering her face with kisses. "Where in the world did you come from?"

"From the Land of Oz," said Dorothy gravely. "And here is Toto, too. And oh, Aunt Em! I'm so glad to be at home again!"

The End

The Marvelous Land of Oz

Preface

The Marvelous Land of Oz
Being an account of the further adventures of the
Scarecrow and Tin Woodman
and also the strange experiences of the highly magnified Woggle-Bug, Jack Pumpkinhead, the Animated Saw-
Horse and the Gump; the story being
A Sequel to The Wizard of Oz
By
L. Frank Baum

Author of Father Goose-His Book; The Wizard of Oz; The Magical Monarch of Mo; The Enchanted Isle of Yew;
The Life and Adventures of Santa Claus; Dot and Tot of Merryland
etc. etc.

Author's Note

AFTER the publication of "The Wonderful Wizard of OZ" I began to receive letters from children, telling me of their pleasure in reading the story and asking me to "write something more" about the Scarecrow and the Tin Woodman. At first I considered these little letters, frank and earnest though they were, in the light of pretty compliments; but the letters continued to come during succeeding months, and even years.

Finally I promised one little girl, who made a long journey to see me and prefer her request,—and she is a "Dorothy," by the way—that when a thousand little girls had written me a thousand little letters asking for the Scarecrow and the Tin Woodman I would write the book, Either little Dorothy was a fairy in disguise, and waved her magic wand, or the success of the stage production of "The Wizard of OZ" made new friends for the story, For the thousand letters reached their destination long since—and many more followed them.

And now, although pleading guilty to long delay, I have kept my promise in this book.

L. FRANK BAUM.
Chicago, June, 1904

Dedication

To those excellent good fellows and comedians David C. Montgomery and Frank A. Stone whose clever personations of the Tin Woodman and the Scarecrow have delighted thousands of children throughout the land, this book is gratefully dedicated
by
THE AUTHOR

LIST OF CHAPTERS

Chapter 1 - Tip Manufactures a Pumpkinhead

In the Country of the Gillikins, which is at the North of the Land of Oz, lived a youth called Tip. There was more to his name than that, for old Mombi often declared that his whole name was Tippetarius; but no one was expected to say such a long word when "Tip" would do just as well.

This boy remembered nothing of his parents, for he had been brought when quite young to be reared by the old woman known as Mombi, whose reputation, I am sorry to say, was none of the best. For the Gillikin people had reason to suspect her of indulging in magical arts, and therefore hesitated to associate with her.

Mombi was not exactly a Witch, because the Good Witch who ruled that part of the Land of Oz had forbidden any other Witch to exist in her dominions. So Tip's guardian, however much she might aspire to working magic, realized it was unlawful to be more than a Sorceress, or at most a Wizardess.

Tip was made to carry wood from the forest, that the old woman might boil her pot. He also worked in the corn-fields, hoeing and husking; and he fed the pigs and milked the four-horned cow that was Mombi's especial pride.

But you must not suppose he worked all the time, for he felt that would be bad for him. When sent to the forest Tip often climbed trees for birds' eggs or amused himself chasing the fleet white rabbits or fishing in the brooks with bent pins. Then he would hastily gather his armful of wood and carry it home. And when he was supposed to be working in the corn-fields, and the tall stalks hid him from Mombi's view, Tip would often dig in the gopher holes, or if the mood seized him—lie upon his back between the rows of corn and take a nap. So, by taking care not to exhaust his strength, he grew as strong and rugged as a boy may be.

Mombi's curious magic often frightened her neighbors, and they treated her shyly, yet respectfully, because of her weird powers. But Tip frankly hated her, and took no pains to hide his feelings. Indeed, he sometimes showed less respect for the old woman than he should have done, considering she was his guardian.

There were pumpkins in Mombi's corn-fields, lying golden red among the rows of green stalks; and these had been planted and carefully tended that the four-horned cow might eat of them in the winter time. But one day, after the corn had all been cut and stacked, and Tip was carrying the pumpkins to the stable, he took a notion to make a "Jack Lantern" and try to give the old woman a fright with it.

So he selected a fine, big pumpkin—one with a lustrous, orange-red color—and began carving it. With the point of his knife he made two round eyes, a three-cornered nose, and been considered strictly beautiful; but it wore a smile so big and broad, and was so Jolly in expression, that even Tip laughed as he looked admiringly at his work.

The child had no playmates, so he did not know that boys often dig out the inside of a "pumpkin-jack," and in the space thus made put a lighted candle to render the face more startling; but he conceived an idea of his own that promised to be quite as effective. He decided to manufacture the form of a man, who would wear this pumpkin head, and to stand it in a place where old Mombi would meet it face to face.

"And then," said Tip to himself, with a laugh, "she'll squeal louder than the brown pig does when I pull her tail, and shiver with fright worse than I did last year when I had the ague!"

He had plenty of time to accomplish this task, for Mombi had gone to a village—to buy groceries, she said—and it was a journey of at least two days.

So he took his axe to the forest, and selected some stout, straight saplings, which he cut down and trimmed of all their twigs and leaves. From these he would make the arms, and legs, and feet of his man. For the body he stripped a sheet of thick bark from around a big tree, and with much labor fashioned it into a cylinder of about the right size, pinning the edges together with wooden pegs. Then, whistling happily as he worked, he carefully jointed the limbs and fastened them to the body with pegs whittled into shape with his knife.

By the time this feat had been accomplished it began to grow dark, and Tip remembered he must milk the cow and feed the pigs. So he picked up his wooden man and carried it back to the house with him.

During the evening, by the light of the fire in the kitchen, Tip carefully rounded all the edges of the joints and smoothed the rough places in a neat and workmanlike manner. Then he stood the figure up against the wall and admired it. It seemed remarkably tall, even for a full-grown man; but that was a good point in a small boy's eyes, and Tip did not object at all to the size of his creation.

Next morning, when he looked at his work again, Tip saw he had forgotten to give the dummy a neck, by means of which he might fasten the pumpkinhead to the body. So he went again to the forest, which was not far away, and chopped from a tree several pieces of wood with which to complete his work. When he returned he fastened a cross-piece to the upper end of the body, making a hole through the center to hold upright the neck. The bit of wood which formed this neck was also sharpened at the upper end, and when all was ready Tip put on the pumpkin head, pressing it well down onto the neck, and found that it fitted very well. The head could be turned to one side or the other, as he pleased, and the hinges of the arms and legs allowed him to place the dummy in any position he desired.

"Now, that," declared Tip, proudly, "is really a very fine man, and it ought to frighten several screeches out of old Mombi! But it would be much more lifelike if it were properly dressed."

To find clothing seemed no easy task; but Tip boldly ransacked the great chest in which Mombi kept all her keepsakes and treasures, and at the very bottom he discovered some purple trousers, a red shirt and a pink vest which was dotted with white spots. These he carried away to his man and succeeded, although the garments did not fit very well, in dressing the creature in a jaunty fashion. Some knit stockings belonging to Mombi and a much worn pair of his own shoes completed the man's apparel, and Tip was so delighted that he danced up and down and laughed aloud in boyish ecstacy.

"I must give him a name!" he cried. "So good a man as this must surely have a name. I believe," he added, after a moment's thought, "I will name the fellow 'Jack Pumpkinhead!'"

Chapter 2 - The Marvelous Powder of Life

After considering the matter carefully, Tip decided that the best place to locate Jack would be at the bend in the road, a little way from the house. So he started to carry his man there, but found him heavy and rather awkward to handle. After dragging the creature a short distance Tip stood him on his feet, and by first bending the joints of one leg, and then those of the other, at the same time pushing from behind, the boy managed to induce Jack to walk to the bend in the road. It was not accomplished without a few tumbles, and Tip really worked harder than he ever had in the fields or forest; but a love of mischief urged him on, and it pleased him to test the cleverness of his workmanship.

"Jack's all right, and works fine!" he said to himself, panting with the unusual exertion. But just then he discovered the man's left arm had fallen off in the journey so he went back to find it, and afterward, by whittling a new and stouter pin for the shoulder-joint, he repaired the injury so successfully that the arm was stronger than before. Tip also noticed that Jack's pumpkin head had twisted around until it faced his back; but this was easily remedied. When, at last, the man was set up facing the turn in the path where old Mombi was to appear, he looked natural enough to be a fair imitation of a Gillikin farmer,—and unnatural enough to startle anyone that came on him unawares.

As it was yet too early in the day to expect the old woman to return home, Tip went down into the valley below the farm-house and began to gather nuts from the trees that grew there.

However, old Mombi returned earlier than usual. She had met a crooked wizard who resided in a lonely cave in the mountains, and had traded several important secrets of magic with him. Having in this way secured three new recipes, four magical powders and a selection of herbs of wonderful power and potency, she hobbled home as fast as she could, in order to test her new sorceries.

So intent was Mombi on the treasures she had gained that when she turned the bend in the road and caught a glimpse of the man, she merely nodded and said:

"Good evening, sir."

But, a moment after, noting that the person did not move or reply, she cast a shrewd glance into his face and discovered his pumpkin head elaborately carved by Tip's jack-knife.

"Heh!" ejaculated Mombi, giving a sort of grunt; "that rascally boy has been playing tricks again! Very good! ve—ry good! I'll beat him black- and-blue for trying to scare me in this fashion!"

Angrily she raised her stick to smash in the grinning pumpkin head of the dummy; but a sudden thought made her pause, the uplifted stick left motionless in the air.

"Why, here is a good chance to try my new powder!" said she, eagerly. "And then I can tell whether that crooked wizard has fairly traded secrets, or whether he has fooled me as wickedly as I fooled him." So she set down her basket and began fumbling in it for one of the precious powders she had obtained.

While Mombi was thus occupied Tip strolled back, with his pockets full of nuts, and discovered the old woman standing beside his man and apparently not the least bit frightened by it.

At first he was generally disappointed; but the next moment he became curious to know what Mombi was going to do. So he hid behind a hedge, where he could see without being seen, and prepared to watch.

After some search the woman drew from her basket an old pepper-box, upon the faded label of which the wizard had written with a lead-pencil:

"Powder of Life."

"Ah—here it is!" she cried, joyfully. "And now let us see if it is potent. The stingy wizard didn't give me much of it, but I guess there's enough for two or three doses."

Tip was much surprised when he overheard this speech. Then he saw old Mombi raise her arm and sprinkle the powder from the box over the pumpkin head of his man Jack. She did this in the same way one would pepper a baked potato, and the powder sifted down from Jack's head and scattered over the red shirt and pink waistcoat and purple trousers Tip had dressed him in, and a portion even fell upon the patched and worn shoes.

Then, putting the pepper-box back into the basket, Mombi lifted her left hand, with its little finger pointed upward, and said:

"Weaugh!"

Then she lifted her right hand, with the thumb pointed upward, and said:

"Teaugh!"

Then she lifted both hands, with all the fingers and thumbs spread out, and cried:

"Peaugh!"

Jack Pumpkinhead stepped back a pace, at this, and said in a reproachful voice:

"Don't yell like that! Do you think I'm deaf?"

Old Mombi danced around him, frantic with delight.

"He lives!" she screamed: "He lives! he lives!"

Then she threw her stick into the air and caught it as it came down; and she hugged herself with both arms, and tried to do a step of a jig; and all the time she repeated, rapturously:

"He lives!—he lives!—he lives!"

Now you may well suppose that Tip observed all this with amazement. At first he was so frightened and horrified that he wanted to run away, but his legs trembled and shook so badly that he couldn't. Then it struck him as a very funny thing for Jack to come to life, especially as the expression on his pumpkin face was so droll and comical it excited laughter on the instant. So, recovering from his first fear, Tip began to laugh; and the merry peals reached old Mombi's ears and made her hobble quickly to the hedge, where she seized Tip's collar and dragged him back to where she had left her basket and the pumpkinheaded man.

"You naughty, sneaking, wicked boy!" she exclaimed, furiously:" I'll teach you to spy out my secrets and to make fun of me!"

"I wasn't making fun of you," protested Tip. "I was laughing at old Pumpkinhead! Look at him! Isn't he a picture, though?"

"I hope you are not reflecting on my personal appearance," said Jack; and it was so funny to hear his grave voice, while his face continued to wear its jolly smile, that Tip again burst into a peal of laughter.

Even Mombi was not without a curious interest in the man her magic had brought to life; for, after staring at him intently, she presently asked:

"What do you know?"

"Well, that is hard to tell," replied Jack. "For although I feel that I know a tremendous lot, I am not yet aware how much there is in the world to find out about. It will take me a little time to discover whether I am very wise or very foolish."

"To be sure," said Mombi, thoughtfully.

"But what are you going to do with him, now he is alive?" asked Tip, wondering.

"I must think it over," answered Mombi. "But we must get home at once, for it is growing dark. Help the Pumpkinhead to walk."

"Never mind me," said Jack; "I can walk as well as you can. Haven't I got legs and feet, and aren't they jointed?"

"Are they?" asked the woman, turning to Tip.

"Of course they are; I made 'em myself," returned the boy, with pride.

So they started for the house, but when they reached the farm yard old Mombi led the pumpkin man to the cow stable and shut him up in an empty stall, fastening the door securely on the outside.

"I've got to attend to you, first," she said, nodding her head at Tip.

Hearing this, the boy became uneasy; for he knew Mombi had a bad and revengeful heart, and would not hesitate to do any evil thing.

They entered the house. It was a round, domeshaped structure, as are nearly all the farm houses in the Land of Oz.

Mombi bade the boy light a candle, while she put her basket in a cupboard and hung her cloak on a peg. Tip obeyed quickly, for he was afraid of her.

After the candle had been lighted Mombi ordered him to build a fire in the hearth, and while Tip was thus engaged the old woman ate her supper. When the flames began to crackle the boy came to her and asked a share of the bread and cheese; but Mombi refused him.

"I'm hungry!" said Tip, in a sulky tone.

"You won't be hungry long," replied Mombi, with a grim look.

The boy didn't like this speech, for it sounded like a threat; but he happened to remember he had nuts in his pocket, so he cracked some of those and ate them while the woman rose, shook the crumbs from her apron, and hung above the fire a small black kettle.

Then she measured out equal parts of milk and vinegar and poured them into the kettle. Next she produced several packets of herbs and powders and began adding a portion of each to the contents of the kettle. Occasionally she would draw near the candle and read from a yellow paper the recipe of the mess she was concocting.

As Tip watched her his uneasiness increased.

"What is that for?" he asked.

"For you," returned Mombi, briefly.

Tip wriggled around upon his stool and stared awhile at the kettle, which was beginning to bubble. Then he would glance at the stern and wrinkled features of the witch and wish he were any place but in that dim and smoky kitchen, where even the shadows cast by the candle upon the wall were enough to give one the horrors. So an hour passed away, during which the silence was only broken by the bubbling of the pot and the hissing of the flames.

Finally, Tip spoke again.

"Have I got to drink that stuff?" he asked, nodding toward the pot.

"Yes," said Mombi.

"What'll it do to me?" asked Tip.

"If it's properly made," replied Mombi, "it will change or transform you into a marble statue."

Tip groaned, and wiped the perspiration from his forehead with his sleeve.

"I don't want to be a marble statue!" he protested.

"That doesn't matter I want you to be one," said the old woman, looking at him severely.

"What use'll I be then?" asked Tip. "There won't be any one to work for you."

"I'll make the Pumpkinhead work for me," said Mombi.

Again Tip groaned.

"Why don't you change me into a goat, or a chicken?" he asked, anxiously. "You can't do anything with a marble statue."

"Oh, yes, I can," returned Mombi. "I'm going to plant a flower garden, next Spring, and I'll put you in the middle of it, for an ornament. I wonder I haven't thought of that before; you've been a bother to me for years."

At this terrible speech Tip felt the beads of perspiration starting all over his body. but he sat still and shivered and looked anxiously at the kettle.

"Perhaps it won't work," he mutttered, in a voice that sounded weak and discouraged.

"Oh, I think it will," answered Mombi, cheerfully. "I seldom make a mistake."

Again there was a period of silence a silence so long and gloomy that when Mombi finally lifted the kettle from the fire it was close to midnight.

"You cannot drink it until it has become quite cold," announced the old witch for in spite of the law she had acknowledged practising witchcraft. "We must both go to bed now, and at daybreak I will call you and at once complete your transformation into a marble statue."

With this she hobbled into her room, bearing the steaming kettle with her, and Tip heard her close and lock the door.

The boy did not go to bed, as he had been commanded to do, but still sat glaring at the embers of the dying fire.

Chapter 3 - The Flight of the Fugitives

Tip reflected.

"It's a hard thing, to be a marble statue," he thought, rebelliously, "and I'm not going to stand it. For years I've been a bother to her, she says; so she's going to get rid of me. Well, there's an easier way than to become a statue. No boy could have any fun forever standing in the middle of a flower garden! I'll run away, that's what I'll do—and I may as well go before she makes me drink that nasty stuff in the kettle." He waited until the snores of the old witch announced she was fast asleep, and then he arose softly and went to the cupboard to find something to eat.

"No use starting on a journey without food," he decided, searching upon the narrow shelves.

He found some crusts of bread; but he had to look into Mombi's basket to find the cheese she had brought from the village. While turning over the contents of the basket he came upon the pepper-box which contained the "Powder of Life."

"I may as well take this with me," he thought, "or Mombi'll be using it to make more mischief with." So he put the box in his pocket, together with the bread and cheese.

Then he cautiously left the house and latched the door behind him. Outside both moon and stars shone brightly, and the night seemed peaceful and inviting after the close and ill-smelling kitchen.

"I'll be glad to get away," said Tip, softly; "for I never did like that old woman. I wonder how I ever came to live with her."

He was walking slowly toward the road when a thought made him pause.

"I don't like to leave Jack Pumpkinhead to the tender mercies of old Mombi," he muttered. "And Jack belongs to me, for I made him even if the old witch did bring him to life."

He retraced his steps to the cow-stable and opened the door of the stall where the pumpkin headed man had been left.

Jack was standing in the middle of the stall, and by the moonlight Tip could see he was smiling just as jovially as ever.

"Come on!" said the boy, beckoning."

"Where to?" asked Jack.

"You'll know as soon as I do," answered Tip, smiling sympathetically into the pumpkin face.

"All we've got to do now is to tramp."

"Very well," returned Jack, and walked awkwardly out of the stable and into the moonlight.

Tip turned toward the road and the man followed him. Jack walked with a sort of limp, and occasionally one of the joints of his legs would turn backward, instead of frontwise, almost causing him to tumble. But the Pumpkinhead was quick to notice this, and began to take more pains to step carefully; so that he met with few accidents.

Tip led him along the path without stopping an instant. They could not go very fast, but they walked steadily; and by the time the moon sank away and the sun peeped over the hills they had travelled so great a distance that the boy had no reason to fear pursuit from the old witch. Moreover, he had turned first into one path, and then into another, so that should anyone follow them it would prove very difficult to guess which way they had gone, or where to seek them.

Fairly satisfied that he had escaped—for a time, at least—being turned into a marble statue, the boy stopped his companion and seated himself upon a rock by the roadside.

"Let's have some breakfast," he said.

Jack Pumpkinhead watched Tip curiously, but refused to join in the repast. "I don't seem to be made the same way you are," he said.

"I know you are not," returned Tip; "for I made you."

"Oh! Did you?" asked Jack.

"Certainly. And put you together. And carved your eyes and nose and ears and mouth," said Tip proudly. "And dressed you."

Jack looked at his body and limbs critically.

"It strikes me you made a very good job of it," he remarked.

"Just so-so," replied Tip, modestly; for he began to see certain defects in the construction of his man. "If I'd known we were going to travel together I might have been a little more particular."

"Why, then," said the Pumpkinhead, in a tone that expressed surprise, "you must be my creator my parent my father!"

"Or your inventor," replied the boy with a laugh. "Yes, my son; I really believe I am!"

"Then I owe you obedience," continued the man, "and you owe me—support."

"That's it, exactly", declared Tip, jumping up. "So let us be off."

"Where are we going?" asked Jack, when they had resumed their journey.

58

"I'm not exactly sure," said the boy; "but I believe we are headed South, and that will bring us, sooner or later, to the Emerald City."

"What city is that?" enquired the Pumpkinhead.

"Why, it's the center of the Land of Oz, and the biggest town in all the country. I've never been there, myself, but I've heard all about its history. It was built by a mighty and wonderful Wizard named Oz, and everything there is of a green color—just as everything in this Country of the Gillikins is of a purple color."

"Is everything here purple?" asked Jack.

"Of course it is. Can't you see?" returned the boy.

"I believe I must be color-blind," said the Pumpkinhead, after staring about him.

"Well, the grass is purple, and the trees are purple, and the houses and fences are purple," explained Tip. "Even the mud in the roads is purple. But in the Emerald City everything is green that is purple here. And in the Country of the Munchkins, over at the East, everything is blue; and in the South country of the Quadlings everything is red; and in the West country of the Winkies, where the Tin Woodman rules, everything is yellow."

"Oh!" said Jack. Then, after a pause, he asked: "Did you say a Tin Woodman rules the Winkies?"

"Yes; he was one of those who helped Dorothy to destroy the Wicked Witch of the West, and the Winkies were so grateful that they invited him to become their ruler,—just as the people of the Emerald City invited the Scarecrow to rule them."

"Dear me!" said Jack. "I'm getting confused with all this history. Who is the Scarecrow?"

"Another friend of Dorothy's," replied Tip.

"And who is Dorothy?"

"She was a girl that came here from Kansas, a place in the big, outside World. She got blown to the Land of Oz by a cyclone, and while she was here the Scarecrow and the Tin Woodman accompanied her on her travels."

"And where is she now?" inquired the Pumpkinhead.

"Glinda the Good, who rules the Quadlings, sent her home again," said the boy.

"Oh. And what became of the Scarecrow?"

"I told you. He rules the Emerald City," answered Tip.

"I thought you said it was ruled by a wonderful Wizard," objected Jack, seeming more and more confused.

"Well, so I did. Now, pay attention, and I'll explain it," said Tip, speaking slowly and looking the smiling Pumpkinhead squarely in the eye. "Dorothy went to the Emerald City to ask the Wizard to send her back to Kansas; and the Scarecrow and the Tin Woodman went with her. But the Wizard couldn't send her back, because he wasn't so much of a Wizard as he might have been. And then they got angry at the Wizard, and threatened to expose him; so the Wizard made a big balloon and escaped in it, and no one has ever seen him since."

"Now, that is very interesting history," said Jack, well pleased; "and I understand it perfectly all but the explanation."

"I'm glad you do," responded Tip. "After the Wizard was gone, the people of the Emerald City made His Majesty, the Scarecrow, their King; "and I have heard that he became a very popular ruler."

"Are we going to see this queer King?" asked Jack, with interest.

"I think we may as well," replied the boy; "unless you have something better to do."

"Oh, no, dear father," said the Pumpkinhead. "I am quite willing to go wherever you please."

Chapter 4 - Tip Makes an Experiment in Magic

The boy, small and rather delicate in appearance seemed somewhat embarrassed at being called "father" by the tall, awkward, pumpkinheaded man, but to deny the relationship would involve another long and tedious explanation; so he changed the subject by asking, abruptly:

"Are you tired?"

"Of course not!" replied the other. "But," he continued, after a pause, "it is quite certain I shall wear out my wooden joints if I keep on walking."

Tip reflected, as they journeyed on, that this was true. He began to regret that he had not constructed the wooden limbs more carefully and substantially. Yet how could he ever have guessed that the man he had made merely to scare old Mombi with would be brought to life by means of a magical powder contained in an old pepper-box?

So he ceased to reproach himself, and began to think how he might yet remedy the deficiencies of Jack's weak joints.

While thus engaged they came to the edge of a wood, and the boy sat down to rest upon an old sawhorse that some woodcutter had left there.

"Why don't you sit down?" he asked the Pumpkinhead.

"Won't it strain my joints?" inquired the other.

"Of course not. It'll rest them," declared the boy.

So Jack tried to sit down; but as soon as he bent his joints farther than usual they gave way altogether, and he came clattering to the ground with such a crash that Tip feared he was entirely ruined.

He rushed to the man, lifted him to his feet, straightened his arms and legs, and felt of his head to see if by chance it had become cracked. But Jack seemed to be in pretty good shape, after all, and Tip said to him:

"I guess you'd better remain standing, hereafter. It seems the safest way."

"Very well, dear father." just as you say, replied the smiling Jack, who had been in no wise confused by his tumble.

Tip sat down again. Presently the Pumpkinhead asked:

"What is that thing you are sitting on?"

"Oh, this is a horse," replied the boy, carelessly.

"What is a horse?" demanded Jack.

"A horse? Why, there are two kinds of horses," returned Tip, slightly puzzled how to explain. "One kind of horse is alive, and has four legs and a head and a tail. And people ride upon its back."

"I understand," said Jack, cheerfully "That's the kind of horse you are now sitting on."

"No, it isn't," answered Tip, promptly.

"Why not? That one has four legs, and a head, and a tail." Tip looked at the saw-horse more carefully, and found that the Pumpkinhead was right. The body had been formed from a tree-trunk, and a branch had been left sticking up at one end that looked very much like a tail. In the other end were two big knots that resembled eyes, and a place had been chopped away that might easily be mistaken for the horse's mouth. As for the legs, they were four straight limbs cut from trees and stuck fast into the body, being spread wide apart so that the saw-horse would stand firmly when a log was laid across it to be sawed.

"This thing resembles a real horse more than I imagined," said Tip, trying to explain. "But a real horse is alive, and trots and prances and eats oats, while this is nothing more than a dead horse, made of wood, and used to saw logs upon."

"If it were alive, wouldn't it trot, and prance, and eat oats?" inquired the Pumpkinhead.

"It would trot and prance, perhaps; but it wouldn't eat oats," replied the boy, laughing at the idea." And of course it can't ever be alive, because it is made of wood."

"So am I," answered the man.

Tip looked at him in surprise.

"Why, so you are!" he exclaimed. "And the magic powder that brought you to life is here in my pocket."

He brought out the pepper box, and eyed it curiously.

"I wonder," said he, musingly, "if it would bring the saw-horse to life."

"If it would," returned Jack, calmly for nothing seemed to surprise him" I could ride on its back, and that would save my joints from wearing out."

"I'll try it!" cried the boy, jumping up. "But I wonder if I can remember the words old Mombi said, and the way she held her hands up."

He thought it over for a minute, and as he had watched carefully from the hedge every motion of the old witch, and listened to her words, he believed he could repeat exactly what she had said and done.

So he began by sprinkling some of the magic Powder of Life from the pepper- box upon the body of the saw-horse. Then he lifted his left hand, with the little finger pointing upward, and said: "Weaugh!"

"What does that mean, dear father?" asked Jack, curiously.

"I don't know," answered Tip. Then he lifted his right hand, with the thumb pointing upward and said: "Teaugh!"

"What's that, dear father?" inquired Jack.

"It means you must keep quiet!" replied the boy, provoked at being interrupted at so important a moment.

"How fast I am learning!" remarked the Pumpkinhead, with his eternal smile.

Tip now lifted both hands above his head, with all the fingers and thumbs spread out, and cried in a loud voice: "Peaugh!"

Immediately the saw-horse moved, stretched its legs, yawned with its chopped-out mouth, and shook a few grains of the powder off its back. The rest of the powder seemed to have vanished into the body of the horse.

"Good!" called Jack, while the boy looked on in astonishment. "You are a very clever sorcerer, dear father!"

Chapter 5 - The Awakening of the Sawhorse

The Saw-Horse, finding himself alive, seemed even more astonished than Tip. He rolled his knotty eyes from side to side, taking a first wondering view of the world in which he had now so important an existence. Then he tried to look at himself; but he had, indeed, no neck to turn; so that in the endeavor to see his body he kept circling around and around, without catching even a glimpse of it. His legs were stiff and awkward, for there were no knee-joints in them; so that presently he bumped against Jack Pumpkinhead and sent that personage tumbling upon the moss that lined the roadside.

Tip became alarmed at this accident, as well as at the persistence of the Saw-Horse in prancing around in a circle; so he called out:

"Whoa! Whoa, there!"

The Saw-Horse paid no attention whatever to this command, and the next instant brought one of his wooden legs down upon Tip's foot so forcibly that the boy danced away in pain to a safer distance, from where he again yelled:

"Whoa! Whoa, I say!"

Jack had now managed to raise himself to a sitting position, and he looked at the Saw-Horse with much interest.

"I don't believe the animal can hear you," he remarked.

"I shout loud enough, don't I?" answered Tip, angrily.

"Yes; but the horse has no ears," said the smiling Pumpkinhead.

"Sure enough!" exclaimed Tip, noting the fact for the first time. "How, then, am I going to stop him?"

But at that instant the Saw-Horse stopped himself, having concluded it was impossible to see his own body. He saw Tip, however, and came close to the boy to observe him more fully.

It was really comical to see the creature walk; for it moved the legs on its right side together, and those on its left side together, as a pacing horse does; and that made its body rock sidewise, like a cradle.

Tip patted it upon the head, and said "Good boy! Good Boy!" in a coaxing tone; and the Saw-Horse pranced away to examine with its bulging eyes the form of Jack Pumpkinhead.

"I must find a halter for him," said Tip; and having made a search in his pocket he produced a roll of strong cord. Unwinding this, he approached the Saw-Horse and tied the cord around its neck, afterward fastening the other end to a large tree. The Saw-Horse, not understanding the action, stepped backward and snapped the string easily; but it made no attempt to run away.

"He's stronger than I thought," said the boy, "and rather obstinate, too."

"Why don't you make him some ears?" asked Jack. "Then you can tell him what to do."

"That's a splendid idea!" said Tip. "How did you happen to think of it?"

"Why, I didn't think of it," answered the Pumpkinhead; "I didn't need to, for it's the simplest and easiest thing to do."

So Tip got out his knife and fashioned some ears out of the bark of a small tree.

"I mustn't make them too big," he said, as he whittled, "or our horse would become a donkey."

"How is that?" inquired Jack, from the roadside.

"Why, a horse has bigger ears than a man; and a donkey has bigger ears than a horse," explained Tip.

"Then, if my ears were longer, would I be a horse?" asked Jack.

"My friend," said Tip, gravely, "you'll never be anything but a Pumpkinhead, no matter how big your ears are."

"Oh," returned Jack, nodding; "I think I understand."

"If you do, you're a wonder," remarked the boy "but there's no harm in thinking you understand. I guess these ears are ready now. Will you hold the horse while I stick them on?"

"Certainly, if you'll help me up," said Jack.

So Tip raised him to his feet, and the Pumpkinhead went to the horse and held its head while the boy bored two holes in it with his knife-blade and inserted the ears.

"They make him look very handsome," said Jack, admiringly.

But those words, spoken close to the Saw-Horse, and being the first sounds he had ever heard, so startled the animal that he made a bound forward and tumbled Tip on one side and Jack on the other. Then he continued to rush forward as if frightened by the clatter of his own foot-steps.

"Whoa!" shouted Tip, picking himself up; "whoa! you idiot whoa!" The Saw-Horse would probably have paid no attention to this, but just then it stepped a leg into a gopher-hole and stumbled head-over-heels to the ground, where it lay upon its back, frantically waving its four legs in the air.

Tip ran up to it.

"You're a nice sort of a horse, I must say!" he exclaimed. "Why didn't you stop when I yelled 'whoa?'"

"Does 'whoa' mean to stop?" asked the Saw-Horse, in a surprised voice, as it rolled its eyes upward to look at the boy.

"Of course it does," answered Tip.

"And a hole in the ground means to stop, also, doesn't it?" continued the horse.

"To be sure; unless you step over it," said Tip.

"What a strange place this is," the creature exclaimed, as if amazed. "What am I doing here, anyway?"

"Why, I've brought you to life," answered the boy "but it won't hurt you any, if you mind me and do as I tell you."

"Then I will do as you tell me," replied the Saw-Horse, humbly. "But what happened to me, a moment ago? I don't seem to be just right, someway."

"You're upside down," explained Tip. "But just keep those legs still a minute and I'll set you right side up again."

"How many sides have I?" asked the creature, wonderingly.

"Several," said Tip, briefly. "But do keep those legs still."

The Saw-Horse now became quiet, and held its legs rigid; so that Tip, after several efforts, was able to roll him over and set him upright.

"Ah, I seem all right now," said the queer animal, with a sigh.

"One of your ears is broken," Tip announced, after a careful examination. "I'll have to make a new one."

Then he led the Saw-Horse back to where Jack was vainly struggling to regain his feet, and after assisting the Pumpkinhead to stand upright Tip whittled out a new ear and fastened it to the horse's head.

"Now," said he, addressing his steed, "pay attention to what I'm going to tell you. 'Whoa!' means to stop; 'Get-Up!' means to walk forward; 'Trot!' means to go as fast as you can. Understand?"

"I believe I do," returned the horse.

"Very good. We are all going on a journey to the Emerald City, to see His Majesty, the Scarecrow; and Jack Pumpkinhead is going to ride on your back, so he won't wear out his joints."

"I don't mind," said the Saw-Horse. "Anything that suits you suits me."

Then Tip assisted Jack to get upon the horse.

"Hold on tight," he cautioned, "or you may fall off and crack your pumpkin head."

"That would be horrible!" said Jack, with a shudder. "What shall I hold on to?"

"Why, hold on to his ears," replied Tip, after a moment's hesitation.

"Don't do that!" remonstrated the Saw-Horse; "for then I can't hear."

That seemed reasonable, so Tip tried to think of something else.

"I'll fix it!" said he, at length. He went into the wood and cut a short length of limb from a young, stout tree. One end of this he sharpened to a point, and then he dug a hole in the back of the Saw-Horse, just behind its head. Next he brought a piece of rock from the road and hammered the post firmly into the animal's back.

"Stop! Stop!" shouted the horse; "you're jarring me terribly."

"Does it hurt?" asked the boy.

"Not exactly hurt," answered the animal; "but it makes me quite nervous to be jarred."

"Well, it's all over now" said Tip, encouragingly. "Now, Jack, be sure to hold fast to this post and then you can't fall off and get smashed."

So Jack held on tight, and Tip said to the horse:

"Get up."

The obedient creature at once walked forward, rocking from side to side as he raised his feet from the ground.

Tip walked beside the Saw-Horse, quite content with this addition to their party. Presently he began to whistle.

"What does that sound mean?" asked the horse.

"Don't pay any attention to it," said Tip. "I'm just whistling, and that only means I'm pretty well satisfied."

"I'd whistle myself, if I could push my lips together," remarked Jack. "I fear, dear father, that in some respects I am sadly lacking."

After journeying on for some distance the narrow path they were following turned into a broad roadway, paved with yellow brick. By the side of the road Tip noticed a sign-post that read:

But it was now growing dark, so he decided to camp for the night by the roadside and to resume the journey next morning by daybreak. He led the Saw- Horse to a grassy mound upon which grew several bushy trees, and carefully assisted the Pumpkinhead to alight.

"I think I'll lay you upon the ground, overnight," said the boy. "You will be safer that way."

"How about me?" asked the Saw-Horse.

"It won't hurt you to stand," replied Tip; "and, as you can't sleep, you may as well watch out and see that no one comes near to disturb us."

Then the boy stretched himself upon the grass beside the Pumpkinhead, and being greatly wearied by the journey was soon fast asleep.

Chapter 6 - Jack Pumpkinhead's Ride to the Emerald City

At daybreak Tip was awakened by the Pumpkinhead. He rubbed the sleep from his eyes, bathed in a little brook, and then ate a portion of his bread and cheese. Having thus prepared for a new day the boy said:

"Let us start at once. Nine miles is quite a distance, but we ought to reach the Emerald City by noon if no accidents happen." So the Pumpkinhead was again perched upon the back of the Saw-Horse and the journey was resumed.

Tip noticed that the purple tint of the grass and trees had now faded to a dull lavender, and before long this lavender appeared to take on a greenish tinge that gradually brightened as they drew nearer to the great City where the Scarecrow ruled.

The little party had traveled but a short two miles upon their way when the road of yellow brick was parted by a broad and swift river. Tip was puzzled how to cross over; but after a time he discovered a man in a ferry-boat approaching from the other side of the stream.

When the man reached the bank Tip asked:

"Will you row us to the other side?"

"Yes, if you have money," returned the ferryman, whose face looked cross and disagreeable.

"But I have no money," said Tip.

"None at all?" inquired the man.

"None at all," answered the boy.

"Then I'll not break my back rowing you over," said the ferryman, decidedly.

"What a nice man!" remarked the Pumpkinhead, smilingly.

The ferryman stared at him, but made no reply. Tip was trying to think, for it was a great disappointment to him to find his journey so suddenly brought to an end.

"I must certainly get to the Emerald City," he said to the boatman; "but how can I cross the river if you do not take me?"

The man laughed, and it was not a nice laugh.

"That wooden horse will float," said he; "and you can ride him across. As for the pumpkinheaded loon who accompanies you, let him sink or swim it won't matter greatly which."

"Don't worry about me," said Jack, smiling pleasantly upon the crabbed ferryman; "I'm sure I ought to float beautifully."

Tip thought the experiment was worth making, and the Saw-Horse, who did not know what danger meant, offered no objections whatever. So the boy led it down into the water and climbed upon its back. Jack also waded in up to his knees and grasped the tail of the horse so that he might keep his pumpkin head above the water.

"Now," said Tip, instructing the Saw-Horse, "if you wiggle your legs you will probably swim; and if you swim we shall probably reach the other side."

The Saw-Horse at once began to wiggle its legs, which acted as oars and moved the adventurers slowly across the river to the opposite side. So successful was the trip that presently they were climbing, wet and dripping, up the grassy bank.

Tip's trouser-legs and shoes were thoroughly soaked; but the Saw-Horse had floated so perfectly that from his knees up the boy was entirely dry. As for the Pumpkinhead, every stitch of his gorgeous clothing dripped water.

"The sun will soon dry us," said Tip "and, anyhow, we are now safely across, in spite of the ferryman, and can continue our journey.

"I didn't mind swimming, at all," remarked the horse.

"Nor did I," added Jack.

They soon regained the road of yellow brick, which proved to be a continuation of the road they had left on the other side, and then Tip once more mounted the Pumpkinhead upon the back of the Saw-Horse.

"If you ride fast," said he, "the wind will help to dry your clothing. I will hold on to the horse's tail and run after you. In this way we all will become dry in a very short time."

"Then the horse must step lively," said Jack.

"I'll do my best," returned the Saw-Horse, cheerfully.

Tip grasped the end of the branch that served as tail to the Saw-Horse, and called loudly: "Get-up!"

The horse started at a good pace, and Tip followed behind. Then he decided they could go faster, so he shouted: "Trot!"

Now, the Saw-Horse remembered that this word was the command to go as fast as he could; so he began rocking along the road at a tremendous pace, and Tip had hard work—running faster than he ever had before in his life—to keep his feet.

Soon he was out of breath, and although he wanted to call "Whoa!" to the horse, he found he could not get the word out of his throat. Then the end of the tail he was clutching, being nothing more than a dead branch, suddenly broke away, and the next minute the boy was rolling in the dust of the road, while the horse and its pumpkin-headed rider dashed on and quickly disappeared in the distance.

By the time Tip had picked himself up and cleared the dust from his throat so he could say "Whoa!" there was no further need of saying it, for the horse was long since out of sight.

So he did the only sensible thing he could do. He sat down and took a good rest, and afterward began walking along the road.

"Some time I will surely overtake them," he reflected; "for the road will end at the gates of the Emerald City, and they can go no further than that."

Meantime Jack was holding fast to the post and the Saw-Horse was tearing along the road like a racer. Neither of them knew Tip was left behind, for the Pumpkinhead did not look around and the Saw-Horse couldn't.

As he rode, Jack noticed that the grass and trees had become a bright emerald-green in color, so he guessed they were nearing the Emerald City even before the tall spires and domes came into sight.

At length a high wall of green stone, studded thick with emeralds, loomed up before them; and fearing the Saw-Horse would not know enough to stop and so might smash them both against this wall, Jack ventured to cry "Whoa!" as loud as he could.

So suddenly did the horse obey that had it not been for his post Jack would have been pitched off head foremost, and his beautiful face ruined.

"That was a fast ride, dear father!" he exclaimed; and then, hearing no reply, he turned around and discovered for the first time that Tip was not there.

This apparent desertion puzzled the Pumpkinhead, and made him uneasy. And while he was wondering what had become of the boy, and what he ought to do next under such trying circumstances, the gateway in the green wall opened and a man came out.

This man was short and round, with a fat face that seemed remarkably good- natured. He was clothed all in green and wore a high, peaked green hat upon his head and green spectacles over his eyes. Bowing before the Pumpkinhead he said:

"I am the Guardian of the Gates of the Emerald City. May I inquire who you are, and what is your business?"

"My name is Jack Pumpkinhead," returned the other, smilingly; "but as to my business, I haven't the least idea in the world what it is."

The Guardian of the Gates looked surprised, and shook his head as if dissatisfied with the reply.

"What are you, a man or a pumpkin?" he asked, politely.

"Both, if you please," answered Jack.

"And this wooden horse—is it alive?" questioned the Guardian.

The horse rolled one knotty eye upward and winked at Jack. Then it gave a prance and brought one leg down on the Guardian's toes.

"Ouch!" cried the man; "I'm sorry I asked that question. But the answer is most convincing. Have you any errand, sir, in the Emerald City?"

"It seems to me that I have," replied the Pumpkinhead, seriously; "but I cannot think what it is. My father knows all about it, but he is not here."

"This is a strange affair very strange!" declared the Guardian. "But you seem harmless. Folks do not smile so delightfully when they mean mischief."

"As for that," said Jack, "I cannot help my smile, for it is carved on my face with a jack-knife."

"Well, come with me into my room," resumed the Guardian, "and I will see what can be done for you."

So Jack rode the Saw-Horse through the gateway into a little room built into the wall. The Guardian pulled a bell-cord, and presently a very tall soldier—clothed in a green uniform—entered from the opposite door. This soldier carried a long green gun over his shoulder and had lovely green whiskers that fell quite to his knees. The Guardian at once addressed him, saying:

"Here is a strange gentleman who doesn't know why he has come to the Emerald City, or what he wants. Tell me, what shall we do with him?"

The Soldier with the Green Whiskers looked at Jack with much care and curiosity. Finally he shook his head so positively that little waves rippled down his whiskers, and then he said:

"I must take him to His Majesty, the Scarecrow."

But what will His Majesty, the Scarecrow, do with him?" asked the Guardian of the Gates.

"That is His Majesty's business," returned the soldier. "I have troubles enough of my own. All outside troubles must be turned over to His Majesty. So put the spectacles on this fellow, and I'll take him to the royal palace."

So the Guardian opened a big box of spectacles and tried to fit a pair to Jack's great round eyes.

"I haven't a pair in stock that will really cover those eyes up," said the little man, with a sigh; "and your head is so big that I shall be obliged to tie the spectacles on."

"But why need I wear spectacles?" asked Jack.

"It's the fashion here," said the Soldier, "and they will keep you from being blinded by the glitter and glare of the gorgeous Emerald City."

"Oh!" exclaimed Jack. "Tie them on, by all means. I don't wish to be blinded."

"Nor I!" broke in the Saw-Horse; so a pair of green spectacles was quickly fastened over the bulging knots that served it for eyes.

Then the Soldier with the Green Whiskers led them through the inner gate and they at once found themselves in the main street of the magnificent Emerald City.

Sparkling green gems ornamented the fronts of the beautiful houses and the towers and turrets were all faced with emeralds. Even the green marble pavement glittered with precious stones, and it was indeed a grand and marvelous sight to one who beheld it for the first time.

However, the Pumpkinhead and the Saw-Horse, knowing nothing of wealth and beauty, paid little attention to the wonderful sights they saw through their green spectacles. They calmly followed after the green soldier and scarcely noticed the crowds of green people who stared at them in surprise. When a green dog ran out and barked at them the Saw- Horse promptly kicked at it with its wooden leg and sent the little animal howling into one of the houses; but nothing more serious than this happened to interrupt their progress to the royal palace.

The Pumpkinhead wanted to ride up the green marble steps and straight into the Scarecrow's presence; but the soldier would not permit that. So Jack dismounted, with much difficulty, and a servant led the Saw-Horse around to the rear while the Soldier with the Green Whiskers escorted the Pumpkinhead into the palace, by the front entrance.

The stranger was left in a handsomely furnished waiting room while the soldier went to announce him. It so happened that at this hour His Majesty was at leisure and greatly bored for want of something to do, so he ordered his visitor to be shown at once into his throne room.

Jack felt no fear or embarrassment at meeting the ruler of this magnificent city, for he was entirely ignorant of all worldly customs. But when he entered the room and saw for the first time His Majesty the Scarecrow seated upon his glittering throne, he stopped short in amazement.

Chapter 7 - His Majesty the Scarecrow

I suppose every reader of this book knows what a scarecrow is; but Jack Pumpkinhead, never having seen such a creation, was more surprised at meeting the remarkable King of the Emerald City than by any other one experience of his brief life.

His Majesty the Scarecrow was dressed in a suit of faded blue clothes, and his head was merely a small sack stuffed with straw, upon which eyes, ears, a nose and a mouth had been rudely painted to represent a face. The clothes were also stuffed with straw, and that so unevenly or carelessly that his Majesty's legs and arms seemed more bumpy than was necessary. Upon his hands were gloves with long fingers, and these were padded with cotton. Wisps of straw stuck out from the monarch's coat and also from his neck and boot-tops. Upon his head he wore a heavy golden crown set thick with sparkling jewels, and the weight of this crown caused his brow to sag in wrinkles, giving a thoughtful expression to the painted face. Indeed, the crown alone betokened majesty; in all else the, Scarecrow King was but a simple scarecrow—flimsy, awkward, and unsubstantial.

But if the strange appearance of his Majesty the Scarecrow seemed startling to Jack, no less wonderful was the form of the Pumpkinhead to the Scarecrow. The purple trousers and pink waistcoat and red shirt hung loosely over the wooden joints Tip had manufactured, and the carved face on the pumpkin grinned perpetually, as if its wearer considered life the jolliest thing imaginable.

At first, indeed, His Majesty thought his queer visitor was laughing at him, and was inclined to resent such a liberty; but it was not without reason that the Scarecrow had attained the reputation of being the wisest personage in the Land of Oz. He made a more careful examination of his visitor, and soon discovered that Jack's features were carved into a smile and that he could not look grave if he wished to.

The King was the first to speak. After regarding Jack for some minutes he said, in a tone of wonder:

"Where on earth did you come from, and how do you happen to be alive?"

"I beg your Majesty's pardon," returned the Pumpkinhead; "but I do not understand you."

"What don't you understand?" asked the Scarecrow.

"Why, I don't understand your language. You see, I came from the Country of the Gillikins, so that I am a foreigner."

"Ah, to be sure!" exclaimed the Scarecrow. "I myself speak the language of the Munchkins, which is also the language of the Emerald City. But you, I suppose, speak the language of the Pumpkinheads?"

"Exactly so, your Majesty" replied the other, bowing; "so it will be impossible for us to understand one another."

"That is unfortunate, certainly," said the Scarecrow, thoughtfully. "We must have an interpreter."

"What is an interpreter?" asked Jack.

"A person who understands both my language and your own. When I say anything, the interpreter can tell you what I mean; and when you say anything the interpreter can tell me what you mean. For the interpreter can speak both languages as well as understand them."

"That is certainly clever," said Jack, greatly pleased at finding so simple a way out of the difficulty.

So the Scarecrow commanded the Soldier with the Green Whiskers to search among his people until he found one who understood the language of the Gillikins as well as the language of the Emerald City, and to bring that person to him at once.

When the Soldier had departed the Scarecrow said:

"Won't you take a chair while we are waiting?"

"Your Majesty forgets that I cannot understand you," replied the Pumpkinhead. "If you wish me to sit down you must make a sign for me to do so." The Scarecrow came down from his throne and rolled an armchair to a position behind the Pumpkinhead. Then he gave Jack a sudden push that sent him sprawling upon the cushions in so awkward a fashion that he doubled up like a jackknife, and had hard work to untangle himself.

"Did you understand that sign?" asked His Majesty, politely.

"Perfectly," declared Jack, reaching up his arms to turn his head to the front, the pumpkin having twisted around upon the stick that supported it.

"You seem hastily made," remarked the Scarecrow, watching Jack's efforts to straighten himself.

"Not more so than your Majesty," was the frank reply.

"There is this difference between us," said the Scarecrow, "that whereas I will bend, but not break, you will break, but not bend."

At this moment the soldier returned leading a young girl by the hand. She seemed very sweet and modest, having a pretty face and beautiful green eyes and hair. A dainty green silk skirt reached to her knees, showing silk stockings embroidered with pea-pods, and green satin slippers with bunches of lettuce for decorations instead of bows or buckles. Upon her silken waist clover leaves were embroidered, and she wore a jaunty little jacket trimmed with sparkling emeralds of a uniform size.

"Why, it's little Jellia Jamb!" exclaimed the Scarecrow, as the green maiden bowed her pretty head before him. "Do you understand the language of the Gillikins, my dear?"

"Yes, your Majesty, she answered, "for I was born in the North Country."

"Then you shall be our interpreter," said the Scarecrow, "and explain to this Pumpkinhead all that I say, and also explain to me all that he says. Is this arrangement satisfactory?" he asked, turning toward his guest.

"Very satisfactory indeed," was the reply.

"Then ask him, to begin with," resumed the Scarecrow, turning to Jellia, "what brought him to the Emerald City"

But instead of this the girl, who had been staring at Jack, said to him:

"You are certainly a wonderful creature. Who made you?"

"A boy named Tip," answered Jack.

"What does he say?" inquired the Scarecrow. "My ears must have deceived me. What did he say?"

"He says that your Majesty's brains seem to have come loose," replied the girl, demurely.

The Scarecrow moved uneasily upon his throne, and felt of his head with his left hand.

"What a fine thing it is to understand two different languages," he said, with a perplexed sigh. "Ask him, my dear, if he has any objection to being put in jail for insulting the ruler of the Emerald City."

"I didn't insult you!" protested Jack, indignantly.

"Tut—tut!" cautioned the Scarecrow "wait, until Jellia translates my speech. What have we got an interpreter for, if you break out in this rash way?"

"All right, I'll wait," replied the Pumpkinhead, in a surly tone—although his face smiled as genially as ever. "Translate the speech, young woman."

"His Majesty inquires if you are hungry, said Jellia.

"Oh, not at all!" answered Jack, more pleasantly, "for it is impossible for me to eat."

"It's the same way with me," remarked the Scarecrow. "What did he say, Jellia, my dear?"

"He asked if you were aware that one of your eyes is painted larger than the other," said the girl, mischievously.

"Don't you believe her, your Majesty, cried Jack.

"Oh, I don't," answered the Scarecrow, calmly. Then, casting a sharp look at the girl, he asked:

"Are you quite certain you understand the languages of both the Gillikins and the Munchkins?"

"Quite certain, your Majesty," said Jellia Jamb, trying hard not to laugh in the face of royalty.

"Then how is it that I seem to understand them myself?" inquired the Scarecrow.

"Because they are one and the same!" declared the girl, now laughing merrily. "Does not your Majesty know that in all the land of Oz but one language is spoken?"

"Is it indeed so?" cried the Scarecrow, much relieved to hear this; "then I might easily have been my own interpreter!"

"It was all my fault, your Majesty," said Jack, looking rather foolish," I thought we must surely speak different languages, since we came from different countries."

"This should be a warning to you never to think," returned the Scarecrow, severely. "For unless one can think wisely it is better to remain a dummy—which you most certainly are."

"I am!—I surely am!" agreed the Pumpkinhead.

"It seems to me," continued the Scarecrow, more mildly, "that your manufacturer spoiled some good pies to create an indifferent man."

"I assure your Majesty that I did not ask to be created," answered Jack.

"Ah! It was the same in my case," said the King, pleasantly. And so, as we differ from all ordinary people, let us become friends."

"With all my heart!" exclaimed Jack.

"What! Have you a heart?" asked the Scarecrow, surprised.

"No; that was only imaginative—I might say, a figure of speech," said the other.

"Well, your most prominent figure seems to be a figure of wood; so I must beg you to restrain an imagination which, having no brains, you have no right to exercise," suggested the Scarecrow, warningly.

"To be sure!" said Jack, without in the least comprehending.

His Majesty then dismissed Jellia Jamb and the Soldier with the Green Whiskers, and when they were gone he took his new friend by the arm and led him into the courtyard to play a game of quoits.

Chapter 8 - Gen. Jinjur's Army of Revolt

Tip was so anxious to rejoin his man Jack and the Saw-Horse that he walked a full half the distance to the Emerald City without stopping to rest. Then he discovered that he was hungry and the crackers and cheese he had provided for the Journey had all been eaten.

While wondering what he should do in this emergency he came upon a girl sitting by the roadside. She wore a costume that struck the boy as being remarkably brilliant: her silken waist being of emerald green and her skirt of four distinct colors—blue in front, yellow at the left side, red at the back and purple at the right side. Fastening the waist in front were four buttons—the top one blue, the next yellow, a third red and the last purple.

The splendor of this dress was almost barbaric; so Tip was fully justified in staring at the gown for some moments before his eyes were attracted by the pretty face above it. Yes, the face was pretty enough, he decided; but it wore an expression of discontent coupled to a shade of defiance or audacity.

While the boy stared the girl looked upon him calmly. A lunch basket stood beside her, and she held a dainty sandwich in one hand and a hard-boiled egg in the other, eating with an evident appetite that aroused Tip's sympathy.

He was just about to ask a share of the luncheon when the girl stood up and brushed the crumbs from her lap.

"There!" said she; "it is time for me to go. Carry that basket for me and help yourself to its contents if you are hungry."

Tip seized the basket eagerly and began to eat, following for a time the strange girl without bothering to ask questions. She walked along before him with swift strides, and there was about her an air of decision and importance that led him to suspect she was some great personage.

Finally, when he had satisfied his hunger, he ran up beside her and tried to keep pace with her swift footsteps—a very difficult feat, for she was much taller than he, and evidently in a hurry.

"Thank you very much for the sandwiches," said Tip, as he trotted along. "May I ask your name?"

"I am General Jinjur," was the brief reply.

"Oh!" said the boy surprised. "What sort of a General?"

"I command the Army of Revolt in this war," answered the General, with unnecessary sharpness.

"Oh!" he again exclaimed. "I didn't know there was a war."

"You were not supposed to know it," she returned, "for we have kept it a secret; and considering that our army is composed entirely of girls," she added, with some pride, "it is surely a remarkable thing that our Revolt is not yet discovered."

"It is, indeed," acknowledged Tip. "But where is your army?"

"About a mile from here," said General Jinjur. "The forces have assembled from all parts of the Land of Oz, at my express command. For this is the day we are to conquer His Majesty the Scarecrow, and wrest from him the throne. The Army of Revolt only awaits my coming to march upon the Emerald City."

"Well!" declared Tip, drawing a long breath, "this is certainly a surprising thing! May I ask why you wish to conquer His Majesty the Scarecrow?"

"Because the Emerald City has been ruled by men long enough, for one reason," said the girl.

"Moreover, the City glitters with beautiful gems, which might far better be used for rings, bracelets and necklaces; and there is enough money in the King's treasury to buy every girl in our Army a dozen new gowns. So we intend to conquer the City and run the government to suit ourselves."

Jinjur spoke these words with an eagerness and decision that proved she was in earnest.

"But war is a terrible thing," said Tip, thoughtfully.

"This war will be pleasant," replied the girl, cheerfully.

"Many of you will be slain!" continued the boy, in an awed voice.

"Oh, no", said Jinjur. "What man would oppose a girl, or dare to harm her? And there is not an ugly face in my entire Army."

Tip laughed.

"Perhaps you are right," said he. "But the Guardian of the Gate is considered a faithful Guardian, and the King's Army will not let the City be conquered without a struggle."

"The Army is old and feeble," replied General Jinjur, scornfully. "His strength has all been used to grow whiskers, and his wife has such a temper that she has already pulled more than half of them out by the roots. When the Wonderful Wizard reigned the Soldier with the Green Whiskers was a very good Royal Army, for people feared the Wizard. But no one is afraid of the Scarecrow, so his Royal Army don't count for much in time of war."

After this conversation they proceeded some distance in silence, and before long reached a large clearing in the forest where fully four hundred young women were assembled. These were laughing and talking together as gaily as if they had gathered for a picnic instead of a war of conquest.

They were divided into four companies, and Tip noticed that all were dressed in costumes similar to that worn by General Jinjur. The only real difference was that while those girls from the Munchkin country had the blue strip in front of their skirts, those from the country of the Quadlings had the red strip in front; and those from the country of the Winkies had the yellow strip in front, and the Gillikin girls wore the purple strip in front. All had green waists, representing the Emerald City they intended to conquer, and the top button on each waist indicated by its color which country the wearer came from. The uniforms were jaunty and becoming, and quite effective when massed together.

Tip thought this strange Army bore no weapons whatever; but in this he was wrong. For each girl had stuck through the knot of her back hair two long, glittering knitting-needles.

General Jinjur immediately mounted the stump of a tree and addressed her army.

"Friends, fellow-citizens, and girls!" she said; "we are about to begin our great Revolt against the men of Oz! We march to conquer the Emerald City—to dethrone the Scarecrow King—to acquire thousands of gorgeous gems—to rifle the royal treasury—and to obtain power over our former oppressors!"

"Hurrah!" said those who had listened; but Tip thought most of the Army was too much engaged in chattering to pay attention to the words of the General.

The command to march was now given, and the girls formed themselves into four bands, or companies, and set off with eager strides toward the Emerald City.

The boy followed after them, carrying several baskets and wraps and packages which various members of the Army of Revolt had placed in his care. It was not long before they came to the green granite walls of the City and halted before the gateway.

The Guardian of the Gate at once came out and looked at them curiously, as if a circus had come to town. He carried a bunch of keys swung round his neck by a golden chain; his hands were thrust carelessly into his pockets, and he seemed to have no idea at all that the City was threatened by rebels. Speaking pleasantly to the girls, he said:

"Good morning, my dears! What can I do for you?"

"Surrender instantly!" answered General Jinjur, standing before him and frowning as terribly as her pretty face would allow her to.

"Surrender!" echoed the man, astounded. "Why, it's impossible. It's against the law! I never heard of such a thing in my life."

"Still, you must surrender!" exclaimed the General, fiercely. "We are revolting!"

"You don't look it," said the Guardian, gazing from one to another, admiringly.

"But we are!" cried Jinjur, stamping her foot, impatiently; "and we mean to conquer the Emerald City!"

"Good gracious!" returned the surprised Guardian of the Gates; "what a nonsensical idea! Go home to your mothers, my good girls, and milk the cows and bake the bread. Don't you know it's a dangerous thing to conquer a city?"

"We are not afraid!" responded the General; and she looked so determined that it made the Guardian uneasy.

So he rang the bell for the Soldier with the Green Whiskers, and the next minute was sorry he had done so. For immediately he was surrounded by a crowd of girls who drew the knitting-needles from their hair and began jabbing them at the Guardian with the sharp points dangerously near his fat cheeks and blinking eyes.

The poor man howled loudly for mercy and made no resistance when Jinjur drew the bunch of keys from around his neck.

Followed by her Army the General now rushed
to the gateway, where she was confronted by the Royal Army of Oz—which was the other name for the Soldier with the Green Whiskers.

"Halt!" he cried, and pointed his long gun full in the face of the leader.

Some of the girls screamed and ran back, but General Jinjur bravely stood her ground and said, reproachfully:

"Why, how now? Would you shoot a poor, defenceless girl?"

"No," replied the soldier. "for my gun isn't loaded."

"Not loaded?"

"No; for fear of accidents. And I've forgotten where I hid the powder and shot to load it with. But if you'll wait a short time I'll try to hunt them up."

"Don't trouble yourself," said Jinjur, cheerfully. Then she turned to her Army and cried:

"Girls, the gun isn't loaded!"

"Hooray," shrieked the rebels, delighted at this good news, and they proceeded to rush upon the Soldier with the Green Whiskers in such a crowd that it was a wonder they didn't stick the knitting-needles into one another.

But the Royal Army of Oz was too much afraid of women to meet the onslaught. He simply turned about and ran with all his might through the gate and toward the royal palace, while General Jinjur and her mob flocked into the unprotected City.

In this way was the Emerald City captured without a drop of blood being spilled. The Army of Revolt had become an Army of Conquerors!

Chapter 9 - The Scarecrow Plans an escape

Tip slipped away from the girls and followed swiftly after the Soldier with the Green Whiskers. The invading army entered the City more slowly, for they stopped to dig emeralds out of the walls and paving-stones with the points of their knitting-needles. So the Soldier and the boy reached the palace before the news had spread that the City was conquered.

The Scarecrow and Jack Pumpkinhead were still playing at quoits in the courtyard when the game was interrupted by the abrupt entrance of the Royal Army of Oz, who came flying in without his hat or gun, his clothes in sad disarray and his long beard floating a yard behind him as he ran.

"Tally one for me," said the Scarecrow, calmly "What's wrong, my man?" he added, addressing the Soldier.

"Oh! your Majesty—your Majesty! The City is conquered!" gasped the Royal Army, who was all out of breath.

"This is quite sudden," said the Scarecrow. "But please go and bar all the doors and windows of the palace, while I show this Pumpkinhead how to throw a quoit."

The Soldier hastened to do this, while Tip, who had arrived at his heels, remained in the courtyard to look at the Scarecrow with wondering eyes.

His Majesty continued to throw the quoits as coolly as if no danger threatened his throne, but the Pumpkinhead, having caught sight of Tip, ambled toward the boy as fast as his wooden legs would go.

"Good afternoon, noble parent!" he cried, delightedly." I'm glad to see you are here. That terrible Saw-Horse ran away with me."

"I suspected it," said Tip. "Did you get hurt? Are you cracked at all?"

"No, I arrived safely," answered Jack, "and his Majesty has been very kind indeed to me.

At this moment the Soldier with the Green Whiskers returned, and the Scarecrow asked:

"By the way, who has conquered me?"

"A regiment of girls, gathered from the four corners of the Land of Oz," replied the Soldier, still pale with fear.

"But where was my Standing Army at the time?" inquired his Majesty, looking at the Soldier, gravely.

"Your Standing Army was running," answered the fellow, honestly; "for no man could face the terrible weapons of the invaders."

"Well," said the Scarecrow, after a moment's thought, "I don't mind much the loss of my throne, for it's a tiresome job to rule over the Emerald City. And this crown is so heavy that it makes my head ache. But I hope the Conquerors have no intention of injuring me, just because I happen to be the King."

"I heard them, say" remarked Tip, with some hesitation, "that they intend to make a rag carpet of your outside and stuff their sofa-cushions with your inside."

"Then I am really in danger," declared his Majesty, positively, "and it will be wise for me to consider a means to escape."

"Where can you go?" asked Jack Pumpkinhead.

"Why, to my friend the Tin Woodman, who rules over the Winkies, and calls himself their Emperor," was the answer. "I am sure he will protect me."

Tip was looking out the window.

"The palace is surrounded by the enemy," said he "It is too late to escape. They would soon tear you to pieces."

The Scarecrow sighed.

"In an emergency," he announced, "it is always a good thing to pause and reflect. Please excuse me while I pause and reflect."

"But we also are in danger," said the Pumpkinhead, anxiously." If any of these girls understand cooking, my end is not far off!"

"Nonsense!" exclaimed the Scarecrow. "they're too busy to cook, even if they know how!"

"But should I remain here a prisoner for any length of time," protested Jack," I'm liable to spoil."

"Ah! then you would not be fit to associate with," returned the Scarecrow. "The matter is more serious than I suspected."

"You," said the Pumpkinhead, gloomily, "are liable to live for many years. My life is necessarily short. So I must take advantage of the few days that remain to me."

"There, there! Don't worry," answered the Scarecrow soothingly; "if you'll keep quiet long enough for me to think, I'll try to find some way for us all to escape."

So the others waited in patient silence while the Scarecrow walked to a corner and stood with his face to the wall for a good five minutes. At the end of that time he faced them with a more cheerful expression upon his painted face.

"Where is the Saw-Horse you rode here?" he asked the Pumpkinhead.

"Why, I said he was a jewel, and so your man locked him up in the royal treasury," said Jack.

"It was the only place I could think of your Majesty," added the Soldier, fearing he had made a blunder.

"It pleases me very much," said the Scarecrow. "Has the animal been fed?"

"Oh, yes; I gave him a heaping peck of sawdust."

"Excellent!" cried the Scarecrow. "Bring the horse here at once."

The Soldier hastened away, and presently they heard the clattering of the horse's wooden legs upon the pavement as he was led into the courtyard.

His Majesty regarded the steed critically. "He doesn't seem especially graceful!" he remarked, musingly. "but I suppose he can run?"

"He can, indeed," said Tip, gazing upon the Saw-Horse admiringly.

"Then, bearing us upon his back, he must make a dash through the ranks of the rebels and carry us to my friend the Tin Woodman," announced the Scarecrow.

"He can't carry four!" objected Tip.

"No, but he may be induced to carry three," said his Majesty. "I shall therefore leave my Royal Army Behind. For, from the ease with which he was conquered, I have little confidence in his powers."

"Still, he can run," declared Tip, laughing.

"I expected this blow" said the Soldier, sulkily; "but I can bear it. I shall disguise myself by cutting off my lovely green whiskers. And, after all, it is no more dangerous to face those reckless girls than to ride this fiery, untamed wooden horse!"

"Perhaps you are right," observed his Majesty. "But, for my part, not being a soldier, I am fond of danger. Now, my boy, you must mount first. And please sit as close to the horse's neck as possible."

Tip climbed quickly to his place, and the Soldier and the Scarecrow managed to hoist the Pumpkinhead to a seat just behind him. There remained so little space for the King that he was liable to fall off as soon as the horse started.

"Fetch a clothesline," said the King to his Army, "and tie us all together. Then if one falls off we will all fall off."

And while the Soldier was gone for the clothesline his Majesty continued, "it is well for me to be careful, for my very existence is in danger."

"I have to be as careful as you do," said Jack.

"Not exactly," replied the Scarecrow. "for if anything happened to me, that would be the end of me. But if anything happened to you, they could use you for seed."

The Soldier now returned with a long line and tied all three firmly together, also lashing them to the body of the Saw-Horse; so there seemed little danger of their tumbling off.

"Now throw open the gates," commanded the Scarecrow, "and we will make a dash to liberty or to death."

The courtyard in which they were standing was located in the center of the great palace, which surrounded it on all sides. But in one place a passage led to an outer gateway, which the Soldier had barred by order of his sovereign. It was through this gateway his Majesty proposed to escape, and the Royal Army now led the Saw-Horse along the passage and unbarred the gate, which swung backward with a loud crash.

"Now," said Tip to the horse, "you must save us all. Run as fast as you can for the gate of the City, and don't let anything stop you."

"All right!" answered the Saw-Horse, gruffly, and dashed away so suddenly that Tip had to gasp for breath and hold firmly to the post he had driven into the creature's neck.

Several of the girls, who stood outside guarding the palace, were knocked over by the Saw-Horse's mad rush. Others ran screaming out of the way, and only one or two jabbed their knitting-needles frantically at the escaping prisoners. Tip got one small prick in his left arm, which smarted for an hour afterward; but the needles had no effect upon the Scarecrow or Jack Pumpkinhead, who never even suspected they were being prodded.

As for the Saw-Horse, he made a wonderful record upsetting a fruit cart, overturning several meek looking men, and finally bowling over the new Guardian of the Gate—a fussy little fat woman appointed by General Jinjur.

Nor did the impetuous charger stop then. Once outside the walls of the Emerald City he dashed along the road to the West with fast and violent leaps that shook the breath out of the boy and filled the Scarecrow with wonder.

Jack had ridden at this mad rate once before, so he devoted every effort to holding, with both hands, his pumpkin head upon its stick, enduring meantime the dreadful jolting with the courage of a philosopher.

"Slow him up! Slow him up!" shouted the Scarecrow. "My straw is all shaking down into my legs."

But Tip had no breath to speak, so the Saw-Horse continued his wild career unchecked and with unabated speed.

Presently they came to the banks of a wide river, and without a pause the wooden steed gave one final leap and launched them all in mid-air.

A second later they were rolling, splashing and bobbing about in the water, the horse struggling frantically to find a rest for its feet and its riders being first plunged beneath the rapid current and then floating upon the surface like corks.

Chapter 10 - The Journey to the Tin Woodman

Tip was well soaked and dripping water from every angle of his body. But he managed to lean forward and shout in the ear of the Saw-Horse:

"Keep still, you fool! Keep still!"

The horse at once ceased struggling and floated calmly upon the surface, its wooden body being as buoyant as a raft.

"What does that word 'fool' mean?" enquired the horse.

"It is a term of reproach," answered Tip, somewhat ashamed of the expression. "I only use it when I am angry."

"Then it pleases me to be able to call you a fool, in return," said the horse. "For I did not make the river, nor put it in our way; so only a term of, reproach is fit for one who becomes angry with me for falling into the water."

"That is quite evident," replied Tip; "so I will acknowledge myself in the wrong." Then he called out to the Pumpkinhead: "are you all right, Jack?"

There was no reply. So the boy called to the King "are you all right, your majesty?"

The Scarecrow groaned.

"I'm all wrong, somehow," he said, in a weak voice. "How very wet this water is!"

Tip was bound so tightly by the cord that he could not turn his head to look at his companions; so he said to the Saw-Horse:

"Paddle with your legs toward the shore."

The horse obeyed, and although their progress was slow they finally reached the opposite river bank at a place where it was low enough to enable the creature to scramble upon dry land.

With some difficulty the boy managed to get his knife out of his pocket and cut the cords that bound the riders to one another and to the wooden horse. He heard the Scarecrow fall to the ground with a mushy sound, and then he himself quickly dismounted and looked at his friend Jack.

The wooden body, with its gorgeous clothing, still sat upright upon the horse's back; but the pumpkin head was gone, and only the sharpened stick that served for a neck was visible. As for the Scarecrow, the straw in his body had shaken down with the jolting and packed itself into his legs and the lower part of his body—which appeared very plump and round while his upper half seemed like an empty sack. Upon his head the Scarecrow still wore the heavy crown, which had been sewed on to prevent his losing it; but the head was now so damp and limp that the weight of the gold and jewels sagged forward and crushed the painted face into a mass of wrinkles that made him look exactly like a Japanese pug dog.

Tip would have laughed—had he not been so anxious about his man Jack. But the Scarecrow, however damaged, was all there, while the pumpkin head that was so necessary to Jack's existence was missing; so the boy seized a long pole that fortunately lay near at hand and anxiously turned again toward the river.

Far out upon the waters he sighted the golden hue of the pumpkin, which gently bobbed up and down with the motion of the waves. At that moment it was quite out of Tip's reach, but after a time it floated nearer and still nearer until the boy was able to reach it with his pole and draw it to the shore. Then he brought it to the top of the bank, carefully wiped the water from its pumpkin face with his handkerchief, and ran with it to Jack and replaced the head upon the man's neck.

"Dear me!" were Jack's first words. "What a dreadful experience! I wonder if water is liable to spoil pumpkins?"

Tip did not think a reply was necessary, for he knew that the Scarecrow also stood in need of his help. So he carefully removed the straw from the King's body and legs, and spread it out in the sun to dry. The wet clothing he hung over the body of the Saw-Horse.

"If water spoils pumpkins," observed Jack, with a deep sigh, "then my days are numbered."

"I've never noticed that water spoils pumpkins," returned Tip; "unless the water happens to be boiling. If your head isn't cracked, my friend, you must be in fairly good condition."

"Oh, my head isn't cracked in the least," declared Jack, more cheerfully.

"Then don't worry," retorted the boy. "Care once killed a cat."

"Then," said Jack, seriously, "I am very glad indeed that I am not a cat."

The sun was fast drying their clothing, and Tip stirred up his Majesty's straw so that the warm rays might absorb the moisture and make it as crisp and dry as ever. When this had been accomplished he stuffed the Scarecrow into symmetrical shape and smoothed out his face so that he wore his usual gay and charming expression.

"Thank you very much," said the monarch, brightly, as he walked about and found himself to be well balanced. "There are several distinct advantages in being a Scarecrow. For if one has friends near at hand to repair damages, nothing very serious can happen to you."

"I wonder if hot sunshine is liable to crack pumpkins," said Jack, with an anxious ring in his voice.

"Not at all—not at all!" replied the Scarecrow, gaily." All you need fear, my boy, is old age. When your golden youth has decayed we shall quickly part company—but you needn't look forward to it; we'll discover the fact ourselves, and notify you. But come! Let us resume our journey. I am anxious to greet my friend the Tin Woodman."

So they remounted the Saw-Horse, Tip holding to the post, the Pumpkinhead clinging to Tip, and the Scarecrow with both arms around the wooden form of Jack.

"Go slowly, for now there is no danger of pursuit," said Tip to his steed.

"All right!" responded the creature, in a voice rather gruff.

"Aren't you a little hoarse?" asked the Pumpkinhead politely.

The Saw-Horse gave an angry prance and rolled one knotty eye backward toward Tip.

"See here," he growled, "can't you protect me from insult?"

"To be sure!" answered Tip, soothingly. "I am sure Jack meant no harm. And it will not do for us to quarrel, you know; we must all remain good friends."

"I'll have nothing more to do with that Pumpkinhead," declared the Saw- Horse, viciously. "he loses his head too easily to suit me."

There seemed no fitting reply to this speech, so for a time they rode along in silence.

After a while the Scarecrow remarked:

"This reminds me of old times. It was upon this grassy knoll that I once saved Dorothy from the Stinging Bees of the Wicked Witch of the West."

"Do Stinging Bees injure pumpkins?" asked Jack, glancing around fearfully.

"They are all dead, so it doesn't matter," replied the Scarecrow." And here is where Nick Chopper destroyed the Wicked Witch's Grey Wolves."

"Who was Nick Chopper?" asked Tip.

"That is the name of my friend the Tin Woodman, answered his Majesty. And here is where the Winged Monkeys captured and bound us, and flew away with little Dorothy," he continued, after they had traveled a little way farther.

"Do Winged Monkeys ever eat pumpkins?" asked Jack, with a shiver of fear.

"I do not know; but you have little cause to, worry, for the Winged Monkeys are now the slaves of Glinda the Good, who owns the Golden Cap that commands their services," said the Scarecrow, reflectively.

Then the stuffed monarch became lost in thought recalling the days of past adventures. And the Saw-Horse rocked and rolled over the flower-strewn fields and carried its riders swiftly upon their way.

Twilight fell, bye and bye, and then the dark shadows of night. So Tip stopped the horse and they all proceeded to dismount.

"I'm tired out," said the boy, yawning wearily; "and the grass is soft and cool. Let us lie down here and sleep until morning."

"I can't sleep," said Jack.

"I never do," said the Scarecrow.

"I do not even know what sleep is," said the Saw-Horse.

"Still, we must have consideration for this poor boy, who is made of flesh and blood and bone, and gets tired," suggested the Scarecrow, in his usual thoughtful manner. "I remember it was the same way with little Dorothy. We always had to sit through the night while she slept."

"I'm sorry," said Tip, meekly, "but I can't help it. And I'm dreadfully hungry, too!"

"Here is a new danger!" remarked Jack, gloomily. "I hope you are not fond of eating pumpkins."

"Not unless they're stewed and made into pies," answered the boy, laughing. "So have no fears of me, friend Jack."

"What a coward that Pumpkinhead is!" said the Saw-Horse, scornfully.

"You might be a coward yourself, if you knew you were liable to spoil!" retorted Jack, angrily.

"There!—there!" interrupted the Scarecrow; "don't let us quarrel. We all have our weaknesses, dear friends; so we must strive to be considerate of one another. And since this poor boy is hungry and has nothing whatever to eat, let us all remain quiet and allow him to sleep; for it is said that in sleep a mortal may forget even hunger."

"Thank you!" exclaimed Tip, gratefully. "Your Majesty is fully as good as you are wise—and that is saying a good deal!"

He then stretched himself upon the grass and, using the stuffed form of the Scarecrow for a pillow, was presently fast asleep.

Chapter 11 - A Nickel-Plated Emperor

Tip awoke soon after dawn, but the Scarecrow had already risen and plucked, with his clumsy fingers, a double-handful of ripe berries from some bushes near by. These the boy ate greedily, finding them an ample breakfast, and afterward the little party resumed its Journey.

After an hour's ride they reached the summit of a hill from whence they espied the City of the Winkies and noted the tall domes of the Emperor's palace rising from the clusters of more modest dwellings.

The Scarecrow became greatly animated at this sight, and exclaimed:

"How delighted I shall be to see my old friend the Tin Woodman again! I hope that he rules his people more successfully than I have ruled mine!"

Is the Tin Woodman the Emperor of the Winkies?" asked the horse.

"Yes, indeed. They invited him to rule over them soon after the Wicked Witch was destroyed; and as Nick Chopper has the best heart in all the world I am sure he has proved an excellent and able emperor."

"I thought that 'Emperor' was the title of a person who rules an empire," said Tip, "and the Country of the Winkies is only a Kingdom."

"Don't mention that to the Tin Woodman!" exclaimed the Scarecrow, earnestly. "You would hurt his feelings terribly. He is a proud man, as he has every reason to be, and it pleases him to be termed Emperor rather than King."

"I'm sure it makes no difference to me," replied the boy.

The Saw-Horse now ambled forward at a pace so fast that its riders had hard work to stick upon its back; so there was little further conversation until they drew up beside the palace steps.

An aged Winkie, dressed in a uniform of silver cloth, came forward to assist them to alight. Said the Scarecrow to his personage:

"Show us at once to your master, the Emperor."

The man looked from one to another of the party in an embarrassed way, and finally answered:

"I fear I must ask you to wait for a time. The Emperor is not receiving this morning."

"How is that?" enquired the Scarecrow, anxiously." I hope nothing has happened to him."

"Oh, no; nothing serious," returned the man. "But this is his Majesty's day for being polished; and just now his august presence is thickly smeared with putz-pomade."

"Oh, I see!" cried the Scarecrow, greatly reassured. "My friend was ever inclined to be a dandy, and I suppose he is now more proud than ever of his personal appearance."

"He is, indeed," said the man, with a polite bow. "Our mighty Emperor has lately caused himself to be nickel-plated."

"Good Gracious!" the Scarecrow exclaimed at hearing this. "If his wit bears the same polish, how sparkling it must be! But show us in—I'm sure the Emperor will receive us, even in his present state"

"The Emperor's state is always magnificent," said the man. "But I will venture to tell him of your arrival, and will receive his commands concerning you."

So the party followed the servant into a splendid ante-room, and the Saw-Horse ambled awkwardly after them, having no knowledge that a horse might be expected to remain outside.

The travelers were at first somewhat awed by their surroundings, and even the Scarecrow seemed impressed as he examined the rich hangings of silver cloth caught up into knots and fastened with tiny silver axes. Upon a handsome center-table stood a large silver oil-can, richly engraved with scenes from the past adventures of the Tin Woodman, Dorothy, the Cowardly Lion and the Scarecrow: the lines of the engraving being traced upon the silver in yellow gold. On the walls hung several portraits, that of the Scarecrow seeming to be the most prominent and carefully executed, while a the large painting of the famous Wizard of Oz, in act of presenting the Tin Woodman with a heart, covered almost one entire end of the room.

While the visitors gazed at these things in silent admiration they suddenly heard a loud voice in the next room exclaim:

"Well! well! well! What a great surprise!"

And then the door burst open and Nick Chopper rushed into their midst and caught the Scarecrow in a close and loving embrace that creased him into many folds and wrinkles.

"My dear old friend! My noble comrade!" cried the Tin Woodman, joyfully. "how delighted!," I am to meet you once again.

And then he released the Scarecrow and held him at arms' length while he surveyed the beloved, painted features.

But, alas! the face of the Scarecrow and many portions of his body bore great blotches of putz-pomade; for the Tin Woodman, in his eagerness to welcome his friend, had quite forgotten the condition of his toilet and had rubbed the thick coating of paste from his own body to that of his comrade.

"Dear me!" said the Scarecrow dolefully. "What a mess I'm in!"

"Never mind, my friend," returned the Tin Woodman," I'll send you to my Imperial Laundry, and you'll come out as good as new."

"Won't I be mangled?" asked the Scarecrow.

"No, indeed!" was the reply. "But tell me, how came your Majesty here? and who are your companions?"

The Scarecrow, with great politeness, introduced Tip and Jack Pumpkinhead, and the latter personage seemed to interest the Tin Woodman greatly.

"You are not very substantial, I must admit," said the Emperor. "but you are certainly unusual, and therefore worthy to become a member of our select society."

"I thank your Majesty, said Jack, humbly.

"I hope you are enjoying good health?" continued the Woodman.

"At present, yes;" replied the Pumpkinhead, with a sigh; "but I am in constant terror of the day when I shall spoil."

"Nonsense!" said the Emperor—but in a kindly, sympathetic tone. "Do not, I beg of you, dampen today's sun with the showers of tomorrow. For before your head has time to spoil you can have it canned, and in that way it may be preserved indefinitely."

Tip, during this conversation, was looking at the Woodman with undisguised amazement, and noticed that the celebrated Emperor of the Winkies was composed entirely of pieces of tin, neatly soldered and riveted together into the form of a man. He rattled and clanked a little, as he moved, but in the main he seemed to be most cleverly constructed, and his appearance was only marred by the thick coating of polishing-paste that covered him from head to foot.

The boy's intent gaze caused the Tin Woodman to remember that he was not in the most presentable condition, so he begged his friends to excuse him while he retired to his private apartment and allowed his servants to polish him. This was accomplished in a short time, and when the emperor returned his nickel-plated body shone so magnificently that the Scarecrow heartily congratulated him on his improved appearance.

"That nickel-plate was, I confess, a happy thought," said Nick; "and it was the more necessary because I had become somewhat scratched during my adventurous experiences. You will observe this engraved star upon my left breast. It not only indicates where my excellent heart lies, but covers very neatly the patch made by the Wonderful Wizard when he placed that valued organ in my breast with his own skillful hands."

"Is your heart, then, a hand-organ?" asked the Pumpkinhead, curiously.

"By no means," responded the emperor, with dignity. "It is, I am convinced, a strictly orthodox heart, although somewhat larger and warmer than most people possess."

Then he turned to the Scarecrow and asked:

"Are your subjects happy and contented, my dear friend?"

"I cannot, say" was the reply. "for the girls of Oz have risen in revolt and driven me out of the emerald City."

"Great Goodness!" cried the Tin Woodman, "What a calamity! They surely do not complain of your wise and gracious rule?"

"No; but they say it is a poor rule that don't work both ways," answered the Scarecrow; "and these females are also of the opinion that men have ruled the land long enough. So they have captured my city, robbed the treasury of all its jewels, and are running things to suit themselves."

"Dear me! What an extraordinary idea!" cried the Emperor, who was both shocked and surprised.

"And I heard some of them say," said Tip, "that they intend to march here and capture the castle and city of the Tin Woodman."

"Ah! we must not give them time to do that," said the Emperor, quickly; "we will go at once and recapture the Emerald City and place the Scarecrow again upon his throne."

"I was sure you would help me," remarked the Scarecrow in a pleased voice. "How large an army can you assemble?"

"We do not need an army," replied the Woodman. "We four, with the aid of my gleaming axe, are enough to strike terror into the hearts of the rebels."

"We five," corrected the Pumpkinhead.

"Five?" repeated the Tin Woodman.

"Yes; the Saw-Horse is brave and fearless," answered Jack, forgetting his recent quarrel with the quadruped.

The Tin Woodman looked around him in a puzzled way, for the Saw-Horse had until now remained quietly standing in a corner, where the Emperor had not noticed him. Tip immediately called the odd-looking creature to them, and it approached so awkwardly that it nearly upset the beautiful center-table and the engraved oil-can.

"I begin to think," remarked the Tin Woodman as he looked earnestly at the Saw-Horse, "that wonders will never cease! How came this creature alive?"

"I did it with a magic powder," modestly asserted the boy. "and the Saw- Horse has been very useful to us."

"He enabled us to escape the rebels," added the Scarecrow.

"Then we must surely accept him as a comrade," declared the emperor. "A live Saw-Horse is a distinct novelty, and should prove an interesting study. Does he know anything?"

"Well, I cannot claim any great experience in life," the Saw-Horse answered for himself. "but I seem to learn very quickly, and often it occurs to me that I know more than any of those around me."

"Perhaps you do," said the emperor; "for experience does not always mean wisdom. But time is precious Just now, so let us quickly make preparations to start upon our Journey.

The emperor called his Lord High Chancellor and instructed him how to run the kingdom during his absence. Meanwhile the Scarecrow was taken apart and the painted sack that served him for a head was carefully laundered and restuffed with the brains originally given him by the great Wizard. His clothes were also cleaned and pressed by the Imperial tailors, and his crown polished and again sewed upon his head, for the Tin Woodman insisted he should not renounce this badge of royalty. The Scarecrow now presented a very respectable appearance, and although in no way addicted to vanity he was quite pleased with himself and strutted a trifle as he walked. While this was being done Tip mended the wooden limbs of Jack Pumpkinhead and made them stronger than before, and the Saw-Horse was also inspected to see if he was in good working order.

Then bright and early the next morning they set out upon the return Journey to the emerald City, the Tin Woodman bearing upon his shoulder a gleaming axe and leading the way, while the Pumpkinhead rode upon the Saw-Horse and Tip and the Scarecrow walked upon either side to make sure that he didn't fall off or become damaged.

Chapter 12 - Mr. H. M. Woggle-Bug, T. E.

Now, General Jinjur—who, you will remember, commanded the Army of Revolt—was rendered very uneasy by the escape of the Scarecrow from the Emerald City. She feared, and with good reason, that if his Majesty and the Tin Woodman Joined forces, it would mean danger to her and her entire army; for the people of Oz had not yet forgotten the deeds of these famous heroes, who had passed successfully through so many startling adventures.

So Jinjur sent post-haste for old Mombi, the witch, and promised her large rewards if she would come to the assistance of the rebel army.

Mombi was furious at the trick Tip had played upon her as well as at his escape and the theft of the precious Powder of Life; so she needed no urging to induce her to travel to the Emerald City to assist Jinjur in defeating the Scarecrow and the Tin Woodman, who had made Tip one of their friends.

Mombi had no sooner arrived at the royal palace than she discovered, by means of her secret magic, that the adventurers were starting upon their Journey to the Emerald City; so she retired to a small room high up in a tower and locked herself in while she practised such arts as she could command to prevent the return of the Scarecrow and his companions.

That was why the Tin Woodman presently stopped and said:

"Something very curious has happened. I ought to know by heart and every step of this Journey, yet I fear we have already lost our way."

"That is quite impossible!" protested the Scarecrow. "Why do you think, my dear friend, that we have gone astray?"

"Why, here before us is a great field of sunflowers—and I never saw this field before in all my life."

At these words they all looked around, only to find that they were indeed surrounded by a field of tall stalks, every stalk bearing at its top a gigantic sunflower. And not only were these flowers almost blinding in their vivid hues of red and gold, but each one whirled around upon its stalk like a miniature wind-mill, completely dazzling the vision of the beholders and so mystifying them that they knew not which way to turn.

"It's witchcraft!" exclaimed Tip.

While they paused, hesitating and wondering, the Tin Woodman uttered a cry of impatience and advanced with swinging axe to cut down the stalks before him. But now the sunflowers suddenly stopped their rapid whirling, and the travelers plainly saw a girl's face appear in the center of each flower. These lovely faces looked upon the astonished band with mocking smiles, and then burst into a chorus of merry laughter at the dismay their appearance caused.

"Stop! stop!" cried Tip, seizing the Woodman's arm; "they're alive! they're girls!"

At that moment the flowers began whirling again, and the faces faded away and were lost in the rapid revolutions.

The Tin Woodman dropped his axe and sat down upon the ground.

"It would be heartless to chop down those pretty creatures," said he, despondently. "and yet I do not know how else we can proceed upon our way"

"They looked to me strangely like the faces of the Army of Revolt," mused the Scarecrow. "But I cannot conceive how the girls could have followed us here so quickly."

"I believe it's magic," said Tip, positively, "and that someone is playing a trick upon us. I've known old Mombi do things like that before. Probably it's nothing more than an illusion, and there are no sunflowers here at all."

"Then let us shut our eyes and walk forward," suggested the Woodman.

"Excuse me," replied the Scarecrow. "My eyes are not painted to shut. Because you happen to have tin eyelids, you must not imagine we are all built in the same way."

"And the eyes of the Saw-Horse are knot eyes," said Jack, leaning forward to examine them.

"Nevertheless, you must ride quickly forward," commanded Tip, "and we will follow after you and so try to escape. My eyes are already so dazzled that I can scarcely see."

So the Pumpkinhead rode boldly forward, and Tip grasped the stub tail of the Saw-Horse and followed with closed eyes. The Scarecrow and the Tin Woodman brought up the rear, and before they had gone many yards a Joyful shout from Jack announced that the way was clear before them.

Then all paused to look backward, but not a trace of the field of sunflowers remained.

More cheerfully, now they proceeded upon their Journey; but old Mombi had so changed the appearance of the landscape that they would surely have been lost had not the Scarecrow wisely concluded to take their direction from the sun. For no witch-craft could change the course of the sun, and it was therefore a safe guide.

However, other difficulties lay before them. The Saw-Horse stepped into a rabbit hole and fell to the ground. The Pumpkinhead was pitched high into the air, and his history would probably have ended at that exact moment had not the Tin Woodman skillfully caught the pumpkin as it descended and saved it from injury.

Tip soon had it fitted to the neck again and replaced Jack upon his feet. But the Saw-Horse did not escape so easily. For when his leg was pulled from the rabbit hole it was found to be broken short off, and must be replaced or repaired before he could go a step farther.

"This is quite serious," said the Tin Woodman." If there were trees near by I might soon manufacture another leg for this animal; but I cannot see even a shrub for miles around."

"And there are neither fences nor houses in this part of the land of Oz," added the Scarecrow, disconsolately.

"Then what shall we do?" enquired the boy.

"I suppose I must start my brains working," replied his Majesty the Scarecrow; "for experience has, taught me that I can do anything if I but take time to think it out."

"Let us all think," said Tip; "and perhaps we shall find a way to repair the Saw-Horse."

So they sat in a row upon the grass and began to think, while the Saw-Horse occupied itself by gazing curiously upon its broken limb.

"Does it hurt?" asked the Tin Woodman, in a soft, sympathetic voice.

"Not in the least," returned the Saw-Horse; "but my pride is injured to find that my anatomy is so brittle."

For a time the little group remained in silent thought. Presently the Tin Woodman raised his head and looked over the fields.

"What sort of creature is that which approaches us?" he asked, wonderingly.

The others followed his gaze, and discovered coming toward them the most extraordinary object they had ever beheld. It advanced quickly and noiselessly over the soft grass and in a few minutes stood before the adventurers and regarded them with an astonishment equal to their own.

The Scarecrow was calm under all circumstances.

"Good morning!" he said, politely.

The stranger removed his hat with a flourish, bowed very low, and then responded:

"Good morning, one and all. I hope you are, as an aggregation, enjoying excellent health. Permit me to present my card."

With this courteous speech it extended a card toward the Scarecrow, who accepted it, turned it over and over, and handed it with a shake of his head to Tip.

The boy read aloud:

"MR. H. M. WOGGLE-BUG, T. E."

"Dear me!" ejaculated the Pumpkinhead, staring somewhat intently.

"How very peculiar!" said the Tin Woodman.

Tip's eyes were round and wondering, and the Saw-Horse uttered a sigh and turned away its head.

"Are you really a Woggle-Bug?" enquired the Scarecrow.

"Most certainly, my dear sir!" answered the stranger, briskly. "Is not my name upon the card?"

"It is," said the Scarecrow. "But may I ask what 'H. M.' stands for?"

"'H. M.' means Highly Magnified," returned the Woggle-Bug, proudly.

"Oh, I see." The Scarecrow viewed the stranger critically. "And are you, in truth, highly magnified?"

"Sir," said the Woggle-Bug, "I take you for a gentleman of judgment and discernment. Does it not occur to you that I am several thousand times greater than any Woggle-Bug you ever saw before? Therefore it is plainly evident that I am Highly Magnified, and there is no good reason why you should doubt the fact."

"Pardon me," returned the Scarecrow. "My brains are slightly mixed since I was last laundered. Would it be improper for me to ask, also, what the 'T.E.' at the end of your name stands for?"

"Those letters express my degree," answered the Woggle-Bug, with a condescending smile. "To be more explicit, the initials mean that I am Thoroughly Educated."

"Oh!" said the Scarecrow, much relieved.

Tip had not yet taken his eyes off this wonderful personage. What he saw was a great, round, buglike body supported upon two slender legs which ended in delicate feet—the toes curling upward. The body of the Woggle-Bug was rather flat, and judging from what could be seen of it was of a glistening dark brown color upon the back, while the front was striped with alternate bands of light brown and white, blending together at the edges. Its arms were fully as slender as its legs, and upon a rather long neck was perched its head—not unlike the head of a man, except that its nose ended in a curling antenna, or "feeler," and its ears from the upper points bore antennae that decorated the sides of its head like two miniature, curling pig tails. It must be admitted that the round, black eyes were rather bulging in appearance; but the expression upon the Woggle-Bug's face was by no means unpleasant.

For dress the insect wore a dark-blue swallowtail coat with a yellow silk lining and a flower in the button-hole; a vest of white duck that stretched tightly across the wide body; knickerbockers of fawn-colored plush, fastened at the knees with gilt buckles; and, perched upon its small head, was jauntily set a tall silk hat.

Standing upright before our amazed friends the Woggle-Bug appeared to be fully as tall as the Tin Woodman; and surely no bug in all the Land of Oz had ever before attained so enormous a size.

"I confess," said the Scarecrow, "that your abrupt appearance has caused me surprise, and no doubt has startled my companions. I hope, however, that this circumstance will not distress you. We shall probably get used to you in time."

"Do not apologize, I beg of you!" returned the Woggle-Bug, earnestly. "It affords me great pleasure to surprise people; for surely I cannot be classed with ordinary insects and am entitled to both curiosity and admiration from those I meet."

"You are, indeed," agreed his Majesty.

"If you will permit me to seat myself in your august company," continued the stranger, "I will gladly relate my history, so that you will be better able to comprehend my unusual—may I say remarkable?—appearance."

"You may say what you please," answered the Tin Woodman, briefly.

So the Woggle-Bug sat down upon the grass, facing the little group of wanderers, and told them the following story:

Chapter 13 - A Highly Magnified History

It is but honest that I should acknowledge at the beginning of my recital that I was born an ordinary Woggle-Bug," began the creature, in a frank and friendly tone. "Knowing no better, I used my arms as well as my legs for walking, and crawled under the edges of stones or hid among the roots of grasses with no thought beyond finding a few insects smaller than myself to feed upon.

"The chill nights rendered me stiff and motionless, for I wore no clothing, but each morning the warm rays of the sun gave me new life and restored me to activity. A horrible existence is this, but you must remember it is the regular ordained existence of Woggle-Bugs, as well as of many other tiny creatures that inhabit the earth.

"But Destiny had singled me out, humble though I was, for a grander fate! One day I crawled near to a country school house, and my curiosity being excited by the monotonous hum of the students within, I made bold to enter and creep along a crack between two boards until I reached the far end, where, in front of a hearth of glowing embers, sat the master at his desk.

"No one noticed so small a creature as a Woggle-Bug, and when I found that the hearth was even warmer and more comfortable than the sunshine, I resolved to establish my future home beside it. So I found a charming nest between two bricks and hid myself therein for many, many months.

"Professor Nowitall is, doubtless, the most famous scholar in the land of Oz, and after a few days I began to listen to the lectures and discourses he gave his pupils. Not one of them was more attentive than the humble, unnoticed Woggle-Bug, and I acquired in this way a fund of knowledge that I will myself confess is simply marvelous. That is why I place 'T.E.' Thoroughly Educated upon my cards; for my greatest pride lies in the fact that the world cannot produce another Woggle-Bug with a tenth part of my own culture and erudition."

"I do not blame you," said the Scarecrow. "Education is a thing to be proud of. I'm educated myself. The mess of brains given me by the Great Wizard is considered by my friends to be unexcelled."

"Nevertheless," interrupted the Tin Woodman, "a good heart is, I believe, much more desirable than education or brains."

"To me," said the Saw-Horse, "a good leg is more desirable than either."

"Could seeds be considered in the light of brains?" enquired the Pumpkinhead, abruptly.

"Keep quiet!" commanded Tip, sternly.

"Very well, dear father," answered the obedient Jack.

The Woggle-Bug listened patiently—even respectfully—to these remarks, and then resumed his story.

"I must have lived fully three years in that secluded school-house hearth," said he, "drinking thirstily of the ever-flowing fount of limpid knowledge before me."

"Quite poetical," commented the Scarecrow, nodding his head approvingly.

"But one, day" continued the Bug, "a marvelous circumstance occurred that altered my very existence and brought me to my present pinnacle of greatness. The Professor discovered me in the act of crawling across the hearth, and before I could escape he had caught me between his thumb and forefinger.

"'My dear children,' said he, 'I have captured a Woggle-Bug—a very rare and interesting specimen. Do any of you know what a Woggle-Bug is?'

"'No!' yelled the scholars, in chorus.

"'Then,' said the Professor, 'I will get out my famous magnifying-glass and throw the insect upon a screen in a highly-magnified condition, that you may all study carefully its peculiar construction and become acquainted with its habits and manner of life.'

"He then brought from a cupboard a most curious instrument, and before I could realize what had happened I found myself thrown upon a screen in a highly-magnified state—even as you now behold me.

"The students stood up on their stools and craned their heads forward to get a better view of me, and two little girls jumped upon the sill of an open window where they could see more plainly.

"'Behold!' cried the Professor, in a loud voice, 'this highly-magnified Woggle-Bug; one of the most curious insects in existence!'

"Being Thoroughly Educated, and knowing what is required of a cultured gentleman, at this juncture I stood upright and, placing my hand upon my bosom, made a very polite bow. My action, being unexpected, must have startled them, for one of the little girls perched upon the window-sill gave a scream and fell backward out the window, drawing her companion with her as she disappeared.

"The Professor uttered a cry of horror and rushed away through the door to see if the poor children were injured by the fall. The scholars followed after him in a wild mob, and I was left alone in the school-room, still in a Highly-Magnified state and free to do as I pleased.

"It immediately occurred to me that this was a good opportunity to escape. I was proud of my great size, and realized that now I could safely travel anywhere in the world, while my superior culture would make me a fit associate for the most learned person I might chance to meet.

"So, while the Professor picked the little girls—who were more frightened than hurt—off the ground, and the pupils clustered around him closely grouped, I calmly walked out of the school-house, turned a corner, and escaped unnoticed to a grove of trees that stood near"

"Wonderful!" exclaimed the Pumpkinhead, admiringly.

"It was, indeed," agreed the Woggle-Bug. "I have never ceased to congratulate myself for escaping while I was Highly Magnified; for even my excessive knowledge would have proved of little use to me had I remained a tiny, insignificant insect."

"I didn't know before," said Tip, looking at the Woggle-Bug with a puzzled expression, "that insects wore clothes."

"Nor do they, in their natural state," returned the stranger. "But in the course of my wanderings I had the good fortune to save the ninth life of a tailor—tailors having, like cats, nine lives, as you probably know. The fellow was exceedingly grateful, for had he lost that ninth life it would have been the end of him; so he begged permission to furnish me with the stylish costume I now wear. It fits very nicely, does it not?" and the Woggle-Bug stood up and turned himself around slowly, that all might examine his person.

"He must have been a good tailor," said the Scarecrow, somewhat enviously.

"He was a good-hearted tailor, at any rate," observed Nick Chopper.

"But where were you going, when you met us?" Tip asked the Woggle-Bug.

"Nowhere in particular," was the reply, "although it is my intention soon to visit the Emerald City and arrange to give a course of lectures to select audiences on the 'Advantages of Magnification.'"

"We are bound for the Emerald City now," said the Tin Woodman; "so, if it pleases you to do so, you are welcome to travel in our company."

The Woggle-Bug bowed with profound grace.

"It will give me great pleasure," said he "to accept your kind invitation; for nowhere in the Land of Oz could I hope to meet with so congenial a company."

"That is true," acknowledged the Pumpkinhead. "We are quite as congenial as flies and honey."

"But—pardon me if I seem inquisitive—are you not all rather—ahem! rather unusual?" asked the Woggle-Bug, looking from one to another with unconcealed interest.

"Not more so than yourself," answered the Scarecrow. "Everything in life is unusual until you get accustomed to it."

"What rare philosophy!" exclaimed the Woggle-Bug, admiringly.

"Yes; my brains are working well today," admitted the Scarecrow, an accent of pride in his voice.

"Then, if you are sufficiently rested and refreshed, let us bend our steps toward the Emerald City," suggested the magnified one.

"We can't," said Tip. "The Saw-Horse has broken a leg, so he can't bend his steps. And there is no wood around to make him a new limb from. And we can't leave the horse behind because the Pumpkinhead is so stiff in his Joints that he has to ride."

"How very unfortunate!" cried the Woggle-Bug. Then he looked the party over carefully and said:

"If the Pumpkinhead is to ride, why not use one of his legs to make a leg for the horse that carries him? I judge that both are made of wood."

"Now, that is what I call real cleverness," said the Scarecrow, approvingly. "I wonder my brains did not think of that long ago! Get to work, my dear Nick, and fit the Pumpkinhead's leg to the Saw-Horse."

Jack was not especially pleased with this idea; but he submitted to having his left leg amputated by the Tin Woodman and whittled down to fit the left leg of the Saw-Horse. Nor was the Saw-Horse especially pleased with the operation, either; for he growled a good deal about being "butchered," as he called it, and afterward declared that the new leg was a disgrace to a respectable Saw-Horse.

"I beg you to be more careful in your speech," said the Pumpkinhead, sharply. "Remember, if you please, that it is my leg you are abusing."

"I cannot forget it," retorted the Saw-Horse, "for it is quite as flimsy as the rest of your person."

"Flimsy! me flimsy!" cried Jack, in a rage. "How dare you call me flimsy?"

"Because you are built as absurdly as a jumping-jack," sneered the horse, rolling his knotty eyes in a vicious manner. "Even your head won't stay straight, and you never can tell whether you are looking backwards or forwards!"

"Friends, I entreat you not to quarrel!" pleaded the Tin Woodman, anxiously." As a matter of fact, we are none of us above criticism; so let us bear with each others' faults."

"An excellent suggestion," said the Woggle-Bug, approvingly. "You must have an excellent heart, my metallic friend."

"I have," returned Nick, well pleased. "My heart is quite the best part of me. But now let us start upon our Journey."

They perched the one-legged Pumpkinhead upon the Saw-Horse, and tied him to his seat with cords, so that he could not possibly fall off.

And then, following the lead of the Scarecrow, they all advanced in the direction of the Emerald City.

Chapter 14 - Old Mombi indulges in Witchcraft

They soon discovered that the Saw-Horse limped, for his new leg was a trifle too long. So they were obliged to halt while the Tin Woodman chopped it down with his axe, after which the wooden steed paced along more comfortably. But the Saw-Horse was not entirely satisfied, even yet.

"It was a shame that I broke my other leg!" it growled.

"On the contrary," airily remarked the Woggle-Bug, who was walking alongside, "you should consider the accident most fortunate. For a horse is never of much use until he has been broken."

"I beg your pardon," said Tip, rather provoked, for he felt a warm interest in both the Saw-Horse and his man Jack; "but permit me to say that your joke is a poor one, and as old as it is poor."

"Still, it is a Joke," declared the Woggle-Bug; firmly, "and a Joke derived from a play upon words is considered among educated people to be eminently proper."

"What does that mean?" enquired the Pumpkinhead, stupidly.

"It means, my dear friend," explained the Woggle-Bug, "that our language contains many words having a double meaning; and that to pronounce a joke that allows both meanings of a certain word, proves the joker a person of culture and refinement, who has, moreover, a thorough command of the language."

"I don't believe that," said Tip, plainly; "anybody can make a pun."

"Not so," rejoined the Woggle-Bug, stiffly. "It requires education of a high order. Are you educated, young sir?"

"Not especially," admitted Tip.

"Then you cannot judge the matter. I myself am Thoroughly Educated, and I say that puns display genius. For instance, were I to ride upon this Saw- Horse, he would not only be an animal he would become an equipage. For he would then be a horse-and-buggy."

At this the Scarecrow gave a gasp and the Tin Woodman stopped short and looked reproachfully at the Woggle-Bug. At the same time the Saw-Horse loudly snorted his derision; and even the Pumpkinhead put up his hand to hide the smile which, because it was carved upon his face, he could not change to a frown.

But the Woggle-Bug strutted along as if he had made some brilliant remark, and the Scarecrow was obliged to say:

"I have heard, my dear friend, that a person can become over-educated; and although I have a high respect for brains, no matter how they may be arranged or classified, I begin to suspect that yours are slightly tangled. In any event, I must beg you to restrain your superior education while in our society."

"We are not very particular," added the Tin Woodman; "and we are exceedingly kind hearted. But if your superior culture gets leaky again—" He did not complete the sentence, but he twirled his gleaming axe so carelessly that the Woggle-Bug looked frightened, and shrank away to a safe distance.

The others marched on in silence, and the Highly Magnified one, after a period of deep thought, said in an humble voice:

"I will endeavor to restrain myself."

"That is all we can expect," returned the Scarecrow pleasantly; and good nature being thus happily restored to the party, they proceeded upon their way.

When they again stopped to allow Tip to rest—the boy being the only one that seemed to tire—the Tin Woodman noticed many small, round holes in the grassy meadow.

"This must be a village of the Field Mice," he said to the Scarecrow." I wonder if my old friend, the Queen of the Mice, is in this neighborhood."

"If she is, she may be of great service to us," answered the Scarecrow, who was impressed by a sudden thought. "See if you can call her, my dear Nick."

So the Tin Woodman blew a shrill note upon a silver whistle that hung around his neck, and presently a tiny grey mouse popped from a near-by hole and advanced fearlessly toward them. For the Tin Woodman had once saved her life, and the Queen of the Field Mice knew he was to be trusted."

"Good day, your Majesty, said Nick, politely addressing the mouse; "I trust you are enjoying good health?"

"Thank you, I am quite well," answered the Queen, demurely, as she sat up and displayed the tiny golden crown upon her head. "Can I do anything to assist my old friends?"

"You can, indeed," replied the Scarecrow, eagerly. "Let me, I intreat you, take a dozen of your subjects with me to the Emerald City."

"Will they be injured in any way?" asked the Queen, doubtfully.

"I think not," replied the Scarecrow. "I will carry them hidden in the straw which stuffs my body, and when I give them the signal by unbuttoning my jacket, they have only to rush out and scamper home again as fast as they can. By doing this they will assist me to regain my throne, which the Army of Revolt has taken from me."

"In that case," said the Queen, "I will not refuse your request. Whenever you are ready, I will call twelve of my most intelligent subjects."

"I am ready now" returned the Scarecrow. Then he lay flat upon the ground and unbuttoned his jacket, displaying the mass of straw with which he was stuffed.

The Queen uttered a little piping call, and in an instant a dozen pretty field mice had emerged from their holes and stood before their ruler, awaiting her orders.

What the Queen said to them none of our travelers could understand, for it was in the mouse language; but the field mice obeyed without hesitation, running one after the other to the Scarecrow and hiding themselves in the straw of his breast.

When all of the twelve mice had thus concealed themselves, the Scarecrow buttoned his Jacket securely and then arose and thanked the Queen for her kindness.

"One thing more you might do to serve us," suggested the Tin Woodman; "and that is to run ahead and show us the way to the Emerald City. For some enemy is evidently trying to prevent us from reaching it."

"I will do that gladly," returned the Queen. "Are you ready?"

The Tin Woodman looked at Tip.

"I'm rested," said the boy. "Let us start."

Then they resumed their journey, the little grey Queen of the Field Mice running swiftly ahead and then pausing until the travelers drew near, when away she would dart again.

Without this unerring guide the Scarecrow and his comrades might never have gained the Emerald City; for many were the obstacles thrown in their way by the arts of old Mombi. Yet not one of the obstacles really existed—all were cleverly contrived deceptions. For when they came to the banks of a rushing river that threatened to bar their way the little Queen kept steadily on, passing through the seeming flood in safety; and our travelers followed her without encountering a single drop of water.

Again, a high wall of granite towered high above their heads and opposed their advance. But the grey Field Mouse walked straight through it, and the others did the same, the wall melting into mist as they passed it.

Afterward, when they had stopped for a moment to allow Tip to rest, they saw forty roads branching off from their feet in forty different directions; and soon these forty roads began whirling around like a mighty wheel, first in one direction and then in the other, completely bewildering their vision.

But the Queen called for them to follow her and darted off in a straight line; and when they had gone a few paces the whirling pathways vanished and were seen no more.

Mombi's last trick was the most fearful of all. She sent a sheet of crackling flame rushing over the meadow to consume them; and for the first time the Scarecrow became afraid and turned to fly.

"If that fire reaches me I will be gone in no time!" said he, trembling until his straw rattled. "It's the most dangerous thing I ever encountered."

"I'm off, too!" cried the Saw-Horse, turning and prancing with agitation; "for my wood is so dry it would burn like kindlings."

"Is fire dangerous to pumpkins?" asked Jack, fearfully.

"You'll be baked like a tart—and so will I!" answered the Woggle-Bug, getting down on all fours so he could run the faster.

But the Tin Woodman, having no fear of fire, averted the stampede by a few sensible words.

"Look at the Field Mouse!" he shouted. "The fire does not burn her in the least. In fact, it is no fire at all, but only a deception."

Indeed, to watch the little Queen march calmly through the advancing flames restored courage to every member of the party, and they followed her without being even scorched.

"This is surely a most extraordinary adventure," said the Woggle-Bug, who was greatly amazed; "for it upsets all the Natural Laws that I heard Professor Nowitall teach in the school-house."

"Of course it does," said the Scarecrow, wisely. "All magic is unnatural, and for that reason is to be feared and avoided. But I see before us the gates of the Emerald City, so I imagine we have now overcome all the magical obstacles that seemed to oppose us."

Indeed, the walls of the City were plainly visible, and the Queen of the Field Mice, who had guided them so faithfully, came near to bid them good- bye.

"We are very grateful to your Majesty for your kind assistance," said the Tin Woodman, bowing before the pretty creature.

"I am always pleased to be of service to my friends," answered the Queen, and in a flash she had darted away upon her journey home.

Chapter 15 - The Prisoners of the Queen

Approaching the gateway of the Emerald City the travelers found it guarded by two girls of the Army of Revolt, who opposed their entrance by drawing the knitting-needles from their hair and threatening to prod the first that came near.

But the Tin Woodman was not afraid."

At the worst they can but scratch my beautiful nickel-plate," he said. "But there will be no 'worst,' for I think I can manage to frighten these absurd soldiers very easily. Follow me closely, all of you!"

Then, swinging his axe in a great circle to right and left before him, he advanced upon the gate, and the others followed him without hesitation.

The girls, who had expected no resistance whatever, were terrified by the sweep of the glittering axe and fled screaming into the city; so that our travelers passed the gates in safety and marched down the green marble pavement of the wide street toward the royal palace.

"At this rate we will soon have your Majesty upon the throne again," said the Tin Woodman, laughing at his easy conquest of the guards.

"Thank you, friend Nick," returned the Scarecrow, gratefully. "Nothing can resist your kind heart and your sharp axe."

As they passed the rows of houses they saw through the open doors that men were sweeping and dusting and washing dishes, while the women sat around in groups, gossiping and laughing.

"What has happened?" the Scarecrow asked a sad-looking man with a bushy beard, who wore an apron and was wheeling a baby-carriage along the sidewalk.

"Why, we've had a revolution, your Majesty as you ought to know very well," replied the man; "and since you went away the women have been running things to suit themselves. I'm glad you have decided to come back and restore order, for doing housework and minding the children is wearing out the strength of every man in the Emerald City."

"Hm!" said the Scarecrow, thoughtfully. "If it is such hard work as you say, how did the women manage it so easily?"

"I really do not know" replied the man, with a deep sigh. "Perhaps the women are made of castiron."

No movement was made, as they passed along the street, to oppose their progress. Several of the women stopped their gossip long enough to cast curious looks upon our friends, but immediately they would turn away with a laugh or a sneer and resume their chatter. And when they met with several girls belonging to the Army of Revolt, those soldiers, instead of being alarmed or appearing surprised, merely stepped out of the way and allowed them to advance without protest.

This action rendered the Scarecrow uneasy."

I'm afraid we are walking into a trap," said he.

"Nonsense!" returned Nick Chopper, confidently; "the silly creatures are conquered already!"

But the Scarecrow shook his head in a way that expressed doubt, and Tip said:

"It's too easy, altogether. Look out for trouble ahead."

"I will," returned his Majesty. Unopposed they reached the royal palace and marched up the marble steps, which had once been thickly crusted with emeralds but were now filled with tiny holes where the jewels had been ruthlessly torn from their settings by the Army of Revolt. And so far not a rebel barred their way.

Through the arched hallways and into the magnificent throne room marched the Tin Woodman and his followers, and here, when the green silken curtains fell behind them, they saw a curious sight.

Seated within the glittering throne was General Jinjur, with the Scarecrow's second-best crown upon her head, and the royal sceptre in her right hand. A box of caramels, from which she was eating, rested in her lap, and the girl seemed entirely at ease in her royal surroundings.

The Scarecrow stepped forward and confronted her, while the Tin Woodman leaned upon his axe and the others formed a half-circle back of his Majesty's person.

"How dare you sit in my throne?" demanded the Scarecrow, sternly eyeing the intruder. "Don't you know you are guilty of treason, and that there is a law against treason?"

"The throne belongs to whoever is able to take it," answered Jinjur, as she slowly ate another caramel. "I have taken it, as you see; so just now I am the Queen, and all who oppose me are guilty of treason, and must be punished by the law you have just mentioned."

This view of the case puzzled the Scarecrow.

"How is it, friend Nick?" he asked, turning to the Tin Woodman.

"Why, when it comes to Law, I have nothing to, say" answered that personage. "for laws were never meant to be understood, and it is foolish to make the attempt."

"Then what shall we do?" asked the Scarecrow, in dismay.

"Why don't you marry the Queen? And then you can both rule," suggested the Woggle-Bug.

Jinjur glared at the insect fiercely. "Why don't you send her back to her mother, where she belongs?" asked Jack Pumpkinhead.

Jinjur frowned.

"Why don't you shut her up in a closet until she behaves herself, and promises to be good?" enquired Tip. Jinjur's lip curled scornfully.

"Or give her a good shaking!" added the Saw-Horse.

"No," said the Tin Woodman, "we must treat the poor girl with gentleness. Let us give her all the Jewels she can carry, and send her away happy and contented."

At this Queen Jinjur laughed aloud, and the next minute clapped her pretty hands together thrice, as if for a signal.

"You are very absurd creatures," said she; "but I am tired of your nonsense and have no time to bother with you longer."

While the monarch and his friends listened in amazement to this impudent speech, a startling thing happened. The Tin Woodman's axe was snatched from his grasp by some person behind him, and he found himself disarmed and helpless. At the same instant a shout of laughter rang in the ears of the devoted band, and turning to see whence this came they found themselves surrounded by the Army of Revolt, the girls bearing in either hand their glistening knitting-needles. The entire throne room seemed to be filled with the rebels, and the Scarecrow and his comrades realized that they were prisoners.

"You see how foolish it is to oppose a woman's wit," said Jinjur, gaily; "and this event only proves that I am more fit to rule the Emerald City than a Scarecrow. I bear you no ill will, I assure you; but lest you should prove troublesome to me in the future I shall order you all to be destroyed. That is, all except the boy, who belongs to old Mombi and must be restored to her keeping. The rest of you are not human, and therefore it will not be wicked to demolish you. The Saw-Horse and the Pumpkinhead's body I will have chopped up for kindling- wood; and the pumpkin shall be made into tarts. The Scarecrow will do nicely to start a bonfire, and the tin man can be cut into small pieces and fed to the goats. As for this immense Woggle-Bug—"

"Highly Magnified, if you please!" interrupted the insect.

"I think I will ask the cook to make green-turtle soup of you," continued the Queen, reflectively.

The Woggle-Bug shuddered.

"Or, if that won't do, we might use you for a Hungarian goulash, stewed and highly spiced," she added, cruelly.

This programme of extermination was so terrible that the prisoners looked upon one another in a panic of fear. The Scarecrow alone did not give way to despair. He stood quietly before the Queen and his brow was wrinkled in deep thought as he strove to find some means to escape.

While thus engaged he felt the straw within his breast move gently. At once his expression changed from sadness to joy, and raising his hand he quickly unbuttoned the front of his jacket.

This action did not pass unnoticed by the crowd of girls clustering about him, but none of them suspected what he was doing until a tiny grey mouse leaped from his bosom to the floor and scampered away between the feet of the Army of Revolt. Another mouse quickly followed; then another and another, in rapid succession. And suddenly such a scream of terror went up from the Army that it might easily have filled the stoutest heart with consternation. The flight that ensued turned to a stampede, and the stampede to a panic.

For while the startled mice rushed wildly about the room the Scarecrow had only time to note a whirl of skirts and a twinkling of feet as the girls disappeared from the palace—pushing and crowding one another in their mad efforts to escape.

The Queen, at the first alarm, stood up on the cushions of the throne and began to dance frantically upon her tiptoes. Then a mouse ran up the cushions, and with a terrified leap poor Jinjur shot clear over the head of the Scarecrow and escaped through an archway—never pausing in her wild career until she had reached the city gates.

So, in less time than I can explain, the throne room was deserted by all save the Scarecrow and his friends, and the Woggle-Bug heaved a deep sigh of relief as he exclaimed:

"Thank goodness, we are saved!"

"For a time, yes;" answered the Tin Woodman. "But the enemy will soon return, I fear."

"Let us bar all the entrances to the palace!" said the Scarecrow. "Then we shall have time to think what is best to be done."

So all except Jack Pumpkinhead, who was still tied fast to the Saw-Horse, ran to the various entrances of the royal palace and closed the heavy doors, bolting and locking them securely. Then, knowing that the Army of Revolt could not batter down the barriers in several days, the adventurers gathered once more in the throne room for a council of war.

Chapter 16 - The Scarecrow Takes Time to Think

It seems to me," began the Scarecrow, when all were again assembled in the throne room, "that the girl Jinjur is quite right in claiming to be Queen. And if she is right, then I am wrong, and we have no business to be occupying her palace."

"But you were the King until she came," said the Woggle-Bug, strutting up and down with his hands in his pockets; "so it appears to me that she is the interloper instead of you."

"Especially as we have just conquered her and put her to flight," added the Pumpkinhead, as he raised his hands to turn his face toward the Scarecrow.

"Have we really conquered her?" asked the Scarecrow, quietly. "Look out of the window, and tell me what you see."

Tip ran to the window and looked out.

"The palace is surrounded by a double row of girl soldiers," he announced.

"I thought so," returned the Scarecrow. "We are as truly their prisoners as we were before the mice frightened them from the palace."

"My friend is right," said Nick Chopper, who had been polishing his breast with a bit of chamois-leather. "Jinjur is still the Queen, and we are her prisoners."

"But I hope she cannot get at us," exclaimed the Pumpkinhead, with a shiver of fear. "She threatened to make tarts of me, you know."

"Don't worry," said the Tin Woodman. "It cannot matter greatly. If you stay shut up here you will spoil in time, anyway. A good tart is far more admirable than a decayed intellect."

"Very true," agreed the Scarecrow.

"Oh, dear!" moaned Jack; "what an unhappy lot is mine! Why, dear father, did you not make me out of tin—or even out of straw—so that I would keep indefinitely."

"Shucks!" returned Tip, indignantly. "You ought to be glad that I made you at all." Then he added, reflectively, "everything has to come to an end, some time."

"But I beg to remind you," broke in the Woggle-Bug, who had a distressed look in his bulging, round eyes, "that this terrible Queen Jinjur suggested making a goulash of me—Me! the only Highly Magnified and Thoroughly Educated Woggle-Bug in the wide, wide world!"

"I think it was a brilliant idea," remarked the Scarecrow, approvingly.

"Don't you imagine he would make a better soup?" asked the Tin Woodman, turning toward his friend.

"Well, perhaps," acknowledged the Scarecrow.

The Woggle-Bug groaned.

"I can see, in my mind's eye," said he, mournfully, "the goats eating small pieces of my dear comrade, the Tin Woodman, while my soup is being cooked on a bonfire built of the Saw-Horse and Jack Pumpkinhead's body, and Queen Jinjur watches me boil while she feeds the flames with my friend the Scarecrow!"

This morbid picture cast a gloom over the entire party, making them restless and anxious.

"It can't happen for some time," said the Tin Woodman, trying to speak cheerfully; "for we shall be able to keep Jinjur out of the palace until she manages to break down the doors."

"And in the meantime I am liable to starve to death, and so is the Woggle- Bug," announced Tip.

"As for me," said the Woggle-Bug, "I think that I could live for some time on Jack Pumpkinhead. Not that I prefer pumpkins for food; but I believe they are somewhat nutritious, and Jack's head is large and plump."

"How heartless!" exclaimed the Tin Woodman, greatly shocked. "Are we cannibals, let me ask? Or are we faithful friends?"

"I see very clearly that we cannot stay shut up in this palace," said the Scarecrow, with decision. "So let us end this mournful talk and try to discover a means to escape."

At this suggestion they all gathered eagerly around the throne, wherein was seated the Scarecrow, and as Tip sat down upon a stool there fell from his pocket a pepper-box, which rolled upon the floor.

"What is this?" asked Nick Chopper, picking up the box.

"Be careful!" cried the boy. "That's my Powder of Life. Don't spill it, for it is nearly gone."

"And what is the Powder of Life?" enquired the Scarecrow, as Tip replaced the box carefully in his pocket.

"It's some magical stuff old Mombi got from a crooked sorcerer," explained the boy. "She brought Jack to life with it, and afterward I used it to bring the Saw-Horse to life. I guess it will make anything live that is sprinkled with it; but there's only about one dose left."

"Then it is very precious," said the Tin Woodman.

"Indeed it is," agreed the Scarecrow. "It may prove our best means of escape from our difficulties. I believe I will think for a few minutes; so I will thank you, friend Tip, to get out your knife and rip this heavy crown from my forehead."

Tip soon cut the stitches that had fastened the crown to the Scarecrow's head, and the former monarch of the Emerald City removed it with a sigh of relief and hung it on a peg beside the throne.

"That is my last memento of royalty" said he; "and I'm glad to get rid of it. The former King of this City, who was named Pastoria, lost the crown to the Wonderful Wizard, who passed it on to me. Now the girl Jinjur claims it, and I sincerely hope it will not give her a headache."

"A kindly thought, which I greatly admire," said the Tin Woodman, nodding approvingly.

"And now I will indulge in a quiet think," continued the Scarecrow, lying back in the throne.

The others remained as silent and still as possible, so as not to disturb him; for all had great confidence in the extraordinary brains of the Scarecrow.

And, after what seemed a very long time indeed to the anxious watchers, the thinker sat up, looked upon his friends with his most whimsical expression, and said:

"My brains work beautifully today. I'm quite proud of them. Now, listen! If we attempt to escape through the doors of the palace we shall surely be captured. And, as we can't escape through the ground, there is only one other thing to be done. We must escape through the air!"

He paused to note the effect of these words; but all his hearers seemed puzzled and unconvinced.

"The Wonderful Wizard escaped in a balloon," he continued. "We don't know how to make a balloon, of course; but any sort of thing that can fly through the air can carry us easily. So I suggest that my friend the Tin Woodman, who is a skillful mechanic, shall build some sort of a machine, with good strong wings, to carry us; and our friend Tip can then bring the Thing to life with his magical powder."

"Bravo!" cried Nick Chopper.

"What splendid brains!" murmured Jack.

"Really quite clever!" said the Educated Woggle-Bug.

"I believe it can be done," declared Tip; "that is, if the Tin Woodman is equal to making the Thing."

"I'll do my best," said Nick, cheerily; "and, as a matter of fact, I do not often fail in what I attempt. But the Thing will have to be built on the roof of the palace, so it can rise comfortably into the air."

"To be sure," said the Scarecrow.

"Then let us search through the palace," continued the Tin Woodman, "and carry all the material we can find to the roof, where I will begin my work."

"First, however," said the Pumpkinhead, "I beg you will release me from this horse, and make me another leg to walk with. For in my present condition I am of no use to myself or to anyone else."

So the Tin Woodman knocked a mahogany center-table to pieces with his axe and fitted one of the legs, which was beautifully carved, on to the body of Jack Pumpkinhead, who was very proud of the acquisition.

"It seems strange," said he, as he watched the Tin Woodman work, "that my left leg should be the most elegant and substantial part of me."

"That proves you are unusual," returned the Scarecrow. "and I am convinced that the only people worthy of consideration in this world are the unusual ones. For the common folks are like the leaves of a tree, and live and die unnoticed."

"Spoken like a philosopher!" cried the Woggle-Bug, as he assisted the Tin Woodman to set Jack upon his feet.

"How do you feel now?" asked Tip, watching the Pumpkinhead stump around to try his new leg."

As good as new" answered Jack, Joyfully, "and quite ready to assist you all to escape."

"Then let us get to work," said the Scarecrow, in a business-like tone.

So, glad to be doing anything that might lead to the end of their captivity, the friends separated to wander over the palace in search of fitting material to use in the construction of their aerial machine.

Chapter 17 - The Astonishing Flight of the Gump

When the adventurers reassembled upon the roof it was found that a remarkably queer assortment of articles had been selected by the various members of the party. No one seemed to have a very clear idea of what was required, but all had brought something.

The Woggle-Bug had taken from its position over the mantle-piece in the great hallway the head of a Gump, which was adorned with wide-spreading antlers; and this, with great care and greater difficulty, the insect had carried up the stairs to the roof. This Gump resembled an Elk's head, only the nose turned upward in a saucy manner and there were whiskers upon its chin, like those of a billy-goat. Why the Woggle-Bug selected this article he could not have explained, except that it had aroused his curiosity.

Tip, with the aid of the Saw-Horse, had brought a large, upholstered sofa to the roof. It was an oldfashioned piece of furniture, with high back and ends, and it was so heavy that even by resting the greatest weight upon the back of the Saw-Horse, the boy found himself out of breath when at last the clumsy sofa was dumped upon the roof.

The Pumpkinhead had brought a broom, which was the first thing he saw. The Scarecrow arrived with a coil of clothes-lines and ropes which he had taken from the courtyard, and in his trip up the stairs he had become so entangled in the loose ends of the ropes that both he and his burden tumbled in a heap upon the roof and might have rolled off if Tip had not rescued him.

The Tin Woodman appeared last. He also had been to the courtyard, where he had cut four great, spreading leaves from a huge palm-tree that was the pride of all the inhabitants of the Emerald City.

"My dear Nick!" exclaimed the Scarecrow, seeing what his friend had done; "you have been guilty of the greatest crime any person can commit in the Emerald City. If I remember rightly, the penalty for chopping leaves from the royal palm-tree is to be killed seven times and afterward imprisoned for life."

"It cannot be helped now" answered the Tin Woodman, throwing down the big leaves upon the roof. "But it may be one more reason why it is necessary for us to escape. And now let us see what you have found for me to work with."

Many were the doubtful looks cast upon the heap of miscellaneous material that now cluttered the roof, and finally the Scarecrow shook his head and remarked:

"Well, if friend Nick can manufacture, from this mess of rubbish, a Thing that will fly through the air and carry us to safety, then I will acknowledge him to be a better mechanic than I suspected."

But the Tin Woodman seemed at first by no means sure of his powers, and only after polishing his forehead vigorously with the chamois-leather did he resolve to undertake the task.

"The first thing required for the machine," said he, "is a body big enough to carry the entire party. This sofa is the biggest thing we have, and might be used for a body. But, should the machine ever tip sideways, we would all slide off and fall to the ground."

"Why not use two sofas?" asked Tip. "There's another one just like this down stairs."

"That is a very sensible suggestion," exclaimed the Tin Woodman. "You must fetch the other sofa at once."

So Tip and the Saw-Horse managed, with much labor, to get the second sofa to the roof; and when the two were placed together, edge to edge, the backs and ends formed a protecting rampart all around the seats.

"Excellent!" cried the Scarecrow. "We can ride within this snug nest quite at our ease."

The two sofas were now bound firmly together with ropes and clothes-lines, and then Nick Chopper fastened the Gump's head to one end.

"That will show which is the front end of the Thing," said he, greatly pleased with the idea." And, really, if you examine it critically, the Gump looks very well as a figure-head. These great palm-leaves, for which I have endangered my life seven times, must serve us as wings."

"Are they strong enough?" asked the boy.

"They are as strong as anything we can get," answered the Woodman; "and although they are not in proportion to the Thing's body, we are not in a position to be very particular."

So he fastened the palm-leaves to the sofas, two on each side.

Said the Woggle-Bug, with considerable admiration:

"The Thing is now complete, and only needs to be brought to life."

"Stop a moment!" exclaimed Jack." Are you not going to use my broom?"

"What for?" asked the Scarecrow.

"Why, it can be fastened to the back end for a tail," answered the Pumpkinhead. "Surely you would not call the Thing complete without a tail."

"Hm!" said the Tin Woodman, "I do not see the use of a tail. We are not trying to copy a beast, or a fish, or a bird. All we ask of the Thing is to carry us through the air.

"Perhaps, after the Thing is brought to life, it can use a tail to steer with," suggested the Scarecrow. "For if it flies through the air it will not be unlike a bird, and I've noticed that all birds have tails, which they use for a rudder while flying."

"Very well," answered Nick, "the broom shall be used for a tail," and he fastened it firmly to the back end of the sofa body.

Tip took the pepper-box from his pocket.

"The Thing looks very big," said he, anxiously; "and I am not sure there is enough powder left to bring all of it to life. But I'll make it go as far as possible."

"Put most on the wings," said Nick Chopper; "for they must be made as strong as possible."

"And don't forget the head!" exclaimed the Woggle-Bug.

"Or the tail!" added Jack Pumpkinhead.

"Do be quiet," said Tip, nervously; "you must give me a chance to work the magic charm in the proper manner."

Very carefully he began sprinkling the Thing with the precious powder. Each of the four wings was first lightly covered with a layer. then the sofas were sprinkled, and the broom given a slight coating.

"The head! The head! Don't, I beg of you, forget the head!" cried the Woggle-Bug, excitedly.

"There's only a little of the powder left," announced Tip, looking within the box." And it seems to me it is more important to bring the legs of the sofas to life than the head."

"Not so," decided the Scarecrow. "Every thing must have a head to direct it; and since this creature is to fly, and not walk, it is really unimportant whether its legs are alive or not."

So Tip abided by this decision and sprinkled the Gump's head with the remainder of the powder.

"Now" said he, "keep silence while I work the, charm!"

Having heard old Mombi pronounce the magic words, and having also succeeded in bringing the Saw-Horse to life, Tip did not hesitate an instant in speaking the three cabalistic words, each accompanied by the peculiar gesture of the hands.

It was a grave and impressive ceremony.

As he finished the incantation the Thing shuddered throughout its huge bulk, the Gump gave the screeching cry that is familiar to those animals, and then the four wings began flopping furiously.

Tip managed to grasp a chimney, else he would have been blown off the roof by the terrible breeze raised by the wings. The Scarecrow, being light in weight, was caught up bodily and borne through the air until Tip luckily seized him by one leg and held him fast. The Woggle-Bug lay flat upon the roof and so escaped harm, and the Tin Woodman, whose weight of tin anchored him firmly, threw both arms around Jack Pumpkinhead and managed to save him. The Saw-Horse toppled over upon his back and lay with his legs waving helplessly above him.

And now, while all were struggling to recover themselves, the Thing rose slowly from the roof and mounted into the air.

"Here! Come back!" cried Tip, in a frightened voice, as he clung to the chimney with one hand and the Scarecrow with the other. "Come back at once, I command you!"

It was now that the wisdom of the Scarecrow, in bringing the head of the Thing to life instead of the legs, was proved beyond a doubt. For the Gump, already high in the air, turned its head at Tip's command and gradually circled around until it could view the roof of the palace.

"Come back!" shouted the boy, again.

And the Gump obeyed, slowly and gracefully waving its four wings in the air until the Thing had settled once more upon the roof and become still.

Chapter 18 - In the Jackdaw's Nest

"This," said the Gump, in a squeaky voice not at all proportioned to the size of its great body, "is the most novel experience I ever heard of. The last thing I remember distinctly is walking through the forest and hearing a loud noise. Something probably killed me then, and it certainly ought to have been the end of me. Yet here I am, alive again, with four monstrous wings and a body which I venture to say would make any respectable animal or fowl weep with shame to own. What does it all mean? Am I a Gump, or am I a juggernaut?" The creature, as it spoke, wiggled its chin whiskers in a very comical manner.

"You're just a Thing," answered Tip, "with a Gump's head on it. And we have made you and brought you to life so that you may carry us through the air wherever we wish to go."

"Very good!" said the Thing. "As I am not a Gump, I cannot have a Gump's pride or independent spirit. So I may as well become your servant as anything else. My only satisfaction is that I do not seem to have a very strong constitution, and am not likely to live long in a state of slavery."

"Don't say that, I beg of you!" cried the Tin Woodman, whose excellent heart was strongly affected by this sad speech." Are you not feeling well today?"

"Oh, as for that," returned the Gump, "it is my first day of existence; so I cannot Judge whether I am feeling well or ill." And it waved its broom tail to and fro in a pensive manner.

"Come, come!" said the Scarecrow, kindly. "do try, to be more cheerful and take life as you find it. We shall be kind masters, and will strive to render your existence as pleasant as possible. Are you willing to carry us through the air wherever we wish to go?"

"Certainly," answered the Gump. "I greatly prefer to navigate the air. For should I travel on the earth and meet with one of my own species, my embarrassment would be something awful!"

"I can appreciate that," said the Tin Woodman, sympathetically.

"And yet," continued the Thing, "when I carefully look you over, my masters, none of you seems to be constructed much more artistically than I am."

"Appearances are deceitful," said the Woggle-Bug, earnestly. "I am both Highly Magnified and Thoroughly Educated."

"Indeed!" murmured the Gump, indifferently.

"And my brains are considered remarkably rare specimens," added the Scarecrow, proudly.

"How strange!" remarked the Gump.

"Although I am of tin," said the Woodman, "I own a heart altogether the warmest and most admirable in the whole world."

"I'm delighted to hear it," replied the Gump, with a slight cough.

"My smile," said Jack Pumpkinhead, "is worthy your best attention. It is always the same."

"Semper idem," explained the Woggle-Bug, pompously; and the Gump turned to stare at him.

"And I," declared the Saw-Horse, filling in an awkward pause, "am only remarkable because I can't help it."

"I am proud, indeed, to meet with such exceptional masters," said the Gump, in a careless tone. "If I could but secure so complete an introduction to myself, I would be more than satisfied."

"That will come in time," remarked the Scarecrow. "To 'Know Thyself' is considered quite an accomplishment, which it has taken us, who are your elders, months to perfect. But now," he added, turning to the others, "let us get aboard and start upon our journey."

"Where shall we go?" asked Tip, as he clambered to a seat on the sofas and assisted the Pumpkinhead to follow him.

"In the South Country rules a very delightful Queen called Glinda the Good, who I am sure will gladly receive us," said the Scarecrow, getting into the Thing clumsily. "Let us go to her and ask her advice."

"That is cleverly thought of," declared Nick Chopper, giving the Woggle-Bug a boost and then toppling the Saw-Horse into the rear end of the cushioned seats." I know Glinda the Good, and believe she will prove a friend indeed."

"Are we all ready?" asked the boy.

"Yes," announced the Tin Woodman, seating himself beside the Scarecrow.

"Then," said Tip, addressing the Gump, "be kind enough to fly with us to the Southward; and do not go higher than to escape the houses and trees, for it makes me dizzy to be up so far."

"All right," answered the Gump, briefly.

It flopped its four huge wings and rose slowly into the air; and then, while our little band of adventurers clung to the backs and sides of the sofas for support, the Gump turned toward the South and soared swiftly and majestically away.

"The scenic effect, from this altitude, is marvelous," commented the educated Woggle-Bug, as they rode along.

"Never mind the scenery," said the Scarecrow. "Hold on tight, or you may get a tumble. The Thing seems to rock badly.'

"It will be dark soon," said Tip, observing that the sun was low on the horizon. "Perhaps we should have waited until morning. I wonder if the Gump can fly in the night."

"I've been wondering that myself," returned the Gump quietly. "You see, this is a new experience to me. I used to have legs that carried me swiftly over the ground. But now my legs feel as if they were asleep."

"They are," said Tip. "We didn't bring 'em to life."

"You're expected to fly," explained the Scarecrow. "not to walk."

"We can walk ourselves," said the Woggle-Bug."

I begin to understand what is required of me," remarked the Gump; "so I will do my best to please you," and he flew on for a time in silence.

Presently Jack Pumpkinhead became uneasy.

"I wonder if riding through the air is liable to spoil pumpkins," he said.

"Not unless you carelessly drop your head over the side," answered the Woggle-Bug. "In that event your head would no longer be a pumpkin, for it would become a squash."

"Have I not asked you to restrain these unfeeling jokes?" demanded Tip, looking at the Woggle-Bug with a severe expression.

"You have; and I've restrained a good many of them," replied the insect. "But there are opportunities for so many excellent puns in our language that, to an educated person like myself, the temptation to express them is almost irresistible."

"People with more or less education discovered those puns centuries ago," said Tip.

"Are you sure?" asked the Woggle-Bug, with a startled look.

"Of course I am," answered the boy. "An educated Woggle-Bug may be a new thing; but a Woggle-Bug education is as old as the hills, judging from the display you make of it."

The insect seemed much impressed by this remark, and for a time maintained a meek silence.

The Scarecrow, in shifting his seat, saw upon the cushions the pepper-box which Tip had cast aside, and began to examine it.

"Throw it overboard," said the boy; "it's quite empty now, and there's no use keeping it."

"Is it really empty?" asked the Scarecrow, looking curiously into the box.

"Of course it is," answered Tip. "I shook out every grain of the powder."

"Then the box has two bottoms," announced the Scarecrow, "for the bottom on the inside is fully an inch away from the bottom on the outside."

"Let me see," said the Tin Woodman, taking the box from his friend. "Yes," he declared, after looking it over, "the thing certainly has a false bottom. Now, I wonder what that is for?"

"Can't you get it apart, and find out?" enquired Tip, now quite interested in the mystery.

"Why, yes; the lower bottom unscrews," said the Tin Woodman. "My fingers are rather stiff; please see if you can open it."

He handed the pepper-box to Tip, who had no difficulty in unscrewing the bottom. And in the cavity below were three silver pills, with a carefully folded paper lying underneath them.

This paper the boy proceeded to unfold, taking care not to spill the pills, and found several lines clearly written in red ink.

"Read it aloud," said the Scarecrow. so Tip read, as follows:

"DR. NIKIDIK'S CELEBRATED WISHING PILLS.

"Directions for Use: Swallow one pill; count seventeen by twos; then make a Wish. The Wish will immediately be granted. CAUTION: Keep in a Dry and Dark Place."

"Why, this is a very valuable discovery!" cried the Scarecrow.

"It is, indeed," replied Tip, gravely. "These pills may be of great use to us. I wonder if old Mombi knew they were in the bottom of the pepper-box. I remember hearing her say that she got the Powder of Life from this same Nikidik."

"He must be a powerful Sorcerer!" exclaimed the Tin Woodman; "and since the powder proved a success we ought to have confidence in the pills."

"But how," asked the Scarecrow, "can anyone count seventeen by twos? Seventeen is an odd number."

"That is true," replied Tip, greatly disappointed. "No one can possibly count seventeen by twos."

"Then the pills are of no use to us," wailed the Pumpkinhead; "and this fact overwhelms me with grief. For I had intended wishing that my head would never spoil."

"Nonsense!" said the Scarecrow, sharply. "If we could use the pills at all we would make far better wishes than that."

"I do not see how anything could be better," protested poor Jack. "If you were liable to spoil at any time you could understand my anxiety."

"For my part," said the Tin Woodman, "I sympathize with you in every respect. But since we cannot count seventeen by twos, sympathy is all you are liable to get."

By this time it had become quite dark, and the voyagers found above them a cloudy sky, through which the rays of the moon could not penetrate.

The Gump flew steadily on, and for some reason the huge sofa-body rocked more and more dizzily every hour.

The Woggle-Bug declared he was sea-sick; and Tip was also pale and somewhat distressed. But the others clung to the backs of the sofas and did not seem to mind the motion as long as they were not tipped out.

Darker and darker grew the night, and on and on sped the Gump through the black heavens. The travelers could not even see one another, and an oppressive silence settled down upon them.

After a long time Tip, who had been thinking deeply, spoke.

"How are we to know when we come to the pallace of Glinda the Good?" he asked.

."It's a long way to Glinda's palace," answered the Woodman; "I've traveled it."

"But how are we to know how fast the Gump is flying?" persisted the boy. "We cannot see a single thing down on the earth, and before morning we may be far beyond the place we want to reach."

"That is all true enough," the Scarecrow replied, a little uneasily. "But I do not see how we can stop just now; for we might alight in a river, or on, the top of a steeple; and that would be a great disaster."

So they permitted the Gump to fly on, with regular flops of its great wings, and waited patiently for morning.

Then Tip's fears were proven to be well founded; for with the first streaks of gray dawn they looked over the sides of the sofas and discovered rolling plains dotted with queer villages, where the houses, instead of being dome- shaped— as they all are in the Land of Oz—had slanting roofs that rose to a peak in the center. Odd looking animals were also moving about upon the open plains, and the country was unfamiliar to both the Tin Woodman and the Scarecrow, who had formerly visited Glinda the Good's domain and knew it well.

"We are lost!" said the Scarecrow, dolefully. "The Gump must have carried us entirely out of the Land of Oz and over the sandy deserts and into the terrible outside world that Dorothy told us about."

"We must get back," exclaimed the Tin Woodman, earnestly. "we must get back as soon as possible!"

"Turn around!" cried Tip to the Gump. "turn as quickly as you can!"

"If I do I shall upset," answered the Gump. "I'm not at all used to flying, and the best plan would be for me to alight in some place, and then I can turn around and take a fresh start."

Just then, however, there seemed to be no stopping-place that would answer their purpose. They flew over a village so big that the Woggle-Bug declared it was a city. and then they came to a range of high mountains with many deep gorges and steep cliffs showing plainly.

"Now is our chance to stop," said the boy, finding they were very close to the mountain tops. Then he turned to the Gump and commanded: "Stop at the first level place you see!"

"Very well," answered the Gump, and settled down upon a table of rock that stood between two cliffs.

But not being experienced in such matters, the Gump did not judge his speed correctly; and instead of coming to a stop upon the flat rock he missed it by half the width of his body, breaking off both his right wings against the sharp edge of the rock and then tumbling over and over down the cliff.

Our friends held on to the sofas as long as they could, but when the Gump caught on a proJecting rock the Thing stopped suddenly—bottom side up—and all were immediately dumped out.

By good fortune they fell only a few feet; for underneath them was a monster nest, built by a colony of Jackdaws in a hollow ledge of rock; so none of them—not even the Pumpkinhead—was injured by the fall. For Jack found his precious head resting on the soft breast of the Scarecrow, which made an excellent cushion; and Tip fell on a mass of leaves and papers, which saved him from injury. The Woggle-Bug had bumped his round head against the Saw-Horse, but without causing him more than a moment's inconvenience.

The Tin Woodman was at first much alarmed; but finding he had escaped without even a scratch upon his beautiful nickle-plate he at once regained his accustomed cheerfulness and turned to address his comrades.

"Our Journey had ended rather suddenly," said he; "and we cannot justly blame our friend the Gump for our accident, because he did the best he could under the circumstances. But how we are ever to escape from this nest I must leave to someone with better brains than I possess."

Here he gazed at the Scarecrow; who crawled to the edge of the nest and looked over. Below them was a sheer precipice several hundred feet in depth. Above them was a smooth cliff unbroken save by the point of rock where the wrecked body of the Gump still hung suspended from the end of one of the sofas. There really seemed to be no means of escape, and as they realized their helpless plight the little band of adventurers gave way to their bewilderment.

"This is a worse prison than the palace," sadly remarked the Woggle-Bug.

"I wish we had stayed there," moaned Jack.

"I'm afraid the mountain air isn't good for pumpkins."

"It won't be when the Jackdaws come back," growled the Saw-Horse, which lay waving its legs in a vain endeavor to get upon its feet again. "Jackdaws are especially fond of pumpkins."

"Do you think the birds will come here?" asked Jack, much distressed.

"Of course they will," said Tip; "for this is their nest. And there must be hundreds of them," he continued, "for see what a lot of things they have brought here!"

Indeed, the nest was half filled with a most curious collection of small articles for which the birds could have no use, but which the thieving Jackdaws had stolen during many years from the homes of men. And as the nest was safely hidden where no human being could reach it, this lost property would never be recovered.

The Woggle-Bug, searching among the rubbish—for the Jackdaws stole useless things as well as valuable ones—turned up with his foot a beautiful diamond necklace. This was so greatly admired by the Tin Woodman that the Woggle-Bug presented it to him with a graceful speech, after which the Woodman hung it around his neck with much pride, rejoicing exceedingly when the big diamonds glittered in the sun's rays.

But now they heard a great jabbering and flopping of wings, and as the sound grew nearer to them Tip exclaimed:

"The Jackdaws are coming! And if they find us here they will surely kill us in their anger."

"I was afraid of this!" moaned the Pumpkinhead. "My time has come!"

"And mine, also!" said the Woggle-Bug; "for Jackdaws are the greatest enemies of my race."

The others were not at all afraid; but the Scarecrow at once decided to save those of the party who were liable to be injured by the angry birds. So he commanded Tip to take off Jack's head and lie down with it in the bottom of the nest, and when this was done he ordered the Woggle-Bug to lie beside Tip. Nick Chopper, who knew from past experience Just what to do, then took the Scarecrow to pieces (all except his head) and scattered the straw over Tip and the Woggle-Bug, completely covering their bodies.

Hardly had this been accomplished when the flock of Jackdaws reached them. Perceiving the intruders in their nest the birds flew down upon them with screams of rage.

Chapter 19 - Dr. Nikidik's Famous Wishing Pills

The Tin Woodman was usually a peaceful man, but when occasion required he could fight as fiercely as a Roman gladiator. So, when the Jackdaws nearly knocked him down in their rush of wings, and their sharp beaks and claws threatened to damage his brilliant plating, the Woodman picked up his axe and made it whirl swiftly around his head.

But although many were beaten off in this way, the birds were so numerous and so brave that they continued the attack as furiously as before. Some of them pecked at the eyes of the Gump, which hung over the nest in a helpless condition; but the Gump's eyes were of glass and could not be injured. Others of the Jackdaws rushed at the Saw-Horse; but that animal, being still upon his back, kicked out so viciously with his wooden legs that he beat off as many assailants as did the Woodman's axe.

Finding themselves thus opposed, the birds fell upon the Scarecrow's straw, which lay at the center of the nest, covering Tip and the Woggle-Bug and Jack's pumpkin head, and began tearing it away and flying off with it, only to let it drop, straw by straw into the great gulf beneath.

The Scarecrow's head, noting with dismay this wanton destruction of his interior, cried to the Tin Woodman to save him; and that good friend responded with renewed energy. His axe fairly flashed among the Jackdaws, and fortunately the Gump began wildly waving the two wings remaining on the left side of its body. The flutter of these great wings filled the Jackdaws with terror, and when the Gump by its exertions freed itself from the peg of rock on which it hung, and sank flopping into the nest, the alarm of the birds knew no bounds and they fled screaming over the mountains.

When the last foe had disappeared, Tip crawled from under the sofas and assisted the Woggle-Bug to follow him.

"We are saved!" shouted the boy, delightedly.

"We are, indeed!" responded the Educated Insect, fairly hugging the stiff head of the Gump in his joy. "and we owe it all to the flopping of the Thing, and the good axe of the Woodman!"

"If I am saved, get me out of here!" called Jack; whose head was still beneath the sofas; and Tip managed to roll the pumpkin out and place it upon its neck again. He also set the Saw-Horse upright, and said to it:

"We owe you many thanks for the gallant fight you made."

"I really think we have escaped very nicely," remarked the Tin Woodman, in a tone of pride.

"Not so!" exclaimed a hollow voice.

At this they all turned in surprise to look at the Scarecrow's head, which lay at the back of the nest.

"I am completely ruined!" declared the Scarecrow, as he noted their astonishment. "For where is the straw that stuffs my body?"

The awful question startled them all. They gazed around the nest with horror, for not a vestige of straw remained. The Jackdaws had stolen it to the last wisp and flung it all into the chasm that yawned for hundreds of feet beneath the nest.

"My poor, poor friend!" said the Tin Woodman, taking up the Scarecrow's head and caressing it tenderly; "whoever could imagine you would come to this untimely end?"

"I did it to save my friends," returned the head; "and I am glad that I perished in so noble and unselfish a manner."

"But why are you all so despondent?" inquired the Woggle-Bug. "The Scarecrow's clothing is still safe."

"Yes," answered the Tin Woodman; "but our friend's clothes are useless without stuffing."

"Why not stuff him with money?" asked Tip.

"Money!" they all cried, in an amazed chorus.

"To be sure," said the boy. "In the bottom of the nest are thousands of dollar bills—and two-dollar bills—and five-dollar bills—and tens, and twenties, and fifties. There are enough of them to stuff a dozen Scarecrows. Why not use the money?"

The Tin Woodman began to turn over the rubbish with the handle of his axe; and, sure enough, what they had first thought only worthless papers were found to be all bills of various denominations, which the mischievous Jackdaws had for years been engaged in stealing from the villages and cities they visited.

There was an immense fortune lying in that inaccessible nest; and Tip's suggestion was, with the Scarecrow's consent, quickly acted upon.

They selected all the newest and cleanest bills and assorted them into various piles. The Scarecrow's left leg and boot were stuffed with five- dollar bills; his right leg was stuffed with ten-dollar bills, and his body so closely filled with fifties, one-hundreds and one-thousands that he could scarcely button his jacket with comfort.

"You are now" said the Woggle-Bug, impressively, when the task had been completed, "the most valuable member of our party; and as you are among faithful friends there is little danger of your being spent."

"Thank you," returned the Scarecrow, gratefully. "I feel like a new man; and although at first glance I might be mistaken for a Safety Deposit Vault, I beg you to remember that my Brains are still composed of the same old material. And these are the possessions that have always made me a person to be depended upon in an emergency."

"Well, the emergency is here," observed Tip; "and unless your brains help us out of it we shall be compelled to pass the remainder of our lives in this nest."

"How about these wishing pills?" enquired the Scarecrow, taking the box from his jacket pocket. "Can't we use them to escape?"

"Not unless we can count seventeen by twos," answered the Tin Woodman. "But our friend the Woggle-Bug claims to be highly educated, so he ought easily to figure out how that can be done."

"It isn't a question of education," returned the Insect; "it's merely a question of mathematics. I've seen the professor work lots of sums on the blackboard, and he claimed anything could be done with x's and y's and a's, and such things, by mixing them up with plenty of plusses and minuses and equals, and so forth. But he never said anything, so far as I can remember, about counting up to the odd number of seventeen by the even numbers of twos."

"Stop! stop!" cried the Pumpkinhead. "You're making my head ache."

"And mine," added the Scarecrow. "Your mathematics seem to me very like a bottle of mixed pickles the more you fish for what you want the less chance you have of getting it. I am certain that if the thing can be accomplished at all, it is in a very simple manner."

"Yes," said Tip. "old Mombi couldn't use x's and minuses, for she never went to school."

"Why not start counting at a half of one?" asked the Saw-Horse, abruptly. "Then anyone can count up to seventeen by twos very easily."

They looked at each other in surprise, for the Saw-Horse was considered the most stupid of the entire party.

"You make me quite ashamed of myself," said the Scarecrow, bowing low to the Saw-Horse.

"Nevertheless, the creature is right," declared the Woggle-Bug; for twice one-half is one, and if you get to one it is easy to count from one up to seventeen by twos."

"I wonder I didn't think of that myself," said the Pumpkinhead.

"I don't," returned the Scarecrow. "You're no wiser than the rest of us, are you? But let us make a wish at once. Who will swallow the first pill?"

"Suppose you do it," suggested Tip.

"I can't," said the Scarecrow.

"Why not? You've a mouth, haven't you?" asked the boy.

"Yes; but my mouth is painted on, and there's no swallow connected with it,' answered the Scarecrow. "In fact," he continued, looking from one to another critically, "I believe the boy and the Woggle-Bug are the only ones in our party that are able to swallow."

Observing the truth of this remark, Tip said:

"Then I will undertake to make the first wish. Give me one of the Silver Pills."

This the Scarecrow tried to do; but his padded gloves were too clumsy to clutch so small an object, and he held the box toward the boy while Tip selected one of the pills and swallowed it.

"Count!" cried the Scarecrow.

"One-half, one, three, five, seven, nine, eleven,!" counted Tip. thirteen, fifteen, seventeen.

"Now wish!" said the Tin Woodman anxiously:

But Just then the boy began to suffer such fearful pains that he became alarmed.

"The pill has poisoned me!" he gasped; "O—h! O-o-o-o-o! Ouch! Murder! Fire! O-o-h!" and here he rolled upon the bottom of the nest in such contortions that he frightened them all.

"What can we do for you. Speak, I beg!" entreated the Tin Woodman, tears of sympathy running down his nickel cheeks.

"I—I don't know!" answered Tip. "O—h! I wish I'd never swallowed that pill!"

Then at once the pain stopped, and the boy rose to his feet again and found the Scarecrow looking with amazement at the end of the pepper-box.

"What's happened?" asked the boy, a little ashamed of his recent exhibition.

"Why, the three pills are in the box again!" said the Scarecrow.

"Of course they are," the Woggle-Bug declared. "Didn't Tip wish that he'd never swallowed one of them? Well, the wish came true, and he didn't swallow one of them. So of course they are all three in the box."

"That may be; but the pill gave me a dreadful pain, just the same," said the boy.

"Impossible!" declared the Woggle-Bug. "If you have never swallowed it, the pill can not have given you a pain. And as your wish, being granted, proves you did not swallow the pill, it is also plain that you suffered no pain."

"Then it was a splendid imitation of a pain," retorted Tip, angrily. "Suppose you try the next pill yourself. We've wasted one wish already."

"Oh, no, we haven't!" protested the Scarecrow. "Here are still three pills in the box, and each pill is good for a wish."

"Now you're making my head ache," said Tip. "I can't understand the thing at all. But I won't take another pill, I promise you!" and with this remark he retired sulkily to the back of the nest.

"Well," said the Woggle-Bug, "it remains for me to save us in my most Highly Magnified and Thoroughly Educated manner; for I seem to be the only one able and willing to make a wish. Let me have one of the pills."

He swallowed it without hesitation, and they all stood admiring his courage while the Insect counted seventeen by twos in the same way that Tip had done. And for some reason—perhaps because Woggle-Bugs have stronger stomachs than boys—the silver pellet caused it no pain whatever.

"I wish the Gump's broken wings mended, and as good as new!" said the Woggle-Bug, in a slow; impressive voice.

All turned to look at the Thing, and so quickly had the wish been granted that the Gump lay before them in perfect repair, and as well able to fly through the air as when it had first been brought to life on the roof of the palace.

Chapter 20 - The Scarecrow Appeals to Glenda the Good

"Hooray!" shouted the Scarecrow, gaily. "We can now leave this miserable Jackdaws' nest whenever we please."

"But it is nearly dark," said the Tin Woodman; "and unless we wait until morning to make our flight we may get into more trouble. I don't like these night trips, for one never knows what will happen."

So it was decided to wait until daylight, and the adventurers amused themselves in the twilight by searching the Jackdaws' nest for treasures.

The Woggle-Bug found two handsome bracelets of wrought gold, which fitted his slender arms very well. The Scarecrow took a fancy for rings, of which there were many in the nest. Before long he had fitted a ring to each finger of his padded gloves, and not being content with that display he added one more to each thumb. As he carefully chose those rings set with sparkling stones, such as rubies, amethysts and sapphires, the Scarecrow's hands now presented a most brilliant appearance.

"This nest would be a picnic for Queen Jinjur," said he, musingly. "for as nearly as I can make out she and her girls conquered me merely to rob my city of its emeralds."

The Tin Woodman was content with his diamond necklace and refused to accept any additional decorations; but Tip secured a fine gold watch, which was attached to a heavy fob, and placed it in his pocket with much pride. He also pinned several jeweled brooches to Jack Pumpkinhead's red waistcoat, and attached a lorgnette, by means of a fine chain, to the neck of the Saw- Horse.

"It's very pretty," said the creature, regarding the lorgnette approvingly; "but what is it for?"

None of them could answer that question, however; so the Saw-Horse decided it was some rare decoration and became very fond of it.

That none of the party might be slighted, they ended by placing several large seal rings upon the points of the Gump's antlers, although that odd personage seemed by no means gratified by the attention.

Darkness soon fell upon them, and Tip and the Woggle-Bug went to sleep while the others sat down to wait patiently for the day.

Next morning they had cause to congratulate themselves upon the useful condition of the Gump; for with daylight a great flock of Jackdaws approached to engage in one more battle for the possession of the nest.

But our adventurers did not wait for the assault. They tumbled into the cushioned seats of the sofas as quickly as possible, and Tip gave the word to the Gump to start.

At once it rose into the air, the great wings flopping strongly and with regular motions, and in a few moments they were so far from the nest that the chattering Jackdaws took possession without any attempt at pursuit.

The Thing flew due North, going in the same direction from whence it had come. At least, that was the Scarecrow's opinion, and the others agreed that the Scarecrow was the best judge of direction. After passing over several cities and villages the Gump carried them high above a broad plain where houses became more and more scattered until they disappeared altogether. Next came the wide, sandy desert separating the rest of the world from the Land of Oz, and before noon they saw the dome-shaped houses that proved they were once more within the borders of their native land.

"But the houses and fences are blue," said the Tin Woodman, "and that indicates we are in the land of the Munchkins, and therefore a long distance from Glinda the Good."

"What shall we do?" asked the boy, turning to their guide.

"I don't know" replied the Scarecrow, frankly. "If we were at the Emerald City we could then move directly southward, and so reach our destination. But we dare not go to the Emerald City, and the Gump is probably carrying us further in the wrong direction with every flop of its wings."

"Then the Woggle-Bug must swallow another pill," said Tip, decidedly, "and wish us headed in the right direction."

"Very well," returned the Highly Magnified one; "I'm willing."

But when the Scarecrow searched in his pocket for the pepper-box containing the two silver Wishing Pills, it was not to be found. Filled with anxiety, the voyagers hunted throughout every inch of the Thing for the precious box; but it had disappeared entirely.

And still the Gump flew onward, carrying them they knew not where.

"I must have left the pepper-box in the Jackdaws' nest," said the Scarecrow, at length.

"It is a great misfortune," the Tin Woodman declared. "But we are no worse off than before we discovered the Wishing Pills."

"We are better off," replied Tip. "for the one pill we used has enabled us to escape from that horrible nest."

"Yet the loss of the other two is serious, and I deserve a good scolding for my carelessness," the Scarecrow rejoined, penitently. "For in such an unusual party as this accidents are liable to happen any moment, and even now we may be approaching a new danger."

No one dared contradict this, and a dismal silence ensued.

The Gump flew steadily on.

Suddenly Tip uttered an exclamation of surprise. "We must have reached the South Country," he cried, "for below us everything is red!"

Immediately they all leaned over the backs of the sofas to look—all except Jack, who was too careful of his pumpkin head to risk its slipping off his neck. Sure enough; the red houses and fences and trees indicated they were within the domain of Glinda the Good; and presently, as they glided rapidly on, the Tin Woodman recognized the roads and buildings they passed, and altered slightly the flight of the Gump so that they might reach the palace of the celebrated Sorceress.

"Good!" cried the Scarecrow, delightedly. "We do not need the lost Wishing Pills now, for we have arrived at our destination."

Gradually the Thing sank lower and nearer to the ground until at length it came to rest within the beautiful gardens of Glinda, settling upon a velvety green lawn close by a fountain which sent sprays of flashing gems, instead of water, high into the air, whence they fell with a soft, tinkling sound into the carved marble basin placed to receive them.

Everything was very gorgeous in Glinda's gardens, and while our voyagers gazed about with admiring eyes a company of soldiers silently appeared and surrounded them. But these soldiers of the great Sorceress were entirely different from those of Jinjur's Army of Revolt, although they were likewise girls. For Glinda's soldiers wore neat uniforms and bore swords and spears; and they marched with a skill and precision that proved them well trained in the arts of war.

The Captain commanding this troop—which was Glinda's private Body Guard - - recognized the Scarecrow and the Tin Woodman at once, and greeted them with respectful salutations.

"Good day!" said the Scarecrow, gallantly removing his hat, while the Woodman gave a soldierly salute; "we have come to request an audience with your fair Ruler."

"Glinda is now within her palace, awaiting you," returned the Captain; "for she saw you coming long before you arrived."

"That is strange!" said Tip, wondering.

"Not at all," answered the Scarecrow, "for Glinda the Good is a mighty Sorceress, and nothing that goes on in the Land of Oz escapes her notice. I suppose she knows why we came as well as we do ourselves."

"Then what was the use of our coming?" asked Jack, stupidly.

"To prove you are a Pumpkinhead!" retorted the Scarecrow. "But, if the Sorceress expects us, we must not keep her waiting."

So they all clambered out of the sofas and followed the Captain toward the palace—even the Saw-Horse taking his place in the queer procession.

Upon her throne of finely wrought gold sat Glinda, and she could scarcely repress a smile as her peculiar visitors entered and bowed before her. Both the Scarecrow and the Tin Woodman she knew and liked; but the awkward Pumpkinhead and Highly Magnified Woggle-Bug were creatures she had never seen before, and they seemed even more curious than the others. As for the Saw-Horse, he looked to be nothing more than an animated chunk of wood; and he bowed so stiffly that his head bumped against the floor, causing a ripple of laughter among the soldiers, in which Glinda frankly joined.

"I beg to announce to your glorious highness," began the Scarecrow, in a solemn voice, "that my Emerald City has been overrun by a crowd of impudent girls with knitting-needles, who have enslaved all the men, robbed the streets and public buildings of all their emerald jewels, and usurped my throne."

"I know it," said Glinda.

"They also threatened to destroy me, as well as all the good friends and allies you see before you," continued the Scarecrow. "and had we not managed to escape their clutches our days would long since have ended."

"I know it," repeated Glinda.

"Therefore I have come to beg your assistance," resumed the Scarecrow, "for I believe you are always glad to succor the unfortunate and oppressed."

"That is true," replied the Sorceress, slowly. "But the Emerald City is now ruled by General Jinjur, who has caused herself to be proclaimed Queen. What right have I to oppose her?"

"Why, she stole the throne from me," said the Scarecrow.

"And how came you to possess the throne?" asked Glinda.

"I got it from the Wizard of Oz, and by the choice of the people," returned the Scarecrow, uneasy at such questioning.

"And where did the Wizard get it?" she continued gravely.

"I am told he took it from Pastoria, the former King," said the Scarecrow, becoming confused under the intent look of the Sorceress.

"Then," declared Glinda, "the throne of the Emerald City belongs neither to you nor to Jinjur, but to this Pastoria from whom the Wizard usurped it."

"That is true," acknowledged the Scarecrow, humbly; "but Pastoria is now dead and gone, and some one must rule in his place."

"Pastoria had a daughter, who is the rightful heir to the throne of the Emerald City. Did you know that?" questioned the Sorceress.

"No," replied the Scarecrow. "But if the girl still lives I will not stand in her way. It will satisfy me as well to have Jinjur turned out, as an impostor, as to regain the throne myself. In fact, it isn't much fun to be King, especially if one has good brains. I have known for some time that I am fitted to occupy a far more exalted position. But where is the girl who owns the throne, and what is her name?"

"Her name is Ozma," answered Glinda. "But where she is I have tried in vain to discover. For the Wizard of Oz, when he stole the throne from Ozma's father, hid the girl in some secret place; and by means of a magical trick with which I am not familiar he also managed to prevent her being discovered—even by so experienced a Sorceress as myself."

"That is strange," interrupted the Woggle-Bug, pompously. "I have been informed that the Wonderful Wizard of Oz was nothing more than a humbug!"

"Nonsense!" exclaimed the Scarecrow, much provoked by this speech. "Didn't he give me a wonderful set of brains?"

"There's no humbug about my heart," announced the Tin Woodman, glaring indignantly at the Woggle-Bug.

"Perhaps I was misinformed," stammered the Insect, shrinking back; "I never knew the Wizard personally."

"Well, we did," retorted the Scarecrow, "and he was a very great Wizard, I assure you. It is true he was guilty of some slight impostures, but unless he was a great Wizard how—let me ask—could he have hidden this girl Ozma so securely that no one can find her?"

"I—I give it up!" replied the Woggle-Bug, meekly.

"That is the most sensible speech you've made," said the Tin Woodman.

"I must really make another effort to discover where this girl is hidden," resumed the Sorceress, thoughtfully. "I have in my library a book in which is inscribed every action of the Wizard while he was in our land of Oz—or, at least, every action that could be observed by my spies. This book I will read carefully tonight, and try to single out the acts that may guide us in discovering the lost Ozma. In the meantime, pray amuse yourselves in my palace and command my servants as if they were your own. I will grant you another audience tomorrow."

With this gracious speech Glinda dismissed the adventurers, and they wandered away through the beautiful gardens, where they passed several hours enjoying all the delightful things with which the Queen of the Southland had surrounded her royal palace.

On the following morning they again appeared before Glinda, who said to them:

"I have searched carefully through the records of the Wizard's actions, and among them I can find but three that appear to have been suspicious. He ate beans with a knife, made three secret visits to old Mombi, and limped slightly on his left foot."

"Ah! that last is certainly suspicious!" exclaimed the Pumpkinhead.

"Not necessarily," said the Scarecrow. "he may, have had corns. Now, it seems to me his eating beans with a knife is more suspicious."

"Perhaps it is a polite custom in Omaha, from which great country the Wizard originally came," suggested the Tin Woodman.

"It may be," admitted the Scarecrow.

"But why," asked Glinda, "did he make three secret visits to old Mombi?"

"Ah! Why, indeed!" echoed the Woggle-Bug, impressively.

"We know that the Wizard taught the old woman many of his tricks of magic," continued Glinda; "and this he would not have done had she not assisted him in some way. So we may suspect with good reason that Mombi aided him to hide the girl Ozma, who was the real heir to the throne of the Emerald City, and a constant danger to the usurper. For, if the people knew that she lived, they would quickly make her their Queen and restore her to her rightful position."

"An able argument!" cried the Scarecrow. "I have no doubt that Mombi was mixed up in this wicked business. But how does that knowledge help us?"

"We must find Mombi," replied Glinda, "and force her to tell where the girl is hidden."

"Mombi is now with Queen Jinjur, in the Emerald, City" said Tip. "It was she who threw so many obstacles in our pathway, and made Jinjur threaten to destroy my friends and give me back into the old witch's power."

"Then," decided Glinda, "I will march with my army to the Emerald City, and take Mombi prisoner. After that we can, perhaps, force her to tell the truth about Ozma."

"She is a terrible old woman!" remarked Tip, with a shudder at the thought of Mombi's black kettle; "and obstinate, too."

"I am quite obstinate myself," returned the Sorceress, with a sweet smile. "so I do not fear Mombi in the least. Today I will make all necessary preparations, and we will march upon the Emerald City at daybreak tomorrow."

Chapter 21 - The Tin Woodman Plucks a Rose

The Army of Glinda the Good looked very grand and imposing when it assembled at daybreak before the palace gates. The uniforms of the girl soldiers were pretty and of gay colors, and their silver-tipped spears were bright and glistening, the long shafts being inlaid with mother-of-pearl. All the officers wore sharp, gleaming swords, and shields edged with peacock- feathers; and it really seemed that no foe could by any possibility defeat such a brilliant army.

The Sorceress rode in a beautiful palanquin which was like the body of a coach, having doors and windows with silken curtains; but instead of wheels, which a coach has, the palanquin rested upon two long, horizontal bars, which were borne upon the shoulders of twelve servants.

The Scarecrow and his comrades decided to ride in the Gump, in order to keep up with the swift march of the army; so, as soon as Glinda had started and her soldiers had marched away to the inspiring strains of music played by the royal band, our friends climbed into the sofas and followed. The Gump flew along slowly at a point directly over the palanquin in which rode the Sorceress.

"Be careful," said the Tin Woodman to the Scarecrow, who was leaning far over the side to look at the army below. "You might fall."

"It wouldn't matter," remarked the educated Woggle-Bug. "he can't get broke so long as he is stuffed with money."

"Didn't I ask you" began Tip, in a reproachful voice.

"You did!" said the Woggle-Bug, promptly. "And I beg your pardon. I will really try to restrain myself."

"You'd better," declared the boy. "That is, if you wish to travel in our company."

"Ah! I couldn't bear to part with you now," murmured the Insect, feelingly; so Tip let the subject drop.

The army moved steadily on, but night had fallen before they came to the walls of the Emerald City. By the dim light of the new moon, however, Glinda's forces silently surrounded the city and pitched their tents of scarlet silk upon the greensward. The tent of the Sorceress was larger than the others, and was composed of pure white silk, with scarlet banners flying above it. A tent was also pitched for the Scarecrow's party; and when these preparations had been made, with military precision and quickness, the army retired to rest.

Great was the amazement of Queen Jinjur next morning when her soldiers came running to inform her of the vast army surrounding them. She at once climbed to a high tower of the royal palace and saw banners waving in every direction and the great white tent of Glinda standing directly before the gates.

"We are surely lost!" cried Jinjur, in despair; "for how can our knitting- needles avail against the long spears and terrible swords of our foes?"

"The best thing we can do," said one of the girls, "is to surrender as quickly as possible, before we get hurt."

"Not so," returned Jinjur, more bravely. "The enemy is still outside the walls, so we must try to gain time by engaging them in parley. Go you with a flag of truce to Glinda and ask her why she has dared to invade my dominions, and what are her demands."

So the girl passed through the gates, bearing a white flag to show she was on a mission of peace, and came to Glinda's tent. "Tell your Queen," said the Sorceress to the girl, "that she must deliver up to me old Mombi, to be my prisoner. If this is done I will not molest her farther."

Now when this message was delivered to the Queen it filled her with dismay, for Mombi was her chief counsellor, and Jinjur was terribly afraid of the old hag. But she sent for Mombi, and told her what Glinda had said.

"I see trouble ahead for all of us," muttered the old witch, after glancing into a magic mirror she carried in her pocket. "But we may even yet escape by deceiving this sorceress, clever as she thinks herself."

"Don't you think it will be safer for me to deliver you into her hands?" asked Jinjur, nervously.

"If you do, it will cost you the throne of the Emerald City!" answered the witch, positively. "But if you will let me have my own way, I can save us both very easily."

"Then do as you please," replied Jinjur, "for it is so aristocratic to be a Queen that I do not wish to be obliged to return home again, to make beds and wash dishes for my mother."

So Mombi called Jellia Jamb to her, and performed a certain magical rite with which she was familiar. As a result of the enchantment Jellia took on the form and features of Mombi, while the old witch grew to resemble the girl so closely that it seemed impossible anyone could guess the deception.

"Now," said old Mombi to the Queen, "let your soldiers deliver up this girl to Glinda. She will think she has the real Mombi in her power, and so will return immediately to her own country in the South."

Therefore Jellia, hobbling along like an aged woman, was led from the city gates and taken before Glinda.

"Here is the person you demanded," said one of the guards, "and our Queen now begs you will go away, as you promised, and leave us in peace."

"That I will surely do," replied Glinda, much pleased; "if this is really the person she seems to be."

"It is certainly old Mombi," said the guard, who believed she was speaking the truth; and then Jinjur's soldiers returned within the city's gates.

The Sorceress quickly summoned the Scarecrow and his friends to her tent, and began to question the supposed Mombi about the lost girl Ozma. But Jellia knew nothing at all of this affair, and presently she grew so nervous under the questioning that she gave way and began to weep, to Glinda's great astonishment.

"Here is some foolish trickery!" said the Sorceress, her eyes flashing with anger. "This is not Mombi at all, but some other person who has been made to resemble her! Tell me," she demanded, turning to the trembling girl, "what is your name?"

This Jellia dared not tell, having been threatened with death by the witch if she confessed the fraud. But Glinda, sweet and fair though she was, understood magic better than any other person in the Land of Oz. So, by uttering a few potent words and making a peculiar gesture, she quickly transformed the girl into her proper shape, while at the same time old Mombi, far away in Jinjur's palace, suddenly resumed her own crooked form and evil features.

"Why, it's Jellia Jamb!" cried the Scarecrow, recognizing in the girl one of his old friends.

"It's our interpreter!" said the Pumpkinhead, smiling pleasantly.

Then Jellia was forced to tell of the trick Mombi

had played and she also begged Glinda's protection, which the Sorceress readily granted. But Glinda was now really angry, and sent word to Jinjur that the fraud was discovered and she must deliver up the real Mombi or suffer terrible consequences. Jinjur was prepared for this message, for the witch well understood, when her natural form was thrust upon her, that Glinda had discovered her trickery. But the wicked old creature had already thought up a new deception, and had made Jinjur promise to carry it out. So the Queen said to Glinda's messenger:

"Tell your mistress that I cannot find Mombi anywhere, but that Glinda is welcome to enter the city and search herself for the old woman. She may also bring her friends with her, if she likes; but if she does not find Mombi by sundown, the Sorceress must promise to go away peaceably and bother us no more."

Glinda agreed to these terms, well knowing that Mombi was somewhere within the city walls. So Jinjur caused the gates to be thrown open, and Glinda marched in at the head of a company of soldiers, followed by the Scarecrow and the Tin Woodman, while Jack Pumpkinhead rode astride the Saw-Horse, and the Educated, Highly Magnified Woggle-Bug sauntered behind in a dignified manner. Tip walked by the side of the Sorceress, for Glinda had conceived a great liking for the boy.

Of course old Mombi had no intention of being found by Glinda; so, while her enemies were marching up the street, the witch transformed herself into a red rose growing upon a bush in the garden of the palace. It was a clever idea, and a trick Glinda did not suspect; so several precious hours were spent in a vain search for Mombi.

As sundown approached the Sorceress realized she had been defeated by the superior cunning of the aged witch; so she gave the command to her people to march out of the city and back to their tents.

The Scarecrow and his comrades happened to be searching in the garden of the palace just then, and they turned with disappointment to obey Glinda's command. But before they left the garden the Tin Woodman, who was fond of flowers, chanced to espy a big red rose growing upon a bush; so he plucked the flower and fastened it securely in the tin buttonhole of his tin bosom.

As he did this he fancied he heard a low moan proceed from the rose; but he paid no attention to the sound, and Mombi was thus carried out of the city and into Glinda's camp without anyone having a suspicion that they had succeeded in their quest.

Chapter 22 - The Transformation of Old Mombi

The Witch was at first frightened at finding herself captured by the enemy; but soon she decided that she was exactly as safe in the Tin Woodman's button-hole as growing upon the bush. For no one knew the rose and Mombi to be one, and now that she was without the gates of the City her chances of escaping altogether from Glinda were much improved.

"But there is no hurry," thought Mombi. "I will wait awhile and enjoy the humiliation of this Sorceress when she finds I have outwitted her." So throughout the night the rose lay quietly on the Woodman's bosom, and in the morning, when Glinda summoned our friends to a consultation, Nick Chopper carried his pretty flower with him to the white silk tent.

"For some reason," said Glinda, "we have failed to find this cunning old Mombi; so I fear our expedition will prove a failure. And for that I am sorry, because without our assistance little Ozma will never be rescued and restored to her rightful position as Queen of the Emerald City"

"Do not let us give up so easily," said the Pumpkinhead. "Let us do something else."

"Something else must really be done," replied Glinda, with a smile. "yet I cannot understand how I have been defeated so easily by an old Witch who knows far less of magic than I do myself."

"While we are on the ground I believe it would be wise for us to conquer the Emerald City for Princess Ozma, and find the girl afterward," said the Scarecrow." And while the girl remains hidden I will gladly rule in her place, for I understand the business of ruling much better than Jinjur does."

"But I have promised not to molest Jinjur," objected Glinda.

"Suppose you all return with me to my kingdom—or Empire, rather," said the Tin Woodman, politely including the entire party in a royal wave of his arm. "It will give me great pleasure to entertain you in my castle, where there is room enough and to spare. And if any of you wish to be nickel- plated, my valet will do it free of all expense."

While the Woodman was speaking Glinda's eyes had been noting the rose in his button-hole, and now she imagined she saw the big red leaves of the flower tremble slightly. This quickly aroused her suspicions, and in a moment more the Sorceress had decided that the seeming rose was nothing else than a transformation of old Mombi. At the same instant Mombi knew she was discovered and must quickly plan an escape, and as transformations were easy to her she immediately took the form of a Shadow and glided along the wall of the tent toward the entrance, thinking thus to disappear.

But Glinda had not only equal cunning, but far more experience than the Witch. So the Sorceress reached the opening of the tent before the Shadow, and with a wave of her hand closed the entrance so securely that Mombi could not find a crack big enough to creep through. The Scarecrow and his friends were greatly surprised at Glinda's actions; for none of them had noted the Shadow. But the Sorceress said to them:

"Remain perfectly quiet, all of you! For the old Witch is even now with us in this tent, and I hope to capture her."

These words so alarmed Mombi that she quickly transformed herself from a shadow to a Black Ant, in which shape she crawled along the ground, seeking a crack or crevice in which to hide her tiny body.

Fortunately, the ground where the tent had been pitched, being Just before the city gates, was hard and smooth; and while the Ant still crawled about, Glinda discovered it and ran quickly forward to effect its capture But, Just as her hand was descending, the Witch, now fairly frantic with fear, made her last transformation, and in the form of a huge Griffin sprang through the wall of the tent—tearing the silk asunder in her rush—and in a moment had darted away with the speed of a whirlwind.

Glinda did not hesitate to follow. She sprang upon the back of the Saw-Horse and cried:

"Now you shall prove that you have a right to be alive! Run—run—run!"

The Saw-Horse ran. Like a flash he followed the Griffin, his wooden legs moving so fast that they twinkled like the rays of a star. Before our friends could recover from their surprise both the Griffin and the Saw-Horse had dashed out of sight.

"Come! Let us follow!" cried the Scarecrow.

They ran to the place where the Gump was lying and quickly tumbled aboard.

"Fly!" commanded Tip, eagerly.

"Where to?" asked the Gump, in its calm voice.

"I don't know," returned Tip, who was very nervous at the delay; "but if you will mount into the air I think we can discover which way Glinda has gone."

"Very well," returned the Gump, quietly; and it spread its great wings and mounted high into the air.

Far away, across the meadows, they could now see two tiny specks, speeding one after the other; and they knew these specks must be the Griffin and the Saw-Horse. So Tip called the Gump's attention to them and bade the creature try to overtake the Witch and the Sorceress. But, swift as was the Gump's flight, the pursued and pursuer moved more swiftly yet, and within a few moments were blotted out against the dim horizon.

"Let us continue to follow them, nevertheless," said the Scarecrow. "for the Land of Oz is of small extent, and sooner or later they must both come to a halt."

Old Mombi had thought herself very wise to choose the form of a Griffin, for its legs were exceedingly fleet and its strength more enduring than that of other animals. But she had not reckoned on the untiring energy of the Saw-Horse, whose wooden limbs could run for days without slacking their speed. Therefore, after an hour's hard running, the Griffin's breath began to fail, and it panted and gasped painfully, and moved more slowly than before. Then it reached the edge of the desert and began racing across the deep sands. But its tired feet sank far into the sand, and in a few minutes the Griffin fell forward, completely exhausted, and lay still upon the desert waste.

Glinda came up a moment later, riding the still vigorous Saw-Horse; and having unwound a slender golden thread from her girdle the Sorceress threw it over the head of the panting and helpless Griffin, and so destroyed the magical power of Mombi's transformation.

For the animal, with one fierce shudder, disappeared from view, while in its place was discovered the form of the old Witch, glaring savagely at the serene and beautiful face of the Sorceress.

Chapter 23 - Princess Ozma of Oz

"You are my prisoner, and it is useless for you to struggle any longer," said Glinda, in her soft, sweet voice. "Lie still a moment, and rest yourself, and then I will carry you back to my tent."

"Why do you seek me?" asked Mombi, still scarce able to speak plainly for lack of breath. "What have I done to you, to be so persecuted?"

"You have done nothing to me," answered the gentle Sorceress; "but I suspect you have been guilty of several wicked actions; and if I find it is true that you have so abused your knowledge of magic, I intend to punish you severely."

"I defy you!" croaked the old hag. "You dare not harm me!"

Just then the Gump flew up to them and alighted upon the desert sands beside Glinda. Our friends were delighted to find that Mombi had finally been captured, and after a hurried consultation it was decided they should all return to the camp in the Gump. So the Saw-Horse was tossed aboard, and then Glinda still holding an end of the golden thread that was around Mombi's neck, forced her prisoner to climb into the sofas. The others now followed, and Tip gave the word to the Gump to return.

The Journey was made in safety, Mombi sitting in her place with a grim and sullen air; for the old hag was absolutely helpless so long as the magical thread encircled her throat. The army hailed Glinda's return with loud cheers, and the party of friends soon gathered again in the royal tent, which had been neatly repaired during their absence.

"Now," said the Sorceress to Mombi, "I want you to tell us why the Wonderful Wizard of Oz paid you three visits, and what became of the child, Ozma, which so curiously disappeared."

The Witch looked at Glinda defiantly, but said not a word.

"Answer me!" cried the Sorceress.

But still Mombi remained silent.

"Perhaps she doesn't know," remarked Jack.

"I beg you will keep quiet," said Tip. "You might spoil everything with your foolishness."

"Very well, dear father!" returned the Pumpkinhead, meekly.

"How glad I am to be a Woggle-Bug!" murmured the Highly Magnified Insect, softly. "No one can expect wisdom to flow from a pumpkin."

"Well," said the Scarecrow, "what shall we do to make Mombi speak? Unless she tells us what we wish to know her capture will do us no good at all."

"Suppose we try kindness," suggested the Tin Woodman. "I've heard that anyone can be conquered with kindness, no matter how ugly they may be."

At this the Witch turned to glare upon him so horribly that the Tin Woodman shrank back abashed.

Glinda had been carefully considering what to do, and now she turned to Mombi and said:

"You will gain nothing, I assure you, by thus defying us. For I am determined to learn the truth about the girl Ozma, and unless you tell me all that you know, I will certainly put you to death."

"Oh, no! Don't do that!" exclaimed the Tin Woodman. "It would be an awful thing to kill anyone—even old Mombi!"

"But it is merely a threat," returned Glinda. "I shall not put Mombi to death, because she will prefer to tell me the truth."

"Oh, I see!" said the tin man, much relieved.

"Suppose I tell you all that you wish to know,". said Mombi, speaking so suddenly that she startled them all. "What will you do with me then?"

"In that case," replied Glinda, "I shall merely ask you to drink a powerful draught which will cause you to forget all the magic you have ever learned."

"Then I would become a helpless old woman!"

"But you would be alive," suggested the Pumpkinhead, consolingly.

"Do try to keep silent!" said Tip, nervously.

"I'll try," responded Jack; "but you will admit that it's a good thing to be alive."

"Especially if one happens to be Thoroughly Educated," added the Woggle-Bug, nodding approval.

"You may make your choice," Glinda said to old Mombi, "between death if you remain silent, and the loss of your magical powers if you tell me the truth. But I think you will prefer to live.

Mombi cast an uneasy glance at the Sorceress, and saw that she was in earnest, and not to be trifled with. So she replied, slowly:

"I will answer your questions."

"That is what I expected," said Glinda, pleasantly. "You have chosen wisely, I assure you."

She then motioned to one of her Captains, who brought her a beautiful golden casket. From this the Sorceress drew an immense white pearl, attached to a slender chain which she placed around her neck in such a way that the pearl rested upon her bosom, directly over her heart.

"Now," said she, "I will ask my first question: Why did the Wizard pay you three visits?"

"Because I would not come to him," answered Mombi.

"That is no answer," said Glinda, sternly. "Tell me the truth."

"Well," returned Mombi, with downcast eyes, "he visited me to learn the way I make tea-biscuits."

"Look up!" commanded the Sorceress.

Mombi obeyed.

"What is the color of my pearl?" demanded Glinda.

"Why—it is black!" replied the old Witch, in a tone of wonder.

"Then you have told me a falsehood!" cried Glinda, angrily. "Only when the truth is spoken will my magic pearl remain a pure white in color."

Mombi now saw how useless it was to try to deceive the Sorceress; so she said, meanwhile scowling at her defeat:

"The Wizard brought to me the girl Ozma, who was then no more than a baby, and begged me to conceal the child."

"That is what I thought," declared Glinda, calmly. "What did he give you for thus serving him?"

"He taught me all the magical tricks he knew. Some were good tricks, and some were only frauds; but I have remained faithful to my promise."

"What did you do with the girl?" asked Glinda; and at this question everyone bent forward and listened eagerly for the reply.

"I enchanted her," answered Mombi.

"In what way?"

"I transformed her into—into—"

"Into what?" demanded Glinda, as the Witch hesitated.

"Into a boy!" said Mombi, in a low tone."

A boy!" echoed every voice; and then, because they knew that this old woman had reared Tip from childhood, all eyes were turned to where the boy stood.

"Yes," said the old Witch, nodding her head; "that is the Princess Ozma—the child brought to me by the Wizard who stole her father's throne. That is the rightful ruler of the Emerald City!" and she pointed her long bony finger straight at the boy.

"I!" cried Tip, in amazement. "Why, I'm no Princess Ozma—I'm not a girl!"

Glinda smiled, and going to Tip she took his small brown hand within her dainty white one.

"You are not a girl just now" said she, gently, "because Mombi transformed you into a boy. But you were born a girl, and also a Princess; so you must resume your proper form, that you may become Queen of the Emerald City."

"Oh, let Jinjur be the Queen!" exclaimed Tip, ready to cry. "I want to stay a boy, and travel with the Scarecrow and the Tin Woodman, and the Woggle- Bug, and Jack—yes! and my friend the Saw-Horse—and the Gump! I don't want to be a girl!"

"Never mind, old chap," said the Tin Woodman, soothingly; "it don't hurt to be a girl, I'm told; and we will all remain your faithful friends just the same. And, to be honest with you, I've always considered girls nicer than boys."

"They're just as nice, anyway," added the Scarecrow, patting Tip affectionately upon the head.

"And they are equally good students," proclaimed the Woggle-Bug. "I should like to become your tutor, when you are transformed into a girl again."

"But—see here!" said Jack Pumpkinhead, with a gasp: "if you become a girl, you can't be my dear father any more!"

"No," answered Tip, laughing in spite of his anxiety. "and I shall not be sorry to escape the relationship." Then he added, hesitatingly, as he turned to Glinda: "I might try it for awhile,-just to see how it seems, you know. But if I don't like being a girl you must promise to change me into a boy again."

"Really," said the Sorceress, "that is beyond my magic. I never deal in transformations, for they are not honest, and no respectable sorceress likes to make things appear to be what they are not. Only unscrupulous witches use the art, and therefore I must ask Mombi to effect your release from her charm, and restore you to your proper form. It will be the last opportunity she will have to practice magic."

Now that the truth about Princes Ozma had been discovered, Mombi did not care what became of Tip; but she feared Glinda's anger, and the boy generously promised to provide for Mombi in her old age if he became the ruler of the Emerald City. So the Witch consented to effect the transformation, and preparations for the event were at once made.

Glinda ordered her own royal couch to be placed in the center of the tent. It was piled high with cushions covered with rose-colored silk, and from a golden railing above hung many folds of pink gossamer, completely concealing the interior of the couch.

The first act of the Witch was to make the boy drink a potion which quickly sent him into a deep and dreamless sleep. Then the Tin Woodman and the Woggle-Bug bore him gently to the couch, placed him upon the soft cushions, and drew the gossamer hangings to shut him from all earthly view.

The Witch squatted upon the ground and kindled a tiny fire of dried herbs, which she drew from her bosom. When the blaze shot up and burned clearly old Mombi scattered a handful of magical powder over the fire, which straightway gave off a rich violet vapor, filling all the tent with its fragrance and forcing the Saw-Horse to sneeze—although he had been warned to keep quiet.

Then, while the others watched her curiously, the hag chanted a rhythmical verse in words which no one understood, and bent her lean body seven times back and forth over the fire. And now the incantation seemed complete, for the Witch stood upright and cried the one word "Yeowa!" in a loud voice.

The vapor floated away; the atmosphere became, clear again; a whiff of fresh air filled the tent, and the pink curtains of the couch trembled slightly, as if stirred from within.

Glinda walked to the canopy and parted the silken hangings. Then she bent over the cushions, reached out her hand, and from the couch arose the form of a young girl, fresh and beautiful as a May morning. Her eyes sparkled as two diamonds, and her lips were tinted like a tourmaline. All adown her back floated tresses of ruddy gold, with a slender jeweled circlet confining them at the brow. Her robes of silken gauze floated around her like a cloud, and dainty satin slippers shod her feet.

At this exquisite vision Tip's old comrades stared in wonder for the space of a full minute, and then every head bent low in honest admiration of the lovely Princess Ozma. The girl herself cast one look into Glinda's bright face, which glowed with pleasure and satisfaction, and then turned upon the others. Speaking the words with sweet diffidence, she said:

"I hope none of you will care less for me than you did before. I'm just the same Tip, you know; only—only—"

"Only you're different!" said the Pumpkinhead; and everyone thought it was the wisest speech he had ever made.

Chapter 24 - The Riches of Content

When the wonderful tidings reached the ears of Queen Jinjur—how Mombi the Witch had been captured; how she had confessed her crime to Glinda; and how the long-lost Princess Ozma had been discovered in no less a personage than the boy Tip—she wept real tears of grief and despair.

"To think," she moaned, "that after having ruled as Queen, and lived in a palace, I must go back to scrubbing floors and churning butter again! It is too horrible to think of! I will never consent!"

So when her soldiers, who spent most of their time making fudge in the palace kitchens, counseled Jinjur to resist, she listened to their foolish prattle and sent a sharp defiance to Glinda the Good and the Princess Ozma. The result was a declaration of war, and the very next day Glinda marched upon the Emerald City with pennants flying and bands playing, and a forest of shining spears, sparkling brightly beneath the sun's rays.

But when it came to the walls this brave assembly made a sudden halt; for Jinjur had closed and barred every gateway, and the walls of the Emerald City were builded high and thick with many blocks of green marble. Finding her advance thus baffled, Glinda bent her brows in deep thought, while the Woggle-Bug said, in his most positive tone:

"We must lay siege to the city, and starve it into submission. It is the only thing we can do."

"Not so," answered the Scarecrow. "We still have the Gump, and the Gump can still fly"

The Sorceress turned quickly at this speech, and her face now wore a bright smile.

"You are right," she exclaimed, "and certainly have reason to be proud of your brains. Let us go to the Gump at once!"

So they passed through the ranks of the army until they came to the place, near the Scarecrow's tent, where the Gump lay. Glinda and Princess Ozma mounted first, and sat upon the sofas. Then the Scarecrow and his friends climbed aboard, and still there was room for a Captain and three soldiers, which Glinda considered sufficient for a guard.

Now, at a word from the Princess, the queer Thing they had called the Gump flopped its palm-leaf wings and rose into the air, carrying the party of adventurers high above the walls. They hovered over the palace, and soon perceived Jinjur reclining in a hammock in the courtyard, where she was comfortably reading a novel with a green cover and eating green chocolates, confident that the walls would protect her from her enemies. Obeying a quick command, the Gump alighted safely in this very courtyard, and before Jinjur had time to do more than scream, the Captain and three soldiers leaped out and made the former Queen a prisoner, locking strong chains upon both her wrists.

That act really ended the war; for the Army of Revolt submitted as soon as they knew Jinjur to be a captive, and the Captain marched in safety through the streets and up to the gates of the city, which she threw wide open. Then the bands played their most stirring music while Glinda's army marched into the city, and heralds proclaimed the conquest of the audacious Jinjur and the accession of the beautiful Princess Ozma to the throne of her royal ancestors.

At once the men of the Emerald City cast off their aprons. And it is said that the women were so tired eating of their husbands' cooking that they all hailed the conquest of Jinjur with Joy. Certain it is that, rushing one and all to the kitchens of their houses, the good wives prepared so delicious a feast for the weary men that harmony was immediately restored in every family.

Ozma's first act was to oblige the Army of Revolt to return to her every emerald or other gem stolen from the public streets and buildings; and so great was the number of precious stones picked from their settings by these vain girls, that every one of the royal jewelers worked steadily for more than a month to replace them in their settings.

Meanwhile the Army of Revolt was disbanded and the girls sent home to their mothers. On promise of good behavior Jinjur was likewise released.

Ozma made the loveliest Queen the Emerald City had ever known; and, although she was so young and inexperienced, she ruled her people with wisdom and Justice. For Glinda gave her good advice on all occasions; and the Woggle- Bug, who was appointed to the important post of Public Educator, was quite helpful to Ozma when her royal duties grew perplexing.

The girl, in her gratitude to the Gump for its services, offered the creature any reward it might name.

"Then," replied the Gump, "please take me to pieces. I did not wish to be brought to life, and I am greatly ashamed of my conglomerate personality. Once I was a monarch of the forest, as my antlers fully prove; but now, in my present upholstered condition of servitude, I am compelled to fly through the air—my legs being of no use to me whatever. Therefore I beg to be dispersed."

So Ozma ordered the Gump taken apart. The antlered head was again hung over the mantle-piece in the hall, and the sofas were untied and placed in the reception parlors. The broom tail resumed its accustomed duties in the kitchen, and finally, the Scarecrow replaced all the clotheslines and ropes on the pegs from which he had taken them on the eventful day when the Thing was constructed.

You might think that was the end of the Gump; and so it was, as a flying- machine. But the head over the mantle-piece continued to talk whenever it took a notion to do so, and it frequently startled, with its abrupt questions, the people who waited in the hall for an audience with the Queen.

The Saw-Horse, being Ozma's personal property, was tenderly cared for; and often she rode the queer creature along the streets of the Emerald City. She had its wooden legs shod with gold, to keep them from wearing out, and the tinkle of these golden shoes upon the pavement always filled the Queen's subjects with awe as they thought upon this evidence of her magical powers.

"The Wonderful Wizard was never so wonderful as Queen Ozma," the people said to one another, in whispers; "for he claimed to do many things he could not do; whereas our new Queen does many things no one would ever expect her to accomplish."

Jack Pumpkinhead remained with Ozma to the end of his days; and he did not spoil as soon as he had feared, although he always remained as stupid as ever. The Woggle-Bug tried to teach him several arts and sciences; but Jack was so poor a student that any attempt to educate him was soon abandoned.

After Glinda's army had marched back home, and peace was restored to the Emerald City, the Tin Woodman announced his intention to return to his own Kingdom of the Winkies.

"It isn't a very big Kingdom," said he to Ozma, "but for that very reason it is easier to rule; and I have called myself an Emperor because I am an Absolute Monarch, and no one interferes in any way with my conduct of public or personal affairs. When I get home I shall have a new coat of nickel plate; for I have become somewhat marred and scratched lately; and then I shall be glad to have you pay me a visit."

"Thank you," replied Ozma. "Some day I may accept the invitation. But what is to become of the Scarecrow?"

"I shall return with my friend the Tin Woodman," said the stuffed one, seriously. "We have decided never to be parted in the future."

"And I have made the Scarecrow my Royal Treasurer," explained the Tin Woodman." For it has occurred to me that it is a good thing to have a Royal Treasurer who is made of money. What do you think?"

"I think," said the little Queen, smiling, "that your friend must be the richest man in all the world."

"I am," returned the Scarecrow. "but not on account of my money. For I consider brains far superior to money, in every way. You may have noticed that if one has money without brains, he cannot use it to advantage; but if one has brains without money, they will enable him to live comfortably to the end of his days."

"At the same time," declared the Tin Woodman, "you must acknowledge that a good heart is a thing that brains can not create, and that money can not buy. Perhaps, after all, it is I who am the richest man in all the world."

"You are both rich, my friends," said Ozma, gently; "and your riches are the only riches worth having—the riches of content!"

The End

Ozma of Oz

Preface

Kansas, the Yellow Hen, the Scarecrow, the Tin Woodman, Tik-tok, the Cowardly Lion and the Hungry Tiger; Besides Other Good People too Numerous to Mention Faithfully Recorded Herein
by
L. Frank Baum
The Author of The Wizard of Oz, The Land of Oz, etc.

Author's Note

My friends the children are responsible for this new "Oz Book," as they were for the last one, which was called The Land of Oz. Their sweet little letters plead to know "more about Dorothy"; and they ask: "What became of the Cowardly Lion?" and "What did Ozma do afterward?"—meaning, of course, after she became the Ruler of Oz. And some of them suggest plots to me, saying: "Please have Dorothy go to the Land of Oz again"; or, "Why don't you make Ozma and Dorothy meet, and have a good time together?" Indeed, could I do all that my little friends ask, I would be obliged to write dozens of books to satisfy their demands. And I wish I could, for I enjoy writing these stories just as much as the children say they enjoy reading them.

Well, here is "more about Dorothy," and about our old friends the Scarecrow and the Tin Woodman, and about the Cowardly Lion, and Ozma, and all the rest of them; and here, likewise, is a good deal about some new folks that are queer and unusual. One little friend, who read this story before it was printed, said to me: "Billina is REAL OZZY, Mr. Baum, and so are Tik-tok and the Hungry Tiger."

If this judgment is unbiased and correct, and the little folks find this new story "real Ozzy," I shall be very glad indeed that I wrote it. But perhaps I shall get some more of those very welcome letters from my readers, telling me just how they like "Ozma of Oz." I hope so, anyway.

L. FRANK BAUM.
MACATAWA, 1907.

LIST OF CHAPTERS

Chapter 1 - The Girl in the Chicken Coop

The wind blew hard and joggled the water of the ocean, sending ripples across its surface.
Then the wind pushed the edges of the ripples until they became waves, and shoved the waves around until they became billows. The billows rolled dreadfully high: higher even than the tops of houses. Some of them, indeed, rolled as high as the tops of tall trees, and seemed like mountains; and the gulfs between the great billows were like deep valleys.

All this mad dashing and splashing of the waters of the big ocean, which the mischievous wind caused without any good reason whatever, resulted in a terrible storm, and a storm on the ocean is liable to cut many queer pranks and do a lot of damage.

At the time the wind began to blow, a ship was sailing far out upon the waters. When the waves began to tumble and toss and to grow bigger and bigger the ship rolled up and down, and tipped sidewise—first one way and then the other—and was jostled around so roughly that even the sailor-men had to hold fast to the ropes and railings to keep themselves from being swept away by the wind or pitched headlong into the sea.

And the clouds were so thick in the sky that the sunlight couldn't get through them; so that the day grew dark as night, which added to the terrors of the storm.

The Captain of the ship was not afraid, because he had seen storms before, and had sailed his ship through them in safety; but he knew that his passengers would be in danger if they tried to stay on deck, so he put them all into the cabin and told them to stay there until after the storm was over, and to keep brave hearts and not be scared, and all would be well with them.

Now, among these passengers was a little Kansas girl named Dorothy Gale, who was going with her Uncle Henry to Australia, to visit some relatives they had never before seen. Uncle Henry, you must know, was not very well, because he had been working so hard on his Kansas farm that his health had given way and left him weak and nervous. So he left Aunt Em at home to watch after the hired men and to take care of the farm, while he traveled far away to Australia to visit his cousins and have a good rest.

Dorothy was eager to go with him on this journey, and Uncle Henry thought she would be good company and help cheer him up; so he decided to take her along. The little girl was quite an experienced traveller, for she had once been carried by a cyclone as far away from home as the marvelous Land of Oz, and she had met with a good many adventures in that strange country before she managed to get back to Kansas again. So she wasn't easily frightened, whatever happened, and when the wind began to howl and whistle, and the waves began to tumble and toss, our little girl didn't mind the uproar the least bit.

"Of course we'll have to stay in the cabin," she said to Uncle Henry and the other passengers, "and keep as quiet as possible until the storm is over. For the Captain says if we go on deck we may be blown overboard."

No one wanted to risk such an accident as that, you may be sure; so all the passengers stayed huddled up in the dark cabin, listening to the shrieking of the storm and the creaking of the masts and rigging and trying to keep from bumping into one another when the ship tipped sidewise.

Dorothy had almost fallen asleep when she was aroused with a start to find that Uncle Henry was missing. She couldn't imagine where he had gone, and as he was not very strong she began to worry about him, and to fear he might have been careless enough to go on deck. In that case he would be in great danger unless he instantly came down again.

The fact was that Uncle Henry had gone to lie down in his little sleeping-berth, but Dorothy did not know that. She only remembered that Aunt Em had cautioned her to take good care of her uncle, so at once she decided to go on deck and find him, in spite of the fact that the tempest was now worse than ever, and the ship was plunging in a really dreadful manner. Indeed, the little girl found it was as much as she could do to mount the stairs to the deck, and as soon as she got there the wind struck her so fiercely that it almost tore away the skirts of her dress. Yet Dorothy felt a sort of joyous excitement in defying the storm, and while she held fast to the railing she peered around through the gloom and thought she saw the dim form of a man clinging to a mast not far away from her. This might be her uncle, so she called as loudly as she could:

"Uncle Henry! Uncle Henry!"

But the wind screeched and howled so madly that she scarce heard her own voice, and the man certainly failed to hear her, for he did not move.

Dorothy decided she must go to him; so she made a dash forward, during a lull in the storm, to where a big square chicken-coop had been lashed to the deck with ropes. She reached this place in safety, but no sooner had she seized fast hold of the slats of the big box in which the chickens were kept than the wind, as if enraged because the little girl dared to resist its power, suddenly redoubled its fury. With a scream like that of an angry giant it tore away the ropes that held the coop and lifted it high into the air, with Dorothy still clinging to the slats. Around and over it whirled, this way and that, and a few moments later the chicken-coop dropped far away into the sea, where the big waves caught it and slid it up-hill to a foaming crest and then down-hill into a deep valley, as if it were nothing more than a plaything to keep them amused.

Dorothy had a good ducking, you may be sure, but she didn't loose her presence of mind even for a second. She kept tight hold of the stout slats and as soon as she could get the water out of her eyes she saw that the wind had ripped the cover from the coop, and the poor chickens were fluttering away in every direction, being blown by the wind until they looked like feather dusters without handles. The bottom of the coop was made of thick boards, so Dorothy found she was clinging to a sort of raft, with sides of slats, which readily bore up her weight. After coughing the water out of her throat and getting her breath again, she managed to climb over the slats and stand upon the firm wooden bottom of the coop, which supported her easily enough.

"Why, I've got a ship of my own!" she thought, more amused than frightened at her sudden change of condition; and then, as the coop climbed up to the top of a big wave, she looked eagerly around for the ship from which she had been blown.

It was far, far away, by this time. Perhaps no one on board had yet missed her, or knew of her strange adventure. Down into a valley between the waves the coop swept her, and when she climbed another crest the ship looked like a toy boat, it was such a long way off. Soon it had entirely disappeared in the gloom, and then Dorothy gave a sigh of regret at parting with Uncle Henry and began to wonder what was going to happen to her next.

Just now she was tossing on the bosom of a big ocean, with nothing to keep her afloat but a miserable wooden hen-coop that had a plank bottom and slatted sides, through which the water constantly splashed and wetted her through to the skin! And there was nothing to eat when she became hungry—as she was sure to do before long—and no fresh water to drink and no dry clothes to put on.

"Well, I declare!" she exclaimed, with a laugh. "You're in a pretty fix, Dorothy Gale, I can tell you! and I haven't the least idea how you're going to get out of it!"

As if to add to her troubles the night was now creeping on, and the gray clouds overhead changed to inky blackness. But the wind, as if satisfied at last with its mischievous pranks, stopped blowing this ocean and hurried away to another part of the world to blow something else; so that the waves, not being joggled any more, began to quiet down and behave themselves.

It was lucky for Dorothy, I think, that the storm subsided; otherwise, brave though she was, I fear she might have perished. Many children, in her place, would have wept and given way to despair; but because Dorothy had encountered so many adventures and come safely through them it did not occur to her at this time to be especially afraid. She was wet and uncomfortable, it is true; but, after sighing that one sigh I told you of, she managed to recall some of her customary cheerfulness and decided to patiently await whatever her fate might be.

By and by the black clouds rolled away and showed a blue sky overhead, with a silver moon shining sweetly in the middle of it and little stars winking merrily at Dorothy when she looked their way. The coop did not toss around any more, but rode the waves more gently—almost like a cradle rocking—so that the floor upon which Dorothy stood was no longer swept by water coming through the slats. Seeing this, and being quite exhausted by the excitement of the past few hours, the little girl decided that sleep would be the best thing to restore her strength and the easiest way in which she could pass the time. The floor was damp and she was herself wringing wet, but fortunately this was a warm climate and she did not feel at all cold.

So she sat down in a corner of the coop, leaned her back against the slats, nodded at the friendly stars before she closed her eyes, and was asleep in half a minute.

Chapter 2 - The Yellow Hen

A strange noise awoke Dorothy, who opened her eyes to find that day had dawned and the sun was shining brightly in a clear sky. She had been dreaming that she was back in Kansas again, and playing in the old barn-yard with the calves and pigs and chickens all around her; and at first, as she rubbed the sleep from her eyes, she really imagined she was there.

"Kut-kut-kut, ka-daw-kut! Kut-kut-kut, ka-daw-kut!"

Ah; here again was the strange noise that had awakened her. Surely it was a hen cackling! But her wide-open eyes first saw, through the slats of the coop, the blue waves of the ocean, now calm and placid, and her thoughts flew back to the past night, so full of danger and discomfort. Also she began to remember that she was a waif of the storm, adrift upon a treacherous and unknown sea.

"Kut-kut-kut, ka-daw-w-w—kut!"

"What's that?" cried Dorothy, starting to her feet.

"Why, I've just laid an egg, that's all," replied a small, but sharp and distinct voice, and looking around her the little girl discovered a yellow hen squatting in the opposite corner of the coop.

"Dear me!" she exclaimed, in surprise; "have YOU been here all night, too?"

"Of course," answered the hen, fluttering her wings and yawning. "When the coop blew away from the ship I clung fast to this corner, with claws and beak, for I knew if I fell into the water I'd surely be drowned. Indeed, I nearly drowned, as it was, with all that water washing over me. I never was so wet before in my life!"

"Yes," agreed Dorothy, "it was pretty wet, for a time, I know. But do you feel comfor'ble now?"

"Not very. The sun has helped to dry my feathers, as it has your dress, and I feel better since I laid my morning egg. But what's to become of us, I should like to know, afloat on this big pond?"

"I'd like to know that, too," said Dorothy. "But, tell me; how does it happen that you are able to talk? I thought hens could only cluck and cackle."

"Why, as for that," answered the yellow hen thoughtfully, "I've clucked and cackled all my life, and never spoken a word before this morning, that I can remember. But when you asked a question, a minute ago, it seemed the most natural thing in the world to answer you. So I spoke, and I seem to keep on speaking, just as you and other human beings do. Strange, isn't it?"

"Very," replied Dorothy. "If we were in the Land of Oz, I wouldn't think it so queer, because many of the animals can talk in that fairy country. But out here in the ocean must be a good long way from Oz."

"How is my grammar?" asked the yellow hen, anxiously. "Do I speak quite properly, in your judgment?"

"Yes," said Dorothy, "you do very well, for a beginner."

"I'm glad to know that," continued the yellow hen, in a confidential tone; "because, if one is going to talk, it's best to talk correctly. The red rooster has often said that my cluck and my cackle were quite perfect; and now it's a comfort to know I am talking properly."

"I'm beginning to get hungry," remarked Dorothy. "It's breakfast time; but there's no breakfast."

"You may have my egg," said the yellow hen. "I don't care for it, you know."

"Don't you want to hatch it?" asked the little girl, in surprise.

"No, indeed; I never care to hatch eggs unless I've a nice snug nest, in some quiet place, with a baker's dozen of eggs under me. That's thirteen, you know, and it's a lucky number for hens. So you may as well eat this egg."

"Oh, I couldn't POSS'BLY eat it, unless it was cooked," exclaimed Dorothy. "But I'm much obliged for your kindness, just the same."

"Don't mention it, my dear," answered the hen, calmly, and began pruning her feathers.

For a moment Dorothy stood looking out over the wide sea. She was still thinking of the egg, though; so presently she asked:

"Why do you lay eggs, when you don't expect to hatch them?"

"It's a habit I have," replied the yellow hen. "It has always been my pride to lay a fresh egg every morning, except when I'm moulting. I never feel like having my morning cackle till the egg is properly laid, and without the chance to cackle I would not be happy."

"It's strange," said the girl, reflectively; "but as I'm not a hen I can't be 'spected to understand that."

"Certainly not, my dear."

Then Dorothy fell silent again. The yellow hen was some company, and a bit of comfort, too; but it was dreadfully lonely out on the big ocean, nevertheless.

After a time the hen flew up and perched upon the topmost slat of the coop, which was a little above Dorothy's head when she was sitting upon the bottom, as she had been doing for some moments past.

"Why, we are not far from land!" exclaimed the hen.

"Where? Where is it?" cried Dorothy, jumping up in great excitement.

"Over there a little way," answered the hen, nodding her head in a certain direction. "We seem to be drifting toward it, so that before noon we ought to find ourselves upon dry land again."

"I shall like that!" said Dorothy, with a little sigh, for her feet and legs were still wetted now and then by the sea-water that came through the open slats.

"So shall I," answered her companion. "There is nothing in the world so miserable as a wet hen."

The land, which they seemed to be rapidly approaching, since it grew more distinct every minute, was quite beautiful as viewed by the little girl in the floating hen-coop. Next to the water was a broad beach of white sand and gravel, and farther back were several rocky hills, while beyond these appeared a strip of green trees that marked the edge of a forest. But there were no houses to be seen, nor any sign of people who might inhabit this unknown land.

"I hope we shall find something to eat," said Dorothy, looking eagerly at the pretty beach toward which they drifted. "It's long past breakfast time, now."

"I'm a trifle hungry, myself," declared the yellow hen.

"Why don't you eat the egg?" asked the child. "You don't need to have your food cooked, as I do."

"Do you take me for a cannibal?" cried the hen, indignantly. "I do not know what I have said or done that leads you to insult me!"

"I beg your pardon, I'm sure Mrs.—Mrs.—by the way, may I inquire your name, ma'am?" asked the little girl.

"My name is Bill," said the yellow hen, somewhat gruffly.

"Bill! Why, that's a boy's name."

"What difference does that make?"

"You're a lady hen, aren't you?"

"Of course. But when I was first hatched out no one could tell whether I was going to be a hen or a rooster; so the little boy at the farm where I was born called me Bill, and made a pet of me because I was the only yellow chicken in the whole brood. When I grew up, and he found that I didn't crow and fight, as all the roosters do, he did not think to change my name, and every creature in the barn-yard, as well as the people in the house, knew me as 'Bill.' So Bill I've always been called, and Bill is my name."

"But it's all wrong, you know," declared Dorothy, earnestly; "and, if you don't mind, I shall call you 'Billina.' Putting the 'eena' on the end makes it a girl's name, you see."

"Oh, I don't mind it in the least," returned the yellow hen. "It doesn't matter at all what you call me, so long as I know the name means ME."

"Very well, Billina. MY name is Dorothy Gale—just Dorothy to my friends and Miss Gale to strangers. You may call me Dorothy, if you like. We're getting very near the shore. Do you suppose it is too deep for me to wade the rest of the way?"

"Wait a few minutes longer. The sunshine is warm and pleasant, and we are in no hurry."

"But my feet are all wet and soggy," said the girl. "My dress is dry enough, but I won't feel real comfor'ble till I get my feet dried."

She waited, however, as the hen advised, and before long the big wooden coop grated gently on the sandy beach and the dangerous voyage was over.

It did not take the castaways long to reach the shore, you may be sure. The yellow hen flew to the sands at once, but Dorothy had to climb over the high slats. Still, for a country girl, that was not much of a feat, and as soon as she was safe ashore Dorothy drew off her wet shoes and stockings and spread them upon the sun-warmed beach to dry.

Then she sat down and watched Billina, who was pick-pecking away with her sharp bill in the sand and gravel, which she scratched up and turned over with her strong claws.

"What are you doing?" asked Dorothy.

"Getting my breakfast, of course," murmured the hen, busily pecking away.

"What do you find?" inquired the girl, curiously.

"Oh, some fat red ants, and some sand-bugs, and once in a while a tiny crab. They are very sweet and nice, I assure you."

"How dreadful!" exclaimed Dorothy, in a shocked voice.

"What is dreadful?" asked the hen, lifting her head to gaze with one bright eye at her companion.

"Why, eating live things, and horrid bugs, and crawly ants. You ought to be 'SHAMED of yourself!"

"Goodness me!" returned the hen, in a puzzled tone; "how queer you are, Dorothy! Live things are much fresher and more wholesome than dead ones, and you humans eat all sorts of dead creatures."

"We don't!" said Dorothy.

"You do, indeed," answered Billina. "You eat lambs and sheep and cows and pigs and even chickens."

"But we cook 'em," said Dorothy, triumphantly.

"What difference does that make?"

"A good deal," said the girl, in a graver tone. "I can't just 'splain the diff'rence, but it's there. And, anyhow, we never eat such dreadful things as BUGS."

"But you eat the chickens that eat the bugs," retorted the yellow hen, with an odd cackle. "So you are just as bad as we chickens are."

This made Dorothy thoughtful. What Billina said was true enough, and it almost took away her appetite for breakfast. As for the yellow hen, she continued to peck away at the sand busily, and seemed quite contented with her bill-of-fare.

Finally, down near the water's edge, Billina stuck her bill deep into the sand, and then drew back and shivered.

"Ow!" she cried. "I struck metal, that time, and it nearly broke my beak."

"It prob'bly was a rock," said Dorothy, carelessly.

"Nonsense. I know a rock from metal, I guess," said the hen. "There's a different feel to it."

"But there couldn't be any metal on this wild, deserted seashore," persisted the girl. "Where's the place? I'll dig it up, and prove to you I'm right,"

Billina showed her the place where she had "stubbed her bill," as she expressed it, and Dorothy dug away the sand until she felt something hard. Then, thrusting in her hand, she pulled the thing out, and discovered it to be a large sized golden key—rather old, but still bright and of perfect shape.

"What did I tell you?" cried the hen, with a cackle of triumph. "Can I tell metal when I bump into it, or is the thing a rock?"

"It's metal, sure enough," answered the child, gazing thoughtfully at the curious thing she had found. "I think it is pure gold, and it must have lain hidden in the sand for a long time. How do you suppose it came there, Billina? And what do you suppose this mysterious key unlocks?"

"I can't say," replied the hen. "You ought to know more about locks and keys than I do."

Dorothy glanced around. There was no sign of any house in that part of the country, and she reasoned that every key must fit a lock and every lock must have a purpose. Perhaps the key had been lost by somebody who lived far away, but had wandered on this very shore.

Musing on these things the girl put the key in the pocket of her dress and then slowly drew on her shoes and stockings, which the sun had fully dried.

"I b'lieve, Billina," she said, "I'll have a look 'round, and see if I can find some breakfast."

Chapter 3 - Letters in the Sand

Walking a little way back from the water's edge, toward the grove of trees, Dorothy came to a flat stretch of white sand that seemed to have queer signs marked upon its surface, just as one would write upon sand with a stick.

"What does it say?" she asked the yellow hen, who trotted along beside her in a rather dignified fashion.

"How should I know?" returned the hen. "I cannot read."

"Oh! Can't you?"

"Certainly not; I've never been to school, you know."

"Well, I have," admitted Dorothy; "but the letters are big and far apart, and it's hard to spell out the words."

But she looked at each letter carefully, and finally discovered that these words were written in the sand:

"BEWARE THE WHEELERS!"

"That's rather strange," declared the hen, when Dorothy had read aloud the words. "What do you suppose the Wheelers are?"

"Folks that wheel, I guess. They must have wheelbarrows, or baby-cabs or hand-carts," said Dorothy.

"Perhaps they're automobiles," suggested the yellow hen. "There is no need to beware of baby-cabs and wheelbarrows; but automobiles are dangerous things. Several of my friends have been run over by them."

"It can't be auto'biles," replied the girl, "for this is a new, wild country, without even trolley-cars or tel'phones. The people here haven't been discovered yet, I'm sure; that is, if there ARE any people. So I don't b'lieve there CAN be any auto'biles, Billina."

"Perhaps not," admitted the yellow hen. "Where are you going now?"

"Over to those trees, to see if I can find some fruit or nuts," answered Dorothy.

She tramped across the sand, skirting the foot of one of the little rocky hills that stood near, and soon reached the edge of the forest.

At first she was greatly disappointed, because the nearer trees were all punita, or cotton-wood or eucalyptus, and bore no fruit or nuts at all. But, bye and bye, when she was almost in despair, the little girl came upon two trees that promised to furnish her with plenty of food.

One was quite full of square paper boxes, which grew in clusters on all the limbs, and upon the biggest and ripest boxes the word "Lunch" could be read, in neat raised letters. This tree seemed to bear all the year around, for there were lunch-box blossoms on some of the branches, and on others tiny little lunch-boxes that were as yet quite green, and evidently not fit to eat until they had grown bigger.

The leaves of this tree were all paper napkins, and it presented a very pleasing appearance to the hungry little girl.

But the tree next to the lunch-box tree was even more wonderful, for it bore quantities of tin dinner-pails, which were so full and heavy that the stout branches bent underneath their weight. Some were small and dark-brown in color; those larger were of a dull tin color; but the really ripe ones were pails of bright tin that shone and glistened beautifully in the rays of sunshine that touched them.

Dorothy was delighted, and even the yellow hen acknowledged that she was surprised.

The little girl stood on tip-toe and picked one of the nicest and biggest lunch-boxes, and then she sat down upon the ground and eagerly opened it. Inside she found, nicely wrapped in white papers, a ham sandwich, a piece of sponge-cake, a pickle, a slice of new cheese and an apple. Each thing had a separate stem, and so had to be picked off the side of the box; but Dorothy found them all to be delicious, and she ate every bit of luncheon in the box before she had finished.

"A lunch isn't zactly breakfast," she said to Billina, who sat beside her curiously watching. "But when one is hungry one can eat even supper in the morning, and not complain."

"I hope your lunch-box was perfectly ripe," observed the yellow hen, in a anxious tone. "So much sickness is caused by eating green things."

"Oh, I'm sure it was ripe," declared Dorothy, "all, that is, 'cept the pickle, and a pickle just HAS to be green, Billina. But everything tasted perfectly splendid, and I'd rather have it than a church picnic. And now I think I'll pick a dinner-pail, to have when I get hungry again, and then we'll start out and 'splore the country, and see where we are."

"Haven't you any idea what country this is?" inquired Billina.

"None at all. But listen: I'm quite sure it's a fairy country, or such things as lunch-boxes and dinner-pails wouldn't be growing upon trees. Besides, Billina, being a hen, you wouldn't be able to talk in any civ'lized country, like Kansas, where no fairies live at all."

"Perhaps we're in the Land of Oz," said the hen, thoughtfully.

"No, that can't be," answered the little girl; because I've been to the Land of Oz, and it's all surrounded by a horrid desert that no one can cross."

"Then how did you get away from there again?" asked Billina.

"I had a pair of silver shoes, that carried me through the air; but I lost them," said Dorothy.

"Ah, indeed," remarked the yellow hen, in a tone of unbelief.

"Anyhow," resumed the girl, "there is no seashore near the Land of Oz, so this must surely be some other fairy country."

While she was speaking she selected a bright and pretty dinner-pail that seemed to have a stout handle, and picked it from its branch. Then, accompanied by the yellow hen, she walked out of the shadow of the trees toward the sea-shore.

They were part way across the sands when Billina suddenly cried, in a voice of terror:

"What's that?"

Dorothy turned quickly around, and saw coming out of a path that led from between the trees the most peculiar person her eyes had ever beheld.

It had the form of a man, except that it walked, or rather rolled, upon all fours, and its legs were the same length as its arms, giving them the appearance of the four legs of a beast. Yet it was no beast that Dorothy had discovered, for the person was clothed most gorgeously in embroidered garments of many colors, and wore a straw hat perched jauntily upon the side of its head. But it differed from human beings in this respect, that instead of hands and feet there grew at the end of its arms and legs round wheels, and by means of these wheels it rolled very swiftly over the level ground. Afterward Dorothy found that these odd wheels were of the same hard substance that our finger-nails and toe-nails are composed of, and she also learned that creatures of this strange race were born in this queer fashion. But when our little girl first caught sight of the first individual of a race that was destined to cause her a lot of trouble, she had an idea that the brilliantly-clothed personage was on roller-skates, which were attached to his hands as well as to his feet.

"Run!" screamed the yellow hen, fluttering away in great fright. "It's a Wheeler!"

"A Wheeler?" exclaimed Dorothy. "What can that be?"

"Don't you remember the warning in the sand: 'Beware the Wheelers'? Run, I tell you—run!"

So Dorothy ran, and the Wheeler gave a sharp, wild cry and came after her in full chase.

Looking over her shoulder as she ran, the girl now saw a great procession of Wheelers emerging from the forest—dozens and dozens of them—all clad in splendid, tight-fitting garments and all rolling swiftly toward her and uttering their wild, strange cries.

"They're sure to catch us!" panted the girl, who was still carrying the heavy dinner-pail she had picked. "I can't run much farther, Billina."

"Climb up this hill,—quick!" said the hen; and Dorothy found she was very near to the heap of loose and jagged rocks they had passed on their way to the forest. The yellow hen was even now fluttering among the rocks, and Dorothy followed as best she could, half climbing and half tumbling up the rough and rugged steep.

She was none too soon, for the foremost Wheeler reached the hill a moment after her; but while the girl scrambled up the rocks the creature stopped short with howls of rage and disappointment.

Dorothy now heard the yellow hen laughing, in her cackling, henny way.

"Don't hurry, my dear," cried Billina. "They can't follow us among these rocks, so we're safe enough now."

Dorothy stopped at once and sat down upon a broad boulder, for she was all out of breath.

The rest of the Wheelers had now reached the foot of the hill, but it was evident that their wheels would not roll upon the rough and jagged rocks, and therefore they were helpless to follow Dorothy and the hen to where they had taken refuge. But they circled all around the little hill, so the child and Billina were fast prisoners and could not come down without being captured.

Then the creatures shook their front wheels at Dorothy in a threatening manner, and it seemed they were able to speak as well as to make their dreadful outcries, for several of them shouted:

"We'll get you in time, never fear! And when we do get you, we'll tear you into little bits!"

"Why are you so cruel to me?" asked Dorothy. "I'm a stranger in your country, and have done you no harm."

"No harm!" cried one who seemed to be their leader. "Did you not pick our lunch-boxes and dinner-pails? Have you not a stolen dinner-pail still in your hand?"

"I only picked one of each," she answered. "I was hungry, and I didn't know the trees were yours."

"That is no excuse," retorted the leader, who was clothed in a most gorgeous suit. "It is the law here that whoever picks a dinner-pail without our permission must die immediately."

"Don't you believe him," said Billina. "I'm sure the trees do not belong to these awful creatures. They are fit for any mischief, and it's my opinion they would try to kill us just the same if you hadn't picked a dinner-pail."

"I think so, too," agreed Dorothy. "But what shall we do now?"

"Stay where we are," advised the yellow hen. "We are safe from the Wheelers until we starve to death, anyhow; and before that time comes a good many things can happen."

Chapter 4 - Tik-tok the Machine Man

After an hour or so most of the band of Wheelers rolled back into the forest, leaving only three of their number to guard the hill. These curled themselves up like big dogs and pretended to go to sleep on the sands; but neither Dorothy nor Billina were fooled by this trick, so they remained in security among the rocks and paid no attention to their cunning enemies.

Finally the hen, fluttering over the mound, exclaimed: "Why, here's a path!"

So Dorothy at once clambered to where Billina sat, and there, sure enough, was a smooth path cut between the rocks. It seemed to wind around the mound from top to bottom, like a cork-screw, twisting here and there between the rough boulders but always remaining level and easy to walk upon.

Indeed, Dorothy wondered at first why the Wheelers did not roll up this path; but when she followed it to the foot of the mound she found that several big pieces of rock had been placed directly across the end of the way, thus preventing any one outside from seeing it and also preventing the Wheelers from using it to climb up the mound.

Then Dorothy walked back up the path, and followed it until she came to the very top of the hill, where a solitary round rock stood that was bigger than any of the others surrounding it. The path came to an end just beside this great rock, and for a moment it puzzled the girl to know why the path had been made at all. But the hen, who had been gravely following her around and was now perched upon a point of rock behind Dorothy, suddenly remarked:

"It looks something like a door, doesn't it?"

"What looks like a door?" enquired the child.

"Why, that crack in the rock, just facing you," replied Billina, whose little round eyes were very sharp and seemed to see everything. "It runs up one side and down the other, and across the top and the bottom."

"What does?"

"Why, the crack. So I think it must be a door of rock, although I do not see any hinges."

"Oh, yes," said Dorothy, now observing for the first time the crack in the rock. "And isn't this a key-hole, Billina?" pointing to a round, deep hole at one side of the door.

"Of course. If we only had the key, now, we could unlock it and see what is there," replied the yellow hen. "May be it's a treasure chamber full of diamonds and rubies, or heaps of shining gold, or—"

"That reminds me," said Dorothy, "of the golden key I picked up on the shore. Do you think that it would fit this key-hole, Billina?"

"Try it and see," suggested the hen.

So Dorothy searched in the pocket of her dress and found the golden key. And when she had put it into the hole of the rock, and turned it, a sudden sharp snap was heard; then, with a solemn creak that made the shivers run down the child's back, the face of the rock fell outward, like a door on hinges, and revealed a small dark chamber just inside.

"Good gracious!" cried Dorothy, shrinking back as far as the narrow path would let her.

For, standing within the narrow chamber of rock, was the form of a man—or, at least, it seemed like a man, in the dim light. He was only about as tall as Dorothy herself, and his body was round as a ball and made out of burnished copper. Also his head and limbs were copper, and these were jointed or hinged to his body in a peculiar way, with metal caps over the joints, like the armor worn by knights in days of old. He stood perfectly still, and where the light struck upon his form it glittered as if made of pure gold.

"Don't be frightened," called Billina, from her perch. "It isn't alive."

"I see it isn't," replied the girl, drawing a long breath.

"It is only made out of copper, like the old kettle in the barn-yard at home," continued the hen, turning her head first to one side and then to the other, so that both her little round eyes could examine the object.

"Once," said Dorothy, "I knew a man made out of tin, who was a woodman named Nick Chopper. But he was as alive as we are, 'cause he was born a real man, and got his tin body a little at a time—first a leg and then a finger and then an ear—for the reason that he had so many accidents with his axe, and cut himself up in a very careless manner."

"Oh," said the hen, with a sniff, as if she did not believe the story.

"But this copper man," continued Dorothy, looking at it with big eyes, "is not alive at all, and I wonder what it was made for, and why it was locked up in this queer place."

"That is a mystery," remarked the hen, twisting her head to arrange her wing-feathers with her bill.

Dorothy stepped inside the little room to get a back view of the copper man, and in this way discovered a printed card that hung between his shoulders, it being suspended from a small copper peg at the back of his neck. She unfastened this card and returned to the path, where the light was better, and sat herself down upon a slab of rock to read the printing.

"What does it say?" asked the hen, curiously.

Dorothy read the card aloud, spelling out the big words with some difficulty; and this is what she read:

SMITH & TINKER'S Patent Double-Action, Extra-Responsive, Thought-Creating, Perfect-Talking MECHANICAL MAN Fitted with our Special Clock-Work Attachment. Thinks, Speaks, Acts, and Does Everything but Live. Manufactured only at our Works at Evna, Land of Ev.

All infringements will be promptly Prosecuted according to Law.

"How queer!" said the yellow hen. "Do you think that is all true, my dear?"

"I don't know," answered Dorothy, who had more to read. "Listen to this, Billina:"

DIRECTIONS FOR USING: For THINKING:—Wind the Clockwork Man under his left arm, (marked No. 1.) For SPEAKING:—Wind the Clockwork Man under his right arm, (marked No. 2.) For WALKING and ACTION:—Wind Clockwork in the middle of his back, (marked No. 3.) N. B.—This Mechanism is guaranteed to work perfectly for a thousand years.

"Well, I declare!" gasped the yellow hen, in amazement; "if the copper man can do half of these things he is a very wonderful machine. But I suppose it is all humbug, like so many other patented articles."

"We might wind him up," suggested Dorothy, "and see what he'll do."

"Where is the key to the clock-work?" asked Billina.

"Hanging on the peg where I found the card."

"Then," said the hen, "let us try him, and find out if he will go. He is warranted for a thousand years, it seems; but we do not know how long he has been standing inside this rock."

Dorothy had already taken the clock key from the peg.

"Which shall I wind up first?" she asked, looking again at the directions on the card.

"Number One, I should think," returned Billina. "That makes him think, doesn't it?"

"Yes," said Dorothy, and wound up Number One, under the left arm.

"He doesn't seem any different," remarked the hen, critically.

"Why, of course not; he is only thinking, now," said Dorothy.

"I wonder what he is thinking about."

"I'll wind up his talk, and then perhaps he can tell us," said the girl.

So she wound up Number Two, and immediately the clock-work man said, without moving any part of his body except his lips:

"Good morn-ing, lit-tle girl. Good morn-ing, Mrs. Hen."

The words sounded a little hoarse and creaky, and they were uttered all in the same tone, without any change of expression whatever; but both Dorothy and Billina understood them perfectly.

"Good morning, sir," they answered, politely.

"Thank you for res-cu-ing me," continued the machine, in the same monotonous voice, which seemed to be worked by a bellows inside of him, like the little toy lambs and cats the children squeeze so that they will make a noise.

"Don't mention it," answered Dorothy. And then, being very curious, she asked: "How did you come to be locked up in this place?"

"It is a long sto-ry," replied the copper man; "but I will tell it to you brief-ly. I was pur-chased from Smith & Tin-ker, my man-u-fac-tur-ers, by a cru-el King of Ev, named Ev-ol-do, who used to beat all his serv-ants un-til they died. How-ev-er, he was not a-ble to kill me, be-cause I was not a-live, and one must first live in or-der to die. So that all his beat-ing did me no harm, and mere-ly kept my cop-per bod-y well pol-ished.

"This cru-el king had a love-ly wife and ten beau-ti-ful chil-dren—five boys and five girls—but in a fit of an-ger he sold them all to the Nome King, who by means of his mag-ic arts changed them all in-to oth-er forms and put them in his un-der-ground pal-ace to or-na-ment the rooms.

"Af-ter-ward the King of Ev re-gret-ted his wick-ed ac-tion, and tried to get his wife and chil-dren a-way from the Nome King, but with-out a-vail. So, in de-spair, he locked me up in this rock, threw the key in-to the o-cean, and then jumped in af-ter it and was drowned."

"How very dreadful!" exclaimed Dorothy.

"It is, in-deed," said the machine. "When I found my-self im-pris-oned I shout-ed for help un-til my voice ran down; and then I walked back and forth in this lit-tle room un-til my ac-tion ran down; and then I stood still and thought un-til my thoughts ran down. Af-ter that I re-mem-ber noth-ing un-til you wound me up a-gain."

"It's a very wonderful story," said Dorothy, "and proves that the Land of Ev is really a fairy land, as I thought it was."

"Of course it is," answered the copper man. "I do not sup-pose such a per-fect ma-chine as I am could be made in an-y place but a fair-y land."

"I've never seen one in Kansas," said Dorothy.

"But where did you get the key to un-lock this door?" asked the clock-work voice.

"I found it on the shore, where it was prob'ly washed up by the waves," she answered. "And now, sir, if you don't mind, I'll wind up your action."

"That will please me ve-ry much," said the machine.

So she wound up Number Three, and at once the copper man in a somewhat stiff and jerky fashion walked out of the rocky cavern, took off his copper hat and bowed politely, and then kneeled before Dorothy. Said he:

"From this time forth I am your o-be-di-ent ser-vant. What-ev-er you com-mand, that I will do will-ing-ly—if you keep me wound up."

"What is your name?" she asked.

"Tik-tok," he replied. "My for-mer mas-ter gave me that name be-cause my clock-work al-ways ticks when it is wound up."

"I can hear it now," said the yellow hen.

"So can I," said Dorothy. And then she added, with some anxiety: "You don't strike, do you?"

"No," answered Tik-tok; "and there is no a-larm con-nec-ted with my ma-chin-er-y. I can tell the time, though, by speak-ing, and as I nev-er sleep I can wak-en you at an-y hour you wish to get up in the morn-ing."

"That's nice," said the little girl; "only I never wish to get up in the morning."

"You can sleep until I lay my egg," said the yellow hen. "Then, when I cackle, Tik-tok will know it is time to waken you."

"Do you lay your egg very early?" asked Dorothy.

"About eight o'clock," said Billina. "And everybody ought to be up by that time, I'm sure."

Chapter 5 - Dorothy Opens the Dinner Pail

"Now Tik-tok," said Dorothy, "the first thing to be done is to find a way for us to escape from these rocks. The Wheelers are down below, you know, and threaten to kill us."

"There is no rea-son to be a-fraid of the Wheel-ers," said Tik-tok, the words coming more slowly than before.

"Why not?" she asked.

"Be-cause they are ag-g-g—gr-gr-r-r-"

He gave a sort of gurgle and stopped short, waving his hands frantically until suddenly he became motionless, with one arm in the air and the other held stiffly before him with all the copper fingers of the hand spread out like a fan.

"Dear me!" said Dorothy, in a frightened tone. "What can the matter be?"

"He's run down, I suppose," said the hen, calmly. "You couldn't have wound him up very tight."

"I didn't know how much to wind him," replied the girl; "but I'll try to do better next time."

She ran around the copper man to take the key from the peg at the back of his neck, but it was not there.

"It's gone!" cried Dorothy, in dismay.

"What's gone?" asked Billina.

"The key."

"It probably fell off when he made that low bow to you," returned the hen. "Look around, and see if you cannot find it again."

Dorothy looked, and the hen helped her, and by and by the girl discovered the clock-key, which had fallen into a crack of the rock.

At once she wound up Tik-tok's voice, taking care to give the key as many turns as it would go around. She found this quite a task, as you may imagine if you have ever tried to wind a clock, but the machine man's first words were to assure Dorothy that he would now run for at least twenty-four hours.

"You did not wind me much, at first," he calmly said, "and I told you that long sto-ry a-bout King Ev-ol-do; so it is no won-der that I ran down."

She next rewound the action clock-work, and then Billina advised her to carry the key to Tik-tok in her pocket, so it would not get lost again.

"And now," said Dorothy, when all this was accomplished, "tell me what you were going to say about the Wheelers."

"Why, they are noth-ing to be fright-en'd at," said the machine. "They try to make folks be-lieve that they are ver-y ter-ri-ble, but as a mat-ter of fact the Wheel-ers are harm-less e-nough to an-y one that dares to fight them. They might try to hurt a lit-tle girl like you, per-haps, be-cause they are ver-y mis-chiev-ous. But if I had a club they would run a-way as soon as they saw me."

"Haven't you a club?" asked Dorothy.

"No," said Tik-tok.

"And you won't find such a thing among these rocks, either," declared the yellow hen.

"Then what shall we do?" asked the girl.

"Wind up my think-works tight-ly, and I will try to think of some oth-er plan," said Tik-tok.

So Dorothy rewound his thought machinery, and while he was thinking she decided to eat her dinner. Billina was already pecking away at the cracks in the rocks, to find something to eat, so Dorothy sat down and opened her tin dinner-pail.

In the cover she found a small tank that was full of very nice lemonade. It was covered by a cup, which might also, when removed, be used to drink the lemonade from. Within the pail were three slices of turkey, two slices of cold tongue, some lobster salad, four slices of bread and butter, a small custard pie, an orange and nine large strawberries, and some nuts and raisins. Singularly enough, the nuts in this dinner-pail grew already cracked, so that Dorothy had no trouble in picking out their meats to eat.

She spread the feast upon the rock beside her and began her dinner, first offering some of it to Tik-tok, who declined because, as he said, he was merely a machine. Afterward she offered to share with Billina, but the hen murmured something about "dead things" and said she preferred her bugs and ants.

"Do the lunch-box trees and the dinner-pail trees belong to the Wheelers?" the child asked Tik-tok, while engaged in eating her meal.

"Of course not," he answered. "They be-long to the roy-al fam-il-y of Ev, on-ly of course there is no roy-al fam-il-y just now be-cause King Ev-ol-do jumped in-to the sea and his wife and ten chil-dren have been trans-formed by the Nome King. So there is no one to rule the Land of Ev, that I can think of. Per-haps it is for this rea-son that the Wheel-ers claim the trees for their own, and pick the lunch-eons and din-ners to eat them-selves. But they be-long to the King, and you will find the roy-al "E" stamped up-on the bot-tom of ev-er-y din-ner pail."

Dorothy turned the pail over, and at once discovered the royal mark upon it, as Tik-tok had said.

"Are the Wheelers the only folks living in the Land of Ev?" enquired the girl.

"No; they on-ly in-hab-it a small por-tion of it just back of the woods," replied the machine. "But they have al-ways been mis-chiev-ous and im-per-ti-nent, and my old mas-ter, King Ev-ol-do, used to car-ry a whip with him, when he walked out, to keep the crea-tures in or-der. When I was first made the Wheel-ers tried to run o-ver me, and butt me with their heads; but they soon found I was built of too sol-id a ma-ter-i-al for them to in-jure."

"You seem very durable," said Dorothy. "Who made you?"

"The firm of Smith & Tin-ker, in the town of Evna, where the roy-al pal-ace stands," answered Tik-tok.

"Did they make many of you?" asked the child.

"No; I am the on-ly au-to-mat-ic me-chan-i-cal man they ev-er com-plet-ed," he replied. "They were ver-y won-der-ful in-ven-tors, were my mak-ers, and quite ar-tis-tic in all they did."

"I am sure of that," said Dorothy. "Do they live in the town of Evna now?"

"They are both gone," replied the machine. "Mr. Smith was an art-ist, as well as an in-vent-or, and he paint-ed a pic-ture of a riv-er which was so nat-ur-al that, as he was reach-ing a-cross it to paint some flow-ers on the op-po-site bank, he fell in-to the wa-ter and was drowned."

"Oh, I'm sorry for that!" exclaimed the little girl.

"Mis-ter Tin-ker," continued Tik-tok, "made a lad-der so tall that he could rest the end of it a-gainst the moon, while he stood on the high-est rung and picked the lit-tle stars to set in the points of the king's crown. But when he got to the moon Mis-ter Tin-ker found it such a love-ly place that he de-cid-ed to live there, so he pulled up the lad-der af-ter him and we have nev-er seen him since."

"He must have been a great loss to this country," said Dorothy, who was by this time eating her custard pie.

"He was," acknowledged Tik-tok. "Also he is a great loss to me. For if I should get out of or-der I do not know of an-y one a-ble to re-pair me, be-cause I am so com-pli-cat-ed. You have no i-de-a how full of ma-chin-er-y I am."

"I can imagine it," said Dorothy, readily.

"And now," continued the machine, "I must stop talk-ing and be-gin think-ing a-gain of a way to es-cape from this rock." So he turned half way around, in order to think without being disturbed.

"The best thinker I ever knew," said Dorothy to the yellow hen, "was a scarecrow."

"Nonsense!" snapped Billina.

"It is true," declared Dorothy. "I met him in the Land of Oz, and he traveled with me to the city of the great Wizard of Oz, so as to get some brains, for his head was only stuffed with straw. But it seemed to me that he thought just as well before he got his brains as he did afterward."

"Do you expect me to believe all that rubbish about the Land of Oz?" enquired Billina, who seemed a little cross—perhaps because bugs were scarce.

"What rubbish?" asked the child, who was now finishing her nuts and raisins.

"Why, your impossible stories about animals that can talk, and a tin woodman who is alive, and a scarecrow who can think."

"They are all there," said Dorothy, "for I have seen them."

"I don't believe it!" cried the hen, with a toss of her head.

"That's 'cause you're so ign'rant," replied the girl, who was a little offended at her friend Billina's speech.

"In the Land of Oz," remarked Tik-tok, turning toward them, "an-y-thing is pos-si-ble. For it is a won-der-ful fair-y coun-try."

"There, Billina! what did I say?" cried Dorothy. And then she turned to the machine and asked in an eager tone: "Do you know the Land of Oz, Tik-tok?"

"No; but I have heard a-bout it," said the cop-per man. "For it is on-ly sep-a-ra-ted from this Land of Ev by a broad des-ert."

Dorothy clapped her hands together delightedly.

"I'm glad of that!" she exclaimed. "It makes me quite happy to be so near my old friends. The scarecrow I told you of, Billina, is the King of the Land of Oz."

"Par-don me. He is not the king now," said Tik-tok.

"He was when I left there," declared Dorothy.

"I know," said Tik-tok, "but there was a rev-o-lu-tion in the Land of Oz, and the Scare-crow was de-posed by a sol-dier wo-man named Gen-er-al Jin-jur. And then Jin-jur was de-posed by a lit-tle girl named Oz-ma, who was the right-ful heir to the throne and now rules the land un-der the ti-tle of Oz-ma of Oz."

"That is news to me," said Dorothy, thoughtfully. "But I s'pose lots of things have happened since I left the Land of Oz. I wonder what has become of the Scarecrow, and of the Tin Woodman, and the Cowardly Lion. And I wonder who this girl Ozma is, for I never heard of her before."

But Tik-tok did not reply to this. He had turned around again to resume his thinking.

Dorothy packed the rest of the food back into the pail, so as not to be wasteful of good things, and the yellow hen forgot her dignity far enough to pick up all of the scattered crumbs, which she ate rather greedily, although she had so lately pretended to despise the things that Dorothy preferred as food.

By this time Tik-tok approached them with his stiff bow.

"Be kind e-nough to fol-low me," he said, "and I will lead you a-way from here to the town of Ev-na, where you will be more com-for-ta-ble, and al-so I will pro-tect you from the Wheel-ers."

"All right," answered Dorothy, promptly. "I'm ready!"

Chapter 6 - The Heads of Langwidere

They walked slowly down the path between the rocks, Tik-tok going first, Dorothy following him, and the yellow hen trotting along last of all.

At the foot of the path the copper man leaned down and tossed aside with ease the rocks that encumbered the way. Then he turned to Dorothy and said:

"Let me car-ry your din-ner-pail."

She placed it in his right hand at once, and the copper fingers closed firmly over the stout handle.

Then the little procession marched out upon the level sands.

As soon as the three Wheelers who were guarding the mound saw them, they began to shout their wild cries and rolled swiftly toward the little group, as if to capture them or bar their way. But when the foremost had approached near enough, Tik-tok swung the tin dinner-pail and struck the Wheeler a sharp blow over its head with the queer weapon.

Perhaps it did not hurt very much, but it made a great noise, and the Wheeler uttered a howl and tumbled over upon its side. The next minute it scrambled to its wheels and rolled away as fast as it could go, screeching with fear at the same time.

"I told you they were harm-less," began Tik-tok; but before he could say more another Wheeler was upon them. Crack! went the dinner-pail against its head, knocking its straw hat a dozen feet away; and that was enough for this Wheeler, also. It rolled away after the first one, and the third did not wait to be pounded with the pail, but joined its fellows as quickly as its wheels would whirl.

The yellow hen gave a cackle of delight, and flying to a perch upon Tik-tok's shoulder, she said:

"Bravely done, my copper friend! and wisely thought of, too. Now we are free from those ugly creatures."

But just then a large band of Wheelers rolled from the forest, and relying upon their numbers to conquer, they advanced fiercely upon Tik-tok. Dorothy grabbed Billina in her arms and held her tight, and the machine embraced the form of the little girl with his left arm, the better to protect her. Then the Wheelers were upon them.

Rattlety, bang! bang! went the dinner-pail in every direction, and it made so much clatter bumping against the heads of the Wheelers that they were much more frightened than hurt and fled in a great panic. All, that is, except their leader. This Wheeler had stumbled against another and fallen flat upon his back, and before he could get his wheels under him to rise again, Tik-tok had fastened his copper fingers into the neck of the gorgeous jacket of his foe and held him fast.

"Tell your peo-ple to go a-way," commanded the machine.

The leader of the Wheelers hesitated to give this order, so Tik-tok shook him as a terrier dog does a rat, until the Wheeler's teeth rattled together with a noise like hailstones on a window pane. Then, as soon as the creature could get its breath, it shouted to the others to roll away, which they immediately did.

"Now," said Tik-tok, "you shall come with us and tell me what I want to know."

"You'll be sorry for treating me in this way," whined the Wheeler. "I'm a terribly fierce person."

"As for that," answered Tik-tok, "I am only a ma-chine, and can-not feel sor-row or joy, no mat-ter what hap-pens. But you are wrong to think your-self ter-ri-ble or fierce."

"Why so?" asked the Wheeler.

"Be-cause no one else thinks as you do. Your wheels make you help-less to in-jure an-y one. For you have no fists and can not scratch or e-ven pull hair. Nor have you an-y feet to kick with. All you can do is to yell and shout, and that does not hurt an-y one at all."

The Wheeler burst into a flood of tears, to Dorothy's great surprise.

"Now I and my people are ruined forever!" he sobbed; "for you have discovered our secret. Being so helpless, our only hope is to make people afraid of us, by pretending we are very fierce and terrible, and writing in the sand warnings to Beware the Wheelers. Until now we have frightened everyone, but since you have discovered our weakness our enemies will fall upon us and make us very miserable and unhappy."

"Oh, no," exclaimed Dorothy, who was sorry to see this beautifully dressed Wheeler so miserable; "Tik-tok will keep your secret, and so will Billina and I. Only, you must promise not to try to frighten children any more, if they come near to you."

"I won't—indeed I won't!" promised the Wheeler, ceasing to cry and becoming more cheerful. "I'm not really bad, you know; but we have to pretend to be terrible in order to prevent others from attacking us."

"That is not ex-act-ly true," said Tik-tok, starting to walk toward the path through the forest, and still holding fast to his prisoner, who rolled slowly along beside him. "You and your peo-ple are full of mis-chief, and like to both-er those who fear you. And you are of-ten im-pu-dent and dis-a-gree-a-ble, too. But if you will try to cure those faults I will not tell any-one how help-less you are."

"I'll try, of course," replied the Wheeler, eagerly. "And thank you, Mr. Tik-tok, for your kindness."

"I am on-ly a ma-chine," said Tik-tok. "I can not be kind an-y more than I can be sor-ry or glad. I can on-ly do what I am wound up to do."

"Are you wound up to keep my secret?" asked the Wheeler, anxiously.

"Yes; if you be-have your-self. But tell me: who rules the Land of Ev now?" asked the machine.

"There is no ruler," was the answer, "because every member of the royal family is imprisoned by the Nome King. But the Princess Langwidere, who is a niece of our late King Evoldo, lives in a part of the royal palace and takes as much money out of the royal treasury as she can spend. The Princess Langwidere is not exactly a ruler, you see, because she doesn't rule; but she is the nearest approach to a ruler we have at present."

"I do not re-mem-ber her," said Tik-tok. "What does she look like?"

"That I cannot say," replied the Wheeler, "although I have seen her twenty times. For the Princess Langwidere is a different person every time I see her, and the only way her subjects can recognize her at all is by means of a beautiful ruby key which she always wears on a chain attached to her left wrist. When we see the key we know we are beholding the Princess."

"That is strange," said Dorothy, in astonishment. "Do you mean to say that so many different princesses are one and the same person?"

"Not exactly," answered the Wheeler. "There is, of course, but one princess; but she appears to us in many forms, which are all more or less beautiful."

"She must be a witch," exclaimed the girl.

"I do not think so," declared the Wheeler. "But there is some mystery connected with her, nevertheless. She is a very vain creature, and lives mostly in a room surrounded by mirrors, so that she can admire herself whichever way she looks."

No one answered this speech, because they had just passed out of the forest and their attention was fixed upon the scene before them—a beautiful vale in which were many fruit trees and green fields, with pretty farm-houses scattered here and there and broad, smooth roads that led in every direction.

In the center of this lovely vale, about a mile from where our friends were standing, rose the tall spires of the royal palace, which glittered brightly against their background of blue sky. The palace was surrounded by charming grounds, full of flowers and shrubbery. Several tinkling fountains could be seen, and there were pleasant walks bordered by rows of white marble statuary.

All these details Dorothy was, of course, unable to notice or admire until they had advanced along the road to a position quite near to the palace, and she was still looking at the pretty sights when her little party entered the grounds and approached the big front door of the king's own apartments. To their disappointment they found the door tightly closed. A sign was tacked to the panel which read as follows:

OWNER ABSENT. Please Knock at the Third Door in the Left Wing.

"Now," said Tik-tok to the captive Wheeler, "you must show us the way to the Left Wing."

"Very well," agreed the prisoner, "it is around here at the right."

"How can the left wing be at the right?" demanded Dorothy, who feared the Wheeler was fooling them.

"Because there used to be three wings, and two were torn down, so the one on the right is the only one left. It is a trick of the Princess Langwidere to prevent visitors from annoying her."

Then the captive led them around to the wing, after which the machine man, having no further use for the Wheeler, permitted him to depart and rejoin his fellows. He immediately rolled away at a great pace and was soon lost to sight.

Tik-tok now counted the doors in the wing and knocked loudly upon the third one.

It was opened by a little maid in a cap trimmed with gay ribbons, who bowed respectfully and asked:

"What do you wish, good people?"

"Are you the Princess Langwidere?" asked Dorothy.

"No, miss; I am her servant," replied the maid.

"May I see the Princess, please?"

"I will tell her you are here, miss, and ask her to grant you an audience," said the maid. "Step in, please, and take a seat in the drawing-room."

So Dorothy walked in, followed closely by the machine. But as the yellow hen tried to enter after them, the little maid cried "Shoo!" and flapped her apron in Billina's face.

"Shoo, yourself!" retorted the hen, drawing back in anger and ruffling up her feathers. "Haven't you any better manners than that?"

"Oh, do you talk?" enquired the maid, evidently surprised.

"Can't you hear me?" snapped Billina. "Drop that apron, and get out of the doorway, so that I may enter with my friends!"

"The Princess won't like it," said the maid, hesitating.

"I don't care whether she likes it or not," replied Billina, and fluttering her wings with a loud noise she flew straight at the maid's face. The little servant at once ducked her head, and the hen reached Dorothy's side in safety.

"Very well," sighed the maid; "if you are all ruined because of this obstinate hen, don't blame me for it. It isn't safe to annoy the Princess Langwidere."

"Tell her we are waiting, if you please," Dorothy requested, with dignity. "Billina is my friend, and must go wherever I go."

Without more words the maid led them to a richly furnished drawing-room, lighted with subdued rainbow tints that came in through beautiful stained-glass windows.

"Remain here," she said. "What names shall I give the Princess?"

"I am Dorothy Gale, of Kansas," replied the child; "and this gentleman is a machine named Tik-tok, and the yellow hen is my friend Billina."

The little servant bowed and withdrew, going through several passages and mounting two marble stairways before she came to the apartments occupied by her mistress.

Princess Langwidere's sitting-room was paneled with great mirrors, which reached from the ceiling to the floor; also the ceiling was composed of mirrors, and the floor was of polished silver that reflected every object upon it. So when Langwidere sat in her easy chair and played soft melodies upon her mandolin, her form was mirrored hundreds of times, in walls and ceiling and floor, and whichever way the lady turned her head she could see and admire her own features. This she loved to do, and just as the maid entered she was saying to herself:

"This head with the auburn hair and hazel eyes is quite attractive. I must wear it more often than I have done of late, although it may not be the best of my collection."

"You have company, Your Highness," announced the maid, bowing low.

"Who is it?" asked Langwidere, yawning.

"Dorothy Gale of Kansas, Mr. Tik-tok and Billina," answered the maid.

"What a queer lot of names!" murmured the Princess, beginning to be a little interested. "What are they like? Is Dorothy Gale of Kansas pretty?"

"She might be called so," the maid replied.

"And is Mr. Tik-tok attractive?" continued the Princess.

"That I cannot say, Your Highness. But he seems very bright. Will Your Gracious Highness see them?"

"Oh, I may as well, Nanda. But I am tired admiring this head, and if my visitor has any claim to beauty I must take care that she does not surpass me. So I will go to my cabinet and change to No. 17, which I think is my best appearance. Don't you?"

"Your No. 17 is exceedingly beautiful," answered Nanda, with another bow.

Again the Princess yawned. Then she said:

"Help me to rise."

So the maid assisted her to gain her feet, although Langwidere was the stronger of the two; and then the Princess slowly walked across the silver floor to her cabinet, leaning heavily at every step upon Nanda's arm.

Now I must explain to you that the Princess Langwidere had thirty heads—as many as there are days in the month. But of course she could only wear one of them at a time, because she had but one neck. These heads were kept in what she called her "cabinet," which was a beautiful dressing-room that lay just between Langwidere's sleeping-chamber and the mirrored sitting-room. Each head was in a separate cupboard lined with velvet. The cupboards ran all around the sides of the dressing-room, and had elaborately carved doors with gold numbers on the outside and jeweled-framed mirrors on the inside of them.

When the Princess got out of her crystal bed in the morning she went to her cabinet, opened one of the velvet-lined cupboards, and took the head it contained from its golden shelf. Then, by the aid of the mirror inside the open door, she put on the head—as neat and straight as could be—and afterward called her maids to robe her for the day. She always wore a simple white costume, that suited all the heads. For, being able to change her face whenever she liked, the Princess had no interest in wearing a variety of gowns, as have other ladies who are compelled to wear the same face constantly.

Of course the thirty heads were in great variety, no two formed alike but all being of exceeding loveliness. There were heads with golden hair, brown hair, rich auburn hair and black hair; but none with gray hair. The heads had eyes of blue, of gray, of hazel, of brown and of black; but there were no red eyes among them, and all were bright and handsome. The noses were Grecian, Roman, retrousse and Oriental, representing all types of beauty; and the mouths were of assorted sizes and shapes, displaying pearly teeth when the heads smiled. As for dimples, they appeared in cheeks and chins, wherever they might be most charming, and one or two heads had freckles upon the faces to contrast the better with the brilliancy of their complexions.

One key unlocked all the velvet cupboards containing these treasures—a curious key carved from a single blood-red ruby—and this was fastened to a strong but slender chain which the Princess wore around her left wrist.

When Nanda had supported Langwidere to a position in front of cupboard No. 17, the Princess unlocked the door with her ruby key and after handing head No. 9, which she had been wearing, to the maid, she took No. 17 from its shelf

123

and fitted it to her neck. It had black hair and dark eyes and a lovely pearl-and-white complexion, and when Langwidere wore it she knew she was remarkably beautiful in appearance.

There was only one trouble with No. 17; the temper that went with it (and which was hidden somewhere under the glossy black hair) was fiery, harsh and haughty in the extreme, and it often led the Princess to do unpleasant things which she regretted when she came to wear her other heads.

But she did not remember this today, and went to meet her guests in the drawing-room with a feeling of certainty that she would surprise them with her beauty.

However, she was greatly disappointed to find that her visitors were merely a small girl in a gingham dress, a copper man that would only go when wound up, and a yellow hen that was sitting contentedly in Langwidere's best work-basket, where there was a china egg used for darning stockings. (It may surprise you to learn that a princess ever does such a common thing as darn stockings. But, if you will stop to think, you will realize that a princess is sure to wear holes in her stockings, the same as other people; only it isn't considered quite polite to mention the matter.)

"Oh!" said Langwidere, slightly lifting the nose of No. 17. "I thought some one of importance had called."

"Then you were right," declared Dorothy. "I'm a good deal of 'portance myself, and when Billina lays an egg she has the proudest cackle you ever heard. As for Tik-tok, he's the—"

"Stop—Stop!" commanded the Princess, with an angry flash of her splendid eyes. "How dare you annoy me with your senseless chatter?"

"Why, you horrid thing!" said Dorothy, who was not accustomed to being treated so rudely.

The Princess looked at her more closely.

"Tell me," she resumed, "are you of royal blood?"

"Better than that, ma'am," said Dorothy. "I came from Kansas."

"Huh!" cried the Princess, scornfully. "You are a foolish child, and I cannot allow you to annoy me. Run away, you little goose, and bother some one else."

Dorothy was so indignant that for a moment she could find no words to reply. But she rose from her chair, and was about to leave the room when the Princess, who had been scanning the girl's face, stopped her by saying, more gently:

"Come nearer to me."

Dorothy obeyed, without a thought of fear, and stood before the Princess while Langwidere examined her face with careful attention.

"You are rather attractive," said the lady, presently. "Not at all beautiful, you understand, but you have a certain style of prettiness that is different from that of any of my thirty heads. So I believe I'll take your head and give you No. 26 for it."

"Well, I b'lieve you won't!" exclaimed Dorothy.

"It will do you no good to refuse," continued the Princess; "for I need your head for my collection, and in the Land of Ev my will is law. I never have cared much for No. 26, and you will find that it is very little worn. Besides, it will do you just as well as the one you're wearing, for all practical purposes."

"I don't know anything about your No. 26, and I don't want to," said Dorothy, firmly. "I'm not used to taking cast-off things, so I'll just keep my own head."

"You refuse?" cried the Princess, with a frown.

"Of course I do," was the reply.

"Then," said Langwidere, "I shall lock you up in a tower until you decide to obey me. Nanda," turning to her maid, "call my army."

Nanda rang a silver bell, and at once a big fat colonel in a bright red uniform entered the room, followed by ten lean soldiers, who all looked sad and discouraged and saluted the princess in a very melancholy fashion.

"Carry that girl to the North Tower and lock her up!" cried the Princess, pointing to Dorothy.

"To hear is to obey," answered the big red colonel, and caught the child by her arm. But at that moment Tik-tok raised his dinner-pail and pounded it so forcibly against the colonel's head that the big officer sat down upon the floor with a sudden bump, looking both dazed and very much astonished.

"Help!" he shouted, and the ten lean soldiers sprang to assist their leader.

There was great excitement for the next few moments, and Tik-tok had knocked down seven of the army, who were sprawling in every direction upon the carpet, when suddenly the machine paused, with the dinner-pail raised for another blow, and remained perfectly motionless.

"My ac-tion has run down," he called to Dorothy. "Wind me up, quick."

She tried to obey, but the big colonel had by this time managed to get upon his feet again, so he grabbed fast hold of the girl and she was helpless to escape.

"This is too bad," said the machine. "I ought to have run six hours lon-ger, at least, but I sup-pose my long walk and my fight with the Wheel-ers made me run down fast-er than us-u-al."

"Well, it can't be helped," said Dorothy, with a sigh.

"Will you exchange heads with me?" demanded the Princess.

"No, indeed!" cried Dorothy.

"Then lock her up," said Langwidere to her soldiers, and they led Dorothy to a high tower at the north of the palace and locked her securely within.

The soldiers afterward tried to lift Tik-tok, but they found the machine so solid and heavy that they could not stir it. So they left him standing in the center of the drawing-room.

"People will think I have a new statue," said Langwidere, "so it won't matter in the least, and Nanda can keep him well polished."

"What shall we do with the hen?" asked the colonel, who had just discovered Billina in the work-basket.

"Put her in the chicken-house," answered the Princess. "Someday I'll have her fried for breakfast."

"She looks rather tough, Your Highness," said Nanda, doubtfully.

"That is a base slander!" cried Billina, struggling frantically in the colonel's arms. "But the breed of chickens I come from is said to be poison to all princesses."

"Then," remarked Langwidere, "I will not fry the hen, but keep her to lay eggs; and if she doesn't do her duty I'll have her drowned in the horse trough."

Chapter 7 - Ozma of Oz to the Rescue

Nanda brought Dorothy bread and water for her supper, and she slept upon a hard stone couch with a single pillow and a silken coverlet.

In the morning she leaned out of the window of her prison in the tower to see if there was any way to escape. The room was not so very high up, when compared with our modern buildings, but it was far enough above the trees and farm houses to give her a good view of the surrounding country.

To the east she saw the forest, with the sands beyond it and the ocean beyond that. There was even a dark speck upon the shore that she thought might be the chicken-coop in which she had arrived at this singular country.

Then she looked to the north, and saw a deep but narrow valley lying between two rocky mountains, and a third mountain that shut off the valley at the further end.

Westward the fertile Land of Ev suddenly ended a little way from the palace, and the girl could see miles and miles of sandy desert that stretched further than her eyes could reach. It was this desert, she thought, with much interest, that alone separated her from the wonderful Land of Oz, and she remembered sorrowfully that she had been told no one had ever been able to cross this dangerous waste but herself. Once a cyclone had carried her across it, and a magical pair of silver shoes had carried her back again. But now she had neither a cyclone nor silver shoes to assist her, and her condition was sad indeed. For she had become the prisoner of a disagreeable princess who insisted that she must exchange her head for another one that she was not used to, and which might not fit her at all.

Really, there seemed no hope of help for her from her old friends in the Land of Oz. Thoughtfully she gazed from her narrow window. On all the desert not a living thing was stirring.

Wait, though! Something surely WAS stirring on the desert—something her eyes had not observed at first. Now it seemed like a cloud; now it seemed like a spot of silver; now it seemed to be a mass of rainbow colors that moved swiftly toward her.

What COULD it be, she wondered?

Then, gradually, but in a brief space of time nevertheless, the vision drew near enough to Dorothy to make out what it was.

A broad green carpet was unrolling itself upon the desert, while advancing across the carpet was a wonderful procession that made the girl open her eyes in amazement as she gazed.

First came a magnificent golden chariot, drawn by a great Lion and an immense Tiger, who stood shoulder to shoulder and trotted along as gracefully as a well-matched team of thoroughbred horses. And standing upright within the chariot was a beautiful girl clothed in flowing robes of silver gauze and wearing a jeweled diadem upon her dainty head. She held in one hand the satin ribbons that guided her astonishing team, and in the other an ivory wand that separated at the top into two prongs, the prongs being tipped by the letters "O" and "Z", made of glistening diamonds set closely together.

The girl seemed neither older nor larger than Dorothy herself, and at once the prisoner in the tower guessed that the lovely driver of the chariot must be that Ozma of Oz of whom she had so lately heard from Tik-tok.

Following close behind the chariot Dorothy saw her old friend the Scarecrow, riding calmly astride a wooden Saw-Horse, which pranced and trotted as naturally as any meat horse could have done.

And then came Nick Chopper, the Tin Woodman, with his funnel-shaped cap tipped carelessly over his left ear, his gleaming axe over his right shoulder, and his whole body sparkling as brightly as it had ever done in the old days when first she knew him.

The Tin Woodman was on foot, marching at the head of a company of twenty-seven soldiers, of whom some were lean and some fat, some short and some tall; but all the twenty-seven were dressed in handsome uniforms of various designs and colors, no two being alike in any respect.

Behind the soldiers the green carpet rolled itself up again, so that there was always just enough of it for the procession to walk upon, in order that their feet might not come in contact with the deadly, life-destroying sands of the desert.

Dorothy knew at once it was a magic carpet she beheld, and her heart beat high with hope and joy as she realized she was soon to be rescued and allowed to greet her dearly beloved friends of Oz—the Scarecrow, the Tin Woodman and the Cowardly Lion.

Indeed, the girl felt herself as good as rescued as soon as she recognized those in the procession, for she well knew the courage and loyalty of her old comrades, and also believed that any others who came from their marvelous country would prove to be pleasant and reliable acquaintances.

As soon as the last bit of desert was passed and all the procession, from the beautiful and dainty Ozma to the last soldier, had reached the grassy meadows of the Land of Ev, the magic carpet rolled itself together and entirely disappeared.

Then the chariot driver turned her Lion and Tiger into a broad roadway leading up to the palace, and the others followed, while Dorothy still gazed from her tower window in eager excitement.

They came quite close to the front door of the palace and then halted, the Scarecrow dismounting from his Saw-Horse to approach the sign fastened to the door, that he might read what it said.

Dorothy, just above him, could keep silent no longer.

"Here I am!" she shouted, as loudly as she could. "Here's Dorothy!"

"Dorothy who?" asked the Scarecrow, tipping his head to look upward until he nearly lost his balance and tumbled over backward.

"Dorothy Gale, of course. Your friend from Kansas," she answered.

"Why, hello, Dorothy!" said the Scarecrow. "What in the world are you doing up there?"

"Nothing," she called down, "because there's nothing to do. Save me, my friend—save me!"

"You seem to be quite safe now," replied the Scarecrow.

"But I'm a prisoner. I'm locked in, so that I can't get out," she pleaded.

"That's all right," said the Scarecrow. "You might be worse off, little Dorothy. Just consider the matter. You can't get drowned, or be run over by a Wheeler, or fall out of an apple-tree. Some folks would think they were lucky to be up there."

"Well, I don't," declared the girl, "and I want to get down immed'i'tly and see you and the Tin Woodman and the Cowardly Lion."

"Very well," said the Scarecrow, nodding. "It shall be just as you say, little friend. Who locked you up?"

"The princess Langwidere, who is a horrid creature," she answered.

At this Ozma, who had been listening carefully to the conversation, called to Dorothy from her chariot, asking:

"Why did the Princess lock you up, my dear?"

"Because," exclaimed Dorothy, "I wouldn't let her have my head for her collection, and take an old, cast-off head in exchange for it."

"I do not blame you," exclaimed Ozma, promptly. "I will see the Princess at once, and oblige her to liberate you."

"Oh, thank you very, very much!" cried Dorothy, who as soon as she heard the sweet voice of the girlish Ruler of Oz knew that she would soon learn to love her dearly.

Ozma now drove her chariot around to the third door of the wing, upon which the Tin Woodman boldly proceeded to knock.

126

As soon as the maid opened the door Ozma, bearing in her hand her ivory wand, stepped into the hall and made her way at once to the drawing-room, followed by all her company, except the Lion and the Tiger. And the twenty-seven soldiers made such a noise and a clatter that the little maid Nanda ran away screaming to her mistress, whereupon the Princess Langwidere, roused to great anger by this rude invasion of her palace, came running into the drawing-room without any assistance whatever.

There she stood before the slight and delicate form of the little girl from Oz and cried out;—

"How dare you enter my palace unbidden? Leave this room at once, or I will bind you and all your people in chains, and throw you into my darkest dungeons!"

"What a dangerous lady!" murmured the Scarecrow, in a soft voice.

"She seems a little nervous," replied the Tin Woodman.

But Ozma only smiled at the angry Princess.

"Sit down, please," she said, quietly. "I have traveled a long way to see you, and you must listen to what I have to say."

"Must!" screamed the Princess, her black eyes flashing with fury—for she still wore her No. 17 head. "Must, to ME!"

"To be sure," said Ozma. "I am Ruler of the Land of Oz, and I am powerful enough to destroy all your kingdom, if I so wish. Yet I did not come here to do harm, but rather to free the royal family of Ev from the thrall of the Nome King, the news having reached me that he is holding the Queen and her children prisoners."

Hearing these words, Langwidere suddenly became quiet.

"I wish you could, indeed, free my aunt and her ten royal children," said she, eagerly. "For if they were restored to their proper forms and station they could rule the Kingdom of Ev themselves, and that would save me a lot of worry and trouble. At present there are at least ten minutes every day that I must devote to affairs of state, and I would like to be able to spend my whole time in admiring my beautiful heads."

"Then we will presently discuss this matter," said Ozma, "and try to find a way to liberate your aunt and cousins. But first you must liberate another prisoner—the little girl you have locked up in your tower."

"Of course," said Langwidere, readily. "I had forgotten all about her. That was yesterday, you know, and a Princess cannot be expected to remember today what she did yesterday. Come with me, and I will release the prisoner at once."

So Ozma followed her, and they passed up the stairs that led to the room in the tower.

While they were gone Ozma's followers remained in the drawing-room, and the Scarecrow was leaning against a form that he had mistaken for a copper statue when a harsh, metallic voice said suddenly in his ear:

"Get off my foot, please. You are scratch-ing my pol-ish."

"Oh, excuse me!" he replied, hastily drawing back. "Are you alive?"

"No," said Tik-tok, "I am on-ly a ma-chine. But I can think and speak and act, when I am pro-per-ly wound up. Just now my ac-tion is run down, and Dor-o-thy has the key to it."

"That's all right," replied the Scarecrow. Dorothy will soon be free, and then she'll attend to your works. But it must be a great misfortune not to be alive. I'm sorry for you."

"Why?" asked Tik-tok.

"Because you have no brains, as I have," said the Scarecrow.

"Oh, yes, I have," returned Tik-tok. "I am fit-ted with Smith & Tin-ker's Im-proved Com-bi-na-tion Steel Brains. They are what make me think. What sort of brains are you fit-ted with?"

"I don't know," admitted the Scarecrow. "They were given to me by the great Wizard of Oz, and I didn't get a chance to examine them before he put them in. But they work splendidly and my conscience is very active. Have you a conscience?"

"No," said Tik-tok.

"And no heart, I suppose?" added the Tin Woodman, who had been listening with interest to this conversation.

"No," said Tik-tok.

"Then," continued the Tin Woodman, "I regret to say that you are greatly inferior to my friend the Scarecrow, and to myself. For we are both alive, and he has brains which do not need to be wound up, while I have an excellent heart that is continually beating in my bosom."

"I con-grat-u-late you," replied Tik-tok. "I can-not help be-ing your in-fer-i-or for I am a mere ma-chine. When I am wound up I do my du-ty by go-ing just as my ma-chin-er-y is made to go. You have no i-de-a how full of ma-chin-er-y I am."

"I can guess," said the Scarecrow, looking at the machine man curiously. "Some day I'd like to take you apart and see just how you are made."

"Do not do that, I beg of you," said Tik-tok; "for you could not put me to-geth-er a-gain, and my use-ful-ness would be de-stroyed."

"Oh! are you useful?" asked the Scarecrow, surprised.

"Ve-ry," said Tik-tok.

"In that case," the Scarecrow kindly promised, "I won't fool with your interior at all. For I am a poor mechanic, and might mix you up."

"Thank you," said Tik-tok.

Just then Ozma re-entered the room, leading Dorothy by the hand and followed closely by the Princess Langwidere.

Chapter 8 - The Hungry Tiger

The first thing Dorothy did was to rush into the embrace of the Scarecrow, whose painted face beamed with delight as he pressed her form to his straw-padded bosom. Then the Tin Woodman embraced her—very gently, for he knew his tin arms might hurt her if he squeezed too roughly.

These greetings having been exchanged, Dorothy took the key to Tik-tok from her pocket and wound up the machine man's action, so that he could bow properly when introduced to the rest of the company. While doing this she told them now useful Tik-tok had been to her, and both the Scarecrow and the Tin Woodman shook hands with the machine once more and thanked him for protecting their friend.

Then Dorothy asked: "Where is Billina?"

"I don't know," said the Scarecrow. "Who is Billina?"

"She's a yellow hen who is another friend of mine," answered the girl, anxiously. "I wonder what has become of her?"

"She is in the chicken house, in the back yard," said the Princess. "My drawing-room is no place for hens."

Without waiting to hear more Dorothy ran to get Billina, and just outside the door she came upon the Cowardly Lion, still hitched to the chariot beside the great Tiger. The Cowardly Lion had a big bow of blue ribbon fastened to the long hair between his ears, and the Tiger wore a bow of red ribbon on his tail, just in front of the bushy end.

In an instant Dorothy was hugging the huge Lion joyfully.

"I'm SO glad to see you again!" she cried.

"I am also glad to see you, Dorothy," said the Lion. "We've had some fine adventures together, haven't we?"

"Yes, indeed," she replied. "How are you?"

"As cowardly as ever," the beast answered in a meek voice. "Every little thing scares me and makes my heart beat fast. But let me introduce to you a new friend of mine, the Hungry Tiger."

"Oh! Are you hungry?" she asked, turning to the other beast, who was just then yawning so widely that he displayed two rows of terrible teeth and a mouth big enough to startle anyone.

"Dreadfully hungry," answered the Tiger, snapping his jaws together with a fierce click.

"Then why don't you eat something?" she asked.

"It's no use," said the Tiger sadly. "I've tried that, but I always get hungry again."

"Why, it is the same with me," said Dorothy. "Yet I keep on eating."

"But you eat harmless things, so it doesn't matter," replied the Tiger. "For my part, I'm a savage beast, and have an appetite for all sorts of poor little living creatures, from a chipmunk to fat babies."

"How dreadful!" said Dorothy.

"Isn't it, though?" returned the Hungry Tiger, licking his lips with his long red tongue. "Fat babies! Don't they sound delicious? But I've never eaten any, because my conscience tells me it is wrong. If I had no conscience I would probably eat the babies and then get hungry again, which would mean that I had sacrificed the poor babies for nothing. No; hungry I was born, and hungry I shall die. But I'll not have any cruel deeds on my conscience to be sorry for."

"I think you are a very good tiger," said Dorothy, patting the huge head of the beast.

"In that you are mistaken," was the reply. "I am a good beast, perhaps, but a disgracefully bad tiger. For it is the nature of tigers to be cruel and ferocious, and in refusing to eat harmless living creatures I am acting as no good tiger has ever before acted. That is why I left the forest and joined my friend the Cowardly Lion."

"But the Lion is not really cowardly," said Dorothy. "I have seen him act as bravely as can be."

"All a mistake, my dear," protested the Lion gravely. "To others I may have seemed brave, at times, but I have never been in any danger that I was not afraid."

"Nor I," said Dorothy, truthfully. "But I must go and set free Billina, and then I will see you again."

She ran around to the back yard of the palace and soon found the chicken house, being guided to it by a loud cackling and crowing and a distracting hubbub of sounds such as chickens make when they are excited.

Something seemed to be wrong in the chicken house, and when Dorothy looked through the slats in the door she saw a group of hens and roosters huddled in one corner and watching what appeared to be a whirling ball of feathers. It bounded here and there about the chicken house, and at first Dorothy could not tell what it was, while the screeching of the chickens nearly deafened her.

But suddenly the bunch of feathers stopped whirling, and then, to her amazement, the girl saw Billina crouching upon the prostrate form of a speckled rooster. For an instant they both remained motionless, and then the yellow hen shook her wings to settle the feathers and walked toward the door with a strut of proud defiance and a cluck of victory, while the speckled rooster limped away to the group of other chickens, trailing his crumpled plumage in the dust as he went.

"Why, Billina!" cried Dorothy, in a shocked voice; "have you been fighting?"

"I really think I have," retorted Billina. "Do you think I'd let that speckled villain of a rooster lord it over ME, and claim to run this chicken house, as long as I'm able to peck and scratch? Not if my name is Bill!"

"It isn't Bill, it's Billina; and you're talking slang, which is very undig'n'fied," said Dorothy, reprovingly. "Come here, Billina, and I'll let you out; for Ozma of Oz is here, and has set us free."

So the yellow hen came to the door, which Dorothy unlatched for her to pass through, and the other chickens silently watched them from their corner without offering to approach nearer.

The girl lifted her friend in her arms and exclaimed:

"Oh, Billina! how dreadful you look. You've lost a lot of feathers, and one of your eyes is nearly pecked out, and your comb is bleeding!"

"That's nothing," said Billina. "Just look at the speckled rooster! Didn't I do him up brown?"

Dorothy shook her head.

"I don't 'prove of this, at all," she said, carrying Billina away toward the palace. "It isn't a good thing for you to 'sociate with those common chickens. They would soon spoil your good manners, and you wouldn't be respec'able any more."

"I didn't ask to associate with them," replied Billina. "It is that cross old Princess who is to blame. But I was raised in the United States, and I won't allow any one-horse chicken of the Land of Ev to run over me and put on airs, as long as I can lift a claw in self-defense."

"Very well, Billina," said Dorothy. "We won't talk about it any more."

Soon they came to the Cowardly Lion and the Hungry Tiger to whom the girl introduced the Yellow Hen.

"Glad to meet any friend of Dorothy's," said the Lion, politely. "To judge by your present appearance, you are not a coward, as I am."

"Your present appearance makes my mouth water," said the Tiger, looking at Billina greedily. "My, my! how good you would taste if I could only crunch you between my jaws. But don't worry. You would only appease my appetite for a moment; so it isn't worth while to eat you."

"Thank you," said the hen, nestling closer in Dorothy's arms.

"Besides, it wouldn't be right," continued the Tiger, looking steadily at Billina and clicking his jaws together.

"Of course not," cried Dorothy, hastily. "Billina is my friend, and you mustn't ever eat her under any circ'mstances."

"I'll try to remember that," said the Tiger; "but I'm a little absent-minded, at times."

Then Dorothy carried her pet into the drawing-room of the palace, where Tik-tok, being invited to do so by Ozma, had seated himself between the Scarecrow and the Tin Woodman. Opposite to them sat Ozma herself and the Princess Langwidere, and beside them there was a vacant chair for Dorothy.

Around this important group was ranged the Army of Oz, and as Dorothy looked at the handsome uniforms of the Twenty-Seven she said:

"Why, they seem to be all officers."

"They are, all except one," answered the Tin Woodman. "I have in my Army eight Generals, six Colonels, seven Majors and five Captains, besides one private for them to command. I'd like to promote the private, for I believe no private should ever be in public life; and I've also noticed that officers usually fight better and are more reliable than common soldiers. Besides, the officers are more important looking, and lend dignity to our army."

"No doubt you are right," said Dorothy, seating herself beside Ozma.

"And now," announced the girlish Ruler of Oz, "we will hold a solemn conference to decide the best manner of liberating the royal family of this fair Land of Ev from their long imprisonment."

Chapter 9 - The Royal Family of Ev

The Tin Woodman was the first to address the meeting.

"To begin with," said he, "word came to our noble and illustrious Ruler, Ozma of Oz, that the wife and ten children—five boys and five girls—of the former King of Ev, by name Evoldo, have been enslaved by the Nome King and are held prisoners in his underground palace. Also that there was no one in Ev powerful enough to release them. Naturally our Ozma wished to undertake the adventure of liberating the poor prisoners; but for a long time she could find no way to cross the great desert between the two countries. Finally she went to a friendly sorceress of our land named Glinda the Good, who heard the story and at once presented Ozma a magic carpet, which would continually unroll beneath our feet and so make a comfortable path for us to cross the desert. As soon as she had received the carpet our gracious Ruler ordered me to assemble our army, which I did. You behold in these bold warriors the pick of all the finest soldiers of Oz; and, if we are obliged to fight the Nome King, every officer as well as the private, will battle fiercely unto death."

Then Tik-tok spoke.

"Why should you fight the Nome King?" he asked. "He has done no wrong."

"No wrong!" cried Dorothy. "Isn't it wrong to imprison a queen mother and her ten children?"

"They were sold to the Nome King by King Ev-ol-do," replied Tik-tok. "It was the King of Ev who did wrong, and when he re-al-ized what he had done he jumped in-to the sea and drowned him-self."

"This is news to me," said Ozma, thoughtfully. "I had supposed the Nome King was all to blame in the matter. But, in any case, he must be made to liberate the prisoners."

"My uncle Evoldo was a very wicked man," declared the Princess Langwidere. "If he had drowned himself before he sold his family, no one would have cared. But he sold them to the powerful Nome King in exchange for a long life, and afterward destroyed the life by jumping into the sea."

"Then," said Ozma, "he did not get the long life, and the Nome King must give up the prisoners. Where are they confined?"

"No one knows, exactly," replied the Princess. "For the king, whose name is Roquat of the Rocks, owns a splendid palace underneath the great mountain which is at the north end of this kingdom, and he has transformed the queen and her children into ornaments and bric-a-brac with which to decorate his rooms."

"I'd like to know," said Dorothy, "who this Nome King is?"

"I will tell you," replied Ozma. "He is said to be the Ruler of the Underground World, and commands the rocks and all that the rocks contain. Under his rule are many thousands of the Nomes, who are queerly shaped but powerful sprites that labor at the furnaces and forges of their king, making gold and silver and other metals which they conceal in the crevices of the rocks, so that those living upon the earth's surface can only find them with great difficulty. Also they make diamonds and rubies and emeralds, which they hide in the ground; so that the kingdom of the Nomes is wonderfully rich, and all we have of precious stones and silver and gold is what we take from the earth and rocks where the Nome King has hidden them."

"I understand," said Dorothy, nodding her little head wisely.

"For the reason that we often steal his treasures," continued Ozma, "the Ruler of the Underground World is not fond of those who live upon the earth's surface, and never appears among us. If we wish to see King Roquat of the Rocks, we must visit his own country, where he is all powerful, and therefore it will be a dangerous undertaking."

"But, for the sake of the poor prisoners," said Dorothy, "we ought to do it."

"We shall do it," replied the Scarecrow, "although it requires a lot of courage for me to go near to the furnaces of the Nome King. For I am only stuffed with straw, and a single spark of fire might destroy me entirely."

"The furnaces may also melt my tin," said the Tin Woodman; "but I am going."

"I can't bear heat," remarked the Princess Langwidere, yawning lazily, "so I shall stay at home. But I wish you may have success in your undertaking, for I am heartily tired of ruling this stupid kingdom, and I need more leisure in which to admire my beautiful heads."

"We do not need you," said Ozma. "For, if with the aid of my brave followers I cannot accomplish my purpose, then it would be useless for you to undertake the journey."

"Quite true," sighed the Princess. "So, if you'll excuse me, I will now retire to my cabinet. I've worn this head quite awhile, and I want to change it for another."

When she had left them (and you may be sure no one was sorry to see her go) Ozma said to Tik-tok:

"Will you join our party?"

"I am the slave of the girl Dor-oth-y, who rescued me from pris-on," replied the machine. "Where she goes I will go."

"Oh, I am going with my friends, of course," said Dorothy, quickly. "I wouldn't miss the fun for anything. Will you go, too, Billina?"

"To be sure," said Billina in a careless tone. She was smoothing down the feathers of her back and not paying much attention.

"Heat is just in her line," remarked the Scarecrow. "If she is nicely roasted, she will be better than ever."

"Then" said Ozma, "we will arrange to start for the Kingdom of the Nomes at daybreak tomorrow. And, in the meantime, we will rest and prepare ourselves for the journey."

Although Princess Langwidere did not again appear to her guests, the palace servants waited upon the strangers from Oz and did everything in their power to make the party comfortable. There were many vacant rooms at their disposal, and the brave Army of twenty-seven was easily provided for and liberally feasted.

The Cowardly Lion and the Hungry Tiger were unharnessed from the chariot and allowed to roam at will throughout the palace, where they nearly frightened the servants into fits, although they did no harm at all. At one time Dorothy found the little maid Nanda crouching in terror in a corner, with the Hungry Tiger standing before her.

"You certainly look delicious," the beast was saying. "Will you kindly give me permission to eat you?"

"No, no, no!" cried the maid in reply.

"Then," said the Tiger, yawning frightfully, "please to get me about thirty pounds of tenderloin steak, cooked rare, with a peck of boiled potatoes on the side, and five gallons of ice-cream for dessert."

"I—I'll do the best I can!" said Nanda, and she ran away as fast as she could go.

"Are you so very hungry?" asked Dorothy, in wonder.

"You can hardly imagine the size of my appetite," replied the Tiger, sadly. "It seems to fill my whole body, from the end of my throat to the tip of my tail. I am very sure the appetite doesn't fit me, and is too large for the size of my body. Some day, when I meet a dentist with a pair of forceps, I'm going to have it pulled."

"What, your tooth?" asked Dorothy.

"No, my appetite," said the Hungry Tiger.

The little girl spent most of the afternoon talking with the Scarecrow and the Tin Woodman, who related to her all that had taken place in the Land of Oz since Dorothy had left it. She was much interested in the story of Ozma, who had been, when a baby, stolen by a wicked old witch and transformed into a boy. She did not know that she had ever been a girl until she was restored to her natural form by a kind sorceress. Then it was found that she was the only child of the former Ruler of Oz, and was entitled to rule in his place. Ozma had many adventures, however, before she regained her father's throne, and in these she was accompanied by a pumpkin-headed man, a highly magnified and thoroughly educated Woggle-Bug, and a wonderful sawhorse that had been brought to life by means of a magic powder. The Scarecrow and the Tin Woodman had also assisted her; but the Cowardly Lion, who ruled the great forest as the King of Beasts, knew nothing of Ozma until after she became the reigning princess of Oz. Then he journeyed to the Emerald City to see her, and on hearing she was about to visit the Land of Ev to set free the royal family of that country, the Cowardly Lion begged to go with her, and brought along his friend, the Hungry Tiger, as well.

Having heard this story, Dorothy related to them her own adventures, and then went out with her friends to find the Sawhorse, which Ozma had caused to be shod with plates of gold, so that its legs would not wear out.

They came upon the Sawhorse standing motionless beside the garden gate, but when Dorothy was introduced to him he bowed politely and blinked his eyes, which were knots of wood, and wagged his tail, which was only the branch of a tree.

"What a remarkable thing, to be alive!" exclaimed Dorothy.

"I quiet agree with you," replied the Sawhorse, in a rough but not unpleasant voice. "A creature like me has no business to live, as we all know. But it was the magic powder that did it, so I cannot justly be blamed."

"Of course not," said Dorothy. "And you seem to be of some use, 'cause I noticed the Scarecrow riding upon your back."

"Oh, yes; I'm of use," returned the Sawhorse; "and I never tire, never have to be fed, or cared for in any way."

"Are you intel'gent?" asked the girl.

"Not very," said the creature. "It would be foolish to waste intelligence on a common Sawhorse, when so many professors need it. But I know enough to obey my masters, and to gid-dup, or whoa, when I'm told to. So I'm pretty well satisfied."

That night Dorothy slept in a pleasant little bed-chamber next to that occupied by Ozma of Oz, and Billina perched upon the foot of the bed and tucked her head under her wing and slept as soundly in that position as did Dorothy upon her soft cushions.

But before daybreak every one was awake and stirring, and soon the adventurers were eating a hasty breakfast in the great dining-room of the palace. Ozma sat at the head of a long table, on a raised platform, with Dorothy on her right hand and the Scarecrow on her left. The Scarecrow did not eat, of course; but Ozma placed him near her so that she might ask his advice about the journey while she ate.

Lower down the table were the twenty-seven warriors of Oz, and at the end of the room the Lion and the Tiger were eating out of a kettle that had been placed upon the floor, while Billina fluttered around to pick up any scraps that might be scattered.

It did not take long to finish the meal, and then the Lion and the Tiger were harnessed to the chariot and the party was ready to start for the Nome King's Palace.

First rode Ozma, with Dorothy beside her in the golden chariot and holding Billina fast in her arms. Then came the Scarecrow on the Sawhorse, with the Tin Woodman and Tik-tok marching side by side just behind him. After these tramped the Army, looking brave and handsome in their splendid uniforms. The generals commanded the colonels and the colonels commanded the majors and the majors commanded the captains and the captains commanded the private, who marched with an air of proud importance because it required so many officers to give him his orders.

And so the magnificent procession left the palace and started along the road just as day was breaking, and by the time the sun came out they had made good progress toward the valley that led to the Nome King's domain.

Chapter 10 - The Giant with the Hammer

The road led for a time through a pretty farm country, and then past a picnic grove that was very inviting. But the procession continued to steadily advance until Billina cried in an abrupt and commanding manner:

"Wait—wait!"

Ozma stopped her chariot so suddenly that the Scarecrow's Sawhorse nearly ran into it, and the ranks of the army tumbled over one another before they could come to a halt. Immediately the yellow hen struggled from Dorothy's arms and flew into a clump of bushes by the roadside.

"What's the matter?" called the Tin Woodman, anxiously.

"Why, Billina wants to lay her egg, that's all," said Dorothy.

"Lay her egg!" repeated the Tin Woodman, in astonishment.

"Yes; she lays one every morning, about this time; and it's quite fresh," said the girl.

"But does your foolish old hen suppose that this entire cavalcade, which is bound on an important adventure, is going to stand still while she lays her egg?" enquired the Tin Woodman, earnestly.

"What else can we do?" asked the girl. "It's a habit of Billina's and she can't break herself of it."

"Then she must hurry up," said the Tin Woodman, impatiently.

"No, no!" exclaimed the Scarecrow. "If she hurries she may lay scrambled eggs."

"That's nonsense," said Dorothy. "But Billina won't be long, I'm sure."

So they stood and waited, although all were restless and anxious to proceed. And by and by the yellow hen came from the bushes saying:

"Kut-kut, kut, ka-daw-kutt! Kut, kut, kut—ka-daw-kut!"

"What is she doing—singing her lay?" asked the Scarecrow.

"For-ward—march!" shouted the Tin Woodman, waving his axe, and the procession started just as Dorothy had once more grabbed Billina in her arms.

"Isn't anyone going to get my egg?" cried the hen, in great excitement.

"I'll get it," said the Scarecrow; and at his command the Sawhorse pranced into the bushes. The straw man soon found the egg, which he placed in his jacket pocket. The cavalcade, having moved rapidly on, was even then far in advance; but it did not take the Sawhorse long to catch up with it, and presently the Scarecrow was riding in his accustomed place behind Ozma's chariot.

"What shall I do with the egg?" he asked Dorothy.

"I do not know," the girl answered. "Perhaps the Hungry Tiger would like it."

"It would not be enough to fill one of my back teeth," remarked the Tiger. "A bushel of them, hard boiled, might take a little of the edge off my appetite; but one egg isn't good for anything at all, that I know of."

"No; it wouldn't even make a sponge cake," said the Scarecrow, thoughtfully. "The Tin Woodman might carry it with his axe and hatch it; but after all I may as well keep it myself for a souvenir." So he left it in his pocket.

They had now reached that part of the valley that lay between the two high mountains which Dorothy had seen from her tower window. At the far end was the third great mountain, which blocked the valley and was the northern edge of the Land of Ev. It was underneath this mountain that the Nome King's palace was said to be; but it would be some time before they reached that place.

The path was becoming rocky and difficult for the wheels of the chariot to pass over, and presently a deep gulf appeared at their feet which was too wide for them to leap. So Ozma took a small square of green cloth from her pocket and threw it upon the ground. At once it became the magic carpet, and unrolled itself far enough for all the cavalcade to walk upon. The chariot now advanced, and the green carpet unrolled before it, crossing the gulf on a level with its banks, so that all passed over in safety.

"That's easy enough," said the Scarecrow. "I wonder what will happen next."

He was not long in making the discovery, for the sides of the mountain came closer together until finally there was but a narrow path between them, along which Ozma and her party were forced to pass in single file.

They now heard a low and deep "thump!—thump!—thump!" which echoed throughout the valley and seemed to grow louder as they advanced. Then, turning a corner of rock, they saw before them a huge form, which towered above the path for more than a hundred feet. The form was that of a gigantic man built out of plates of cast iron, and it stood with one foot on either side of the narrow road and swung over its right shoulder an immense iron mallet, with which it constantly pounded the earth. These resounding blows explained the thumping sounds they had heard, for the mallet was much bigger than a barrel, and where it struck the path between the rocky sides of the mountain it filled all the space through which our travelers would be obliged to pass.

Of course they at once halted, a safe distance away from the terrible iron mallet. The magic carpet would do them no good in this case, for it was only meant to protect them from any dangers upon the ground beneath their feet, and not from dangers that appeared in the air above them.

"Wow!" said the Cowardly Lion, with a shudder. "It makes me dreadfully nervous to see that big hammer pounding so near my head. One blow would crush me into a door-mat."

"The ir-on gi-ant is a fine fel-low," said Tik-tok, "and works as stead-i-ly as a clock. He was made for the Nome King by Smith & Tin-ker, who made me, and his du-ty is to keep folks from find-ing the un-der-ground pal-ace. Is he not a great work of art?"

"Can he think, and speak, as you do?" asked Ozma, regarding the giant with wondering eyes.

"No," replied the machine; "he is on-ly made to pound the road, and has no think-ing or speak-ing at-tach-ment. But he pounds ve-ry well, I think."

"Too well," observed the Scarecrow. "He is keeping us from going farther. Is there no way to stop his machinery?"

"On-ly the Nome King, who has the key, can do that," answered Tik-tok.

"Then," said Dorothy, anxiously, "what shall we do?"

"Excuse me for a few minutes," said the Scarecrow, "and I will think it over."

He retired, then, to a position in the rear, where he turned his painted face to the rocks and began to think.

Meantime the giant continued to raise his iron mallet high in the air and to strike the path terrific blows that echoed through the mountains like the roar of a cannon. Each time the mallet lifted, however, there was a moment when the path beneath the monster was free, and perhaps the Scarecrow had noticed this, for when he came back to the others he said:

"The matter is a very simple one, after all. We have but to run under the hammer, one at a time, when it is lifted, and pass to the other side before it falls again."

"It will require quick work, if we escape the blow," said the Tin Woodman, with a shake of his head. "But it really seems the only thing to be done. Who will make the first attempt?"

They looked at one another hesitatingly for a moment. Then the Cowardly Lion, who was trembling like a leaf in the wind, said to them:

"I suppose the head of the procession must go first—and that's me. But I'm terribly afraid of the big hammer!"

"What will become of me?" asked Ozma. "You might rush under the hammer yourself, but the chariot would surely be crushed."

133

"We must leave the chariot," said the Scarecrow. "But you two girls can ride upon the backs of the Lion and the Tiger."

So this was decided upon, and Ozma, as soon as the Lion was unfastened from the chariot, at once mounted the beast's back and said she was ready.

"Cling fast to his mane," advised Dorothy. "I used to ride him myself, and that's the way I held on."

So Ozma clung fast to the mane, and the lion crouched in the path and eyed the swinging mallet carefully until he knew just the instant it would begin to rise in the air.

Then, before anyone thought he was ready, he made a sudden leap straight between the iron giant's legs, and before the mallet struck the ground again the Lion and Ozma were safe on the other side.

The Tiger went next. Dorothy sat upon his back and locked her arms around his striped neck, for he had no mane to cling to. He made the leap straight and true as an arrow from a bow, and ere Dorothy realized it she was out of danger and standing by Ozma's side.

Now came the Scarecrow on the Sawhorse, and while they made the dash in safety they were within a hair's breadth of being caught by the descending hammer.

Tik-tok walked up to the very edge of the spot the hammer struck, and as it was raised for the next blow he calmly stepped forward and escaped its descent. That was an idea for the Tin Woodman to follow, and he also crossed in safety while the great hammer was in the air. But when it came to the twenty-six officers and the private, their knees were so weak that they could not walk a step.

"In battle we are wonderfully courageous," said one of the generals, "and our foes find us very terrible to face. But war is one thing and this is another. When it comes to being pounded upon the head by an iron hammer, and smashed into pancakes, we naturally object."

"Make a run for it," urged the Scarecrow.

"Our knees shake so that we cannot run," answered a captain. "If we should try it we would all certainly be pounded to a jelly."

"Well, well," sighed the Cowardly Lion, "I see, friend Tiger, that we must place ourselves in great danger to rescue this bold army. Come with me, and we will do the best we can."

So, Ozma and Dorothy having already dismounted from their backs, the Lion and the Tiger leaped back again under the awful hammer and returned with two generals clinging to their necks. They repeated this daring passage twelve times, when all the officers had been carried beneath the giant's legs and landed safely on the further side. By that time the beasts were very tired, and panted so hard that their tongues hung out of their great mouths.

"But what is to become of the private?" asked Ozma.

"Oh, leave him there to guard the chariot," said the Lion. "I'm tired out, and won't pass under that mallet again."

The officers at once protested that they must have the private with them, else there would be no one for them to command. But neither the Lion or the Tiger would go after him, and so the Scarecrow sent the Sawhorse.

Either the wooden horse was careless, or it failed to properly time the descent of the hammer, for the mighty weapon caught it squarely upon its head, and thumped it against the ground so powerfully that the private flew off its back high into the air, and landed upon one of the giant's cast-iron arms. Here he clung desperately while the arm rose and fell with each one of the rapid strokes.

The Scarecrow dashed in to rescue his Sawhorse, and had his left foot smashed by the hammer before he could pull the creature out of danger. They then found that the Sawhorse had been badly dazed by the blow; for while the hard wooden knot of which his head was formed could not be crushed by the hammer, both his ears were broken off and he would be unable to hear a sound until some new ones were made for him. Also his left knee was cracked, and had to be bound up with a string.

Billina having fluttered under the hammer, it now remained only to rescue the private who was riding upon the iron giant's arm, high in the air.

The Scarecrow lay flat upon the ground and called to the man to jump down upon his body, which was soft because it was stuffed with straw. This the private managed to do, waiting until a time when he was nearest the ground and then letting himself drop upon the Scarecrow. He accomplished the feat without breaking any bones, and the Scarecrow declared he was not injured in the least.

Therefore, the Tin Woodman having by this time fitted new ears to the Sawhorse, the entire party proceeded upon its way, leaving the giant to pound the path behind them.

Chapter 11 - The Nome King

By and by, when they drew near to the mountain that blocked their path and which was the furthermost edge of the Kingdom of Ev, the way grew dark and gloomy for the reason that the high peaks on either side shut out the sunshine. And it was very silent, too, as there were no birds to sing or squirrels to chatter, the trees being left far behind them and only the bare rocks remaining.

Ozma and Dorothy were a little awed by the silence, and all the others were quiet and grave except the Sawhorse, which, as it trotted along with the Scarecrow upon his back, hummed a queer song, of which this was the chorus:

"Would a wooden horse in a woodland go? Aye, aye! I sigh, he would, although Had he not had a wooden head He'd mount the mountain top instead."

But no one paid any attention to this because they were now close to the Nome King's dominions, and his splendid underground palace could not be very far away.

Suddenly they heard a shout of jeering laughter, and stopped short. They would have to stop in a minute, anyway, for the huge mountain barred their further progress and the path ran close up to a wall of rock and ended.

"Who was that laughing?" asked Ozma.

There was no reply, but in the gloom they could see strange forms flit across the face of the rock. Whatever the creations might be they seemed very like the rock itself, for they were the color of rocks and their shapes were as rough and rugged as if they had been broken away from the side of the mountain. They kept close to the steep cliff facing our friends, and glided up and down, and this way and that, with a lack of regularity that was quite confusing. And they seemed not to need places to rest their feet, but clung to the surface of the rock as a fly does to a window-pane, and were never still for a moment.

"Do not mind them," said Tik-tok, as Dorothy shrank back. "They are on-ly the Nomes."

"And what are Nomes?" asked the girl, half frightened.

"They are rock fair-ies, and serve the Nome King," replied the machine. "But they will do us no harm. You must call for the King, be-cause with-out him you can ne-ver find the en-trance to the pal-ace."

"YOU call," said Dorothy to Ozma.

Just then the Nomes laughed again, and the sound was so weird and disheartening that the twenty-six officers commanded the private to "right-about-face!" and they all started to run as fast as they could.

The Tin Woodman at once pursued his army and cried "halt!" and when they had stopped their flight he asked: "Where are you going?"

"I—I find I've forgotten the brush for my whiskers," said a general, trembling with fear. "S-s-so we are g-going back after it!"

"That is impossible," replied the Tin Woodman. "For the giant with the hammer would kill you all if you tried to pass him."

"Oh! I'd forgotten the giant," said the general, turning pale.

"You seem to forget a good many things," remarked the Tin Woodman. "I hope you won't forget that you are brave men."

"Never!" cried the general, slapping his gold-embroidered chest.

"Never!" cried all the other officers, indignantly slapping their chests.

"For my part," said the private, meekly, "I must obey my officers; so when I am told to run, I run; and when I am told to fight, I fight."

"That is right," agreed the Tin Woodman. "And now you must all come back to Ozma, and obey HER orders. And if you try to run away again I will have her reduce all the twenty-six officers to privates, and make the private your general."

This terrible threat so frightened them that they at once returned to where Ozma was standing beside the Cowardly Lion.

Then Ozma cried out in a loud voice:

"I demand that the Nome King appear to us!"

There was no reply, except that the shifting Nomes upon the mountain laughed in derision.

"You must not command the Nome King," said Tik-tok, "for you do not rule him, as you do your own peo-ple."

So Ozma called again, saying:

"I request the Nome King to appear to us."

Only the mocking laughter replied to her, and the shadowy Nomes continued to flit here and there upon the rocky cliff.

"Try en-treat-y," said Tik-tok to Ozma. "If he will not come at your re-quest, then the Nome King may list-en to your plead-ing."

Ozma looked around her proudly.

"Do you wish your ruler to plead with this wicked Nome King?" she asked. "Shall Ozma of Oz humble herself to a creature who lives in an underground kingdom?"

"No!" they all shouted, with big voices; and the Scarecrow added:

"If he will not come, we will dig him out of his hole, like a fox, and conquer his stubbornness. But our sweet little ruler must always maintain her dignity, just as I maintain mine."

"I'm not afraid to plead with him," said Dorothy. "I'm only a little girl from Kansas, and we've got more dignity at home than we know what to do with. I'LL call the Nome King."

"Do," said the Hungry Tiger; "and if he makes hash of you I'll willingly eat you for breakfast tomorrow morning."

So Dorothy stepped forward and said:

"PLEASE Mr. Nome King, come here and see us."

The Nomes started to laugh again; but a low growl came from the mountain, and in a flash they had all vanished from sight and were silent.

Then a door in the rock opened, and a voice cried:

"Enter!"

"Isn't it a trick?" asked the Tin Woodman.

"Never mind," replied Ozma. "We came here to rescue the poor Queen of Ev and her ten children, and we must run some risks to do so."

"The Nome King is hon-est and good na-tured," said Tik-tok. "You can trust him to do what is right."

So Ozma led the way, hand in hand with Dorothy, and they passed through the arched doorway of rock and entered a long passage which was lighted by jewels set in the walls and having lamps behind them. There was no one to escort them, or to show them the way, but all the party pressed through the passage until they came to a round, domed cavern that was grandly furnished.

In the center of this room was a throne carved out of a solid boulder of rock, rude and rugged in shape but glittering with great rubies and diamonds and emeralds on every part of its surface. And upon the throne sat the Nome King.

This important monarch of the Underground World was a little fat man clothed in gray-brown garments that were the exact color of the rock throne in which he was seated. His bushy hair and flowing beard were also colored like the rocks, and so was his face. He wore no crown of any sort, and his only ornament was a broad, jewel-studded belt that encircled his fat little body. As for his features, they seemed kindly and good humored, and his eyes were turned merrily upon his visitors as Ozma and Dorothy stood before him with their followers ranged in close order behind them.

"Why, he looks just like Santa Claus—only he isn't the same color!" whispered Dorothy to her friend; but the Nome King heard the speech, and it made him laugh aloud.

"'He had a red face and a round little belly That shook when he laughed like a bowl full of jelly!'"

quoth the monarch, in a pleasant voice; and they could all see that he really did shake like jelly when he laughed.

Both Ozma and Dorothy were much relieved to find the Nome King so jolly, and a minute later he waved his right hand and the girls each found a cushioned stool at her side.

"Sit down, my dears," said the King, "and tell me why you have come all this way to see me, and what I can do to make you happy."

While they seated themselves the Nome King picked up a pipe, and taking a glowing red coal out of his pocket he placed it in the bowl of the pipe and began puffing out clouds of smoke that curled in rings above his head. Dorothy thought this made the little monarch look more like Santa Claus than ever; but Ozma now began speaking, and every one listened intently to her words.

"Your Majesty," said she, "I am the ruler of the Land of Oz, and I have come here to ask you to release the good Queen of Ev and her ten children, whom you have enchanted and hold as your prisoners."

"Oh, no; you are mistaken about that," replied the King. "They are not my prisoners, but my slaves, whom I purchased from the King of Ev."

"But that was wrong," said Ozma.

"According to the laws of Ev, the king can do no wrong," answered the monarch, eying a ring of smoke he had just blown from his mouth; "so that he had a perfect right to sell his family to me in exchange for a long life."

"You cheated him, though," declared Dorothy; "for the King of Ev did not have a long life. He jumped into the sea and was drowned."

"That was not my fault," said the Nome King, crossing his legs and smiling contentedly. "I gave him the long life, all right; but he destroyed it."

"Then how could it be a long life?" asked Dorothy.

"Easily enough," was the reply. "Now suppose, my dear, that I gave you a pretty doll in exchange for a lock of your hair, and that after you had received the doll you smashed it into pieces and destroyed it. Could you say that I had not given you a pretty doll?"

"No," answered Dorothy.

"And could you, in fairness, ask me to return to you the lock of hair, just because you had smashed the doll?"

"No," said Dorothy, again.

"Of course not," the Nome King returned. "Nor will I give up the Queen and her children because the King of Ev destroyed his long life by jumping into the sea. They belong to me and I shall keep them."

"But you are treating them cruelly," said Ozma, who was much distressed by the King's refusal.

"In what way?" he asked.

"By making them your slaves," said she.

"Cruelty," remarked the monarch, puffing out wreaths of smoke and watching them float into the air, "is a thing I can't abide. So, as slaves must work hard, and the Queen of Ev and her children were delicate and tender, I transformed them all into articles of ornament and bric-a-brac and scattered them around the various rooms of my palace. Instead of being obliged to labor, they merely decorate my apartments, and I really think I have treated them with great kindness."

"But what a dreadful fate is theirs!" exclaimed Ozma, earnestly. "And the Kingdom of Ev is in great need of its royal family to govern it. If you will liberate them, and restore them to their proper forms, I will give you ten ornaments to replace each one you lose."

The Nome King looked grave.

"Suppose I refuse?" he asked.

"Then," said Ozma, firmly, "I am here with my friends and my army to conquer your kingdom and oblige you to obey my wishes."

The Nome King laughed until he choked; and he choked until he coughed; and he coughed until his face turned from grayish-brown to bright red. And then he wiped his eyes with a rock-colored handkerchief and grew grave again.

"You are as brave as you are pretty, my dear," he said to Ozma. "But you have little idea of the extent of the task you have undertaken. Come with me for a moment."

He arose and took Ozma's hand, leading her to a little door at one side of the room. This he opened and they stepped out upon a balcony, from whence they obtained a wonderful view of the Underground World.

A vast cave extended for miles and miles under the mountain, and in every direction were furnaces and forges glowing brightly and Nomes hammering upon precious metals or polishing gleaming jewels. All around the walls of the cave were thousands of doors of silver and gold, built into the solid rock, and these extended in rows far away into the distance, as far as Ozma's eyes could follow them.

While the little maid from Oz gazed wonderingly upon this scene the Nome King uttered a shrill whistle, and at once all the silver and gold doors flew open and solid ranks of Nome soldiers marched out from every one. So great were their numbers that they quickly filled the immense underground cavern and forced the busy workmen to abandon their tasks.

Although this tremendous army consisted of rock-colored Nomes, all squat and fat, they were clothed in glittering armor of polished steel, inlaid with beautiful gems. Upon his brow each wore a brilliant electric light, and they bore sharp spears and swords and battle-axes of solid bronze. It was evident they were perfectly trained, for they stood in straight rows, rank after rank, with their weapons held erect and true, as if awaiting but the word of command to level them upon their foes.

"This," said the Nome King, "is but a small part of my army. No ruler upon Earth has ever dared to fight me, and no ruler ever will, for I am too powerful to oppose."

He whistled again, and at once the martial array filed through the silver and gold doorways and disappeared, after which the workmen again resumed their labors at the furnaces.

Then, sad and discouraged, Ozma of Oz turned to her friends, and the Nome King calmly reseated himself on his rock throne.

"It would be foolish for us to fight," the girl said to the Tin Woodman. "For our brave Twenty-Seven would be quickly destroyed. I'm sure I do not know how to act in this emergency.

"Ask the King where his kitchen is," suggested the Tiger. "I'm hungry as a bear."

"I might pounce upon the King and tear him in pieces," remarked the Cowardly Lion.

"Try it," said the monarch, lighting his pipe with another hot coal which he took from his pocket.

The Lion crouched low and tried to spring upon the Nome King; but he hopped only a little way into the air and came down again in the same place, not being able to approach the throne by even an inch.

"It seems to me," said the Scarecrow, thoughtfully, "that our best plan is to wheedle his Majesty into giving up his slaves, since he is too great a magician to oppose."

"This is the most sensible thing any of you have suggested," declared the Nome King. "It is folly to threaten me, but I'm so kind-hearted that I cannot stand coaxing or wheedling. If you really wish to accomplish anything by your journey, my dear Ozma, you must coax me."

"Very well," said Ozma, more cheerfully. "Let us be friends, and talk this over in a friendly manner."

"To be sure," agreed the King, his eyes twinkling merrily.

"I am very anxious," she continued, "to liberate the Queen of Ev and her children who are now ornaments and bric-a-brac in your Majesty's palace, and to restore them to their people. Tell me, sir, how this may be accomplished."

The king remained thoughtful for a moment, after which he asked:

"Are you willing to take a few chances and risks yourself, in order to set free the people of Ev?"

"Yes, indeed!" answered Ozma, eagerly.

"Then," said the Nome King, "I will make you this offer: You shall go alone and unattended into my palace and examine carefully all that the rooms contain. Then you shall have permission to touch eleven different objects, pronouncing at the time the word 'Ev,' and if any one of them, or more than one, proves to be the transformation of the Queen of Ev or any of her ten children, then they will instantly be restored to their true forms and may leave my palace and my kingdom in your company, without any objection whatever. It is possible for you, in this way, to free the entire eleven; but if you do not guess all the objects correctly, and some of the slaves remain transformed, then each one of your friends and followers may, in turn, enter the palace and have the same privileges I grant you."

"Oh, thank you! thank you for this kind offer!" said Ozma, eagerly.

"I make but one condition," added the Nome King, his eyes twinkling.

"What is it?" she enquired.

"If none of the eleven objects you touch proves to be the transformation of any of the royal family of Ev, then, instead of freeing them, you will yourself become enchanted, and transformed into an article of bric-a-brac or an ornament. This is only fair and just, and is the risk you declared you were willing to take."

Chapter 12 - The Eleven Guesses

Hearing this condition imposed by the Nome King, Ozma became silent and thoughtful, and all her friends looked at her uneasily.

"Don't you do it!" exclaimed Dorothy. "If you guess wrong, you will be enslaved yourself."

"But I shall have eleven guesses," answered Ozma. "Surely I ought to guess one object in eleven correctly; and, if I do, I shall rescue one of the royal family and be safe myself. Then the rest of you may attempt it, and soon we shall free all those who are enslaved."

"What if we fail?" enquired the Scarecrow. "I'd look nice as a piece of bric-a-brac, wouldn't I?"

"We must not fail!" cried Ozma, courageously. "Having come all this distance to free these poor people, it would be weak and cowardly in us to abandon the adventure. Therefore I will accept the Nome King's offer, and go at once into the royal palace."

"Come along, then, my dear," said the King, climbing down from his throne with some difficulty, because he was so fat; "I'll show you the way."

He approached a wall of the cave and waved his hand. Instantly an opening appeared, through which Ozma, after a smiling farewell to her friends, boldly passed.

She found herself in a splendid hall that was more beautiful and grand than anything she had ever beheld. The ceilings were composed of great arches that rose far above her head, and all the walls and floors were of polished marble exquisitely tinted in many colors. Thick velvet carpets were on the floor and heavy silken draperies covered the arches leading to the various rooms of the palace. The furniture was made of rare old woods richly carved and covered with delicate satins, and the entire palace was lighted by a mysterious rosy glow that seemed to come from no particular place but flooded each apartment with its soft and pleasing radiance.

Ozma passed from one room to another, greatly delighted by all she saw. The lovely palace had no other occupant, for the Nome King had left her at the entrance, which closed behind her, and in all the magnificent rooms there appeared to be no other person.

Upon the mantels, and on many shelves and brackets and tables, were clustered ornaments of every description, seemingly made out of all sorts of metals, glass, china, stones and marbles. There were vases, and figures of men and animals, and graven platters and bowls, and mosaics of precious gems, and many other things. Pictures, too, were on the walls, and the underground palace was quite a museum of rare and curious and costly objects.

After her first hasty examination of the rooms Ozma began to wonder which of all the numerous ornaments they contained were the transformations of the royal family of Ev. There was nothing to guide her, for everything seemed without a spark of life. So she must guess blindly; and for the first time the girl came to realize how dangerous was her task, and how likely she was to lose her own freedom in striving to free others from the bondage of the Nome King. No wonder the cunning monarch laughed good naturedly with his visitors, when he knew how easily they might be entrapped.

But Ozma, having undertaken the venture, would not abandon it. She looked at a silver candelabra that had ten branches, and thought: "This may be the Queen of Ev and her ten children." So she touched it and uttered aloud the word "Ev," as the Nome King had instructed her to do when she guessed. But the candelabra remained as it was before.

Then she wandered into another room and touched a china lamb, thinking it might be one of the children she sought. But again she was unsuccessful. Three guesses; four guesses; five, six, seven, eight, nine and ten she made, and still not one of them was right!

The girl shivered a little and grew pale even under the rosy light; for now but one guess remained, and her own fate depended upon the result.

She resolved not to be hasty, and strolled through all the rooms once more, gazing earnestly upon the various ornaments and trying to decide which she would touch. Finally, in despair, she decided to leave it entirely to chance. She faced the doorway of a room, shut her eyes tightly, and then, thrusting aside the heavy draperies, she advanced blindly with her right arm outstretched before her.

Slowly, softly she crept forward until her hand came in contact with an object upon a small round table. She did not know what it was, but in a low voice she pronounced the word "Ev."

The rooms were quite empty of life after that. The Nome King had gained a new ornament. For upon the edge of the table rested a pretty grasshopper, that seemed to have been formed from a single emerald. It was all that remained of Ozma of Oz.

In the throne room just beyond the palace the Nome King suddenly looked up and smiled.

"Next!" he said, in his pleasant voice.

Dorothy, the Scarecrow, and the Tin Woodman, who had been sitting in anxious silence, each gave a start of dismay and stared into one another's eyes.

"Has she failed?" asked Tik-tok.

"So it seems," answered the little monarch, cheerfully. "But that is no reason one of you should not succeed. The next may have twelve guesses, instead of eleven, for there are now twelve persons transformed into ornaments. Well, well! Which of you goes next?"

"I'll go," said Dorothy.

"Not so," replied the Tin Woodman. "As commander of Ozma's army, it is my privilege to follow her and attempt her rescue."

"Away you go, then," said the Scarecrow. "But be careful, old friend."

"I will," promised the Tin Woodman; and then he followed the Nome King to the entrance to the palace and the rock closed behind him.

Chapter 13 - The Nome King Laughs

In a moment the King returned to his throne and relighted his pipe, and the rest of the little band of adventurers settled themselves for another long wait. They were greatly disheartened by the failure of their girl Ruler, and the knowledge that she was now an ornament in the Nome King's palace—a dreadful, creepy place in spite of all its magnificence. Without their little leader they did not know what to do next, and each one, down to the trembling private of the army, began to fear he would soon be more ornamental than useful.

Suddenly the Nome King began laughing.

"Ha, ha, ha! He, he, he! Ho, ho, ho!"

"What's happened?" asked the Scarecrow.

"Why, your friend, the Tin Woodman, has become the funniest thing you can imagine," replied the King, wiping the tears of merriment from his eyes. "No one would ever believe he could make such an amusing ornament. Next!"

They gazed at each other with sinking hearts. One of the generals began to weep dolefully.

"What are you crying for?" asked the Scarecrow, indignant at such a display of weakness.

"He owed me six weeks back pay," said the general, "and I hate to lose him."

"Then you shall go and find him," declared the Scarecrow.

"Me!" cried the general, greatly alarmed.

"Certainly. It is your duty to follow your commander. March!"

"I won't," said the general. "I'd like to, of course; but I just simply WON'T."

The Scarecrow looked enquiringly at the Nome King.

"Never mind," said the jolly monarch. "If he doesn't care to enter the palace and make his guesses I'll throw him into one of my fiery furnaces."

"I'll go!—of course I'm going," yelled the general, as quick as scat. "Where is the entrance—where is it? Let me go at once!"

So the Nome King escorted him into the palace, and again returned to await the result. What the general did, no one can tell; but it was not long before the King called for the next victim, and a colonel was forced to try his fortune.

Thus, one after another, all of the twenty-six officers filed into the palace and made their guesses—and became ornaments.

Meantime the King ordered refreshments to be served to those waiting, and at his command a rudely shaped Nome entered, bearing a tray. This Nome was not unlike the others that Dorothy had seen, but he wore a heavy gold chain around his neck to show that he was the Chief Steward of the Nome King, and he assumed an air of much importance, and even told his majesty not to eat too much cake late at night, or he would be ill.

Dorothy, however, was hungry, and she was not afraid of being ill; so she ate several cakes and found them good, and also she drank a cup of excellent coffee made of a richly flavored clay, browned in the furnaces and then ground fine, and found it most refreshing and not at all muddy.

Of all the party which had started upon this adventure, the little Kansas girl was now left alone with the Scarecrow, Tik-tok, and the private for counsellors and companions. Of course the Cowardly Lion and the Hungry Tiger were still there, but they, having also eaten some of the cakes, had gone to sleep at one side of the cave, while upon the other side stood the Sawhorse, motionless and silent, as became a mere thing of wood. Billina had quietly walked around and picked up the crumbs of cake which had been scattered, and now, as it was long after bed-time, she tried to find some dark place in which to go to sleep.

Presently the hen espied a hollow underneath the King's rocky throne, and crept into it unnoticed. She could still hear the chattering of those around her, but it was almost dark underneath the throne, so that soon she had fallen fast asleep.

"Next!" called the King, and the private, whose turn it was to enter the fatal palace, shook hands with Dorothy and the Scarecrow and bade them a sorrowful good-bye, and passed through the rocky portal.

They waited a long time, for the private was in no hurry to become an ornament and made his guesses very slowly. The Nome King, who seemed to know, by some magical power, all that took place in his beautiful rooms of his palace, grew impatient finally and declared he would sit up no longer.

"I love ornaments," said he, "but I can wait until tomorrow to get more of them; so, as soon as that stupid private is transformed, we will all go to bed and leave the job to be finished in the morning."

"Is it so very late?" asked Dorothy.

"Why, it is after midnight," said the King, "and that strikes me as being late enough. There is neither night nor day in my kingdom, because it is under the earth's surface, where the sun does not shine. But we have to sleep, just the same as the up-stairs people do, and for my part I'm going to bed in a few minutes."

Indeed, it was not long after this that the private made his last guess. Of course he guessed wrongly, and of course he at once became an ornament. So the King was greatly pleased, and clapped his hands to summon his Chief Steward.

"Show these guests to some of the sleeping apartments," he commanded, "and be quick about it, too, for I'm dreadfully sleepy myself."

"You've no business to sit up so late," replied the Steward, gruffly. "You'll be as cross as a griffin tomorrow morning."

His Majesty made no answer to this remark, and the Chief Steward led Dorothy through another doorway into a long hall, from which several plain but comfortable sleeping rooms opened. The little girl was given the first room, and the Scarecrow and Tik-tok the next—although they never slept—and the Lion and the Tiger the third. The Sawhorse hobbled after the Steward into a fourth room, to stand stiffly in the center of it until morning. Each night was rather a bore to the Scarecrow, Tik-tok and the Sawhorse; but they had learned from experience to pass the time patiently and quietly, since all their friends who were made of flesh had to sleep and did not like to be disturbed.

When the Chief Steward had left them alone the Scarecrow remarked, sadly:

"I am in great sorrow over the loss of my old comrade, the Tin Woodman. We have had many dangerous adventures together, and escaped them all, and now it grieves me to know he has become an ornament, and is lost to me forever."

"He was al-ways an or-na-ment to so-ci-e-ty," said Tik-tok.

"True; but now the Nome King laughs at him, and calls him the funniest ornament in all the palace. It will hurt my poor friend's pride to be laughed at," continued the Scarecrow, sadly.

"We will make rath-er ab-surd or-na-ments, our-selves, to-mor-row," observed the machine, in his monotonous voice.

Just then Dorothy ran into their room, in a state of great anxiety, crying:

"Where's Billina? Have you seen Billina? Is she here?"

"No," answered the Scarecrow.

"Then what has become of her?" asked the girl.

"Why, I thought she was with you," said the Scarecrow. "Yet I do not remember seeing the yellow hen since she picked up the crumbs of cake."

"We must have left her in the room where the King's throne is," decided Dorothy, and at once she turned and ran down the hall to the door through which they had entered. But it was fast closed and locked on the other side, and the heavy slab of rock proved to be so thick that no sound could pass through it. So Dorothy was forced to return to her chamber.

The Cowardly Lion stuck his head into her room to try to console the girl for the loss of her feathered friend.

"The yellow hen is well able to take care of herself," said he; "so don't worry about her, but try to get all the sleep you can. It has been a long and weary day, and you need rest."

"I'll prob'ly get lots of rest tomorrow, when I become an orn'ment," said Dorothy, sleepily. But she lay down upon her couch, nevertheless, and in spite of all her worries was soon in the land of dreams.

Chapter 14 - Dorothy Tries to be Brave

Meantime the Chief Steward had returned to the throne room, where he said to the King:

"You are a fool to waste so much time upon these people."

"What!" cried his Majesty, in so enraged a voice that it awoke Billina, who was asleep under his throne. "How dare you call me a fool?"

"Because I like to speak the truth," said the Steward. "Why didn't you enchant them all at once, instead of allowing them to go one by one into the palace and guess which ornaments are the Queen of Ev and her children?"

"Why, you stupid rascal, it is more fun this way," returned the King, "and it serves to keep me amused for a long time."

"But suppose some of them happen to guess aright," persisted the Steward; "then you would lose your old ornaments and these new ones, too."

"There is no chance of their guessing aright," replied the monarch, with a laugh. "How could they know that the Queen of Ev and her family are all ornaments of a royal purple color?"

"But there are no other purple ornaments in the palace," said the Steward.

"There are many other colors, however, and the purple ones are scattered throughout the rooms, and are of many different shapes and sizes. Take my word for it, Steward, they will never think of choosing the purple ornaments."

Billina, squatting under the throne, had listened carefully to all this talk, and now chuckled softly to herself as she heard the King disclose his secret.

"Still, you are acting foolishly by running the chance," continued the Steward, roughly; "and it is still more foolish of you to transform all those people from Oz into green ornaments."

"I did that because they came from the Emerald City," replied the King; "and I had no green ornaments in my collection until now. I think they will look quite pretty, mixed with the others. Don't you?"

The Steward gave an angry grunt.

"Have your own way, since you are the King," he growled. "But if you come to grief through your carelessness, remember that I told you so. If I wore the magic belt which enables you to work all your transformations, and gives you so much other power, I am sure I would make a much wiser and better King than you are."

"Oh, cease your tiresome chatter!" commanded the King, getting angry again. "Because you are my Chief Steward you have an idea you can scold me as much as you please. But the very next time you become impudent, I will send you to work in the furnaces, and get another Nome to fill your place. Now follow me to my chamber, for I am going to bed. And see that I am wakened early tomorrow morning. I want to enjoy the fun of transforming the rest of these people into ornaments."

"What color will you make the Kansas girl?" asked the Steward.

"Gray, I think," said his Majesty.

"And the Scarecrow and the machine man?"

"Oh, they shall be of solid gold, because they are so ugly in real life."

Then the voices died away, and Billina knew that the King and his Steward had left the room. She fixed up some of her tail feathers that were not straight, and then tucked her head under her wing again and went to sleep.

In the morning Dorothy and the Lion and Tiger were given their breakfast in their rooms, and afterward joined the King in his throne room. The Tiger complained bitterly that he was half starved, and begged to go into the palace and become an ornament, so that he would no longer suffer the pangs of hunger.

"Haven't you had your breakfast?" asked the Nome King.

"Oh, I had just a bite," replied the beast. "But what good is a bite, to a hungry tiger?"

"He ate seventeen bowls of porridge, a platter full of fried sausages, eleven loaves of bread and twenty-one mince pies," said the Steward.

"What more do you want?" demanded the King.

"A fat baby. I want a fat baby," said the Hungry Tiger. "A nice, plump, juicy, tender, fat baby. But, of course, if I had one, my conscience would not allow me to eat it. So I'll have to be an ornament and forget my hunger."

"Impossible!" exclaimed the King. "I'll have no clumsy beasts enter my palace, to overturn and break all my pretty nick-nacks. When the rest of your friends are transformed you can return to the upper world, and go about your business."

"As for that, we have no business, when our friends are gone," said the Lion. "So we do not care much what becomes of us."

Dorothy begged to be allowed to go first into the palace, but Tik-tok firmly maintained that the slave should face danger before the mistress. The Scarecrow agreed with him in that, so the Nome King opened the door for the machine man, who tramped into the palace to meet his fate. Then his Majesty returned to his throne and puffed his pipe so contentedly that a small cloud of smoke formed above his head.

Bye and bye he said:

"I'm sorry there are so few of you left. Very soon, now, my fun will be over, and then for amusement I shall have nothing to do but admire my new ornaments."

"It seems to me," said Dorothy, "that you are not so honest as you pretend to be."

"How's that?" asked the King.

"Why, you made us think it would be easy to guess what ornaments the people of Ev were changed into."

"It IS easy," declared the monarch, "if one is a good guesser. But it appears that the members of your party are all poor guessers."

"What is Tik-tok doing now?" asked the girl, uneasily.

"Nothing," replied the King, with a frown. "He is standing perfectly still, in the middle of a room."

"Oh, I expect he's run down," said Dorothy. "I forgot to wind him up this morning. How many guesses has he made?"

"All that he is allowed except one," answered the King. "Suppose you go in and wind him up, and then you can stay there and make your own guesses."

"All right," said Dorothy.

"It is my turn next," declared the Scarecrow.

"Why, you don't want to go away and leave me all alone, do you?" asked the girl. "Besides, if I go now I can wind up Tik-tok, so that he can make his last guess."

"Very well, then," said the Scarecrow, with a sigh. "Run along, little Dorothy, and may good luck go with you!"

So Dorothy, trying to be brave in spite of her fears, passed through the doorway into the gorgeous rooms of the palace. The stillness of the place awed her, at first, and the child drew short breaths, and pressed her hand to her heart, and looked all around with wondering eyes.

Yes, it was a beautiful place; but enchantments lurked in every nook and corner, and she had not yet grown accustomed to the wizardries of these fairy countries, so different from the quiet and sensible common-places of her own native land.

Slowly she passed through several rooms until she came upon Tik-tok, standing motionless. It really seemed, then, that she had found a friend in this mysterious palace, so she hastened to wind up the machine man's action and speech and thoughts.

"Thank you, Dor-oth-y," were his first words. "I have now one more guess to make."

"Oh, be very careful, Tik-tok; won't you?" cried the girl.

"Yes. But the Nome King has us in his power, and he has set a trap for us. I fear we are all lost." he answered.

"I fear so, too," said Dorothy, sadly.

"If Smith & Tin-ker had giv-en me a guess-ing clock-work at-tach-ment," continued Tik-tok, "I might have de-fied the Nome King. But my thoughts are plain and sim-ple, and are not of much use in this case."

"Do the best you can," said Dorothy, encouragingly, "and if you fail I will watch and see what shape you are changed into."

So Tik-tok touched a yellow glass vase that had daisies painted on one side, and he spoke at the same time the word "Ev."

In a flash the machine man had disappeared, and although the girl looked quickly in every direction, she could not tell which of the many ornaments the room contained had a moment before been her faithful friend and servant.

So all she could do was to accept the hopeless task set her, and make her guesses and abide by the result.

"It can't hurt very much," she thought, "for I haven't heard any of them scream or cry out—not even the poor officers. Dear me! I wonder if Uncle Henry or Aunt Em will ever know I have become an orn'ment in the Nome King's palace, and must stand forever and ever in one place and look pretty—'cept when I'm moved to be dusted. It isn't the way I thought I'd turn out, at all; but I s'pose it can't be helped."

She walked through all the rooms once more, and examined with care all the objects they contained; but there were so many, they bewildered her, and she decided, after all, as Ozma had done, that it could be only guess work at the best, and that the chances were much against her guessing aright.

Timidly she touched an alabaster bowl and said: "Ev."

"That's one failure, anyhow," she thought. "But how am I to know which thing is enchanted, and which is not?"

Next she touched the image of a purple kitten that stood on the corner of a mantel, and as she pronounced the word "Ev" the kitten disappeared, and a pretty, fair-haired boy stood beside her. At the same time a bell rang somewhere in the distance, and as Dorothy started back, partly in surprise and partly in joy, the little one exclaimed:

"Where am I? And who are you? And what has happened to me?"

"Well, I declare!" said Dorothy. "I've really done it."

"Done what?" asked the boy.

"Saved myself from being an ornament," replied the girl, with a laugh, "and saved you from being forever a purple kitten."

"A purple kitten?" he repeated. "There IS no such thing."

"I know," she answered. "But there was, a minute ago. Don't you remember standing on a corner of the mantel?"

"Of course not. I am a Prince of Ev, and my name is Evring," the little one announced, proudly. "But my father, the King, sold my mother and all her children to the cruel ruler of the Nomes, and after that I remember nothing at all."

"A purple kitten can't be 'spected to remember, Evring," said Dorothy. "But now you are yourself again, and I'm going to try to save some of your brothers and sisters, and perhaps your mother, as well. So come with me."

She seized the child's hand and eagerly hurried here and there, trying to decide which object to choose next. The third guess was another failure, and so was the fourth and the fifth.

Little Evring could not imagine what she was doing, but he trotted along beside her very willingly, for he liked the new companion he had found.

Dorothy's further quest proved unsuccessful; but after her first disappointment was over, the little girl was filled with joy and thankfulness to think that after all she had been able to save one member of the royal family of Ev, and could restore the little Prince to his sorrowing country. Now she might return to the terrible Nome King in safety, carrying with her the prize she had won in the person of the fair-haired boy.

So she retraced her steps until she found the entrance to the palace, and as she approached, the massive doors of rock opened of their own accord, allowing both Dorothy and Evring to pass the portals and enter the throne room.

Chapter 15 - Billina Frightens the Nome King

Now when Dorothy had entered the palace to make her guesses and the Scarecrow was left with the Nome King, the two sat in moody silence for several minutes. Then the monarch exclaimed, in a tone of satisfaction:

"Very good!"

"Who is very good?" asked the Scarecrow.

"The machine man. He won't need to be wound up any more, for he has now become a very neat ornament. Very neat, indeed."

"How about Dorothy?" the Scarecrow enquired.

"Oh, she will begin to guess, pretty soon," said the King, cheerfully. "And then she will join my collection, and it will be your turn."

The good Scarecrow was much distressed by the thought that his little friend was about to suffer the fate of Ozma and the rest of their party; but while he sat in gloomy reverie a shrill voice suddenly cried:

"Kut, kut, kut—ka-daw-kutt! Kut, kut, kut—ka-daw-kutt!"

The Nome King nearly jumped off his seat, he was so startled.

"Good gracious! What's that?" he yelled.

"Why, it's Billina," said the Scarecrow.

"What do you mean by making a noise like that?" shouted the King, angrily, as the yellow hen came from under the throne and strutted proudly about the room.

"I've got a right to cackle, I guess," replied Billina. "I've just laid my egg."

"What! Laid an egg! In my throne room! How dare you do such a thing?" asked the King, in a voice of fury.

"I lay eggs wherever I happen to be," said the hen, ruffling her feathers and then shaking them into place.

"But—thunder-ation! Don't you know that eggs are poison?" roared the King, while his rock-colored eyes stuck out in great terror.

"Poison! well, I declare," said Billina, indignantly. "I'll have you know all my eggs are warranted strictly fresh and up to date. Poison, indeed!"

"You don't understand," retorted the little monarch, nervously. "Eggs belong only to the outside world—to the world on the earth's surface, where you came from. Here, in my underground kingdom, they are rank poison, as I said, and we Nomes can't bear them around."

"Well, you'll have to bear this one around," declared Billina; "for I've laid it."

"Where?" asked the King.

"Under your throne," said the hen.

The King jumped three feet into the air, so anxious was he to get away from the throne.

"Take it away! Take it away at once!" he shouted.

"I can't," said Billina. "I haven't any hands."

"I'll take the egg," said the Scarecrow. "I'm making a collection of Billina's eggs. There's one in my pocket now, that she laid yesterday."

Hearing this, the monarch hastened to put a good distance between himself and the Scarecrow, who was about to reach under the throne for the egg when the hen suddenly cried:

"Stop!"

"What's wrong?" asked the Scarecrow.

"Don't take the egg unless the King will allow me to enter the palace and guess as the others have done," said Billina.

"Pshaw!" returned the King. "You're only a hen. How could you guess my enchantments?"

"I can try, I suppose," said Billina. "And, if I fail, you will have another ornament."

"A pretty ornament you'd make, wouldn't you?" growled the King. "But you shall have your way. It will properly punish you for daring to lay an egg in my presence. After the Scarecrow is enchanted you shall follow him into the palace. But how will you touch the objects?"

"With my claws," said the hen; "and I can speak the word 'Ev' as plainly as anyone. Also I must have the right to guess the enchantments of my friends, and to release them if I succeed."

"Very well," said the King. "You have my promise."

"Then," said Billina to the Scarecrow, "you may get the egg."

He knelt down and reached underneath the throne and found the egg, which he placed in another pocket of his jacket, fearing that if both eggs were in one pocket they would knock together and get broken.

Just then a bell above the throne rang briskly, and the King gave another nervous jump.

"Well, well!" said he, with a rueful face; "the girl has actually done it."

"Done what?" asked the Scarecrow.

"She has made one guess that is right, and broken one of my neatest enchantments. By ricketty, it's too bad! I never thought she would do it."

"Do I understand that she will now return to us in safety?" enquired the Scarecrow, joyfully wrinkling his painted face into a broad smile.

"Of course," said the King, fretfully pacing up and down the room. "I always keep my promises, no matter how foolish they are. But I shall make an ornament of the yellow hen to replace the one I have just lost."

"Perhaps you will, and perhaps you won't," murmured Billina, calmly. "I may surprise you by guessing right."

"Guessing right?" snapped the King. "How could you guess right, where your betters have failed, you stupid fowl?"

Billina did not care to answer this question, and a moment later the doors flew open and Dorothy entered, leading the little Prince Evring by the hand.

The Scarecrow welcomed the girl with a close embrace, and he would have embraced Evring, too, in his delight. But the little Prince was shy, and shrank away from the painted Scarecrow because he did not yet know his many excellent qualities.

But there was little time for the friends to talk, because the Scarecrow must now enter the palace. Dorothy's success had greatly encouraged him, and they both hoped he would manage to make at least one correct guess.

However, he proved as unfortunate as the others except Dorothy, and although he took a good deal of time to select his objects, not one did the poor Scarecrow guess aright.

So he became a solid gold card-receiver, and the beautiful but terrible palace awaited it's next visitor.

"It's all over," remarked the King, with a sigh of satisfaction; "and it has been a very amusing performance, except for the one good guess the Kansas girl made. I am richer by a great many pretty ornaments.

"It is my turn, now," said Billina, briskly.

"Oh, I'd forgotten you," said the King. "But you needn't go if you don't wish to. I will be generous, and let you off."

"No you won't," replied the hen. "I insist upon having my guesses, as you promised."

"Then go ahead, you absurd feathered fool!" grumbled the King, and he caused the opening that led to the palace to appear once more.

"Don't go, Billina," said Dorothy, earnestly. "It isn't easy to guess those orn'ments, and only luck saved me from being one myself. Stay with me and we'll go back to the Land of Ev together. I'm sure this little Prince will give us a home."

"Indeed I will," said Evring, with much dignity.

"Don't worry, my dear," cried Billina, with a cluck that was meant for a laugh. "I may not be human, but I'm no fool, if I AM a chicken."

"Oh, Billina!" said Dorothy, "you haven't been a chicken in a long time. Not since you—you've been—grown up."

"Perhaps that's true," answered Billina, thoughtfully. "But if a Kansas farmer sold me to some one, what would he call me?—a hen or a chicken!"

"You are not a Kansas farmer, Billina," replied the girl, "and you said—"

"Never mind that, Dorothy. I'm going. I won't say good-bye, because I'm coming back. Keep up your courage, for I'll see you a little later."

Then Billina gave several loud "cluck-clucks" that seemed to make the fat little King MORE nervous than ever, and marched through the entrance into the enchanted palace.

"I hope I've seen the last of THAT bird," declared the monarch, seating himself again in his throne and mopping the perspiration from his forehead with his rock-colored handkerchief. "Hens are bothersome enough at their best, but when they can talk they're simply dreadful."

"Billina's my friend," said Dorothy quietly. "She may not always be 'zactly polite; but she MEANS well, I'm sure."

Chapter 16 - Purple, Green, and Gold

The yellow hen, stepping high and with an air of vast importance, walked slowly over the rich velvet carpets of the splendid palace, examining everything she met with her sharp little eyes.

Billina had a right to feel important; for she alone shared the Nome King's secret and knew how to tell the objects that were transformations from those that had never been alive. She was very sure that her guesses would be correct, but before she began to make them she was curious to behold all the magnificence of this underground palace, which was perhaps one of the most splendid and beautiful places in any fairyland.

As she went through the rooms she counted the purple ornaments; and although some were small and hidden in queer places, Billina spied them all, and found the entire ten scattered about the various rooms. The green ornaments she did not bother to count, for she thought she could find them all when the time came.

Finally, having made a survey of the entire palace and enjoyed its splendor, the yellow hen returned to one of the rooms where she had noticed a large purple footstool. She placed a claw upon this and said "Ev," and at once the footstool vanished and a lovely lady, tall and slender and most beautifully robed, stood before her.

The lady's eyes were round with astonishment for a moment, for she could not remember her transformation, nor imagine what had restored her to life.

"Good morning, ma'am," said Billina, in her sharp voice. "You're looking quite well, considering your age."

"Who speaks?" demanded the Queen of Ev, drawing herself up proudly.

"Why, my name's Bill, by rights," answered the hen, who was now perched upon the back of a chair; "although Dorothy has put scollops on it and made it Billina. But the name doesn't matter. I've saved you from the Nome King, and you are a slave no longer."

"Then I thank you for the gracious favor," said the Queen, with a graceful courtesy. "But, my children—tell me, I beg of you—where are my children?" and she clasped her hands in anxious entreaty.

"Don't worry," advised Billina, pecking at a tiny bug that was crawling over the chair back. "Just at present they are out of mischief and perfectly safe, for they can't even wiggle."

"What mean you, O kindly stranger?" asked the Queen, striving to repress her anxiety.

"They're enchanted," said Billina, "just as you have been—all, that is, except the little fellow Dorothy picked out. And the chances are that they have been good boys and girls for some time, because they couldn't help it."

"Oh, my poor darlings!" cried the Queen, with a sob of anguish.

"Not at all," returned the hen. "Don't let their condition make you unhappy, ma'am, because I'll soon have them crowding 'round to bother and worry you as naturally as ever. Come with me, if you please, and I'll show you how pretty they look."

She flew down from her perch and walked into the next room, the Queen following. As she passed a low table a small green grasshopper caught her eye, and instantly Billina pounced upon it and snapped it up in her sharp bill. For grasshoppers are a favorite food with hens, and they usually must be caught quickly, before they can hop away. It might easily have been the end of Ozma of Oz, had she been a real grasshopper instead of an emerald one. But Billina found the grasshopper hard and lifeless, and suspecting it was not good to eat she quickly dropped it instead of letting it slide down her throat.

"I might have known better," she muttered to herself, "for where there is no grass there can be no live grasshoppers. This is probably one of the King's transformations."

A moment later she approached one of the purple ornaments, and while the Queen watched her curiously the hen broke the Nome King's enchantment and a sweet-faced girl, whose golden hair fell in a cloud over her shoulders, stood beside them.

"Evanna!" cried the Queen, "my own Evanna!" and she clasped the girl to her bosom and covered her face with kisses.

"That's all right," said Billina, contentedly. "Am I a good guesser, Mr. Nome King? Well, I guess!"

Then she disenchanted another girl, whom the Queen addressed as Evrose, and afterwards a boy named Evardo, who was older than his brother Evring. Indeed, the yellow hen kept the good Queen exclaiming and embracing for some time, until five Princesses and four Princes, all looking very much alike except for the difference in size, stood in a row beside their happy mother.

The Princesses were named, Evanna, Evrose, Evella, Evirene and Evedna, while the Princes were Evrob, Evington, Evardo and Evroland. Of these Evardo was the eldest and would inherit his father's throne and be crowned King of Ev when he returned to his own country. He was a grave and quiet youth, and would doubtless rule his people wisely and with justice.

Billina, having restored all of the royal family of Ev to their proper forms, now began to select the green ornaments which were the transformations of the people of Oz. She had little trouble in finding these, and before long all the twenty-six officers, as well as the private, were gathered around the yellow hen, joyfully congratulating her upon their release. The thirty-seven people who were now alive in the rooms of the palace knew very well that they owed their freedom to the cleverness of the yellow hen, and they were earnest in thanking her for saving them from the magic of the Nome King.

"Now," said Billina, "I must find Ozma. She is sure to be here, somewhere, and of course she is green, being from Oz. So look around, you stupid soldiers, and help me in my search."

For a while, however, they could discover nothing more that was green. But the Queen, who had kissed all her nine children once more and could now find time to take an interest in what was going on, said to the hen:

"Mayhap, my gentle friend, it is the grasshopper whom you seek."

"Of course it's the grasshopper!" exclaimed Billina. "I declare, I'm nearly as stupid as these brave soldiers. Wait here for me, and I'll go back and get it."

So she went into the room where she had seen the grasshopper, and presently Ozma of Oz, as lovely and dainty as ever, entered and approached the Queen of Ev, greeting her as one high born princess greets another.

"But where are my friends, the Scarecrow and the Tin Woodman?" asked the girl Ruler, when these courtesies had been exchanged.

"I'll hunt them up," replied Billina. "The Scarecrow is solid gold, and so is Tik-tok; but I don't exactly know what the Tin Woodman is, because the Nome King said he had been transformed into something funny."

Ozma eagerly assisted the hen in her quest, and soon the Scarecrow and the machine man, being ornaments of shining gold, were discovered and restored to their accustomed forms. But, search as they might, in no place could they find a funny ornament that might be the transformation of the Tin Woodman.

"Only one thing can be done," said Ozma, at last, "and that is to return to the Nome King and oblige him to tell us what has become of our friend."

"Perhaps he won't," suggested Billina.

"He must," returned Ozma, firmly. "The King has not treated us honestly, for under the mask of fairness and good nature he entrapped us all, and we would have been forever enchanted had not our wise and clever friend, the yellow hen, found a way to save us."

"The King is a villain," declared the Scarecrow.

"His laugh is worse than another man's frown," said the private, with a shudder.

"I thought he was hon-est, but I was mis-tak-en," remarked Tik-tok. "My thoughts are us-u-al-ly cor-rect, but it is Smith & Tin-ker's fault if they some-times go wrong or do not work prop-er-ly."

"Smith & Tinker made a very good job of you," said Ozma, kindly. "I do not think they should be blamed if you are not quite perfect."

"Thank you," replied Tik-tok.

"Then," said Billina, in her brisk little voice, "let us all go back to the Nome King, and see what he has to say for himself."

So they started for the entrance, Ozma going first, with the Queen and her train of little Princes and Princesses following. Then came Tik-tok, and the Scarecrow with Billina perched upon his straw-stuffed shoulder. The twenty-seven officers and the private brought up the rear.

As they reached the hall the doors flew open before them; but then they all stopped and stared into the domed cavern with faces of astonishment and dismay. For the room was filled with the mail-clad warriors of the Nome King, rank after rank standing in orderly array. The electric lights upon their brows gleamed brightly, their battle-axes were poised as if to strike down their foes; yet they remained motionless as statues, awaiting the word of command.

And in the center of this terrible army sat the little King upon his throne of rock. But he neither smiled nor laughed. Instead, his face was distorted with rage, and most dreadful to behold.

Chapter 17 - The Scarecrow Wins the Fight

After Billina had entered the palace Dorothy and Evring sat down to await the success or failure of her mission, and the Nome King occupied his throne and smoked his long pipe for a while in a cheerful and contented mood.

Then the bell above the throne, which sounded whenever an enchantment was broken, began to ring, and the King gave a start of annoyance and exclaimed, "Rocketty-ricketts!"

When the bell rang a second time the King shouted angrily, "Smudge and blazes!" and at a third ring he screamed in a fury, "Hippikaloric!" which must be a dreadful word because we don't know what it means.

After that the bell went on ringing time after time; but the King was now so violently enraged that he could not utter a word, but hopped out of his throne and all around the room in a mad frenzy, so that he reminded Dorothy of a jumping-jack.

The girl was, for her part, filled with joy at every peal of the bell, for it announced the fact that Billina had transformed one more ornament into a living person. Dorothy was also amazed at Billina's success, for she could not imagine how the yellow hen was able to guess correctly from all the bewildering number of articles clustered in the rooms of the palace. But after she had counted ten, and the bell continued to ring, she knew that not only the royal family of Ev, but Ozma and her followers also, were being restored to their natural forms, and she was so delighted that the antics of the angry King only made her laugh merrily.

Perhaps the little monarch could not be more furious than he was before, but the girl's laughter nearly drove him frantic, and he roared at her like a savage beast. Then, as he found that all his enchantments were likely to be dispelled and his victims every one set free, he suddenly ran to the little door that opened upon the balcony and gave the shrill whistle that summoned his warriors.

At once the army filed out of the gold and silver doors in great numbers, and marched up a winding stairs and into the throne room, led by a stern featured Nome who was their captain. When they had nearly filled the throne room they formed ranks in the big underground cavern below, and then stood still until they were told what to do next.

Dorothy had pressed back to one side of the cavern when the warriors entered, and now she stood holding little Prince Evring's hand while the great Lion crouched upon one side and the enormous Tiger crouched on the other side.

"Seize that girl!" shouted the King to his captain, and a group of warriors sprang forward to obey. But both the Lion and Tiger snarled so fiercely and bared their strong, sharp teeth so threateningly, that the men drew back in alarm.

"Don't mind them!" cried the Nome King; "they cannot leap beyond the places where they now stand."

"But they can bite those who attempt to touch the girl," said the captain.

"I'll fix that," answered the King. "I'll enchant them again, so that they can't open their jaws."

He stepped out of the throne to do this, but just then the Sawhorse ran up behind him and gave the fat monarch a powerful kick with both his wooden hind legs.

"Ow! Murder! Treason!" yelled the King, who had been hurled against several of his warriors and was considerably bruised. "Who did that?"

"I did," growled the Sawhorse, viciously. "You let Dorothy alone, or I'll kick you again."

"We'll see about that," replied the King, and at once he waved his hand toward the Sawhorse and muttered a magical word. "Aha!" he continued; "NOW let us see you move, you wooden mule!"

But in spite of the magic the Sawhorse moved; and he moved so quickly toward the King, that the fat little man could not get out of his way. Thump—BANG! came the wooden heels, right against his round body, and the King flew into the air and fell upon the head of his captain, who let him drop flat upon the ground.

"Well, well!" said the King, sitting up and looking surprised. "Why didn't my magic belt work, I wonder?"

"The creature is made of wood," replied the captain. "Your magic will not work on wood, you know."

"Ah, I'd forgotten that," said the King, getting up and limping to his throne. "Very well, let the girl alone. She can't escape us, anyway."

The warriors, who had been rather confused by these incidents, now formed their ranks again, and the Sawhorse pranced across the room to Dorothy and took a position beside the Hungry Tiger.

At that moment the doors that led to the palace flew open and the people of Ev and the people of Oz were disclosed to view. They paused, astonished, at sight of the warriors and the angry Nome King, seated in their midst.

"Surrender!" cried the King, in a loud voice. "You are my prisoners."

"Go 'long!" answered Billina, from the Scarecrow's shoulder. "You promised me that if I guessed correctly my friends and I might depart in safety. And you always keep your promises."

"I said you might leave the palace in safety," retorted the King; "and so you may, but you cannot leave my dominions. You are my prisoners, and I will hurl you all into my underground dungeons, where the volcanic fires glow and the molten lava flows in every direction, and the air is hotter than blue blazes."

"That will be the end of me, all right," said the Scarecrow, sorrowfully. "One small blaze, blue or green, is enough to reduce me to an ash-heap."

"Do you surrender?" demanded the King.

Billina whispered something in the Scarecrow's ear that made him smile and put his hands in his jacket pockets.

"No!" returned Ozma, boldly answering the King. Then she said to her army:

"Forward, my brave soldiers, and fight for your Ruler and yourselves, unto death!"

"Pardon me, Most Royal Ozma," replied one of her generals; "but I find that I and my brother officers all suffer from heart disease, and the slightest excitement might kill us. If we fight we may get excited. Would it not be well for us to avoid this grave danger?"

"Soldiers should not have heart disease," said Ozma.

"Private soldiers are not, I believe, afflicted that way," declared another general, twirling his moustache thoughtfully. "If your Royal Highness desires, we will order our private to attack yonder warriors."

"Do so," replied Ozma.

"For-ward—march!" cried all the generals, with one voice. "For-ward—march!" yelled the colonels. "For-ward—march!" shouted the majors. "For-ward—march!" commanded the captains.

And at that the private leveled his spear and dashed furiously upon the foe.

The captain of the Nomes was so surprised by this sudden onslaught that he forgot to command his warriors to fight, so that the ten men in the first row, who stood in front of the private's spear, fell over like so many toy soldiers. The spear could not go through their steel armor, however, so the warriors scrambled to their feet again, and by that time the private had knocked over another row of them.

Then the captain brought down his battle-axe with such a strong blow that the private's spear was shattered and knocked from his grasp, and he was helpless to fight any longer.

The Nome King had left his throne and pressed through his warriors to the front ranks, so he could see what was going on; but as he faced Ozma and her friends the Scarecrow, as if aroused to action by the valor of the private, drew one of Billina's eggs from his right jacket pocket and hurled it straight at the little monarch's head.

It struck him squarely in his left eye, where the egg smashed and scattered, as eggs will, and covered his face and hair and beard with its sticky contents.

"Help, help!" screamed the King, clawing with his fingers at the egg, in a struggle to remove it.

"An egg! an egg! Run for your lives!" shouted the captain of the Nomes, in a voice of horror.

And how they DID run! The warriors fairly tumbled over one another in their efforts to escape the fatal poison of that awful egg, and those who could not rush down the winding stair fell off the balcony into the great cavern beneath, knocking over those who stood below them.

Even while the King was still yelling for help his throne room became emptied of every one of his warriors, and before the monarch had managed to clear the egg away from his left eye the Scarecrow threw the second egg against his right eye, where it smashed and blinded him entirely. The King was unable to flee because he could not see which way to run; so he stood still and howled and shouted and screamed in abject fear.

While this was going on, Billina flew over to Dorothy, and perching herself upon the Lion's back the hen whispered eagerly to the girl:

"Get his belt! Get the Nome King's jeweled belt! It unbuckles in the back. Quick, Dorothy—quick!"

Chapter 18 - The Fate of the Tin Woodman

Dorothy obeyed. She ran at once behind the Nome King, who was still trying to free his eyes from the egg, and in a twinkling she had unbuckled his splendid jeweled belt and carried it away with her to her place beside the Tiger and Lion, where, because she did not know what else to do with it, she fastened it around her own slim waist.

Just then the Chief Steward rushed in with a sponge and a bowl of water, and began mopping away the broken eggs from his master's face. In a few minutes, and while all the party stood looking on, the King regained the use of his eyes, and the first thing he did was to glare wickedly upon the Scarecrow and exclaim:

"I'll make you suffer for this, you hay-stuffed dummy! Don't you know eggs are poison to Nomes?"

"Really," said the Scarecrow, "they DON'T seem to agree with you, although I wonder why."

"They were strictly fresh and above suspicion," said Billina. "You ought to be glad to get them."

"I'll transform you all into scorpions!" cried the King, angrily, and began waving his arms and muttering magic words.

But none of the people became scorpions, so the King stopped and looked at them in surprise.

"What's wrong?" he asked.

"Why, you are not wearing your magic belt," replied the Chief Steward, after looking the King over carefully. "Where is it? What have you done with it?"

The Nome King clapped his hand to his waist, and his rock colored face turned white as chalk.

"It's gone," he cried, helplessly. "It's gone, and I am ruined!"

Dorothy now stepped forward and said:

"Royal Ozma, and you, Queen of Ev, I welcome you and your people back to the land of the living. Billina has saved you from your troubles, and now we will leave this drea'ful place, and return to Ev as soon as poss'ble."

While the child spoke they could all see that she wore the magic belt, and a great cheer went up from all her friends, which was led by the voices of the Scarecrow and the private. But the Nome King did not join them. He crept back onto his throne like a whipped dog, and lay there bitterly bemoaning his defeat.

"But we have not yet found my faithful follower, the Tin Woodman," said Ozma to Dorothy, "and without him I do not wish to go away."

"Nor I," replied Dorothy, quickly. "Wasn't he in the palace?"

"He must be there," said Billina; "but I had no clue to guide me in guessing the Tin Woodman, so I must have missed him."

"We will go back into the rooms," said Dorothy. "This magic belt, I am sure, will help us to find our dear old friend."

So she re-entered the palace, the doors of which still stood open, and everyone followed her except the Nome King, the Queen of Ev and Prince Evring. The mother had taken the little Prince in her lap and was fondling and kissing him lovingly, for he was her youngest born.

But the others went with Dorothy, and when she came to the middle of the first room the girl waved her hand, as she had seen the King do, and commanded the Tin Woodman, whatever form he might then have, to resume his proper shape. No result followed this attempt, so Dorothy went into another room and repeated it, and so through all the rooms of the palace. Yet the Tin Woodman did not appear to them, nor could they imagine which among the thousands of ornaments was their transformed friend.

Sadly they returned to the throne room, where the King, seeing that they had met with failure, jeered at Dorothy, saying:

"You do not know how to use my belt, so it is of no use to you. Give it back to me and I will let you go free—you and all the people who came with you. As for the royal family of Ev, they are my slaves, and shall remain here."

"I shall keep the belt," said Dorothy.

"But how can you escape, without my consent?" asked the King.

"Easily enough," answered the girl. "All we need to do is to walk out the way that we came in."

"Oh, that's all, is it?" sneered the King. "Well, where is the passage through which you entered this room?"

They all looked around, but could not discover the place, for it had long since been closed. Dorothy, however, would not be dismayed. She waved her hand toward the seemingly solid wall of the cavern and said:

"I command the passage to open!"

Instantly the order was obeyed; the opening appeared and the passage lay plainly before them.

The King was amazed, and all the others overjoyed.

"Why, then, if the belt obeys you, were we unable to discover the Tin Woodman?" asked Ozma.

"I can't imagine," said Dorothy.

"See here, girl," proposed the King, eagerly; "give me the belt, and I will tell you what shape the Tin Woodman was changed into, and then you can easily find him."

Dorothy hesitated, but Billina cried out:

"Don't you do it! If the Nome King gets the belt again he will make every one of us prisoners, for we will be in his power. Only by keeping the belt, Dorothy, will you ever be able to leave this place in safety."

"I think that is true," said the Scarecrow. "But I have another idea, due to my excellent brains. Let Dorothy transform the King into a goose-egg unless he agrees to go into the palace and bring out to us the ornament which is our friend Nick Chopper, the Tin Woodman."

"A goose-egg!" echoed the horrified King. "How dreadful!"

"Well, a goose-egg you will be unless you go and fetch us the ornament we want," declared Billina, with a joyful chuckle.

"You can see for yourself that Dorothy is able to use the magic belt all right," added the Scarecrow.

The Nome King thought it over and finally consented, for he did not want to be a goose-egg. So he went into the palace to get the ornament which was the transformation of the Tin Woodman, and they all awaited his return with considerable impatience, for they were anxious to leave this underground cavern and see the sunshine once more. But when the Nome King came back he brought nothing with him except a puzzled and anxious expression upon his face.

"He's gone!" he said. "The Tin Woodman is nowhere in the palace."

"Are you sure?" asked Ozma, sternly.

"I'm very sure," answered the King, trembling, "for I know just what I transformed him into, and exactly where he stood. But he is not there, and please don't change me into a goose-egg, because I've done the best I could."

They were all silent for a time, and then Dorothy said:

"There is no use punishing the Nome King any more, and I'm 'fraid we'll have to go away without our friend."

"If he is not here, we cannot rescue him," agreed the Scarecrow, sadly. "Poor Nick! I wonder what has become of him."

"And he owed me six weeks back pay!" said one of the generals, wiping the tears from his eyes with his gold-laced coat sleeve.

Very sorrowfully they determined to return to the upper world without their former companion, and so Ozma gave the order to begin the march through the passage.

The army went first, and then the royal family of Ev, and afterward came Dorothy, Ozma, Billina, the Scarecrow and Tik-tok.

They left the Nome King scowling at them from his throne, and had no thought of danger until Ozma chanced to look back and saw a large number of the warriors following them in full chase, with their swords and spears and axes raised to strike down the fugitives as soon as they drew near enough.

Evidently the Nome King had made this last attempt to prevent their escaping him; but it did him no good, for when Dorothy saw the danger they were in she stopped and waved her hand and whispered a command to the magic belt.

Instantly the foremost warriors became eggs, which rolled upon the floor of the cavern in such numbers that those behind could not advance without stepping upon them. But, when they saw the eggs, all desire to advance departed from the warriors, and they turned and fled madly into the cavern, and refused to go back again.

Our friends had no further trouble in reaching the end of the passage, and soon were standing in the outer air upon the gloomy path between the two high mountains. But the way to Ev lay plainly before them, and they fervently hoped that they had seen the last of the Nome King and of his dreadful palace.

The cavalcade was led by Ozma, mounted on the Cowardly Lion, and the Queen of Ev, who rode upon the back of the Tiger. The children of the Queen walked behind her, hand in hand. Dorothy rode the Sawhorse, while the Scarecrow walked and commanded the army in the absence of the Tin Woodman.

Presently the way began to lighten and more of the sunshine to come in between the two mountains. And before long they heard the "thump! thump! thump!" of the giant's hammer upon the road.

"How may we pass the monstrous man of iron?" asked the Queen, anxious for the safety of her children. But Dorothy solved the problem by a word to the magic belt.

The giant paused, with his hammer held motionless in the air, thus allowing the entire party to pass between his cast-iron legs in safety.

Chapter 19 - The King of Ev

If there were any shifting, rock-colored Nomes on the mountain side now, they were silent and respectful, for our adventurers were not annoyed, as before, by their impudent laughter. Really the Nomes had nothing to laugh at, since the defeat of their King.

On the other side they found Ozma's golden chariot, standing as they had left it. Soon the Lion and the Tiger were harnessed to the beautiful chariot, in which was enough room for Ozma and the Queen and six of the royal children.

Little Evring preferred to ride with Dorothy upon the Sawhorse, which had a long back. The Prince had recovered from his shyness and had become very fond of the girl who had rescued him, so they were fast friends and chatted pleasantly together as they rode along. Billina was also perched upon the head of the wooden steed, which seemed not to mind the added weight in the least, and the boy was full of wonder that a hen could talk, and say such sensible things.

When they came to the gulf, Ozma's magic carpet carried them all over in safety; and now they began to pass the trees, in which birds were singing; and the breeze that was wafted to them from the farms of Ev was spicy with flowers and new-mown hay; and the sunshine fell full upon them, to warm them and drive away from their bodies the chill and dampness of the underground kingdom of the Nomes.

"I would be quite content," said the Scarecrow to Tik-tok, "were only the Tin Woodman with us. But it breaks my heart to leave him behind."

"He was a fine fel-low," replied Tik-tok, "al-though his ma-ter-i-al was not ve-ry du-ra-ble."

"Oh, tin is an excellent material," the Scarecrow hastened to say; "and if anything ever happened to poor Nick Chopper he was always easily soldered. Besides, he did not have to be wound up, and was not liable to get out of order."

"I some-times wish," said Tik-tok, "that I was stuffed with straw, as you are. It is hard to be made of cop-per."

"I have no reason to complain of my lot," replied the Scarecrow. "A little fresh straw, now and then, makes me as good as new. But I can never be the polished gentleman that my poor departed friend, the Tin Woodman, was."

You may be sure the royal children of Ev and their Queen mother were delighted at seeing again their beloved country; and when the towers of the palace of Ev came into view they could not forbear cheering at the sight. Little Evring, riding in front of Dorothy, was so overjoyed that he took a curious tin whistle from his pocket and blew a shrill blast that made the Sawhorse leap and prance in sudden alarm.

"What is that?" asked Billina, who had been obliged to flutter her wings in order to keep her seat upon the head of the frightened Sawhorse.

"That's my whistle," said Prince Evring, holding it out upon his hand.

It was in the shape of a little fat pig, made of tin and painted green. The whistle was in the tail of the pig.

"Where did you get it?" asked the yellow hen, closely examining the toy with her bright eyes.

"Why, I picked it up in the Nome King's palace, while Dorothy was making her guesses, and I put it in my pocket," answered the little Prince.

Billina laughed; or at least she made the peculiar cackle that served her for a laugh.

"No wonder I couldn't find the Tin Woodman," she said; "and no wonder the magic belt didn't make him appear, or the King couldn't find him, either!"

"What do you mean?" questioned Dorothy.

"Why, the Prince had him in his pocket," cried Billina, cackling again.

"I did not!" protested little Evring. "I only took the whistle."

"Well, then, watch me," returned the hen, and reaching out a claw she touched the whistle and said "Ev."

Swish!

"Good afternoon," said the Tin Woodman, taking off his funnel cap and bowing to Dorothy and the Prince. "I think I must have been asleep for the first time since I was made of tin, for I do not remember our leaving the Nome King."

"You have been enchanted," answered the girl, throwing an arm around her old friend and hugging him tight in her joy. "But it's all right, now."

"I want my whistle!" said the little Prince, beginning to cry.

"Hush!" cautioned Billina. "The whistle is lost, but you may have another when you get home."

The Scarecrow had fairly thrown himself upon the bosom of his old comrade, so surprised and delighted was he to see him again, and Tik-tok squeezed the Tin Woodman's hand so earnestly that he dented some of his fingers. Then they had to make way for Ozma to welcome the tin man, and the army caught sight of him and set up a cheer, and everybody was delighted and happy.

For the Tin Woodman was a great favorite with all who knew him, and his sudden recovery after they had thought he was lost to them forever was indeed a pleasant surprise.

Before long the cavalcade arrived at the royal palace, where a great crowd of people had gathered to welcome their Queen and her ten children. There was much shouting and cheering, and the people threw flowers in their path, and every face wore a happy smile.

They found the Princess Langwidere in her mirrored chamber, where she was admiring one of her handsomest heads—one with rich chestnut hair, dreamy walnut eyes and a shapely hickorynut nose. She was very glad to be relieved of her duties to the people of Ev, and the Queen graciously permitted her to retain her rooms and her cabinet of heads as long as she lived.

Then the Queen took her eldest son out upon a balcony that overlooked the crowd of subjects gathered below, and said to them:

"Here is your future ruler, King Evardo Fifteenth. He is fifteen years of age, has fifteen silver buckles on his jacket and is the fifteenth Evardo to rule the land of Ev."

The people shouted their approval fifteen times, and even the Wheelers, some of whom were present, loudly promised to obey the new King.

So the Queen placed a big crown of gold, set with rubies, upon Evardo's head, and threw an ermine robe over his shoulders, and proclaimed him King; and he bowed gratefully to all his subjects and then went away to see if he could find any cake in the royal pantry.

Ozma of Oz and her people, as well as Dorothy, Tik-tok and Billina, were splendidly entertained by the Queen mother, who owed all her happiness to their kind offices; and that evening the yellow hen was publicly presented with a beautiful necklace of pearls and sapphires, as a token of esteem from the new King.

Chapter 20 - The Emerald City

Dorothy decided to accept Ozma's invitation to return with her to the Land of Oz. There was no greater chance of her getting home from Ev than from Oz, and the little girl was anxious to see once more the country where she had encountered such wonderful adventures. By this time Uncle Henry would have reached Australia in his ship, and had probably given her up for lost; so he couldn't worry any more than he did if she stayed away from him a while longer. So she would go to Oz.

They bade good-bye to the people of Ev, and the King promised Ozma that he would ever be grateful to her and render the Land of Oz any service that might lie within his power.

And then they approached the edge of the dangerous desert, and Ozma threw down the magic carpet, which at once unrolled far enough for all of them to walk upon it without being crowded.

Tik-tok, claiming to be Dorothy's faithful follower because he belonged to her, had been permitted to join the party, and before they started the girl wound up his machinery as far as possible, and the copper man stepped off as briskly as any one of them.

Ozma also invited Billina to visit the Land of Oz, and the yellow hen was glad enough to go where new sights and scenes awaited her.

They began the trip across the desert early in the morning, and as they stopped only long enough for Billina to lay her daily egg, before sunset they espied the green slopes and wooded hills of the beautiful Land of Oz. They entered it in the Munchkin territory, and the King of the Munchkins met them at the border and welcomed Ozma with great respect, being very pleased by her safe return. For Ozma of Oz ruled the King of the Munchkins, the King of the Winkies, the King of the Quadlings and the King of the Gillikins just as those kings ruled their own people; and this supreme ruler of the Land of Oz lived in a great town of her own, called the Emerald City, which was in the exact center of the four kingdoms of the Land of Oz.

The Munchkin king entertained them at his palace that night, and in the morning they set out for the Emerald City, travelling over a road of yellow brick that led straight to the jewel-studded gates. Everywhere the people turned out to greet their beloved Ozma, and to hail joyfully the Scarecrow, the Tin Woodman and the Cowardly Lion, who were popular favorites. Dorothy, too, remembered some of the people, who had befriended her on the occasion of her first visit to Oz, and they were well pleased to see the little Kansas girl again, and showered her with compliments and good wishes.

At one place, where they stopped to refresh themselves, Ozma accepted a bowl of milk from the hands of a pretty dairy-maid. Then she looked at the girl more closely, and exclaimed:

"Why, it's Jinjur—isn't it!"

"Yes, your Highness," was the reply, as Jinjur dropped a low curtsy. And Dorothy looked wonderingly at this lively appearing person, who had once assembled an army of women and driven the Scarecrow from the throne of the Emerald City, and even fought a battle with the powerful army of Glinda the Sorceress.

"I've married a man who owns nine cows," said Jinjur to Ozma, "and now I am happy and contented and willing to lead a quiet life and mind my own business."

"Where is your husband?" asked Ozma.

"He is in the house, nursing a black eye," replied Jinjur, calmly. "The foolish man would insist upon milking the red cow when I wanted him to milk the white one; but he will know better next time, I am sure."

Then the party moved on again, and after crossing a broad river on a ferry and passing many fine farm houses that were dome shaped and painted a pretty green color, they came in sight of a large building that was covered with flags and bunting.

"I don't remember that building," said Dorothy. "What is it?"

"That is the College of Art and Athletic Perfection," replied Ozma. "I had it built quite recently, and the Woggle-Bug is it's president. It keeps him busy, and the young men who attend the college are no worse off than they were before. You see, in this country are a number of youths who do not like to work, and the college is an excellent place for them."

And now they came in sight of the Emerald City, and the people flocked out to greet their lovely ruler. There were several bands and many officers and officials of the realm, and a crowd of citizens in their holiday attire.

Thus the beautiful Ozma was escorted by a brilliant procession to her royal city, and so great was the cheering that she was obliged to constantly bow to the right and left to acknowledge the greetings of her subjects.

That evening there was a grand reception in the royal palace, attended by the most important persons of Oz, and Jack Pumpkinhead, who was a little overripe but still active, read an address congratulating Ozma of Oz upon the success of her generous mission to rescue the royal family of a neighboring kingdom.

Then magnificent gold medals set with precious stones were presented to each of the twenty-six officers; and the Tin Woodman was given a new axe studded with diamonds; and the Scarecrow received a silver jar of complexion powder. Dorothy was presented with a pretty coronet and made a Princess of Oz, and Tik-tok received two bracelets set with eight rows of very clear and sparkling emeralds.

Afterward they sat down to a splendid feast, and Ozma put Dorothy at her right and Billina at her left, where the hen sat upon a golden roost and ate from a jeweled platter. Then were placed the Scarecrow, the Tin Woodman and Tik-tok, with baskets of lovely flowers before them, because they did not require food. The twenty-six officers were at the lower end of the table, and the Lion and the Tiger also had seats, and were served on golden platters, that held a half a bushel at one time.

The wealthiest and most important citizens of the Emerald City were proud to wait upon these famous adventurers, and they were assisted by a sprightly little maid named Jellia Jamb, whom the Scarecrow pinched upon her rosy cheeks and seemed to know very well.

During the feast Ozma grew thoughtful, and suddenly she asked:

"Where is the private?"

"Oh, he is sweeping out the barracks," replied one of the generals, who was busy eating a leg of a turkey. "But I have ordered him a dish of bread and molasses to eat when his work is done."

"Let him be sent for," said the girl ruler.

While they waited for this command to be obeyed, she enquired:

"Have we any other privates in the armies?"

"Oh, yes," replied the Tin Woodman, "I believe there are three, altogether."

The private now entered, saluting his officers and the royal Ozma very respectfully.

"What is your name, my man?" asked the girl.

"Omby Amby," answered the private.

"Then, Omby Amby," said she, "I promote you to be Captain General of all the armies of my kingdom, and especially to be Commander of my Body Guard at the royal palace."

"It is very expensive to hold so many offices," said the private, hesitating. "I have no money with which to buy uniforms."

"You shall be supplied from the royal treasury," said Ozma.

Then the private was given a seat at the table, where the other officers welcomed him cordially, and the feasting and merriment were resumed.

Suddenly Jellia Jamb exclaimed:

"There is nothing more to eat! The Hungry Tiger has consumed everything!"

"But that is not the worst of it," declared the Tiger, mournfully. "Somewhere or somehow, I've actually lost my appetite!"

Chapter 21 - Dorothy's Magic Belt

Dorothy passed several very happy weeks in the Land of Oz as the guest of the royal Ozma, who delighted to please and interest the little Kansas girl. Many new acquaintances were formed and many old ones renewed, and wherever she went Dorothy found herself among friends.

One day, however, as she sat in Ozma's private room, she noticed hanging upon the wall a picture which constantly changed in appearance, at one time showing a meadow and at another time a forest, a lake or a village.

"How curious!" she exclaimed, after watching the shifting scenes for a few moments.

"Yes," said Ozma, "that is really a wonderful invention in magic. If I wish to see any part of the world or any person living, I need only express the wish and it is shown in the picture."

"May I use it?" asked Dorothy, eagerly.

"Of course, my dear."

"Then I'd like to see the old Kansas farm, and Aunt Em," said the girl.

Instantly the well remembered farmhouse appeared in the picture, and Aunt Em could be seen quite plainly. She was engaged in washing dishes by the kitchen window and seemed quite well and contented. The hired men and the teams were in the harvest fields behind the house, and the corn and wheat seemed to the child to be in prime condition. On the side porch Dorothy's pet dog, Toto, was lying fast asleep in the sun, and to her surprise old Speckles was running around with a brood of twelve new chickens trailing after her.

"Everything seems all right at home," said Dorothy, with a sigh of relief. "Now I wonder what Uncle Henry is doing."

The scene in the picture at once shifted to Australia, where, in a pleasant room in Sydney, Uncle Henry was seated in an easy chair, solemnly smoking his briar pipe. He looked sad and lonely, and his hair was now quite white and his hands and face thin and wasted.

"Oh!" cried Dorothy, in an anxious voice, "I'm sure Uncle Henry isn't getting any better, and it's because he is worried about me. Ozma, dear, I must go to him at once!"

"How can you?" asked Ozma.

"I don't know," replied Dorothy; "but let us go to Glinda the Good. I'm sure she will help me, and advise me how to get to Uncle Henry."

Ozma readily agreed to this plan and caused the Sawhorse to be harnessed to a pretty green and pink phaeton, and the two girls rode away to visit the famous sorceress.

Glinda received them graciously, and listened to Dorothy's story with attention.

"I have the magic belt, you know," said the little girl. "If I buckled it around my waist and commanded it to take me to Uncle Henry, wouldn't it do it?"

"I think so," replied Glinda, with a smile.

"And then," continued Dorothy, "if I ever wanted to come back here again, the belt would bring me."

"In that you are wrong," said the sorceress. "The belt has magical powers only while it is in some fairy country, such as the Land of Oz, or the Land of Ev. Indeed, my little friend, were you to wear it and wish yourself in Australia, with your uncle, the wish would doubtless be fulfilled, because it was made in fairyland. But you would not find the magic belt around you when you arrived at your destination."

"What would become of it?" asked the girl.

"It would be lost, as were your silver shoes when you visited Oz before, and no one would see it again. It seems too bad to destroy the use of the magic belt in that way, doesn't it?"

"Then," said Dorothy, after a moment's thought, "I will give the magic belt to Ozma, for she can use it in her own country. And she can wish me transported to Uncle Henry without losing the belt."

"That is a wise plan," replied Glinda.

So they rode back to the Emerald City, and on the way it was arranged that every Saturday morning Ozma would look at Dorothy in her magic picture, wherever the little girl might chance to be. And, if she saw Dorothy make a certain signal, then Ozma would know that the little Kansas girl wanted to revisit the Land of Oz, and by means of the Nome King's magic belt would wish that she might instantly return.

This having been agreed upon, Dorothy bade good-bye to all her friends. Tik-tok wanted to go to Australia; too, but Dorothy knew that the machine man would never do for a servant in a civilized country, and the chances were that his machinery wouldn't work at all. So she left him in Ozma's care.

Billina, on the contrary, preferred the Land of Oz to any other country, and refused to accompany Dorothy.

"The bugs and ants that I find here are the finest flavored in the world," declared the yellow hen, "and there are plenty of them. So here I shall end my days; and I must say, Dorothy, my dear, that you are very foolish to go back into that stupid, humdrum world again."

"Uncle Henry needs me," said Dorothy, simply; and every one except Billina thought it was right that she should go.

All Dorothy's friends of the Land of Oz—both old and new—gathered in a group in front of the palace to bid her a sorrowful good-bye and to wish her long life and happiness. After much hand shaking, Dorothy kissed Ozma once more, and then handed her the Nome King's magic belt, saying:

"Now, dear Princess, when I wave my handkerchief, please wish me with Uncle Henry. I'm aw'fly sorry to leave you—and the Scarecrow—and the Tin Woodman—and the Cowardly Lion—and Tik-tok—and—and everybody—but I do want my Uncle Henry! So good-bye, all of you."

Then the little girl stood on one of the big emeralds which decorated the courtyard, and after looking once again at each of her friends, waved her handkerchief.

"No," said Dorothy, "I wasn't drowned at all. And I've come to nurse you and take care of you, Uncle Henry, and you must promise to get well as soon as poss'ble."

Uncle Henry smiled and cuddled his little niece close in his lap.

"I'm better already, my darling," said he.

The End

Dorothy and the Wizard of Oz

Introduction

A Faithful Record of Their Amazing Adventures in an Underground World; and How with the Aid of Their Friends Zeb Hugson, Eureka the Kitten, and Jim the Cab-Horse, they Finally Reached the Wonderful Land of Oz.

By

L. Frank Baum "Royal Historian of Oz"

To My Readers

It's no use; no use at all. The children won't let me stop telling tales of the Land of Oz. I know lots of other stories, and I hope to tell them, some time or another; but just now my loving tyrants won't allow me. They cry: "Oz—Oz! more about Oz, Mr. Baum!" and what can I do but obey their commands?

This is Our Book—mine and the children's. For they have flooded me with thousands of suggestions in regard to it, and I have honestly tried to adopt as many of these suggestions as could be fitted into one story.

After the wonderful success of "Ozma of Oz" it is evident that Dorothy has become a firm fixture in these Oz stories. The little ones all love Dorothy, and as one of my small friends aptly states: "It isn't a real Oz story without her." So here she is again, as sweet and gentle and innocent as ever, I hope, and the heroine of another strange adventure.

There were many requests from my little correspondents for "more about the Wizard." It seems the jolly old fellow made hosts of friends in the first Oz book, in spite of the fact that he frankly acknowledged himself "a humbug." The children had heard how he mounted into the sky in a balloon and they were all waiting for him to come down again. So what could I do but tell "what happened to the Wizard afterward"? You will find him in these pages, just the same humbug Wizard as before.

There was one thing the children demanded which I found it impossible to do in this present book: they bade me introduce Toto, Dorothy's little black dog, who has many friends among my readers. But you will see, when you begin to read the story, that Toto was in Kansas while Dorothy was in California, and so she had to start on her adventure without him. In this book Dorothy had to take her kitten with her instead of her dog; but in the next Oz book, if I am permitted to write one, I intend to tell a good deal about Toto's further history.

Princess Ozma, whom I love as much as my readers do, is again introduced in this story, and so are several of our old friends of Oz. You will also become acquainted with Jim the Cab-Horse, the Nine Tiny Piglets, and Eureka, the Kitten. I am sorry the kitten was not as well behaved as she ought to have been; but perhaps she wasn't brought up properly. Dorothy found her, you see, and who her parents were nobody knows.

I believe, my dears, that I am the proudest story-teller that ever lived. Many a time tears of pride and joy have stood in my eyes while I read the tender, loving, appealing letters that came to me in almost every mail from my little readers. To have pleased you, to have interested you, to have won your friendship, and perhaps your love, through my stories, is to my mind as great an achievement as to become President of the United States. Indeed, I would much rather be your story-teller, under these conditions, than to be the President. So you have helped me to fulfill my life's ambition, and I am more grateful to you, my dears, than I can express in words.

I try to answer every letter of my young correspondents; yet sometimes there are so many letters that a little time must pass before you get your answer. But be patient, friends, for the answer will surely come, and by writing to me you more than repay me for the pleasant task of preparing these books. Besides, I am proud to acknowledge that the books are partly yours, for your suggestions often guide me in telling the stories, and I am sure they would not be half so good without your clever and thoughtful assistance.

L. FRANK BAUM Coronado, 1908.

LIST OF CHAPTERS

Chapter 1 - The Earthquake

The train from 'Frisco was very late. It should have arrived at Hugson's Siding at midnight, but it was already five o'clock and the gray dawn was breaking in the east when the little train slowly rumbled up to the open shed that served for the station-house. As it came to a stop the conductor called out in a loud voice:

"Hugson's Siding!"

At once a little girl rose from her seat and walked to the door of the car, carrying a wicker suit-case in one hand and a round bird-cage covered up with newspapers in the other, while a parasol was tucked under her arm. The conductor helped her off the car and then the engineer started his train again, so that it puffed and groaned and moved slowly away up the track. The reason he was so late was because all through the night there were times when the solid earth shook and trembled under him, and the engineer was afraid that at any moment the rails might spread apart and an accident happen to his passengers. So he moved the cars slowly and with caution.

The little girl stood still to watch until the train had disappeared around a curve; then she turned to see where she was.

The shed at Hugson's Siding was bare save for an old wooden bench, and did not look very inviting. As she peered through the soft gray light not a house of any sort was visible near the station, nor was any person in sight; but after a while the child discovered a horse and buggy standing near a group of trees a short distance away. She walked toward it and found the horse tied to a tree and standing motionless, with its head hanging down almost to the ground. It was a big horse, tall and bony, with long legs and large knees and feet. She could count his ribs easily where they showed through the skin of his body, and his head was long and seemed altogether too big for him, as if it did not fit. His tail was short and scraggly, and his harness had been broken in many places and fastened together again with cords and bits of wire. The buggy seemed almost new, for it had a shiny top and side curtains. Getting around in front, so that she could look inside, the girl saw a boy curled up on the seat, fast asleep.

She set down the bird-cage and poked the boy with her parasol. Presently he woke up, rose to a sitting position and rubbed his eyes briskly.

"Hello!" he said, seeing her, "are you Dorothy Gale?"

"Yes," she answered, looking gravely at his tousled hair and blinking gray eyes. "Have you come to take me to Hugson's Ranch?"

"Of course," he answered. "Train in?"

"I couldn't be here if it wasn't," she said.

He laughed at that, and his laugh was merry and frank. Jumping out of the buggy he put Dorothy's suit-case under the seat and her bird-cage on the floor in front.

"Canary-birds?" he asked.

"Oh no; it's just Eureka, my kitten. I thought that was the best way to carry her."

The boy nodded.

"Eureka's a funny name for a cat," he remarked.

"I named my kitten that because I found it," she explained. "Uncle Henry says 'Eureka' means 'I have found it.'"

"All right; hop in."

She climbed into the buggy and he followed her. Then the boy picked up the reins, shook them, and said "Gid-dap!"

The horse did not stir. Dorothy thought he just wiggled one of his drooping ears, but that was all.

"Gid-dap!" called the boy, again.

The horse stood still.

"Perhaps," said Dorothy, "if you untied him, he would go."

The boy laughed cheerfully and jumped out.

"Guess I'm half asleep yet," he said, untying the horse. "But Jim knows his business all right—don't you, Jim?" patting the long nose of the animal.

Then he got into the buggy again and took the reins, and the horse at once backed away from the tree, turned slowly around, and began to trot down the sandy road which was just visible in the dim light.

"Thought that train would never come," observed the boy. "I've waited at that station for five hours."

"We had a lot of earthquakes," said Dorothy. "Didn't you feel the ground shake?"

"Yes; but we're used to such things in California," he replied. "They don't scare us much."

"The conductor said it was the worst quake he ever knew."

"Did he? Then it must have happened while I was asleep," he said thoughtfully.

"How is Uncle Henry?" she enquired, after a pause during which the horse continued to trot with long, regular strides.

"He's pretty well. He and Uncle Hugson have been having a fine visit."

"Is Mr. Hugson your uncle?" she asked.

"Yes. Uncle Bill Hugson married your Uncle Henry's wife's sister; so we must be second cousins," said the boy, in an amused tone. "I work for Uncle Bill on his ranch, and he pays me six dollars a month and my board."

"Isn't that a great deal?" she asked, doubtfully.

"Why, it's a great deal for Uncle Hugson, but not for me. I'm a splendid worker. I work as well as I sleep," he added, with a laugh.

"What is your name?" said Dorothy, thinking she liked the boy's manner and the cheery tone of his voice.

"Not a very pretty one," he answered, as if a little ashamed. "My whole name is Zebediah; but folks just call me 'Zeb.' You've been to Australia, haven't you?"

"Yes; with Uncle Henry," she answered. "We got to San Francisco a week ago, and Uncle Henry went right on to Hugson's Ranch for a visit while I stayed a few days in the city with some friends we had met."

"How long will you be with us?" he asked.

"Only a day. Tomorrow Uncle Henry and I must start back for Kansas. We've been away for a long time, you know, and so we're anxious to get home again."

The boy flicked the big, boney horse with his whip and looked thoughtful. Then he started to say something to his little companion, but before he could speak the buggy began to sway dangerously from side to side and the earth seemed to rise up before them. Next minute there was a roar and a sharp crash, and at her side Dorothy saw the ground open in a wide crack and then come together again.

"Goodness!" she cried, grasping the iron rail of the seat. "What was that?"

"That was an awful big quake," replied Zeb, with a white face. "It almost got us that time, Dorothy."

The horse had stopped short, and stood firm as a rock. Zeb shook the reins and urged him to go, but Jim was stubborn. Then the boy cracked his whip and touched the animal's flanks with it, and after a low moan of protest Jim stepped slowly along the road.

Neither the boy nor the girl spoke again for some minutes. There was a breath of danger in the very air, and every few moments the earth would shake violently. Jim's ears were standing erect upon his head and every muscle of his big body was tense as he trotted toward home. He was not going very fast, but on his flanks specks of foam began to appear and at times he would tremble like a leaf.

The sky had grown darker again and the wind made queer sobbing sounds as it swept over the valley.

Suddenly there was a rending, tearing sound, and the earth split into another great crack just beneath the spot where the horse was standing. With a wild neigh of terror the animal fell bodily into the pit, drawing the buggy and its occupants after him.

Dorothy grabbed fast hold of the buggy top and the boy did the same. The sudden rush into space confused them so that they could not think.

Blackness engulfed them on every side, and in breathless silence they waited for the fall to end and crush them against jagged rocks or for the earth to close in on them again and bury them forever in its dreadful depths.

The horrible sensation of falling, the darkness and the terrifying noises, proved more than Dorothy could endure and for a few moments the little girl lost consciousness. Zeb, begin a boy, did not faint, but he was badly frightened, and clung to the buggy seat with a tight grip, expecting every moment would be his last.

Chapter 2 - The Glass City

When Dorothy recovered her senses they were still falling, but not so fast. The top of the buggy caught the air like a parachute or an umbrella filled with wind, and held them back so that they floated downward with a gentle motion that was not so very disagreeable to bear. The worst thing was their terror of reaching the bottom of this great crack in the earth, and the natural fear that sudden death was about to overtake them at any moment. Crash after crash echoed far above their heads, as the earth came together where it had split, and stones and chunks of clay rattled around them on every side. These they could not see, but they could feel them pelting the buggy top, and Jim screamed almost like a human being when a stone overtook him and struck his boney body. They did not really hurt the poor horse, because everything was falling together; only the stones and rubbish fell faster than the horse and buggy, which were held back by the pressure of the air, so that the terrified animal was actually more frightened than he was injured.

How long this state of things continued Dorothy could not even guess, she was so greatly bewildered. But bye and bye, as she stared ahead into the black chasm with a beating heart, she began to dimly see the form of the horse Jim—his head up in the air, his ears erect and his long legs sprawling in every direction as he tumbled through space. Also, turning her head, she found that she could see the boy beside her, who had until now remained as still and silent as she herself.

Dorothy sighed and commenced to breathe easier. She began to realize that death was not in store for her, after all, but that she had merely started upon another adventure, which promised to be just as queer and unusual as were those she had before encountered.

With this thought in mind the girl took heart and leaned her head over the side of the buggy to see where the strange light was coming from. Far below her she found six great glowing balls suspended in the air. The central and largest one was white, and reminded her of the sun. Around it were arranged, like the five points of a star, the other five brilliant balls; one being rose colored, one violet, one yellow, one blue and one orange. This splendid group of colored suns sent rays darting in every direction, and as the horse and buggy—with Dorothy and Zeb—sank steadily downward and came nearer to the lights, the rays began to take on all the delicate tintings of a rainbow, growing more and more distinct every moment until all the space was brilliantly illuminated.

Dorothy was too dazed to say much, but she watched one of Jim's big ears turn to violet and the other to rose, and wondered that his tail should be yellow and his body striped with blue and orange like the stripes of a zebra. Then she looked at Zeb, whose face was blue and whose hair was pink, and gave a little laugh that sounded a bit nervous.

"Isn't it funny?" she said.

The boy was startled and his eyes were big. Dorothy had a green streak through the center of her face where the blue and yellow lights came together, and her appearance seemed to add to his fright.

"I—I don't s-s-see any-thing funny—'bout it!" he stammered.

Just then the buggy tipped slowly over upon its side, the body of the horse tipping also. But they continued to fall, all together, and the boy and girl had no difficulty in remaining upon the seat, just as they were before. Then they turned bottom side up, and continued to roll slowly over until they were right side up again. During this time Jim struggled frantically, all his legs kicking the air; but on finding himself in his former position the horse said, in a relieved tone of voice:

"Well, that's better!"

Dorothy and Zeb looked at one another in wonder.

"Can your horse talk?" she asked.

"Never knew him to, before," replied the boy.

"Those were the first words I ever said," called out the horse, who had overheard them, "and I can't explain why I happened to speak then. This is a nice scrape you've got me into, isn't it?"

"As for that, we are in the same scrape ourselves," answered Dorothy, cheerfully. "But never mind; something will happen pretty soon."

"Of course," growled the horse, "and then we shall be sorry it happened."

Zeb gave a shiver. All this was so terrible and unreal that he could not understand it at all, and so had good reason to be afraid.

Swiftly they drew near to the flaming colored suns, and passed close beside them. The light was then so bright that it dazzled their eyes, and they covered their faces with their hands to escape being blinded. There was no heat in the colored suns, however, and after they had passed below them the top of the buggy shut out many of the piercing rays so that the boy and girl could open their eyes again.

"We've got to come to the bottom some time," remarked Zeb, with a deep sigh. "We can't keep falling forever, you know."

"Of course not," said Dorothy. "We are somewhere in the middle of the earth, and the chances are we'll reach the other side of it before long. But it's a big hollow, isn't it?"

"Awful big!" answered the boy.

"We're coming to something now," announced the horse.

At this they both put their heads over the side of the buggy and looked down. Yes; there was land below them; and not so very far away, either. But they were floating very, very slowly—so slowly that it could no longer be called a fall—and the children had ample time to take heart and look about them.

They saw a landscape with mountains and plains, lakes and rivers, very like those upon the earth's surface; but all the scene was splendidly colored by the variegated lights from the six suns. Here and there were groups of houses that seemed made of clear glass, because they sparkled so brightly.

"I'm sure we are in no danger," said Dorothy, in a sober voice. "We are falling so slowly that we can't be dashed to pieces when we land, and this country that we are coming to seems quite pretty."

"We'll never get home again, though!" declared Zeb, with a groan.

"Oh, I'm not so sure of that," replied the girl. "But don't let us worry over such things, Zeb; we can't help ourselves just now, you know, and I've always been told it's foolish to borrow trouble."

The boy became silent, having no reply to so sensible a speech, and soon both were fully occupied in staring at the strange scenes spread out below them. They seemed to be falling right into the middle of a big city which had many tall buildings with glass domes and sharp-pointed spires. These spires were like great spear-points, and if they tumbled upon one of them they were likely to suffer serious injury.

Jim the horse had seen these spires, also, and his ears stood straight up with fear, while Dorothy and Zeb held their breaths in suspense. But no; they floated gently down upon a broad, flat roof, and came to a stop at last.

When Jim felt something firm under his feet the poor beast's legs trembled so much that he could hardly stand; but Zeb at once leaped out of the buggy to the roof, and he was so awkward and hasty that he kicked over Dorothy's bird-cage, which rolled out upon the roof so that the bottom came off. At once a pink kitten crept out of the upset cage, sat down upon the glass roof, and yawned and blinked its round eyes.

"Oh," said Dorothy. "There's Eureka."

"First time I ever saw a pink cat," said Zeb.

"Eureka isn't pink; she's white. It's this queer light that gives her that color."

"Where's my milk?" asked the kitten, looking up into Dorothy's face. "I'm 'most starved to death."

"Oh, Eureka! Can you talk?"

"Talk! Am I talking? Good gracious, I believe I am. Isn't it funny?" asked the kitten.

"It's all wrong." said Zeb, gravely. "Animals ought not to talk. But even old Jim has been saying things since we had our accident."

"I can't see that it's wrong," remarked Jim, in his gruff tones. "At least, it isn't as wrong as some other things. What's going to become of us now?"

"I don't know," answered the boy, looking around him curiously.

The houses of the city were all made of glass, so clear and transparent that one could look through the walls as easily as through a window. Dorothy saw, underneath the roof on which she stood, several rooms used for rest chambers, and even thought she could make out a number of queer forms huddled into the corners of these rooms.

The roof beside them had a great hole smashed through it, and pieces of glass were lying scattered in every direction. A nearby steeple had been broken off short and the fragments lay heaped beside it. Other buildings were cracked in places or had corners chipped off from them; but they must have been very beautiful before these accidents had happened to mar their perfection. The rainbow tints from the colored suns fell upon the glass city softly and gave to the buildings many delicate, shifting hues which were very pretty to see.

But not a sound had broken the stillness since the strangers had arrived, except that of their own voices. They began to wonder if there were no people to inhabit this magnificent city of the inner world.

Suddenly a man appeared through a hole in the roof next to the one they were on and stepped into plain view. He was not a very large man, but was well formed and had a beautiful face—calm and serene as the face of a fine portrait. His clothing fitted his form snugly and was gorgeously colored in brilliant shades of green, which varied as the sunbeams touched them but was not wholly influenced by the solar rays.

The man had taken a step or two across the glass roof before he noticed the presence of the strangers; but then he stopped abruptly. There was no expression of either fear or surprise upon his tranquil face, yet he must have been both astonished and afraid; for after his eyes had rested upon the ungainly form of the horse for a moment he walked rapidly to the furthest edge of the roof, his head turned back over his shoulder to gaze at the strange animal.

"Look out!" cried Dorothy, who noticed that the beautiful man did not look where he was going; "be careful, or you'll fall off!"

But he paid no attention to her warning. He reached the edge of the tall roof, stepped one foot out into the air, and walked into space as calmly as if he were on firm ground.

The girl, greatly astonished, ran to lean over the edge of the roof, and saw the man walking rapidly through the air toward the ground. Soon he reached the street and disappeared through a glass doorway into one of the glass buildings.

"How strange!" she exclaimed, drawing a long breath.

"Yes; but it's lots of fun, if it IS strange," remarked the small voice of the kitten, and Dorothy turned to find her pet walking in the air a foot or so away from the edge of the roof.

"Come back, Eureka!" she called, in distress, "you'll certainly be killed."

"I have nine lives," said the kitten, purring softly as it walked around in a circle and then came back to the roof; "but I can't lose even one of them by falling in this country, because I really couldn't manage to fall if I wanted to."

"Does the air bear up your weight?" asked the girl.

"Of course; can't you see?" and again the kitten wandered into the air and back to the edge of the roof.

"It's wonderful!" said Dorothy.

"Suppose we let Eureka go down to the street and get some one to help us," suggested Zeb, who had been even more amazed than Dorothy at these strange happenings.

"Perhaps we can walk on the air ourselves," replied the girl.

Zeb drew back with a shiver.

"I wouldn't dare try," he said.

"Maybe Jim will go," continued Dorothy, looking at the horse.

"And maybe he won't!" answered Jim. "I've tumbled through the air long enough to make me contented on this roof."

"But we didn't tumble to the roof," said the girl; "by the time we reached here we were floating very slowly, and I'm almost sure we could float down to the street without getting hurt. Eureka walks on the air all right."

"Eureka weights only about half a pound," replied the horse, in a scornful tone, "while I weigh about half a ton."

"You don't weigh as much as you ought to, Jim," remarked the girl, shaking her head as she looked at the animal. "You're dreadfully skinny."

"Oh, well; I'm old," said the horse, hanging his head despondently, "and I've had lots of trouble in my day, little one. For a good many years I drew a public cab in Chicago, and that's enough to make anyone skinny."

"He eats enough to get fat, I'm sure," said the boy, gravely.

"Do I? Can you remember any breakfast that I've had today?" growled Jim, as if he resented Zeb's speech.

"None of us has had breakfast," said the boy; "and in a time of danger like this it's foolish to talk about eating."

"Nothing is more dangerous than being without food," declared the horse, with a sniff at the rebuke of his young master; "and just at present no one can tell whether there are any oats in this queer country or not. If there are, they are liable to be glass oats!"

"Oh, no!" exclaimed Dorothy. "I can see plenty of nice gardens and fields down below us, at the edge of this city. But I wish we could find a way to get to the ground."

"Why don't you walk down?" asked Eureka. "I'm as hungry as the horse is, and I want my milk."

"Will you try it, Zeb" asked the girl, turning to her companion.

Zeb hesitated. He was still pale and frightened, for this dreadful adventure had upset him and made him nervous and worried. But he did not wish the little girl to think him a coward, so he advanced slowly to the edge of the roof.

Dorothy stretched out a hand to him and Zeb put one foot out and let it rest in the air a little over the edge of the roof. It seemed firm enough to walk upon, so he took courage and put out the other foot. Dorothy kept hold of his hand and followed him, and soon they were both walking through the air, with the kitten frisking beside them.

"Come on, Jim!" called the boy. "It's all right."

Jim had crept to the edge of the roof to look over, and being a sensible horse and quite experienced, he made up his mind that he could go where the others did. So, with a snort and a neigh and a whisk of his short tail he trotted off the roof into the air and at once began floating downward to the street. His great weight made him fall faster than the children walked, and he passed them on the way down; but when he came to the glass pavement he alighted upon it so softly that he was not even jarred.

"Well, well!" said Dorothy, drawing a long breath, "What a strange country this is."

People began to come out of the glass doors to look at the new arrivals, and pretty soon quite a crowd had assembled. There were men and women, but no children at all, and the folks were all beautifully formed and attractively dressed and had wonderfully handsome faces. There was not an ugly person in all the throng, yet Dorothy was not especially pleased by the appearance of these people because their features had no more expression than the faces of dolls. They did not smile nor did they frown, or show either fear or surprise or curiosity or friendliness. They simply started at the strangers, paying most attention to Jim and Eureka, for they had never before seen either a horse or a cat and the children bore an outward resemblance to themselves.

Pretty soon a man joined the group who wore a glistening star in the dark hair just over his forehead. He seemed to be a person of authority, for the others pressed back to give him room. After turning his composed eyes first upon the animals and then upon the children he said to Zeb, who was a little taller than Dorothy:

"Tell me, intruder, was it you who caused the Rain of Stones?"

For a moment the boy did not know what he meant by this question. Then, remembering the stones that had fallen with them and passed them long before they had reached this place, he answered:

"No, sir; we didn't cause anything. It was the earthquake."

The man with the star stood for a time quietly thinking over this speech. Then he asked:

"What is an earthquake?"

"I don't know," said Zeb, who was still confused. But Dorothy, seeing his perplexity, answered:

"It's a shaking of the earth. In this quake a big crack opened and we fell through—horse and buggy, and all—and the stones got loose and came down with us."

The man with the star regarded her with his calm, expressionless eyes.

"The Rain of Stones has done much damage to our city," he said; "and we shall hold you responsible for it unless you can prove your innocence."

"How can we do that?" asked the girl.

"That I am not prepared to say. It is your affair, not mine. You must go to the House of the Sorcerer, who will soon discover the truth."

"Where is the House of the Sorcerer?" the girl enquired.

"I will lead you to it. Come!"

He turned and walked down the street, and after a moment's hesitation Dorothy caught Eureka in her arms and climbed into the buggy. The boy took his seat beside her and said: "Gid-dap Jim."

As the horse ambled along, drawing the buggy, the people of the glass city made way for them and formed a procession in their rear. Slowly they moved down one street and up another, turning first this way and then that, until they came to an open square in the center of which was a big glass palace having a central dome and four tall spires on each corner.

Chapter 3 - The Arrival of the Wizard

The doorway of the glass palace was quite big enough for the horse and buggy to enter, so Zeb drove straight through it and the children found themselves in a lofty hall that was very beautiful. The people at once followed and formed a circle around the sides of the spacious room, leaving the horse and buggy and the man with the star to occupy the center of the hall.

"Come to us, oh, Gwig!" called the man, in a loud voice.

Instantly a cloud of smoke appeared and rolled over the floor; then it slowly spread and ascended into the dome, disclosing a strange personage seated upon a glass throne just before Jim's nose. He was formed just as were the other inhabitants of this land and his clothing only differed from theirs in being bright yellow. But he had no hair at all, and all over his bald head and face and upon the backs of his hands grew sharp thorns like those found on the branches of rose-bushes. There was even a thorn upon the tip of his nose and he looked so funny that Dorothy laughed when she saw him.

The Sorcerer, hearing the laugh, looked toward the little girl with cold, cruel eyes, and his glance made her grow sober in an instant.

"Why have you dared to intrude your unwelcome persons into the secluded Land of the Mangaboos?" he asked, sternly.

"'Cause we couldn't help it," said Dorothy.

"Why did you wickedly and viciously send the Rain of Stones to crack and break our houses?" he continued.

"We didn't," declared the girl.

"Prove it!" cried the Sorcerer.

"We don't have to prove it," answered Dorothy, indignantly. "If you had any sense at all you'd known it was the earthquake."

"We only know that yesterday came a Rain of Stones upon us, which did much damage and injured some of our people. Today came another Rain of Stones, and soon after it you appeared among us."

164

"By the way," said the man with the star, looking steadily at the Sorcerer, "you told us yesterday that there would not be a second Rain of Stones. Yet one has just occurred that was even worse than the first. What is your sorcery good for if it cannot tell us the truth?"

"My sorcery does tell the truth!" declared the thorn-covered man. "I said there would be but one Rain of Stones. This second one was a Rain of People-and-Horse-and-Buggy. And some stones came with them."

"Will there be any more Rains?" asked the man with the star.

"No, my Prince."

"Neither stones nor people?"

"No, my Prince."

"Are you sure?"

"Quite sure, my Prince. My sorcery tells me so."

Just then a man came running into the hall and addressed the Prince after making a low bow.

"More wonders in the air, my Lord," said he.

Immediately the Prince and all of his people flocked out of the hall into the street, that they might see what was about to happen. Dorothy and Zeb jumped out of the buggy and ran after them, but the Sorcerer remained calmly in his throne.

Far up in the air was an object that looked like a balloon. It was not so high as the glowing star of the six colored suns, but was descending slowly through the air—so slowly that at first it scarcely seemed to move.

The throng stood still and waited. It was all they could do, for to go away and leave that strange sight was impossible; nor could they hurry its fall in any way. The earth children were not noticed, being so near the average size of the Mangaboos, and the horse had remained in the House of the Sorcerer, with Eureka curled up asleep on the seat of the buggy.

Gradually the balloon grew bigger, which was proof that it was settling down upon the Land of the Mangaboos. Dorothy was surprised to find how patient the people were, for her own little heart was beating rapidly with excitement. A balloon meant to her some other arrival from the surface of the earth, and she hoped it would be some one able to assist her and Zeb out of their difficulties.

In an hour the balloon had come near enough for her to see a basket suspended below it; in two hours she could see a head looking over the side of the basket; in three hours the big balloon settled slowly into the great square in which they stood and came to rest on the glass pavement.

Then a little man jumped out of the basket, took off his tall hat, and bowed very gracefully to the crowd of Mangaboos around him. He was quite an old little man and his head was long and entirely bald.

"Why," cried Dorothy, in amazement, "it's Oz!"

The little man looked toward her and seemed as much surprised as she was. But he smiled and bowed as he answered:

"Yes, my dear; I am Oz, the Great and Terrible. Eh? And you are little Dorothy, from Kansas. I remember you very well."

"Who did you say it was?" whispered Zeb to the girl.

"It's the wonderful Wizard of Oz. Haven't you heard of him?"

Just then the man with the star came and stood before the Wizard.

"Sir," said he, "why are you here, in the Land of the Mangaboos?"

"Didn't know what land it was, my son," returned the other, with a pleasant smile; "and, to be honest, I didn't mean to visit you when I started out. I live on top of the earth, your honor, which is far better than living inside it; but yesterday I went up in a balloon, and when I came down I fell into a big crack in the earth, caused by an earthquake. I had let so much gas out of my balloon that I could not rise again, and in a few minutes the earth closed over my head. So I continued to descend until I reached this place, and if you will show me a way to get out of it, I'll go with pleasure. Sorry to have troubled you; but it couldn't be helped."

The Prince had listened with attention. Said he:

"This child, who is from the crust of the earth, like yourself, called you a Wizard. Is not a Wizard something like a Sorcerer?"

"It's better," replied Oz, promptly. "One Wizard is worth three Sorcerers."

"Ah, you shall prove that," said the Prince. "We Mangaboos have, at the present time, one of the most wonderful Sorcerers that ever was picked from a bush; but he sometimes makes mistakes. Do you ever make mistakes?"

"Never!" declared the Wizard, boldly.

"Oh, Oz!" said Dorothy; "you made a lot of mistakes when you were in the marvelous Land of Oz."

"Nonsense!" said the little man, turning red—although just then a ray of violet sunlight was on his round face.

165

"Come with me," said the Prince to him. "I wish to meet our Sorcerer."

The Wizard did not like this invitation, but he could not refuse to accept it. So he followed the Prince into the great domed hall, and Dorothy and Zeb came after them, while the throng of people trooped in also.

There sat the thorny Sorcerer in his chair of state, and when the Wizard saw him he began to laugh, uttering comical little chuckles.

"What an absurd creature!" he exclaimed.

"He may look absurd," said the Prince, in his quiet voice; "but he is an excellent Sorcerer. The only fault I find with him is that he is so often wrong."

"I am never wrong," answered the Sorcerer.

"Only a short time ago you told me there would be no more Rain of Stones or of People," said the Prince.

"Well, what then?"

"Here is another person descended from the air to prove you were wrong."

"One person cannot be called 'people,'" said the Sorcerer. "If two should come out of the sky you might with justice say I was wrong; but unless more than this one appears I will hold that I was right."

"Very clever," said the Wizard, nodding his head as if pleased. "I am delighted to find humbugs inside the earth, just the same as on top of it. Were you ever with a circus, brother?"

"No," said the Sorcerer.

"You ought to join one," declared the little man seriously. "I belong to Bailum & Barney's Great Consolidated Shows—three rings in one tent and a menagerie on the side. It's a fine aggregation, I assure you."

"What do you do?" asked the Sorcerer.

"I go up in a balloon, usually, to draw the crowds to the circus. But I've just had the bad luck to come out of the sky, skip the solid earth, and land lower down than I intended. But never mind. It isn't everybody who gets a chance to see your Land of the Gabazoos."

"Mangaboos," said the Sorcerer, correcting him. "If you are a Wizard you ought to be able to call people by their right names."

"Oh, I'm a Wizard; you may be sure of that. Just as good a Wizard as you are a Sorcerer."

"That remains to be seen," said the other.

"If you are able to prove that you are better," said the Prince to the little man, "I will make you the Chief Wizard of this domain. Otherwise—"

"What will happen otherwise?" asked the Wizard.

"I will stop you from living and forbid you to be planted," returned the Prince.

"That does not sound especially pleasant," said the little man, looking at the one with the star uneasily. "But never mind. I'll beat Old Prickly, all right."

"My name is Gwig," said the Sorcerer, turning his heartless, cruel eyes upon his rival. "Let me see you equal the sorcery I am about to perform."

He waved a thorny hand and at once the tinkling of bells was heard, playing sweet music. Yet, look where she would, Dorothy could discover no bells at all in the great glass hall.

The Mangaboo people listened, but showed no great interest. It was one of the things Gwig usually did to prove he was a sorcerer.

Now was the Wizard's turn, so he smiled upon the assemblage and asked:

"Will somebody kindly loan me a hat?"

No one did, because the Mangaboos did not wear hats, and Zeb had lost his, somehow, in his flight through the air.

"Ahem!" said the Wizard, "will somebody please loan me a handkerchief?"

But they had no handkerchiefs, either.

"Very good," remarked the Wizard. "I'll use my own hat, if you please. Now, good people, observe me carefully. You see, there is nothing up my sleeve and nothing concealed about my person. Also, my hat is quite empty." He took off his hat and held it upside down, shaking it briskly.

"Let me see it," said the Sorcerer.

He took the hat and examined it carefully, returning it afterward to the Wizard.

"Now," said the little man, "I will create something out of nothing."

He placed the hat upon the glass floor, made a pass with his hand, and then removed the hat, displaying a little white piglet no bigger than a mouse, which began to run around here and there and to grunt and squeal in a tiny, shrill voice.

The people watched it intently, for they had never seen a pig before, big or little. The Wizard reached out, caught the wee creature in his hand, and holding its head between one thumb and finger and its tail between the other thumb and finger he pulled it apart, each of the two parts becoming a whole and separate piglet in an instant.

He placed one upon the floor, so that it could run around, and pulled apart the other, making three piglets in all; and then one of these was pulled apart, making four piglets. The Wizard continued this surprising performance until nine tiny piglets were running about at his feet, all squealing and grunting in a very comical way.

"Now," said the Wizard of Oz, "having created something from nothing, I will make something nothing again."

With this he caught up two of the piglets and pushed them together, so that the two were one. Then he caught up another piglet and pushed it into the first, where it disappeared. And so, one by one, the nine tiny piglets were pushed together until but a single one of the creatures remained. This the Wizard placed underneath his hat and made a mystic sign above it. When he removed his hat the last piglet had disappeared entirely.

The little man gave a bow to the silent throng that had watched him, and then the Prince said, in his cold, calm voice:

"You are indeed a wonderful Wizard, and your powers are greater than those of my Sorcerer."

"He will not be a wonderful Wizard long," remarked Gwig.

"Why not?" enquired the Wizard.

"Because I am going to stop your breath," was the reply. "I perceive that you are curiously constructed, and that if you cannot breathe you cannot keep alive."

The little man looked troubled.

"How long will it take you to stop my breath?" he asked.

"About five minutes. I'm going to begin now. Watch me carefully."

He began making queer signs and passes toward the Wizard; but the little man did not watch him long. Instead, he drew a leathern case from his pocket and took from it several sharp knives, which he joined together, one after another, until they made a long sword. By the time he had attached a handle to this sword he was having much trouble to breathe, as the charm of the Sorcerer was beginning to take effect.

So the Wizard lost no more time, but leaping forward he raised the sharp sword, whirled it once or twice around his head, and then gave a mighty stroke that cut the body of the Sorcerer exactly in two.

Dorothy screamed and expected to see a terrible sight; but as the two halves of the Sorcerer fell apart on the floor she saw that he had no bones or blood inside of him at all, and that the place where he was cut looked much like a sliced turnip or potato.

"Why, he's vegetable!" cried the Wizard, astonished.

"Of course," said the Prince. "We are all vegetable, in this country. Are you not vegetable, also?"

"No," answered the Wizard. "People on top of the earth are all meat. Will your Sorcerer die?"

"Certainly, sir. He is really dead now, and will wither very quickly. So we must plant him at once, that other Sorcerers may grow upon his bush," continued the Prince.

"What do you mean by that?" asked the little Wizard, greatly puzzled.

"If you will accompany me to our public gardens," replied the Prince, "I will explain to you much better than I can here the mysteries of our Vegetable Kingdom."

Chapter 4 - The Vegetable Kingdom

After the Wizard had wiped the dampness from his sword and taken it apart and put the pieces into their leathern case again, the man with the star ordered some of his people to carry the two halves of the Sorcerer to the public gardens.

Jim pricked up his ears when he heard they were going to the gardens, and wanted to join the party, thinking he might find something proper to eat; so Zeb put down the top of the buggy and invited the Wizard to ride with them. The seat was amply wide enough for the little man and the two children, and when Jim started to leave the hall the kitten jumped upon his back and sat there quite contentedly.

So the procession moved through the streets, the bearers of the Sorcerer first, the Prince next, then Jim drawing the buggy with the strangers inside of it, and last the crowd of vegetable people who had no hearts and could neither smile nor frown.

The glass city had several fine streets, for a good many people lived there; but when the procession had passed through these it came upon a broad plain covered with gardens and watered by many pretty brooks that flowed through it. There were paths through these gardens, and over some of the brooks were ornamental glass bridges.

Dorothy and Zeb now got out of the buggy and walked beside the Prince, so that they might see and examine the flowers and plants better.

"Who built these lovely bridges?" asked the little girl.

"No one built them," answered the man with the star. "They grow."

"That's queer," said she. "Did the glass houses in your city grow, too?"

"Of course," he replied. "But it took a good many years for them to grow as large and fine as they are now. That is why we are so angry when a Rain of Stones comes to break our towers and crack our roofs."

"Can't you mend them?" she enquired.

"No; but they will grow together again, in time, and we must wait until they do."

They first passed through many beautiful gardens of flowers, which grew nearest the city; but Dorothy could hardly tell what kind of flowers they were, because the colors were constantly changing under the shifting lights of the six suns. A flower would be pink one second, white the next, then blue or yellow; and it was the same way when they came to the plants, which had broad leaves and grew close to the ground.

When they passed over a field of grass Jim immediately stretched down his head and began to nibble.

"A nice country this is," he grumbled, "where a respectable horse has to eat pink grass!"

"It's violet," said the Wizard, who was in the buggy.

"Now it's blue," complained the horse. "As a matter of fact, I'm eating rainbow grass."

"How does it taste?" asked the Wizard.

"Not bad at all," said Jim. "If they give me plenty of it I'll not complain about its color."

By this time the party had reached a freshly plowed field, and the Prince said to Dorothy:

"This is our planting-ground."

Several Mangaboos came forward with glass spades and dug a hole in the ground. Then they put the two halves of the Sorcerer into it and covered him up. After that other people brought water from a brook and sprinkled the earth.

"He will sprout very soon," said the Prince, "and grow into a large bush, from which we shall in time be able to pick several very good sorcerers."

"Do all your people grow on bushes?" asked the boy.

"Certainly," was the reply. "Do not all people grow upon bushes where you came from, on the outside of the earth?"

"Not that I ever hear of."

"How strange! But if you will come with me to one of our folk gardens I will show you the way we grow in the Land of the Mangaboos."

It appeared that these odd people, while they were able to walk through the air with ease, usually moved upon the ground in the ordinary way. There were no stairs in their houses, because they did not need them, but on a level surface they generally walked just as we do.

The little party of strangers now followed the Prince across a few more of the glass bridges and along several paths until they came to a garden enclosed by a high hedge. Jim had refused to leave the field of grass, where he was engaged in busily eating; so the Wizard got out of the buggy and joined Zeb and Dorothy, and the kitten followed demurely at their heels.

Inside the hedge they came upon row after row of large and handsome plants with broad leaves gracefully curving until their points nearly reached the ground. In the center of each plant grew a daintily dressed Mangaboo, for the clothing of all these creatures grew upon them and was attached to their bodies.

The growing Mangaboos were of all sizes, from the blossom that had just turned into a wee baby to the full-grown and almost ripe man or woman. On some of the bushes might be seen a bud, a blossom, a baby, a half-grown person and a ripe one; but even those ready to pluck were motionless and silent, as if devoid of life. This sight explained to Dorothy why she had seen no children among the Mangaboos, a thing she had until now been unable to account for.

"Our people do not acquire their real life until they leave their bushes," said the Prince. "You will notice they are all attached to the plants by the soles of their feet, and when they are quite ripe they are easily separated from the stems and at once attain the powers of motion and speech. So while they grow they cannot be said to really live, and they must be picked before they can become good citizens."

"How long do you live, after you are picked?" asked Dorothy.

"That depends upon the care we take of ourselves," he replied. "If we keep cool and moist, and meet with no accidents, we often live for five years. I've been picked over six years, but our family is known to be especially long lived."

"Do you eat?" asked the boy.

"Eat! No, indeed. We are quite solid inside our bodies, and have no need to eat, any more than does a potato."

"But the potatoes sometimes sprout," said Zeb.

"And sometimes we do," answered the Prince; "but that is considered a great misfortune, for then we must be planted at once."

"Where did you grow?" asked the Wizard.

"I will show you," was the reply. "Step this way, please."

He led them within another but smaller circle of hedge, where grew one large and beautiful bush.

"This," said he, "is the Royal Bush of the Mangaboos. All of our Princes and Rulers have grown upon this one bush from time immemorial."

They stood before it in silent admiration. On the central stalk stood poised the figure of a girl so exquisitely formed and colored and so lovely in the expression of her delicate features that Dorothy thought she had never seen so sweet and adorable a creature in all her life. The maiden's gown was soft as satin and fell about her in ample folds, while dainty lace-like traceries trimmed the bodice and sleeves. Her flesh was fine and smooth as polished ivory, and her poise expressed both dignity and grace.

"Who is this?" asked the Wizard, curiously.

The Prince had been staring hard at the girl on the bush. Now he answered, with a touch of uneasiness in his cold tones:

"She is the Ruler destined to be my successor, for she is a Royal Princess. When she becomes fully ripe I must abandon the sovereignty of the Mangaboos to her."

"Isn't she ripe now?" asked Dorothy.

He hesitated.

"Not quite," said he, finally. "It will be several days before she needs to be picked, or at least that is my judgment. I am in no hurry to resign my office and be planted, you may be sure."

"Probably not," declared the Wizard, nodding.

"This is one of the most unpleasant things about our vegetable lives," continued the Prince, with a sigh, "that while we are in our full prime we must give way to another, and be covered up in the ground to sprout and grow and give birth to other people."

"I'm sure the Princess is ready to be picked," asserted Dorothy, gazing hard at the beautiful girl on the bush. "She's as perfect as she can be."

"Never mind," answered the Prince, hastily, "she will be all right for a few days longer, and it is best for me to rule until I can dispose of you strangers, who have come to our land uninvited and must be attended to at once."

"What are you going to do with us?" asked Zeb.

"That is a matter I have not quite decided upon," was the reply. "I think I shall keep this Wizard until a new Sorcerer is ready to pick, for he seems quite skillful and may be of use to us. But the rest of you must be destroyed in some way, and you cannot be planted, because I do not wish horses and cats and meat people growing all over our country."

"You needn't worry," said Dorothy. "We wouldn't grow under ground, I'm sure."

"But why destroy my friends?" asked the little Wizard. "Why not let them live?"

"They do not belong here," returned the Prince. "They have no right to be inside the earth at all."

"We didn't ask to come down here; we fell," said Dorothy.

"That is no excuse," declared the Prince, coldly.

The children looked at each other in perplexity, and the Wizard sighed. Eureka rubbed her paw on her face and said in her soft, purring voice:

"He won't need to destroy ME, for if I don't get something to eat pretty soon I shall starve to death, and so save him the trouble."

"If he planted you, he might grow some cat-tails," suggested the Wizard.

"Oh, Eureka! perhaps we can find you some milk-weeds to eat," said the boy.

"Phoo!" snarled the kitten; "I wouldn't touch the nasty things!"

"You don't need milk, Eureka," remarked Dorothy; "you are big enough now to eat any kind of food."

"If I can get it," added Eureka.

"I'm hungry myself," said Zeb. "But I noticed some strawberries growing in one of the gardens, and some melons in another place. These people don't eat such things, so perhaps on our way back they will let us get them."

"Never mind your hunger," interrupted the Prince. "I shall order you destroyed in a few minutes, so you will have no need to ruin our pretty melon vines and berry bushes. Follow me, please, to meet your doom."

Chapter 5 - Dorothy Picks the Princess

The words of the cold and moist vegetable Prince were not very comforting, and as he spoke them he turned away and left the enclosure. The children, feeling sad and despondent, were about to follow him when the Wizard touched Dorothy softly on her shoulder.

"Wait!" he whispered.

"What for?" asked the girl.

"Suppose we pick the Royal Princess," said the Wizard. "I'm quite sure she's ripe, and as soon as she comes to life she will be the Ruler, and may treat us better than that heartless Prince intends to."

"All right!" exclaimed Dorothy, eagerly. "Let's pick her while we have the chance, before the man with the star comes back."

So together they leaned over the great bush and each of them seized one hand of the lovely Princess.

"Pull!" cried Dorothy, and as they did so the royal lady leaned toward them and the stems snapped and separated from her feet. She was not at all heavy, so the Wizard and Dorothy managed to lift her gently to the ground.

The beautiful creature passed her hands over her eyes an instant, tucked in a stray lock of hair that had become disarranged, and after a look around the garden made those present a gracious bow and said, in a sweet but even toned voice:

"I thank you very much."

"We salute your Royal Highness!" cried the Wizard, kneeling and kissing her hand.

Just then the voice of the Prince was heard calling upon them to hasten, and a moment later he returned to the enclosure, followed by a number of his people.

Instantly the Princess turned and faced him, and when he saw that she was picked the Prince stood still and began to tremble.

"Sir," said the Royal Lady, with much dignity, "you have wronged me greatly, and would have wronged me still more had not these strangers come to my rescue. I have been ready for picking all the past week, but because you were selfish and desired to continue your unlawful rule, you left me to stand silent upon my bush."

"I did not know that you were ripe," answered the Prince, in a low voice.

"Give me the Star of Royalty!" she commanded.

Slowly he took the shining star from his own brow and placed it upon that of the Princess. Then all the people bowed low to her, and the Prince turned and walked away alone. What became of him afterward our friends never knew.

The people of Mangaboo now formed themselves into a procession and marched toward the glass city to escort their new ruler to her palace and to perform those ceremonies proper to the occasion. But while the people in the procession walked upon the ground the Princess walked in the air just above their heads, to show that she was a superior being and more exalted than her subjects.

No one now seemed to pay any attention to the strangers, so Dorothy and Zeb and the Wizard let the train pass on and then wandered by themselves into the vegetable gardens. They did not bother to cross the bridges over the brooks, but when they came to a stream they stepped high and walked in the air to the other side. This was a very interesting experience to them, and Dorothy said:

"I wonder why it is that we can walk so easily in the air."

"Perhaps," answered the Wizard, "it is because we are close to the center of the earth, where the attraction of gravitation is very slight. But I've noticed that many queer things happen in fairy countries."

"Is this a fairy country?" asked the boy.

"Of course it is," returned Dorothy promptly. "Only a fairy country could have veg'table people; and only in a fairy country could Eureka and Jim talk as we do."

"That's true," said Zeb, thoughtfully.

In the vegetable gardens they found the strawberries and melons, and several other unknown but delicious fruits, of which they ate heartily. But the kitten bothered them constantly by demanding milk or meat, and called the Wizard names because he could not bring her a dish of milk by means of his magical arts.

As they sat upon the grass watching Jim, who was still busily eating, Eureka said:

"I don't believe you are a Wizard at all!"

"No," answered the little man, "you are quite right. In the strict sense of the word I am not a Wizard, but only a humbug."

"The Wizard of Oz has always been a humbug," agreed Dorothy. "I've known him for a long time."

"If that is so," said the boy, "how could he do that wonderful trick with the nine tiny piglets?"

"Don't know," said Dorothy, "but it must have been humbug."

"Very true," declared the Wizard, nodding at her. "It was necessary to deceive that ugly Sorcerer and the Prince, as well as their stupid people; but I don't mind telling you, who are my friends, that the thing was only a trick."

"But I saw the little pigs with my own eyes!" exclaimed Zeb.

"So did I," purred the kitten.

"To be sure," answered the Wizard. "You saw them because they were there. They are in my inside pocket now. But the pulling of them apart and pushing them together again was only a sleight-of-hand trick."

"Let's see the pigs," said Eureka, eagerly.

The little man felt carefully in his pocket and pulled out the tiny piglets, setting them upon the grass one by one, where they ran around and nibbled the tender blades.

"They're hungry, too," he said.

"Oh, what cunning things!" cried Dorothy, catching up one and petting it.

"Be careful!" said the piglet, with a squeal, "you're squeezing me!"

"Dear me!" murmured the Wizard, looking at his pets in astonishment. "They can actually talk!"

"May I eat one of them?" asked the kitten, in a pleading voice. "I'm awfully hungry."

"Why, Eureka," said Dorothy, reproachfully, "what a cruel question! It would be dreadful to eat these dear little things."

"I should say so!" grunted another of the piglets, looking uneasily at the kitten; "cats are cruel things."

"I'm not cruel," replied the kitten, yawning. "I'm just hungry."

"You cannot eat my piglets, even if you are starving," declared the little man, in a stern voice. "They are the only things I have to prove I'm a wizard."

"How did they happen to be so little?" asked Dorothy. "I never saw such small pigs before."

"They are from the Island of Teenty-Weent," said the Wizard, "where everything is small because it's a small island. A sailor brought them to Los Angeles and I gave him nine tickets to the circus for them."

"But what am I going to eat?" wailed the kitten, sitting in front of Dorothy and looking pleadingly into her face. "There are no cows here to give milk; or any mice, or even grasshoppers. And if I can't eat the piglets you may as well plant me at once and raise catsup."

"I have an idea," said the Wizard, "that there are fishes in these brooks. Do you like fish?"

"Fish!" cried the kitten. "Do I like fish? Why, they're better than piglets—or even milk!"

"Then I'll try to catch you some," said he.

"But won't they be veg'table, like everything else here?" asked the kitten.

"I think not. Fishes are not animals, and they are as cold and moist as the vegetables themselves. There is no reason, that I can see, why they may not exist in the waters of this strange country."

Then the Wizard bent a pin for a hook and took a long piece of string from his pocket for a fish-line. The only bait he could find was a bright red blossom from a flower; but he knew fishes are easy to fool if anything bright attracts their attention, so he decided to try the blossom. Having thrown the end of his line in the water of a nearby brook he soon felt a sharp tug that told him a fish had bitten and was caught on the bent pin; so the little man drew in the string and, sure enough, the fish came with it and was landed safely on the shore, where it began to flop around in great excitement.

The fish was fat and round, and its scales glistened like beautifully cut jewels set close together; but there was no time to examine it closely, for Eureka made a jump and caught it between her claws, and in a few moments it had entirely disappeared.

"Oh, Eureka!" cried Dorothy, "did you eat the bones?"

"If it had any bones, I ate them," replied the kitten, composedly, as it washed its face after the meal. "But I don't think that fish had any bones, because I didn't feel them scratch my throat."

"You were very greedy," said the girl.

"I was very hungry," replied the kitten.

The little pigs had stood huddled in a group, watching this scene with frightened eyes.

"Cats are dreadful creatures!" said one of them.

"I'm glad we are not fishes!" said another.

"Don't worry," Dorothy murmured, soothingly, "I'll not let the kitten hurt you."

Then she happened to remember that in a corner of her suit-case were one or two crackers that were left over from her luncheon on the train, and she went to the buggy and brought them. Eureka stuck up her nose at such food, but the tiny piglets squealed delightedly at the sight of the crackers and ate them up in a jiffy.

"Now let us go back to the city," suggested the Wizard. "That is, if Jim has had enough of the pink grass."

The cab-horse, who was browsing near, lifted his head with a sigh.

"I've tried to eat a lot while I had the chance," said he, "for it's likely to be a long while between meals in this strange country. But I'm ready to go, now, at any time you wish."

So, after the Wizard had put the piglets back into his inside pocket, where they cuddled up and went to sleep, the three climbed into the buggy and Jim started back to the town.

"Where shall we stay?" asked the girl.

"I think I shall take possession of the House of the Sorcerer," replied the Wizard; "for the Prince said in the presence of his people that he would keep me until they picked another Sorcerer, and the new Princess won't know but that we belong there."

They agreed to this plan, and when they reached the great square Jim drew the buggy into the big door of the domed hall.

"It doesn't look very homelike," said Dorothy, gazing around at the bare room. "But it's a place to stay, anyhow."

"What are those holes up there?" enquired the boy, pointing to some openings that appeared near the top of the dome.

"They look like doorways," said Dorothy; "only there are no stairs to get to them."

"You forget that stairs are unnecessary," observed the Wizard. "Let us walk up, and see where the doors lead to."

With this he began walking in the air toward the high openings, and Dorothy and Zeb followed him. It was the same sort of climb one experiences when walking up a hill, and they were nearly out of breath when they came to the row of openings, which they perceived to be doorways leading into halls in the upper part of the house. Following these halls they discovered many small rooms opening from them, and some were furnished with glass benches, tables and chairs. But there were no beds at all.

"I wonder if these people never sleep," said the girl.

"Why, there seems to be no night at all in this country," Zeb replied. "Those colored suns are exactly in the same place they were when we came, and if there is no sunset there can be no night."

"Very true," agreed the Wizard. "But it is a long time since I have had any sleep, and I'm tired. So I think I shall lie down upon one of these hard glass benches and take a nap."

"I will, too," said Dorothy, and chose a little room at the end of the hall.

Zeb walked down again to unharness Jim, who, when he found himself free, rolled over a few times and then settled down to sleep, with Eureka nestling comfortably beside his big, boney body. Then the boy returned to one of the upper rooms, and in spite of the hardness of the glass bench was soon deep in slumberland.

Chapter 6 - The Mangaboos Prove Dangerous

When the Wizard awoke the six colored suns were shining down upon the Land of the Mangaboos just as they had done ever since his arrival. The little man, having had a good sleep, felt rested and refreshed, and looking through the glass partition of the room he saw Zeb sitting up on his bench and yawning. So the Wizard went in to him.

"Zeb," said he, "my balloon is of no further use in this strange country, so I may as well leave it on the square where it fell. But in the basket-car are some things I would like to keep with me. I wish you would go and fetch my satchel, two lanterns, and a can of kerosene oil that is under the seat. There is nothing else that I care about."

So the boy went willingly upon the errand, and by the time he had returned Dorothy was awake. Then the three held a counsel to decide what they should do next, but could think of no way to better their condition.

"I don't like these veg'table people," said the little girl. "They're cold and flabby, like cabbages, in spite of their prettiness."

"I agree with you. It is because there is no warm blood in them," remarked the Wizard.

"And they have no hearts; so they can't love anyone—not even themselves," declared the boy.

"The Princess is lovely to look at," continued Dorothy, thoughtfully; "but I don't care much for her, after all. If there was any other place to go, I'd like to go there."

"But IS there any other place?" asked the Wizard.

"I don't know," she answered.

Just then they heard the big voice of Jim the cab-horse calling to them, and going to the doorway leading to the dome they found the Princess and a throng of her people had entered the House of the Sorcerer.

So they went down to greet the beautiful vegetable lady, who said to them:

"I have been talking with my advisors about you meat people, and we have decided that you do not belong in the Land of the Mangaboos and must not remain here."

"How can we go away?" asked Dorothy.

"Oh, you cannot go away, of course; so you must be destroyed," was the answer.

"In what way?" enquired the Wizard.

"We shall throw you three people into the Garden of the Twining Vines," said the Princess, "and they will soon crush you and devour your bodies to make themselves grow bigger. The animals you have with you we will drive to the mountains and put into the Black Pit. Then our country will be rid of all its unwelcome visitors."

"But you are in need of a Sorcerer," said the Wizard, "and not one of those growing is yet ripe enough to pick. I am greater than any thorn-covered sorcerer that every grew in your garden. Why destroy me?"

"It is true we need a Sorcerer," acknowledged the Princess, "but I am informed that one of our own will be ready to pick in a few days, to take the place of Gwig, whom you cut in two before it was time for him to be planted. Let us see your arts, and the sorceries you are able to perform. Then I will decide whether to destroy you with the others or not."

At this the Wizard made a bow to the people and repeated his trick of producing the nine tiny piglets and making them disappear again. He did it very cleverly, indeed, and the Princess looked at the strange piglets as if she were as truly astonished as any vegetable person could be. But afterward she said:

"I have heard of this wonderful magic. But it accomplishes nothing of value. What else can you do?"

The Wizard tried to think. Then he jointed together the blades of his sword and balanced it very skillfully upon the end of his nose. But even that did not satisfy the Princess.

Just then his eye fell upon the lanterns and the can of kerosene oil which Zeb had brought from the car of his balloon, and he got a clever idea from those commonplace things.

"Your Highness," said he, "I will now proceed to prove my magic by creating two suns that you have never seen before; also I will exhibit a Destroyer much more dreadful that your Clinging Vines."

So he placed Dorothy upon one side of him and the boy upon the other and set a lantern upon each of their heads.

"Don't laugh," he whispered to them, "or you will spoil the effect of my magic."

Then, with much dignity and a look of vast importance upon his wrinkled face, the Wizard got out his match-box and lighted the two lanterns. The glare they made was very small when compared with the radiance of the six great colored suns; but still they gleamed steadily and clearly. The Mangaboos were much impressed because they had never before seen any light that did not come directly from their suns.

Next the Wizard poured a pool of oil from the can upon the glass floor, where it covered quite a broad surface. When he lighted the oil a hundred tongues of flame shot up, and the effect was really imposing.

"Now, Princess," exclaimed the Wizard, "those of your advisors who wished to throw us into the Garden of Clinging Vines must step within this circle of light. If they advised you well, and were in the right, they will not be injured in any way. But if any advised you wrongly, the light will wither him."

The advisors of the Princess did not like this test; but she commanded them to step into the flame and one by one they did so, and were scorched so badly that the air was soon filled with an odor like that of baked potatoes. Some of the Mangaboos fell down and had to be dragged from the fire, and all were so withered that it would be necessary to plant them at once.

"Sir," said the Princess to the Wizard, "you are greater than any Sorcerer we have ever known. As it is evident that my people have advised me wrongly, I will not cast you three people into the dreadful Garden of the Clinging Vines; but your animals must be driven into the Black Pit in the mountain, for my subjects cannot bear to have them around."

The Wizard was so pleased to have saved the two children and himself that he said nothing against this decree; but when the Princess had gone both Jim and Eureka protested they did not want to go to the Black Pit, and Dorothy promised she would do all that she could to save them from such a fate.

For two or three days after this—if we call days the periods between sleep, there being no night to divide the hours into days—our friends were not disturbed in any way. They were even permitted to occupy the House of the Sorcerer in peace, as if it had been their own, and to wander in the gardens in search of food.

Once they came near to the enclosed Garden of the Clinging Vines, and walking high into the air looked down upon it with much interest. They saw a mass of tough green vines all matted together and writhing and twisting around like a nest of great snakes. Everything the vines touched they crushed, and our adventurers were indeed thankful to have escaped being cast among them.

Whenever the Wizard went to sleep he would take the nine tiny piglets from his pocket and let them run around on the floor of his room to amuse themselves and get some exercise; and one time they found his glass door ajar and wandered into the hall and then into the bottom part of the great dome, walking through the air as easily as Eureka could. They knew the kitten, by this time, so they scampered over to where she lay beside Jim and commenced to frisk and play with her.

The cab-horse, who never slept long at a time, sat upon his haunches and watched the tiny piglets and the kitten with much approval.

"Don't be rough!" he would call out, if Eureka knocked over one of the round, fat piglets with her paw; but the pigs never minded, and enjoyed the sport very greatly.

Suddenly they looked up to find the room filled with the silent, solemn-eyed Mangaboos. Each of the vegetable folks bore a branch covered with sharp thorns, which was thrust defiantly toward the horse, the kitten and the piglets.

"Here—stop this foolishness!" Jim roared, angrily; but after being pricked once or twice he got upon his four legs and kept out of the way of the thorns.

The Mangaboos surrounded them in solid ranks, but left an opening to the doorway of the hall; so the animals slowly retreated until they were driven from the room and out upon the street. Here were more of the vegetable people with thorns,and silently they urged the now frightened creatures down the street. Jim had to be careful not to step upon the tiny piglets, who scampered under his feet grunting and squealing, while Eureka, snarling and biting at the thorns pushed toward her, also tried to protect the pretty little things from injury. Slowly but steadily the heartless Mangaboos drove them on, until they had passed through the city and the gardens and come to the broad plains leading to the mountain.

"What does all this mean, anyhow?" asked the horse, jumping to escape a thorn.

"Why, they are driving us toward the Black Pit, into which they threatened to cast us," replied the kitten. "If I were as big as you are, Jim, I'd fight these miserable turnip-roots!"

"What would you do?" enquired Jim.

"I'd kick out with those long legs and iron-shod hoofs."

"All right," said the horse; "I'll do it."

An instant later he suddenly backed toward the crowd of Mangaboos and kicked out his hind legs as hard as he could. A dozen of them smashed together and tumbled to the ground, and seeing his success Jim kicked again and again, charging into the vegetable crowd, knocking them in all directions and sending the others scattering to escape his iron heels. Eureka helped him by flying into the faces of the enemy and scratching and biting furiously, and the kitten ruined so many vegetable complexions that the Mangaboos feared her as much as they did the horse.

But the foes were too many to be repulsed for long. They tired Jim and Eureka out, and although the field of battle was thickly covered with mashed and disabled Mangaboos, our animal friends had to give up at last and allow themselves to be driven to the mountain.

Chapter 7 - In the Black Pit and Out Again

When they came to the mountain it proved to be a rugged, towering chunk of deep green glass, and looked dismal and forbidding in the extreme. Half way up the steep was a yawning cave, black as night beyond the point where the rainbow rays of the colored suns reached into it.

The Mangaboos drove the horse and the kitten and the piglets into this dark hole and then, having pushed the buggy in after them—for it seemed some of them had dragged it all the way from the domed hall—they began to pile big glass rocks within the entrance, so that the prisoners could not get out again.

"This is dreadful!" groaned Jim. "It will be about the end of our adventures, I guess."

"If the Wizard was here," said one of the piglets, sobbing bitterly, "he would not see us suffer so."

"We ought to have called him and Dorothy when we were first attacked," added Eureka. "But never mind; be brave, my friends, and I will go and tell our masters where you are, and get them to come to your rescue."

The mouth of the hole was nearly filled up now, but the kitten gave a leap through the remaining opening and at once scampered up into the air. The Mangaboos saw her escape, and several of them caught up their thorns and gave chase, mounting through the air after her. Eureka, however, was lighter than the Mangaboos, and while they could mount only about a hundred feet above the earth the kitten found she could go nearly two hundred feet. So she ran along over their heads until she had left them far behind and below and had come to the city and the House of the Sorcerer. There she entered in at Dorothy's window in the dome and aroused her from her sleep.

As soon as the little girl knew what had happened she awakened the Wizard and Zeb, and at once preparations were made to go to the rescue of Jim and the piglets. The Wizard carried his satchel, which was quite heavy, and Zeb carried the two lanterns and the oil can. Dorothy's wicker suit-case was still under the seat of the buggy, and by good fortune the boy had also placed the harness in the buggy when he had taken it off from Jim to let the horse lie down and rest. So there was nothing for the girl to carry but the kitten, which she held close to her bosom and tried to comfort, for its little heart was still beating rapidly.

Some of the Mangaboos discovered them as soon as they left the House of the Sorcerer; but when they started toward the mountain the vegetable people allowed them to proceed without interference, yet followed in a crowd behind them so that they could not go back again.

Before long they neared the Black Pit, where a busy swarm of Mangaboos, headed by their Princess, was engaged in piling up glass rocks before the entrance.

"Stop, I command you!" cried the Wizard, in an angry tone, and at once began pulling down the rocks to liberate Jim and the piglets. Instead of opposing him in this they stood back in silence until he had made a good-sized hole in the barrier, when by order of the Princess they all sprang forward and thrust out their sharp thorns.

Dorothy hopped inside the opening to escape being pricked, and Zeb and the Wizard, after enduring a few stabs from the thorns, were glad to follow her. At once the Mangaboos began piling up the rocks of glass again, and as the little man realized that they were all about to be entombed in the mountain he said to the children:

"My dears, what shall we do? Jump out and fight?"

"What's the use?" replied Dorothy. "I'd as soon die here as live much longer among these cruel and heartless people."

"That's the way I feel about it," remarked Zeb, rubbing his wounds. "I've had enough of the Mangaboos."

"All right," said the Wizard; "I'm with you, whatever you decide. But we can't live long in this cavern, that's certain."

Noticing that the light was growing dim he picked up his nine piglets, patted each one lovingly on its fat little head, and placed them carefully in his inside pocket.

Zeb struck a match and lighted one of the lanterns. The rays of the colored suns were now shut out from them forever, for the last chinks had been filled up in the wall that separated their prison from the Land of the Mangaboos.

"How big is this hole?" asked Dorothy.

"I'll explore it and see," replied the boy.

So he carried the lantern back for quite a distance, while Dorothy and the Wizard followed at his side. The cavern did not come to an end, as they had expected it would, but slanted upward through the great glass mountain, running in a direction that promised to lead them to the side opposite the Mangaboo country.

"It isn't a bad road," observed the Wizard, "and if we followed it it might lead us to some place that is more comfortable than this black pocket we are now in. I suppose the vegetable folk were always afraid to enter this cavern because it is dark; but we have our lanterns to light the way, so I propose that we start out and discover where this tunnel in the mountain leads to."

The others agreed readily to this sensible suggestion, and at once the boy began to harness Jim to the buggy. When all was in readiness the three took their seats in the buggy and Jim started cautiously along the way, Zeb driving while the Wizard and Dorothy each held a lighted lantern so the horse could see where to go.

Sometimes the tunnel was so narrow that the wheels of the buggy grazed the sides; then it would broaden out as wide as a street; but the floor was usually smooth, and for a long time they travelled on without any accident. Jim stopped sometimes to rest, for the climb was rather steep and tiresome.

"We must be nearly as high as the six colored suns, by this time," said Dorothy. "I didn't know this mountain was so tall."

"We are certainly a good distance away from the Land of the Mangaboos," added Zeb; "for we have slanted away from it ever since we started."

But they kept steadily moving, and just as Jim was about tired out with his long journey the way suddenly grew lighter, and Zeb put out the lanterns to save the oil.

To their joy they found it was a white light that now greeted them, for all were weary of the colored rainbow lights which, after a time, had made their eyes ache with their constantly shifting rays. The sides of the tunnel showed before them like the inside of a long spy-glass, and the floor became more level. Jim hastened his lagging steps at this assurance of a quick relief from the dark passage, and in a few moments more they had emerged from the mountain and found themselves face to face with a new and charming country.

Chapter 8 - The Valley of Voices

By journeying through the glass mountain they had reached a delightful valley that was shaped like the hollow of a great cup, with another rugged mountain showing on the other side of it, and soft and pretty green hills at the ends. It was all laid out into lovely lawns and gardens, with pebble paths leading through them and groves of beautiful and stately trees dotting the landscape here and there. There were orchards, too, bearing luscious fruits that are all unknown in our world. Alluring brooks of crystal water flowed sparkling between their flower-strewn banks, while scattered over the valley were dozens of the quaintest and most picturesque cottages our travelers had ever beheld. None of them were in clusters, such as villages or towns, but each had ample grounds of its own, with orchards and gardens surrounding it.

As the new arrivals gazed upon this exquisite scene they were enraptured by its beauties and the fragrance that permeated the soft air, which they breathed so gratefully after the confined atmosphere of the tunnel. Several minutes were consumed in silent admiration before they noticed two very singular and unusual facts about this valley. One was that it was lighted from some unseen source; for no sun or moon was in the arched blue sky, although every object was flooded with a clear and perfect light. The second and even more singular fact was the absence of any inhabitant of this splendid place. From their elevated position they could overlook the entire valley, but not a single moving object could they see. All appeared mysteriously deserted.

The mountain on this side was not glass, but made of a stone similar to granite. With some difficulty and danger Jim drew the buggy over the loose rocks until he reached the green lawns below, where the paths and orchards and gardens began. The nearest cottage was still some distance away.

"Isn't it fine?" cried Dorothy, in a joyous voice, as she sprang out of the buggy and let Eureka run frolicking over the velvety grass.

"Yes, indeed!" answered Zeb. "We were lucky to get away from those dreadful vegetable people."

"It wouldn't be so bad," remarked the Wizard, gazing around him, "if we were obliged to live here always. We couldn't find a prettier place, I'm sure."

He took the piglets from his pocket and let them run on the grass, and Jim tasted a mouthful of the green blades and declared he was very contented in his new surroundings.

"We can't walk in the air here, though," called Eureka, who had tried it and failed; but the others were satisfied to walk on the ground, and the Wizard said they must be nearer the surface of the earth then they had been in the Mangaboo country, for everything was more homelike and natural.

"But where are the people?" asked Dorothy.

The little man shook his bald head.

"Can't imagine, my dear," he replied.

They heard the sudden twittering of a bird, but could not find the creature anywhere. Slowly they walked along the path toward the nearest cottage, the piglets racing and gambolling beside them and Jim pausing at every step for another mouthful of grass.

Presently they came to a low plant which had broad, spreading leaves, in the center of which grew a single fruit about as large as a peach. The fruit was so daintily colored and so fragrant, and looked so appetizing and delicious that Dorothy stopped and exclaimed:

"What is it, do you s'pose?"

The piglets had smelled the fruit quickly, and before the girl could reach out her hand to pluck it every one of the nine tiny ones had rushed in and commenced to devour it with great eagerness.

"It's good, anyway," said Zeb, "or those little rascals wouldn't have gobbled it up so greedily."

"Where are they?" asked Dorothy, in astonishment.

They all looked around, but the piglets had disappeared.

"Dear me!" cried the Wizard; "they must have run away. But I didn't see them go; did you?"

"No!" replied the boy and the girl, together.

"Here,—piggy, piggy, piggy!" called their master, anxiously.

Several squeals and grunts were instantly heard at his feet, but the Wizard could not discover a single piglet.

"Where are you?" he asked.

"Why, right beside you," spoke a tiny voice. "Can't you see us?"

"No," answered the little man, in a puzzled tone.

"We can see you," said another of the piglets.

The Wizard stooped down and put out his hand, and at once felt the small fat body of one of his pets. He picked it up, but could not see what he held.

"It is very strange," said he, soberly. "The piglets have become invisible, in some curious way."

"I'll bet it's because they ate that peach!" cried the kitten.

"It wasn't a peach, Eureka," said Dorothy. "I only hope it wasn't poison."

"It was fine, Dorothy," called one of the piglets.

"We'll eat all we can find of them," said another.

"But WE mus'n't eat them," the Wizard warned the children, "or we too may become invisible, and lose each other. If we come across another of the strange fruit we must avoid it."

Calling the piglets to him he picked them all up, one by one, and put them away in his pocket; for although he could not see them he could feel them, and when he had buttoned his coat he knew they were safe for the present.

The travellers now resumed their walk toward the cottage, which they presently reached. It was a pretty place, with vines growing thickly over the broad front porch. The door stood open and a table was set in the front room, with four chairs drawn up to it. On the table were plates, knives and forks, and dishes of bread, meat and fruits. The meat was smoking hot and the knives and forks were performing strange antics and jumping here and there in quite a puzzling way. But not a single person appeared to be in the room.

"How funny!" exclaimed Dorothy, who with Zeb and the Wizard now stood in the doorway.

A peal of merry laughter answered her, and the knives and forks fell to the plates with a clatter. One of the chairs pushed back from the table, and this was so astonishing and mysterious that Dorothy was almost tempted to run away in fright.

"Here are strangers, mama!" cried the shrill and childish voice of some unseen person.

"So I see, my dear," answered another voice, soft and womanly.

"What do you want?" demanded a third voice, in a stern, gruff accent.

"Well, well!" said the Wizard; "are there really people in this room?"

"Of course," replied the man's voice.

"And—pardon me for the foolish question—but, are you all invisible?"

"Surely," the woman answered, repeating her low, rippling laughter. "Are you surprised that you are unable to see the people of Voe?"

"Why, yes," stammered the Wizard. "All the people I have ever met before were very plain to see."

"Where do you come from, then?" asked the woman, in a curious tone.

"We belong upon the face of the earth," explained the Wizard, "but recently, during an earthquake, we fell down a crack and landed in the Country of the Mangaboos."

"Dreadful creatures!" exclaimed the woman's voice. "I've heard of them."

"They walled us up in a mountain," continued the Wizard; "but we found there was a tunnel through to this side, so we came here. It is a beautiful place. What do you call it?"

"It is the Valley of Voe."

"Thank you. We have seen no people since we arrived, so we came to this house to enquire our way."

"Are you hungry?" asked the woman's voice.

"I could eat something," said Dorothy.

"So could I," added Zeb.

"But we do not wish to intrude, I assure you," the Wizard hastened to say.

"That's all right," returned the man's voice, more pleasantly than before. "You are welcome to what we have."

As he spoke the voice came so near to Zeb that he jumped back in alarm. Two childish voices laughed merrily at this action, and Dorothy was sure they were in no danger among such light-hearted folks, even if those folks couldn't be seen.

"What curious animal is that which is eating the grass on my lawn?" enquired the man's voice.

"That's Jim," said the girl. "He's a horse."

"What is he good for?" was the next question.

"He draws the buggy you see fastened to him, and we ride in the buggy instead of walking," she explained.

"Can he fight?" asked the man's voice.

"No! he can kick pretty hard with his heels, and bite a little; but Jim can't 'zactly fight," she replied.

"Then the bears will get him," said one of the children's voices.

"Bears!" exclaimed Dorothy. "Are these bears here?"

"That is the one evil of our country," answered the invisible man. "Many large and fierce bears roam in the Valley of Voe, and when they can catch any of us they eat us up; but as they cannot see us, we seldom get caught."

"Are the bears invis'ble, too?" asked the girl.

"Yes; for they eat of the dama-fruit, as we all do, and that keeps them from being seen by any eye, whether human or animal."

"Does the dama-fruit grow on a low bush, and look something like a peach?" asked the Wizard.

"Yes," was the reply.

"If it makes you invis'ble, why do you eat it?" Dorothy enquired.

"For two reasons, my dear," the woman's voice answered. "The dama-fruit is the most delicious thing that grows, and when it makes us invisible the bears cannot find us to eat us up. But now, good wanderers, your luncheon is on the table, so please sit down and eat as much as you like."

Chapter 9 - They Fight the Invisible Bears

The strangers took their seats at the table willingly enough, for they were all hungry and the platters were now heaped with good things to eat. In front of each place was a plate bearing one of the delicious dama-fruit, and the perfume that rose from these was so enticing and sweet that they were sorely tempted to eat of them and become invisible.

But Dorothy satisfied her hunger with other things, and her companions did likewise, resisting the temptation.

"Why do you not eat the damas?" asked the woman's voice.

"We don't want to get invis'ble," answered the girl.

"But if you remain visible the bears will see you and devour you," said a girlish young voice, that belonged to one of the children. "We who live here much prefer to be invisible; for we can still hug and kiss one another, and are quite safe from the bears."

"And we do not have to be so particular about our dress," remarked the man.

"And mama can't tell whether my face is dirty or not!" added the other childish voice, gleefully.

"But I make you wash it, every time I think of it," said the mother; "for it stands to reason your face is dirty, Ianu, whether I can see it or not."

Dorothy laughed and stretched out her hands.

"Come here, please—Ianu and your sister—and let me feel of you," she requested.

They came to her willingly, and Dorothy passed her hands over their faces and forms and decided one was a girl of about her own age and the other a boy somewhat smaller. The girl's hair was soft and fluffy and her skin as smooth as satin. When Dorothy gently touched her nose and ears and lips they seemed to be well and delicately formed.

"If I could see you I am sure you would be beautiful," she declared.

The girl laughed, and her mother said:

"We are not vain in the Valley of Voe, because we can not display our beauty, and good actions and pleasant ways are what make us lovely to our companions. Yet we can see and appreciate the beauties of nature, the dainty flowers and trees, the green fields and the clear blue of the sky."

"How about the birds and beasts and fishes?" asked Zeb.

"The birds we cannot see, because they love to eat of the damas as much as we do; yet we hear their sweet songs and enjoy them. Neither can we see the cruel bears, for they also eat the fruit. But the fishes that swim in our brooks we can see, and often we catch them to eat."

"It occurs to me you have a great deal to make you happy, even while invisible," remarked the Wizard. "Nevertheless, we prefer to remain visible while we are in your valley."

Just then Eureka came in, for she had been until now wandering outside with Jim; and when the kitten saw the table set with food she cried out:

"Now you must feed me, Dorothy, for I'm half starved."

The children were inclined to be frightened by the sight of the small animal, which reminded them of the bears; but Dorothy reassured them by explaining that Eureka was a pet and could do no harm even if she wished to. Then, as the others had by this time moved away from the table, the kitten sprang upon the chair and put her paws upon the cloth to see what there was to eat. To her surprise an unseen hand clutched her and held her suspended in the air. Eureka was frantic with terror, and tried to scratch and bite, so the next moment she was dropped to the floor,

"Did you see that, Dorothy?" she gasped.

"Yes, dear," her mistress replied; "there are people living in this house, although we cannot see them. And you must have better manners, Eureka, or something worse will happen to you."

She placed a plate of food upon the floor and the kitten ate greedily.

"Give me that nice-smelling fruit I saw on the table," she begged, when she had cleaned the plate.

"Those are damas," said Dorothy, "and you must never even taste them, Eureka, or you'll get invis'ble, and then we can't see you at all."

The kitten gazed wistfully at the forbidden fruit.

"Does it hurt to be invis'ble?" she asked.

"I don't know," Dorothy answered; "but it would hurt me dre'fully to lose you."

"Very well, I won't touch it," decided the kitten; "but you must keep it away from me, for the smell is very tempting."

"Can you tell us, sir or ma'am," said the Wizard, addressing the air because he did not quite know where the unseen people stood, "if there is any way we can get out of your beautiful Valley, and on top of the Earth again."

"Oh, one can leave the Valley easily enough," answered the man's voice; "but to do so you must enter a far less pleasant country. As for reaching the top of the earth, I have never heard that it is possible to do that, and if you succeeded in getting there you would probably fall off."

"Oh, no," said Dorothy, "we've been there, and we know."

"The Valley of Voe is certainly a charming place," resumed the Wizard; "but we cannot be contented in any other land than our own, for long. Even if we should come to unpleasant places on our way it is necessary, in order to reach the earth's surface, to keep moving on toward it."

"In that case," said the man, "it will be best for you to cross our Valley and mount the spiral staircase inside the Pyramid Mountain. The top of that mountain is lost in the clouds, and when you reach it you will be in the awful Land of Naught, where the Gargoyles live."

"What are Gargoyles?" asked Zeb.

"I do not know, young sir. Our greatest Champion, Overman-Anu, once climbed the spiral stairway and fought nine days with the Gargoyles before he could escape them and come back; but he could never be induced to describe the dreadful creatures, and soon afterward a bear caught him and ate him up."

The wanders were rather discouraged by this gloomy report, but Dorothy said with a sigh:

"If the only way to get home is to meet the Gurgles, then we've got to meet 'em. They can't be worse than the Wicked Witch or the Nome King."

"But you must remember you had the Scarecrow and the Tin Woodman to help you conquer those enemies," suggested the Wizard. "Just now, my dear, there is not a single warrior in your company."

"Oh, I guess Zeb could fight if he had to. Couldn't you, Zeb?" asked the little girl.

"Perhaps; if I had to," answered Zeb, doubtfully.

"And you have the jointed sword that you chopped the veg'table Sorcerer in two with," the girl said to the little man.

"True," he replied; "and in my satchel are other useful things to fight with."

"What the Gargoyles most dread is a noise," said the man's voice. "Our Champion told me that when he shouted his battle-cry the creatures shuddered and drew back, hesitating to continue the combat. But they were in great numbers, and the Champion could not shout much because he had to save his breath for fighting."

"Very good," said the Wizard; "we can all yell better than we can fight, so we ought to defeat the Gargoyles."

"But tell me," said Dorothy, "how did such a brave Champion happen to let the bears eat him? And if he was invis'ble, and the bears invis'ble, who knows that they really ate him up?"

"The Champion had killed eleven bears in his time," returned the unseen man; "and we know this is true because when any creature is dead the invisible charm of the dama-fruit ceases to be active, and the slain one can be plainly seen by all eyes. When the Champion killed a bear everyone could see it; and when the bears killed the Champion we all saw several pieces of him scattered about, which of course disappeared again when the bears devoured them."

They now bade farewell to the kind but unseen people of the cottage, and after the man had called their attention to a high, pyramid-shaped mountain on the opposite side of the Valley, and told them how to travel in order to reach it, they again started upon their journey.

They followed the course of a broad stream and passed several more pretty cottages; but of course they saw no one, nor did any one speak to them. Fruits and flowers grew plentifully all about, and there were many of the delicious damas that the people of Voe were so fond of.

About noon they stopped to allow Jim to rest in the shade of a pretty orchard, and while they plucked and ate some of the cherries and plums that grew there a soft voice suddenly said to them:

"There are bears near by. Be careful."

The Wizard got out his sword at once, and Zeb grabbed the horse-whip. Dorothy climbed into the buggy, although Jim had been unharnessed from it and was grazing some distance away.

The owner of the unseen voice laughed lightly and said:

"You cannot escape the bears that way."

"How CAN we 'scape?" asked Dorothy, nervously, for an unseen danger is always the hardest to face.

"You must take to the river," was the reply. "The bears will not venture upon the water."

"But we would be drowned!" exclaimed the girl.

"Oh, there is no need of that," said the voice, which from its gentle tones seemed to belong to a young girl. "You are strangers in the Valley of Voe, and do not seem to know our ways; so I will try to save you."

The next moment a broad-leaved plant was jerked from the ground where it grew and held suspended in the air before the Wizard.

"Sir," said the voice, "you must rub these leaves upon the soles of all your feet, and then you will be able to walk upon the water without sinking below the surface. It is a secret the bears do not know, and we people of Voe usually walk upon the water when we travel, and so escape our enemies."

"Thank you!" cried the Wizard, joyfully, and at once rubbed a leaf upon the soles of Dorothy's shoes and then upon his own. The girl took a leaf and rubbed it upon the kitten's paws, and the rest of the plant was handed to Zeb, who, after applying it to his own feet, carefully rubbed it upon all four of Jim's hoofs and then upon the tires of the buggy-wheels. He had nearly finished this last task when a low growling was suddenly heard and the horse began to jump around and kick viciously with his heels.

"Quick! To the water or you are lost!" cried their unseen friend, and without hesitation the Wizard drew the buggy down the bank and out upon the broad river, for Dorothy was still seated in it with Eureka in her arms. They did not sink at all, owing to the virtues of the strange plant they had used, and when the buggy was in the middle of the stream the Wizard returned to the bank to assist Zeb and Jim.

The horse was plunging madly about, and two or three deep gashes appeared upon its flanks, from which the blood flowed freely.

"Run for the river!" shouted the Wizard, and Jim quickly freed himself from his unseen tormenters by a few vicious kicks and then obeyed. As soon as he trotted out upon the surface of the river he found himself safe from pursuit, and Zeb was already running across the water toward Dorothy.

As the little Wizard turned to follow them he felt a hot breath against his cheek and heard a low, fierce growl. At once he began stabbing at the air with his sword, and he knew that he had struck some substance because when he drew back the blade it was dripping with blood. The third time that he thrust out the weapon there was a loud roar and a fall, and suddenly at his feet appeared the form of a great red bear, which was nearly as big as the horse and much stronger and fiercer. The beast was quite dead from the sword thrusts, and after a glance at its terrible claws and sharp teeth the little man turned in a panic and rushed out upon the water, for other menacing growls told him more bears were near.

On the river, however, the adventurers seemed to be perfectly safe. Dorothy and the buggy had floated slowly down stream with the current of the water, and the others made haste to join her. The Wizard opened his satchel and got out some sticking-plaster with which he mended the cuts Jim had received from the claws of the bears.

"I think we'd better stick to the river, after this," said Dorothy. "If our unknown friend hadn't warned us, and told us what to do, we would all be dead by this time."

"That is true," agreed the Wizard, "and as the river seems to be flowing in the direction of the Pyramid Mountain it will be the easiest way for us to travel."

Zeb hitched Jim to the buggy again, and the horse trotted along and drew them rapidly over the smooth water. The kitten was at first dreadfully afraid of getting wet, but Dorothy let her down and soon Eureka was frisking along beside the buggy without being scared a bit. Once a little fish swam too near the surface, and the kitten grabbed it in her mouth and ate it up as quick as a wink; but Dorothy cautioned her to be careful what she ate in this valley of enchantments, and no more fishes were careless enough to swim within reach.

After a journey of several hours they came to a point where the river curved, and they found they must cross a mile or so of the Valley before they came to the Pyramid Mountain. There were few houses in this part, and few orchards or flowers; so our friends feared they might encounter more of the savage bears, which they had learned to dread with all their hearts.

"You'll have to make a dash, Jim," said the Wizard, "and run as fast as you can go."

"All right," answered the horse; "I'll do my best. But you must remember I'm old, and my dashing days are past and gone."

All three got into the buggy and Zeb picked up the reins, though Jim needed no guidance of any sort. The horse was still smarting from the sharp claws of the invisible bears, and as soon as he was on land and headed toward the mountain the thought that more of those fearsome creatures might be near acted as a spur and sent him galloping along in a way that made Dorothy catch her breath.

Then Zeb, in a spirit of mischief, uttered a growl like that of the bears, and Jim pricked up his ears and fairly flew. His boney legs moved so fast they could scarcely be seen, and the Wizard clung fast to the seat and yelled "Whoa!" at the top of his voice.

"I—I'm 'fraid he's—he's running away!" gasped Dorothy.

"I KNOW he is," said Zeb; "but no bear can catch him if he keeps up that gait—and the harness or the buggy don't break."

Jim did not make a mile a minute; but almost before they were aware of it he drew up at the foot of the mountain, so suddenly that the Wizard and Zeb both sailed over the dashboard and landed in the soft grass—where they rolled over several times before they stopped. Dorothy nearly went with them, but she was holding fast to the iron rail of the seat, and that saved her. She squeezed the kitten, though, until it screeched; and then the old cab-horse made several curious sounds that led the little girl to suspect he was laughing at them all.

Chapter 10 - The Braided Man of Pyramid Mountains

The mountain before them was shaped like a cone and was so tall that its point was lost in the clouds. Directly facing the place where Jim had stopped was an arched opening leading to a broad stairway. The stairs were cut in the rock inside the mountain, and they were broad and not very steep, because they circled around like a cork-screw, and at the arched opening where the flight began the circle was quite big. At the foot of the stairs was a sign reading:

WARNING. These steps lead to the Land of the Gargoyles. DANGER! KEEP OUT.

"I wonder how Jim is ever going to draw the buggy up so many stairs," said Dorothy, gravely.

"No trouble at all," declared the horse, with a contemptuous neigh. "Still, I don't care to drag any passengers. You'll all have to walk."

"Suppose the stairs get steeper?" suggested Zeb, doubtfully.

"Then you'll have to boost the buggy-wheels, that's all," answered Jim.

"We'll try it, anyway," said the Wizard. "It's the only way to get out of the Valley of Voe."

So they began to ascend the stairs, Dorothy and the Wizard first, Jim next, drawing the buggy, and then Zeb to watch that nothing happened to the harness.

The light was dim, and soon they mounted into total darkness, so that the Wizard was obliged to get out his lanterns to light the way. But this enabled them to proceed steadily until they came to a landing where there was a rift in the side of the mountain that let in both light and air. Looking through this opening they could see the Valley of Voe lying far below them, the cottages seeming like toy houses from that distance.

After resting a few moments they resumed their climb, and still the stairs were broad and low enough for Jim to draw the buggy easily after him. The old horse panted a little, and had to stop often to get his breath. At such times they were all glad to wait for him, for continually climbing up stairs is sure to make one's legs ache.

They wound about, always going upward, for some time. The lights from the lanterns dimly showed the way, but it was a gloomy journey, and they were pleased when a broad streak of light ahead assured them they were coming to a second landing.

Here one side of the mountain had a great hole in it, like the mouth of a cavern, and the stairs stopped at the near edge of the floor and commenced ascending again at the opposite edge.

The opening in the mountain was on the side opposite to the Valley of Voe, and our travellers looked out upon a strange scene. Below them was a vast space, at the bottom of which was a black sea with rolling billows, through which little tongues of flame constantly shot up. Just above them, and almost on a level with their platform, were banks of rolling clouds which constantly shifted position and changed color. The blues and greys were very beautiful, and Dorothy noticed that on the cloud banks sat or reclined fleecy, shadowy forms of beautiful beings who must have been the Cloud Fairies. Mortals who stand upon the earth and look up at the sky cannot often distinguish these forms, but our friends were now so near to the clouds that they observed the dainty fairies very clearly.

"Are they real?" asked Zeb, in an awed voice.

"Of course," replied Dorothy, softly. "They are the Cloud Fairies."

"They seem like open-work," remarked the boy, gazing intently. "If I should squeeze one, there wouldn't be anything left of it."

In the open space between the clouds and the black, bubbling sea far beneath, could be seen an occasional strange bird winging its way swiftly through the air. These birds were of enormous size, and reminded Zeb of the rocs he had read about in the Arabian Nights. They had fierce eyes and sharp talons and beaks, and the children hoped none of them would venture into the cavern.

"Well, I declare!" suddenly exclaimed the little Wizard. "What in the world is this?"

They turned around and found a man standing on the floor in the center of the cave, who bowed very politely when he saw he had attracted their attention. He was a very old man, bent nearly double; but the queerest thing about him was his white hair and beard. These were so long that they reached to his feet, and both the hair and the beard were carefully plaited into many braids, and the end of each braid fastened with a bow of colored ribbon.

"Where did you come from?" asked Dorothy, wonderingly.

"No place at all," answered the man with the braids; "that is, not recently. Once I lived on top the earth, but for many years I have had my factory in this spot—half way up Pyramid Mountain."

"Are we only half way up?" enquired the boy, in a discouraged tone.

"I believe so, my lad," replied the braided man. "But as I have never been in either direction, down or up, since I arrived, I cannot be positive whether it is exactly half way or not."

"Have you a factory in this place?" asked the Wizard, who had been examining the strange personage carefully.

"To be sure," said the other. "I am a great inventor, you must know, and I manufacture my products in this lonely spot."

"What are your products?" enquired the Wizard.

"Well, I make Assorted Flutters for flags and bunting, and a superior grade of Rustles for ladies' silk gowns."

"I thought so," said the Wizard, with a sigh. "May we examine some of these articles?"

"Yes, indeed; come into my shop, please," and the braided man turned and led the way into a smaller cave, where he evidently lived. Here, on a broad shelf, were several card-board boxes of various sizes, each tied with cotton cord.

"This," said the man, taking up a box and handling it gently, "contains twelve dozen rustles—enough to last any lady a year. Will you buy it, my dear?" he asked, addressing Dorothy.

"My gown isn't silk," she said, smiling.

"Never mind. When you open the box the rustles will escape, whether you are wearing a silk dress or not," said the man, seriously. Then he picked up another box. "In this," he continued, "are many assorted flutters. They are invaluable to make flags flutter on a still day, when there is no wind. You, sir," turning to the Wizard, "ought to have this assortment. Once you have tried my goods I am sure you will never be without them."

"I have no money with me," said the Wizard, evasively.

"I do not want money," returned the braided man, "for I could not spend it in this deserted place if I had it. But I would like very much a blue hair-ribbon. You will notice my braids are tied with yellow, pink, brown, red, green, white and black; but I have no blue ribbons."

"I'll get you one!" cried Dorothy, who was sorry for the poor man; so she ran back to the buggy and took from her suit-case a pretty blue ribbon. It did her good to see how the braided man's eyes sparkled when he received this treasure.

"You have made me very, very happy, my dear!" he exclaimed; and then he insisted on the Wizard taking the box of flutters and the little girl accepting the box of rustles.

"You may need them, some time," he said, "and there is really no use in my manufacturing these things unless somebody uses them."

"Why did you leave the surface of the earth?" enquired the Wizard.

"I could not help it. It is a sad story, but if you will try to restrain your tears I will tell you about it. On earth I was a manufacturer of Imported Holes for American Swiss Cheese, and I will acknowledge that I supplied a superior article, which was in great demand. Also I made pores for porous plasters and high-grade holes for doughnuts and buttons. Finally I invented a new Adjustable Post-hole, which I thought would make my fortune. I manufactured a large quantity of these post-holes, and having no room in which to store them I set them all end to end and put the top one in the ground. That made an extraordinary long hole, as you may imagine, and reached far down into the earth; and, as I leaned over it to try to see to the bottom, I lost my balance and tumbled in. Unfortunately, the hole led directly into the vast space you see outside this mountain; but I managed to catch a point of rock that projected from this cavern, and so saved myself from tumbling headlong into the black waves beneath, where the tongues of flame that dart out would certainly have consumed me. Here, then, I made my home; and although it is a lonely place I amuse myself making rustles and flutters, and so get along very nicely."

When the braided man had completed this strange tale Dorothy nearly laughed, because it was all so absurd; but the Wizard tapped his forehead significantly, to indicate that he thought the poor man was crazy. So they politely bade him good day, and went back to the outer cavern to resume their journey.

Chapter 11 - They Meet the Wooden Gargoyles

Another breathless climb brought our adventurers to a third landing where there was a rift in the mountain. On peering out all they could see was rolling banks of clouds, so thick that they obscured all else.

But the travellers were obliged to rest, and while they were sitting on the rocky floor the Wizard felt in his pocket and brought out the nine tiny piglets. To his delight they were now plainly visible, which proved that they had passed beyond the influence of the magical Valley of Voe.

"Why, we can see each other again!" cried one, joyfully.

"Yes," sighed Eureka; "and I also can see you again, and the sight makes me dreadfully hungry. Please, Mr. Wizard, may I eat just one of the fat little piglets? You'd never miss ONE of them, I'm sure!"

"What a horrid, savage beast!" exclaimed a piglet; "and after we've been such good friends, too, and played with one another!"

"When I'm not hungry, I love to play with you all," said the kitten, demurely; "but when my stomach is empty it seems that nothing would fill it so nicely as a fat piglet."

"And we trusted you so!" said another of the nine, reproachfully.

"And thought you were respectable!" said another.

"It seems we were mistaken," declared a third, looking at the kitten timorously, "no one with such murderous desires should belong to our party, I'm sure."

"You see, Eureka," remarked Dorothy, reprovingly, "you are making yourself disliked. There are certain things proper for a kitten to eat; but I never heard of a kitten eating a pig, under ANY cir'stances."

"Did you ever see such little pigs before?" asked the kitten. "They are no bigger than mice, and I'm sure mice are proper for me to eat."

"It isn't the bigness, dear; its the variety," replied the girl. "These are Mr. Wizard's pets, just as you are my pet, and it wouldn't be any more proper for you to eat them than it would be for Jim to eat you."

"And that's just what I shall do if you don't let those little balls of pork alone," said Jim, glaring at the kitten with his round, big eyes. "If you injure any one of them I'll chew you up instantly."

The kitten looked at the horse thoughtfully, as if trying to decide whether he meant it or not.

"In that case," she said, "I'll leave them alone. You haven't many teeth left, Jim, but the few you have are sharp enough to make me shudder. So the piglets will be perfectly safe, hereafter, as far as I am concerned."

"That is right, Eureka," remarked the Wizard, earnestly. "Let us all be a happy family and love one another."

Eureka yawned and stretched herself.

"I've always loved the piglets," she said; "but they don't love me."

"No one can love a person he's afraid of," asserted Dorothy. "If you behave, and don't scare the little pigs, I'm sure they'll grow very fond of you."

The Wizard now put the nine tiny ones back into his pocket and the journey was resumed.

"We must be pretty near the top, now," said the boy, as they climbed wearily up the dark, winding stairway.

"The Country of the Gurgles can't be far from the top of the earth," remarked Dorothy. "It isn't very nice down here. I'd like to get home again, I'm sure."

No one replied to this, because they found they needed all their breath for the climb. The stairs had become narrower and Zeb and the Wizard often had to help Jim pull the buggy from one step to another, or keep it from jamming against the rocky walls.

At last, however, a dim light appeared ahead of them, which grew clearer and stronger as they advanced.

"Thank goodness we're nearly there!" panted the little Wizard.

Jim, who was in advance, saw the last stair before him and stuck his head above the rocky sides of the stairway. Then he halted, ducked down and began to back up, so that he nearly fell with the buggy onto the others.

"Let's go down again!" he said, in his hoarse voice.

"Nonsense!" snapped the tired Wizard. "What's the matter with you, old man?"

"Everything," grumbled the horse. "I've taken a look at this place, and it's no fit country for real creatures to go to. Everything's dead, up there—no flesh or blood or growing thing anywhere."

"Never mind;. we can't turn back," said Dorothy; "and we don't intend to stay there, anyhow."

"It's dangerous," growled Jim, in a stubborn tone.

"See here, my good steed," broke in the Wizard, "little Dorothy and I have been in many queer countries in our travels, and always escaped without harm. We've even been to the marvelous Land of Oz—haven't we, Dorothy?—so we don't much care what the Country of the Gargoyles is like. Go ahead, Jim, and whatever happens we'll make the best of it."

"All right," answered the horse; "this is your excursion, and not mine; so if you get into trouble don't blame me."

With this speech he bent forward and dragged the buggy up the remaining steps. The others followed and soon they were all standing upon a broad platform and gazing at the most curious and startling sight their eyes had ever beheld.

"The Country of the Gargoyles is all wooden!" exclaimed Zeb; and so it was. The ground was sawdust and the pebbles scattered around were hard knots from trees, worn smooth in course of time. There were odd wooden houses, with carved wooden flowers in the front yards. The tree-trunks were of coarse wood, but the leaves of the trees were shavings. The patches of grass were splinters of wood, and where neither grass nor sawdust showed was a solid wooden flooring. Wooden birds fluttered among the trees and wooden cows were browsing upon the wooden grass; but the most amazing things of all were the wooden people—the creatures known as Gargoyles.

These were very numerous, for the place was thickly inhabited, and a large group of the queer people clustered near, gazing sharply upon the strangers who had emerged from the long spiral stairway.

The Gargoyles were very small of stature, being less than three feet in height. Their bodies were round, their legs short and thick and their arms extraordinarily long and stout. Their heads were too big for their bodies and their faces were decidedly ugly to look upon. Some had long, curved noses and chins, small eyes and wide, grinning mouths. Others had flat noses, protruding eyes, and ears that were shaped like those of an elephant. There were many types, indeed, scarcely two being alike; but all were equally disagreeable in appearance. The tops of their heads had no hair, but were carved into a variety of fantastic shapes, some having a row of points or balls around the top, others designs resembling flowers or vegetables, and still others having squares that looked like waffles cut criss-cross on their heads. They all wore short wooden wings which were fastened to their wooden bodies by means of wooden hinges with wooden screws, and with these wings they flew swiftly and noiselessly here and there, their legs being of little use to them.

This noiseless motion was one of the most peculiar things about the Gargoyles. They made no sounds at all, either in flying or trying to speak, and they conversed mainly by means of quick signals made with their wooden fingers or lips. Neither was there any sound to be heard anywhere throughout the wooden country. The birds did not sing, nor did the cows moo; yet there was more than ordinary activity everywhere.

The group of these queer creatures which was discovered clustered near the stairs at first remained staring and motionless, glaring with evil eyes at the intruders who had so suddenly appeared in their land. In turn the Wizard and the children, the horse and the kitten, examined the Gargoyles with the same silent attention.

"There's going to be trouble, I'm sure," remarked the horse. "Unhitch those tugs, Zeb, and set me free from the buggy, so I can fight comfortably."

"Jim's right," sighed the Wizard. "There's going to be trouble, and my sword isn't stout enough to cut up those wooden bodies—so I shall have to get out my revolvers."

He got his satchel from the buggy and, opening it, took out two deadly looking revolvers that made the children shrink back in alarm just to look at.

"What harm can the Gurgles do?" asked Dorothy. "They have no weapons to hurt us with."

"Each of their arms is a wooden club," answered the little man, "and I'm sure the creatures mean mischief, by the looks of their eyes. Even these revolvers can merely succeed in damaging a few of their wooden bodies, and after that we will be at their mercy."

"But why fight at all, in that case?" asked the girl.

"So I may die with a clear conscience," returned the Wizard, gravely. "It's every man's duty to do the best he knows how; and I'm going to do it."

"Wish I had an axe," said Zeb, who by now had unhitched the horse.

"If we had known we were coming we might have brought along several other useful things," responded the Wizard. "But we dropped into this adventure rather unexpectedly."

The Gargoyles had backed away a distance when they heard the sound of talking, for although our friends had spoken in low tones their words seemed loud in the silence surrounding them. But as soon as the conversation ceased, the grinning, ugly creatures arose in a flock and flew swiftly toward the strangers, their long arms stretched out before them like the bowsprits of a fleet of sail-boats. The horse had especially attracted their notice, because it was the biggest and strangest creature they had ever seen; so it became the center of their first attack.

But Jim was ready for them, and when he saw them coming he turned his heels toward them and began kicking out as hard as he could. Crack! crash! bang! went his iron-shod hoofs against the wooden bodies of the Gargoyles, and they were battered right and left with such force that they scattered like straws in the wind. But the noise and clatter seemed as dreadful to them as Jim's heels, for all who were able swiftly turned and flew away to a great distance. The others picked themselves up from the ground one by one and quickly rejoined their fellows, so for a moment the horse thought he had won the fight with ease.

But the Wizard was not so confident.

"Those wooden things are impossible to hurt," he said, "and all the damage Jim has done to them is to knock a few splinters from their noses and ears. That cannot make them look any uglier, I'm sure, and it is my opinion they will soon renew the attack."

"What made them fly away?" asked Dorothy.

"The noise, of course. Don't you remember how the Champion escaped them by shouting his battle-cry?"

"Suppose we escape down the stairs, too," suggested the boy. "We have time, just now, and I'd rather face the invis'ble bears than those wooden imps."

"No," returned Dorothy, stoutly, "it won't do to go back, for then we would never get home. Let's fight it out."

"That is what I advise," said the Wizard. "They haven't defeated us yet, and Jim is worth a whole army."

But the Gargoyles were clever enough not to attack the horse the next time. They advanced in a great swarm, having been joined by many more of their kind, and they flew straight over Jim's head to where the others were standing.

The Wizard raised one of his revolvers and fired into the throng of his enemies, and the shot resounded like a clap of thunder in that silent place.

Some of the wooden beings fell flat upon the ground, where they quivered and trembled in every limb; but most of them managed to wheel and escape again to a distance.

Zeb ran and picked up one of the Gargoyles that lay nearest to him. The top of its head was carved into a crown and the Wizard's bullet had struck it exactly in the left eye, which was a hard wooden knot. Half of the bullet stuck in the wood and half stuck out, so it had been the jar and the sudden noise that had knocked the creature down, more than the fact that it was really hurt. Before this crowned Gargoyle had recovered himself Zeb had wound a strap several times around its body, confining its wings and arms so that it could not move. Then, having tied the wooden creature securely, the boy buckled the strap and tossed his prisoner into the buggy. By that time the others had all retired.

Chapter 12 - A Wonderful Escape

For a while the enemy hesitated to renew the attack. Then a few of them advanced until another shot from the Wizard's revolver made them retreat.

"That's fine," said Zeb. "We've got 'em on the run now, sure enough."

"But only for a time," replied the Wizard, shaking his head gloomily. "These revolvers are good for six shots each, but when those are gone we shall be helpless."

The Gargoyles seemed to realize this, for they sent a few of their band time after time to attack the strangers and draw the fire from the little man's revolvers. In this way none of them was shocked by the dreadful report more than once, for the main band kept far away and each time a new company was sent into the battle. When the Wizard had fired all of his twelve bullets he had caused no damage to the enemy except to stun a few by the noise, and so he as no nearer to victory than in the beginning of the fray.

"What shall we do now?" asked Dorothy, anxiously.

"Let's yell—all together," said Zeb.

"And fight at the same time," added the Wizard. "We will get near Jim, so that he can help us, and each one must take some weapon and do the best he can. I'll use my sword, although it isn't much account in this affair. Dorothy must take her parasol and open it suddenly when the wooden folks attack her. I haven't anything for you, Zeb."

"I'll use the king," said the boy, and pulled his prisoner out of the buggy. The bound Gargoyle's arms extended far out beyond its head, so by grasping its wrists Zeb found the king made a very good club. The boy was strong for one of his years, having always worked upon a farm; so he was likely to prove more dangerous to the enemy than the Wizard.

When the next company of Gargoyles advanced, our adventurers began yelling as if they had gone mad. Even the kitten gave a dreadfully shrill scream and at the same time Jim the cab-horse neighed loudly. This daunted the enemy for a time, but the defenders were soon out of breath. Perceiving this, as well as the fact that there were no more of the awful "bangs" to come from the revolvers, the Gargoyles advanced in a swarm as thick as bees, so that the air was filled with them.

Dorothy squatted upon the ground and put up her parasol, which nearly covered her and proved a great protection. The Wizard's sword-blade snapped into a dozen pieces at the first blow he struck against the wooden people. Zeb pounded away with the Gargoyle he was using as a club until he had knocked down dozens of foes; but at the last they clustered so thickly about him that he no longer had room in which to swing his arms. The horse performed some wonderful kicking and even Eureka assisted when she leaped bodily upon the Gargoyles and scratched and bit at them like a wild-cat.

But all this bravery amounted to nothing at all. The wooden things wound their long arms around Zeb and the Wizard and held them fast. Dorothy was captured in the same way, and numbers of the Gargoyles clung to Jim's legs, so weighting him down that the poor beast was helpless. Eureka made a desperate dash to escape and scampered along the ground like a streak; but a grinning Gargoyle flew after her and grabbed her before she had gone very far.

All of them expected nothing less than instant death; but to their surprise the wooden creatures flew into the air with them and bore them far away, over miles and miles of wooden country, until they came to a wooden city. The houses of this city had many corners, being square and six-sided and eight-sided. They were tower-like in shape and the best of them seemed old and weather-worn; yet all were strong and substantial.

To one of these houses which had neither doors nor windows, but only one broad opening far up underneath the roof, the prisoners were brought by their captors. The Gargoyles roughly pushed them into the opening, where there was a platform, and then flew away and left them. As they had no wings the strangers could not fly away, and if they jumped down from such a height they would surely be killed. The creatures had sense enough to reason that way, and the only mistake they made was in supposing the earth people were unable to overcome such ordinary difficulties.

Jim was brought with the others, although it took a good many Gargoyles to carry the big beast through the air and land him on the high platform, and the buggy was thrust in after him because it belonged to the party and the wooden folks had no idea what it was used for or whether it was alive or not. When Eureka's captor had thrown the kitten after the others the last Gargoyle silently disappeared, leaving our friends to breathe freely once more.

"What an awful fight!" said Dorothy, catching her breath in little gasps.

"Oh, I don't know," purred Eureka, smoothing her ruffled fur with her paw; "we didn't manage to hurt anybody, and nobody managed to hurt us."

"Thank goodness we are together again, even if we are prisoners," sighed the little girl.

"I wonder why they didn't kill us on the spot," remarked Zeb, who had lost his king in the struggle.

"They are probably keeping us for some ceremony," the Wizard answered, reflectively; "but there is no doubt they intend to kill us as dead as possible in a short time."

"As dead as poss'ble would be pretty dead, wouldn't it?" asked Dorothy.

"Yes, my dear. But we have no need to worry about that just now. Let us examine our prison and see what it is like."

186

The space underneath the roof, where they stood, permitted them to see on all sides of the tall building, and they looked with much curiosity at the city spread out beneath them. Everything visible was made of wood, and the scene seemed stiff and extremely unnatural.

From their platform a stair descended into the house, and the children and the Wizard explored it after lighting a lantern to show them the way. Several stories of empty rooms rewarded their search, but nothing more; so after a time they came back to the platform again. Had there been any doors or windows in the lower rooms, or had not the boards of the house been so thick and stout, escape could have been easy; but to remain down below was like being in a cellar or the hold of a ship, and they did not like the darkness or the damp smell.

In this country, as in all others they had visited underneath the earth's surface, there was no night, a constant and strong light coming from some unknown source. Looking out, they could see into some of the houses near them, where there were open windows in abundance, and were able to mark the forms of the wooden Gargoyles moving about in their dwellings.

"This seems to be their time of rest," observed the Wizard. "All people need rest, even if they are made of wood, and as there is no night here they select a certain time of the day in which to sleep or doze."

"I feel sleepy myself," remarked Zeb, yawning.

"Why, where's Eureka?" cried Dorothy, suddenly.

They all looked around, but the kitten was no place to be seen.

"She's gone out for a walk," said Jim, gruffly.

"Where? On the roof?" asked the girl.

"No; she just dug her claws into the wood and climbed down the sides of this house to the ground."

"She couldn't climb DOWN, Jim," said Dorothy. "To climb means to go up."

"Who said so?" demanded the horse.

"My school-teacher said so; and she knows a lot, Jim."

"To 'climb down' is sometimes used as a figure of speech," remarked the Wizard.

"Well, this was a figure of a cat," said Jim, "and she WENT down, anyhow, whether she climbed or crept."

"Dear me! how careless Eureka is," exclaimed the girl, much distressed. "The Gurgles will get her, sure!"

"Ha, ha!" chuckled the old cab-horse; "they're not 'Gurgles,' little maid; they're Gargoyles."

"Never mind; they'll get Eureka, whatever they're called."

"No they won't," said the voice of the kitten, and Eureka herself crawled over the edge of the platform and sat down quietly upon the floor.

"Wherever have you been, Eureka?" asked Dorothy, sternly.

"Watching the wooden folks. They're too funny for anything, Dorothy. Just now they are all going to bed, and—what do you think?—they unhook the hinges of their wings and put them in a corner until they wake up again."

"What, the hinges?"

"No; the wings."

"That," said Zeb, "explains why this house is used by them for a prison. If any of the Gargoyles act badly, and have to be put in jail, they are brought here and their wings unhooked and taken away from them until they promise to be good."

The Wizard had listened intently to what Eureka had said.

"I wish we had some of those loose wings," he said.

"Could we fly with them?" asked Dorothy.

"I think so. If the Gargoyles can unhook the wings then the power to fly lies in the wings themselves, and not in the wooden bodies of the people who wear them. So, if we had the wings, we could probably fly as well as they do—as least while we are in their country and under the spell of its magic."

"But how would it help us to be able to fly?" questioned the girl.

"Come here," said the little man, and took her to one of the corners of the building. "Do you see that big rock standing on the hillside yonder?" he continued, pointing with his finger.

"Yes; it's a good way off, but I can see it," she replied.

"Well, inside that rock, which reaches up into the clouds, is an archway very much like the one we entered when we climbed the spiral stairway from the Valley of Voe. I'll get my spy-glass, and then you can see it more plainly."

He fetched a small but powerful telescope, which had been in his satchel, and by its aid the little girl clearly saw the opening.

"Where does it lead to?" she asked.

"That I cannot tell," said the Wizard; "but we cannot now be far below the earth's surface, and that entrance may lead to another stairway that will bring us on top of our world again, where we belong. So, if we had the wings, and could escape the Gargoyles, we might fly to that rock and be saved."

"I'll get you the wings," said Zeb, who had thoughtfully listened to all this. "That is, if the kitten will show me where they are."

"But how can you get down?" enquired the girl, wonderingly.

For answer Zeb began to unfasten Jim's harness, strap by strap, and to buckle one piece to another until he had made a long leather strip that would reach to the ground.

"I can climb down that, all right," he said.

"No you can't," remarked Jim, with a twinkle in his round eyes. "You may GO down, but you can only CLIMB up."

"Well, I'll climb up when I get back, then," said the boy, with a laugh. "Now, Eureka, you'll have to show me the way to those wings."

"You must be very quiet," warned the kitten; "for if you make the least noise the Gargoyles will wake up. They can hear a pin drop."

"I'm not going to drop a pin," said Zeb.

He had fastened one end of the strap to a wheel of the buggy, and now he let the line dangle over the side of the house.

"Be careful," cautioned Dorothy, earnestly.

"I will," said the boy, and let himself slide over the edge.

The girl and the Wizard leaned over and watched Zeb work his way carefully downward, hand over hand, until he stood upon the ground below. Eureka clung with her claws to the wooden side of the house and let herself down easily. Then together they crept away to enter the low doorway of a neighboring dwelling.

The watchers waited in breathless suspense until the boy again appeared, his arms now full of the wooden wings.

When he came to where the strap was hanging he tied the wings all in a bunch to the end of the line, and the Wizard drew them up. Then the line was let down again for Zeb to climb up by. Eureka quickly followed him, and soon they were all standing together upon the platform, with eight of the much prized wooden wings beside them.

The boy was no longer sleepy, but full of energy and excitement. He put the harness together again and hitched Jim to the buggy. Then, with the Wizard's help, he tried to fasten some of the wings to the old cab-horse.

This was no easy task, because half of each one of the hinges of the wings was missing, it being still fastened to the body of the Gargoyle who had used it. However, the Wizard went once more to his satchel— which seemed to contain a surprising variety of odds and ends—and brought out a spool of strong wire, by means of which they managed to fasten four of the wings to Jim's harness, two near his head and two near his tail. They were a bit wiggley, but secure enough if only the harness held together.

The other four wings were then fastened to the buggy, two on each side, for the buggy must bear the weight of the children and the Wizard as it flew through the air.

These preparations had not consumed a great deal of time, but the sleeping Gargoyles were beginning to wake up and move around, and soon some of them would be hunting for their missing wings. So the prisoners resolved to leave their prison at once.

They mounted into the buggy, Dorothy holding Eureka safe in her lap. The girl sat in the middle of the seat, with Zeb and the Wizard on each side of her. When all was ready the boy shook the reins and said:

"Fly away, Jim!"

"Which wings must I flop first?" asked the cab-horse, undecidedly.

"Flop them all together," suggested the Wizard.

"Some of them are crooked," objected the horse.

"Never mind; we will steer with the wings on the buggy," said Zeb. "Just you light out and make for that rock, Jim; and don't waste any time about it, either."

So the horse gave a groan, flopped its four wings all together, and flew away from the platform. Dorothy was a little anxious about the success of their trip, for the way Jim arched his long neck and spread out his bony legs as he fluttered and floundered through the air was enough to make anybody nervous. He groaned, too, as if frightened, and the wings creaked dreadfully because the Wizard had forgotten to oil them; but they kept fairly good time with the wings of the buggy, so that they made excellent progress from the start. The only thing that anyone could complain of with justice was the fact that they wobbled first up and then down, as if the road were rocky instead of being as smooth as the air could make it.

The main point, however, was that they flew, and flew swiftly, if a bit unevenly, toward the rock for which they had headed.

Some of the Gargoyles saw them, presently, and lost no time in collecting a band to pursue the escaping prisoners; so that when Dorothy happened to look back she saw them coming in a great cloud that almost darkened the sky.

Chapter 13 - The Den of the Dragonettes

Our friends had a good start and were able to maintain it, for with their eight wings they could go just as fast as could the Gargoyles. All the way to the great rock the wooden people followed them, and when Jim finally alighted at the mouth of the cavern the pursuers were still some distance away.

"But, I'm afraid they'll catch us yet," said Dorothy, greatly excited.

"No; we must stop them," declared the Wizard. "Quick Zeb, help me pull off these wooden wings!"

They tore off the wings, for which they had no further use, and the Wizard piled them in a heap just outside the entrance to the cavern. Then he poured over them all the kerosene oil that was left in his oil-can, and lighting a match set fire to the pile.

The flames leaped up at once and the bonfire began to smoke and roar and crackle just as the great army of wooden Gargoyles arrived. The creatures drew back at once, being filled with fear and horror; for such as dreadful thing as a fire they had never before known in all the history of their wooden land.

Inside the archway were several doors, leading to different rooms built into the mountain, and Zeb and the Wizard lifted these wooden doors from their hinges and tossed them all on the flames.

"That will prove a barrier for some time to come," said the little man, smiling pleasantly all over his wrinkled face at the success of their stratagem. "Perhaps the flames will set fire to all that miserable wooden country, and if it does the loss will be very small and the Gargoyles never will be missed. But come, my children; let us explore the mountain and discover which way we must go in order to escape from this cavern, which is getting to be almost as hot as a bake-oven."

To their disappointment there was within this mountain no regular flight of steps by means of which they could mount to the earth's surface. A sort of inclined tunnel led upward for a way, and they found the floor of it both rough and steep. Then a sudden turn brought them to a narrow gallery where the buggy could not pass. This delayed and bothered them for a while, because they did not wish to leave the buggy behind them. It carried their baggage and was useful to ride in wherever there were good roads, and since it had accompanied them so far in their travels they felt it their duty to preserve it. So Zeb and the Wizard set to work and took off the wheels and the top, and then they put the buggy edgewise, so it would take up the smallest space. In this position they managed, with the aid of the patient cab-horse, to drag the vehicle through the narrow part of the passage. It was not a great distance, fortunately, and when the path grew broader they put the buggy together again and proceeded more comfortably. But the road was nothing more than a series of rifts or cracks in the mountain, and it went zig-zag in every direction, slanting first up and then down until they were puzzled as to whether they were any nearer to the top of the earth than when they had started, hours before.

"Anyhow," said Dorothy, "we've 'scaped those awful Gurgles, and that's ONE comfort!"

"Probably the Gargoyles are still busy trying to put out the fire," returned the Wizard. "But even if they succeeded in doing that it would be very difficult for them to fly amongst these rocks; so I am sure we need fear them no longer."

Once in a while they would come to a deep crack in the floor, which made the way quite dangerous; but there was still enough oil in the lanterns to give them light, and the cracks were not so wide but that they were able to jump over them. Sometimes they had to climb over heaps of loose rock, where Jim could scarcely drag the buggy. At such times Dorothy, Zeb and the Wizard all pushed behind, and lifted the wheels over the roughest places; so they managed, by dint of hard work, to keep going. But the little party was both weary and discouraged when at last, on turning a sharp corner, the wanderers found themselves in a vast cave arching high over their heads and having a smooth, level floor.

The cave was circular in shape, and all around its edge, near to the ground, appeared groups of dull yellow lights, two of them being always side by side. These were motionless at first, but soon began to flicker more brightly and to sway slowly from side to side and then up and down.

"What sort of place is this?" asked the boy, trying to see more clearly through the gloom.

"I cannot imagine, I'm sure," answered the Wizard, also peering about.

"Woogh!" snarled Eureka, arching her back until her hair stood straight on end; "it's den of alligators, or crocodiles, or some other dreadful creatures! Don't you see their terrible eyes?"

"Eureka sees better in the dark than we can," whispered Dorothy. "Tell us, dear, what do the creatures look like?" she asked, addressing her pet.

"I simply can't describe 'em," answered the kitten, shuddering. "Their eyes are like pie-plates and their mouths like coal-scuttles. But their bodies don't seem very big."

"Where are they?" enquired the girl.

"They are in little pockets all around the edge of this cavern. Oh, Dorothy—you can't imagine what horrid things they are! They're uglier than the Gargoyles."

"Tut-tut! be careful how you criticise your neighbors," spoke a rasping voice near by. "As a matter of fact you are rather ugly-looking creatures yourselves, and I'm sure mother has often told us we were the loveliest and prettiest things in all the world."

Hearing these words our friends turned in the direction of the sound, and the Wizard held his lanterns so that their light would flood one of the little pockets in the rock.

"Why, it's a dragon!" he exclaimed.

"No," answered the owner of the big yellow eyes which were blinking at them so steadily; "you are wrong about that. We hope to grow to be dragons some day, but just now we're only dragonettes."

"What's that?" asked Dorothy, gazing fearfully at the great scaley head, the yawning mouth and the big eyes.

"Young dragons, of course; but we are not allowed to call ourselves real dragons until we get our full growth," was the reply. "The big dragons are very proud, and don't think children amount to much; but mother says that some day we will all be very powerful and important."

"Where is your mother?" asked the Wizard, anxiously looking around.

"She has gone up to the top of the earth to hunt for our dinner. If she has good luck she will bring us an elephant, or a brace of rhinoceri, or perhaps a few dozen people to stay our hunger."

"Oh; are you hungry?" enquired Dorothy, drawing back.

"Very," said the dragonette, snapping its jaws.

"And—and—do you eat people?"

"To be sure, when we can get them. But they've been very scarce for a few years and we usually have to be content with elephants or buffaloes," answered the creature, in a regretful tone.

"How old are you?" enquired Zeb, who stared at the yellow eyes as if fascinated.

"Quite young, I grieve to say; and all of my brothers and sisters that you see here are practically my own age. If I remember rightly, we were sixty-six years old the day before yesterday."

"But that isn't young!" cried Dorothy, in amazement.

"No?" drawled the dragonette; "it seems to me very babyish."

"How old is your mother?" asked the girl.

"Mother's about two thousand years old; but she carelessly lost track of her age a few centuries ago and skipped several hundreds. She's a little fussy, you know, and afraid of growing old, being a widow and still in her prime."

"I should think she would be," agreed Dorothy. Then, after a moment's thought, she asked: "Are we friends or enemies? I mean, will you be good to us, or do you intend to eat us?"

"As for that, we dragonettes would love to eat you, my child; but unfortunately mother has tied all our tails around the rocks at the back of our individual caves, so that we can not crawl out to get you. If you choose to come nearer we will make a mouthful of you in a wink; but unless you do you will remain quite safe."

There was a regretful accent in the creature's voice, and at the words all the other dragonettes sighed dismally.

Dorothy felt relieved. Presently she asked:

"Why did your mother tie your tails?"

"Oh, she is sometimes gone for several weeks on her hunting trips, and if we were not tied we would crawl all over the mountain and fight with each other and get into a lot of mischief. Mother usually knows what she is about, but she made a mistake this time; for you are sure to escape us unless you come too near, and you probably won't do that."

"No, indeed!" said the little girl. "We don't wish to be eaten by such awful beasts."

"Permit me to say," returned the dragonette, "that you are rather impolite to call us names, knowing that we cannot resent your insults. We consider ourselves very beautiful in appearance, for mother has told us so, and she knows. And we are of an excellent family and have a pedigree that I challenge any humans to equal, as it extends back about twenty thousand years, to the time of the famous Green Dragon of Atlantis, who lived in a time when humans had not yet been created. Can you match that pedigree, little girl?"

"Well," said Dorothy, "I was born on a farm in Kansas, and I guess that's being just as 'spectable and haughty as living in a cave with your tail tied to a rock. If it isn't I'll have to stand it, that's all."

"Tastes differ," murmured the dragonette, slowly drooping its scaly eyelids over its yellow eyes, until they looked like half-moons.

Being reassured by the fact that the creatures could not crawl out of their rock-pockets, the children and the Wizard now took time to examine them more closely. The heads of the dragonettes were as big as barrels and covered with hard, greenish scales that glittered brightly under the light of the lanterns. Their front legs, which grew just back of their heads, were also strong and big; but their bodies were smaller around than their heads, and dwindled away in a long line until their tails were slim as a shoe-string. Dorothy thought, if it had taken them sixty-six years to grow to this size, that it would be fully a hundred years more before they could hope to call themselves dragons, and that seemed like a good while to wait to grow up.

"It occurs to me," said the Wizard, "that we ought to get out of this place before the mother dragon comes back."

"Don't hurry," called one of the dragonettes; "mother will be glad to meet you, I'm sure."

"You may be right," replied the Wizard, "but we're a little particular about associating with strangers. Will you kindly tell us which way your mother went to get on top the earth?"

"That is not a fair question to ask us," declared another dragonette. "For, if we told you truly, you might escape us altogether; and if we told you an untruth we would be naughty and deserve to be punished."

"Then," decided Dorothy, "we must find our way out the best we can."

They circled all around the cavern, keeping a good distance away from the blinking yellow eyes of the dragonettes, and presently discovered that there were two paths leading from the wall opposite to the place where they had entered. They selected one of these at a venture and hurried along it as fast as they could go, for they had no idea when the mother dragon would be back and were very anxious not to make her acquaintance.

Chapter 14 - Ozma Uses the Magic Belt

For a considerable distance the way led straight upward in a gentle incline, and the wanderers made such good progress that they grew hopeful and eager, thinking they might see sunshine at any minute. But at length they came unexpectedly upon a huge rock that shut off the passage and blocked them from proceeding a single step farther.

This rock was separate from the rest of the mountain and was in motion, turning slowly around and around as if upon a pivot. When first they came to it there was a solid wall before them; but presently it revolved until there was exposed a wide, smooth path across it to the other side. This appeared so unexpectedly that they were unprepared to take advantage of it at first, and allowed the rocky wall to swing around again before they had decided to pass over. But they knew now that there was a means of escape and so waited patiently until the path appeared for the second time.

The children and the Wizard rushed across the moving rock and sprang into the passage beyond, landing safely though a little out of breath. Jim the cab-horse came last, and the rocky wall almost caught him; for just as he leaped to the floor of the further passage the wall swung across it and a loose stone that the buggy wheels knocked against fell into the narrow crack where the rock turned, and became wedged there.

They heard a crunching, grinding sound, a loud snap, and the turn-table came to a stop with its broadest surface shutting off the path from which they had come.

"Never mind," said Zeb, "we don't want to get back, anyhow."

"I'm not so sure of that," returned Dorothy. "The mother dragon may come down and catch us here."

"It is possible," agreed the Wizard, "if this proves to be the path she usually takes. But I have been examining this tunnel, and I do not see any signs of so large a beast having passed through it."

"Then we're all right," said the girl, "for if the dragon went the other way she can't poss'bly get to us now."

"Of course not, my dear. But there is another thing to consider. The mother dragon probably knows the road to the earth's surface, and if she went the other way then we have come the wrong way," said the Wizard, thoughtfully.

"Dear me!" cried Dorothy. "That would be unlucky, wouldn't it?"

"Very. Unless this passage also leads to the top of the earth," said Zeb. "For my part, if we manage to get out of here I'll be glad it isn't the way the dragon goes."

"So will I," returned Dorothy. "It's enough to have your pedigree flung in your face by those saucy dragonettes. No one knows what the mother might do."

They now moved on again, creeping slowly up another steep incline. The lanterns were beginning to grow dim, and the Wizard poured the remaining oil from one into the other, so that the one light would last longer. But their journey was almost over, for in a short time they reached a small cave from which there was no further outlet.

They did not realize their ill fortune at first, for their hearts were gladdened by the sight of a ray of sunshine coming through a small crack in the roof of the cave, far overhead. That meant that their world—the real world—was not very far away, and that the succession of perilous adventures they had encountered had at last brought them near the earth's surface, which meant home to them. But when the adventurers looked more carefully around them they discovered that there were in a strong prison from which there was no hope of escape.

"But we're ALMOST on earth again," cried Dorothy, "for there is the sun—the most BEAU'FUL sun that shines!" and she pointed eagerly at the crack in the distant roof.

"Almost on earth isn't being there," said the kitten, in a discontented tone. "It wouldn't be possible for even me to get up to that crack—or through it if I got there."

"It appears that the path ends here," announced the Wizard, gloomily.

"And there is no way to go back," added Zeb, with a low whistle of perplexity.

"I was sure it would come to this, in the end," remarked the old cab-horse. "Folks don't fall into the middle of the earth and then get back again to tell of their adventures—not in real life. And the whole thing has been unnatural because that cat and I are both able to talk your language, and to understand the words you say."

"And so can the nine tiny piglets," added Eureka. "Don't forget them, for I may have to eat them, after all."

"I've heard animals talk before," said Dorothy, "and no harm came of it."

"Were you ever before shut up in a cave, far under the earth, with no way of getting out?" enquired the horse, seriously.

"No," answered Dorothy. "But don't you lose heart, Jim, for I'm sure this isn't the end of our story, by any means."

The reference to the piglets reminded the Wizard that his pets had not enjoyed much exercise lately, and must be tired of their prison in his pocket. So he sat down upon the floor of the cave, brought the piglets out one by one, and allowed them to run around as much as they pleased.

"My dears," he said to them, "I'm afraid I've got you into a lot of trouble, and that you will never again be able to leave this gloomy cave."

"What's wrong?" asked a piglet. "We've been in the dark quite a while, and you may as well explain what has happened."

The Wizard told them of the misfortune that had overtaken the wanderers.

"Well," said another piglet, "you are a wizard, are you not?"

"I am," replied the little man.

"Then you can do a few wizzes and get us out of this hole," declared the tiny one, with much confidence.

"I could if I happened to be a real wizard," returned the master sadly. "But I'm not, my piggy-wees; I'm a humbug wizard."

"Nonsense!" cried several of the piglets, together.

"You can ask Dorothy," said the little man, in an injured tone.

"It's true enough," returned the girl, earnestly. "Our friend Oz is merely a humbug wizard, for he once proved it to me. He can do several very wonderful things—if he knows how. But he can't wiz a single thing if he hasn't the tools and machinery to work with."

"Thank you, my dear, for doing me justice," responded the Wizard, gratefully. "To be accused of being a real wizard, when I'm not, is a slander I will not tamely submit to. But I am one of the greatest humbug wizards that ever lived, and you will realize this when we have all starved together and our bones are scattered over the floor of this lonely cave."

"I don't believe we'll realize anything, when it comes to that," remarked Dorothy, who had been deep in thought. "But I'm not going to scatter my bones just yet, because I need them, and you prob'ly need yours, too."

"We are helpless to escape," sighed the Wizard.

"WE may be helpless," answered Dorothy, smiling at him, "but there are others who can do more than we can. Cheer up, friends. "I'm sure Ozma will help us."

"Ozma!" exclaimed the Wizard. "Who is Ozma?"

"The girl that rules the marvelous Land of Oz," was the reply. "She's a friend of mine, for I met her in the Land of Ev, not long ago, and went to Oz with her."

"For the second time?" asked the Wizard, with great interest.

"Yes. The first time I went to Oz I found you there, ruling the Emerald City. After you went up in a balloon, and escaped us, I got back to Kansas by means of a pair of magical silver shoes."

"I remember those shoes," said the little man, nodding. "They once belonged to the Wicked Witch. Have you them here with you?"

"No; I lost them somewhere in the air," explained the child. "But the second time I went to the Land of Oz I owned the Nome King's Magic Belt, which is much more powerful than were the Silver Shoes."

"Where is that Magic Belt?" enquired the Wizard, who had listened with great interest.

"Ozma has it; for its powers won't work in a common, ordinary country like the United States. Anyone in a fairy country like the Land of Oz can do anything with it; so I left it with my friend the Princess Ozma, who used it to wish me in Australia with Uncle Henry."

"And were you?" asked Zeb, astonished at what he heard.

"Of course; in just a jiffy. And Ozma has an enchanted picture hanging in her room that shows her the exact scene where any of her friends may be, at any time she chooses. All she has to do is to say: 'I wonder what So-and-so is doing,' and at once the picture shows where her friend is and what the friend is doing. That's REAL magic, Mr. Wizard; isn't it? Well, every day at four o'clock Ozma has promised to look at me in that picture, and if I am in need of help I am to make her a certain sign and she will put on the Nome King's Magic Belt and wish me to be with her in Oz."

"Do you mean that Princess Ozma will see this cave in her enchanted picture, and see all of us here, and what we are doing?" demanded Zeb.

"Of course; when it is four o'clock," she replied, with a laugh at his startled expression.

"And when you make a sign she will bring you to her in the Land of Oz?" continued the boy.

"That's it, exactly; by means of the Magic Belt."

"Then," said the Wizard, "you will be saved, little Dorothy; and I am very glad of it. The rest of us will die much more cheerfully when we know you have escaped our sad fate."

"I won't die cheerfully!" protested the kitten. "There's nothing cheerful about dying that I could ever see, although they say a cat has nine lives, and so must die nine times."

"Have you ever died yet?" enquired the boy.

"No, and I'm not anxious to begin," said Eureka.

"Don't worry, dear," Dorothy exclaimed, "I'll hold you in my arms, and take you with me."

"Take us, too!" cried the nine tiny piglets, all in one breath.

"Perhaps I can," answered Dorothy. "I'll try."

"Couldn't you manage to hold me in your arms?" asked the cab-horse.

Dorothy laughed.

"I'll do better than that," she promised, "for I can easily save you all, once I am myself in the Land of Oz."

"How?" they asked.

"By using the Magic Belt. All I need do is to wish you with me, and there you'll be—safe in the royal palace!"

"Good!" cried Zeb.

"I built that palace, and the Emerald City, too," remarked the Wizard, in a thoughtful tone, "and I'd like to see them again, for I was very happy among the Munchkins and Winkies and Quadlings and Gillikins."

"Who are they?" asked the boy.

"The four nations that inhabit the Land of Oz," was the reply. "I wonder if they would treat me nicely if I went there again."

"Of course they would!" declared Dorothy. "They are still proud of their former Wizard, and often speak of you kindly."

"Do you happen to know whatever became of the Tin Woodman and the Scarecrow?" he enquired.

"They live in Oz yet," said the girl, "and are very important people."

"And the Cowardly Lion?"

"Oh, he lives there too, with his friend the Hungry Tiger; and Billina is there, because she liked the place better than Kansas, and wouldn't go with me to Australia."

"I'm afraid I don't know the Hungry Tiger and Billina," said the Wizard, shaking his head. "Is Billina a girl?"

"No; she's a yellow hen, and a great friend of mine. You're sure to like Billina, when you know her," asserted Dorothy.

"Your friends sound like a menagerie," remarked Zeb, uneasily. "Couldn't you wish me in some safer place than Oz."

"Don't worry," replied the girl. "You'll just love the folks in Oz, when you get acquainted. What time is it, Mr. Wizard?"

The little man looked at his watch—a big silver one that he carried in his vest pocket.

"Half-past three," he said.

"Then we must wait for half an hour," she continued; "but it won't take long, after that, to carry us all to the Emerald City."

They sat silently thinking for a time. Then Jim suddenly asked:

"Are there any horses in Oz?"

"Only one," replied Dorothy, "and he's a sawhorse."

"A what?"

"A sawhorse. Princess Ozma once brought him to life with a witch-powder, when she was a boy."

"Was Ozma once a boy?" asked Zeb, wonderingly.

"Yes; a wicked witch enchanted her, so she could not rule her kingdom. But she's a girl now, and the sweetest, loveliest girl in all the world."

"A sawhorse is a thing they saw boards on," remarked Jim, with a sniff.

"It is when it's not alive," acknowledged the girl. "But this sawhorse can trot as fast as you can, Jim; and he's very wise, too."

"Pah! I'll race the miserable wooden donkey any day in the week!" cried the cab-horse.

Dorothy did not reply to that. She felt that Jim would know more about the Saw-Horse later on.

The time dragged wearily enough to the eager watchers, but finally the Wizard announced that four o'clock had arrived, and Dorothy caught up the kitten and began to make the signal that had been agreed upon to the far-away invisible Ozma.

"Nothing seems to happen," said Zeb, doubtfully.

"Oh, we must give Ozma time to put on the Magic Belt," replied the girl.

She had scarcely spoken the words then she suddenly disappeared from the cave, and with her went the kitten. There had been no sound of any kind and no warning. One moment Dorothy sat beside them with the kitten in her lap, and a moment later the horse, the piglets, the Wizard and the boy were all that remained in the underground prison.

"I believe we will soon follow her," announced the Wizard, in a tone of great relief; "for I know something about the magic of the fairyland that is called the Land of Oz. Let us be ready, for we may be sent for any minute."

He put the piglets safely away in his pocket again and then he and Zeb got into the buggy and sat expectantly upon the seat.

"Will it hurt?" asked the boy, in a voice that trembled a little.

"Not at all," replied the Wizard. "It will all happen as quick as a wink."

And that was the way it did happen.

The cab-horse gave a nervous start and Zeb began to rub his eyes to make sure he was not asleep. For they were in the streets of a beautiful emerald-green city, bathed in a grateful green light that was especially pleasing to their eyes, and surrounded by merry faced people in gorgeous green-and-gold costumes of many extraordinary designs.

Before them were the jewel-studded gates of a magnificent palace, and now the gates opened slowly as if inviting them to enter the courtyard, where splendid flowers were blooming and pretty fountains shot their silvery sprays into the air.

Zeb shook the reins to rouse the cab-horse from his stupor of amazement, for the people were beginning to gather around and stare at the strangers.

"Gid-dap!" cried the boy, and at the word Jim slowly trotted into the courtyard and drew the buggy along the jewelled driveway to the great entrance of the royal palace.

Chapter 15 - Old Friends are Reunited

Many servants dressed in handsome uniforms stood ready to welcome the new arrivals, and when the Wizard got out of the buggy a pretty girl in a green gown cried out in surprise:

"Why, it's Oz, the Wonderful Wizard, come back again!"

The little man looked at her closely and then took both the maiden's hands in his and shook them cordially.

"On my word," he exclaimed, "it's little Jellia Jamb—as pert and pretty as ever!"

"Why not, Mr. Wizard?" asked Jellia, bowing low. "But I'm afraid you cannot rule the Emerald City, as you used to, because we now have a beautiful Princess whom everyone loves dearly."

"And the people will not willingly part with her," added a tall soldier in a Captain-General's uniform.

The Wizard turned to look at him.

"Did you not wear green whiskers at one time?" he asked.

"Yes," said the soldier; "but I shaved them off long ago, and since then I have risen from a private to be the Chief General of the Royal Armies."

"That's nice," said the little man. "But I assure you, my good people, that I do not wish to rule the Emerald City," he added, earnestly.

"In that case you are very welcome!" cried all the servants, and it pleased the Wizard to note the respect with which the royal retainers bowed before him. His fame had not been forgotten in the Land of Oz, by any means.

"Where is Dorothy?" enquired Zeb, anxiously, as he left the buggy and stood beside his friend the little Wizard.

"She is with the Princess Ozma, in the private rooms of the palace," replied Jellia Jamb. "But she has ordered me to make you welcome and to show you to your apartments."

The boy looked around him with wondering eyes. Such magnificence and wealth as was displayed in this palace was more than he had ever dreamed of, and he could scarcely believe that all the gorgeous glitter was real and not tinsel.

"What's to become of me?" asked the horse, uneasily. He had seen considerable of life in the cities in his younger days, and knew that this regal palace was no place for him.

It perplexed even Jellia Jamb, for a time, to know what to do with the animal. The green maiden was much astonished at the sight of so unusual a creature, for horses were unknown in this Land; but those who lived in the Emerald City were apt to be astonished by queer sights, so after inspecting the cab-horse and noting the mild look in his big eyes the girl decided not to be afraid of him.

"There are no stables here," said the Wizard, "unless some have been built since I went away."

"We have never needed them before," answered Jellia; "for the Sawhorse lives in a room of the palace, being much smaller and more natural in appearance than this great beast you have brought with you."

"Do you mean that I'm a freak?" asked Jim, angrily.

"Oh, no," she hastened to say, "there may be many more like you in the place you came from, but in Oz any horse but a Sawhorse is unusual."

This mollified Jim a little, and after some thought the green maiden decided to give the cab-horse a room in the palace, such a big building having many rooms that were seldom in use.

So Zeb unharnessed Jim, and several of the servants then led the horse around to the rear, where they selected a nice large apartment that he could have all to himself.

Then Jellia said to the Wizard:

"Your own room—which was back of the great Throne Room—has been vacant ever since you left us. Would you like it again?"

"Yes, indeed!" returned the little man. "It will seem like being at home again, for I lived in that room for many, many years."

He knew the way to it, and a servant followed him, carrying his satchel. Zeb was also escorted to a room—so grand and beautiful that he almost feared to sit in the chairs or lie upon the bed, lest he might dim their splendor. In the closets he discovered many fancy costumes of rich velvets and brocades, and one of the attendants told him to dress himself in any of the clothes that pleased him and to be prepared to dine with the Princess and Dorothy in an hour's time.

Opening from the chamber was a fine bathroom having a marble tub with perfumed water; so the boy, still dazed by the novelty of his surroundings, indulged in a good bath and then selected a maroon velvet costume with silver buttons to replace his own soiled and much worn clothing. There were silk stockings and soft leather slippers with diamond buckles to accompany his new costume, and when he was fully dressed Zeb looked much more dignified and imposing than ever before in his life.

He was all ready when an attendant came to escort him to the presence of the Princess; he followed bashfully and was ushered into a room more dainty and attractive than it was splendid. Here he found Dorothy seated beside a young girl so marvelously beautiful that the boy stopped suddenly with a gasp of admiration.

But Dorothy sprang up and ran to seize her friend's hand drawing him impulsively toward the lovely Princess, who smiled most graciously upon her guest. Then the Wizard entered, and his presence relieved the boy's embarrassment. The little man was clothed in black velvet, with many sparkling emerald ornaments decorating his breast; but his bald head and wrinkled features made him appear more amusing than impressive.

Ozma had been quite curious to meet the famous man who had built the Emerald City and united the Munchkins, Gillikins, Quadlings and Winkies into one people; so when they were all four seated at the dinner table the Princess said:

"Please tell me, Mr. Wizard, whether you called yourself Oz after this great country, or whether you believe my country is called Oz after you. It is a matter that I have long wished to enquire about, because you are of a strange race and my own name is Ozma. No, one, I am sure, is better able to explain this mystery than you."

"That is true," answered the little Wizard; "therefore it will give me pleasure to explain my connection with your country. In the first place, I must tell you that I was born in Omaha, and my father, who was a politician, named me Oscar Zoroaster Phadrig Isaac Norman Henkle Emmannuel Ambroise Diggs, Diggs being the last name because he could think of no more to go before it. Taken altogether, it was a dreadfully long name to weigh down a poor innocent child, and one of the hardest lessons I ever learned was to remember my own name. When I grew up I just called myself O. Z., because the other initials were P-I-N-H-E-A-D; and that spelled 'pinhead,' which was a reflection on my intelligence."

"Surely no one could blame you for cutting your name short," said Ozma, sympathetically. "But didn't you cut it almost too short?"

"Perhaps so," replied the Wizard. "When a young man I ran away from home and joined a circus. I used to call myself a Wizard, and do tricks of ventriloquism."

"What does that mean?" asked the Princess.

"Throwing my voice into any object I pleased, to make it appear that the object was speaking instead of me. Also I began to make balloon ascensions. On my balloon and on all the other articles I used in the circus I painted the two initials: 'O. Z.', to show that those things belonged to me.

"One day my balloon ran away with me and brought me across the deserts to this beautiful country. When the people saw me come from the sky they naturally thought me some superior creature, and bowed down before me. I told them I was a Wizard, and showed them some easy tricks that amazed them; and when they saw the initials painted on the balloon they called me Oz."

"Now I begin to understand," said the Princess, smiling.

"At that time," continued the Wizard, busily eating his soup while talking, "there were four separate countries in this Land, each one of the four being ruled by a Witch. But the people thought my power was greater than that of the Witches; and perhaps the Witches thought so too, for they never dared oppose me. I ordered the Emerald City to be built just where the four countries cornered together, and when it was completed I announced myself the Ruler of the Land of Oz, which included all the four countries of the Munchkins, the Gillikins, the Winkies and the Quadlings. Over this Land I ruled in peace for many years, until I grew old and longed to see my native city once again. So when Dorothy was first blown to this place by a cyclone I arranged to go away with her in a balloon; but the balloon escaped too soon and carried me back alone. After many adventures I reached Omaha, only to find that all my old friends were dead or had moved away. So, having nothing else to do, I joined a circus again, and made my balloon ascensions until the earthquake caught me."

"That is quite a history," said Ozma; "but there is a little more history about the Land of Oz that you do not seem to understand—perhaps for the reason that no one ever told it you. Many years before you came here this Land was united under one Ruler, as it is now, and the Ruler's name was always 'Oz,' which means in our language 'Great and Good'; or, if the Ruler happened to be a woman, her name was always 'Ozma.' But once upon a time four Witches leagued together to depose the king and rule the four parts of the kingdom themselves; so when the Ruler, my grandfather, was hunting one day, one Wicked Witch named Mombi stole him and carried him away, keeping him a close prisoner. Then the Witches divided up the kingdom, and ruled the four parts of it until you came here. That was why the people were so glad to see you, and why they thought from your initials that you were their rightful ruler."

"But, at that time," said the Wizard, thoughtfully, "there were two Good Witches and two Wicked Witches ruling in the land."

"Yes," replied Ozma, "because a good Witch had conquered Mombi in the North and Glinda the Good had conquered the evil Witch in the South. But Mombi was still my grandfather's jailor, and afterward my father's jailor. When I was born she transformed me into a boy, hoping that no one would ever recognize me and know that I was the rightful Princess of the Land of Oz. But I escaped from her and am now the Ruler of my people."

"I am very glad of that," said the Wizard, "and hope you will consider me one of your most faithful and devoted subjects."

"We owe a great deal to the Wonderful Wizard," continued the Princess, "for it was you who built this splendid Emerald City."

"Your people built it," he answered. "I only bossed the job, as we say in Omaha."

"But you ruled it wisely and well for many years," said she, "and made the people proud of your magical art. So, as you are now too old to wander abroad and work in a circus, I offer you a home here as long as you live. You shall be the Official Wizard of my kingdom, and be treated with every respect and consideration."

"I accept your kind offer with gratitude, gracious Princess," the little man said, in a soft voice, and they could all see that tear-drops were standing in his keen old eyes. It meant a good deal to him to secure a home like this.

"He's only a humbug Wizard, though," said Dorothy, smiling at him.

"And that is the safest kind of a Wizard to have," replied Ozma, promptly.

"Oz can do some good tricks, humbug or no humbug," announced Zeb, who was now feeling more at ease.

"He shall amuse us with his tricks tomorrow," said the Princess. "I have sent messengers to summon all of Dorothy's old friends to meet her and give her welcome, and they ought to arrive very soon, now."

Indeed, the dinner was no sooner finished than in rushed the Scarecrow, to hug Dorothy in his padded arms and tell her how glad he was to see her again. The Wizard was also most heartily welcomed by the straw man, who was an important personage in the Land of Oz.

"How are your brains?" enquired the little humbug, as he grasped the soft, stuffed hands of his old friend.

"Working finely," answered the Scarecrow. "I'm very certain, Oz, that you gave me the best brains in the world, for I can think with them day and night, when all other brains are fast asleep."

"How long did you rule the Emerald City, after I left here?" was the next question.

"Quite awhile, until I was conquered by a girl named General Jinjur. But Ozma soon conquered her, with the help of Glinda the Good, and after that I went to live with Nick Chopper, the Tin Woodman."

Just then a loud cackling was heard outside; and, when a servant threw open the door with a low bow, a yellow hen strutted in. Dorothy sprang forward and caught the fluffy fowl in her arms, uttering at the same time a glad cry.

"Oh, Billina!" she said; "how fat and sleek you've grown."

"Why shouldn't I?" asked the hen, in a sharp, clear voice. "I live on the fat of the land—don't I, Ozma?"

"You have everything you wish for," said the Princess.

Around Billina's neck was a string of beautiful pearls, and on her legs were bracelets of emeralds. She nestled herself comfortably in Dorothy's lap until the kitten gave a snarl of jealous anger and leaped up with a sharp claw fiercely bared to strike Billina a blow. But the little girl gave the angry kitten such a severe cuff that it jumped down again without daring to scratch.

"How horrid of you, Eureka!" cried Dorothy. "Is that the way to treat my friends?"

"You have queer friends, seems to me," replied the kitten, in a surly tone.

"Seems to me the same way," said Billina, scornfully, "if that beastly cat is one of them."

"Look here!" said Dorothy, sternly. "I won't have any quarrelling in the Land of Oz, I can tell you! Everybody lives in peace here, and loves everybody else; and unless you two, Billina and Eureka, make up and be friends, I'll take my Magic Belt and wish you both home again, IMMEJITLY. So, there!"

They were both much frightened at the threat, and promised meekly to be good. But it was never noticed that they became very warm friends, for all of that.

And now the Tin Woodman arrived, his body most beautifully nickle-plated, so that it shone splendidly in the brilliant light of the room. The Tin Woodman loved Dorothy most tenderly, and welcomed with joy the return of the little old Wizard.

"Sir," said he to the latter, "I never can thank you enough for the excellent heart you once gave me. It has made me many friends, I assure you, and it beats as kindly and lovingly today as it every did."

"I'm glad to hear that," said the Wizard. "I was afraid it would get moldy in that tin body of yours."

"Not at all," returned Nick Chopper. "It keeps finely, being preserved in my air-tight chest."

Zeb was a little shy when first introduced to these queer people; but they were so friendly and sincere that he soon grew to admire them very much, even finding some good qualities in the yellow hen. But he became nervous again when the next visitor was announced.

"This," said Princess Ozma, "is my friend Mr. H. M. Woggle-Bug, T. E., who assisted me one time when I was in great distress, and is now the Dean of the Royal College of Athletic Science."

"Ah," said the Wizard; "I'm pleased to meet so distinguished a personage."

"H. M.," said the Woggle-Bug, pompously, "means Highly Magnified; and T. E. means Thoroughly Educated. I am, in reality, a very big bug, and doubtless the most intelligent being in all this broad domain."

"How well you disguise it," said the Wizard. "But I don't doubt your word in the least."

"Nobody doubts it, sir," replied the Woggle-Bug, and drawing a book from its pocket the strange insect turned its back on the company and sat down in a corner to read.

Nobody minded this rudeness, which might have seemed more impolite in one less thoroughly educated; so they straightway forgot him and joined in a merry conversation that kept them well amused until bed-time arrived.

Chapter 16 - Jim, The Cab-Horse

Jim the Cab-horse found himself in possession of a large room with a green marble floor and carved marble wainscoting, which was so stately in its appearance that it would have awed anyone else. Jim accepted it as a mere detail, and at his command the attendants gave his coat a good rubbing, combed his mane and tail, and washed his hoofs and fetlocks. Then they told him dinner would be served directly and he replied that they could not serve it too quickly to suit his convenience. First they brought him a steaming bowl of soup, which the horse eyed in dismay.

"Take that stuff away!" he commanded. "Do you take me for a salamander?"

They obeyed at once, and next served a fine large turbot on a silver platter, with drawn gravy poured over it.

"Fish!" cried Jim, with a sniff. "Do you take me for a tom-cat? Away with it!"

The servants were a little discouraged, but soon they brought in a great tray containing two dozen nicely roasted quail on toast.

"Well, well!" said the horse, now thoroughly provoked. "Do you take me for a weasel? How stupid and ignorant you are, in the Land of Oz, and what dreadful things you feed upon! Is there nothing that is decent to eat in this palace?"

The trembling servants sent for the Royal Steward, who came in haste and said:

"What would your Highness like for dinner?"

"Highness!" repeated Jim, who was unused to such titles.

"You are at least six feet high, and that is higher than any other animal in this country," said the Steward.

"Well, my Highness would like some oats," declared the horse.

"Oats? We have no whole oats," the Steward replied, with much deference. "But there is any quantity of oatmeal, which we often cook for breakfast. Oatmeal is a breakfast dish," added the Steward, humbly.

"I'll make it a dinner dish," said Jim. "Fetch it on, but don't cook it, as you value your life."

You see, the respect shown the worn-out old cab-horse made him a little arrogant, and he forgot he was a guest, never having been treated otherwise than as a servant since the day he was born, until his arrival in the Land of Oz. But the royal attendants did not heed the animal's ill temper. They soon mixed a tub of oatmeal with a little water, and Jim ate it with much relish.

Then the servants heaped a lot of rugs upon the floor and the old horse slept on the softest bed he had ever known in his life.

In the morning, as soon as it was daylight, he resolved to take a walk and try to find some grass for breakfast; so he ambled calmly through the handsome arch of the doorway, turned the corner of the palace, wherein all seemed asleep, and came face to face with the Sawhorse.

Jim stopped abruptly, being startled and amazed. The Sawhorse stopped at the same time and stared at the other with its queer protruding eyes, which were mere knots in the log that formed its body. The legs of the Sawhorse were four sticks driving into holes bored in the log; its tail was a small branch that had been left by accident and its mouth a place chopped in one end of the body which projected a little and served as a head. The ends of the wooden legs were shod with plates of solid gold, and the saddle of the Princess Ozma, which was of red leather set with sparkling diamonds, was strapped to the clumsy body.

Jim's eyes stuck out as much as those of the Sawhorse, and he stared at the creature with his ears erect and his long head drawn back until it rested against his arched neck.

In this comical position the two horses circled slowly around each other for a while, each being unable to realize what the singular thing might be which it now beheld for the first time. Then Jim exclaimed:

"For goodness sake, what sort of a being are you?"

"I'm a Sawhorse," replied the other.

"Oh; I believe I've heard of you," said the cab-horse; "but you are unlike anything that I expected to see."

"I do not doubt it," the Sawhorse observed, with a tone of pride. "I am considered quite unusual."

"You are, indeed. But a rickety wooden thing like you has no right to be alive."

"I couldn't help it," returned the other, rather crestfallen. "Ozma sprinkled me with a magic powder, and I just had to live. I know I'm not much account; but I'm the only horse in all the Land of Oz, so they treat me with great respect."

"You, a horse!"

"Oh, not a real one, of course. There are no real horses here at all. But I'm a splendid imitation of one."

Jim gave an indignant neigh.

"Look at me!" he cried. "Behold a real horse!"

The wooden animal gave a start, and then examined the other intently.

"Is it possible that you are a Real Horse?" he murmured.

"Not only possible, but true," replied Jim, who was gratified by the impression he had created. "It is proved by my fine points. For example, look at the long hairs on my tail, with which I can whisk away the flies."

"The flies never trouble me," said the Saw-Horse.

"And notice my great strong teeth, with which I nibble the grass."

"It is not necessary for me to eat," observed the Sawhorse.

"Also examine my broad chest, which enables me to draw deep, full breaths," said Jim, proudly.

"I have no need to breathe," returned the other.

"No; you miss many pleasures," remarked the cab-horse, pityingly. "You do not know the relief of brushing away a fly that has bitten you, nor the delight of eating delicious food, nor the satisfaction of drawing a long breath of fresh, pure air. You may be an imitation of a horse, but you're a mighty poor one."

"Oh, I cannot hope ever to be like you," sighed the Sawhorse. "But I am glad to meet a last a Real Horse. You are certainly the most beautiful creature I ever beheld."

This praise won Jim completely. To be called beautiful was a novelty in his experience. Said he:

"Your chief fault, my friend, is in being made of wood, and that I suppose you cannot help. Real horses, like myself, are made of flesh and blood and bones."

"I can see the bones all right," replied the Sawhorse, "and they are admirable and distinct. Also I can see the flesh. But the blood, I suppose is tucked away inside."

"Exactly," said Jim.

"What good is it?" asked the Sawhorse.

Jim did not know, but he would not tell the Sawhorse that.

"If anything cuts me," he replied, "the blood runs out to show where I am cut. You, poor thing! cannot even bleed when you are hurt."

"But I am never hurt," said the Sawhorse. "Once in a while I get broken up some, but I am easily repaired and put in good order again. And I never feel a break or a splinter in the least."

Jim was almost tempted to envy the wooden horse for being unable to feel pain; but the creature was so absurdly unnatural that he decided he would not change places with it under any circumstances.

"How did you happen to be shod with gold?" he asked.

"Princess Ozma did that," was the reply; "and it saves my legs from wearing out. We've had a good many adventures together, Ozma and I, and she likes me."

The cab-horse was about to reply when suddenly he gave a start and a neigh of terror and stood trembling like a leaf. For around the corner had come two enormous savage beasts, treading so lightly that they were upon him before he was aware of their presence. Jim was in the act of plunging down the path to escape when the Sawhorse cried out:

"Stop, my brother! Stop, Real Horse! These are friends, and will do you no harm."

Jim hesitated, eyeing the beasts fearfully. One was an enormous Lion with clear, intelligent eyes, a tawney mane bushy and well kept, and a body like yellow plush. The other was a great Tiger with purple stripes around his lithe body, powerful limbs, and eyes that showed through the half closed lids like coals of fire. The huge forms of these monarchs of the forest and jungle were enough to strike terror to the stoutest heart, and it is no wonder Jim was afraid to face them.

But the Sawhorse introduced the stranger in a calm tone, saying:

"This, noble Horse, is my friend the Cowardly Lion, who is the valiant King of the Forest, but at the same time a faithful vassal of Princess Ozma. And this is the Hungry Tiger, the terror of the jungle, who longs to devour fat babies but is prevented by his conscience from doing so. These royal beasts are both warm friends of little Dorothy and have come to the Emerald City this morning to welcome her to our fairyland."

Hearing these words Jim resolved to conquer his alarm. He bowed his head with as much dignity as he could muster toward the savage looking beasts, who in return nodded in a friendly way.

"Is not the Real Horse a beautiful animal?" asked the Sawhorse admiringly.

"That is doubtless a matter of taste," returned the Lion. "In the forest he would be thought ungainly, because his face is stretched out and his neck is uselessly long. His joints, I notice, are swollen and overgrown, and he lacks flesh and is old in years."

"And dreadfully tough," added the Hungry Tiger, in a sad voice. "My conscience would never permit me to eat so tough a morsel as the Real Horse."

"I'm glad of that," said Jim; "for I, also, have a conscience, and it tells me not to crush in your skull with a blow of my powerful hoof."

If he thought to frighten the striped beast by such language he was mistaken. The Tiger seemed to smile, and winked one eye slowly.

"You have a good conscience, friend Horse," it said, "and if you attend to its teachings it will do much to protect you from harm. Some day I will let you try to crush in my skull, and afterward you will know more about tigers than you do now."

"Any friend of Dorothy," remarked the Cowardly Lion, "must be our friend, as well. So let us cease this talk of skull crushing and converse upon more pleasant subjects. Have you breakfasted, Sir Horse?"

"Not yet," replied Jim. "But here is plenty of excellent clover, so if you will excuse me I will eat now."

"He's a vegetarian," remarked the Tiger, as the horse began to munch the clover. "If I could eat grass I would not need a conscience, for nothing could then tempt me to devour babies and lambs."

Just then Dorothy, who had risen early and heard the voices of the animals, ran out to greet her old friends. She hugged both the Lion and the Tiger with eager delight, but seemed to love the King of Beasts a little better than she did his hungry friend, having known him longer.

By this time they had indulged in a good talk and Dorothy had told them all about the awful earthquake and her recent adventures, the breakfast bell rang from the palace and the little girl went inside to join her human comrades. As she entered the great hall a voice called out, in a rather harsh tone:

"What! are YOU here again?"

"Yes, I am," she answered, looking all around to see where the voice came from.

"What brought you back?" was the next question, and Dorothy's eye rested on an antlered head hanging on the wall just over the fireplace, and caught its lips in the act of moving.

"Good gracious!" she exclaimed. "I thought you were stuffed."

"So I am," replied the head. "But once on a time I was part of the Gump, which Ozma sprinkled with the Powder of Life. I was then for a time the Head of the finest Flying Machine that was ever known to exist, and we did many wonderful things. Afterward the Gump was taken apart and I was put back on this wall; but I can still talk when I feel in the mood, which is not often."

"It's very strange," said the girl. "What were you when you were first alive?"

"That I have forgotten," replied the Gump's Head, "and I do not think it is of much importance. But here comes Ozma; so I'd better hush up, for the Princess doesn't like me to chatter since she changed her name from Tip to Ozma."

Just then the girlish Ruler of Oz opened the door and greeted Dorothy with a good-morning kiss. The little Princess seemed fresh and rosy and in good spirits.

"Breakfast is served, dear," she said, "and I am hungry. So don't let us keep it waiting a single minute."

Chapter 17 - The Nine Tiny Piglets

After breakfast Ozma announced that she had ordered a holiday to be observed throughout the Emerald City, in honor of her visitors. The people had learned that their old Wizard had returned to them and all were anxious to see him again, for he had always been a rare favorite. So first there was to be a grand procession through the streets, after which the little old man was requested to perform some of his wizardries in the great Throne Room of the palace. In the afternoon there were to be games and races.

The procession was very imposing. First came the Imperial Cornet Band of Oz, dressed in emerald velvet uniforms with slashes of pea-green satin and buttons of immense cut emeralds. They played the National air called "The Oz Spangled Banner," and behind them were the standard bearers with the Royal flag. This flag was divided into four quarters, one being colored sky-blue, another pink, a third lavender and a fourth white. In the center was a large emerald-green star, and all over the four quarters were sewn spangles that glittered beautifully in the sunshine. The colors represented the four countries of Oz, and the green star the Emerald City.

Just behind the royal standard-bearers came the Princess Ozma in her royal chariot, which was of gold encrusted with emeralds and diamonds set in exquisite designs. The chariot was drawn on this occasion by the Cowardly Lion and the Hungry Tiger, who were decorated with immense pink and blue bows. In the chariot rode Ozma and Dorothy, the former in splendid raiment and wearing her royal coronet, while the little Kansas girl wore around her waist the Magic Belt she had once captured from the Nome King.

Following the chariot came the Scarecrow mounted on the Sawhorse, and the people cheered him almost as loudly as they did their lovely Ruler. Behind him stalked with regular, jerky steps, the famous machine-man called Tik-tok, who had been wound up by Dorothy for the occasion. Tik-tok moved by clockwork, and was made all of burnished copper. He really belonged to the Kansas girl, who had much respect for his thoughts after they had been properly wound and set going; but as the copper man would be useless in any place but a fairy country Dorothy had left him in charge of Ozma, who saw that he was suitably cared for.

There followed another band after this, which was called the Royal Court Band, because the members all lived in the palace. They wore white uniforms with real diamond buttons and played "What is Oz without Ozma" very sweetly.

Then came Professor Woggle-Bug, with a group of students from the Royal College of Scientific Athletics. The boys wore long hair and striped sweaters and yelled their college yell every other step they took, to the great satisfaction of the populace, which was glad to have this evidence that their lungs were in good condition.

The brilliantly polished Tin Woodman marched next, at the head of the Royal Army of Oz which consisted of twenty-eight officers, from Generals down to Captains. There were no privates in the army because all were so courageous and skillful that they had been promoted one by one until there were no privates left. Jim and the buggy followed, the old cab-horse being driven by Zeb while the Wizard stood up on the seat and bowed his bald head right and left in answer to the cheers of the people, who crowded thick about him.

Taken altogether the procession was a grand success, and when it had returned to the palace the citizens crowded into the great Throne Room to see the Wizard perform his tricks.

The first thing the little humbug did was to produce a tiny white piglet from underneath his hat and pretend to pull it apart, making two. This act he repeated until all of the nine tiny piglets were visible, and they were so glad to get out of his pocket that they ran around in a very lively manner. The pretty little creatures would have been a novelty anywhere, so the people were as amazed and delighted at their appearance as even the Wizard could have desired. When he had made them all disappear again Ozma declared she was sorry they were gone, for she wanted one of them to pet and play with. So the Wizard pretended to take one of the piglets out of the hair of the Princess (while really he slyly took it from his inside pocket) and Ozma smiled joyously as the creature nestled in her arms, and she promised to have an emerald collar made for its fat neck and to keep the little squealer always at hand to amuse her.

Afterward it was noticed that the Wizard always performed his famous trick with eight piglets, but it seemed to please the people just as well as if there had been nine of them.

In his little room back of the Throne Room the Wizard had found a lot of things he had left behind him when he went away in the balloon, for no one had occupied the apartment in his absence. There was enough material there to enable him to prepare several new tricks which he had learned from some of the jugglers in the circus, and he had passed part of the night in getting them ready. So he followed the trick of the nine tiny piglets with several other wonderful feats that greatly delighted his audience and the people did not seem to care a bit whether the little man was a humbug Wizard or not, so long as he succeeded in amusing them. They applauded all his tricks and at the end of the performance begged him earnestly not to go away again and leave them.

"In that case," said the little man, gravely, "I will cancel all of my engagements before the crowned heads of Europe and America and devote myself to the people of Oz, for I love you all so well that I can deny you nothing."

After the people had been dismissed with this promise our friends joined Princess Ozma at an elaborate luncheon in the palace, where even the Tiger and the Lion were sumptuously fed and Jim the Cab-horse ate his oatmeal out of a golden bowl with seven rows of rubies, sapphires and diamonds set around the rim of it.

In the afternoon they all went to a great field outside the city gates where the games were to be held. There was a beautiful canopy for Ozma and her guests to sit under and watch the people run races and jump and wrestle. You may be sure the folks of Oz did their best with such a distinguished company watching them, and finally Zeb offered to wrestle with a little Munchkin who seemed to be the champion. In appearance he was twice as old as Zeb, for he had long pointed whiskers and wore a peaked hat with little bells all around the brim of it, which tinkled gaily as he moved. But although the Munchkin was hardly tall enough to come to Zeb's shoulder he was so strong and clever that he laid the boy three times on his back with apparent ease.

Zeb was greatly astonished at his defeat, and when the pretty Princess joined her people in laughing at him he proposed a boxing-match with the Munchkin, to which the little Ozite readily agreed. But the first time that Zeb managed to give him a sharp box on the ears the Munchkin sat down upon the ground and cried until the tears ran down his whiskers, because he had been hurt. This made Zeb laugh, in turn, and the boy felt comforted to find that Ozma laughed as merrily at her weeping subject as she had at him.

Just then the Scarecrow proposed a race between the Sawhorse and the Cab-horse; and although all the others were delighted at the suggestion the Sawhorse drew back, saying:

"Such a race would not be fair."

"Of course not," added Jim, with a touch of scorn; "those little wooden legs of yours are not half as long as my own."

"It isn't that," said the Sawhorse, modestly; "but I never tire, and you do."

"Bah!" cried Jim, looking with great disdain at the other; "do you imagine for an instant that such a shabby imitation of a horse as you are can run as fast as I?"

"I don't know, I'm sure," replied the Sawhorse.

"That is what we are trying to find out," remarked the Scarecrow. "The object of a race is to see who can win it—or at least that is what my excellent brains think."

"Once, when I was young," said Jim, "I was a race horse, and defeated all who dared run against me. I was born in Kentucky, you know, where all the best and most aristocratic horses come from."

"But you're old, now, Jim," suggested Zeb.

"Old! Why, I feel like a colt today," replied Jim. "I only wish there was a real horse here for me to race with. I'd show the people a fine sight, I can tell you."

"Then why not race with the Sawhorse?" enquired the Scarecrow.

"He's afraid," said Jim.

"Oh, no," answered the Sawhorse. "I merely said it wasn't fair. But if my friend the Real Horse is willing to undertake the race I am quite ready."

So they unharnessed Jim and took the saddle off the Sawhorse, and the two queerly matched animals were stood side by side for the start.

"When I say 'Go!'" Zeb called to them, "you must dig out and race until you reach those three trees you see over yonder. Then circle 'round them and come back again. The first one that passes the place where the Princess sits shall be named the winner. Are you ready?"

"I suppose I ought to give the wooden dummy a good start of me," growled Jim.

"Never mind that," said the Sawhorse. "I'll do the best I can."

"Go!" cried Zeb; and at the word the two horses leaped forward and the race was begun.

Jim's big hoofs pounded away at a great rate, and although he did not look very graceful he ran in a way to do credit to his Kentucky breeding. But the Sawhorse was swifter than the wind. Its wooden legs moved so fast that their twinkling could scarcely be seen, and although so much smaller than the cab-horse it covered the ground much faster. Before they had reached the trees the Sawhorse was far ahead, and the wooden animal returned to the starting place and was being lustily cheered by the Ozites before Jim came panting up to the canopy where the Princess and her friends were seated.

I am sorry to record the fact that Jim was not only ashamed of his defeat but for a moment lost control of his temper. As he looked at the comical face of the Sawhorse he imagined that the creature was laughing at him; so in a fit of unreasonable anger he turned around and made a vicious kick that sent his rival tumbling head over heels upon the ground, and broke off one of its legs and its left ear.

An instant later the Tiger crouched and launched its huge body through the air swift and resistless as a ball from a cannon. The beast struck Jim full on his shoulder and sent the astonished cab-horse rolling over and over, amid shouts of delight from the spectators, who had been horrified by the ungracious act he had been guilty of.

When Jim came to himself and sat upon his haunches he found the Cowardly Lion crouched on one side of him and the Hungry Tiger on the other, and their eyes were glowing like balls of fire.

"I beg your pardon, I'm sure," said Jim, meekly. "I was wrong to kick the Sawhorse, and I am sorry I became angry at him. He has won the race, and won it fairly; but what can a horse of flesh do against a tireless beast of wood?"

Hearing this apology the Tiger and the Lion stopped lashing their tails and retreated with dignified steps to the side of the Princess.

"No one must injure one of our friends in our presence," growled the Lion; and Zeb ran to Jim and whispered that unless he controlled his temper in the future he would probably be torn to pieces.

Then the Tin Woodman cut a straight and strong limb from a tree with his gleaming axe and made a new leg and a new ear for the Sawhorse; and when they had been securely fastened in place Princess Ozma took the coronet from her own head and placed it upon that of the winner of the race. Said she:

"My friend, I reward you for your swiftness by proclaiming you Prince of Horses, whether of wood or of flesh; and hereafter all other horses—in the Land of Oz, at least—must be considered imitations, and you the real Champion of your race."

There was more applause at this, and then Ozma had the jewelled saddle replaced upon the Sawhorse and herself rode the victor back to the city at the head of the grand procession.

"I ought to be a fairy," grumbled Jim, as he slowly drew the buggy home; "for to be just an ordinary horse in a fairy country is to be of no account whatever. It's no place for us, Zeb."

"It's lucky we got here, though," said the boy; and Jim thought of the dark cave, and agreed with him.

Chapter 18 - The Trial of Eureka the Kitten

Several days of festivity and merry-making followed, for such old friends did not often meet and there was much to be told and talked over between them, and many amusements to be enjoyed in this delightful country.

Ozma was happy to have Dorothy beside her, for girls of her own age with whom it was proper for the Princess to associate were very few, and often the youthful Ruler of Oz was lonely for lack of companionship.

It was the third morning after Dorothy's arrival, and she was sitting with Ozma and their friends in a reception room, talking over old times, when the Princess said to her maid:

"Please go to my boudoir, Jellia, and get the white piglet I left on the dressing-table. I want to play with it."

Jellia at once departed on the errand, and she was gone so long that they had almost forgotten her mission when the green robed maiden returned with a troubled face.

"The piglet is not there, your Highness," said she.

"Not there!" exclaimed Ozma. "Are you sure?"

"I have hunted in every part of the room," the maid replied.

"Was not the door closed?" asked the Princess.

"Yes, your Highness; I am sure it was; for when I opened it Dorothy's white kitten crept out and ran up the stairs."

Hearing this, Dorothy and the Wizard exchanged startled glances, for they remembered how often Eureka had longed to eat a piglet. The little girl jumped up at once.

"Come, Ozma," she said, anxiously; "let us go ourselves to search for the piglet."

So the two went to the dressing-room of the Princess and searched carefully in every corner and among the vases and baskets and ornaments that stood about the pretty boudoir. But not a trace could they find of the tiny creature they sought.

Dorothy was nearly weeping, by this time, while Ozma was angry and indignant. When they returned to the others the Princess said:

"There is little doubt that my pretty piglet has been eaten by that horrid kitten, and if that is true the offender must be punished."

"I don't b'lieve Eureka would do such a dreadful thing!" cried Dorothy, much distressed. "Go and get my kitten, please, Jellia, and we'll hear what she has to say about it."

The green maiden hastened away, but presently returned and said:

"The kitten will not come. She threatened to scratch my eyes out if I touched her."

"Where is she?" asked Dorothy.

"Under the bed in your own room," was the reply.

So Dorothy ran to her room and found the kitten under the bed.

"Come here, Eureka!" she said.

"I won't," answered the kitten, in a surly voice.

"Oh, Eureka! Why are you so bad?"

The kitten did not reply.

"If you don't come to me, right away," continued Dorothy, getting provoked, "I'll take my Magic Belt and wish you in the Country of the Gurgles."

"Why do you want me?" asked Eureka, disturbed by this threat.

"You must go to Princess Ozma. She wants to talk to you."

"All right," returned the kitten, creeping out. "I'm not afraid of Ozma—or anyone else."

Dorothy carried her in her arms back to where the others sat in grieved and thoughtful silence.

"Tell me, Eureka," said the Princess, gently: "did you eat my pretty piglet?"

"I won't answer such a foolish question," asserted Eureka, with a snarl.

"Oh, yes you will, dear," Dorothy declared. "The piglet is gone, and you ran out of the room when Jellia opened the door. So, if you are innocent, Eureka, you must tell the Princess how you came to be in her room, and what has become of the piglet."

"Who accuses me?" asked the kitten, defiantly.

"No one," answered Ozma. "Your actions alone accuse you. The fact is that I left my little pet in my dressing-room lying asleep upon the table; and you must have stolen in without my knowing it. When next the door was opened you ran out and hid yourself—and the piglet was gone."

"That's none of my business," growled the kitten.

"Don't be impudent, Eureka," admonished Dorothy.

"It is you who are impudent," said Eureka, "for accusing me of such a crime when you can't prove it except by guessing."

Ozma was now greatly incensed by the kitten's conduct. She summoned her Captain-General, and when the long, lean officer appeared she said:

"Carry this cat away to prison, and keep her in safe confinement until she is tried by law for the crime of murder."

So the Captain-General took Eureka from the arms of the now weeping Dorothy and in spite of the kitten's snarls and scratches carried it away to prison.

"What shall we do now?" asked the Scarecrow, with a sigh, for such a crime had cast a gloom over all the company.

"I will summon the Court to meet in the Throne Room at three o'clock," replied Ozma. "I myself will be the judge, and the kitten shall have a fair trial."

"What will happen if she is guilty?" asked Dorothy.

"She must die," answered the Princess.

"Nine times?" enquired the Scarecrow.

"As many times as is necessary," was the reply. "I will ask the Tin Woodman to defend the prisoner, because he has such a kind heart I am sure he will do his best to save her. And the Woggle-Bug shall be the Public Accuser, because he is so learned that no one can deceive him."

"Who will be the jury?" asked the Tin Woodman.

"There ought to be several animals on the jury," said Ozma, "because animals understand each other better than we people understand them. So the jury shall consist of the Cowardly Lion, the Hungry Tiger, Jim the Cab-horse, the Yellow Hen, the Scarecrow, the Wizard, Tik-tok the Machine Man, the Sawhorse and Zeb of Hugson's Ranch. That makes the nine which the law requires, and all my people shall be admitted to hear the testimony."

They now separated to prepare for the sad ceremony; for whenever an appeal is made to law sorrow is almost certain to follow—even in a fairyland like Oz. But is must be stated that the people of that Land were generally so well-behaved that there was not a single lawyer amongst them, and it had been years since any Ruler had sat in judgment upon an offender of the law. The crime of murder being the most dreadful crime of all, tremendous excitement prevailed in the Emerald City when the news of Eureka's arrest and trial became known.

The Wizard, when he returned to his own room, was exceedingly thoughtful. He had no doubt Eureka had eaten his piglet, but he realized that a kitten cannot be depended upon at all times to act properly, since its nature is to destroy small animals and even birds for food, and the tame cat that we keep in our houses today is descended from the wild cat of the jungle—a very ferocious creature, indeed. The Wizard knew that if Dorothy's pet was found guilty and condemned to death the little girl would be made very unhappy; so, although he grieved over the piglet's sad fate as much as any of them, he resolved to save Eureka's life.

Sending for the Tin Woodman the Wizard took him into a corner and whispered:

"My friend, it is your duty to defend the white kitten and try to save her, but I fear you will fail because Eureka has long wished to eat a piglet, to my certain knowledge, and my opinion is that she has been unable to resist the temptation. Yet her disgrace and death would not bring back the piglet, but only serve to make Dorothy unhappy. So I intend to prove the kitten's innocence by a trick."

He drew from his inside pocket one of the eight tiny piglets that were remaining and continued:

"This creature you must hide in some safe place, and if the jury decides that Eureka is guilty you may then produce this piglet and claim it is the one that was lost. All the piglets are exactly alike, so no one can dispute your word. This deception will save Eureka's life, and then we may all be happy again."

"I do not like to deceive my friends," replied the Tin Woodman; "still, my kind heart urges me to save Eureka's life, and I can usually trust my heart to do the right thing. So I will do as you say, friend Wizard."

After some thought he placed the little pig inside his funnel-shaped hat, and then put the hat upon his head and went back to his room to think over his speech to the jury.

Chapter 19 - The Wizard Performas Another Trick

At three o'clock the Throne Room was crowded with citizens, men, women and children being eager to witness the great trial.

Princess Ozma, dressed in her most splendid robes of state, sat in the magnificent emerald throne, with her jewelled sceptre in her hand and her sparkling coronet upon her fair brow. Behind her throne stood the twenty-eight officers of her army and many officials of the royal household. At her right sat the queerly assorted Jury—animals, animated dummies and people—all gravely prepared to listen to what was said. The kitten had been placed in a large cage just before the throne, where she sat upon her haunches and gazed through the bars at the crowds around her, with seeming unconcern.

And now, at a signal from Ozma, the Woggle-Bug arose and addressed the jury. His tone was pompous and he strutted up and down in an absurd attempt to appear dignified.

"Your Royal Highness and Fellow Citizens," he began; "the small cat you see a prisoner before you is accused of the crime of first murdering and then eating our esteemed Ruler's fat piglet—or else first eating and then murdering it. In either case a grave crime has been committed which deserves a grave punishment."

"Do you mean my kitten must be put in a grave?" asked Dorothy.

"Don't interrupt, little girl," said the Woggle-Bug. "When I get my thoughts arranged in good order I do not like to have anything upset them or throw them into confusion."

"If your thoughts were any good they wouldn't become confused," remarked the Scarecrow, earnestly. "My thoughts are always—"

"Is this a trial of thoughts, or of kittens?" demanded the Woggle-Bug.

"It's a trial of one kitten," replied the Scarecrow; "but your manner is a trial to us all."

"Let the Public Accuser continue," called Ozma from her throne, "and I pray you do not interrupt him."

"The criminal who now sits before the court licking her paws," resumed the Woggle-Bug, "has long desired to unlawfully eat the fat piglet, which was no bigger than a mouse. And finally she made a wicked plan to satisfy her depraved appetite for pork. I can see her, in my mind's eye—"

"What's that?" asked the Scarecrow.

"I say I can see her in my mind's eye—"

"The mind has no eye," declared the Scarecrow. "It's blind."

"Your Highness," cried the Woggle-Bug, appealing to Ozma, "have I a mind's eye, or haven't I?"

"If you have, it is invisible," said the Princess.

"Very true," returned the Woggle-Bug, bowing. "I say I see the criminal, in my mind's eye, creeping stealthily into the room of our Ozma and secreting herself, when no one was looking, until the Princess had gone away and the door was closed. Then the murderer was alone with her helpless victim, the fat piglet, and I see her pounce upon the innocent creature and eat it up—"

"Are you still seeing with your mind's eye?" enquired the Scarecrow.

"Of course; how else could I see it? And we know the thing is true, because since the time of that interview there is no piglet to be found anywhere."

"I suppose, if the cat had been gone, instead of the piglet, your mind's eye would see the piglet eating the cat," suggested the Scarecrow.

"Very likely," acknowledged the Woggle-Bug. "And now, Fellow Citizens and Creatures of the Jury, I assert that so awful a crime deserves death, and in the case of the ferocious criminal before you—who is now washing her face— the death penalty should be inflicted nine times."

There was great applause when the speaker sat down. Then the Princess spoke in a stern voice:

"Prisoner, what have you to say for yourself? Are you guilty, or not guilty?"

"Why, that's for you to find out," replied Eureka. "If you can prove I'm guilty, I'll be willing to die nine times, but a mind's eye is no proof, because the Woggle-Bug has no mind to see with."

"Never mind, dear," said Dorothy.

Then the Tin Woodman arose and said:

"Respected Jury and dearly beloved Ozma, I pray you not to judge this feline prisoner unfeelingly. I do not think the innocent kitten can be guilty, and surely it is unkind to accuse a luncheon of being a murder. Eureka is the sweet pet of a lovely little girl whom we all admire, and gentleness and innocence are her chief virtues. Look at the kitten's intelligent eyes;" (here Eureka closed her eyes sleepily) "gaze at her smiling countenance!" (here Eureka snarled and showed her teeth) "mark the tender pose of her soft, padded little hands!" (Here Eureka bared her sharp claws and scratched at the bars of the cage.) "Would such a gentle animal be guilty of eating a fellow creature? No; a thousand times, no!"

"Oh, cut it short," said Eureka; "you've talked long enough."

"I'm trying to defend you," remonstrated the Tin Woodman.

"Then say something sensible," retorted the kitten. "Tell them it would be foolish for me to eat the piglet, because I had sense enough to know it would raise a row if I did. But don't try to make out I'm too innocent to eat a fat piglet if I could do it and not be found out. I imagine it would taste mighty good."

"Perhaps it would, to those who eat," remarked the Tin Woodman. "I myself, not being built to eat, have no personal experience in such matters. But I remember that our great poet once said:

"'To eat is sweet When hunger's seat Demands a treat Of savory meat.'

"Take this into consideration, friends of the Jury, and you will readily decide that the kitten is wrongfully accused and should be set at liberty."

When the Tin Woodman sat down no one applauded him, for his arguments had not been very convincing and few believed that he had proved Eureka's innocence. As for the Jury, the members whispered to each other for a few minutes and then they appointed the Hungry Tiger their spokesman. The huge beast slowly arose and said:

"Kittens have no consciences, so they eat whatever pleases them. The jury believes the white kitten known as Eureka is guilty of having eaten the piglet owned by Princess Ozma, and recommends that she be put to death in punishment of the crime."

The judgment of the jury was received with great applause, although Dorothy was sobbing miserably at the fate of her pet. The Princess was just about to order Eureka's head chopped off with the Tin Woodman's axe when that brilliant personage once more arose and addressed her.

"Your Highness," said he, "see how easy it is for a jury to be mistaken. The kitten could not have eaten your piglet—for here it is!"

He took off his funnel hat and from beneath it produced a tiny white piglet, which he held aloft that all might see it clearly.

Ozma was delighted and exclaimed, eagerly:

"Give me my pet, Nick Chopper!"

And all the people cheered and clapped their hands, rejoicing that the prisoner had escaped death and been proved to be innocent.

As the Princess held the white piglet in her arms and stroked its soft hair she said: "Let Eureka out of the cage, for she is no longer a prisoner, but our good friend. Where did you find my missing pet, Nick Chopper?"

"In a room of the palace," he answered.

"Justice," remarked the Scarecrow, with a sigh, "is a dangerous thing to meddle with. If you hadn't happened to find the piglet, Eureka would surely have been executed."

"But justice prevailed at the last," said Ozma, "for here is my pet, and Eureka is once more free."

"I refuse to be free," cried the kitten, in a sharp voice, "unless the Wizard can do his trick with eight piglets. If he can produce but seven, then this is not the piglet that was lost, but another one."

"Hush, Eureka!" warned the Wizard.

"Don't be foolish," advised the Tin Woodman, "or you may be sorry for it."

"The piglet that belonged to the Princess wore an emerald collar," said Eureka, loudly enough for all to hear.

"So it did!" exclaimed Ozma. "This cannot be the one the Wizard gave me."

"Of course not; he had nine of them, altogether," declared Eureka; "and I must say it was very stingy of him not to let me eat just a few. But now that this foolish trial is ended, I will tell you what really became of your pet piglet."

At this everyone in the Throne Room suddenly became quiet, and the kitten continued, in a calm, mocking tone of voice:

"I will confess that I intended to eat the little pig for my breakfast; so I crept into the room where it was kept while the Princess was dressing and hid myself under a chair. When Ozma went away she closed the door and left her pet on the table. At once I jumped up and told the piglet not to make a fuss, for he would be inside of me in half a second; but no one can teach one of these creatures to be reasonable. Instead of keeping still, so I could eat him comfortably, he trembled so with fear that he fell off the table into a big vase that was standing on the floor. The vase had a very small neck, and spread out at the top like a bowl. At first the piglet stuck in the neck of the vase and I thought I should get him, after all, but he wriggled himself through and fell down into the deep bottom part—and I suppose he's there yet."

All were astonished at this confession, and Ozma at once sent an officer to her room to fetch the vase. When he returned the Princess looked down the narrow neck of the big ornament and discovered her lost piglet, just as Eureka had said she would.

There was no way to get the creature out without breaking the vase, so the Tin Woodman smashed it with his axe and set the little prisoner free.

Then the crowd cheered lustily and Dorothy hugged the kitten in her arms and told her how delighted she was to know that she was innocent.

"But why didn't you tell us at first?" she asked.

"It would have spoiled the fun," replied the kitten, yawning.

Ozma gave the Wizard back the piglet he had so kindly allowed Nick Chopper to substitute for the lost one, and then she carried her own into the apartments of the palace where she lived. And now, the trial being over, the good citizens of the Emerald City scattered to their homes, well content with the day's amusement.

Chapter 20 - Zeb Returns to the Ranch

Eureka was much surprised to find herself in disgrace; but she was, in spite of the fact that she had not eaten the piglet. For the folks of Oz knew the kitten had tried to commit the crime, and that only an accident had prevented her from doing so; therefore even the Hungry Tiger preferred not to associate with her. Eureka was forbidden to wander around the palace and was made to stay in confinement in Dorothy's room; so she began to beg her mistress to send her to some other place where she could enjoy herself better.

Dorothy was herself anxious to get home, so she promised Eureka they would not stay in the Land of Oz much longer.

The next evening after the trial the little girl begged Ozma to allow her to look in the enchanted picture, and the Princess readily consented. She took the child to her room and said: "Make your wish, dear, and the picture will show the scene you desire to behold."

Then Dorothy found, with the aid of the enchanted picture, that Uncle Henry had returned to the farm in Kansas, and she also saw that both he and Aunt Em were dressed in mourning, because they thought their little niece had been killed by the earthquake.

"Really," said the girl, anxiously, "I must get back as soon as poss'ble to my own folks."

Zeb also wanted to see his home, and although he did not find anyone morning for him, the sight of Hugson's Ranch in the picture made him long to get back there.

"This is a fine country, and I like all the people that live in it," he told Dorothy. "But the fact is, Jim and I don't seem to fit into a fairyland, and the old horse has been begging me to go home again ever since he lost the race. So, if you can find a way to fix it, we'll be much obliged to you."

"Ozma can do it, easily," replied Dorothy. "Tomorrow morning I'll go to Kansas and you can go to Californy."

That last evening was so delightful that the boy will never forget it as long as he lives. They were all together (except Eureka) in the pretty rooms of the Princess, and the Wizard did some new tricks, and the Scarecrow told stories, and the Tin Woodman sang a love song in a sonorous, metallic voice, and everybody laughed and had a good time. Then Dorothy wound up Tik-tok and he danced a jig to amuse the company, after which the Yellow Hen related some of her adventures with the Nome King in the Land of Ev.

The Princess served delicious refreshments to those who were in the habit of eating, and when Dorothy's bed time arrived the company separated after exchanging many friendly sentiments.

Next morning they all assembled for the final parting, and many of the officials and courtiers came to look upon the impressive ceremonies.

Dorothy held Eureka in her arms and bade her friends a fond good-bye.

"You must come again, some time," said the little Wizard; and she promised she would if she found it possible to do so.

"But Uncle Henry and Aunt Em need me to help them," she added, "so I can't ever be very long away from the farm in Kansas."

Ozma wore the Magic Belt; and, when she had kissed Dorothy farewell and had made her wish, the little girl and her kitten disappeared in a twinkling.

"Where is she?" asked Zeb, rather bewildered by the suddenness of it.

"Greeting her uncle and aunt in Kansas, by this time," returned Ozma, with a smile.

Then Zeb brought out Jim, all harnessed to the buggy, and took his seat.

"I'm much obliged for all your kindness," said the boy, "and very grateful to you for saving my life and sending me home again after all the good times I've had. I think this is the loveliest country in the world; but not being fairies Jim and I feel we ought to be where we belong—and that's at the ranch. Good-bye, everybody!"

He gave a start and rubbed his eyes. Jim was trotting along the well-known road, shaking his ears and whisking his tail with a contented motion. Just ahead of them were the gates of Hugson's Ranch, and Uncle Hugson now came out and stood with uplifted arms and wide open mouth, staring in amazement.

"Goodness gracious! It's Zeb—and Jim, too!" he exclaimed. "Where in the world have you been, my lad?"

"Why, in the world, Uncle," answered Zeb, with a laugh.

The End

The Road to Oz

Introduction

In which is related how Dorothy Gale of Kansas, The Shaggy Man, Button Bright, and Polychrome the Rainbow's Daughter met on an Enchanted Road and followed it all the way to the
Marvelous Land of Oz.

    by
L. Frank Baum
"Royal Historian of Oz"

To My Readers

    Well, my dears, here is what you have asked for: another "Oz Book" about Dorothy's strange adventures. Toto is in this story, because you wanted him to be there, and many other characters which you will recognize are in the story, too. Indeed, the wishes of my little correspondents have been considered as carefully as possible, and if the story is not exactly as you would have written it yourselves, you must remember that a story has to be a story before it can be written down, and the writer cannot change it much without spoiling it.

    In the preface to "Dorothy and the Wizard of Oz" I said I would like to write some stories that were not "Oz" stories, because I thought I had written about Oz long enough; but since that volume was published I have been fairly deluged with letters from children imploring me to "write more about Dorothy," and "more about Oz," and since I write only to please the children I shall try to respect their wishes.

    There are some new characters in this book that ought to win your live. I'm very fond of the shaggy man myself, and I think you will like him, too. As for Polychrome—the Rainbow's Daughter—and stupid little Button-Bright, they seem to have brought a new element of fun into these Oz stories, and I am glad I discovered them. Yet I am anxious to have you write and tell me how you like them.

    Since this book was written I have received some very remarkable News from The Land of Oz, which has greatly astonished me. I believe it will astonish you, too, my dears, when you hear it. But it is such a long and exciting story that it must be saved for another book—and perhaps that book will be the last story that will ever be told about the Land of Oz.

L. FRANK BAUM
Coronado, 1909.

LIST OF CHAPTERS

Chapter 1 - The Way to Butterfield

"Please, miss," said the shaggy man, "can you tell me the road to Butterfield?"

Dorothy looked him over. Yes, he was shaggy, all right, but there was a twinkle in his eye that seemed pleasant.

"Oh yes," she replied; "I can tell you. But it isn't this road at all."

"No?"

"You cross the ten-acre lot, follow the lane to the highway, go north to the five branches, and take—let me see—"

"To be sure, miss; see as far as Butterfield, if you like," said the shaggy man.

"You take the branch next the willow stump, I b'lieve; or else the branch by the gopher holes; or else—"

"Won't any of 'em do, miss?"

"'Course not, Shaggy Man. You must take the right road to get to Butterfield."

"And is that the one by the gopher stump, or—"

"Dear me!" cried Dorothy. "I shall have to show you the way, you're so stupid. Wait a minute till I run in the house and get my sunbonnet."

The shaggy man waited. He had an oat-straw in his mouth, which he chewed slowly as if it tasted good; but it didn't. There was an apple-tree beside the house, and some apples had fallen to the ground. The shaggy man thought they would taste better than the oat-straw, so he walked over to get some. A little black dog with bright brown eyes dashed out of the farm-house and ran madly toward the shaggy man, who had already picked up three apples and put them in one of the big wide pockets of his shaggy coat. The little dog barked and made a dive for the shaggy man's leg; but he grabbed the dog by the neck and put it in his big pocket along with the apples. He took more apples, afterward, for many were on the ground; and each one that he tossed into his pocket hit the little dog somewhere upon the head or back, and made him growl. The little dog's name was Toto, and he was sorry he had been put in the shaggy man's pocket.

Pretty soon Dorothy came out of the house with her sunbonnet, and she called out:

"Come on, Shaggy Man, if you want me to show you the road to Butterfield." She climbed the fence into the ten-acre lot and he followed her, walking slowly and stumbling over the little hillocks in the pasture as if he was thinking of something else and did not notice them.

"My, but you're clumsy!" said the little girl. "Are your feet tired?"

"No, miss; it's my whiskers; they tire very easily in this warm weather," said he. "I wish it would snow, don't you?"

"'Course not, Shaggy Man," replied Dorothy, giving him a severe look. "If it snowed in August it would spoil the corn and the oats and the wheat; and then Uncle Henry wouldn't have any crops; and that would make him poor; and—"

"Never mind," said the shaggy man. "It won't snow, I guess. Is this the lane?"

"Yes," replied Dorothy, climbing another fence; "I'll go as far as the highway with you."

"Thankee, miss; you're very kind for your size, I'm sure," said he gratefully.

"It isn't everyone who knows the road to Butterfield," Dorothy remarked as she tripped along the lane; "but I've driven there many a time with Uncle Henry, and so I b'lieve I could find it blindfolded."

"Don't do that, miss," said the shaggy man earnestly; "you might make a mistake."

"I won't," she answered, laughing. "Here's the highway. Now it's the second—no, the third turn to the left—or else it's the fourth. Let's see. The first one is by the elm tree, and the second is by the gopher holes; and then—"

"Then what?" he inquired, putting his hands in his coat pockets. Toto grabbed a finger and bit it; the shaggy man took his hand out of that pocket quickly, and said "Oh!"

Dorothy did not notice. She was shading her eyes from the sun with her arm, looking anxiously down the road.

"Come on," she commanded. "It's only a little way farther, so I may as well show you."

After a while, they came to the place where five roads branched in different directions; Dorothy pointed to one, and said:

"That's it, Shaggy Man."

"I'm much obliged, miss," he said, and started along another road.

"Not that one!" she cried; "you're going wrong."

He stopped.

"I thought you said that other was the road to Butterfield," said he, running his fingers through his shaggy whiskers in a puzzled way.

"So it is."

"But I don't want to go to Butterfield, miss."

"You don't?"

"Of course not. I wanted you to show me the road, so I shouldn't go there by mistake."

"Oh! Where DO you want to go, then?"

"I'm not particular, miss."

This answer astonished the little girl; and it made her provoked, too, to think she had taken all this trouble for nothing.

"There are a good many roads here," observed the shaggy man, turning slowly around, like a human windmill. "Seems to me a person could go 'most anywhere, from this place."

Dorothy turned around too, and gazed in surprise. There WERE a good many roads; more than she had ever seen before. She tried to count them, knowing there ought to be five, but when she had counted seventeen she grew bewildered and stopped, for the roads were as many as the spokes of a wheel and ran in every direction from the place where they stood; so if she kept on counting she was likely to count some of the roads twice.

"Dear me!" she exclaimed. "There used to be only five roads, highway and all. And now—why, where's the highway, Shaggy Man?"

"Can't say, miss," he responded, sitting down upon the ground as if tired with standing. "Wasn't it here a minute ago?"

"I thought so," she answered, greatly perplexed. "And I saw the gopher holes, too, and the dead stump; but they're not here now. These roads are all strange—and what a lot of them there are! Where do you suppose they all go to?"

"Roads," observed the shaggy man, "don't go anywhere. They stay in one place, so folks can walk on them."

He put his hand in his side-pocket and drew out an apple—quick, before Toto could bite him again. The little dog got his head out this time and said "Bow-wow!" so loudly that it made Dorothy jump.

"O, Toto!" she cried; "where did you come from?"

"I brought him along," said the shaggy man.

"What for?" she asked.

"To guard these apples in my pocket, miss, so no one would steal them."

With one hand the shaggy man held the apple, which he began eating, while with the other hand he pulled Toto out of his pocket and dropped him to the ground. Of course Toto made for Dorothy at once, barking joyfully at his release from the dark pocket. When the child had patted his head lovingly, he sat down before her, his red tongue hanging out one side of his mouth, and looked up into her face with his bright brown eyes, as if asking her what they should do next.

Dorothy didn't know. She looked around her anxiously for some familiar landmark; but everything was strange. Between the branches of the many roads were green meadows and a few shrubs and trees, but she couldn't see anywhere the farm-house from which she had just come, or anything she had ever seen before—except the shaggy man and Toto. Besides this, she had turned around and around so many times trying to find out where she was, that now she couldn't even tell which direction the farm-house ought to be in; and this began to worry her and make her feel anxious.

"I'm 'fraid, Shaggy Man," she said, with a sigh, "that we're lost!"

"That's nothing to be afraid of," he replied, throwing away the core of his apple and beginning to eat another one. "Each of these roads must lead somewhere, or it wouldn't be here. So what does it matter?"

"I want to go home again," she said.

"Well, why don't you?" said he.

"I don't know which road to take."

"That is too bad," he said, shaking his shaggy head gravely. "I wish I could help you; but I can't. I'm a stranger in these parts."

"Seems as if I were, too," she said, sitting down beside him. "It's funny. A few minutes ago I was home, and I just came to show you the way to Butterfield—"

"So I shouldn't make a mistake and go there—"

"And now I'm lost myself and don't know how to get home!"

"Have an apple," suggested the shaggy man, handing her one with pretty red cheeks.

"I'm not hungry," said Dorothy, pushing it away.

"But you may be, to-morrow; then you'll be sorry you didn't eat the apple," said he.

"If I am, I'll eat the apple then," promised Dorothy.

"Perhaps there won't be any apple then," he returned, beginning to eat the red-cheeked one himself. "Dogs sometimes can find their way home better than people," he went on; "perhaps your dog can lead you back to the farm."

"Will you, Toto?" asked Dorothy.

Toto wagged his tail vigorously.

"All right," said the girl; "let's go home."

Toto looked around a minute and dashed up one of the roads.

"Good-bye, Shaggy Man," called Dorothy, and ran after Toto. The little dog pranced briskly along for some distance; when he turned around and looked at his mistress questioningly.

"Oh, don't 'spect ME to tell you anything; I don't know the way," she said. "You'll have to find it yourself."

But Toto couldn't. He wagged his tail, and sneezed, and shook his ears, and trotted back where they had left the shaggy man. From here he started along another road; then came back and tried another; but each time he found the way strange and decided it would not take them to the farm-house. Finally, when Dorothy had begun to tire with chasing after him, Toto sat down panting beside the shaggy man and gave up.

Dorothy sat down, too, very thoughtful. The little girl had encountered some queer adventures since she came to live at the farm; but this was the queerest of them all. To get lost in fifteen minutes, so near to her home and in the unromantic State of Kansas, was an experience that fairly bewildered her.

"Will your folks worry?" asked the shaggy man, his eyes twinkling in a pleasant way.

"I s'pose so," answered Dorothy with a sigh. "Uncle Henry says there's ALWAYS something happening to me; but I've always come home safe at the last. So perhaps he'll take comfort and think I'll come home safe this time."

"I'm sure you will," said the shaggy man, smilingly nodding at her. "Good little girls never come to any harm, you know. For my part, I'm good, too; so nothing ever hurts me."

Dorothy looked at him curiously. His clothes were shaggy, his boots were shaggy and full of holes, and his hair and whiskers were shaggy. But his smile was sweet and his eyes were kind.

"Why didn't you want to go to Butterfield?" she asked.

"Because a man lives there who owes me fifteen cents, and if I went to Butterfield and he saw me he'd want to pay me the money. I don't want money, my dear."

"Why not?" she inquired.

"Money," declared the shaggy man, "makes people proud and haughty. I don't want to be proud and haughty. All I want is to have people love me; and as long as I own the Love Magnet, everyone I meet is sure to love me dearly."

"The Love Magnet! Why, what's that?"

"I'll show you, if you won't tell any one," he answered, in a low, mysterious voice.

"There isn't any one to tell, 'cept Toto," said the girl.

The shaggy man searched in one pocket, carefully; and in another pocket; and in a third. At last he drew out a small parcel wrapped in crumpled paper and tied with a cotton string. He unwound the string, opened the parcel, and took out a bit of metal shaped like a horseshoe. It was dull and brown, and not very pretty.

"This, my dear," said he, impressively, "is the wonderful Love Magnet. It was given me by an Eskimo in the Sandwich Islands—where there are no sandwiches at all—and as long as I carry it every living thing I meet will love me dearly."

"Why didn't the Eskimo keep it?" she asked, looking at the Magnet with interest.

"He got tired of being loved and longed for some one to hate him. So he gave me the Magnet and the very next day a grizzly bear ate him."

"Wasn't he sorry then?" she inquired.

"He didn't say," replied the shaggy man, wrapping and tying the Love Magnet with great care and putting it away in another pocket. "But the bear didn't seem sorry a bit," he added.

"Did you know the bear?" asked Dorothy.

"Yes; we used to play ball together in the Caviar Islands. The bear loved me because I had the Love Magnet. I couldn't blame him for eating the Eskimo, because it was his nature to do so."

"Once," said Dorothy, "I knew a Hungry Tiger who longed to eat fat babies, because it was his nature to; but he never ate any because he had a Conscience."

"This bear," replied the shaggy man, with a sigh, "had no Conscience, you see."

The shaggy man sat silent for several minutes, apparently considering the cases of the bear and the tiger, while Toto watched him with an air of great interest. The little dog was doubtless thinking of his ride in the shaggy man's pocket and planning to keep out of reach in the future.

At last the shaggy man turned and inquired, "What's your name, little girl?"

213

"My name's Dorothy," said she, jumping up again, "but what are we going to do? We can't stay here forever, you know."

"Let's take the seventh road," he suggested. "Seven is a lucky number for little girls named Dorothy."

"The seventh from where?"

"From where you begin to count."

So she counted seven roads, and the seventh looked just like all the others; but the shaggy man got up from the ground where he had been sitting and started down this road as if sure it was the best way to go; and Dorothy and Toto followed him.

Chapter 2 - Dorothy Meets Button-Bright

The seventh road was a good road, and curved this way and that—winding through green meadows and fields covered with daisies and buttercups and past groups of shady trees. There were no houses of any sort to be seen, and for some distance they met with no living creature at all.

Dorothy began to fear they were getting a good way from the farm-house, since here everything was strange to her; but it would do no good at all to go back where the other roads all met, because the next one they chose might lead her just as far from home.

She kept on beside the shaggy man, who whistled cheerful tunes to beguile the journey, until by and by they followed a turn in the road and saw before them a big chestnut tree making a shady spot over the highway. In the shade sat a little boy dressed in sailor clothes, who was digging a hole in the earth with a bit of wood. He must have been digging some time, because the hole was already big enough to drop a football into.

Dorothy and Toto and the shaggy man came to a halt before the little boy, who kept on digging in a sober and persistent fashion.

"Who are you?" asked the girl.

He looked up at her calmly. His face was round and chubby and his eyes were big, blue and earnest.

"I'm Button-Bright," said he.

"But what's your real name?" she inquired.

"Button-Bright."

"That isn't a really-truly name!" she exclaimed.

"Isn't it?" he asked, still digging.

"'Course not. It's just a—a thing to call you by. You must have a name."

"Must I?"

"To be sure. What does your mama call you?"

He paused in his digging and tried to think.

"Papa always said I was bright as a button; so mama always called me Button-Bright," he said.

"What is your papa's name?"

"Just Papa."

"What else?"

"Don't know."

"Never mind," said the shaggy man, smiling. "We'll call the boy Button-Bright, as his mama does. That name is as good as any, and better than some."

Dorothy watched the boy dig.

"Where do you live?" she asked.

"Don't know," was the reply.

"How did you come here?"

"Don't know," he said again.

"Don't you know where you came from?"

"No," said he.

"Why, he must be lost," she said to the shaggy man. She turned to the boy once more.

"What are you going to do?" she inquired.

"Dig," said he.

"But you can't dig forever; and what are you going to do then?" she persisted.

"Don't know," said the boy.

"But you MUST know SOMETHING," declared Dorothy, getting provoked.

"Must I?" he asked, looking up in surprise.

"Of course you must."

"What must I know?"

"What's going to become of you, for one thing," she answered.

"Do YOU know what's going to become of me?" he asked.

"Not—not 'zactly," she admitted.

"Do you know what's going to become of YOU?" he continued, earnestly.

"I can't say I do," replied Dorothy, remembering her present difficulties.

The shaggy man laughed.

"No one knows everything, Dorothy," he said.

"But Button-Bright doesn't seem to know ANYthing," she declared. "Do you, Button-Bright?"

He shook his head, which had pretty curls all over it, and replied with perfect calmness:

"Don't know."

Never before had Dorothy met with anyone who could give her so little information. The boy was evidently lost, and his people would be sure to worry about him. He seemed two or three years younger than Dorothy, and was prettily dressed, as if someone loved him dearly and took much pains to make him look well. How, then, did he come to be in this lonely road? she wondered.

Near Button-Bright, on the ground, lay a sailor hat with a gilt anchor on the band. His sailor trousers were long and wide at the bottom, and the broad collar of his blouse had gold anchors sewed on its corners. The boy was still digging at his hole.

"Have you ever been to sea?" asked Dorothy.

"To see what?" answered Button-Bright.

"I mean, have you ever been where there's water?"

"Yes," said Button-Bright; "there's a well in our back yard."

"You don't understand," cried Dorothy. "I mean, have you ever been on a big ship floating on a big ocean?"

"Don't know," said he.

"Then why do you wear sailor clothes?"

"Don't know," he answered, again.

Dorothy was in despair.

"You're just AWFUL stupid, Button-Bright," she said.

"Am I?" he asked.

"Yes, you are."

"Why?" looking up at her with big eyes.

She was going to say: "Don't know," but stopped herself in time.

"That's for you to answer," she replied.

"It's no use asking Button-Bright questions," said the shaggy man, who had been eating another apple; "but someone ought to take care of the poor little chap, don't you think? So he'd better come along with us."

Toto had been looking with great curiosity in the hole which the boy was digging, and growing more and more excited every minute, perhaps thinking that Button-Bright was after some wild animal. The little dog began barking loudly and jumped into the hole himself, where he began to dig with his tiny paws, making the earth fly in all directions. It spattered over the boy. Dorothy seized him and raised him to his feet, brushing his clothes with her hand.

"Stop that, Toto!" she called. "There aren't any mice or woodchucks in that hole, so don't be foolish."

Toto stopped, sniffed at the hole suspiciously, and jumped out of it, wagging his tail as if he had done something important.

"Well," said the shaggy man, "let's start on, or we won't get anywhere before night comes."

"Where do you expect to get to?" asked Dorothy.

"I'm like Button-Bright. I don't know," answered the shaggy man, with a laugh. "But I've learned from long experience that every road leads somewhere, or there wouldn't be any road; so it's likely that if we travel long enough, my dear, we will come to some place or another in the end. What place it will be we can't even guess at this moment, but we're sure to find out when we get there."

"Why, yes," said Dorothy; "that seems reas'n'ble, Shaggy Man."

Chapter 3 - A Queer Village

Button-Bright took the shaggy man's hand willingly; for the shaggy man had the Love
Magnet, you know, which was the reason Button-Bright had loved him at once. They started on, with Dorothy on one side, and Toto on the other, the little party trudging along more cheerfully than you might have supposed. The girl was getting used to queer adventures, which interested her very much. Wherever Dorothy went Toto was sure to go, like Mary's little lamb. Button-Bright didn't seem a bit afraid or worried because he was lost, and the shaggy man had no home, perhaps, and was as happy in one place as in another.

Before long they saw ahead of them a fine big arch spanning the road, and when they came nearer they found that the arch was beautifully carved and decorated with rich colors. A row of peacocks with spread tails ran along the top of it, and all the feathers were gorgeously painted. In the center was a large fox's head, and the fox wore a shrewd and knowing expression and had large spectacles over its eyes and a small golden crown with shiny points on top of its head.

While the travelers were looking with curiosity at this beautiful arch there suddenly marched out of it a company of soldiers—only the soldiers were all foxes dressed in uniforms. They wore green jackets and yellow pantaloons, and their little round caps and their high boots were a bright red color. Also, there was a big red bow tied about the middle of each long, bushy tail. Each soldier was armed with a wooden sword having an edge of sharp teeth set in a row, and the sight of these teeth at first caused Dorothy to shudder.

A captain marched in front of the company of fox-soldiers, his uniform embroidered with gold braid to make it handsomer than the others.

Almost before our friends realized it the soldiers had surrounded them on all sides, and the captain was calling out in a harsh voice:

"Surrender! You are our prisoners."

"What's a pris'ner?" asked Button-Bright.

"A prisoner is a captive," replied the fox-captain, strutting up and down with much dignity.

"What's a captive?" asked Button-Bright.

"You're one," said the captain.

That made the shaggy man laugh

"Good afternoon, captain," he said, bowing politely to all the foxes and very low to their commander. "I trust you are in good health, and that your families are all well?"

The fox-captain looked at the shaggy man, and his sharp features grew pleasant and smiling.

"We're pretty well, thank you, Shaggy Man," said he; and Dorothy knew that the Love Magnet was working and that all the foxes now loved the shaggy man because of it. But Toto didn't know this, for he began barking angrily and tried to bite the captain's hairy leg where it showed between his red boots and his yellow pantaloons.

"Stop, Toto!" cried the little girl, seizing the dog in her arms. "These are our friends."

"Why, so we are!" remarked the captain in tones of astonishment. "I thought at first we were enemies, but it seems you are friends instead. You must come with me to see King Dox."

"Who's he?" asked Button-Bright, with earnest eyes.

"King Dox of Foxville; the great and wise sovereign who rules over our community."

"What's sov'rin, and what's c'u'nity?" inquired Button-Bright.

"Don't ask so many questions, little boy."

"Why?"

"Ah, why indeed?" exclaimed the captain, looking at Button-Bright admiringly. "If you don't ask questions you will learn nothing. True enough. I was wrong. You're a very clever little boy, come to think of it—very clever indeed. But now, friends, please come with me, for it is my duty to escort you at once to the royal palace."

The soldiers marched back through the arch again, and with them marched the shaggy man, Dorothy, Toto, and Button-Bright. Once through the opening they found a fine, big city spread out before them, all the houses of carved marble in beautiful colors. The decorations were mostly birds and other fowl, such as peacocks, pheasants, turkeys, prairie-chickens, ducks, and geese. Over each doorway was carved a head representing the fox who lived in that house, this effect being quite pretty and unusual.

As our friends marched along, some of the foxes came out on the porches and balconies to get a view of the strangers. These foxes were all handsomely dressed, the girl-foxes and women-foxes wearing gowns of feathers woven together effectively and colored in bright hues which Dorothy thought were quite artistic and decidedly attractive.

Button-Bright stared until his eyes were big and round, and he would have stumbled and fallen more than once had not the shaggy man grasped his hand tightly. They were all interested, and Toto was so excited he wanted to bark every minute and to chase and fight every fox he caught sight of; but Dorothy held his little wiggling body fast in her arms and commanded him to be good and behave himself. So he finally quieted down, like a wise doggy, deciding there were too many foxes in Foxville to fight at one time.

By-and-by they came to a big square, and in the center of the square stood the royal palace. Dorothy knew it at once because it had over its great door the carved head of a fox just like the one she had seen on the arch, and this fox was the only one who wore a golden crown.

There were many fox-soldiers guarding the door, but they bowed to the captain and admitted him without question. The captain led them through many rooms, where richly dressed foxes were sitting on beautiful chairs or sipping tea, which was being passed around by fox-servants in white aprons. They came to a big doorway covered with heavy curtains of cloth of gold.

Beside this doorway stood a huge drum. The fox-captain went to this drum and knocked his knees against it—first one knee and then the other—so that the drum said: "Boom-boom."

"You must all do exactly what I do," ordered the captain; so the shaggy man pounded the drum with his knees, and so did Dorothy and so did Button-Bright. The boy wanted to keep on pounding it with his little fat knees, because he liked the sound of it; but the captain stopped him. Toto couldn't pound the drum with his knees and he didn't know enough to wag his tail against it, so Dorothy pounded the drum for him and that made him bark, and when the little dog barked the fox-captain scowled.

The golden curtains drew back far enough to make an opening, through which marched the captain with the others.

The broad, long room they entered was decorated in gold with stained-glass windows of splendid colors. In the corner of the room upon a richly carved golden throne, sat the fox-king, surrounded by a group of other foxes, all of whom wore great spectacles over their eyes, making them look solemn and important.

Dorothy knew the King at once, because she had seen his head carved on the arch and over the doorway of the palace. Having met with several other kings in her travels, she knew what to do, and at once made a low bow before the throne. The shaggy man bowed, too, and Button-Bright bobbed his head and said "Hello."

"Most wise and noble Potentate of Foxville," said the captain, addressing the King in a pompous voice, "I humbly beg to report that I found these strangers on the road leading to your Foxy Majesty's dominions, and have therefore brought them before you, as is my duty."

"So—so," said the King, looking at them keenly. "What brought you here, strangers?"

"Our legs, may it please your Royal Hairiness," replied the shaggy man.

"What is your business here?" was the next question.

"To get away as soon as possible," said the shaggy man.

The King didn't know about the Magnet, of course; but it made him love the shaggy man at once.

"Do just as you please about going away," he said; "but I'd like to show you the sights of my city and to entertain your party while you are here. We feel highly honored to have little Dorothy with us, I assure you, and we appreciate her kindness in making us a visit. For whatever country Dorothy visits is sure to become famous."

This speech greatly surprised the little girl, who asked:

"How did your Majesty know my name?"

"Why, everybody knows you, my dear," said the Fox-King. "Don't you realize that? You are quite an important personage since Princess Ozma of Oz made you her friend."

"Do you know Ozma?" she asked, wondering.

"I regret to say that I do not," he answered, sadly; "but I hope to meet her soon. You know the Princess Ozma is to celebrate her birthday on the twenty-first of this month."

"Is she?" said Dorothy. "I didn't know that."

"Yes; it is to be the most brilliant royal ceremony ever held in any city in Fairyland, and I hope you will try to get me an invitation."

Dorothy thought a moment.

"I'm sure Ozma would invite you if I asked her," she said; "but how could you get to the Land of Oz and the Emerald City? It's a good way from Kansas."

"Kansas!" he exclaimed, surprised.

"Why, yes; we are in Kansas now, aren't we?" she returned.

"What a queer notion!" cried the Fox-King, beginning to laugh. "Whatever made you think this is Kansas?"

"I left Uncle Henry's farm only about two hours ago; that's the reason," she said, rather perplexed.

"But, tell me, my dear, did you ever see so wonderful a city as Foxville in Kansas?" he questioned.

"No, your Majesty."

"And haven't you traveled from Oz to Kansas in less than half a jiffy, by means of the Silver Shoes and the Magic Belt?"

"Yes, your Majesty," she acknowledged.

"Then why do you wonder that an hour or two could bring you to Foxville, which is nearer to Oz than it is to Kansas?"

"Dear me!" exclaimed Dorothy; "is this another fairy adventure?"

"It seems to be," said the Fox-King, smiling.

Dorothy turned to the shaggy man, and her face was grave and reproachful.

"Are you a magician? or a fairy in disguise?" she asked. "Did you enchant me when you asked the way to Butterfield?"

The shaggy man shook his head.

"Who ever heard of a shaggy fairy?" he replied. "No, Dorothy, my dear; I'm not to blame for this journey in any way, I assure you. There's been something strange about me ever since I owned the Love Magnet; but I don't know what it is any more than you do. I didn't try to get you away from home, at all. If you want to find your way back to the farm I'll go with you willingly, and do my best to help you."

"Never mind," said the little girl, thoughtfully. "There isn't so much to see in Kansas as there is here, and I guess Aunt Em won't be VERY much worried; that is, if I don't stay away too long."

"That's right," declared the Fox-King, nodding approval. "Be contented with your lot, whatever it happens to be, if you are wise. Which reminds me that you have a new companion on this adventure—he looks very clever and bright."

"He is," said Dorothy; and the shaggy man added:

"That's his name, your Royal Foxiness—Button-Bright."

Chapter 4 - King Dox

It was amusing to note the expression on the face of King Dox as he looked the boy over, from his sailor hat to his stubby shoes, and it was equally diverting to watch Button-Bright stare at the King in return. No fox ever beheld a fresher, fairer child's face, and no child had ever before heard a fox talk, or met with one who dressed so handsomely and ruled so big a city. I am sorry to say that no one had ever told the little boy much about fairies of any kind; this being the case, it is easy to understand how much this strange experience startled and astonished him.

"How do you like us?" asked the King.

"Don't know," said Button-Bright.

"Of course you don't. It's too short an acquaintance," returned his Majesty. "What do you suppose my name is?"

"Don't know," said Button-Bright.

"How should you? Well, I'll tell you. My private name is Dox, but a King can't be called by his private name; he has to take one that is official. Therefore my official name is King Renard the Fourth. Ren-ard with the accent on the 'Ren'."

"What's 'ren'?" asked Button-Bright.

"How clever!" exclaimed the King, turning a pleased face toward his counselors. "This boy is indeed remarkably bright. 'What's 'ren'?' he asks; and of course 'ren' is nothing at all, all by itself. Yes, he's very bright indeed."

"That question is what your Majesty might call foxy," said one of the counselors, an old grey fox.

"So it is," declared the King. Turning again to Button-Bright, he asked:

"Having told you my name, what would you call me?"

"King Dox," said the boy.

"Why?"

"'Cause 'ren''s nothing at all," was the reply.

"Good! Very good indeed! You certainly have a brilliant mind. Do you know why two and two make four?"

"No," said Button-Bright.

"Clever! clever indeed! Of course you don't know. Nobody knows why; we only know it's so, and can't tell why it's so. Button-Bright, those curls and blue eyes do not go well with so much wisdom. They make you look too youthful, and hide your real cleverness. Therefore, I will do you a great favor. I will confer upon you the head of a fox, so that you may hereafter look as bright as you really are."

As he spoke the King waved his paw toward the boy, and at once the pretty curls and fresh round face and big blue eyes were gone, while in their place a fox's head appeared upon Button-Bright's shoulders—a hairy head with a sharp nose, pointed ears, and keen little eyes.

"Oh, don't do that!" cried Dorothy, shrinking back from her transformed companion with a shocked and dismayed face.

"Too late, my dear; it's done. But you also shall have a fox's head if you can prove you're as clever as Button-Bright."

"I don't want it; it's dreadful!" she exclaimed; and, hearing this verdict, Button-Bright began to boo-hoo just as if he were still a little boy.

"How can you call that lovely head dreadful?" asked the King. "It's a much prettier face than he had before, to my notion, and my wife says I'm a good judge of beauty. Don't cry, little fox-boy. Laugh and be proud, because you are so highly favored. How do you like the new head, Button-Bright?"

"D-d-don't n-n-n-know!" sobbed the child.

"Please, PLEASE change him back again, your Majesty!" begged Dorothy.

King Renard IV shook his head.

"I can't do that," he said; "I haven't the power, even if I wanted to. No, Button-Bright must wear his fox head, and he'll be sure to love it dearly as soon as he gets used to it."

Both the shaggy man and Dorothy looked grave and anxious, for they were sorrowful that such a misfortune had overtaken their little companion. Toto barked at the fox-boy once or twice, not realizing it was his former friend who now wore the animal head; but Dorothy cuffed the dog and made him stop. As for the foxes, they all seemed to think Button-Bright's new head very becoming and that their King had conferred a great honor on this little stranger. It was funny to see the boy reach up to feel of his sharp nose and wide mouth, and wail afresh with grief. He wagged his ears in a comical manner and tears were in his little black eyes. But Dorothy couldn't laugh at her friend just yet, because she felt so sorry.

Just then three little fox-princesses, daughters of the King, entered the room, and when they saw Button-Bright one exclaimed: "How lovely he is!" and the next one cried in delight: "How sweet he is!" and the third princess clapped her hands with pleasure and said, "How beautiful he is!"

Button-Bright stopped crying and asked timidly:

"Am I?"

"In all the world there is not another face so pretty," declared the biggest fox-princess.

"You must live with us always, and be our brother," said the next.

"We shall all love you dearly," the third said.

This praise did much to comfort the boy, and he looked around and tried to smile. It was a pitiful attempt, because the fox face was new and stiff, and Dorothy thought his expression more stupid than before the transformation.

"I think we ought to be going now," said the shaggy man, uneasily, for he didn't know what the King might take into his head to do next.

"Don't leave us yet, I beg of you," pleaded King Renard. "I intend to have several days of feasting and merry-making in honor of your visit."

"Have it after we're gone, for we can't wait," said Dorothy, decidedly. But seeing this displeased the King, she added: "If I'm going to get Ozma to invite you to her party I'll have to find her as soon as poss'ble, you know."

In spite of all the beauty of Foxville and the gorgeous dresses of its inhabitants, both the girl and the shaggy man felt they were not quite safe there, and would be glad to see the last of it.

"But it is now evening," the King reminded them, "and you must stay with us until morning, anyhow. Therefore, I invite you to be my guests at dinner, and to attend the theater afterward and sit in the royal box. To-morrow morning, if you really insist upon it, you may resume your journey."

They consented to this, and some of the fox-servants led them to a suite of lovely rooms in the big palace.

Button-Bright was afraid to be left alone, so Dorothy took him into her own room. While a maid-fox dressed the little girl's hair—which was a bit tangled—and put some bright, fresh ribbons in it, another maid-fox combed the hair on poor Button-Bright's face and head and brushed it carefully, tying a pink bow to each of his pointed ears. The maids wanted to dress the children in fine costumes of woven feathers, such as all the foxes wore; but neither of them consented to that.

"A sailor suit and a fox head do not go well together," said one of the maids, "for no fox was ever a sailor that I can remember."

"I'm not a fox!" cried Button-Bright.

"Alas, no," agreed the maid. "But you've got a lovely fox head on your skinny shoulders, and that's ALMOST as good as being a fox."

The boy, reminded of his misfortune, began to cry again. Dorothy petted and comforted him and promised to find some way to restore him his own head.

"If we can manage to get to Ozma," she said, "the Princess will change you back to yourself in half a second; so you just wear that fox head as comft'bly as you can, dear, and don't worry about it at all. It isn't nearly as pretty as your own head, no matter what the foxes say; but you can get along with it for a little while longer, can't you?"

"Don't know," said Button-Bright, doubtfully; but he didn't cry any more after that.

Dorothy let the maids pin ribbons to her shoulders, after which they were ready for the King's dinner. When they met the shaggy man in the splendid drawing room of the palace they found him just the same as before. He had refused to give up his shaggy clothes for new ones, because if he did that he would no longer be the shaggy man, he said, and he might have to get acquainted with himself all over again.

He told Dorothy he had brushed his shaggy hair and whiskers; but she thought he must have brushed them the wrong way, for they were quite as shaggy as before.

As for the company of foxes assembled to dine with the strangers, they were most beautifully costumed, and their rich dresses made Dorothy's simple gown and Button-Bright's sailor suit and the shaggy man's shaggy clothes look commonplace. But they treated their guests with great respect and the King's dinner was a very good dinner indeed. Foxes, as you know, are fond of chicken and other fowl; so they served chicken soup and roasted turkey and stewed duck and fried grouse and broiled quail and goose pie, and as the cooking was excellent the King's guests enjoyed the meal and ate heartily of the various dishes.

The party went to the theater, where they saw a play acted by foxes dressed in costumes of brilliantly colored feathers. The play was about a fox-girl who was stolen by some wicked wolves and carried to their cave; and just as they were about to kill her and eat her a company of fox-soldiers marched up, saved the girl, and put all the wicked wolves to death.

"How do you like it?" the King asked Dorothy.

"Pretty well," she answered. "It reminds me of one of Mr. Aesop's fables."

"Don't mention Aesop to me, I beg of you!" exclaimed King Dox. "I hate that man's name. He wrote a good deal about foxes, but always made them out cruel and wicked, whereas we are gentle and kind, as you may see."

"But his fables showed you to be wise and clever, and more shrewd than other animals," said the shaggy man, thoughtfully.

"So we are. There is no question about our knowing more than men do," replied the King, proudly. "But we employ our wisdom to do good, instead of harm; so that horrid Aesop did not know what he was talking about."

They did not like to contradict him, because they felt he ought to know the nature of foxes better than men did; so they sat still and watched the play, and Button-Bright became so interested that for the time he forgot he wore a fox head.

Afterward they went back to the palace and slept in soft beds stuffed with feathers; for the foxes raised many fowl for food, and used their feathers for clothing and to sleep upon.

Dorothy wondered why the animals living in Foxville did not wear just their own hairy skins as wild foxes do; when she mentioned it to King Dox he said they clothed themselves because they were civilized.

"But you were born without clothes," she observed, "and you don't seem to me to need them."

"So were human beings born without clothes," he replied; "and until they became civilized they wore only their natural skins. But to become civilized means to dress as elaborately and prettily as possible, and to make a show of your clothes so your neighbors will envy you, and for that reason both civilized foxes and civilized humans spend most of their time dressing themselves."

"I don't," declared the shaggy man.

"That is true," said the King, looking at him carefully; "but perhaps you are not civilized."

After a sound sleep and a good night's rest they had their breakfast with the King and then bade his Majesty good-bye.

"You've been kind to us—'cept poor Button-Bright," said Dorothy, "and we've had a nice time in Foxville."

"Then," said King Dox, "perhaps you'll be good enough to get me an invitation to Princess Ozma's birthday celebration."

"I'll try," she promised; "if I see her in time."

"It's on the twenty-first, remember," he continued; "and if you'll just see that I'm invited I'll find a way to cross the Dreadful Desert into the marvelous Land of Oz. I've always wanted to visit the Emerald City, so I'm sure it was fortunate you arrived here just when you did, you being Princess Ozma's friend and able to assist me in getting the invitation."

"If I see Ozma I'll ask her to invite you," she replied.

The Fox-King had a delightful luncheon put up for them, which the shaggy man shoved in his pocket, and the fox-captain escorted them to an arch at the side of the village opposite the one by which they had entered. Here they found more soldiers guarding the road.

"Are you afraid of enemies?" asked Dorothy.

"No; because we are watchful and able to protect ourselves," answered the captain. "But this road leads to another village peopled by big, stupid beasts who might cause us trouble if they thought we were afraid of them."

"What beasts are they?" asked the shaggy man.

The captain hesitated to answer. Finally, he said:

"You will learn all about them when you arrive at their city. But do not be afraid of them. Button-Bright is so wonderfully clever and has now such an intelligent face that I'm sure he will manage to find a way to protect you."

This made Dorothy and the shaggy man rather uneasy, for they had not so much confidence in the fox-boy's wisdom as the captain seemed to have. But as their escort would say no more about the beasts, they bade him good-bye and proceeded on their journey.

Chapter 5 - The Rainbow's Daughter

Toto, now allowed to run about as he pleased, was glad to be free again and able to bark at the birds and chase the butterflies. The country around them was charming, yet in the pretty fields of wild-flowers and groves of leafy trees were no houses whatever, or sign of any inhabitants. Birds flew through the air and cunning white rabbits darted amongst the tall grasses and green bushes; Dorothy noticed even the ants toiling busily along the roadway, bearing gigantic loads of clover seed; but of people there were none at all.

They walked briskly on for an hour or two, for even little Button-Bright was a good walker and did not tire easily. At length as they turned a curve in the road they beheld just before them a curious sight.

A little girl, radiant and beautiful, shapely as a fairy and exquisitely dressed, was dancing gracefully in the middle of the lonely road, whirling slowly this way and that, her dainty feet twinkling in sprightly fashion. She was clad in flowing, fluffy robes of soft material that reminded Dorothy of woven cobwebs, only it was colored in soft tintings of violet, rose, topaz, olive, azure, and white, mingled together most harmoniously in stripes which melted one into the other with soft blendings. Her hair was like spun gold and flowed around her in a cloud, no strand being fastened or confined by either pin or ornament or ribbon.

Filled with wonder and admiration our friends approached and stood watching this fascinating dance. The girl was no taller than Dorothy, although more slender; nor did she seem any older than our little heroine.

Suddenly she paused and abandoned the dance, as if for the first time observing the presence of strangers. As she faced them, shy as a frightened fawn, poised upon one foot as if to fly the next instant, Dorothy was astonished to see tears flowing from her violet eyes and trickling down her lovely rose-hued cheeks. That the dainty maiden should dance and weep at the same time was indeed surprising; so Dorothy asked in a soft, sympathetic voice:

"Are you unhappy, little girl?"

"Very!" was the reply; "I am lost."

"Why, so are we," said Dorothy, smiling; "but we don't cry about it."

"Don't you? Why not?"

"'Cause I've been lost before, and always got found again," answered Dorothy simply.

"But I've never been lost before," murmured the dainty maiden, "and I'm worried and afraid."

"You were dancing," remarked Dorothy, in a puzzled tone of voice.

"Oh, that was just to keep warm," explained the maiden, quickly. "It was not because I felt happy or gay, I assure you."

Dorothy looked at her closely. Her gauzy flowing robes might not be very warm, yet the weather wasn't at all chilly, but rather mild and balmy, like a spring day.

"Who are you, dear?" she asked, gently.

"I'm Polychrome," was the reply.

"Polly whom?"

"Polychrome. I'm the Daughter of the Rainbow."

"Oh!" said Dorothy with a gasp; "I didn't know the Rainbow had children. But I MIGHT have known it, before you spoke. You couldn't really be anything else."

"Why not?" inquired Polychrome, as if surprised.

"Because you're so lovely and sweet."

The little maiden smiled through her tears, came up to Dorothy, and placed her slender fingers in the Kansas girl's chubby hand.

"You'll be my friend—won't you?" she said, pleadingly.

"Of course."

"And what is your name?"

"I'm Dorothy; and this is my friend Shaggy Man, who owns the Love Magnet; and this is Button-Bright—only you don't see him as he really is because the Fox-King carelessly changed his head into a fox head. But the real Button-Bright is good to look at, and I hope to get him changed back to himself, some time."

The Rainbow's Daughter nodded cheerfully, no longer afraid of her new companions.

"But who is this?" she asked, pointing to Toto, who was sitting before her wagging his tail in the most friendly manner and admiring the pretty maid with his bright eyes. "Is this, also, some enchanted person?"

"Oh no, Polly—I may call you Polly, mayn't I? Your whole name's awful hard to say."

"Call me Polly if you wish, Dorothy."

"Well, Polly, Toto's just a dog; but he has more sense than Button-Bright, to tell the truth; and I'm very fond of him."

"So am I," said Polychrome, bending gracefully to pat Toto's head.

"But how did the Rainbow's Daughter ever get on this lonely road, and become lost?" asked the shaggy man, who had listened wonderingly to all this.

"Why, my father stretched his rainbow over here this morning, so that one end of it touched this road," was the reply; "and I was dancing upon the pretty rays, as I love to do, and never noticed I was getting too far over the bend in the circle. Suddenly I began to slide, and I went faster and faster until at last I bumped on the ground, at the very end. Just then father lifted the rainbow again, without noticing me at all, and though I tried to seize the end of it and hold fast, it melted away entirely and I was left alone and helpless on the cold, hard earth!"

"It doesn't seem cold to me, Polly," said Dorothy; "but perhaps you're not warmly dressed."

"I'm so used to living nearer the sun," replied the Rainbow's Daughter, "that at first I feared I would freeze down here. But my dance has warmed me some, and now I wonder how I am ever to get home again."

"Won't your father miss you, and look for you, and let down another rainbow for you?"

"Perhaps so, but he's busy just now because it rains in so many parts of the world at this season, and he has to set his rainbow in a lot of different places. What would you advise me to do, Dorothy?"

"Come with us," was the answer. "I'm going to try to find my way to the Emerald City, which is in the fairy Land of Oz. The Emerald City is ruled by a friend of mine, the Princess Ozma, and if we can manage to get there I'm sure she will know a way to send you home to your father again."

"Do you really think so?" asked Polychrome, anxiously.

"I'm pretty sure."

"Then I'll go with you," said the little maid; "for travel will help keep me warm, and father can find me in one part of the world as well as another—if he gets time to look for me."

"Come along, then," said the shaggy man, cheerfully; and they started on once more. Polly walked beside Dorothy a while, holding her new friend's hand as if she feared to let it go; but her nature seemed as light and buoyant as her fleecy robes, for suddenly she darted ahead and whirled round in a giddy dance. Then she tripped back to them with sparkling eyes and smiling cheeks, having regained her usual happy mood and forgotten all her worry about being lost.

They found her a charming companion, and her dancing and laughter—for she laughed at times like the tinkling of a silver bell—did much to enliven their journey and keep them contented.

Chapter 6 - The City of Beasts

When noon came they opened the Fox-King's basket of luncheon, and found a nice roasted turkey with cranberry sauce and some slices of bread and butter. As they sat on the grass by the roadside the shaggy man cut up the turkey with his pocket-knife and passed slices of it around.

"Haven't you any dewdrops, or mist-cakes, or cloudbuns?" asked Polychrome, longingly.

"'Course not," replied Dorothy. "We eat solid things, down here on the earth. But there's a bottle of cold tea. Try some, won't you?"

The Rainbow's Daughter watched Button-Bright devour one leg of the turkey.

"Is it good?" she asked.

He nodded.

"Do you think I could eat it?"

"Not this," said Button-Bright.

"But I mean another piece?"

"Don't know," he replied.

"Well, I'm going to try, for I'm very hungry," she decided, and took a thin slice of the white breast of turkey which the shaggy man cut for her, as well as a bit of bread and butter. When she tasted it Polychrome thought the turkey was good—better even than mist-cakes; but a little satisfied her hunger and she finished with a tiny sip of cold tea.

"That's about as much as a fly would eat," said Dorothy, who was making a good meal herself. "But I know some people in Oz who eat nothing at all."

"Who are they?" inquired the shaggy man.

"One is a scarecrow who's stuffed with straw, and the other a woodman made out of tin. They haven't any appetites inside of 'em, you see; so they never eat anything at all."

"Are they alive?" asked Button-Bright.

"Oh yes," replied Dorothy; "and they're very clever and very nice, too. If we get to Oz I'll introduce them to you."

"Do you really expect to get to Oz?" inquired the shaggy man, taking a drink of cold tea.

"I don't know just what to 'spect," answered the child, seriously; "but I've noticed if I happen to get lost I'm almost sure to come to the Land of Oz in the end, somehow 'r other; so I may get there this time. But I can't promise, you know; all I can do is wait and see."

"Will the Scarecrow scare me?" asked Button-Bright.

"No; 'cause you're not a crow," she returned. "He has the loveliest smile you ever saw—only it's painted on and he can't help it."

Luncheon being over they started again upon their journey, the shaggy man, Dorothy and Button-Bright walking soberly along, side by side, and the Rainbow's Daughter dancing merrily before them.

Sometimes she darted along the road so swiftly that she was nearly out of sight, then she came tripping back to greet them with her silvery laughter. But once she came back more sedately, to say:

"There's a city a little way off."

"I 'spected that," returned Dorothy; "for the fox-people warned us there was one on this road. It's filled with stupid beasts of some sort, but we musn't be afraid of 'em 'cause they won't hurt us."

"All right," said Button-Bright; but Polychrome didn't know whether it was all right or not.

"It's a big city," she said, "and the road runs straight through it."

"Never mind," said the shaggy man; "as long as I carry the Love Magnet every living thing will love me, and you may be sure I shan't allow any of my friends to be harmed in any way."

This comforted them somewhat, and they moved on again. Pretty soon they came to a signpost that read:

HAF A MYLE TO DUNKITON.

"Oh," said the shaggy man, "if they're donkeys, we've nothing to fear at all."

"They may kick," said Dorothy, doubtfully.

"Then we will cut some switches, and make them behave," he replied. At the first tree he cut himself a long, slender switch from one of the branches, and shorter switches for the others.

"Don't be afraid to order the beasts around," he said; "they're used to it."

Before long the road brought them to the gates of the city. There was a high wall all around, which had been whitewashed, and the gate just before our travelers was a mere opening in the wall, with no bars across it. No towers or steeples or domes showed above the enclosure, nor was any living thing to be seen as our friends drew near.

Suddenly, as they were about to boldly enter through the opening, there arose a harsh clamor of sound that swelled and echoed on every side, until they were nearly deafened by the racket and had to put their fingers to their ears to keep the noise out.

It was like the firing of many cannon, only there were no cannon-balls or other missiles to be seen; it was like the rolling of mighty thunder, only not a cloud was in the sky; it was like the roar of countless breakers on a rugged seashore, only there was no sea or other water anywhere about.

They hesitated to advance; but, as the noise did no harm, they entered through the whitewashed wall and quickly discovered the cause of the turmoil. Inside were suspended many sheets of tin or thin iron, and against these metal sheets a row of donkeys were pounding their heels with vicious kicks.

The shaggy man ran up to the nearest donkey and gave the beast a sharp blow with his switch.

"Stop that noise!" he shouted; and the donkey stopped kicking the metal sheet and turned its head to look with surprise at the shaggy man. He switched the next donkey, and made him stop, and then the next, so that gradually the rattling of heels ceased and the awful noise subsided. The donkeys stood in a group and eyed the strangers with fear and trembling.

"What do you mean by making such a racket?" asked the shaggy man, sternly.

"We were scaring away the foxes," said one of the donkeys, meekly. "Usually they run fast enough when they hear the noise, which makes them afraid."

"There are no foxes here," said the shaggy man.

"I beg to differ with you. There's one, anyhow," replied the donkey, sitting upright on its haunches and waving a hoof toward Button-Bright. "We saw him coming and thought the whole army of foxes was marching to attack us."

"Button-Bright isn't a fox," explained the shaggy man. "He's only wearing a fox head for a time, until he can get his own head back."

"Oh, I see," remarked the donkey, waving its left ear reflectively. "I'm sorry we made such a mistake, and had all our work and worry for nothing."

The other donkeys by this time were sitting up and examining the strangers with big, glassy eyes. They made a queer picture, indeed; for they wore wide, white collars around their necks and the collars had many scallops and points. The gentlemen-donkeys wore high pointed caps set between their great ears, and the lady-donkeys wore sunbonnets with holes cut in the top for the ears to stick through. But they had no other clothing except their hairy skins, although many wore gold and silver bangles on their front wrists and bands of different metals on their rear ankles. When they were kicking they had braced themselves with their front legs, but now they all stood or sat upright on their hind legs and used the front ones as arms. Having no fingers or hands the beasts were rather clumsy, as you may guess; but Dorothy was surprised to observe how many things they could do with their stiff, heavy hoofs.

Some of the donkeys were white, some were brown, or gray, or black, or spotted; but their hair was sleek and smooth and their broad collars and caps gave them a neat, if whimsical, appearance.

"This is a nice way to welcome visitors, I must say!" remarked the shaggy man, in a reproachful tone.

"Oh, we did not mean to be impolite," replied a grey donkey which had not spoken before. "But you were not expected, nor did you send in your visiting cards, as it is proper to do."

"There is some truth in that," admitted the shaggy man; "but, now you are informed that we are important and distinguished travelers, I trust you will accord us proper consideration."

These big words delighted the donkeys, and made them bow to the shaggy man with great respect. Said the grey one:

"You shall be taken before his great and glorious Majesty King Kik-a-bray, who will greet you as becomes your exalted stations."

"That's right," answered Dorothy. "Take us to some one who knows something."

"Oh, we all know something, my child, or we shouldn't be donkeys," asserted the grey one, with dignity. "The word 'donkey' means 'clever,' you know."

"I didn't know it," she replied. "I thought it meant 'stupid'."

"Not at all, my child. If you will look in the Encyclopedia Donkaniara you will find I'm correct. But come; I will myself lead you before our splendid, exalted, and most intellectual ruler."

All donkeys love big words, so it is no wonder the grey one used so many of them.

Chapter 7 - The Shaggy Man's Transformation

They found the houses of the town all low and square and built of bricks, neatly whitewashed inside and out. The houses were not set in rows, forming regular streets, but placed here and there in a haphazard manner which made it puzzling for a stranger to find his way.

"Stupid people must have streets and numbered houses in their cities, to guide them where to go," observed the grey donkey, as he walked before the visitors on his hind legs, in an awkward but comical manner; "but clever donkeys know their way about without such absurd marks. Moreover, a mixed city is much prettier than one with straight streets."

Dorothy did not agree with this, but she said nothing to contradict it. Presently she saw a sign on a house that read: "Madam de Fayke, Hoofist," and she asked their conductor:

"What's a 'hoofist,' please?"

"One who reads your fortune in your hoofs," replied the grey donkey.

"Oh, I see," said the little girl. "You are quite civilized here."

"Dunkiton," he replied, "is the center of the world's highest civilization."

They came to a house where two youthful donkeys were whitewashing the wall, and Dorothy stopped a moment to watch them. They dipped the ends of their tails, which were much like paint-brushes, into a pail of whitewash, backed up against the house, and wagged their tails right and left until the whitewash was rubbed on the wall, after which they dipped these funny brushes in the pail again and repeated the performance.

"That must be fun," said Button-Bright.

"No, it's work," replied the old donkey; "but we make our youngsters do all the whitewashing, to keep them out of mischief."

"Don't they go to school?" asked Dorothy.

"All donkeys are born wise," was the reply, "so the only school we need is the school of experience. Books are only for those who know nothing, and so are obliged to learn things from other people."

"In other words, the more stupid one is, the more he thinks he knows," observed the shaggy man. The grey donkey paid no attention to this speech because he had just stopped before a house which had painted over the doorway a pair of hoofs, with a donkey tail between them and a rude crown and sceptre above.

"I'll see if his magnificent Majesty King Kik-a-bray is at home," said he. He lifted his head and called "Whee-haw! whee-haw! whee-haw!" three times, in a shocking voice, turning about and kicking with his heels against the panel of the door. For a time there was no reply; then the door opened far enough to permit a donkey's head to stick out and look at them.

It was a white head, with big, awful ears and round, solemn eyes.

"Have the foxes gone?" it asked, in a trembling voice.

"They haven't been here, most stupendous Majesty," replied the grey one. "The new arrivals prove to be travelers of distinction."

"Oh," said the King, in a relieved tone of voice. "Let them come in."

He opened the door wide, and the party marched into a big room, which, Dorothy thought, looked quite unlike a king's palace. There were mats of woven grasses on the floor and the place was clean and neat; but his Majesty had no other furniture at all—perhaps because he didn't need it. He squatted down in the center of the room and a little brown donkey ran and brought a big gold crown which it placed on the monarch's head, and a golden staff with a jeweled ball at the end of it, which the King held between his front hoofs as he sat upright.

"Now then," said his Majesty, waving his long ears gently to and fro, "tell me why you are here, and what you expect me to do for you." He eyed Button-Bright rather sharply, as if afraid of the little boy's queer head, though it was the shaggy man who undertook to reply.

"Most noble and supreme ruler of Dunkiton," he said, trying not to laugh in the solemn King's face, "we are strangers traveling through your dominions and have entered your magnificent city because the road led through it, and there was no way to go around. All we desire is to pay our respects to your Majesty—the cleverest king in all the world, I'm sure—and then to continue on our way."

This polite speech pleased the King very much; indeed, it pleased him so much that it proved an unlucky speech for the shaggy man. Perhaps the Love Magnet helped to win his Majesty's affections as well as the flattery, but however this may be, the white donkey looked kindly upon the speaker and said:

"Only a donkey should be able to use such fine, big words, and you are too wise and admirable in all ways to be a mere man. Also, I feel that I love you as well as I do my own favored people, so I will bestow upon you the greatest gift within my power—a donkey's head."

As he spoke he waved his jeweled staff. Although the shaggy man cried out and tried to leap backward and escape, it proved of no use. Suddenly his own head was gone and a donkey head appeared in its place—a brown, shaggy head so absurd and droll that Dorothy and Polly both broke into merry laughter, and even Button-Bright's fox face wore a smile.

"Dear me! dear me!" cried the shaggy man, feeling of his shaggy new head and his long ears. "What a misfortune—what a great misfortune! Give me back my own head, you stupid king—if you love me at all!"

"Don't you like it?" asked the King, surprised.

"Hee-haw! I hate it! Take it away, quick!" said the shaggy man.

"But I can't do that," was the reply. "My magic works only one way. I can DO things, but I can't UNdo them. You'll have to find the Truth Pond, and bathe in its water, in order to get back your own head. But I advise you not to do that. This head is much more beautiful than the old one."

"That's a matter of taste," said Dorothy.

"Where is the Truth Pond?" asked the shaggy man, earnestly.

"Somewhere in the Land of Oz; but just the exact location of it I can not tell," was the answer.

"Don't worry, Shaggy Man," said Dorothy, smiling because her friend wagged his new ears so comically. "If the Truth Pond is in Oz, we'll be sure to find it when we get there."

"Oh! Are you going to the Land of Oz?" asked King Kik-a-bray.

"I don't know," she replied, "but we've been told we are nearer the Land of Oz than to Kansas, and if that's so, the quickest way for me to get home is to find Ozma."

"Haw-haw! Do you know the mighty Princess Ozma?" asked the King, his tone both surprised and eager.

"'Course I do; she's my friend," said Dorothy.

"Then perhaps you'll do me a favor," continued the white donkey, much excited.

"What is it?" she asked.

"Perhaps you can get me an invitation to Princess Ozma's birthday celebration, which will be the grandest royal function ever held in Fairyland. I'd love to go."

"Hee-haw! You deserve punishment, rather than reward, for giving me this dreadful head," said the shaggy man, sorrowfully.

"I wish you wouldn't say 'hee-haw' so much," Polychrome begged him; "it makes cold chills run down my back."

"But I can't help it, my dear; my donkey head wants to bray continually," he replied. "Doesn't your fox head want to yelp every minute?" he asked Button-Bright.

"Don't know," said the boy, still staring at the shaggy man's ears. These seemed to interest him greatly, and the sight also made him forget his own fox head, which was a comfort.

"What do you think, Polly? Shall I promise the donkey king an invitation to Ozma's party?" asked Dorothy of the Rainbow's Daughter, who was flitting about the room like a sunbeam because she could never keep still.

"Do as you please, dear," answered Polychrome. "He might help to amuse the guests of the Princess."

"Then, if you will give us some supper and a place to sleep to-night, and let us get started on our journey early to-morrow morning," said Dorothy to the King, "I'll ask Ozma to invite you—if I happen to get to Oz."

"Good! Hee-haw! Excellent!" cried Kik-a-bray, much pleased. "You shall all have fine suppers and good beds. What food would you prefer, a bran mash or ripe oats in the shell?"

"Neither one," replied Dorothy, promptly.

"Perhaps plain hay, or some sweet juicy grass would suit you better," suggested Kik-a-bray, musingly.

"Is that all you have to eat?" asked the girl.

"What more do you desire?"

"Well, you see we're not donkeys," she explained, "and so we're used to other food. The foxes gave us a nice supper in Foxville."

"We'd like some dewdrops and mist-cakes," said Polychrome.

"I'd prefer apples and a ham sandwich," declared the shaggy man, "for although I've a donkey head, I still have my own particular stomach."

"I want pie," said Button-Bright.

"I think some beefsteak and chocolate layer-cake would taste best," said Dorothy.

"Hee-haw! I declare!" exclaimed the King. "It seems each one of you wants a different food. How queer all living creatures are, except donkeys!"

"And donkeys like you are queerest of all," laughed Polychrome.

"Well," decided the King, "I suppose my Magic Staff will produce the things you crave; if you are lacking in good taste it is not my fault."

With this, he waved his staff with the jeweled ball, and before them instantly appeared a tea-table, set with linen and pretty dishes, and on the table were the very things each had wished for. Dorothy's beefsteak was smoking hot, and the shaggy man's apples were plump and rosy-cheeked. The King had not thought to provide chairs, so they all stood in their places around the table and ate with good appetite, being hungry. The Rainbow's Daughter found three tiny dewdrops on a crystal plate, and Button-Bright had a big slice of apple pie, which he devoured eagerly.

Afterward the King called the brown donkey, which was his favorite servant, and bade it lead his guests to the vacant house where they were to pass the night. It had only one room and no furniture except beds of clean straw and a few mats of woven grasses; but our travelers were contented with these simple things because they realized it was the best the Donkey-King had to offer them. As soon as it was dark they lay down on the mats and slept comfortably until morning.

At daybreak there was a dreadful noise throughout the city. Every donkey in the place brayed. When he heard this the shaggy man woke up and called out "Hee-haw!" as loud as he could.

"Stop that!" said Button-Bright, in a cross voice. Both Dorothy and Polly looked at the shaggy man reproachfully.

"I couldn't help it, my dears," he said, as if ashamed of his bray; "but I'll try not to do it again."

Of coursed they forgave him, for as he still had the Love Magnet in his pocket they were all obliged to love him as much as ever.

They did not see the King again, but Kik-a-bray remembered them; for a table appeared again in their room with the same food upon it as on the night before.

"Don't want pie for breakfus'," said Button-Bright.

"I'll give you some of my beefsteak," proposed Dorothy; "there's plenty for us all."

That suited the boy better, but the shaggy man said he was content with his apples and sandwiches, although he ended the meal by eating Button-Bright's pie. Polly liked her dewdrops and mist-cakes better than any other food, so they all enjoyed an excellent breakfast. Toto had the scraps left from the beefsteak, and he stood up nicely on his hind legs while Dorothy fed them to him.

Breakfast ended, they passed through the village to the side opposite that by which they had entered, the brown servant-donkey guiding them through the maze of scattered houses. There was the road again, leading far away into the unknown country beyond.

"King Kik-a-bray says you must not forget his invitation," said the brown donkey, as they passed through the opening in the wall.

"I shan't," promised Dorothy.

Perhaps no one ever beheld a more strangely assorted group than the one which now walked along the road, through pretty green fields and past groves of feathery pepper-trees and fragrant mimosa. Polychrome, her beautiful gauzy robes floating around her like a rainbow cloud, went first, dancing back and forth and darting now here to pluck a wild-flower or there to watch a beetle crawl across the path. Toto ran after her at times, barking joyously the while, only to become sober again and trot along at Dorothy's heels. The little Kansas girl walked holding Button-Bright's hand clasped in her own, and the wee boy with his fox head covered by the sailor hat presented an odd appeaance. Strangest of all, perhaps, was the shaggy man, with his shaggy donkey head, who shuffled along in the rear with his hands thrust deep in his big pockets.

None of the party was really unhappy. All were straying in an unknown land and had suffered more or less annoyance and discomfort; but they realized they were having a fairy adventure in a fairy country, and were much interested in finding out what would happen next.

Chapter 8 - The Musicker

About the middle of the forenoon they began to go up a long hill. By-and-by this hill suddenly dropped down into a pretty valley, where the travelers saw, to their surprise, a small house standing by the road-side.

It was the first house they had seen, and they hastened into the valley to discover who lived there. No one was in sight as they approached, but when they began to get nearer the house they heard queer sounds coming from it. They could not make these out at first, but as they became louder our friends thought they heard a sort of music like that made by a wheezy hand-organ; the music fell upon their ears in this way:

Tiddle-widdle-iddle oom pom-pom! Oom, pom-pom! oom, pom-pom! Tiddle-tiddle-tiddle oom pom-pom! Oom, pom-pom—pah!

"What is it, a band or a mouth-organ?" asked Dorothy.

"Don't know," said Button-Bright.

"Sounds to me like a played-out phonograph," said the shaggy man, lifting his enormous ears to listen.

"Oh, there just COULDN'T be a funnygraf in Fairyland!" cried Dorothy.

"It's rather pretty, isn't it?" asked Polychrome, trying to dance to the strains.

Tiddle-widdle-iddle, oom pom-pom, Oom pom-pom; oom pom-pom!

came the music to their ears, more distinctly as they drew nearer the house. Presently, they saw a little fat man sitting on a bench before the door. He wore a red, braided jacket that reached to his waist, a blue waistcoat, and white trousers with gold stripes down the sides. On his bald head was perched a little, round, red cap held in place by a rubber elastic underneath his chin. His face was round, his eyes a faded blue, and he wore white cotton gloves. The man leaned on a stout gold-headed cane, bending forward on his seat to watch his visitors approach.

Singularly enough, the musical sounds they had heard seemed to come from the inside of the fat man himself; for he was playing no instrument nor was any to be seen near him.

They came up and stood in a row, staring at him, and he stared back while the queer sounds came from him as before:

Tiddle-iddle-iddle, oom pom-pom, Oom, pom-pom; oom pom-pom! Tiddle-widdle-iddle, oom pom-pom, Oom, pom-pom—pah!

Why, he's a reg'lar musicker!" said Button-Bright.

"What's a musicker?" asked Dorothy.

"Him!" said the boy.

Hearing this, the fat man sat up a little stiffer than before, as if he had received a compliment, and still came the sounds:

Tiddle-widdle-iddle, oom pom-pom, Oom pom-pom, oom—

"Stop it!" cried the shaggy man, earnestly. "Stop that dreadful noise."

The fat man looked at him sadly and began his reply. When he spoke the music changed and the words seemed to accompany the notes. He said—or rather sang:

It isn't a noise that you hear, But Music, harmonic and clear. My breath makes me play Like an organ, all day— That bass note is in my left ear.

"How funny!" exclaimed Dorothy; "he says his breath makes the music."

"That's all nonsense," declared the shaggy man; but now the music began again, and they all listened carefully.

My lungs are full of reeds like those In organs, therefore I suppose, If I breathe in or out my nose, The reeds are bound to play.

So as I breathe to live, you know, I squeeze out music as I go; I'm very sorry this is so—Forgive my piping, pray!

"Poor man," said Polychrome; "he can't help it. What a great misfortune it is!"

"Yes," replied the shaggy man; "we are only obliged to hear this music a short time, until we leave him and go away; but the poor fellow must listen to himself as long as he lives, and that is enough to drive him crazy. Don't you think so?"

"Don't know," said Button-Bright. Toto said, "Bow-wow!" and the others laughed.

"Perhaps that's why he lives all alone," suggested Dorothy.

"Yes; if he had neighbors, they might do him an injury," responded the shaggy man.

All this while the little fat musicker was breathing the notes:

Tiddle-tiddle-iddle, oom, pom-pom,

and they had to speak loud in order to hear themselves. The shaggy man said:

"Who are you, sir?"

The reply came in the shape of this sing-song:

I'm Allegro da Capo, a very famous man; Just find another, high or low, to match me if you can. Some people try, but can't, to play And have to practice every day; But I've been musical always, since first my life began.

"Why, I b'lieve he's proud of it," exclaimed Dorothy; "and seems to me I've heard worse music than he makes."

"Where?" asked Button-Bright.

"I've forgotten, just now. But Mr. Da Capo is certainly a strange person—isn't he?—and p'r'aps he's the only one of his kind in all the world."

This praise seemed to please the little fat musicker, for he swelled out his chest, looked important and sang as follows:

I wear no band around me, And yet I am a band! I do not strain to make my strains But, on the other hand, My toot is always destitute Of flats or other errors; To see sharp and be natural are For me but minor terrors.

"I don't quite understand that," said Polychrome, with a puzzled look; "but perhaps it's because I'm accustomed only to the music of the spheres."

"What's that?" asked Button-Bright.

"Oh, Polly means the atmosphere and hemisphere, I s'pose," explained Dorothy.

"Oh," said Button-Bright.

"Bow-wow!" said Toto.

But the musicker was still breathing his constant

Oom, pom-pom; Oom pom-pom—

and it seemed to jar on the shaggy man's nerves.

"Stop it, can't you?" he cried angrily; "or breathe in a whisper; or put a clothes-pin on your nose. Do something, anyhow!"

But the fat one, with a sad look, sang this answer:

Music hath charms, and it may Soothe even the savage, they say; So if savage you feel Just list to my reel, For sooth to say that's the real way.

The shaggy man had to laugh at this, and when he laughed he stretched his donkey mouth wide open. Said Dorothy:

"I don't know how good his poetry is, but it seems to fit the notes, so that's all that can be 'xpected."

"I like it," said Button-Bright, who was staring hard at the musicker, his little legs spread wide apart. To the surprise of his companions, the boy asked this long question:

"If I swallowed a mouth-organ, what would I be?"

"An organette," said the shaggy man. "But come, my dears; I think the best thing we can do is to continue on our journey before Button-Bright swallows anything. We must try to find that Land of Oz, you know."

Hearing this speech the musicker sang, quickly:

If you go to the Land of Oz Please take me along, because On Ozma's birthday I'm anxious to play The loveliest song ever was.

"No thank you," said Dorothy; "we prefer to travel alone. But if I see Ozma I'll tell her you want to come to her birthday party."

"Let's be going," urged the shaggy man, anxiously.

Polly was already dancing along the road, far in advance, and the others turned to follow her. Toto did not like the fat musicker and made a grab for his chubby leg. Dorothy quickly caught up the growling little dog and hurried after her companions, who were walking faster than usual in order to get out of hearing. They had to climb a hill, and until they got to the top they could not escape the musicker's monotonous piping:

Oom, pom-pom; oom, pom-pom; Tiddle-iddle-widdle, oom, pom-pom; Oom, pom-pom—pah!

As they passed the brow of the hill, however, and descended on the other side, the sounds gradually died away, whereat they all felt much relieved.

"I'm glad I don't have to live with the organ-man; aren't you, Polly?" said Dorothy.

"Yes indeed," answered the Rainbow's Daughter.

"He's nice," declared Button-Bright, soberly.

"I hope your Princess Ozma won't invite him to her birthday celebration," remarked the shaggy man; "for the fellow's music would drive her guests all crazy. You've given me an idea, Button-Bright; I believe the musicker must have swallowed an accordeon in his youth."

"What's 'cordeon?" asked the boy.

"It's a kind of pleating," explained Dorothy, putting down the dog.

"Bow-wow!" said Toto, and ran away at a mad gallop to chase a bumble-bee.

Chapter 9 - Facing the Scoodlers

The country wasn't so pretty now. Before the travelers appeared a rocky plain covered with hills on which grew nothing green. They were nearing some low mountains, too, and the road, which before had been smooth and pleasant to walk upon, grew rough and uneven.

Button-Bright's little feet stumbled more than once, and Polychrome ceased her dancing because the walking was now so difficult that she had no trouble to keep warm.

It had become afternoon, yet there wasn't a thing for their luncheon except two apples which the shaggy man had taken from the breakfast table. He divided these into four pieces and gave a portion to each of his companions. Dorothy and Button-Bright were glad to get theirs; but Polly was satisfied with a small bite, and Toto did not like apples.

"Do you know," asked the Rainbow's Daughter, "if this is the right road to the Emerald City?"

"No, I don't," replied Dorothy, "but it's the only road in this part of the country, so we may as well go to the end of it."

"It looks now as if it might end pretty soon," remarked the shaggy man; "and what shall we do if it does?"

"Don't know," said Button-Bright.

"If I had my Magic Belt," replied Dorothy, thoughtfully, "it could do us a lot of good just now."

"What is your Magic Belt?" asked Polychrome.

"It's a thing I captured from the Nome King one day, and it can do 'most any wonderful thing. But I left it with Ozma, you know; 'cause magic won't work in Kansas, but only in fairy countries."

"Is this a fairy country?" asked Button-Bright.

"I should think you'd know," said the little girl, gravely. "If it wasn't a fairy country you couldn't have a fox head and the shaggy man couldn't have a donkey head, and the Rainbow's Daughter would be invis'ble."

"What's that?" asked the boy.

"You don't seem to know anything, Button-Bright. Invis'ble is a thing you can't see."

"Then Toto's invis'ble," declared the boy, and Dorothy found he was right. Toto had disappeared from view, but they could hear him barking furiously among the heaps of grey rock ahead of them.

They moved forward a little faster to see what the dog was barking at, and found perched upon a point of rock by the roadside a curious creature. It had the form of a man, middle-sized and rather slender and graceful; but as it sat silent and motionless upon the peak they could see that its face was black as ink, and it wore a black cloth costume made like a union suit and fitting tight to its skin. Its hands were black, too, and its toes curled down, like a bird's. The creature was black all over except its hair, which was fine, and yellow, banged in front across the black forehead and cut close at the sides. The eyes, which were fixed steadily upon the barking dog, were small and sparkling and looked like the eyes of a weasel.

"What in the world do you s'pose that is?" asked Dorothy in a hushed voice, as the little group of travelers stood watching the strange creature.

"Don't know," said Button-Bright.

The thing gave a jump and turned half around, sitting in the same place but with the other side of its body facing them. Instead of being black, it was now pure white, with a face like that of a clown in a circus and hair of a brilliant purple. The creature could bend either way, and its white toes now curled the same way the black ones on the other side had done.

"It has a face both front and back," whispered Dorothy, wonderingly; "only there's no back at all, but two fronts."

Having made the turn, the being sat motionless as before, while Toto barked louder at the white man than he had done at the black one.

"Once," said the shaggy man, "I had a jumping jack like that, with two faces."

"Was it alive?" asked Button-Bright.

"No," replied the shaggy man; "it worked on strings and was made of wood."

"Wonder if this works with strings," said Dorothy; but Polychrome cried "Look!" for another creature just like the first had suddenly appeared sitting on another rock, its black side toward them. The two twisted their heads around and showed a black face on the white side of one and a white face on the black side of the other.

"How curious," said Polychrome; "and how loose their heads seem to be! Are they friendly to us, do you think?"

"Can't tell, Polly," replied Dorothy. "Let's ask 'em."

The creatures flopped first one way and then the other, showing black or white by turns; and now another joined them, appearing on another rock. Our friends had come to a little hollow in the hills, and the place where they now stood was surrounded by jagged peaks of rock, except where the road ran through.

"Now there are four of them," said the shaggy man.

"Five," declared Polychrome.

"Six," said Dorothy.

"Lots of 'em!" cried Button-Bright; and so there were—quite a row of the two-sided black and white creatures sitting on the rocks all around.

Toto stopped barking and ran between Dorothy's feet, where he crouched down as if afraid. The creatures did not look pleasant or friendly, to be sure, and the shaggy man's donkey face became solemn, indeed.

"Ask 'em who they are, and what they want," whispered Dorothy; so the shaggy man called out in a loud voice:

"Who are you?"

"Scoodlers!" they yelled in chorus, their voices sharp and shrill.

"What do you want?" called the shaggy man.

"You!" they yelled, pointing their thin fingers at the group; and they all flopped around, so they were white, and then all flopped back again, so they were black.

"But what do you want us for?" asked the shaggy man, uneasily.

"Soup!" they all shouted, as if with one voice.

"Goodness me!" said Dorothy, trembling a little; "the Scoodlers must be reg'lar cannibals."

"Don't want to be soup," protested Button-Bright, beginning to cry.

"Hush, dear," said the little girl, trying to comfort him; "we don't any of us want to be soup. But don't worry; the shaggy man will take care of us."

"Will he?" asked Polychrome, who did not like the Scoodlers at all, and kept close to Dorothy.

"I'll try," promised the shaggy man; but he looked worried.

Happening just then to feel the Love Magnet in his pocket, he said to the creatures, with more confidence:

"Don't you love me?"

"Yes!" they shouted, all together.

"Then you mustn't harm me, or my friends," said the shaggy man, firmly.

"We love you in soup!" they yelled, and in a flash turned their white sides to the front.

"How dreadful!" said Dorothy. "This is a time, Shaggy Man, when you get loved too much."

"Don't want to be soup!" wailed Button-Bright again; and Toto began to whine dismally, as if he didn't want to be soup, either.

"The only thing to do," said the shaggy man to his friends, in a low tone, "is to get out of this pocket in the rocks as soon as we can, and leave the Scoodlers behind us. Follow me, my dears, and don't pay any attention to what they do or say."

With this, he began to march along the road to the opening in the rocks ahead, and the others kept close behind him. But the Scoodlers closed up in front, as if to bar their way, and so the shaggy man stooped down and picked up a loose stone, which he threw at the creatures to scare them from the path.

At this the Scoodlers raised a howl. Two of them picked their heads from their shoulders and hurled them at the shaggy man with such force that he fell over in a heap, greatly astonished. The two now ran forward with swift leaps, caught up their heads, and put them on again, after which they sprang back to their positions on the rocks.

Chapter 10 - Escaping the Soup-Kettle

The shaggy man got up and felt of himself to see if he was hurt; but he was not. One of the heads had struck his breast and the other his left shoulder; yet though they had knocked him down, the heads were not hard enough to bruise him.

"Come on," he said firmly; "we've got to get out of here some way," and forward he started again.

The Scoodlers began yelling and throwing their heads in great numbers at our frightened friends. The shaggy man was knocked over again, and so was Button-Bright, who kicked his heels against the ground and howled as loud as he could, although he was not hurt a bit. One head struck Toto, who first yelped and then grabbed the head by an ear and started running away with it.

The Scoodlers who had thrown their heads began to scramble down and run to pick them up, with wonderful quickness; but the one whose head Toto had stolen found it hard to get it back again. The head couldn't see the body with either pair of its eyes, because the dog was in the way, so the headless Scoodler stumbled around over the rocks and tripped on them more than once in its effort to regain its top. Toto was trying to get outside the rocks and roll the head down the hill; but some of the other Scoodlers came to the rescue of their unfortunate comrade and pelted the dog with their own heads until he was obliged to drop his burden and hurry back to Dorothy.

The little girl and the Rainbow's Daughter had both escaped the shower of heads, but they saw now that it would be useless to try to run away from the dreadful Scoodlers.

"We may as well submit," declared the shaggy man, in a rueful voice, as he got upon his feet again. He turned toward their foes and asked:

"What do you want us to do?"

"Come!" they cried, in a triumphant chorus, and at once sprang from the rocks and surrounded their captives on all sides. One funny thing about the Scoodlers was they could walk in either direction, coming or going, without turning around; because they had two faces and, as Dorothy said, "two front sides," and their feet were shaped like the letter T upside down. They moved with great rapidity and there was something about their glittering eyes and contrasting colors and removable heads that inspired the poor prisoners with horror, and made them long to escape.

But the creatures led their captives away from the rocks and the road, down the hill by a side path until they came before a low mountain of rock that looked like a huge bowl turned upside down. At the edge of this mountain was a deep gulf—so deep that when you looked into it there was nothing but blackness below. Across the gulf was a narrow bridge of rock, and at the other end of the bridge was an arched opening that led into the mountain.

Over this bridge the Scoodlers led their prisoners, through the opening into the mountain, which they found to be an immense hollow dome lighted by several holes in the roof. All around the circular space were built rock houses, set close together, each with a door in the front wall. None of these houses was more than six feet wide, but the Scoodlers were thin people sidewise and did not need much room. So vast was the dome that there was a large space in the middle of the cave, in front of all these houses, where the creatures might congregate as in a great hall.

It made Dorothy shudder to see a huge iron kettle suspended by a stout chain in the middle of the place, and underneath the kettle a great heap of kindling wood and shavings, ready to light.

"What's that?" asked the shaggy man, drawing back as they approached this place, so that they were forced to push him forward.

"The Soup Kettle!" yelled the Scoodlers, and then they shouted in the next breath:

"We're hungry!"

Button-Bright, holding Dorothy's hand in one chubby fist and Polly's hand in the other, was so affected by this shout that he began to cry again, repeating the protest:

"Don't want to be soup, I don't!"

"Never mind," said the shaggy man, consolingly; "I ought to make enough soup to feed them all, I'm so big; so I'll ask them to put me in the kettle first."

"All right," said Button-Bright, more cheerfully.

But the Scoodlers were not ready to make soup yet. They led the captives into a house at the farthest side of the cave—a house somewhat wider than the others.

"Who lives here?" asked the Rainbow's Daughter. The Scoodlers nearest her replied:

"The Queen."

It made Dorothy hopeful to learn that a woman ruled over these fierce creatures, but a moment later they were ushered by two or three of the escort into a gloomy, bare room—and her hope died away.

For the Queen of the Scoodlers proved to be much more dreadful in appearance than any of her people. One side of her was fiery red, with jet-black hair and green eyes and the other side of her was bright yellow, with crimson hair and black eyes. She wore a short skirt of red and yellow and her hair, instead of being banged, was a tangle of short curls upon which rested a circular crown of silver—much dented and twisted because the Queen had thrown her head at so many things so many times. Her form was lean and bony and both her faces were deeply wrinkled.

"What have we here?" asked the Queen sharply, as our friends were made to stand before her.

"Soup!" cried the guard of Scoodlers, speaking together.

"We're not!" said Dorothy, indignantly; "we're nothing of the sort."

"Ah, but you will be soon," retorted the Queen, a grim smile making her look more dreadful than before.

"Pardon me, most beautiful vision," said the shaggy man, bowing before the queen politely. "I must request your Serene Highness to let us go our way without being made into soup. For I own the Love Magnet, and whoever meets me must love me and all my friends."

"True," replied the Queen. "We love you very much; so much that we intend to eat your broth with real pleasure. But tell me, do you think I am so beautiful?"

"You won't be at all beautiful if you eat me," he said, shaking his head sadly. "Handsome is as handsome does, you know."

The Queen turned to Button-Bright.

"Do YOU think I'm beautiful?" she asked.

"No," said the boy; "you're ugly."

"I think you're a fright," said Dorothy.

"If you could see yourself you'd be terribly scared," added Polly.

The Queen scowled at them and flopped from her red side to her yellow side.

"Take them away," she commanded the guard, "and at six o'clock run them through the meat chopper and start the soup kettle boiling. And put plenty of salt in the broth this time, or I'll punish the cooks severely."

"Any onions, your Majesty?" asked one of the guard.

"Plenty of onions and garlic and a dash of red pepper. Now, go!"

The Scoodlers led the captives away and shut them up in one of the houses, leaving only a single Scoodler to keep guard.

The place was a sort of store-house; containing bags of potatoes and baskets of carrots, onions and turnips.

"These," said their guard, pointing to the vegetables, "we use to flavor our soups with."

The prisoners were rather disheartened by this time, for they saw no way to escape and did not know how soon it would be six o'clock and time for the meatchopper to begin work. But the shaggy man was brave and did not intend to submit to such a horrid fate without a struggle.

"I'm going to fight for our lives," he whispered to the children, "for if I fail we will be no worse off than before, and to sit here quietly until we are made into soup would be foolish and cowardly."

The Scoodler on guard stood near the doorway, turning first his white side toward them and then his black side, as if he wanted to show to all of his greedy four eyes the sight of so many fat prisoners. The captives sat in a sorrowful group at the other end of the room—except Polychrome, who danced back and forth in the little place to keep herself warm, for she felt the chill of the cave. Whenever she approached the shaggy man he would whisper something in her ear, and Polly would nod her pretty head as if she understood.

The shaggy man told Dorothy and Button-Bright to stand before him while he emptied the potatoes out of one of the sacks. When this had been secretly done, little Polychrome, dancing near to the guard, suddenly reached out her hand and slapped his face, the next instant whirling away from him quickly to rejoin her friends.

The angry Scoodler at once picked off his head and hurled it at the Rainbow's Daughter; but the shaggy man was expecting that, and caught the head very neatly, putting it in the sack, which he tied at the mouth. The body of the guard, not having the eyes of its head to guide it, ran here and there in an aimless manner, and the shaggy man easily dodged it and opened the door. Fortunately, there was no one in the big cave at that moment, so he told Dorothy and Polly to run as fast as they could for the entrance, and out across the narrow bridge.

"I'll carry Button-Bright," he said, for he knew the little boy's legs were too short to run fast.

Dorothy picked up Toto and then seized Polly's hand and ran swiftly toward the entrance to the cave. The shaggy man perched Button-Bright on his shoulders and ran after them. They moved so quickly and their escape was so wholly unexpected that they had almost reached the bridge when one of the Scoodlers looked out of his house and saw them.

The creature raised a shrill cry that brought all of its fellows bounding out of the numerous doors, and at once they started in chase. Dorothy and Polly had reached the bridge and crossed it when the Scoodlers began throwing their heads. One of the queer missiles struck the shaggy man on his back and nearly knocked him over; but he was at the mouth of the cave now, so he set down Button-Bright and told the boy to run across the bridge to Dorothy.

Then the shaggy man turned around and faced his enemies, standing just outside the opening, and as fast as they threw their heads at him he caught them and tossed them into the black gulf below. The headless bodies of the foremost Scoodlers kept the others from running close up, but they also threw their heads in an effort to stop the escaping prisoners. The shaggy man caught them all and sent them whirling down into the black gulf. Among them he noticed the crimson and yellow head of the Queen, and this he tossed after the others with right good will.

Presently every Scoodler of the lot had thrown its head, and every head was down in the deep gulf, and now the helpless bodies of the creatures were mixed together in the cave and wriggling around in a vain attempt to discover what had become of their heads. The shaggy man laughed and walked across the bridge to rejoin his companions.

"It's lucky I learned to play base-ball when I was young," he remarked, "for I caught all those heads easily and never missed one. But come along, little ones; the Scoodlers will never bother us or anyone else any more."

Button-Bright was still frightened and kept insisting, "I don't want to be soup!" for the victory had been gained so suddenly that the boy could not realize they were free and safe. But the shaggy man assured him that all danger of their being made into soup was now past, as the Scoodlers would be unable to eat soup for some time to come.

So now, anxious to get away from the horrid gloomy cave as soon as possible, they hastened up the hillside and regained the road just beyond the place where they had first met the Scoodlers; and you may be sure they were glad to find their feet on the old familiar path again.

Chapter 11 - Johnny Doit Does It

"It's getting awful rough walking," said Dorothy, as they trudged along. Button-Bright gave a deep sigh and said he was hungry. Indeed, all were hungry, and thirsty, too; for they had eaten nothing but the apples since breakfast; so their steps lagged and they grew silent and weary. At last they slowly passed over the crest of a barren hill and saw before them a line of green trees with a strip of grass at their feet. An agreeable fragrance was wafted toward them.

Our travelers, hot and tired, ran forward on beholding this refreshing sight and were not long in coming to the trees. Here they found a spring of pure bubbling water, around which the grass was full of wild strawberry plants, their pretty red berries ripe and ready to eat. Some of the trees bore yellow oranges and some russet pears, so the hungry adventurers suddenly found themselves provided with plenty to eat and to drink. They lost no time in picking the biggest strawberries and ripest oranges and soon had feasted to their hearts' content. Walking beyond the line of trees they saw before them a fearful, dismal desert, everywhere gray sand. At the edge of this awful waste was a large, white sign with black letters neatly painted upon it and the letters made these words:

ALL PERSONS ARE WARNED NOT TO VENTURE UPON THIS DESERT

For the Deadly Sands will Turn Any Living Flesh to Dust in an instant.

Beyond This Barrier is the

LAND OF OZ

But no one can Reach that Beautiful Country because of these Destroying Sands

"Oh," said Dorothy, when the shaggy man had read the sign aloud; "I've seen this desert before, and it's true no one can live who tries to walk upon the sands."

"Then we musn't try it," answered the shaggy man thoughtfully. "But as we can't go ahead and there's no use going back, what shall we do next?"

"Don't know," said Button-Bright.

"I'm sure I don't know, either," added Dorothy, despondently.

"I wish father would come for me," sighed the pretty Rainbow's Daughter, "I would take you all to live upon the rainbow, where you could dance along its rays from morning till night, without a care or worry of any sort. But I suppose father's too busy just now to search the world for me."

"Don't want to dance," said Button-Bright, sitting down wearily upon the soft grass.

"It's very good of you, Polly," said Dorothy; "but there are other things that would suit me better than dancing on rainbows. I'm 'fraid they'd be kind of soft an' squashy under foot, anyhow, although they're so pretty to look at."

This didn't help to solve the problem, and they all fell silent and looked at one another questioningly.

"Really, I don't know what to do," muttered the shaggy man, gazing hard at Toto; and the little dog wagged his tail and said "Bow-wow!" just as if he could not tell, either, what to do. Button-Bright got a stick and began to dig in the earth, and the others watched him for a while in deep thought. Finally, the shaggy man said:

"It's nearly evening, now; so we may as well sleep in this pretty place and get rested; perhaps by morning we can decide what is best to be done."

There was little chance to make beds for the children, but the leaves of the trees grew thickly and would serve to keep off the night dews, so the shaggy man piled soft grasses in the thickest shade and when it was dark they lay down and slept peacefully until morning.

Long after the others were asleep, however, the shaggy man sat in the starlight by the spring, gazing thoughtfully into its bubbling waters. Suddenly he smiled and nodded to himself as if he had found a good thought, after which he, too, laid himself down under a tree and was soon lost in slumber.

In the bright morning sunshine, as they ate of the strawberries and sweet juicy pears, Dorothy said:

"Polly, can you do any magic?"

"No dear," answered Polychrome, shaking her dainty head.

"You ought to know SOME magic, being the Rainbow's Daughter," continued Dorothy, earnestly.

"But we who live on the rainbow among the fleecy clouds have no use for magic," replied Polychrome.

"What I'd like," said Dorothy, "is to find some way to cross the desert to the Land of Oz and its Emerald City. I've crossed it already, you know, more than once. First a cyclone carried my house over, and some Silver Shoes brought me back again—in half a second. Then Ozma took me over on her Magic Carpet, and the Nome King's Magic Belt took me home that time. You see it was magic that did it every time 'cept the first, and we can't 'spect a cyclone to happen along and take us to the Emerald City now."

"No indeed," returned Polly, with a shudder, "I hate cyclones, anyway."

"That's why I wanted to find out if you could do any magic," said the little Kansas girl. "I'm sure I can't; and I'm sure Button-Bright can't; and the only magic the shaggy man has is the Love Magnet, which won't help us much."

"Don't be too sure of that, my dear," spoke the shaggy man, a smile on his donkey face. "I may not be able to do magic myself, but I can call to us a powerful friend who loves me because I own the Love Magnet, and this friend surely will be able to help us."

"Who is your friend?" asked Dorothy.

"Johnny Dooit."

"What can Johnny do?"

"Anything," answered the shaggy man, with confidence.

"Ask him to come," she exclaimed, eagerly.

The shaggy man took the Love Magnet from his pocket and unwrapped the paper that surrounded it. Holding the charm in the palm of his hand he looked at it steadily and said these words:

"Dear Johnny Dooit, come to me. I need you bad as bad can be."

"Well, here I am," said a cheery little voice; "but you shouldn't say you need me bad, 'cause I'm always, ALWAYS, good."

At this they quickly whirled around to find a funny little man sitting on a big copper chest, puffing smoke from a long pipe. His hair was grey, his whiskers were grey; and these whiskers were so long that he had wound the ends of them around his waist and tied them in a hard knot underneath the leather apron that reached from his chin nearly to his feet, and which was soiled and scratched as if it had been used a long time. His nose was broad, and stuck up a little; but his eyes were twinkling and merry. The little man's hands and arms were as hard and tough as the leather in his apron, and Dorothy thought Johnny Dooit looked as if he had done a lot of hard work in his lifetime.

"Good morning, Johnny," said the shaggy man. "Thank you for coming to me so quickly."

"I never waste time," said the newcomer, promptly. "But what's happened to you? Where did you get that donkey head? Really, I wouldn't have known you at all, Shaggy Man, if I hadn't looked at your feet."

The shaggy man introduced Johnny Dooit to Dorothy and Toto and Button-Bright and the Rainbow's Daughter, and told him the story of their adventures, adding that they were anxious now to reach the Emerald City in the Land of Oz, where Dorothy had friends who would take care of them and send them safe home again.

"But," said he, "we find that we can't cross this desert, which turns all living flesh that touches it into dust; so I have asked you to come and help us."

Johnny Dooit puffed his pipe and looked carefully at the dreadful desert in front of them—stretching so far away they could not see its end.

"You must ride," he said, briskly.

"What in?" asked the shaggy man.

"In a sand-boat, which has runners like a sled and sails like a ship. The wind will blow you swiftly across the desert and the sand cannot touch your flesh to turn it into dust."

"Good!" cried Dorothy, clapping her hands delightedly. "That was the way the Magic Carpet took us across. We didn't have to touch the horrid sand at all."

"But where is the sand-boat?" asked the shaggy man, looking all around him.

"I'll make you one," said Johnny Dooit.

As he spoke, he knocked the ashes from his pipe and put it in his pocket. Then he unlocked the copper chest and lifted the lid, and Dorothy saw it was full of shining tools of all sorts and shapes.

Johnny Dooit moved quickly now—so quickly that they were astonished at the work he was able to accomplish. He had in his chest a tool for everything he wanted to do, and these must have been magic tools because they did their work so fast and so well.

The man hummed a little song as he worked, and Dorothy tried to listen to it. She thought the words were something like these:

The only way to do a thing Is do it when you can, And do it cheerfully, and sing And work and think and plan. The only real unhappy one Is he who dares to shirk; The only really happy one Is he who cares to work.

Whatever Johnny Dooit was singing he was certainly doing things, and they all stood by and watched him in amazement.

He seized an axe and in a couple of chops felled a tree. Next he took a saw and in a few minutes sawed the tree-trunk into broad, long boards. He then nailed the boards together into the shape of a boat, about twelve feet long and four feet wide. He cut from another tree a long, slender pole which, when trimmed of its branches and fastened upright in the center of the boat, served as a mast. From the chest he drew a coil of rope and a big bundle of canvas, and with these—still humming his song—he rigged up a sail, arranging it so it could be raised or lowered upon the mast.

Dorothy fairly gasped with wonder to see the thing grow so speedily before her eyes, and both Button-Bright and Polly looked on with the same absorbed interest.

"It ought to be painted," said Johnny Dooit, tossing his tools back into the chest, "for that would make it look prettier. But 'though I can paint it for you in three seconds it would take an hour to dry, and that's a waste of time."

"We don't care how it looks," said the shaggy man, "if only it will take us across the desert."

"It will do that," declared Johnny Dooit. "All you need worry about is tipping over. Did you ever sail a ship?"

"I've seen one sailed," said the shaggy man.

"Good. Sail this boat the way you've seen a ship sailed, and you'll be across the sands before you know it."

With this he slammed down the lid of the chest, and the noise made them all wink. While they were winking the workman disappeared, tools and all.

Chapter 12 - The Deadly Desert Crossed

"Oh, that's too bad!" cried Dorothy; "I wanted to thank Johnny Dooit for all his kindness to us."

"He hasn't time to listen to thanks," replied the shaggy man; "but I'm sure he knows we are grateful. I suppose he is already at work in some other part of the world."

They now looked more carefully at the sand-boat, and saw that the bottom was modeled with two sharp runners which would glide through the sand. The front of the sand-boat was pointed like the bow of a ship, and there was a rudder at the stern to steer by.

It had been built just at the edge of the desert, so that all its length lay upon the gray sand except the after part, which still rested on the strip of grass.

"Get in, my dears," said the shaggy man; "I'm sure I can manage this boat as well as any sailor. All you need do is sit still in your places."

Dorothy got in, Toto in her arms, and sat on the bottom of the boat just in front of the mast. Button-Bright sat in front of Dorothy, while Polly leaned over the bow. The shaggy man knelt behind the mast. When all were ready he raised the sail half-way. The wind caught it. At once the sand-boat started forward—slowly at first, then with added speed. The shaggy man pulled the sail way up, and they flew so fast over the Deadly Desert that every one held fast to the sides of the boat and scarcely dared to breathe.

The sand lay in billows, and was in places very uneven, so that the boat rocked dangerously from side to side; but it never quite tipped over, and the speed was so great that the shaggy man himself became frightened and began to wonder how he could make the ship go slower.

"It we're spilled in this sand, in the middle of the desert," Dorothy thought to herself, "we'll be nothing but dust in a few minutes, and that will be the end of us."

But they were not spilled, and by-and-by Polychrome, who was clinging to the bow and looking straight ahead, saw a dark line before them and wondered what it was. It grew plainer every second, until she discovered it to be a row of jagged rocks at the end of the desert, while high above these rocks she could see a tableland of green grass and beautiful trees.

"Look out!" she screamed to the shaggy man. "Go slowly, or we shall smash into the rocks."

He heard her, and tried to pull down the sail; but the wind would not let go of the broad canvas and the ropes had become tangled.

Nearer and nearer they drew to the great rocks, and the shaggy man was in despair because he could do nothing to stop the wild rush of the sand-boat.

They reached the edge of the desert and bumped squarely into the rocks. There was a crash as Dorothy, Button-Bright, Toto and Polly flew up in the air in a curve like a skyrocket's, one after another landing high upon the grass, where they rolled and tumbled for a time before they could stop themselves.

The shaggy man flew after them, head first, and lighted in a heap beside Toto, who, being much excited at the time, seized one of the donkey ears between his teeth and shook and worried it as hard as he could, growling angrily. The shaggy man made the little dog let go, and sat up to look around him.

Dorothy was feeling one of her front teeth, which was loosened by knocking against her knee as she fell. Polly was looking sorrowfully at a rent in her pretty gauze gown, and Button-Bright's fox head had stuck fast in a gopher hole and he was wiggling his little fat legs frantically in an effort to get free.

Otherwise they were unhurt by the adventure; so the shaggy man stood up and pulled Button-Bright out of the hole and went to the edge of the desert to look at the sand-boat. It was a mere mass of splinters now, crushed out of shape against the rocks. The wind had torn away the sail and carried it to the top of a tall tree, where the fragments of it fluttered like a white flag.

"Well," he said, cheerfully, "we're here; but where the here is I don't know."

"It must be some part of the Land of Oz," observed Dorothy, coming to his side.

"Must it?"

"'Course it must. We're across the desert, aren't we? And somewhere in the middle of Oz is the Emerald City."

"To be sure," said the shaggy man, nodding. "Let's go there."

"But I don't see any people about, to show us the way," she continued.

"Let's hunt for them," he suggested. "There must be people somewhere; but perhaps they did not expect us, and so are not at hand to give us a welcome."

Chapter 13 - The Truth Pond

They now made a more careful examination of the country around them. All was fresh and beautiful after the sultriness of the desert, and the sunshine and sweet, crisp air were delightful to the wanderers. Little mounds of yellowish green were away at the right, while on the left waved a group of tall leafy trees bearing yellow blossoms that looked like tassels and pompoms. Among the grasses carpeting the ground were pretty buttercups and cowslips and marigolds. After looking at these a moment Dorothy said reflectively:

"We must be in the Country of the Winkies, for the color of that country is yellow, and you will notice that 'most everything here is yellow that has any color at all."

"But I thought this was the Land of Oz," replied the shaggy man, as if greatly disappointed.

"So it is," she declared; "but there are four parts to the Land of Oz. The North Country is purple, and it's the Country of the Gillikins. The East Country is blue, and that's the Country of the Munchkins. Down at the South is the red Country of the Quadlings, and here, in the West, the yellow Country of the Winkies. This is the part that is ruled by the Tin Woodman, you know."

"Who's he?" asked Button-Bright.

"Why, he's the tin man I told you about. His name is Nick Chopper, and he has a lovely heart given him by the wonderful Wizard."

"Where does HE live?" asked the boy.

"The Wizard? Oh, he lives in the Emerald City, which is just in the middle of Oz, where the corners of the four countries meet."

"Oh," said Button-Bright, puzzled by this explanation.

"We must be some distance from the Emerald City," remarked the shaggy man.

"That's true," she replied; "so we'd better start on and see if we can find any of the Winkies. They're nice people," she continued, as the little party began walking toward the group of trees, "and I came here once with my friends the Scarecrow, and the Tin Woodman, and the Cowardly Lion, to fight a wicked witch who had made all the Winkies her slaves."

"Did you conquer her?" asked Polly.

"Why, I melted her with a bucket of water, and that was the end of her," replied Dorothy. "After that the people were free, you know, and they made Nick Chopper—that's the Tin Woodman—their Emp'ror."

"What's that?" asked Button-Bright.

"Emp'ror? Oh, it's something like an alderman, I guess."

"Oh," said the boy.

"But I thought Princess Ozma ruled Oz," said the shaggy man.

"So she does; she rules the Emerald City and all the four countries of Oz; but each country has another little ruler, not so big as Ozma. It's like the officers of an army, you see; the little rulers are all captains, and Ozma's the general."

By this time they had reached the trees, which stood in a perfect circle and just far enough apart so that their thick branches touched—or "shook hands," as Button-Bright remarked. Under the shade of the trees they found, in the center of the circle, a crystal pool, its water as still as glass. It must have been deep, too, for when Polychrome bent over it she gave a little sigh of pleasure.

"Why, it's a mirror!" she cried; for she could see all her pretty face and fluffy, rainbow-tinted gown reflected in the pool, as natural as life.

Dorothy bent over, too, and began to arrange her hair, blown by the desert wind into straggling tangles. Button-Bright leaned over the edge next, and then began to cry, for the sight of his fox head frightened the poor little fellow.

"I guess I won't look," remarked the shaggy man, sadly, for he didn't like his donkey head, either. While Polly and Dorothy tried to comfort Button-Bright, the shaggy man sat down near the edge of the pool, where his image could not be reflected, and stared at the water thoughtfully. As he did this he noticed a silver plate fastened to a rock just under the surface of the water, and on the silver plate was engraved these words:

THE TRUTH POND

"Ah!" cried the shaggy man, springing to his feet with eager joy; "we've found it at last."

"Found what?" asked Dorothy, running to him.

"The Truth Pond. Now, at last, I may get rid of this frightful head; for we were told, you remember, that only the Truth Pond could restore to me my proper face."

"Me, too!" shouted Button-Bright, trotting up to them.

"Of course," said Dorothy. "It will cure you both of your bad heads, I guess. Isn't it lucky we found it?"

"It is, indeed," replied the shaggy man. "I hated dreadfully to go to Princess Ozma looking like this; and she's to have a birthday celebration, too."

Just then a splash startled them, for Button-Bright, in his anxiety to see the pool that would "cure" him, had stepped too near the edge and tumbled heels over head into the water. Down he went, out of sight entirely, so that only his sailor hat floated on the top of the Truth Pond.

He soon bobbed up, and the shaggy man seized him by his sailor collar and dragged him to the shore, dripping and gasping for breath. They all looked upon the boy wonderingly, for the fox head with its sharp nose and pointed ears was gone, and in its place appeared the chubby round face and blue eyes and pretty curls that had belonged to Button-Bright before King Dox of Foxville transformed him.

"Oh, what a darling!" cried Polly, and would have hugged the little one had he not been so wet.

Their joyful exclamations made the child rub the water out of his eyes and look at his friends questioningly.

"You're all right now, dear," said Dorothy. "Come and look at yourself." She led him to the pool, and although there were still a few ripples on the surface of the water he could see his reflection plainly.

"It's me!" he said, in a pleased yet awed whisper.

"'Course it is," replied the girl, "and we're all as glad as you are, Button-Bright."

"Well," announced the shaggy man, "it's my turn next." He took off his shaggy coat and laid it on the grass and dived head first into the Truth Pond.

When he came up the donkey head had disappeared, and the shaggy man's own shaggy head was in its place, with the water dripping in little streams from his shaggy whiskers. He scrambled ashore and shook himself to get off some of the wet, and then leaned over the pool to look admiringly at his reflected face.

"I may not be strictly beautiful, even now," he said to his companions, who watched him with smiling faces; "but I'm so much handsomer than any donkey that I feel as proud as I can be."

"You're all right, Shaggy Man," declared Dorothy. "And Button-Bright is all right, too. So let's thank the Truth Pond for being so nice, and start on our journey to the Emerald City."

"I hate to leave it," murmured the shaggy man, with a sigh. "A truth pond wouldn't be a bad thing to carry around with us." But he put on his coat and started with the others in search of some one to direct them on their way.

Chapter 14 - Tik-Tok and Billina

They had not walked far across the flower-strewn meadows when they came upon a fine road leading toward the northwest and winding gracefully among the pretty yellow hills.

"That way," said Dorothy, "must be the direction of the Emerald City. We'd better follow the road until we meet some one or come to a house."

The sun soon dried Button-Bright's sailor suit and the shaggy man's shaggy clothes, and so pleased were they at regaining their own heads that they did not mind at all the brief discomfort of getting wet.

"It's good to be able to whistle again," remarked the shaggy man, "for those donkey lips were so thick I could not whistle a note with them." He warbled a tune as merrily as any bird.

"You'll look more natural at the birthday celebration, too," said Dorothy, happy in seeing her friends so happy.

Polychrome was dancing ahead in her usual sprightly manner, whirling gaily along the smooth, level road, until she passed from sight around the curve of one of the mounds. Suddenly they heard her exclaim "Oh!" and she appeared again, running toward them at full speed.

"What's the matter, Polly?" asked Dorothy, perplexed.

There was no need for the Rainbow's Daughter to answer, for turning the bend in the road there came advancing slowly toward them a funny round man made of burnished copper, gleaming brightly in the sun. Perched on the copper man's shoulder sat a yellow hen, with fluffy feathers and a pearl necklace around her throat.

"Oh, Tik-tok!" cried Dorothy, running forward. When she came to him, the copper man lifted the little girl in his copper arms and kissed her cheek with his copper lips.

"Oh, Billina!" cried Dorothy, in a glad voice, and the yellow hen flew to her arms, to be hugged and petted by turns.

The others were curiously crowding around the group, and the girl said to them:

"It's Tik-tok and Billina; and oh! I'm so glad to see them again."

"Wel-come to Oz," said the copper man in a monotonous voice.

Dorothy sat right down in the road, the yellow hen in her arms, and began to stroke Billina's back. Said the hen:

"Dorothy, dear, I've got some wonderful news to tell you."

"Tell it quick, Billina!" said the girl.

Just then Toto, who had been growling to himself in a cross way, gave a sharp bark and flew at the yellow hen, who ruffled her feathers and let out such an angry screech that Dorothy was startled.

"Stop, Toto! Stop that this minute!" she commanded. "Can't you see that Billina is my friend?" In spite of this warning had she not grabbed Toto quickly by the neck the little dog would have done the yellow hen a mischief, and even now he struggled madly to escape Dorothy's grasp. She slapped his ears once or twice and told him to behave, and the yellow hen flew to Tik-tok's shoulder again, where she was safe.

"What a brute!" croaked Billina, glaring down at the little dog.

"Toto isn't a brute," replied Dorothy, "but at home Uncle Henry has to whip him sometimes for chasing the chickens. Now look here, Toto," she added, holding up her finger and speaking sternly to him, "you've got to understand that Billina is one of my dearest friends, and musn't be hurt—now or ever."

Toto wagged his tail as if he understood.

"The miserable thing can't talk," said Billina, with a sneer.

"Yes, he can," replied Dorothy; "he talks with his tail, and I know everything he says. If you could wag your tail, Billina, you wouldn't need words to talk with."

"Nonsense!" said Billina.

"It isn't nonsense at all. Just now Toto says he's sorry, and that he'll try to love you for my sake. Don't you, Toto?"

"Bow-wow!" said Toto, wagging his tail again.

"But I've such wonderful news for you, Dorothy," cried the yellow hen; "I've—"

"Wait a minute, dear," interrupted the little girl; "I've got to introduce you all, first. That's manners, Billina. This," turning to her traveling companions, "is Mr. Tik-tok, who works by machinery 'cause his thoughts wind up, and his talk winds up, and his action winds up—like a clock."

"Do they all wind up together?" asked the shaggy man.

"No; each one separate. But he works just lovely, and Tik-tok was a good friend to me once, and saved my life—and Billina's life, too."

"Is he alive?" asked Button-Bright, looking hard at the copper man.

"Oh, no, but his machinery makes him just as good as alive." She turned to the copper man and said politely: "Mr. Tik-tok, these are my new friends: the shaggy man, and Polly the Rainbow's Daughter, and Button-Bright, and Toto. Only Toto isn't a new friend, 'cause he's been to Oz before."

The copper man bowed low, removing his copper hat as he did so.

"I'm ve-ry pleased to meet Dor-o-thy's fr-r-r-r—-" Here he stopped short.

"Oh, I guess his speech needs winding!" said the little girl, running behind the copper man to get the key off a hook at his back. She wound him up at a place under his right arm and he went on to say:

"Par-don me for run-ning down. I was a-bout to say I am pleased to meet Dor-o-thy's friends, who must be my friends." The words were somewhat jerky, but plain to understand.

"And this is Billina," continued Dorothy, introducing the yellow hen, and they all bowed to her in turn.

"I've such wonderful news," said the hen, turning her head so that one bright eye looked full at Dorothy.

"What is it, dear?" asked the girl.

"I've hatched out ten of the loveliest chicks you ever saw."

"Oh, how nice! And where are they, Billina?"

"I left them at home. But they're beauties, I assure you, and all wonderfully clever. I've named them Dorothy."

"Which one?" asked the girl.

"All of them," replied Billina.

"That's funny. Why did you name them all with the same name?"

"It was so hard to tell them apart," explained the hen. "Now, when I call 'Dorothy,' they all come running to me in a bunch; it's much easier, after all, than having a separate name for each."

"I'm just dying to see 'em, Billina," said Dorothy, eagerly. "But tell me, my friends, how did you happen to be here, in the Country of the Winkies, the first of all to meet us?"

"I'll tell you," answered Tik-tok, in his monotonous voice, all the sounds of his words being on one level—"Prin-cess Oz-ma saw you in her mag-ic pic-ture, and knew you were com-ing here; so she sent Bil-lin-a and me to wel-come you as she could not come her-self; so that—fiz-i-dig-le cum-so-lut-ing hy-ber-gob-ble in-tu-zib-ick—"

"Good gracious! Whatever's the matter now?" cried Dorothy, as the copper man continued to babble these unmeaning words, which no one could understand at all because they had no sense.

"Don't know," said Button-Bright, who was half scared. Polly whirled away to a distance and turned to look at the copper man in a fright.

"His thoughts have run down, this time," remarked Billina composedly, as she sat on Tik-tok's shoulder and pruned her sleek feathers. "When he can't think, he can't talk properly, any more than you can. You'll have to wind up his thoughts, Dorothy, or else I'll have to finish his story myself."

Dorothy ran around and got the key again and wound up Tik-tok under his left arm, after which he could speak plainly again.

"Par-don me," he said, "but when my thoughts run down, my speech has no mean-ing, for words are formed on-ly by thought. I was a-bout to say that Oz-ma sent us to wel-come you and in-vite you to come straight to the Em-er-ald Ci-ty. She was too bus-y to come her-self, for she is pre-par-ing for her birth-day cel-e-bra-tion, which is to be a grand af-fair."

"I've heard of it," said Dorothy, "and I'm glad we've come in time to attend. Is it far from here to the Emerald City?"

"Not ve-ry far," answered Tik-tok, "and we have plen-ty of time. To-night we will stop at the pal-ace of the Tin Wood-man, and to-mor-row night we will ar-rive at the Em-er-ald Ci-ty."

"Goody!" cried Dorothy. "I'd like to see dear Nick Chopper again. How's his heart?"

"It's fine," said Billina; "the Tin Woodman says it gets softer and kindlier every day. He's waiting at his castle to welcome you, Dorothy; but he couldn't come with us because he's getting polished as bright as possible for Ozma's party."

"Well then," said Dorothy, "let's start on, and we can talk more as we go."

They proceeded on their journey in a friendly group, for Polychrome had discovered that the copper man was harmless and was no longer afraid of him. Button-Bright was also reassured, and took quite a fancy to Tik-tok. He wanted the clockwork man to open himself, so that he might see the wheels go round; but that was a thing Tik-tok could not do. Button-Bright then wanted to wind up the copper man, and Dorothy promised he should do so as soon as any part of the machinery ran down. This pleased Button-Bright, who held fast to one of Tik-tok's copper hands as he trudged along the road, while Dorothy walked on the other side of her old friend and Billina perched by turns upon his shoulder or his copper hat. Polly once more joyously danced ahead and Toto ran after her, barking with glee. The shaggy man was left to walk behind; but he didn't seem to mind that a bit,and whistled merrily or looked curiously upon the pretty scenes they passed.

At last they came to a hilltop from which the tin castle of Nick Chopper could plainly be seen, its towers glistening magnificently under the rays of the declining sun.

"How pretty!" exclaimed Dorothy. "I've never seen the Emp'ror's new house before."

"He built it because the old castle was damp, and likely to rust his tin body," said Billina. "All those towers and steeples and domes and gables took a lot of tin, as you can see."

"Is it a toy?" asked Button-Bright softly.

"No, dear," answered Dorothy; "it's better than that. It's the fairy dwelling of a fairy prince."

Chapter 15 - The Emporer's Tin Castler

The grounds around Nick Chopper's new house were laid out in pretty flower-beds, with fountains of crystal water and statues of tin representing the Emperor's personal friends. Dorothy was astonished and delighted to find a tin statue of herself standing on a tin pedestal at a bend in the avenue leading up to the entrance. It was life-size and showed her in her sunbonnet with her basket on her arm, just as she had first appeared in the Land of Oz.

"Oh, Toto—you're there too!" she exclaimed; and sure enough there was the tin figure of Toto lying at the tin Dorothy's feet.

Also, Dorothy saw figures of the Scarecrow, and the Wizard, and Ozma, and of many others, including Tik-tok. They reached the grand tin entrance to the tin castle, and the Tin Woodman himself came running out of the door to embrace little Dorothy and give her a glad welcome. He welcomed her friends as well, and the Rainbow's Daughter he declared to be the loveliest vision his tin eyes had ever beheld. He patted Button-Bright's curly head tenderly, for he was fond of children, and turned to the shaggy man and shook both his hands at the same time.

Nick Chopper, the Emperor of the Winkies, who was also known throughout the Land of Oz as the Tin Woodman, was certainly a remarkable person. He was neatly made, all of tin, nicely soldered at the joints, and his various limbs were cleverly hinged to his body so that he could use them nearly as well as if they had been common flesh. Once, he told the shaggy man, he had been made all of flesh and bones, as other people are, and then he chopped wood in the forests to earn his living. But the axe slipped so often and cut off parts of him—which he had replaced with tin—that finally there was no flesh left, nothing but tin; so he became a real tin woodman. The wonderful Wizard of Oz had given him an excellent heart to replace his old one, and he didn't at all mind being tin. Every one loved him, he loved every one; and he was therefore as happy as the day was long.

The Emperor was proud of his new tin castle, and showed his visitors through all the rooms. Every bit of the furniture was made of brightly polished tin—the tables, chairs, beds, and all—even the floors and walls were of tin.

"I suppose," said he, "that there are no cleverer tinsmiths in all the world than the Winkies. It would be hard to match this castle in Kansas; wouldn't it, little Dorothy?"

"Very hard," replied the child, gravely.

"It must have cost a lot of money," remarked the shaggy man.

"Money! Money in Oz!" cried the Tin Woodman. "What a queer idea! Did you suppose we are so vulgar as to use money here?"

"Why not?" asked the shaggy man.

"If we used money to buy things with, instead of love and kindness and the desire to please one another, then we should be no better than the rest of the world," declared the Tin Woodman. "Fortunately money is not known in the Land of Oz at all. We have no rich, and no poor; for what one wishes the others all try to give him, in order to make him happy, and no one in all Oz cares to have more than he can use."

"Good!" cried the shaggy man, greatly pleased to hear this. "I also despise money—a man in Butterfield owes me fifteen cents, and I will not take it from him. The Land of Oz is surely the most favored land in all the world, and its people the happiest. I should like to live here always."

The Tin Woodman listened with respectful attention. Already he loved the shaggy man, although he did not yet know of the Love Magnet. So he said:

"If you can prove to the Princess Ozma that you are honest and true and worthy of our friendship, you may indeed live here all your days, and be as happy as we are."

"I'll try to prove that," said the shaggy man, earnestly.

"And now," continued the Emperor, "you must all go to your rooms and prepare for dinner, which will presently be served in the grand tin dining-hall. I am sorry, Shaggy Man, that I can not offer you a change of clothing; but I dress only in tin, myself, and I suppose that would not suit you."

"I care little about dress," said the shaggy man, indifferently.

"So I should imagine," replied the Emperor, with true politeness.

They were shown to their rooms and permitted to make such toilets as they could, and soon they assembled again in the grand tin dining-hall, even Toto being present. For the Emperor was fond of Dorothy's little dog, and the girl explained to her friends that in Oz all animals were treated with as much consideration as the people—"if they behave themselves," she added.

Toto behaved himself, and sat in a tin high-chair beside Dorothy and ate his dinner from a tin platter.

Indeed, they all ate from tin dishes, but these were of pretty shapes and brightly polished; Dorothy thought they were just as good as silver.

Button-Bright looked curiously at the man who had "no appetite inside him," for the Tin Woodman, although he had prepared so fine a feast for his guests, ate not a mouthful himself, sitting patiently in his place to see that all built so they could eat were well and plentifully served.

What pleased Button-Bright most about the dinner was the tin orchestra that played sweet music while the company ate. The players were not tin, being just ordinary Winkies; but the instruments they played upon were all tin—tin trumpets, tin fiddles, tin drums and cymbals and flutes and horns and all. They played so nicely the "Shining Emperor Waltz," composed expressly in honor of the Tin Woodman by Mr. H. M. Wogglebug, T.E., that Polly could not resist dancing to it. After she had tasted a few dewdrops, freshly gathered for her, she danced gracefully to the music while the others finished their repast; and when she whirled until her fleecy draperies of rainbow hues enveloped her like a cloud, the Tin Woodman was so delighted that he clapped his tin hands until the noise of them drowned the sound of the cymbals.

Altogether it was a merry meal, although Polychrome ate little and the host nothing at all.

"I'm sorry the Rainbow's Daughter missed her mist-cakes," said the Tin Woodman to Dorothy; "but by a mistake Miss Polly's mist-cakes were mislaid and not missed until now. I'll try to have some for her breakfast."

They spent the evening telling stories, and the next morning left the splendid tin castle and set out upon the road to the Emerald City. The Tin Woodman went with them, of course, having by this time been so brightly polished that he sparkled like silver. His axe, which he always carried with him, had a steel blade that was tin plated and a handle covered with tin plate beautifully engraved and set with diamonds.

The Winkies assembled before the castle gates and cheered their Emperor as he marched away, and it was easy to see that they all loved him dearly.

Chapter 16 - Visiting the Pumpkin Field

Dorothy let Button-Bright wind up the clockwork in the copper man this morning—his thinking machine first, then his speech, and finally his action; so he would doubtless run perfectly until they had reached the Emerald City. The copper man and the tin man were good friends, and not so much alike as you might think. For one was alive and the other moved by means of machinery; one was tall and angular and the other short and round. You could love the Tin Woodman because he had a fine nature, kindly and simple; but the machine man you could only admire without loving, since to love such a thing as he was as impossible as to love a sewing-machine or an automobile. Yet Tik-tok was popular with the people of Oz because he was so trustworthy, reliable and true; he was sure to do exactly what he was wound up to do, at all times and in all circumstances. Perhaps it is better to be a machine that does its duty than a flesh-and-blood person who will not, for a dead truth is better than a live falsehood.

About noon the travelers reached a large field of pumpkins—a vegetable quite appropriate to the yellow country of the Winkies—and some of the pumpkins which grew there were of remarkable size. Just before they entered upon this field they saw three little mounds that looked like graves, with a pretty headstone to each one of them.

"What is this?" asked Dorothy, in wonder.

"It's Jack Pumpkinhead's private graveyard," replied the Tin Woodman.

"But I thought nobody ever died in Oz," she said.

"Nor do they; although if one is bad, he may be condemned and killed by the good citizens," he answered.

Dorothy ran over to the little graves and read the words engraved upon the tombstones. The first one said:

Here Lies the Mortal Part of JACK PUMPKINHEAD Which Spoiled April 9th.

She then went to the next stone, which read:

Here Lies the Mortal Part of JACK PUMPKINHEAD Which Spoiled October 2nd.

On the third stone were carved these words:

Here Lies the Mortal Part of JACK PUMPKINHEAD Which Spoiled January 24th.

"Poor Jack!" sighed Dorothy. "I'm sorry he had to die in three parts, for I hoped to see him again."

"So you shall," declared the Tin Woodman, "since he is still alive. Come with me to his house, for Jack is now a farmer and lives in this very pumpkin field."

They walked over to a monstrous big, hollow pumpkin which had a door and windows cut through the rind. There was a stovepipe running through the stem, and six steps had been built leading up to the front door.

They walked up to this door and looked in. Seated on a bench was a man clothed in a spotted shirt, a red vest, and faded blue trousers, whose body was merely sticks of wood, jointed clumsily together. On his neck was set a round, yellow pumpkin, with a face carved on it such as a boy often carves on a jack-lantern.

This queer man was engaged in snapping slippery pumpkin-seeds with his wooden fingers, trying to hit a target on the other side of the room with them. He did not know he had visitors until Dorothy exclaimed:

"Why, it's Jack Pumpkinhead himself!"

He turned and saw them, and at once came forward to greet the little Kansas girl and Nick Chopper, and to be introduced to their new friends.

Button-Bright was at first rather shy with the quaint Pumpkinhead, but Jack's face was so jolly and smiling—being carved that way—that the boy soon grew to like him.

"I thought a while ago that you were buried in three parts," said Dorothy, "but now I see you're just the same as ever."

"Not quite the same, my dear, for my mouth is a little more one-sided than it used to be; but pretty nearly the same. I've a new head, and this is the fourth one I've owned since Ozma first made me and brought me to life by sprinkling me with the Magic Powder."

"What became of the other heads, Jack?"

"They spoiled and I buried them, for they were not even fit for pies. Each time Ozma has carved me a new head just like the old one, and as my body is by far the largest part of me, I am still Jack Pumpkinhead, no matter how often I change my upper end. Once we had a dreadful time to find another pumpkin, as they were out of season, and so I was obliged to wear my old head a little longer than was strictly healthy. But after this sad experience I resolved to raise pumpkins myself, so as never to be caught again without one handy; and now I have this fine field that you see before you. Some grow pretty big—too big to be used for heads—so I dug out this one and use it for a house."

"Isn't it damp?" asked Dorothy.

"Not very. There isn't much left but the shell, you see, and it will last a long time yet."

"I think you are brighter than you used to be, Jack," said the Tin Woodman. "Your last head was a stupid one."

"The seeds in this one are better," was the reply.

"Are you going to Ozma's party?" asked Dorothy.

"Yes," said he, "I wouldn't miss it for anything. Ozma's my parent, you know, because she built my body and carved my pumpkin head. I'll follow you to the Emerald City to-morrow, where we shall meet again. I can't go to-day, because I have to plant fresh pumpkin-seeds and water the young vines. But give my love to Ozma, and tell her I'll be there in time for the jubilation."

"We will," she promised; and then they all left him and resumed their journey.

Chapter 17 - The Royal Chariot Arrives

The neat yellow houses of the Winkies were now to be seen standing here and there along the roadway, giving the country a more cheerful and civilized look. They were farm-houses, though, and set far apart; for in the Land of Oz there were no towns or villages except the magnificent Emerald City in its center.

Hedges of evergreen or of yellow roses bordered the broad highway and the farms showed the care of their industrious inhabitants. The nearer the travelers came to the great city the more prosperous the country became, and they crossed many bridges over the sparkling streams and rivulets that watered the lands.

As they walked leisurely along the shaggy man said to the Tin Woodman:

"What sort of a Magic Powder was it that made your friend the Pumpkinhead live?"

"It was called the Powder of Life," was the answer; "and it was invented by a crooked Sorcerer who lived in the mountains of the North Country. A Witch named Mombi got some of this powder from the crooked Sorcerer and took it home with her. Ozma lived with the Witch then, for it was before she became our Princess, while Mombi had transformed her into the shape of a boy. Well, while Mombi was gone to the crooked Sorcerer's, the boy made this pumpkin-headed man to amuse himself, and also with the hope of frightening the Witch with it when she returned. But Mombi was not scared, and she sprinkled the Pumpkinhead with her Magic Powder of Life, to see if the Powder would work. Ozma was watching, and saw the Pumpkinhead come to life; so that night she took the pepper-box containing the Powder and ran away with it and with Jack, in search of adventures.

"Next day they found a wooden Saw-Horse standing by the roadside, and sprinkled it with the Powder. It came to life at once, and Jack Pumpkinhead rode the Saw-Horse to the Emerald City."

"What became of the Saw-Horse, afterward?" asked the shaggy man, much interested in this story.

"Oh, it's alive yet, and you will probably meet it presently in the Emerald City. Afterward, Ozma used the last of the Powder to bring the Flying Gump to life; but as soon as it had carried her away from her enemies the Gump was taken apart, so it doesn't exist any more."

"It's too bad the Powder of Life was all used up," remarked the shaggy man; "it would be a handy thing to have around."

"I am not so sure of that, sir," answered the Tin Woodman. "A while ago the crooked Sorcerer who invented the Magic Powder fell down a precipice and was killed. All his possessions went to a relative—an old woman named Dyna, who lives in the Emerald City. She went to the mountains where the Sorcerer had lived and brought away everything she thought of value. Among them was a small bottle of the Powder of Life; but of course Dyna didn't know it was a Magic Powder, at all. It happened she had once had a big blue bear for a pet; but the bear choked to death on a fishbone one day, and she loved it so dearly that Dyna made a rug of its skin, leaving the head and four paws on the hide. She kept the rug on the floor of her front parlor."

"I've seen rugs like that," said the shaggy man, nodding, "but never one made from a blue bear."

"Well," continued the Tin Woodman, "the old woman had an idea that the Powder in the bottle must be moth-powder, because it smelled something like moth-powder; so one day she sprinkled it on her bear rug to keep the moths out of it. She said, looking lovingly at the skin: 'I wish my dear bear were alive again!' To her horror, the bear rug at once came to life, having been sprinkled with the Magic Powder; and now this live bear rug is a great trial to her, and makes her a lot of trouble."

"Why?" asked the shaggy man.

"Well, it stands up on its four feet and walks all around, and gets in the way; and that spoils it for a rug. It can't speak, although it is alive; for, while its head might say words, it has no breath in a solid body to push the words out of its mouth. It's a very slimpsy affair altogether, that bear rug, and the old woman is sorry it came to life. Every day she has to scold it, and make it lie down flat on the parlor floor to be walked upon; but sometimes when she goes to market the rug will hump up its back skin, and stand on its four feet, and trot along after her."

"I should think Dyna would like that," said Dorothy.

"Well, she doesn't; because every one knows it isn't a real bear, but just a hollow skin, and so of no actual use in the world except for a rug," answered the Tin Woodman. "Therefore I believe it is a good thing that all the Magic Powder of Life is now used up, as it can not cause any more trouble."

"Perhaps you're right," said the shaggy man, thoughtfully.

At noon they stopped at a farmhouse, where it delighted the farmer and his wife to be able to give them a good luncheon. The farm people knew Dorothy, having seen her when she was in the country before, and they treated the little girl with as much respect as they did the Emperor, because she was a friend of the powerful Princess Ozma.

They had not proceeded far after leaving this farm-house before coming to a high bridge over a broad river. This river, the Tin Woodman informed them, was the boundary between the Country of the Winkies and the territory of the Emerald City. The city itself was still a long way off, but all around it was a green meadow as pretty as a well-kept lawn, and in this were neither houses nor farms to spoil the beauty of the scene.

From the top of the high bridge they could see far away the magnificent spires and splendid domes of the superb city, sparkling like brilliant jewels as they towered above the emerald walls. The shaggy man drew a deep breath of awe and amazement, for never had he dreamed that such a grand and beautiful place could exist—even in the fairyland of Oz.

Polly was so pleased that her violet eyes sparkled like amethysts, and she danced away from her companions across the bridge and into a group of feathery trees lining both the roadsides. These trees she stopped to look at with pleasure and surprise, for their leaves were shaped like ostrich plumes, their feather edges beautifully curled; and all the plumes were tinted in the same dainty rainbow hues that appeared in Polychrome's own pretty gauze gown.

"Father ought to see these trees," she murmured; "they are almost as lovely as his own rainbows."

Then she gave a start of terror, for beneath the trees came stalking two great beasts, either one big enough to crush the little Daughter of the Rainbow with one blow of his paws, or to eat her up with one snap of his enormous jaws. One was a tawny lion, as tall as a horse, nearly; the other a striped tiger almost the same size.

Polly was too frightened to scream or to stir; she stood still with a wildly beating heart until Dorothy rushed past her and with a glad cry threw her arms around the huge lion's neck, hugging and kissing the beast with evident joy.

"Oh, I'm SO glad to see you again!" cried the little Kansas girl. "And the Hungry Tiger, too! How fine you're both looking. Are you well and happy?"

"We certainly are, Dorothy," answered the Lion, in a deep voice that sounded pleasant and kind; "and we are greatly pleased that you have come to Ozma's party. It's going to be a grand affair, I promise you."

"There will be lots of fat babies at the celebration, I hear," remarked the Hungry Tiger, yawning so that his mouth opened dreadfully wide and showed all his big, sharp teeth; "but of course I can't eat any of 'em."

"Is your Conscience still in good order?" asked Dorothy, anxiously.

"Yes; it rules me like a tyrant," answered the Tiger, sorrowfully. "I can imagine nothing more unpleasant than to own a Conscience," and he winked slyly at his friend the Lion.

"You're fooling me!" said Dorothy, with a laugh. "I don't b'lieve you'd eat a baby if you lost your Conscience. Come here, Polly," she called, "and be introduced to my friends."

Polly advanced rather shyly.

"You have some queer friends, Dorothy," she said.

"The queerness doesn't matter so long as they're friends," was the answer. "This is the Cowardly Lion, who isn't a coward at all, but just thinks he is. The Wizard gave him some courage once, and he has part of it left."

The Lion bowed with great dignity to Polly.

"You are very lovely, my dear," said he. "I hope we shall be friends when we are better acquainted."

"And this is the Hungry Tiger," continued Dorothy. "He says he longs to eat fat babies; but the truth is he is never hungry at all, 'cause he gets plenty to eat; and I don't s'pose he'd hurt anybody even if he WAS hungry."

"Hush, Dorothy," whispered the Tiger; "you'll ruin my reputation if you are not more discreet. It isn't what we are, but what folks think we are, that counts in this world. And come to think of it Miss Polly would make a fine variegated breakfast, I'm sure."

Chapter 18 - The Emerald City

The others now came up, and the Tin Woodman greeted the Lion and the Tiger

cordially. Button-Bright yelled with fear when Dorothy first took his hand and led him toward the great beasts; but the girl insisted they were kind and good, and so the boy mustered up courage enough to pat their heads; after they had spoken to him gently and he had looked into their intelligent eyes his fear vanished entirely and he was so delighted with the animals that he wanted to keep close to them and stroke their soft fur every minute.

As for the shaggy man, he might have been afraid if he had met the beasts alone, or in any other country, but so many were the marvels in; the Land of Oz that he was no longer easily surprised, and Dorothy's friendship for the Lion and Tiger was enough to assure him they were safe companions. Toto barked at the Cowardly Lion in joyous greeting, for he knew the beast of old and loved him, and it was funny to see how gently the Lion raised his huge paw to pat Toto's head. The little dog smelled of the Tiger's nose, and the Tiger politely shook paws with him; so they were quite likely to become firm friends.

Tik-tok and Billina knew the beasts well, so merely bade them good day and asked after their healths and inquired about the Princess Ozma.

Now it was seen that the Cowardly Lion and the Hungry Tiger were drawing behind them a splendid golden chariot, to which they were harnessed by golden cords. The body of the chariot was decorated on the outside with designs in clusters of sparkling emeralds, while inside it was lined with a green and gold satin, and the cushions of the seats were of green plush embroidered in gold with a crown, underneath which was a monogram.

"Why, it's Ozma's own royal chariot!" exclaimed Dorothy.

"Yes," said the Cowardly Lion; "Ozma sent us to meet you here, for she feared you would be weary with your long walk and she wished you to enter the City in a style becoming your exalted rank."

"What!" cried Polly, looking at Dorothy curiously. "Do you belong to the nobility?"

"Just in Oz I do," said the child, "'cause Ozma made me a Princess, you know. But when I'm home in Kansas I'm only a country girl, and have to help with the churning and wipe the dishes while Aunt Em washes 'em. Do you have to help wash dishes on the rainbow, Polly?"

"No, dear," answered Polychrome, smiling.

"Well, I don't have to work any in Oz, either," said Dorothy. "It's kind of fun to be a Princess once in a while; don't you think so?"

"Dorothy and Polychrome and Button-Bright are all to ride in the chariot," said the Lion. "So get in, my dears, and be careful not to mar the gold or put your dusty feet on the embroidery."

Button-Bright was delighted to ride behind such a superb team, and he told Dorothy it made him feel like an actor in a circus. As the strides of the animals brought them nearer to the Emerald City every one bowed respectfully to the children, as well as to the Tin Woodman, Tik-tok, and the shaggy man, who were following behind.

The Yellow Hen had perched upon the back of the chariot, where she could tell Dorothy more about her wonderful chickens as they rode. And so the grand chariot came finally to the high wall surrounding the City, and paused before the magnificent jewel-studded gates.

These were opened by a cheerful-looking little man who wore green spectacles over his eyes. Dorothy introduced him to her friends as the Guardian of the Gates, and they noticed a big bunch of keys suspended on the golden chain that hung around his neck. The chariot passed through the outer gates into a fine arched chamber built in the thick wall, and through the inner gates into the streets of the Emerald City.

Polychrome exclaimed in rapture at the wondrous beauty that met her eyes on every side as they rode through this stately and imposing City, the equal of which has never been discovered, even in Fairyland. Button-Bright could only say "My!" so amazing was the sight; but his eyes were wide open and he tried to look in every direction at the same time, so as not to miss anything.

The shaggy man was fairly astounded at what he saw, for the graceful and handsome buildings were covered with plates of gold and set with emeralds so splendid and valuable that in any other part of the world any one of them would have been worth a fortune to its owner. The sidewalks were superb marble slabs polished as smooth as glass, and the curbs that separated the walks from the broad street were also set thick with clustered emeralds. There were many people on these walks—men, women and children—all dressed in handsome garments of silk or satin or velvet, with beautiful jewels. Better even than this: all seemed happy and contented, for their faces were smiling and free from care, and music and laughter might be heard on every side.

"Don't they work at all?" asked the shaggy man.

"To be sure they work," replied the Tin Woodman; "this fair city could not be built or cared for without labor, nor could the fruit and vegetables and other food be provided for the inhabitants to eat. But no one works more than half his time, and the people of Oz enjoy their labors as much as they do their play."

"It's wonderful!" declared the shaggy man. "I do hope Ozma will let me live here."

The chariot, winding through many charming streets, paused before a building so vast and noble and elegant that even Button-Bright guessed at once that it was the Royal Palace. Its gardens and ample grounds were surrounded by a separate wall, not so high or thick as the wall around the City, but more daintily designed and built all of green marble. The gates flew open as the chariot appeared before them, and the Cowardly Lion and Hungry Tiger trotted up a jeweled driveway to the front door of the palace and stopped short.

"Here we are!" said Dorothy, gaily, and helped Button-Bright from the chariot. Polychrome leaped out lightly after them, and they were greeted by a crowd of gorgeously dressed servants who bowed low as the visitors mounted the marble steps. At their head was a pretty little maid with dark hair and eyes, dressed all in green embroidered with silver. Dorothy ran up to her with evident pleasure, and exclaimed:

"O, Jellia Jamb! I'm so glad to see you again. Where's Ozma?"

"In her room, your Highness," replied the little maid demurely, for this was Ozma's favorite attendant. "She wishes you to come to her as soon as you have rested and changed your dress, Princess Dorothy. And you and your friends are to dine with her this evening."

"When is her birthday, Jellia?" asked the girl.

"Day after to-morrow, your Highness."

"And where's the Scarecrow?"

"He's gone into the Munchkin country to get some fresh straw to stuff himself with, in honor of Ozma's celebration," replied the maid. "He returns to the Emerald City to-morrow, he said."

By this time, Tok-tok, the Tin Woodman, and the shaggy man had arrived and the chariot had gone around to the back of the palace, Billina going with the Lion and Tiger to see her chickens after her absence from them. But Toto stayed close beside Dorothy.

"Come in, please," said Jellia Jamb; "it shall be our pleasant duty to escort all of you to the rooms prepared for your use."

The shaggy man hesitated. Dorothy had never known him to be ashamed of his shaggy looks before, but now that he was surrounded by so much magnificence and splendor the shaggy man felt sadly out of place.

Dorothy assured him that all her friends were welcome at Ozma's palace, so he carefully dusted his shaggy shoes with his shaggy handkerchief and entered the grand hall after the others.

Tik-tok lived at the Royal Palace and the Tin Woodman always had the same room whenever he visited Ozma, so these two went at once to remove the dust of the journey from their shining bodies. Dorothy also had a pretty suite of rooms which she always occupied when in the Emerald City; but several servants walked ahead politely to show the way, although she was quite sure she could find the rooms herself. She took Button-Bright with her, because he seemed too small to be left alone in such a big palace; but Jellia Jamb herself ushered the beautiful Daughter of the Rainbow to her apartments, because it was easy to see that Polychrome was used to splendid palaces and was therefore entitled to especial attention.

Chapter 19 - The Shaggy Man's Welcome

The shaggy man stood in the great hall, his shaggy hat in his hands, wondering what would become of him. He had never been a guest in a fine palace before; perhaps he had never been a guest anywhere. In the big, cold, outside world people did not invite shaggy men to their homes, and this shaggy man of ours had slept more in hay-lofts and stables than in comfortable rooms. When the others left the great hall he eyed the splendidly dressed servants of the Princess Ozma as if he expected to be ordered out; but one of them bowed before him as respectfully as if he had been a prince, and said:

"Permit me, sir, to conduct you to your apartments."

The shaggy man drew a long breath and took courage.

"Very well," he answered. "I'm ready."

Through the big hall they went, up the grand staircase carpeted thick with velvet, and so along a wide corridor to a carved doorway. Here the servant paused, and opening the door said with polite deference:

"Be good enough to enter, sir, and make yourself at home in the rooms our Royal Ozma has ordered prepared for you. Whatever you see is for you to use and enjoy, as if your own. The Princess dines at seven, and I shall be here in time to lead you to the drawing-room, where you will be privileged to meet the lovely Ruler of Oz. Is there any command, in the meantime, with which you desire to honor me?"

"No," said the shaggy man; "but I'm much obliged."

He entered the room and shut the door, and for a time stood in bewilderment, admiring the grandeur before him.

He had been given one of the handsomest apartments in the most magnificent palace in the world, and you can not wonder that his good fortune astonished and awed him until he grew used to his surroundings.

The furniture was upholstered in cloth of gold, with the royal crown embroidered upon it in scarlet. The rug upon the marble floor was so thick and soft that he could not hear the sound of his own footsteps, and upon the walls were splendid tapestries woven with scenes from the Land of Oz. Books and ornaments were scattered about in profusion, and the shaggy man thought he had never seen so many pretty things in one place before. In one corner played a tinkling fountain of perfumed water, and in another was a table bearing a golden tray loaded with freshly gathered fruit, including several of the red-cheeked apples that the shaggy man loved.

At the farther end of this charming room was an open doorway, and he crossed over to find himself in a bedroom containing more comforts than the shaggy man had ever before imagined. The bedstead was of gold and set with many brilliant diamonds, and the coverlet had designs of pearls and rubies sewed upon it. At one side of the bedroom was a dainty dressing-room with closets containing a large assortment of fresh clothing; and beyond this was the bath—a large room having a marble pool big enough to swim in, with white marble steps leading down to the water. Around the edge of the pool were set rows of fine emeralds as large as door-knobs, while the water of the bath was clear as crystal.

For a time the shaggy man gazed upon all this luxury with silent amazement. Then he decided, being wise in his way, to take advantage of his good fortune. He removed his shaggy boots and his shaggy clothing, and bathed in the pool with rare enjoyment. After he had dried himself with the soft towels he went into the dressing-room and took fresh linen from the drawers and put it on, finding that everything fitted him exactly. He examined the contents of the closets and selected an elegant suit of clothing. Strangely enough, everything about it was shaggy, although so new and beautiful, and he sighed with contentment to realize that he could now be finely dressed and still be the shaggy man. His coat was of rose-colored velvet, trimmed with shags and bobtails, with buttons of blood-red rubies and golden shags around the edges. His vest was a shaggy satin of a delicate cream color, and his knee-breeches of rose velvet trimmed like the coat. Shaggy creamy stockings of silk, and shaggy slippers of rose leather with ruby buckles, completed his costume, and when he was thus attired the shaggy man looked at himself in a long mirror with great admiration. On a table he found a mother-of-pearl chest decorated with delicate silver vines and flowers of clustered rubies, and on the cover was a silver plate engraved with these words:

THE SHAGGY MAN: HIS BOX OF ORNAMENTS

The chest was not locked, so he opened it and was almost dazzled by the brilliance of the rich jewels it contained. After admiring the pretty things, he took out a fine golden watch with a big chain, several handsome finger-rings, and an ornament of rubies to pin upon the breast of his shaggy shirt-bosom. Having carefully brushed his hair and whiskers all the wrong way to make them look as shaggy as possible, the shaggy man breathed a deep sigh of joy and decided he was ready to meet the Royal Princess as soon as she sent for him. While he waited he returned to the beautiful sitting room and ate several of the red-cheeked apples to pass away the time.

Meanwhile, Dorothy had dressed herself in a pretty gown of soft grey embroidered with silver, and put a blue-and-gold suit of satin upon little Button-Bright, who looked as sweet as a cherub in it. Followed by the boy and Toto—the dog with a new green ribbon around his neck—she hastened down to the splendid drawing-room of the palace, where, seated upon an exquisite throne of carved malachite and nestled amongst its green satin cushions was the lovely Princess Ozma, waiting eagerly to welcome her friend.

Chapter 20 - Princess Ozma of Oz

The royal historians of Oz, who are fine writers and know any number of big words, have often tried to describe the rare beauty of Ozma and failed because the words were not good enough. So of course I cannot hope to tell you how great was the charm of this little Princess, or how her loveliness put to shame all the sparkling jewels and magnificent luxury that surrounded her in this her royal palace. Whatever else was beautiful or dainty or delightful of itself faded to dullness when contrasted with Ozma's bewitching face, and it has often been said by those who know that no other ruler in all the world can ever hope to equal the gracious charm of her manner.

Everything about Ozma attracted one, and she inspired love and the sweetest affection rather than awe or ordinary admiration. Dorothy threw her arms around her little friend and hugged and kissed her rapturously, and Toto barked joyfully and Button-Bright smiled a happy smile and consented to sit on the soft cushions close beside the Princess.

"Why didn't you send me word you were going to have a birthday party?" asked the little Kansas girl, when the first greetings were over.

"Didn't I?" asked Ozma, her pretty eyes dancing with merriment.

"Did you?" replied Dorothy, trying to think.

"Who do you imagine, dear, mixed up those roads, so as to start you wandering in the direction of Oz?" inquired the Princess.

"Oh! I never 'spected YOU of that," cried Dorothy.

"I've watched you in my Magic Picture all the way here," declared Ozma, "and twice I thought I should have to use the Magic Belt to save you and transport you to the Emerald City. Once was when the Scoodlers caught you, and again when you reached the Deadly Desert. But the shaggy man was able to help you out both times, so I did not interfere."

"Do you know who Button-Bright is?" asked Dorothy.

"No; I never saw him until you found him in the road, and then only in my Magic Picture."

"And did you send Polly to us?"

"No, dear; the Rainbow's Daughter slid from her father's pretty arch just in time to meet you."

"Well," said Dorothy, "I've promised King Dox of Foxville and King Kik-a-bray of Dunkiton that I'd ask you to invite them to your party."

"I have already done that," returned Ozma, "because I thought it would please you to favor them."

"Did you 'vite the Musicker?" asked Button-Bright.

"No; because he would be too noisy, and might interfere with the comfort of others. When music is not very good, and is indulged in all the time, it is better that the performer should be alone," said the Princess.

"I like the Musicker's music," declared the boy, gravely.

"But I don't," said Dorothy.

"Well, there will be plenty of music at my celebration," promised Ozma; "so I've an idea Button-Bright won't miss the Musicker at all."

Just then Polychrome danced in, and Ozma rose to greet the Rainbow's Daughter in her sweetest and most cordial manner.

Dorothy thought she had never seen two prettier creatures together than these lovely maidens; but Polly knew at once her own dainty beauty could not match that of Ozma, yet was not a bit jealous because this was so.

The Wizard of Oz was announced, and a dried-up, little, old man, clothed all in black, entered the drawing-room. His face was cheery and his eyes twinkling with humor, so Polly and Button-Bright were not at all afraid of the wonderful personage whose fame as a humbug magician had spread throughout the world. After greeting Dorothy with much affection, he stood modestly behind Ozma's throne and listened to the lively prattle of the young people.

Now the shaggy man appeared, and so startling was his appearance, all clad in shaggy new rainment, that Dorothy cried "Oh!" and clasped her hands impulsively as she examined her friend with pleased eyes.

"He's still shaggy, all right," remarked Button-Bright; and Ozma nodded brightly because she had meant the shaggy man to remain shaggy when she provided his new clothes for him.

Dorothy led him toward the throne, as he was shy in such fine company, and presented him gracefully to the Princess, saying:

"This, your Highness, is my friend, the shaggy man, who owns the Love Magnet."

"You are welcome to Oz," said the girl Ruler, in gracious accents. "But tell me, sir, where did you get the Love Magnet which you say you own?"

The shaggy man grew red and looked downcast, as he answered in a low voice:

"I stole it, your Majesty."

"Oh, Shaggy Man!" cried Dorothy. "How dreadful! And you told me the Eskimo gave you the Love Magnet."

He shuffled first on one foot and then on the other, much embarrassed.

"I told you a falsehood, Dorothy," he said; "but now, having bathed in the Truth Pond, I must tell nothing but the truth."

"Why did you steal it?" asked Ozma, gently.

"Because no one loved me, or cared for me," said the shaggy man, "and I wanted to be loved a great deal. It was owned by a girl in Butterfield who was loved too much, so that the young men quarreled over her, which made her unhappy. After I had stolen the Magnet from her, only one young man continued to love the girl, and she married him and regained her happiness."

"Are you sorry you stole it?" asked the Princess.

"No, your Highness; I'm glad," he answered; "for it has pleased me to be loved, and if Dorothy had not cared for me I could not have accompanied her to this beautiful Land of Oz, or met its kind-hearted Ruler. Now that I'm here, I hope to remain, and to become one of your Majesty's most faithful subjects."

"But in Oz we are loved for ourselves alone, and for our kindness to one another, and for our good deeds," she said.

"I'll give up the Love Magnet," said the shaggy man, eagerly; "Dorothy shall have it."

"But every one loves Dorothy already," declared the Wizard.

"Then Button-Bright shall have it."

"Don't want it," said the boy, promptly.

"Then I'll give it to the Wizard, for I'm sure the lovely Princess Ozma does not need it."

"All my people love the Wizard, too," announced the Princess, laughing; "so we will hang the Love Magnet over the gates of the Emerald City, that whoever shall enter or leave the gates may be loved and loving."

"That is a good idea," said the shaggy man; "I agree to it most willingly."

Those assembled now went in to dinner, which you can imagine was a grand affair; and afterward Ozma asked the Wizard to give them an exhibition of his magic.

The Wizard took eight tiny white piglets from an inside pocket and set them on the table. One was dressed like a clown, and performed funny antics, and the others leaped over the spoons and dishes and ran around the table like race-horses, and turned hand-springs and were so sprightly and amusing that they kept the company in one roar of merry laughter. The Wizard had trained these pets to do many curious things, and they were so little and so cunning and soft that Polychrome loved to pick them up as they passed near her place and fondle them as if they were kittens.

It was late when the entertainment ended, and they separated to go to their rooms.

"To-morrow," said Ozma, "my invited guests will arrive, and you will find among them some interesting and curious people, I promise you. The next day will be my birthday, and the festivities will be held on the broad green just outside the gates of the City, where all my people can assemble without being crowded."

"I hope the Scarecrow won't be late," said Dorothy, anxiously.

"Oh, he is sure to return to-morrow," answered Ozma. "He wanted new straw to stuff himself with, so he went to the Munchkin Country, where straw is plentiful."

With this the Princess bade her guests good night and went to her own room.

Chapter 21 - Dorothy Received the Guests

Next morning Dorothy's breakfast was served in her own pretty sitting room, and she sent to invite Polly and the shaggy man to join her and Button-Bright at the meal. They came gladly, and Toto also had breakfast with them, so that the little party that had traveled together to Oz was once more reunited.

No sooner had they finished eating than they heard the distant blast of many trumpets, and the sound of a brass band playing martial music; so they all went out upon the balcony. This was at the front of the palace and overlooked the streets of the City, being higher than the wall that shut in the palace grounds. They saw approaching down the street a band of musicians, playing as hard and loud as they could, while the people of the Emerald City crowded the sidewalks and cheered so lustily that they almost drowned the noise of the drums and horns.

Dorothy looked to see what they were cheering at, and discovered that behind the band was the famous Scarecrow, riding proudly upon the back of a wooden Saw-Horse which pranced along the street almost as gracefully as if it had been made of flesh. Its hoofs, or rather the ends of its wooden legs, were shod with plates of solid gold, and the saddle strapped to the wooden body was richly embroidered and glistened with jewels.

As he reached the palace the Scarecrow looked up and saw Dorothy, and at once waved his peaked hat at her in greeting. He rode up to the front door and dismounted, and the band stopped playing and went away and the crowds of people returned to their dwellings.

By the time Dorothy and her friends had re-entered her room, the Scarecrow was there, and he gave the girl a hearty embrace and shook the hands of the others with his own squashy hands, which were white gloves filled with straw.

The shaggy man, Button-Bright, and Polychrome stared hard at this celebrated person, who was acknowledged to be the most popular and most beloved man in all the Land of Oz.

"Why, your face has been newly painted!" exclaimed Dorothy, when the first greetings were over.

"I had it touched up a bit by the Munchkin farmer who first made me," answered the Scarecrow, pleasantly. "My complexion had become a bit grey and faded, you know, and the paint had peeled off one end of my mouth, so I couldn't talk quite straight. Now I feel like myself again, and I may say without immodesty that my body is stuffed with the loveliest oat-straw in all Oz." He pushed against his chest. "Hear me crunkle?" he asked.

"Yes," said Dorothy; "you sound fine."

Button-Bright was wonderfully attracted by the strawman, and so was Polly. The shaggy man treated him with great respect, because he was so queerly made.

Jellia Jamb now came to say that Ozma wanted Princess Dorothy to receive the invited guests in the Throne-Room, as they arrived. The Ruler was herself busy ordering the preparations for the morrow's festivities, so she wished her friend to act in her place.

Dorothy willingly agreed, being the only other Princess in the Emerald City; so she went to the great Throne-Room and sat in Ozma's seat, placing Polly on one side of her and Button-Bright on the other. The Scarecrow stood at the left of the throne and the Tin Woodman at the right, while the Wonderful Wizard and the shaggy man stood behind.

The Cowardly Lion and the Hungry Tiger came in, with bright new bows of ribbon on their collars and tails. After greeting Dorothy affectionately the huge beasts lay down at the foot of the throne.

While they waited, the Scarecrow, who was near the little boy, asked:

"Why are you called Button-Bright?"

"Don't know," was the answer.

"Oh yes, you do, dear," said Dorothy. "Tell the Scarecrow how you got your name."

"Papa always said I was bright as a button, so mama always called me Button-Bright," announced the boy.

"Where is your mama?" asked the Scarecrow.

"Don't know," said Button-Bright.

"Where is your home?" asked the Scarecrow.

"Don't know," said Button-Bright.

"Don't you want to find your mama again?" asked the Scarecrow.

"Don't know," said Button-Bright, calmly.

The Scarecrow looked thoughtful.

"Your papa may have been right," he observed; "but there are many kinds of buttons, you see. There are silver and gold buttons, which are highly polished and glitter brightly. There are pearl and rubber buttons, and other kinds, with surfaces more or less bright. But there is still another sort of button which is covered with dull cloth, and that must be the sort your papa meant when he said you were bright as a button. Don't you think so?"

"Don't know," said Button-Bright.

Jack Pumpkinhead arrived, wearing a pair of new, white kid gloves; and he brought a birthday present for Ozma consisting of a necklace of pumpkin-seeds. In each seed was set a sparkling carolite, which is considered the rarest and most beautiful gem that exists. The necklace was in a plush case and Jellia Jamb put it on a table with the Princess Ozma's other presents.

Next came a tall, beautiful woman clothed in a splendid trailing gown, trimmed with exquisite lace as fine as cobweb. This was the important Sorceress known as Glinda the Good, who had been of great assistance to both Ozma and Dorothy. There was no humbug about her magic, you may be sure, and Glinda was as kind as she was powerful. She greeted Dorothy most lovingly, and kissed Button-Bright and Polly, and smiled upon the shaggy man, after which Jellia Jamb led the Sorceress to one of the most magnificent rooms of the royal palace and appointed fifty servants to wait upon her.

The next arrival was Mr. H. M. Woggle-Bug, T.E.; the "H. M." meaning Highly Magnified and the "T.E." meaning Thoroughly Educated. The Woggle-Bug was head professor at the Royal College of Oz, and he had composed a fine Ode in honor of Ozma's birthday. This he wanted to read to them; but the Scarecrow wouldn't let him.

Soon they heard a clucking sound and a chorus of "cheep! cheep!" and a servant threw open the door to allow Billina and her ten fluffy chicks to enter the Throne-Room. As the Yellow Hen marched proudly at the head of her family, Dorothy cried, "Oh, you lovely things!" and ran down from her seat to pet the little yellow downy balls. Billina wore a pearl necklace, and around the neck of each chicken was a tiny gold chain holding a locket with the letter "D" engraved upon the outside.

"Open the lockets, Dorothy," said Billina. The girl obeyed and found a picture of herself in each locket. "They were named after you, my dear," continued the Yellow Hen, "so I wanted all my chickens to wear your picture. Cluck—cluck! come here, Dorothy—this minute!" she cried, for the chickens were scattered and wandering all around the big room.

They obeyed the call at once, and came running as fast as they could, fluttering their fluffy wings in a laughable way.

It was lucky that Billina gathered the little ones under her soft breast just then, for Tik-tok came in and tramped up to the throne on his flat copper feet.

"I am all wound up and work-ing fine-ly," said the clock-work man to Dorothy.

"I can hear him tick," declared Button-Bright.

"You are quite the polished gentleman," said the Tin Woodman. "Stand up here beside the shaggy man, Tik-tok, and help receive the company."

Dorothy placed soft cushions in a corner for Billina and her chicks, and had just returned to the Throne and seated herself when the playing of the royal band outside the palace announced the approach of distinguished guests.

And my, how they did stare when the High Chamberlain threw open the doors and the visitors entered the Throne-Room!

First walked a gingerbread man neatly formed and baked to a lovely brown tint. He wore a silk hat and carried a candy cane prettily striped with red and yellow. His shirt-front and cuffs were white frosting, and the buttons on his coat were licorice drops.

Behind the gingerbread man came a child with flaxen hair and merry blue eyes, dressed in white pajamas, with sandals on the soles of its pretty bare feet. The child looked around smiling and thrust its hands into the pockets of the pajamas. Close after it came a big rubber bear, walking erect on its hind feet. The bear had twinkling black eyes, and its body looked as if it had been pumped full of air.

Following these curious visitors were two tall, thin men and two short, fat men, all four dressed in gorgeous uniforms.

Ozma's High Chamberlain now hurried forward to announce the names of the new arrivals, calling out in a loud voice:

"His Gracious and Most Edible Majesty, King Dough the First, Ruler of the Two Kingdoms of Hiland and Loland. Also the Head Boolywag of his Majesty, known as Chick the Cherub, and their faithful friend Para Bruin, the rubber bear."

These great personages bowed low as their names were called, and Dorothy hastened to introduce them to the assembled company. They were the first foreign arrivals, and the friends of Princess Ozma were polite to them and tried to make them feel that they were welcome.

Chick the Cherub shook hands with every one, including Billina, and was so joyous and frank and full of good spirits that John Dough's Head Booleywag at once became a prime favorite.

"Is it a boy or a girl?" whispered Dorothy.

"Don't know," said Button-Bright.

"Goodness me! what a queer lot of people you are," exclaimed the rubber bear, looking at the assembled company.

"So're you," said Button-Bright, gravely. "Is King Dough good to eat?"

"He's too good to eat," laughed Chick the Cherub.

"I hope none of you are fond of gingerbread," said the King, rather anxiously.

"We should never think of eating our visitors, if we were," declared the Scarecrow; "so please do not worry, for you will be perfectly safe while you remain in Oz."

"Why do they call you Chick?" the Yellow Hen asked the child.

"Because I'm an Incubator Baby, and never had any parents," replied the Head Booleywag.

"My chicks have a parent, and I'm it," said Billina.

"I'm glad of that," answered the Cherub, "because they'll have more fun worrying you than if they were brought up in an Incubator. The Incubator never worries, you know."

King John Dough had brought for Ozma's birthday present a lovely gingerbread crown, with rows of small pearls around it and a fine big pearl in each of its five points. After this had been received by Dorothy with proper thanks and placed on the table with the other presents, the visitors from Hiland and Loland were escorted to their rooms by the High Chamberlain.

They had no sooner departed than the band before the palace began to play again, announcing more arrivals, and as these were doubtless from foreign parts the High Chamberlain hurried back to receive them in his most official manner.

Chapter 22 - Important Arrivals

First entered a band of Ryls from the Happy Valley, all merry little sprites like fairy elves. A dozen crooked Knooks followed from the great Forest of Burzee. They had long whiskers and pointed caps and curling toes, yet were no taller than Button-Bright's shoulder. With this group came a man so easy to recognize and so important and dearly beloved throughout the known world, that all present rose to their feet and bowed their heads in respectful homage, even before the High Chamberlain knelt to announce his name.

"The most Mighty and Loyal Friend of Children, His Supreme Highness—Santa Claus!" said the Chamberlain, in an awed voice.

"Well, well, well! Glad to see you—glad to meet you all!" cried Santa Claus, briskly, as he trotted up the long room.

He was round as an apple, with a fresh rosy face, laughing eyes, and a bushy beard as white as snow. A red cloak trimmed with beautiful ermine hung from his shoulders and upon his back was a basket filled with pretty presents for the Princess Ozma.

"Hello, Dorothy; still having adventures?" he asked in his jolly way, as he took the girl's hand in both his own.

"How did you know my name, Santa?" she replied, feeling more shy in the presence of this immortal saint than she ever had before in her young life.

"Why, don't I see you every Christmas Eve, when you're asleep?" he rejoined, pinching her blushing cheek.

"Oh, do you?"

"And here's Button-Bright, I declare!" cried Santa Claus, holding up the boy to kiss him. "What a long way from home you are; dear me!"

"Do you know Button-Bright, too?" questioned Dorothy, eagerly.

"Indeed I do. I've visited his home several Christmas Eves."

"And do you know his father?" asked the girl.

"Certainly, my dear. Who else do you suppose brings him his Christmas neckties and stockings?" with a sly wink at the Wizard.

"Then where does he live? We're just crazy to know, 'cause Button-Bright's lost," she said.

Santa laughed and laid his finger aside of his nose as if thinking what to reply. He leaned over and whispered something in the Wizard's ear, at which the Wizard smiled and nodded as if he understood.

Now Santa Claus spied Polychrome, and trotted over to where she stood.

"Seems to me the Rainbow's Daughter is farther from home than any of you," he observed, looking at the pretty maiden admiringly. "I'll have to tell your father where you are, Polly, and send him to get you."

"Please do, dear Santa Claus," implored the little maid, beseechingly.

"But just now we must all have a jolly good time at Ozma's party," said the old gentleman, turning to put his presents on the table with the others already there. "It isn't often I find time to leave my castle, as you know; but Ozma invited me and I just couldn't help coming to celebrate the happy occasion."

"I'm so glad!" exclaimed Dorothy.

"These are my Ryls," pointing to the little sprites squatting around him. "Their business is to paint the colors of the flowers when they bud and bloom; but I brought the merry fellows along to see Oz, and they've left their paint-pots behind them. Also I brought these crooked Knooks, whom I love. My dears, the Knooks are much nicer than they look, for their duty is to water and care for the young trees of the forest, and they do their work faithfully and well. It's hard work, though, and it makes my Knooks crooked and gnarled, like the trees themselves; but their hearts are big and kind, as are the hearts of all who do good in our beautiful world."

"I've read of the Ryls and Knooks," said Dorothy, looking upon these little workers with interest.

Santa Claus turned to talk with the Scarecrow and the Tin Woodman, and he also said a kind word to the shaggy man, and afterward went away to ride the Saw-Horse around the Emerald City. "For," said he, "I must see all the grand sights while I am here and have the chance, and Ozma has promised to let me ride the Saw-Horse because I'm getting fat and short of breath."

"Where are your reindeer?" asked Polychrome.

"I left them at home, for it is too warm for them in this sunny country," he answered. "They're used to winter weather when they travel."

In a flash he was gone, and the Ryls and Knooks with him; but they could all hear the golden hoofs of the Saw-Horse ringing on the marble pavement outside, as he pranced away with his noble rider.

Presently the band played again, and the High Chamberlain announced:

"Her Gracious Majesty, the Queen of Merryland."

They looked earnestly to discover whom this queen might be, and saw advancing up the room an exquisite wax doll dressed in dainty fluffs and ruffles and spangled gown. She was almost as big as Button-Bright, and her cheeks and mouth and eyebrow were prettily painted in delicate colors. Her blue eyes stared a bit, being of glass, yet the expression upon her Majesty's face was quite pleasant and decidedly winning. With the Queen of Merryland were four wooden soldiers, two stalking ahead of her with much dignity and two following behind, like a royal bodyguard. The soldiers were painted in bright colors and carried wooden guns, and after them came a fat little man who attracted attention at once, although he seemed modest and retiring. For he was made of candy, and carried a tin sugar-sifter filled with powdered sugar, with which he dusted himself frequently so that he wouldn't stick to things if he touched them. The High Chamberlain had called him "The Candy Man of Merryland," and Dorothy saw that one of his thumbs looked as if it had been bitten off by some one who was fond of candy and couldn't resist the temptation.

The wax doll Queen spoke prettily to Dorothy and the others, and sent her loving greetings to Ozma before she retired to the rooms prepared for her. She had brought a birthday present wrapped in tissue paper and tied with pink and blue ribbons, and one of the wooden soldiers placed it on the table with the other gifts. But the Candy Man did not go to his room, because he said he preferred to stay and talk with the Scarecrow and Tik-tok and the Wizard and Tin Woodman, whom he declared the queerest people he had ever met. Button-Bright was glad the Candy Man stayed in the Throne Room, because the boy thought this guest smelled deliciously of wintergreen and maple sugar.

The Braided Man now entered the room, having been fortunate enough to receive an invitation to the Princess Ozma's party. He was from a cave halfway between the Invisible Valley and the Country of the Gargoyles, and his hair and whiskers were so long that he was obliged to plait them into many braids that hung to his feet, and every braid was tied with a bow of colored ribbon.

"I've brought Princess Ozma a box of flutters for her birthday," said the Braided Man, earnestly; "and I hope she will like them, for they are the finest quality I have ever made."

"I'm sure she will be greatly pleased," said Dorothy, who remembered the Braided Man well; and the Wizard introduced the guest to the rest of the company and made him sit down in a chair and keep quiet, for, if allowed, he would talk continually about his flutters.

The band then played a welcome to another set of guests, and into the Throne-Room swept the handsome and stately Queen of Ev. Beside her was young King Evardo, and following them came the entire royal family of five Princesses and four Princes of Ev. The Kingdom of Ev lay just across the Deadly Desert to the North of Oz, and once Ozma and her people had rescued the Queen of Ev and her ten children from the Nome King, who had enslaved them. Dorothy had been present on this adventure, so she greeted the royal family cordially; and all the visitors were delighted to meet the little Kansas girl again. They knew Tik-tok and Billina, too, and the Scarecrow and Tin Woodman, as well as the Lion and Tiger; so there was a joyful reunion, as you may imagine, and it was fully an hour before the Queen and her train retired to their rooms. Perhaps they would not have gone then had not the band begun to play to announce new arrivals; but before they left the great Throne-Room King Evardo added to Ozma's birthday presents a diadem of diamonds set in radium.

The next comer proved to be King Renard of Foxville; or King Dox, as he preferred to be called. He was magnificently dressed in a new feather costume and wore white kid mittens over his paws and a flower in his button-hole and had his hair parted in the middle.

King Dox thanked Dorothy fervently for getting him the invitation to come to Oz, which he all his life longed to visit. He strutted around rather absurdly as he was introduced to all the famous people assembled in the Throne-Room, and when he learned that Dorothy was a Princess of Oz the Fox King insisted on kneeling at her feet and afterward retired backward—a dangerous thing to do, as he might have stubbed his paw and tumbled over.

No sooner was he gone than the blasts of bugles and clatter of drums and cymbals announced important visitors, and the High Chamberlain assumed his most dignified tone as he threw open the door and said proudly:

"Her Sublime and Resplendent Majesty, Queen Zixi of Ix! His Serene and Tremendous Majesty, King Bud of Noland. Her Royal Highness, the Princess Fluff."

That three such high and mighty royal personages should arrive at once was enough to make Dorothy and her companions grow solemn and assume their best company manners; but when the exquisite beauty of Queen Zixi met their eyes they thought they had never beheld anything so charming. Dorothy decided that Zixi must be about sixteen years old, but the Wizard whispered to her that this wonderful queen had lived thousands of years, but knew the secret of remaining always fresh and beautiful.

King Bud of Noland and his dainty fair-haired sister, the Princess Fluff, were friends of Zixi, as their kingdoms were adjoining, so they had traveled together from their far-off domains to do honor to Ozma of Oz on the occasion of her birthday. They brought many splendid gifts; so the table was now fairly loaded down with presents.

Dorothy and Polly loved the Princess Fluff the moment they saw her, and little King Bud was so frank and boyish that Button-Bright accepted him as a chum at once and did not want him to go away. But it was after noon now, and the royal guests must prepare their toilets for the grand banquet at which they were to assemble that evening to meet the reigning Princess of this Fairyland; so Queen Zixi was shown to her room by a troop of maidens led by Jellia Jamb, and Bud and Fluff presently withdrew to their own apartments.

"My! what a big party Ozma is going to have," exclaimed Dorothy. "I guess the palace will be chock full, Button-Bright; don't you think so?"

"Don't know," said the boy.

"But we must go to our rooms, pretty soon, to dress for the banquet," continued the girl.

"I don't have to dress," said the Candy Man from Merryland. "All I need do is to dust myself with fresh sugar."

"Tik-tok always wears the same suits of clothes," said the Tin Woodman; "and so does our friend the Scarecrow."

"My feathers are good enough for any occasion," cried Billina, from her corner.

"Then I shall leave you four to welcome any new guests that come," said Dorothy; "for Button-Bright and I must look our very best at Ozma's banquet."

"Who is still to come?" asked the Scarecrow.

"Well, there's King Kik-a-bray of Dunkiton, and Johnny Dooit, and the Good Witch of the North. But Johnny Dooit may not get here until late, he's so very busy."

"We will receive them and give them a proper welcome," promised the Scarecrow. "So run along, little Dorothy, and get yourself dressed."

Chapter 23 - The Grand Banquet

I wish I could tell you how fine the company was that assembled that evening at Ozma's royal banquet. A long table was spread in the center of the great dining-hall of the palace and the splendor of the decorations and the blaze of lights and jewels was acknowledged to be the most magnificent sight that any of the guests had ever seen.

The jolliest person present, as well as the most important, was of course old Santa Claus; so he was given the seat of honor at one end of the table while at the other end sat Princess Ozma, the hostess.

John Dough, Queen Zixi, King Bud, the Queen of Ev and her son Evardo, and the Queen of Merryland had golden thrones to sit in, while the others were supplied with beautiful chairs.

At the upper end of the banquet room was a separate table provided for the animals. Toto sat at one end of this table with a bib tied around his neck and a silver platter to eat from. At the other end was placed a small stand, with a low rail around the edge of it, for Billina and her chicks. The rail kept the ten little Dorothys from falling off the stand, while the Yellow Hen could easily reach over and take her food from her tray upon the table. At other places sat the Hungry Tiger, the Cowardly Lion, the Saw-Horse, the Rubber Bear, the Fox King and the Donkey King; they made quite a company of animals.

At the lower end of the great room was another table, at which sat the Ryls and Knooks who had come with Santa Claus, the wooden soldiers who had come with the Queen of Merryland, and the Hilanders and Lolanders who had come with John Dough. Here were also seated the officers of the royal palace and of Ozma's army.

The splendid costumes of those at the three tables made a gorgeous and glittering display that no one present was ever likely to forget; perhaps there has never been in any part of the world at any time another assemblage of such wonderful people as that which gathered this evening to honor the birthday of the Ruler of Oz.

When all members of ethe company were in their places an orchestra of five hundred pieces, in a balcony overlooking the banquet room, began to play sweet and delightful music. Then a door draped with royal green opened, and in came the fair and girlish Princess Ozma, who now greeted her guests in person for the first time.

As she stood by her throne at the head of the banquet table every eye was turned eagerly upon the lovely Princess, who was as dignified as she was bewitching, and who smiled upon all her old and new friends in a way that touched their hearts and brought an answering smile to every face.

Each guest had been served with a crystal goblet filled with lacasa, which is a sort of nectar famous in Oz and nicer to drink than soda-water or lemonade. Santa now made a pretty speech in verse, congratulating Ozma on having a birthday, and asking every one present to drink to the health and happiness of their dearly beloved hostess. This was done with great enthusiasm by those who were made so they could drink at all, and those who could not drink politely touched the rims of their goblets to their lips. All seated themselves at the tables and the servants of the Princess began serving the feast.

I am quite sure that only in Fairyland could such a delicious repast be prepared. The dishes were of precious metals set with brilliant jewels and the good things to eat which were placed upon them were countless in number and of exquisite flavor. Several present, such as the Candy Man, the Rubber Bear, Tik-tok, and the Scarecrow, were not made so they could eat, and the Queen of Merryland contented herself with a small dish of sawdust; but these enjoyed the pomp and glitter of the gorgeous scene as much as did those who feasted.

The Woggle-Bug read his "Ode to Ozma," which was written in very good rhythm and was well received by the company. The Wizard added to the entertainment by making a big pie appear before Dorothy, and when the little girl cut the pie the nine tiny piglets leaped out of it and danced around the table, while the orchestra played a merry tune. This amused the company very much, but they were even more pleased when Polychrome, whose hunger had been easily satisfied, rose from the table and performed her graceful and bewildering Rainbow Dance for them. When it was ended, the people clapped their hands and the animals clapped their paws, while Billina cackled and the Donkey King brayed approval.

Johnny Dooit was present, and of course he proved he could do wonders in the way of eating, as well as in everything else that he undertook to do; the Tin Woodman sang a love song, every one joining in the chorus; and the wooden soldiers from Merryland gave an exhibition of a lightning drill with their wooden muskets; the Ryls and Knooks danced the Fairy Circle; and the Rubber Bear bounced himself all around the room. There was laughter and merriment on every side, and everybody was having a royal good time. Button-Bright was so excited and interested that he paid little attention to his fine dinner and a great deal of attention to his queer companions; and perhaps he was wise to do this, because he could eat at any other time.

The feasting and merrymaking continued until late in the evening, when they separated to meet again the next morning and take part in the birthday celebration, to which this royal banquet was merely the introduction.

Chapter 24 - The Birthday Celebration

A clear, perfect day, with a gentle breeze and a sunny sky, greeted Princess Ozma as she wakened next morning, the anniversary of her birth. While it was yet early all the city was astir and crowds of people came from all parts of the Land of Oz to witness the festivities in honor of their girl Ruler's birthday.

The noted visitors from foreign countries, who had all been transported to the Emerald City by means of the Magic Belt, were as much a show to the Ozites as were their own familiar celebrities, and the streets leading from the royal palace to the jeweled gates were thronged with men, women, and children to see the procession as it passed out to the green fields where the ceremonies were to take place.

And what a great procession it was!

First came a thousand young girls—the prettiest in the land—dressed in white muslin, with green sashes and hair ribbons, bearing green baskets of red roses. As they walked they scattered these flowers upon the marble pavements, so that the way was carpeted thick with roses for the procession to walk upon.

Then came the Rulers of the four Kingdoms of Oz: the Emperor of the Winkies, the Monarch of the Munchkins, the King of the Quadlings and the Sovereign of the Gillikins, each wearing a long chain of emeralds around his neck to show that he was a vassal of the Ruler of the Emerald City.

Next marched the Emerald City Cornet Band, clothed in green-and-gold uniforms and playing the "Ozma Two-Step." The Royal Army of Oz followed, consisting of twenty-seven officers, from the Captain-General down to the Lieutenants. There were no privates in Ozma's Army because soldiers were not needed to fight battles, but only to look important, and an officer always looks more imposing than a private.

While the people cheered and waved their hats and handkerchiefs, there came walking the Royal Princess Ozma, looking so pretty and sweet that it is no wonder her people love her so dearly. She had decided she would not ride in her chariot that day, as she preferred to walk in the procession with her favored subjects and her guests. Just in front of her trotted the living Blue Bear Rug owned by old Dyna, which wobbled clumsily on its four feet because there was nothing but the skin to support them, with a stuffed head at one end and a stubby tail at the other. But whenever Ozma paused in her walk the Bear Rug would flop down flat upon the ground for the princess to stand upon until she resumed her progress.

Following the Princess stalked her two enormous beasts, the Cowardly Lion and the Hungry Tiger, and even if the Army had not been there these two would have been powerful enough to guard their mistress from any harm.

Next marched the invited guests, who were loudly cheered by the people of Oz along the road, and were therefore obliged to bow to right and left almost every step of the way. First was Santa Claus, who, because he was fat and not used to walking, rode the wonderful Saw-Horse. The merry old gentleman had a basket of small toys with him, and he tossed the toys one by one to the children as he passed by. His Ryls and Knooks marched close behind him.

Queen Zixi of Ix came after; then John Dough and the Cherub, with the rubber bear named Para Bruin strutting between them on its hind legs; then the Queen of Merryland, escorted by her wooden soldiers; then King Bud of Noland and his sister, the Princess Fluff; then the Queen of Ev and her ten royal children; then the Braided Man and the Candy Man, side by side; then King Dox of Foxville and King Kik-a-bray of Dunkiton, who by this time had become good friends; and finally Johnny Dooit, in his leather apron, smoking his long pipe.

These wonderful personages were not more heartily cheered by the people than were those who followed after them in the procession. Dorothy was a general favorite, and she walked arm in arm with the Scarecrow, who was beloved by all. Then came Polychrome and Button-Bright, and the people loved the Rainbow's pretty Daughter and the beautiful blue-eyed boy as soon as they saw them. The shaggy man in his shaggy new suit attracted much attention because he was such a novelty. With regular steps tramped the machine-man Tik-tok, and there was more cheering when the Wizard of Oz followed in the procession. The Woggle-Bug and Jack Pumpkinhead were next, and behind them Glinda the Sorceress and the Good Witch of the North. Finally came Billina, with her brood of chickens to whom she clucked anxiously to keep them together and to hasten them along so they would not delay the procession.

Another band followed, this time the Tin Band of the Emperor of the Winkies, playing a beautiful march called, "There's No Plate Like Tin." Then came the servants of the Royal Palace, in a long line, and behind them all the people joined the procession and marched away through the emerald gates and out upon the broad green.

Here had been erected a splendid pavilion, with a grandstand big enough to seat all the royal party and those who had taken part in the procession. Over the pavilion, which was of green silk and cloth of gold, countless banners waved in the breeze. Just in front of this, and connected with it by a runway had been built a broad platform, so that all the spectators could see plainly the entertainment provided for them.

The Wizard now became Master of Ceremonies, as Ozma had placed the conduct of the performance in his hands. After the people had all congregated about the platform and the royal party and the visitors were seated in the grandstand, the Wizard skillfully performed some feats of juggling glass balls and lighted candles. He tossed a dozen or so of them high in the air and caught them one by one as they came down, without missing any.

Then he introduced the Scarecrow, who did a sword-swallowing act that aroused much interest. After this the Tin Woodman gave an exhibition of Swinging the Axe, which he made to whirl around him so rapidly that the eye could scarcely follow the motion of the gleaming blade. Glinda the Sorceress then stepped upon the platform, and by her magic made a big tree grow in the middle of the space, made blossoms appear upon the tree, and made the blossoms become delicious fruit called tamornas, and so great was the quantity of fruit produced that when the servants climbed the tree and tossed it down to the crowd, there was enough to satisfy every person present.

Para Bruin, the rubber bear, climbed to a limb of the big tree, rolled himself into a ball, and dropped to the platform, whence he bounded up again to the limb. He repeated this bouncing act several times, to the great delight of all the children present. After he had finished, and bowed, and returned to his seat, Glinda waved her wand and the tree disappeared; but its fruit still remained to be eaten.

The Good Witch of the North amused the people by transforming ten stones into ten birds, the ten birds into ten lambs, and the ten lambs into ten little girls, who gave a pretty dance and were then transformed into ten stones again, just as they were in the beginning.

Johnny Dooit next came on the platform with his tool-chest, and in a few minutes built a great flying machine; then put his chest in the machine and the whole thing flew away together—Johnny and all—after he had bid good-bye to those present and thanked the Princess for her hospitality.

The Wizard then announced the last act of all, which was considered really wonderful. He had invented a machine to blow huge soap-bubbles, as big as balloons, and this machine was hidden under the platform so that only the rim of the big clay pipe to produce the bubbles showed above the flooring. The tank of soapsuds, and the air-pumps to inflate the bubbles, were out of sight beneath, so that when the bubbles began to grow upon the floor of the platform it really seemed like magic to the people of Oz, who knew nothing about even the common soap-bubbles that our children blow with a penny clay pipe and a basin of soap-and-water.

The Wizard had invented another thing. Usually, soap-bubbles are frail and burst easily, lasting only a few moments as they float in the air; but the Wizard added a sort of glue to his soapsuds, which made his bubbles tough; and, as the glue dried rapidly when exposed to the air, the Wizard's bubbles were strong enough to float for hours without breaking.

He began by blowing—by means of his machinery and air-pumps—several large bubbles which he allowed to float upward into the sky, where the sunshine fell upon them and gave them iridescent hues that were most beautiful. This aroused much wonder and delight because it was a new amusement to every one present—except perhaps Dorothy and Button-Bright, and even they had never seen such big, strong bubbles before.

The Wizard then blew a bunch of small bubbles and afterward blew a big bubble around them so they were left in the center of it; then he allowed the whole mass of pretty globes to float into the air and disappear in the far distant sky.

"That is really fine!" declared Santa Claus, who loved toys and pretty things. "I think, Mr. Wizard, I shall have you blow a bubble around me; then I can float away home and see the country spread out beneath me as I travel. There isn't a spot on earth that I haven't visited, but I usually go in the night-time, riding behind my swift reindeer. Here is a good chance to observe the country by daylight, while I am riding slowly and at my ease."

"Do you think you will be able to guide the bubble?" asked the Wizard.

"Oh yes; I know enough magic to do that," replied Santa Claus. "You blow the bubble, with me inside of it, and I'll be sure to get home in safety."

"Please send me home in a bubble, too!" begged the Queen of Merryland.

"Very well, madam; you shall try the journey first," politely answered old Santa.

The pretty wax doll bade good-bye to the Princess Ozma and the others and stood on the platform while the Wizard blew a big soap-bubble around her. When completed, he allowed the bubble to float slowly upward, and there could be seen the little Queen of Merryland standing in the middle of it and blowing kisses from her fingers to those below. The bubble took a southerly direction, quickly floating out of sight.

"That's a very nice way to travel," said Princess Fluff. "I'd like to go home in a bubble, too."

So the Wizard blew a big bubble around Princess Fluff, and another around King Bud, her brother, and a third one around Queen Zixi; and soon these three bubbles had mounted into the sky and were floating off in a group in the direction of the kingdom of Noland.

The success of these ventures induced the other guests from foreign lands to undertake bubble journeys, also; so the Wizard put them one by one inside his bubbles, and Santa Claus directed the way they should go, because he knew exactly where everybody lived.

Finally, Button-Bright said:

"I want to go home, too."

"Why, so you shall!" cried Santa; "for I'm sure your father and mother will be glad to see you again. Mr. Wizard, please blow a big, fine bubble for Button-Bright to ride in, and I'll agree to send him home to his family as safe as safe can be."

"I'm sorry," said Dorothy with a sigh, for she was fond of her little comrade; "but p'raps it's best for Button-Bright to get home; 'cause his folks must be worrying just dreadful."

She kissed the boy, and Ozma kissed him, too, and all the others waved their hands and said good-bye and wished him a pleasant journey.

"Are you glad to leave us, dear?" asked Dorothy, a little wistfully.

"Don't know," said Button-Bright.

He sat down cross-legged on the platform, with his sailor hat tipped back on his head, and the Wizard blew a beautiful bubble all around him.

A minute later it had mounted into the sky, sailing toward the west, and the last they saw of Button-Bright he was still sitting in the middle of the shining globe and waving his sailor hat at those below.

"Will you ride in a bubble, or shall I send you and Toto home by means of the Magic Belt?" the Princess asked Dorothy.

"Guess I'll use the Belt," replied the little girl. "I'm sort of 'fraid of those bubbles."

"Bow-wow!" said Toto, approvingly. He loved to bark at the bubbles as they sailed away, but he didn't care to ride in one.

Santa Claus decided to go next. He thanked Ozma for her hospitality and wished her many happy returns of the day. Then the Wizard blew a bubble around his chubby little body and smaller bubbles around each of his Ryls and Knooks.

As the kind and generous friend of children mounted into the air the people all cheered at the top of their voices, for they loved Santa Claus dearly; and the little man heard them through the walls of his bubble and waved his hands in return as he smiled down upon them. The band played bravely while every one watched the bubble until it was completely out of sight.

"How 'bout you, Polly?" Dorothy asked her friend. "Are you 'fraid of bubbles, too?"

"No," answered Polychrome, smiling; "but Santa Claus promised to speak to my father as he passed through the sky. So perhaps I shall get home an easier way."

Indeed, the little maid had scarcely made this speech when a sudden radiance filled the air, and while the people looked on in wonder the end of a gorgeous rainbow slowly settled down upon the platform.

With a glad cry, the Rainbow's Daughter sprang from her seat and danced along the curve of the bow, mounting gradually upward, while the folds of her gauzy gown whirled and floated around her like a cloud and blended with the colors of the rainbow itself.

"Good-bye Ozma! Good-bye Dorothy!" cried a voice they knew belonged to Polychrome; but now the little maiden's form had melted wholly into the rainbow, and their eyes could no longer see her.

Suddenly, the end of the rainbow lifted and its colors slowly faded like mist before a breeze. Dorothy sighed deeply and turned to Ozma.

"I'm sorry to lose Polly," she said; "but I guess she's better off with her father; 'cause even the Land of Oz couldn't be like home to a cloud fairy."

"No indeed," replied the Princess; "but it has been delightful for us to know Polychrome for a little while, and—who knows?—perhaps we may meet the Rainbow's Daughter again, some day."

The entertainment being now ended, all left the pavilion and formed their gay procession back to the Emerald City again. Of Dorothy's recent traveling companions only Toto and the shaggy man remained, and Ozma had decided to allow the latter to live in Oz for a time, at least. If he proved honest and true she promised to let him live there always, and the shaggy man was anxious to earn this reward.

They had a nice quiet dinner together and passed a pleasant evening with the Scarecrow, the Tin Woodman, Tik-tok, and the Yellow Hen for company.

When Dorothy bade them good-night, she kissed them all good-bye at the same time. For Ozma had agreed that while Dorothy slept she and Toto should be transported by means of the Magic Belt to her own little bed in the Kansas farm-house and the little girl laughed as she thought how astonished Uncle Henry and Aunt Em would be when she came down to breakfast with them next morning.

Quite content to have had so pleasant an adventure, and a little tired by all the day's busy scenes, Dorothy clasped Toto in her arms and lay down upon the pretty white bed in her room in Ozma's royal palace.

Presently she was sound asleep.

The End

The Emerald City of Oz

Preface

Perhaps I should admit on the title page that this book is "By L. Frank Baum and his correspondents," for I have used many suggestions conveyed to me in letters from children. Once on a time I really imagined myself "an author of fairy tales," but now I am merely an editor or private secretary for a host of youngsters whose ideas I am requested to weave into the thread of my stories.

These ideas are often clever. They are also logical and interesting. So I have used them whenever I could find an opportunity, and it is but just that I acknowledge my indebtedness to my little friends.

My, what imaginations these children have developed! Sometimes I am fairly astounded by their daring and genius. There will be no lack of fairy-tale authors in the future, I am sure. My readers have told me what to do with Dorothy, and Aunt Em and Uncle Henry, and I have obeyed their mandates. They have also given me a variety of subjects to write about in the future: enough, in fact, to keep me busy for some time. I am very proud of this alliance. Children love these stories because children have helped to create them. My readers know what they want and realize that I try to please them. The result is very satisfactory to the publishers, to me, and (I am quite sure) to the children.

I hope, my dears, it will be a long time before we are obliged to dissolve partnership.

L. FRANK BAUM.
Coronado, 1910

LIST OF CHAPTERS

Chapter 1 - How the Nome King became Angry

The Nome King was in an angry mood, and at such times he was very disagreeable.

Every one kept away from him, even his Chief Steward Kaliko.

Therefore the King stormed and raved all by himself, walking up and down in his jewel-studded cavern and getting angrier all the time. Then he remembered that it was no fun being angry unless he had some one to frighten and make miserable, and he rushed to his big gong and made it clatter as loud as he could.

In came the Chief Steward, trying not to show the Nome King how frightened he was.

"Send the Chief Counselor here!" shouted the angry monarch.

Kaliko ran out as fast as his spindle legs could carry his fat, round body, and soon the Chief Counselor entered the cavern. The King scowled and said to him:

"I'm in great trouble over the loss of my Magic Belt. Every little while I want to do something magical, and find I can't because the Belt is gone. That makes me angry, and when I'm angry I can't have a good time. Now, what do you advise?"

"Some people," said the Chief Counselor, "enjoy getting angry."

"But not all the time," declared the King. "To be angry once in a while is really good fun, because it makes others so miserable. But to be angry morning, noon and night, as I am, grows monotonous and prevents my gaining any other pleasure in life. Now what do you advise?"

"Why, if you are angry because you want to do magical things and can't, and if you don't want to get angry at all, my advice is not to want to do magical things."

Hearing this, the King glared at his Counselor with a furious expression and tugged at his own long white whiskers until he pulled them so hard that he yelled with pain.

"You are a fool!" he exclaimed.

"I share that honor with your Majesty," said the Chief Counselor.

The King roared with rage and stamped his foot.

"Ho, there, my guards!" he cried. "Ho" is a royal way of saying, "Come here." So, when the guards had hoed, the King said to them:

"Take this Chief Counselor and throw him away."

Then the guards took the Chief Counselor, and bound him with chains to prevent his struggling, and threw him away. And the King paced up and down his cavern more angry than before.

Finally he rushed to his big gong and made it clatter like a fire alarm. Kaliko appeared again, trembling and white with fear.

"Fetch my pipe!" yelled the King.

"Your pipe is already here, your Majesty," replied Kaliko.

"Then get my tobacco!" roared the King.

"The tobacco is in your pipe, your Majesty," returned the Steward.

"Then bring a live coal from the furnace!" commanded the King.

"The tobacco is lighted, and your Majesty is already smoking your pipe," answered the Steward.

"Why, so I am!" said the King, who had forgotten this fact; "but you are very rude to remind me of it."

"I am a lowborn, miserable villain," declared the Chief Steward, humbly.

The Nome King could think of nothing to say next, so he puffed away at his pipe and paced up and down the room. Finally, he remembered how angry he was, and cried out:

"What do you mean, Kaliko, by being so contented when your monarch is unhappy?"

"What makes you unhappy?" asked the Steward.

"I've lost my Magic Belt. A little girl named Dorothy, who was here with Ozma of Oz, stole my Belt and carried it away with her," said the King, grinding his teeth with rage.

"She captured it in a fair fight," Kaliko ventured to say.

"But I want it! I must have it! Half my power is gone with that Belt!" roared the King.

"You will have to go to the Land of Oz to recover it, and your Majesty can't get to the Land of Oz in any possible way," said the Steward, yawning because he had been on duty ninety-six hours, and was sleepy.

"Why not?" asked the King.

"Because there is a deadly desert all around that fairy country, which no one is able to cross. You know that fact as well as I do, your Majesty. Never mind the lost Belt. You have plenty of power left, for you rule this underground kingdom like a tyrant, and thousands of Nomes obey your commands. I advise you to drink a glass of melted silver, to quiet your nerves, and then go to bed."

The King grabbed a big ruby and threw it at Kaliko's head. The Steward ducked to escape the heavy jewel, which crashed against the door just over his left ear.

"Get out of my sight! Vanish! Go away—and send General Blug here," screamed the Nome King.

Kaliko hastily withdrew, and the Nome King stamped up and down until the General of his armies appeared.

This Nome was known far and wide as a terrible fighter and a cruel, desperate commander. He had fifty thousand Nome soldiers, all well drilled, who feared nothing but their stern master. Yet General Blug was a trifle uneasy when he arrived and saw how angry the Nome King was.

"Ha! So you're here!" cried the King.

"So I am," said the General.

"March your army at once to the Land of Oz, capture and destroy the Emerald City, and bring back to me my Magic Belt!" roared the King.

"You're crazy," calmly remarked the General.

"What's that? What's that? What's that?" And the Nome King danced around on his pointed toes, he was so enraged.

"You don't know what you're talking about," continued the General, seating himself upon a large cut diamond. "I advise you to stand in a corner and count sixty before you speak again. By that time you may be more sensible."

The King looked around for something to throw at General Blug, but as nothing was handy he began to consider that perhaps the man was right and he had been talking foolishly. So he merely threw himself into his glittering throne and tipped his crown over his ear and curled his feet up under him and glared wickedly at Blug.

"In the first place," said the General, "we cannot march across the deadly desert to the Land of Oz. And if we could, the Ruler of that country, Princess Ozma, has certain fairy powers that would render my army helpless. Had you not lost your Magic Belt we might have some chance of defeating Ozma; but the Belt is gone."

"I want it!" screamed the King. "I must have it."

"Well, then, let us try in a sensible way to get it," replied the General. "The Belt was captured by a little girl named Dorothy, who lives in Kansas, in the United States of America."

"But she left it in the Emerald City, with Ozma," declared the King.

"How do you know that?" asked the General.

"One of my spies, who is a Blackbird, flew over the desert to the Land of Oz, and saw the Magic Belt in Ozma's palace," replied the King with a groan.

"Now that gives me an idea," said General Blug, thoughtfully. "There are two ways to get to the Land of Oz without traveling across the sandy desert."

"What are they?" demanded the King, eagerly.

"One way is OVER the desert, through the air; and the other way is UNDER the desert, through the earth."

Hearing this the Nome King uttered a yell of joy and leaped from his throne, to resume his wild walk up and down the cavern.

"That's it, Blug!" he shouted. "That's the idea, General! I'm King of the Under World, and my subjects are all miners. I'll make a secret tunnel under the desert to the Land of Oz—yes! right up to the Emerald City—and you will march your armies there and capture the whole country!"

"Softly, softly, your Majesty. Don't go too fast," warned the General. "My Nomes are good fighters, but they are not strong enough to conquer the Emerald City."

"Are you sure?" asked the King.

"Absolutely certain, your Majesty."

"Then what am I to do?"

"Give up the idea and mind your own business," advised the General. "You have plenty to do trying to rule your underground kingdom."

"But I want the Magic Belt—and I'm going to have it!" roared the Nome King.

"I'd like to see you get it," replied the General, laughing maliciously.

The King was by this time so exasperated that he picked up his scepter, which had a heavy ball, made from a sapphire, at the end of it, and threw it with all his force at General Blug. The sapphire hit the General upon his forehead and knocked him flat upon the ground, where he lay motionless. Then the King rang his gong and told his guards to drag out the General and throw him away; which they did.

This Nome King was named Roquat the Red, and no one loved him. He was a bad man and a powerful monarch, and he had resolved to destroy the Land of Oz and its magnificent Emerald City, to enslave Princess Ozma and little Dorothy and all the Oz people, and recover his Magic Belt. This same Belt had once enabled Roquat the Red to carry out many wicked plans; but that was before Ozma and her people marched to the underground cavern and captured it. The Nome King could not forgive Dorothy or Princess Ozma, and he had determined to be revenged upon them.

But they, for their part, did not know they had so dangerous an enemy. Indeed, Ozma and Dorothy had both almost forgotten that such a person as the Nome King yet lived under the mountains of the Land of Ev—which lay just across the deadly desert to the south of the Land of Oz.

An unsuspected enemy is doubly dangerous.

Chapter 2 - How Uncle Henry Got into Trouble

Dorothy Gale lived on a farm in Kansas, with her Aunt Em and her Uncle Henry.

It was not a big farm, nor a very good one, because sometimes the rain did not come when the crops needed it, and then everything withered and dried up. Once a cyclone had carried away Uncle Henry's house, so that he was obliged to build another; and as he was a poor man he had to mortgage his farm to get the money to pay for the new house. Then his health became bad and he was too feeble to work. The doctor ordered him to take a sea voyage and he went to Australia and took Dorothy with him. That cost a lot of money, too.

Uncle Henry grew poorer every year, and the crops raised on the farm only bought food for the family. Therefore the mortgage could not be paid. At last the banker who had loaned him the money said that if he did not pay on a certain day, his farm would be taken away from him.

This worried Uncle Henry a good deal, for without the farm he would have no way to earn a living. He was a good man, and worked in the field as hard as he could; and Aunt Em did all the housework, with Dorothy's help. Yet they did not seem to get along.

This little girl, Dorothy, was like dozens of little girls you know. She was loving and usually sweet-tempered, and had a round rosy face and earnest eyes. Life was a serious thing to Dorothy, and a wonderful thing, too, for she had encountered more strange adventures in her short life than many other girls of her age.

Aunt Em once said she thought the fairies must have marked Dorothy at her birth, because she had wandered into strange places and had always been protected by some unseen power. As for Uncle Henry, he thought his little niece merely a dreamer, as her dead mother had been, for he could not quite believe all the curious stories Dorothy told them of the Land of Oz, which she had several times visited. He did not think that she tried to deceive her uncle and aunt, but he imagined that she had dreamed all of those astonishing adventures, and that the dreams had been so real to her that she had come to believe them true.

Whatever the explanation might be, it was certain that Dorothy had been absent from her Kansas home for several long periods, always disappearing unexpectedly, yet always coming back safe and sound, with amazing tales of where she had been and the unusual people she had met. Her uncle and aunt listened to her stories eagerly and in spite of their doubts began to feel that the little girl had gained a lot of experience and wisdom that were unaccountable in this age, when fairies are supposed no longer to exist.

Most of Dorothy's stories were about the Land of Oz, with its beautiful Emerald City and a lovely girl Ruler named Ozma, who was the most faithful friend of the little Kansas girl. When Dorothy told about the riches of this fairy country Uncle Henry would sigh, for he knew that a single one of the great emeralds that were so common there would pay all his debts and leave his farm free. But Dorothy never brought any jewels home with her, so their poverty became greater every year.

When the banker told Uncle Henry that he must pay the money in thirty days or leave the farm, the poor man was in despair, as he knew he could not possibly get the money. So he told his wife, Aunt Em, of his trouble, and she first cried a little and then said that they must be brave and do the best they could, and go away somewhere and try to earn an honest living. But they were getting old and feeble and she feared that they could not take care of Dorothy as well as they had formerly done. Probably the little girl would also be obliged to go to work.

They did not tell their niece the sad news for several days, not wishing to make her unhappy; but one morning the little girl found Aunt Em softly crying while Uncle Henry tried to comfort her. Then Dorothy asked them to tell her what was the matter.

"We must give up the farm, my dear," replied her uncle sadly, "and wander away into the world to work for our living."

The girl listened quite seriously, for she had not known before how desperately poor they were.

"We don't mind for ourselves," said her aunt, stroking the little girl's head tenderly; "but we love you as if you were our own child, and we are heart-broken to think that you must also endure poverty, and work for a living before you have grown big and strong."

"What could I do to earn money?" asked Dorothy.

"You might do housework for some one, dear, you are so handy; or perhaps you could be a nurse-maid to little children. I'm sure I don't know exactly what you CAN do to earn money, but if your uncle and I are able to support you we will do it willingly, and send you to school. We fear, though, that we shall have much trouble in earning a living for ourselves. No one wants to employ old people who are broken down in health, as we are."

Dorothy smiled.

"Wouldn't it be funny," she said, "for me to do housework in Kansas, when I'm a Princess in the Land of Oz?"

"A Princess!" they both exclaimed, astonished.

"Yes; Ozma made me a Princess some time ago, and she has often begged me to come and live always in the Emerald City," said the child.

Her uncle and aunt looked at her in amazement. Then the man said:

"Do you suppose you could manage to return to your fairyland, my dear?"

"Oh yes," replied Dorothy; "I could do that easily."

"How?" asked Aunt Em.

"Ozma sees me every day at four o'clock, in her Magic Picture. She can see me wherever I am, no matter what I am doing. And at that time, if I make a certain secret sign, she will send for me by means of the Magic Belt, which I once captured from the Nome King. Then, in the wink of an eye, I shall be with Ozma in her palace."

The elder people remained silent for some time after Dorothy had spoken. Finally, Aunt Em said, with another sigh of regret:

"If that is the case, Dorothy, perhaps you'd better go and live in the Emerald City. It will break our hearts to lose you from our lives, but you will be so much better off with your fairy friends that it seems wisest and best for you to go."

"I'm not so sure about that," remarked Uncle Henry, shaking his gray head doubtfully. "These things all seem real to Dorothy, I know; but I'm afraid our little girl won't find her fairyland just what she had dreamed it to be. It would make me very unhappy to think that she was wandering among strangers who might be unkind to her."

Dorothy laughed merrily at this speech, and then she became very sober again, for she could see how all this trouble was worrying her aunt and uncle, and knew that unless she found a way to help them their future lives would be quite miserable and unhappy. She knew that she COULD help them. She had thought of a way already. Yet she did not tell them at once what it was, because she must ask Ozma's consent before she would be able to carry out her plans.

So she only said:

"If you will promise not to worry a bit about me, I'll go to the Land of Oz this very afternoon. And I'll make a promise, too; that you shall both see me again before the day comes when you must leave this farm."

"The day isn't far away, now," her uncle sadly replied. "I did not tell you of our trouble until I was obliged to, dear Dorothy, so the evil time is near at hand. But if you are quite sure your fairy friends will give you a home, it will be best for you to go to them, as your aunt says."

That was why Dorothy went to her little room in the attic that afternoon, taking with her a small dog named Toto. The dog had curly black hair and big brown eyes and loved Dorothy very dearly.

The child had kissed her uncle and aunt affectionately before she went upstairs, and now she looked around her little room rather wistfully, gazing at the simple trinkets and worn calico and gingham dresses, as if they were old friends. She was tempted at first to make a bundle of them, yet she knew very well that they would be of no use to her in her future life.

She sat down upon a broken-backed chair—the only one the room contained—and holding Toto in her arms waited patiently until the clock struck four.

Then she made the secret signal that had been agreed upon between her and Ozma.

Uncle Henry and Aunt Em waited downstairs. They were uneasy and a good deal excited, for this is a practical humdrum world, and it seemed to them quite impossible that their little niece could vanish from her home and travel instantly to fairyland.

So they watched the stairs, which seemed to be the only way that Dorothy could get out of the farmhouse, and they watched them a long time. They heard the clock strike four but there was no sound from above.

Half-past four came, and now they were too impatient to wait any longer. Softly, they crept up the stairs to the door of the little girl's room.

"Dorothy! Dorothy!" they called.

There was no answer.

They opened the door and looked in.

The room was empty.

Chapter 3 - How Ozma Granted Dorothy's Request

I suppose you have read so much about the magnificent Emerald City that there is little need for me to describe it here. It is the Capital City of the Land of Oz, which is justly considered the most attractive and delightful fairyland in all the world.

The Emerald City is built all of beautiful marbles in which are set a profusion of emeralds, every one exquisitely cut and of very great size. There are other jewels used in the decorations inside the houses and palaces, such as rubies, diamonds, sapphires, amethysts and turquoises. But in the streets and upon the outside of the buildings only emeralds appear, from which circumstance the place is named the Emerald City of Oz. It has nine thousand, six hundred and fifty-four buildings, in which lived fifty-seven thousand three hundred and eighteen people, up to the time my story opens.

All the surrounding country, extending to the borders of the desert which enclosed it upon every side, was full of pretty and comfortable farmhouses, in which resided those inhabitants of Oz who preferred country to city life.

Altogether there were more than half a million people in the Land of Oz—although some of them, as you will soon learn, were not made of flesh and blood as we are—and every inhabitant of that favored country was happy and prosperous.

No disease of any sort was ever known among the Ozites, and so no one ever died unless he met with an accident that prevented him from living. This happened very seldom, indeed. There were no poor people in the Land of Oz, because there was no such thing as money, and all property of every sort belonged to the Ruler. The people were her children, and she cared for them. Each person was given freely by his neighbors whatever he required for his use, which is as much as any one may reasonably desire. Some tilled the lands and raised great crops of grain, which was divided equally among the entire population, so that all had enough. There were many tailors and dressmakers and shoemakers and the like, who made things that any who desired them might wear. Likewise there were jewelers who made ornaments for the person, which pleased and beautified the people, and these ornaments also were free to those who asked for them. Each man and woman, no matter what he or she produced for the good of the community, was supplied by the neighbors with food and clothing and a house and furniture and ornaments and games. If by chance the supply ever ran short, more was taken from the great storehouses of the Ruler, which were afterward filled up again when there was more of any article than the people needed.

Every one worked half the time and played half the time, and the people enjoyed the work as much as they did the play, because it is good to be occupied and to have something to do. There were no cruel overseers set to watch them, and no one to rebuke them or to find fault with them. So each one was proud to do all he could for his friends and neighbors, and was glad when they would accept the things he produced.

You will know by what I have here told you, that the Land of Oz was a remarkable country. I do not suppose such an arrangement would be practical with us, but Dorothy assures me that it works finely with the Oz people.

Oz being a fairy country, the people were, of course, fairy people; but that does not mean that all of them were very unlike the people of our own world. There were all sorts of queer characters among them, but not a single one who was evil, or who possessed a selfish or violent nature. They were peaceful, kind hearted, loving and merry, and every inhabitant adored the beautiful girl who ruled them and delighted to obey her every command.

In spite of all I have said in a general way, there were some parts of the Land of Oz not quite so pleasant as the farming country and the Emerald City which was its center. Far away in the South Country there lived in the mountains a band of strange people called Hammer-Heads, because they had no arms and used their flat heads to pound any one who came near them. Their necks were like rubber, so that they could shoot out their heads to quite a distance, and afterward draw them back again to their shoulders. The Hammer-Heads were called the "Wild People," but never harmed any but those who disturbed them in the mountains where they lived.

In some of the dense forests there lived great beasts of every sort; yet these were for the most part harmless and even sociable, and conversed agreeably with those who visited their haunts. The Kalidahs—beasts with bodies like bears and heads like tigers—had once been fierce and bloodthirsty, but even they were now nearly all tamed, although at times one or another of them would get cross and disagreeable.

Not so tame were the Fighting Trees, which had a forest of their own. If any one approached them these curious trees would bend down their branches, twine them around the intruders, and hurl them away.

But these unpleasant things existed only in a few remote parts of the Land of Oz. I suppose every country has some drawbacks, so even this almost perfect fairyland could not be quite perfect. Once there had been wicked witches in the land, too; but now these had all been destroyed; so, as I said, only peace and happiness reigned in Oz.

For some time Ozma had ruled over this fair country, and never was Ruler more popular or beloved. She is said to be the most beautiful girl the world has ever known, and her heart and mind are as lovely as her person.

Dorothy Gale had several times visited the Emerald City and experienced adventures in the Land of Oz, so that she and Ozma had now become firm friends. The girl Ruler had even made Dorothy a Princess of Oz, and had often implored her to come to Ozma's stately palace and live there always; but Dorothy had been loyal to her Aunt Em and Uncle Henry, who had cared for her since she was a baby, and she had refused to leave them because she knew they would be lonely without her.

However, Dorothy now realized that things were going to be different with her uncle and aunt from this time forth, so after giving the matter deep thought she decided to ask Ozma to grant her a very great favor.

A few seconds after she had made the secret signal in her little bedchamber, the Kansas girl was seated in a lovely room in Ozma's palace in the Emerald City of Oz. When the first loving kisses and embraces had been exchanged, the fair Ruler inquired:

"What is the matter, dear? I know something unpleasant has happened to you, for your face was very sober when I saw it in my Magic Picture. And whenever you signal me to transport you to this safe place, where you are always welcome, I know you are in danger or in trouble."

Dorothy sighed.

"This time, Ozma, it isn't I," she replied. "But it's worse, I guess, for Uncle Henry and Aunt Em are in a heap of trouble, and there seems no way for them to get out of it—anyhow, not while they live in Kansas."

"Tell me about it, Dorothy," said Ozma, with ready sympathy.

"Why, you see Uncle Henry is poor; for the farm in Kansas doesn't 'mount to much, as farms go. So one day Uncle Henry borrowed some money, and wrote a letter saying that if he didn't pay the money back they could take his farm for pay. Course he 'spected to pay by making money from the farm; but he just couldn't. An' so they're going to take the farm, and Uncle Henry and Aunt Em won't have any place to live. They're pretty old to do much hard work, Ozma; so I'll have to work for them, unless—"

Ozma had been thoughtful during the story, but now she smiled and pressed her little friend's hand.

"Unless what, dear?" she asked.

Dorothy hesitated, because her request meant so much to them all.

"Well," said she, "I'd like to live here in the Land of Oz, where you've often 'vited me to live. But I can't, you know, unless Uncle Henry and Aunt Em could live here too."

"Of course not," exclaimed the Ruler of Oz, laughing gaily. "So, in order to get you, little friend, we must invite your Uncle and Aunt to live in Oz, also."

"Oh, will you, Ozma?" cried Dorothy, clasping her chubby little hands eagerly. "Will you bring them here with the Magic Belt, and give them a nice little farm in the Munchkin Country, or the Winkie Country—or some other place?"

"To be sure," answered Ozma, full of joy at the chance to please her little friend. "I have long been thinking of this very thing, Dorothy dear, and often I have had it in my mind to propose it to you. I am sure your uncle and aunt must be good and worthy people, or you would not love them so much; and for YOUR friends, Princess, there is always room in the Land of Oz."

Dorothy was delighted, yet not altogether surprised, for she had clung to the hope that Ozma would be kind enough to grant her request. When, indeed, had her powerful and faithful friend refused her anything?

"But you must not call me 'Princess'," she said; "for after this I shall live on the little farm with Uncle Henry and Aunt Em, and princesses ought not to live on farms."

"Princess Dorothy will not," replied Ozma with her sweet smile. "You are going to live in your own rooms in this palace, and be my constant companion."

"But Uncle Henry—" began Dorothy.

"Oh, he is old, and has worked enough in his lifetime," interrupted the girl Ruler; "so we must find a place for your uncle and aunt where they will be comfortable and happy and need not work more than they care to. When shall we transport them here, Dorothy?"

"I promised to go and see them again before they were turned out of the farmhouse," answered Dorothy; "so—perhaps next Saturday—"

"But why wait so long?" asked Ozma. "And why make the journey back to Kansas again? Let us surprise them, and bring them here without any warning."

"I'm not sure that they believe in the Land of Oz," said Dorothy, "though I've told 'em 'bout it lots of times."

"They'll believe when they see it," declared Ozma; "and if they are told they are to make a magical journey to our fairyland, it may make them nervous. I think the best way will be to use the Magic Belt without warning them, and when they have arrived you can explain to them whatever they do not understand."

"Perhaps that's best," decided Dorothy. "There isn't much use in their staying at the farm until they are put out, 'cause it's much nicer here."

"Then to-morrow morning they shall come here," said Princess Ozma. "I will order Jellia Jamb, who is the palace housekeeper, to have rooms all prepared for them, and after breakfast we will get the Magic Belt and by its aid transport your uncle and aunt to the Emerald City."

"Thank you, Ozma!" cried Dorothy, kissing her friend gratefully.

"And now," Ozma proposed, "let us take a walk in the gardens before we dress for dinner. Come, Dorothy dear!"

Chapter 4 - How the Nome King Planned Revenge

The reason most people are bad is because they do not try to be good. Now, the Nome King had never tried to be good, so he was very bad indeed. Having decided to conquer the Land of Oz and to destroy the Emerald City and enslave all its people, King Roquat the Red kept planning ways to do this dreadful thing, and the more he planned the more he believed he would be able to accomplish it.

About the time Dorothy went to Ozma the Nome King called his Chief Steward to him and said:

"Kaliko, I think I shall make you the General of my armies."

"I think you won't," replied Kaliko, positively.

"Why not?" inquired the King, reaching for his scepter with the big sapphire.

"Because I'm your Chief Steward and know nothing of warfare," said Kaliko, preparing to dodge if anything were thrown at him. "I manage all the affairs of your kingdom better than you could yourself, and you'll never find another Steward as good as I am. But there are a hundred Nomes better fitted to command your army, and your Generals get thrown away so often that I have no desire to be one of them."

"Ah, there is some truth in your remarks, Kaliko," remarked the King, deciding not to throw the scepter. "Summon my army to assemble in the Great Cavern."

Kaliko bowed and retired, and in a few minutes returned to say that the army was assembled. So the King went out upon a balcony that overlooked the Great Cavern, where fifty thousand Nomes, all armed with swords and pikes, stood marshaled in military array.

When they were not required as soldiers all these Nomes were metal workers and miners, and they had hammered so much at the forges and dug so hard with pick and shovel that they had acquired great muscular strength. They were strangely formed creatures, rather round and not very tall. Their toes were curly and their ears broad and flat.

In time of war every Nome left his forge or mine and became part of the great army of King Roquat. The soldiers wore rock-colored uniforms and were excellently drilled.

The King looked upon this tremendous army, which stood silently arrayed before him, and a cruel smile curled the corners of his mouth, for he saw that his legions were very powerful. Then he addressed them from the balcony, saying:

"I have thrown away General Blug, because he did not please me. So I want another General to command this army. Who is next in command?"

"I am," replied Colonel Crinkle, a dapper-looking Nome, as he stepped forward to salute his monarch.

The King looked at him carefully and said:

"I want you to march this army through an underground tunnel, which I am going to bore, to the Emerald City of Oz. When you get there I want you to conquer the Oz people, destroy them and their city, and bring all their gold and silver and precious stones back to my cavern. Also you are to recapture my Magic Belt and return it to me. Will you do this, General Crinkle?"

"No, your Majesty," replied the Nome; "for it can't be done."

"Oh indeed!" exclaimed the King. Then he turned to his servants and said: "Please take General Crinkle to the torture chamber. There you will kindly slice him into thin slices. Afterward you may feed him to the seven-headed dogs."

"Anything to oblige your Majesty," replied the servants, politely, and led the condemned man away.

When they had gone, the King addressed the army again.

"Listen!" said he. "The General who is to command my armies must promise to carry out my orders. If he fails he will share the fate of poor Crinkle. Now, then, who will volunteer to lead my hosts to the Emerald City?"

For a time no one moved and all were silent. Then an old Nome with white whiskers so long that they were tied around his waist to prevent their tripping him up, stepped out of the ranks and saluted the King.

"I'd like to ask a few questions, your Majesty," he said.

"Go ahead," replied the King.

"These Oz people are quite good, are they not?"

"As good as apple pie," said the King.

"And they are happy, I suppose?" continued the old Nome.

"Happy as the day is long," said the King.

"And contented and prosperous?" inquired the Nome.

"Very much so," said the King.

"Well, your Majesty," remarked he of the white whiskers, "I think I should like to undertake the job, so I'll be your General. I hate good people; I detest happy people; I'm opposed to any one who is contented and prosperous. That is why I am so fond of your Majesty. Make me your General and I'll promise to conquer and destroy the Oz people. If I fail I'm ready to be sliced thin and fed to the seven-headed dogs."

"Very good! Very good, indeed! That's the way to talk!" cried Roquat the Red, who was greatly pleased. "What is your name, General?"

"I'm called Guph, your Majesty."

"Well, Guph, come with me to my private cave, and we'll talk it over." Then he turned to the army. "Nomes and soldiers," said he, "you are to obey the commands of General Guph until he becomes dog-feed. Any man who fails to obey his new General will be promptly thrown away. You are now dismissed."

Guph went to the King's private cave and sat down upon an amethyst chair and put his feet on the arm of the King's ruby throne. Then he lighted his pipe and threw the live coal he had taken from his pocket upon the King's left foot and puffed the smoke into the King's eyes and made himself comfortable. For he was a wise old Nome, and he knew that the best way to get along with Roquat the Red was to show that he was not afraid of him.

"I'm ready for the talk, your Majesty," he said.

The King coughed and looked at his new General fiercely.

"Do you not tremble to take such liberties with your monarch?" he asked.

"Oh no," replied Guph, calmly, and he blew a wreath of smoke that curled around the King's nose and made him sneeze. "You want to conquer the Emerald City, and I'm the only Nome in all your dominions who can conquer it. So you will be very careful not to hurt me until I have carried out your wishes. After that—"

"Well, what then?" inquired the King.

"Then you will be so grateful to me that you won't care to hurt me," replied the General.

"That is a very good argument," said Roquat. "But suppose you fail?"

"Then it's the slicing machine. I agree to that," announced Guph. "But if you do as I tell you there will be no failure. The trouble with you, Roquat, is that you don't think carefully enough. I do. You would go ahead and march through your tunnel into Oz, and get defeated and driven back. I won't. And the reason I won't is because when I march I'll have all my plans made, and a host of allies to assist my Nomes."

"What do you mean by that?" asked the King.

"I'll explain, King Roquat. You're going to attack a fairy country, and a mighty fairy country, too. They haven't much of an army in Oz, but the Princess who ruled them has a fairy wand; and the little girl Dorothy has your Magic Belt; and at the North of the Emerald City lives a clever sorceress called Glinda the Good, who commands the spirits of the air. Also I have heard that there is a wonderful Wizard in Ozma's palace, who is so skillful that people used to pay him money in America to see him perform. So you see it will be no easy thing to overcome all this magic."

"We have fifty thousand soldiers!" cried the King proudly.

269

"Yes; but they are Nomes," remarked Guph, taking a silk handkerchief from the King's pocket and wiping his own pointed shoes with it. "Nomes are immortals, but they are not strong on magic. When you lost your famous Belt the greater part of your own power was gone from you. Against Ozma you and your Nomes would have no show at all."

Roquat's eyes flashed angrily.

"Then away you go to the slicing machine!" he cried.

"Not yet," said the General, filling his pipe from the King's private tobacco pouch.

"What do you propose to do?" asked the monarch.

"I propose to obtain the power we need," answered Guph. "There are a good many evil creatures who have magic powers sufficient to destroy and conquer the Land of Oz. We will get them on our side, band them all together, and then take Ozma and her people by surprise. It's all very simple and easy when you know how. Alone, we should be helpless to injure the Ruler of Oz, but with the aid of the evil powers we can summon we shall easily succeed."

King Roquat was delighted with this idea, for he realized how clever it was.

"Surely, Guph, you are the greatest General I have ever had!" he exclaimed, his eyes sparkling with joy. "You must go at once and make arrangements with the evil powers to assist us, and meantime I'll begin to dig the tunnel."

"I thought you'd agree with me, Roquat," replied the new General. "I'll start this very afternoon to visit the Chief of the Whimsies."

Chapter 5 - How Dorothy Became a Princess

When the people of the Emerald City heard that Dorothy had returned to them every one was eager to see her, for the little girl was a general favorite in the Land of Oz. From time to time some of the folk from the great outside world had found their way into this fairyland, but all except one had been companions of Dorothy and had turned out to be very agreeable people. The exception I speak of was the wonderful Wizard of Oz, a sleight-of-hand performer from Omaha who went up in a balloon and was carried by a current of air to the Emerald City. His queer and puzzling tricks made the people of Oz believe him a great wizard for a time, and he ruled over them until Dorothy arrived on her first visit and showed the Wizard to be a mere humbug. He was a gentle, kind-hearted little man, and Dorothy grew to like him afterward. When, after an absence, the Wizard returned to the Land of Oz, Ozma received him graciously and gave him a home in a part of the palace.

In addition to the Wizard two other personages from the outside world had been allowed to make their home in the Emerald City. The first was a quaint Shaggy Man, whom Ozma had made the Governor of the Royal Storehouses, and the second a Yellow Hen named Billina, who had a fine house in the gardens back of the palace, where she looked after a large family. Both these had been old comrades of Dorothy, so you see the little girl was quite an important personage in Oz, and the people thought she had brought them good luck, and loved her next best to Ozma. During her several visits this little girl had been the means of destroying two wicked witches who oppressed the people, and she had discovered a live scarecrow who was now one of the most popular personages in all the fairy country. With the Scarecrow's help she had rescued Nick Chopper, a Tin Woodman, who had rusted in a lonely forest, and the tin man was now the Emperor of the Country of the Winkies and much beloved because of his kind heart. No wonder the people thought Dorothy had brought them good luck! Yet, strange as it may seem, she had accomplished all these wonders not because she was a fairy or had any magical powers whatever, but because she was a simple, sweet and true little girl who was honest to herself and to all whom she met. In this world in which we live simplicity and kindness are the only magic wands that work wonders, and in the Land of Oz Dorothy found these same qualities had won for her the love and admiration of the people. Indeed, the little girl had made many warm friends in the fairy country, and the only real grief the Ozites had ever experienced was when Dorothy left them and returned to her Kansas home.

Now she received a joyful welcome, although no one except Ozma knew at first that she had finally come to stay for good and all.

That evening Dorothy had many callers, and among them were such important people as Tik-tok, a machine man who thought and spoke and moved by clockwork; her old companion the genial Shaggy Man; Jack Pumpkinhead, whose body was brush-wood and whose head was a ripe pumpkin with a face carved upon it; the Cowardly Lion and the Hungry Tiger, two great beasts from the forest, who served Princess Ozma, and Professor H. M. Wogglebug, T.E. This wogglebug was a remarkable creature. He had once been a tiny little bug, crawling around in a school-room, but he was discovered and highly magnified so that he could be seen more plainly, and while in this magnified condition he had escaped. He had always remained big, and he dressed like a dandy and was so full of knowledge and information (which are distinct acquirements) that he had been made a Professor and the head of the Royal College.

Dorothy had a nice visit with these old friends, and also talked a long time with the Wizard, who was little and old and withered and dried up, but as merry and active as a child. Afterward, she went to see Billina's fast-growing family of chicks.

Toto, Dorothy's little black dog, also met with a cordial reception. Toto was an especial friend of the Shaggy Man, and he knew every one else. Being the only dog in the Land of Oz, he was highly respected by the people, who believed animals entitled to every consideration if they behaved themselves properly.

Dorothy had four lovely rooms in the palace, which were always reserved for her use and were called "Dorothy's rooms." These consisted of a beautiful sitting room, a dressing room, a dainty bedchamber and a big marble bathroom. And in these rooms were everything that heart could desire, placed there with loving thoughtfulness by Ozma for her little friend's use. The royal dressmakers had the little girl's measure, so they kept the closets in her dressing room filled with lovely dresses of every description and suitable for every occasion. No wonder Dorothy had refrained from bringing with her her old calico and gingham dresses! Here everything that was dear to a little girl's heart was supplied in profusion, and nothing so rich and beautiful could ever have been found in the biggest department stores in America. Of course Dorothy enjoyed all these luxuries, and the only reason she had heretofore preferred to live in Kansas was because her uncle and aunt loved her and needed her with them.

Now, however, all was to be changed, and Dorothy was really more delighted to know that her dear relatives were to share in her good fortune and enjoy the delights of the Land of Oz, than she was to possess such luxury for herself.

Next morning, at Ozma's request, Dorothy dressed herself in a pretty sky-blue gown of rich silk, trimmed with real pearls. The buckles of her shoes were set with pearls, too, and more of these priceless gems were on a lovely coronet which she wore upon her forehead. "For," said her friend Ozma, "from this time forth, my dear, you must assume your rightful rank as a Princess of Oz, and being my chosen companion you must dress in a way befitting the dignity of your position."

Dorothy agreed to this, although she knew that neither gowns nor jewels could make her anything else than the simple, unaffected little girl she had always been.

As soon as they had breakfasted—the girls eating together in Ozma's pretty boudoir—the Ruler of Oz said:

"Now, dear friend, we will use the Magic Belt to transport your uncle and aunt from Kansas to the Emerald City. But I think it would be fitting, in receiving such distinguished guests, for us to sit in my Throne Room."

"Oh, they're not very 'stinguished, Ozma," said Dorothy. "They're just plain people, like me."

"Being your friends and relatives, Princess Dorothy, they are certainly distinguished," replied the Ruler, with a smile.

"They—they won't hardly know what to make of all your splendid furniture and things," protested Dorothy, gravely. "It may scare 'em to see your grand Throne Room, an' p'raps we'd better go into the back yard, Ozma, where the cabbages grow an' the chickens are playing. Then it would seem more natural to Uncle Henry and Aunt Em."

"No; they shall first see me in my Throne Room," replied Ozma, decidedly; and when she spoke in that tone Dorothy knew it was not wise to oppose her, for Ozma was accustomed to having her own way.

So together they went to the Throne Room, an immense domed chamber in the center of the palace. Here stood the royal throne, made of solid gold and encrusted with enough precious stones to stock a dozen jewelry stores in our country.

Ozma, who was wearing the Magic Belt, seated herself in the throne, and Dorothy sat at her feet. In the room were assembled many ladies and gentlemen of the court, clothed in rich apparel and wearing fine jewelry. Two immense animals squatted, one on each side of the throne—the Cowardly Lion and the Hungry Tiger. In a balcony high up in the dome an orchestra played sweet music, and beneath the dome two electric fountains sent sprays of colored perfumed water shooting up nearly as high as the arched ceiling.

"Are you ready, Dorothy?" asked the Ruler.

"I am," replied Dorothy; "but I don't know whether Aunt Em and Uncle Henry are ready."

"That won't matter," declared Ozma. "The old life can have very little to interest them, and the sooner they begin the new life here the happier they will be. Here they come, my dear!"

As she spoke, there before the throne appeared Uncle Henry and Aunt Em, who for a moment stood motionless, glaring with white and startled faces at the scene that confronted them. If the ladies and gentlemen present had not been so polite I am sure they would have laughed at the two strangers.

Aunt Em had her calico dress skirt "tucked up," and she wore a faded, blue-checked apron. Her hair was rather straggly and she had on a pair of Uncle Henry's old slippers. In one hand she held a dish-towel and in the other a cracked earthenware plate, which she had been engaged in wiping when so suddenly transported to the Land of Oz.

Uncle Henry, when the summons came, had been out in the barn "doin' chores." He wore a ragged and much soiled straw hat, a checked shirt without any collar and blue overalls tucked into the tops of his old cowhide boots.

"By gum!" gasped Uncle Henry, looking around as if bewildered.

"Well, I swan!" gurgled Aunt Em in a hoarse, frightened voice. Then her eyes fell upon Dorothy, and she said: "D-d-d-don't that look like our little girl—our Dorothy, Henry?"

"Hi, there—look out, Em!" exclaimed the old man, as Aunt Em advanced a step; "take care o' the wild beastses, or you're a goner!"

But now Dorothy sprang forward and embraced and kissed her aunt and uncle affectionately, afterward taking their hands in her own.

"Don't be afraid," she said to them. "You are now in the Land of Oz, where you are to live always, and be comfer'ble an' happy. You'll never have to worry over anything again, 'cause there won't be anything to worry about. And you owe it all to the kindness of my friend Princess Ozma."

Here she led them before the throne and continued:

"Your Highness, this is Uncle Henry. And this is Aunt Em. They want to thank you for bringing them here from Kansas."

Aunt Em tried to "slick" her hair, and she hid the dish-towel and dish under her apron while she bowed to the lovely Ozma. Uncle Henry took off his straw hat and held it awkwardly in his hands.

But the Ruler of Oz rose and came from her throne to greet her newly arrived guests, and she smiled as sweetly upon them as if they had been a king and queen.

"You are very welcome here, where I have brought you for Princess Dorothy's sake," she said, graciously, "and I hope you will be quite happy in your new home." Then she turned to her courtiers, who were silently and gravely regarding the scene, and added: "I present to my people our Princess Dorothy's beloved Uncle Henry and Aunt Em, who will hereafter be subjects of our kingdom. It will please me to have you show them every kindness and honor in your power, and to join me in making them happy and contented."

Hearing this, all those assembled bowed low and respectfully to the old farmer and his wife, who bobbed their own heads in return.

"And now," said Ozma to them, "Dorothy will show you the rooms prepared for you. I hope you will like them, and shall expect you to join me at luncheon."

So Dorothy led her relatives away, and as soon as they were out of the Throne Room and alone in the corridor, Aunt Em squeezed Dorothy's hand and said:

"Child, child! How in the world did we ever get here so quick? And is it all real? And are we to stay here, as she says? And what does it all mean, anyhow?"

Dorothy laughed.

"Why didn't you tell us what you were goin' to do?" inquired Uncle Henry, reproachfully. "If I'd known about it, I'd 'a put on my Sunday clothes."

"I'll 'splain ever'thing as soon as we get to your rooms," promised Dorothy. "You're in great luck, Uncle Henry and Aunt Em; an' so am I! And oh! I'm so happy to have got you here, at last!"

As he walked by the little girl's side, Uncle Henry stroked his whiskers thoughtfully. "'Pears to me, Dorothy, we won't make bang-up fairies," he remarked.

"An' my back hair looks like a fright!" wailed Aunt Em.

"Never mind," returned the little girl, reassuringly. "You won't have anything to do now but to look pretty, Aunt Em; an' Uncle Henry won't have to work till his back aches, that's certain."

"Sure?" they asked, wonderingly, and in the same breath.

"Course I'm sure," said Dorothy. "You're in the Fairyland of Oz, now; an' what's more, you belong to it!"

Chapter 6 - How Guph Visited the Whimsies

The new General of the Nome King's army knew perfectly well that to fail in his plans meant death for him. Yet he was not at all anxious or worried. He hated every one who was good and longed to make all who were happy unhappy. Therefore he had accepted this dangerous position as General quite willingly, feeling sure in his evil mind that he would be able to do a lot of mischief and finally conquer the Land of Oz.

Yet Guph determined to be careful, and to lay his plans well, so as not to fail. He argued that only careless people fail in what they attempt to do.

The mountains underneath which the Nome King's extensive caverns were located lay grouped just north of the Land of Ev, which lay directly across the deadly desert to the east of the Land of Oz. As the mountains were also on the edge of the desert the Nome King found that he had only to tunnel underneath the desert to reach Ozma's dominions. He did not wish his armies to appear above ground in the Country of the Winkies, which was the part of the Land of Oz nearest to King Roquat's own country, as then the people would give the alarm and enable Ozma to fortify the Emerald City and assemble an army. He wanted to take all the Oz people by surprise; so he decided to run the tunnel clear through to the Emerald City, where he and his hosts could break through the ground without warning and conquer the people before they had time to defend themselves.

Roquat the Red began work at once upon his tunnel, setting a thousand miners at the task and building it high and broad enough for his armies to march through it with ease. The Nomes were used to making tunnels, as all the kingdom in which they lived was under ground; so they made rapid progress.

While this work was going on General Guph started out alone to visit the Chief of the Whimsies.

These Whimsies were curious people who lived in a retired country of their own. They had large, strong bodies, but heads so small that they were no bigger than door-knobs. Of course, such tiny heads could not contain any great amount of brains, and the Whimsies were so ashamed of their personal appearance and lack of commonsense that they wore big heads made of pasteboard, which they fastened over their own little heads. On these pasteboard heads they sewed sheep's wool for hair, and the wool was colored many tints—pink, green and lavender being the favorite colors. The faces of these false heads were painted in many ridiculous ways, according to the whims of the owners, and these big, burly creatures looked so whimsical and absurd in their queer masks that they were called "Whimsies." They foolishly imagined that no one would suspect the little heads that were inside the imitation ones, not knowing that it is folly to try to appear otherwise than as nature has made us.

The Chief of the Whimsies had as little wisdom as the others, and had been chosen chief merely because none among them was any wiser or more capable of ruling. The Whimsies were evil spirits and could not be killed. They were hated and feared by every one and were known as terrible fighters because they were so strong and muscular and had not sense enough to know when they were defeated.

General Guph thought the Whimsies would be a great help to the Nomes in the conquest of Oz, for under his leadership they could be induced to fight as long so they could stand up. So he traveled to their country and asked to see the Chief, who lived in a house that had a picture of his grotesque false head painted over the doorway.

The Chief's false head had blue hair, a turned-up nose, and a mouth that stretched half across the face. Big green eyes had been painted upon it, but in the center of the chin were two small holes made in the pasteboard, so that the Chief could see through them with his own tiny eyes; for when the big head was fastened upon his shoulders the eyes in his own natural head were on a level with the false chin.

Said General Guph to the Chief of the Whimsies:

"We Nomes are going to conquer the Land of Oz and capture our King's Magic Belt, which the Oz people stole from him. Then we are going to plunder and destroy the whole country. And we want the Whimsies to help us."

"Will there be any fighting?" asked the Chief.

"Plenty," replied Guph.

That must have pleased the Chief, for he got up and danced around the room three times. Then he seated himself again, adjusted his false head, and said:

"We have no quarrel with Ozma of Oz."

"But you Whimsies love to fight, and here is a splendid chance to do so," urged Guph.

"Wait till I sing a song," said the Chief. Then he lay back in his chair and sang a foolish song that did not seem to the General to mean anything, although he listened carefully. When he had finished, the Chief Whimsie looked at him through the holes in his chin and asked:

"What reward will you give us if we help you?"

The General was prepared for this question, for he had been thinking the matter over on his journey. People often do a good deed without hope of reward, but for an evil deed they always demand payment.

"When we get our Magic Belt," he made reply, "our King, Roquat the Red, will use its power to give every Whimsie a natural head as big and fine as the false head he now wears. Then you will no longer be ashamed because your big strong bodies have such teenty-weenty heads."

"Oh! Will you do that?" asked the Chief, eagerly.

"We surely will," promised the General.

"I'll talk to my people," said the Chief.

So he called a meeting of all the Whimsies and told them of the offer made by the Nomes. The creatures were delighted with the bargain, and at once agreed to fight for the Nome King and help him to conquer Oz.

One Whimsie alone seemed to have a glimmer of sense, for he asked:

"Suppose we fail to capture the Magic Belt? What will happen then, and what good will all our fighting do?"

But they threw him into the river for asking foolish questions, and laughed when the water ruined his pasteboard head before he could swim out again.

So the compact was made and General Guph was delighted with his success in gaining such powerful allies.

But there were other people, too, just as important as the Whimsies, whom the clever old Nome had determined to win to his side.

Chapter 7 - How Aunt Em Conquered the Lion

"These are your rooms," said Dorothy, opening a door.

Aunt Em drew back at the sight of the splendid furniture and draperies.

"Ain't there any place to wipe my feet?" she asked.

"You will soon change your slippers for new shoes," replied Dorothy. "Don't be afraid, Aunt Em. Here is where you are to live, so walk right in and make yourself at home."

Aunt Em advanced hesitatingly.

"It beats the Topeka Hotel!" she cried admiringly. "But this place is too grand for us, child. Can't we have some back room in the attic, that's more in our class?"

"No," said Dorothy. "You've got to live here, 'cause Ozma says so. And all the rooms in this palace are just as fine as these, and some are better. It won't do any good to fuss, Aunt Em. You've got to be swell and high-toned in the Land of Oz, whether you want to or not; so you may as well make up your mind to it."

"It's hard luck," replied her aunt, looking around with an awed expression; "but folks can get used to anything, if they try. Eh, Henry?"

"Why, as to that," said Uncle Henry, slowly, "I b'lieve in takin' what's pervided us, an' askin' no questions. I've traveled some, Em, in my time, and you hain't; an' that makes a difference atween us."

Then Dorothy showed them through the rooms. The first was a handsome sitting-room, with windows opening upon the rose gardens. Then came separate bedrooms for Aunt Em and Uncle Henry, with a fine bathroom between them. Aunt Em had a pretty dressing room, besides, and Dorothy opened the closets and showed several exquisite costumes that had been provided for her aunt by the royal dressmakers, who had worked all night to get them ready. Everything that Aunt Em could possibly need was in the drawers and closets, and her dressing-table was covered with engraved gold toilet articles.

Uncle Henry had nine suits of clothes, cut in the popular Munchkin fashion, with knee-breeches, silk stockings, and low shoes with jeweled buckles. The hats to match these costumes had pointed tops and wide brims with small gold bells around the edges. His shirts were of fine linen with frilled bosoms, and his vests were richly embroidered with colored silks.

Uncle Henry decided that he would first take a bath and then dress himself in a blue satin suit that had caught his fancy. He accepted his good fortune with calm composure and refused to have a servant to assist him. But Aunt Em was "all of a flutter," as she said, and it took Dorothy and Jellia Jamb, the housekeeper, and two maids a long time to dress her and do up her hair and get her "rigged like a popinjay," as she quaintly expressed it. She wanted to stop and admire everything that caught her eye, and she sighed continually and declared that such finery was too good for an old country woman, and that she never thought she would have to "put on airs" at her time of life.

Finally she was dressed, and when she went into the sitting-room there was Uncle Henry in his blue satin, walking gravely up and down the room. He had trimmed his beard and mustache and looked very dignified and respectable.

"Tell me, Dorothy," he said; "do all the men here wear duds like these?"

"Yes," she replied; "all 'cept the Scarecrow and the Shaggy Man—and of course the Tin Woodman and Tik-tok, who are made of metal. You'll find all the men at Ozma's court dressed just as you are—only perhaps a little finer."

"Henry, you look like a play-actor," announced Aunt Em, looking at her husband critically.

"An' you, Em, look more highfalutin' than a peacock," he replied.

"I guess you're right," she said regretfully; "but we're helpless victims of high-toned royalty."

Dorothy was much amused.

"Come with me," she said, "and I'll show you 'round the palace."

She took them through the beautiful rooms and introduced them to all the people they chanced to meet. Also she showed them her own pretty rooms, which were not far from their own.

"So it's all true," said Aunt Em, wide-eyed with amazement, "and what Dorothy told us of this fairy country was plain facts instead of dreams! But where are all the strange creatures you used to know here?"

"Yes, where's the Scarecrow?" inquired Uncle Henry.

"Why, he's just now away on a visit to the Tin Woodman, who is Emp'ror of the Winkie Country," answered the little girl. "You'll see him when he comes back, and you're sure to like him."

"And where's the Wonderful Wizard?" asked Aunt Em.

"You'll see him at Ozma's luncheon, for he lives here in this palace," was the reply.

"And Jack Pumpkinhead?"

"Oh, he lives a little way out of town, in his own pumpkin field. We'll go there some time and see him, and we'll call on Professor Wogglebug, too. The Shaggy Man will be at the luncheon, I guess, and Tik-tok. And now I'll take you out to see Billina, who has a house of her own."

So they went into the back yard, and after walking along winding paths some distance through the beautiful gardens they came to an attractive little house where the Yellow Hen sat on the front porch sunning herself.

"Good morning, my dear Mistress," called Billina, fluttering down to meet them. "I was expecting you to call, for I heard you had come back and brought your uncle and aunt with you."

"We're here for good and all, this time, Billina," cried Dorothy, joyfully. "Uncle Henry and Aunt Em belong to Oz now as much as I do!"

"Then they are very lucky people," declared Billina; "for there couldn't be a nicer place to live. But come, my dear; I must show you all my Dorothys. Nine are living and have grown up to be very respectable hens; but one took cold at Ozma's birthday party and died of the pip, and the other two turned out to be horrid roosters, so I had to change their names from Dorothy to Daniel. They all had the letter 'D' engraved upon their gold lockets, you remember, with your picture inside, and 'D' stands for Daniel as well as for Dorothy."

"Did you call both the roosters Daniel?" asked Uncle Henry.

"Yes, indeed. I've nine Dorothys and two Daniels; and the nine Dorothys have eighty-six sons and daughters and over three hundred grandchildren," said Billina, proudly.

"What names do you give 'em all, dear?" inquired the little girl.

"Oh, they are all Dorothys and Daniels, some being Juniors and some Double-Juniors. Dorothy and Daniel are two good names, and I see no object in hunting for others," declared the Yellow Hen. "But just think, Dorothy, what a big chicken family we've grown to be, and our numbers increase nearly every day! Ozma doesn't know what to do with all the eggs we lay, and we are never eaten or harmed in any way, as chickens are in your country. They give us everything to make us contented and happy, and I, my dear, am the acknowledged Queen and Governor of every chicken in Oz, because I'm the eldest and started the whole colony."

"You ought to be very proud, ma'am," said Uncle Henry, who was astonished to hear a hen talk so sensibly.

"Oh, I am," she replied. "I've the loveliest pearl necklace you ever saw. Come in the house and I'll show it to you. And I've nine leg bracelets and a diamond pin for each wing. But I only wear them on state occasions."

They followed the Yellow Hen into the house, which Aunt Em declared was neat as a pin. They could not sit down, because all Billina's chairs were roosting-poles made of silver; so they had to stand while the hen fussily showed them her treasures.

Then they had to go into the back rooms occupied by Billina's nine Dorothys and two Daniels, who were all plump yellow chickens and greeted the visitors very politely. It was easy to see that they were well bred and that Billina had looked after their education.

In the yards were all the children and grandchildren of these eleven elders and they were of all sizes, from well-grown hens to tiny chickens just out of the shell. About fifty fluffy yellow youngsters were at school, being taught good manners and good grammar by a young hen who wore spectacles. They sang in chorus a patriotic song of the Land of Oz, in honor of their visitors, and Aunt Em was much impressed by these talking chickens.

Dorothy wanted to stay and play with the young chickens for awhile, but Uncle Henry and Aunt Em had not seen the palace grounds and gardens yet and were eager to get better acquainted with the marvelous and delightful land in which they were to live.

"I'll stay here, and you can go for a walk," said Dorothy. "You'll be perfec'ly safe anywhere, and may do whatever you want to. When you get tired, go back to the palace and find your rooms, and I'll come to you before luncheon is ready."

So Uncle Henry and Aunt Em started out alone to explore the grounds, and Dorothy knew that they couldn't get lost, because all the palace grounds were enclosed by a high wall of green marble set with emeralds.

It was a rare treat to these simple folk, who had lived in the country all their lives and known little enjoyment of any sort, to wear beautiful clothes and live in a palace and be treated with respect and consideration by all around them. They were very happy indeed as they strolled up the shady walks and looked upon the gorgeous flowers and shrubs, feeling that their new home was more beautiful than any tongue could describe.

Suddenly, as they turned a corner and walked through a gap in a high hedge, they came face to face with an enormous Lion, which crouched upon the green lawn and seemed surprised by their appearance.

They stopped short, Uncle Henry trembling with horror and Aunt Em too terrified to scream. Next moment the poor woman clasped her husband around the neck and cried:

"Save me, Henry, save me!"

"Can't even save myself, Em," he returned, in a husky voice, "for the animile looks as if it could eat both of us an' lick its chops for more! If I only had a gun—"

"Haven't you, Henry? Haven't you?" she asked anxiously.

"Nary gun, Em. So let's die as brave an' graceful as we can. I knew our luck couldn't last!"

"I won't die. I won't be eaten by a lion!" wailed Aunt Em, glaring upon the huge beast. Then a thought struck her, and she whispered, "Henry, I've heard as savage beastses can be conquered by the human eye. I'll eye that lion out o' countenance an' save our lives."

"Try it, Em," he returned, also in a whisper. "Look at him as you do at me when I'm late to dinner."

Aunt Em turned upon the Lion a determined countenance and a wild dilated eye. She glared at the immense beast steadily, and the Lion, who had been quietly blinking at them, began to appear uneasy and disturbed.

"Is anything the matter, ma'am?" he asked, in a mild voice.

At this speech from the terrible beast Aunt Em and Uncle Henry both were startled, and then Uncle Henry remembered that this must be the Lion they had seen in Ozma's Throne Room.

"Hold on, Em!" he exclaimed. "Quit the eagle eye conquest an' take courage. I guess this is the same Cowardly Lion Dorothy has told us about."

"Oh, is it?" she cried, much relieved.

"When he spoke, I got the idea; and when he looked so 'shamed like, I was sure of it," Uncle Henry continued.

Aunt Em regarded the animal with new interest.

"Are you the Cowardly Lion?" she inquired. "Are you Dorothy's friend?"

"Yes'm," answered the Lion, meekly. "Dorothy and I are old chums and are very fond of each other. I'm the King of Beasts, you know, and the Hungry Tiger and I serve Princess Ozma as her body guards."

"To be sure," said Aunt Em, nodding. "But the King of Beasts shouldn't be cowardly."

"I've heard that said before," remarked the Lion, yawning till he showed two great rows of sharp white teeth; "but that does not keep me from being frightened whenever I go into battle."

"What do you do, run?" asked Uncle Henry.

"No; that would be foolish, for the enemy would run after me," declared the Lion. "So I tremble with fear and pitch in as hard as I can; and so far I have always won my fight."

"Ah, I begin to understand," said Uncle Henry.

"Were you scared when I looked at you just now?" inquired Aunt Em.

"Terribly scared, madam," answered the Lion, "for at first I thought you were going to have a fit. Then I noticed you were trying to overcome me by the power of your eye, and your glance was so fierce and penetrating that I shook with fear."

This greatly pleased the lady, and she said quite cheerfully:

"Well, I won't hurt you, so don't be scared any more. I just wanted to see what the human eye was good for."

"The human eye is a fearful weapon," remarked the Lion, scratching his nose softly with his paw to hide a smile. "Had I not known you were Dorothy's friends I might have torn you both into shreds in order to escape your terrible gaze."

Aunt Em shuddered at hearing this, and Uncle Henry said hastily:

"I'm glad you knew us. Good morning, Mr. Lion; we'll hope to see you again—by and by—some time in the future."

"Good morning," replied the Lion, squatting down upon the lawn again. "You are likely to see a good deal of me, if you live in the Land of Oz."

Chapter 8 - How the Grand Gallipoot Joined the Nomes

After leaving the Whimsies, Guph continued on his journey and penetrated far into the Northwest. He wanted to get to the Country of the Growleywogs, and in order to do that he must cross the Ripple Land, which was a hard thing to do. For the Ripple Land was a succession of hills and valleys, all very steep and rocky, and they changed places constantly by rippling. While Guph was climbing a hill it sank down under him and became a valley, and while he was descending into a valley it rose up and carried him to the top of a hill. This was very perplexing to the traveler, and a stranger might have thought he could never cross the Ripple Land at all. But Guph knew that if he kept steadily on he would get to the end at last; so he paid no attention to the changing hills and valleys and plodded along as calmly as if walking upon the level ground.

The result of this wise persistence was that the General finally reached firmer soil and, after penetrating a dense forest, came to the Dominion of the Growleywogs.

No sooner had he crossed the border of this domain when two guards seized him and carried him before the Grand Gallipoot of the Growleywogs, who scowled upon him ferociously and asked him why he dared intrude upon his territory.

"I'm the Lord High General of the Invincible Army of the Nomes, and my name is Guph," was the reply. "All the world trembles when that name is mentioned."

The Growleywogs gave a shout of jeering laughter at this, and one of them caught the Nome in his strong arms and tossed him high into the air. Guph was considerably shaken when he fell upon the hard ground, but he appeared to take no notice of the impertinence and composed himself to speak again to the Grand Gallipoot.

"My master, King Roquat the Red, has sent me here to confer with you. He wishes your assistance to conquer the Land of Oz."

Here the General paused, and the Grand Gallipoot scowled upon him more terribly than ever and said:

"Go on!"

The voice of the Grand Gallipoot was partly a roar and partly a growl. He mumbled his words badly and Guph had to listen carefully in order to understand him.

These Growleywogs were certainly remarkable creatures. They were of gigantic size, yet were all bone and skin and muscle, there being no meat or fat upon their bodies at all. Their powerful muscles lay just underneath their skins, like bunches of tough rope, and the weakest Growleywog was so strong that he could pick up an elephant and toss it seven miles away.

It seems unfortunate that strong people are usually so disagreeable and overbearing that no one cares for them. In fact, to be different from your fellow creatures is always a misfortune. The Growleywogs knew that they were disliked and avoided by every one, so they had become surly and unsociable even among themselves. Guph knew that they hated all people, including the Nomes; but he hoped to win them over, nevertheless, and knew that if he succeeded they would afford him very powerful assistance.

"The Land of Oz is ruled by a namby-pamby girl who is disgustingly kind and good," he continued. "Her people are all happy and contented and have no care or worries whatever."

"Go on!" growled the Grand Gallipoot.

"Once the Nome King enslaved the Royal Family of Ev—another goody-goody lot that we detest," said the General. "But Ozma interfered, although it was none of her business, and marched her army against us. With her was a Kansas girl named Dorothy, and a Yellow Hen, and they marched directly into the Nome King's cavern. There they liberated our slaves from Ev and stole King Roquat's Magic Belt, which they carried away with them. So now our King is making a tunnel under the deadly desert, so we can march through it to the Emerald City. When we get there we mean to conquer and destroy all the land and recapture the Magic Belt."

Again he paused, and again the Grand Gallipoot growled:

"Go on!"

Guph tried to think what to say next, and a happy thought soon occurred to him.

"We want you to help us in this conquest," he announced, "for we need the mighty aid of the Growleywogs in order to make sure that we shall not be defeated. You are the strongest people in all the world, and you hate good and happy creatures as much as we Nomes do. I am sure it will be a real pleasure to you to tear down the beautiful Emerald City, and in return for your valuable assistance we will allow you to bring back to your country ten thousand people of Oz, to be your slaves."

"Twenty thousand!" growled the Grand Gallipoot.

"All right, we promise you twenty thousand," agreed the General.

The Gallipoot made a signal and at once his attendants picked up General Guph and carried him away to a prison, where the jailer amused himself by sticking pins in the round fat body of the old Nome, to see him jump and hear him yell.

But while this was going on the Grand Gallipoot was talking with his counselors, who were the most important officials of the Growleywogs. When he had stated to them the proposition of the Nome King, he said:

"My advice is to offer to help them. Then, when we have conquered the Land of Oz, we will take not only our twenty thousand prisoners but all the gold and jewels we want."

"Let us take the Magic Belt, too," suggested one counselor.

"And rob the Nome King and make him our slave," said another.

"That is a good idea," declared the Grand Gallipoot. "I'd like King Roquat for my own slave. He could black my boots and bring me my porridge every morning while I am in bed."

"There is a famous Scarecrow in Oz. I'll take him for my slave," said a counselor.

"I'll take Tik-tok, the machine man," said another.

"Give me the Tin Woodman," said a third.

They went on for some time, dividing up the people and the treasure of Oz in advance of the conquest. For they had no doubt at all that they would be able to destroy Ozma's domain. Were they not the strongest people in all the world?

"The deadly desert has kept us out of Oz before," remarked the Grand Gallipoot, "but now that the Nome King is building a tunnel we shall get into the Emerald City very easily. So let us send the little fat General back to his King with our promise to assist him. We will not say that we intend to conquer the Nomes after we have conquered Oz, but we will do so, just the same."

This plan being agreed upon, they all went home to dinner, leaving General Guph still in prison. The Nome had no idea that he had succeeded in his mission, for finding himself in prison he feared the Growleywogs intended to put him to death.

By this time the jailer had tired of sticking pins in the General, and was amusing himself by carefully pulling the Nome's whiskers out by the roots, one at a time. This enjoyment was interrupted by the Grand Gallipoot sending for the prisoner.

"Wait a few hours," begged the jailer. "I haven't pulled out a quarter of his whiskers yet."

"If you keep the Grand Gallipoot waiting, he'll break your back," declared the messenger.

"Perhaps you're right," sighed the jailer. "Take the prisoner away, if you will, but I advise you to kick him at every step he takes. It will be good fun, for he is as soft as a ripe peach."

So Guph was led away to the royal castle, where the Grand Gallipoot told him that the Growleywogs had decided to assist the Nomes in conquering the Land of Oz.

"Whenever you are ready," he added, "send me word and I will march with eighteen thousand of my most powerful warriors to your aid."

Guph was so delighted that he forgot all the smarting caused by the pins and the pulling of whiskers. He did not even complain of the treatment he had received, but thanked the Grand Gallipoot and hurried away upon his journey.

He had now secured the assistance of the Whimsies and the Growleywogs; but his success made him long for still more allies. His own life depended upon his conquering Oz, and he said to himself:

"I'll take no chances. I'll be certain of success. Then, when Oz is destroyed, perhaps I shall be a greater man than old Roquat, and I can throw him away and be King of the Nomes myself. Why not? The Whimsies are stronger than the Nomes, and they also are my friends. There are some people still stronger than the Growleywogs, and if I can but induce them to aid me I shall have nothing more to fear."

Chapter 9 - How the Woggleburg Taught Atletics

It did not take Dorothy long to establish herself in her new home, for she knew the people and the manners and customs of the Emerald City just as well as she knew the old Kansas farm.

But Uncle Henry and Aunt Em had some trouble in getting used to the finery and pomp and ceremony of Ozma's palace, and felt uneasy because they were obliged to be "dressed up" all the time. Yet every one was very courteous and kind to them and endeavored to make them happy. Ozma, especially, made much of Dorothy's relatives, for her little friend's sake, and she well knew that the awkwardness and strangeness of their new mode of life would all wear off in time.

The old people were chiefly troubled by the fact that there was no work for them to do.

"Ev'ry day is like Sunday, now," declared Aunt Em, solemnly, "and I can't say I like it. If they'd only let me do up the dishes after meals, or even sweep an' dust my own rooms, I'd be a deal happier. Henry don't know what to do with himself either, and once when he stole out an' fed the chickens Billina scolded him for letting 'em eat between meals. I never knew before what a hardship it is to be rich and have everything you want."

These complaints began to worry Dorothy; so she had a long talk with Ozma upon the subject.

"I see I must find them something to do," said the girlish Ruler of Oz, seriously. "I have been watching your uncle and aunt, and I believe they will be more contented if occupied with some light tasks. While I am considering this matter, Dorothy, you might make a trip with them through the Land of Oz, visiting some of the odd corners and introducing your relatives to some of our curious people."

"Oh, that would be fine!" exclaimed Dorothy, eagerly.

"I will give you an escort befitting your rank as a Princess," continued Ozma; "and you may go to some of the places you have not yet visited yourself, as well as some others that you know. I will mark out a plan of the trip for you and have everything in readiness for you to start to-morrow morning. Take your time, dear, and be gone as long as you wish. By the time you return I shall have found some occupation for Uncle Henry and Aunt Em that will keep them from being restless and dissatisfied."

Dorothy thanked her good friend and kissed the lovely Ruler gratefully. Then she ran to tell the joyful news to her uncle and aunt.

Next morning, after breakfast, everything was found ready for their departure.

The escort included Omby Amby, the Captain General of Ozma's army, which consisted merely of twenty-seven officers besides the Captain General. Once Omby Amby had been a private soldier—the only private in the army—but as there was never any fighting to do Ozma saw no need of a private, so she made Omby Amby the highest officer of them all. He was very tall and slim and wore a gay uniform and a fierce mustache. Yet the mustache was the only fierce thing about Omby Amby, whose nature was as gentle as that of a child.

The wonderful Wizard had asked to join the party, and with him came his friend the Shaggy Man, who was shaggy but not ragged, being dressed in fine silks with satin shags and bobtails. The Shaggy Man had shaggy whiskers and hair, but a sweet disposition and a soft, pleasant voice.

There was an open wagon, with three seats for the passengers, and the wagon was drawn by the famous wooden Sawhorse which had once been brought to life by Ozma by means of a magic powder. The Sawhorse wore wooden shoes to keep his wooden legs from wearing away, and he was strong and swift. As this curious creature was Ozma's own favorite steed, and very popular with all the people of the Emerald City, Dorothy knew that she had been highly favored by being permitted to use the Sawhorse on her journey.

In the front seat of the wagon sat Dorothy and the Wizard. Uncle Henry and Aunt Em sat in the next seat and the Shaggy Man and Omby Amby in the third seat. Of course Toto was with the party, curled up at Dorothy's feet, and just as they were about to start, Billina came fluttering along the path and begged to be taken with them. Dorothy readily agreed, so the Yellow Hen flew up and perched herself upon the dashboard. She wore her pearl necklace and three bracelets upon each leg, in honor of the occasion.

Dorothy kissed Ozma good-bye, and all the people standing around waved their handkerchiefs, and the band in an upper balcony struck up a military march. Then the Wizard clucked to the Sawhorse and said: "Gid-dap!" and the wooden animal pranced away and drew behind him the big red wagon and all the passengers, without any effort at all. A servant threw open a gate of the palace enclosure, that they might pass out; and so, with music and shouts following them, the journey was begun.

"It's almost like a circus," said Aunt Em, proudly. "I can't help feelin' high an' mighty in this kind of a turn-out."

Indeed, as they passed down the street, all the people cheered them lustily, and the Shaggy Man and the Wizard and the Captain General all took off their hats and bowed politely in acknowledgment.

When they came to the great wall of the Emerald City, the gates were opened by the Guardian who always tended them. Over the gateway hung a dull-colored metal magnet shaped like a horse-shoe, placed against a shield of polished gold.

"That," said the Shaggy Man, impressively, "is the wonderful Love Magnet. I brought it to the Emerald City myself, and all who pass beneath this gateway are both loving and beloved."

"It's a fine thing," declared Aunt Em, admiringly. "If we'd had it in Kansas I guess the man who held a mortgage on the farm wouldn't have turned us out."

"Then I'm glad we didn't have it," returned Uncle Henry. "I like Oz better than Kansas, even; an' this little wood Sawhorse beats all the critters I ever saw. He don't have to be curried, or fed, or watered, an' he's strong as an ox. Can he talk, Dorothy?"

"Yes, Uncle," replied the child. "But the Sawhorse never says much. He told me once that he can't talk and think at the same time, so he prefers to think."

"Which is very sensible," declared the Wizard, nodding approvingly. "Which way do we go, Dorothy?"

"Straight ahead into the Quadling Country," she answered. "I've got a letter of interduction to Miss Cuttenclip."

"Oh!" exclaimed the Wizard, much interested. "Are we going there? Then I'm glad I came, for I've always wanted to meet the Cuttenclips."

"Who are they?" inquired Aunt Em.

"Wait till we get there," replied Dorothy, with a laugh; "then you'll see for yourself. I've never seen the Cuttenclips, you know, so I can't 'zactly 'splain 'em to you."

Once free of the Emerald City the Sawhorse dashed away at tremendous speed. Indeed, he went so fast that Aunt Em had hard work to catch her breath, and Uncle Henry held fast to the seat of the red wagon.

"Gently—gently, my boy!" called the Wizard, and at this the Sawhorse slackened his speed.

"What's wrong?" asked the animal, slightly turning his wooden head to look at the party with one eye, which was a knot of wood.

"Why, we wish to admire the scenery, that's all," answered the Wizard.

"Some of your passengers," added the Shaggy Man, "have never been out of the Emerald City before, and the country is all new to them."

"If you go too fast you'll spoil all the fun," said Dorothy. "There's no hurry."

"Very well; it is all the same to me," observed the Sawhorse; and after that he went at a more moderate pace.

Uncle Henry was astonished.

"How can a wooden thing be so intelligent?" he asked.

"Why, I gave him some sawdust brains the last time I fitted his head with new ears," explained the Wizard. "The sawdust was made from hard knots, and now the Sawhorse is able to think out any knotty problem he meets with."

"I see," said Uncle Henry.

"I don't," remarked Aunt Em; but no one paid any attention to this statement.

Before long they came to a stately building that stood upon a green plain with handsome shade trees grouped here and there.

"What is that?" asked Uncle Henry.

"That," replied the Wizard, "is the Royal Athletic College of Oz, which is directed by Professor H. M. Wogglebug, T.E."

"Let's stop and make a call," suggested Dorothy.

So the Sawhorse drew up in front of the great building and they were met at the door by the learned Wogglebug himself. He seemed fully as tall as the Wizard, and was dressed in a red and white checked vest and a blue swallow-tailed coat, and had yellow knee breeches and purple silk stockings upon his slender legs. A tall hat was jauntily set upon his head and he wore spectacles over his big bright eyes.

"Welcome, Dorothy," said the Wogglebug; "and welcome to all your friends. We are indeed pleased to receive you at this great Temple of Learning."

"I thought it was an Athletic College," said the Shaggy Man.

"It is, my dear sir," answered the Wogglebug, proudly. "Here it is that we teach the youth of our great land scientific College Athletics—in all their purity."

"Don't you teach them anything else?" asked Dorothy. "Don't they get any reading, writing and 'rithmetic?"

"Oh, yes; of course. They get all those, and more," returned the Professor. "But such things occupy little of their time. Please follow me and I will show you how my scholars are usually occupied. This is a class hour and they are all busy."

They followed him to a big field back of the college building, where several hundred young Ozites were at their classes. In one place they played football, in another baseball. Some played tennis, some golf; some were swimming in a big pool. Upon a river which wound through the grounds several crews in racing boats were rowing with great enthusiasm. Other groups of students played basketball and cricket, while in one place a ring was roped in to permit boxing and wrestling by the energetic youths. All the collegians seemed busy and there was much laughter and shouting.

"This college," said Professor Wogglebug, complacently, "is a great success. Its educational value is undisputed, and we are turning out many great and valuable citizens every year."

"But when do they study?" asked Dorothy.

"Study?" said the Wogglebug, looking perplexed at the question.

"Yes; when do they get their 'rithmetic, and jogerfy, and such things?"

"Oh, they take doses of those every night and morning," was the reply.

"What do you mean by doses?" Dorothy inquired, wonderingly.

"Why, we use the newly invented School Pills, made by your friend the Wizard. These pills we have found to be very effective, and they save a lot of time. Please step this way and I will show you our Laboratory of Learning."

He led them to a room in the building where many large bottles were standing in rows upon shelves.

"These are the Algebra Pills," said the Professor, taking down one of the bottles. "One at night, on retiring, is equal to four hours of study. Here are the Geography Pills—one at night and one in the morning. In this next bottle are the Latin Pills—one three times a day. Then we have the Grammar Pills—one before each meal—and the Spelling Pills, which are taken whenever needed."

"Your scholars must have to take a lot of pills," remarked Dorothy, thoughtfully. "How do they take 'em, in applesauce?"

"No, my dear. They are sugar-coated and are quickly and easily swallowed. I believe the students would rather take the pills than study, and certainly the pills are a more effective method. You see, until these School Pills were invented we wasted a lot of time in study that may now be better employed in practicing athletics."

"Seems to me the pills are a good thing," said Omby Amby, who remembered how it used to make his head ache as a boy to study arithmetic.

"They are, sir," declared the Wogglebug, earnestly. "They give us an advantage over all other colleges, because at no loss of time our boys become thoroughly conversant with Greek and Latin, Mathematics and Geography, Grammar and Literature. You see they are never obliged to interrupt their games to acquire the lesser branches of learning."

"It's a great invention, I'm sure," said Dorothy, looking admiringly at the Wizard, who blushed modestly at this praise.

"We live in an age of progress," announced Professor Wogglebug, pompously. "It is easier to swallow knowledge than to acquire it laboriously from books. Is it not so, my friends?"

"Some folks can swallow anything," said Aunt Em, "but to me this seems too much like taking medicine."

"Young men in college always have to take their medicine, one way or another," observed the Wizard, with a smile; "and, as our Professor says, these School Pills have proved to be a great success. One day while I was making them I happened to drop one of them, and one of Billina's chickens gobbled it up. A few minutes afterward this chick got upon a roost and recited 'The Boy Stood on the Burning Deck' without making a single mistake. Then it recited 'The Charge of the Light Brigade' and afterwards 'Excelsior.' You see, the chicken had eaten an Elocution Pill."

They now bade good-bye to the Professor, and thanking him for his kind reception mounted again into the red wagon and continued their journey.

Chapter 10 - How the Cuttenclips Lived

The travelers had taken no provisions with them because they knew that they would be welcomed wherever they might go in the Land of Oz, and that the people would feed and lodge them with genuine hospitality. So about noon they stopped at a farm-house and were given a delicious luncheon of bread and milk, fruits and wheat cakes with maple syrup. After resting a while and strolling through the orchards with their host—a round, jolly farmer—they got into the wagon and again started the Sawhorse along the pretty, winding road.

There were signposts at all the corners, and finally they came to one which read:

TAKE THIS ROAD TO THE CUTTENCLIPS

There was also a hand pointing in the right direction, so they turned the Sawhorse that way and found it a very good road, but seemingly little traveled.

"I've never seen the Cuttenclips before," remarked Dorothy.

"Nor I," said the Captain General.

"Nor I," said the Wizard.

"Nor I," said Billina.

"I've hardly been out of the Emerald City since I arrived in this country," added the Shaggy Man.

"Why, none of us has been there, then," exclaimed the little girl. "I wonder what the Cuttenclips are like."

"We shall soon find out," said the Wizard, with a sly laugh. "I've heard they are rather flimsy things."

The farm-houses became fewer as they proceeded, and the path was at times so faint that the Sawhorse had hard work to keep in the road. The wagon began to jounce, too; so they were obliged to go slowly.

After a somewhat wearisome journey they came in sight of a high wall, painted blue with pink ornaments. This wall was circular, and seemed to enclose a large space. It was so high that only the tops of the trees could be seen above it.

The path led up to a small door in the wall, which was closed and latched. Upon the door was a sign in gold letters reading as follows:

VISITORS are requested to MOVE SLOWLY and CAREFULLY, and to avoid COUGHING or making any BREEZE or DRAUGHT.

"That's strange," said the Shaggy Man, reading the sign aloud. "Who ARE the Cuttenclips, anyhow?"

"Why, they're paper dolls," answered Dorothy. "Didn't you know that?"

"Paper dolls! Then let's go somewhere else," said Uncle Henry. "We're all too old to play with dolls, Dorothy."

"But these are different," declared the girl. "They're alive."

"Alive!" gasped Aunt Em, in amazement.

"Yes. Let's go in," said Dorothy.

So they all got out of the wagon, since the door in the wall was not big enough for them to drive the Sawhorse and wagon through it.

"You stay here, Toto!" commanded Dorothy, shaking her finger at the little dog. "You're so careless that you might make a breeze if I let you inside."

Toto wagged his tail as if disappointed at being left behind; but he made no effort to follow them. The Wizard unlatched the door, which opened outward, and they all looked eagerly inside.

Just before the entrance was drawn up a line of tiny soldiers, with uniforms brightly painted and paper guns upon their shoulders. They were exactly alike, from one end of the line to the other, and all were cut out of paper and joined together in the centers of their bodies.

As the visitors entered the enclosure the Wizard let the door swing back into place, and at once the line of soldiers tumbled over, fell flat upon their backs, and lay fluttering upon the ground.

"Hi there!" called one of them; "what do you mean by slamming the door and blowing us over?"

"I beg your pardon, I'm sure," said the Wizard, regretfully. "I didn't know you were so delicate."

"We're not delicate!" retorted another soldier, raising his head from the ground. "We are strong and healthy; but we can't stand draughts."

"May I help you up?" asked Dorothy.

"If you please," replied the end soldier. "But do it gently, little girl."

Dorothy carefully stood up the line of soldiers, who first dusted their painted clothes and then saluted the visitors with their paper muskets. From the end it was easy to see that the entire line had been cut out of paper, although from the front the soldiers looked rather solid and imposing.

"I've a letter of introduction from Princess Ozma to Miss Cuttenclip," announced Dorothy.

"Very well," said the end soldier, and blew upon a paper whistle that hung around his neck. At once a paper soldier in a Captain's uniform came out of a paper house near by and approached the group at the entrance. He was not very big, and he walked rather stiffly and uncertainly on his paper legs; but he had a pleasant face, with very red cheeks and very blue eyes, and he bowed so low to the strangers that Dorothy laughed, and the breeze from her mouth nearly blew the Captain over. He wavered and struggled and finally managed to remain upon his feet.

"Take care, Miss!" he said, warningly. "You're breaking the rules, you know, by laughing."

"Oh, I didn't know that," she replied.

"To laugh in this place is nearly as dangerous as to cough," said the Captain. "You'll have to breathe very quietly, I assure you."

"We'll try to," promised the girl. "May we see Miss Cuttenclip, please?"

"You may," promptly returned the Captain. "This is one of her reception days. Be good enough to follow me."

He turned and led the way up a path, and as they followed slowly, because the paper Captain did not move very swiftly, they took the opportunity to gaze around them at this strange paper country.

Beside the path were paper trees, all cut out very neatly and painted a brilliant green color. And back of the trees were rows of cardboard houses, painted in various colors but most of them having green blinds. Some were large and some small, and in the front yards were beds of paper flowers quite natural in appearance. Over some of the porches paper vines were twined, giving them a cozy and shady look.

As the visitors passed along the street a good many paper dolls came to the doors and windows of their houses to look at them curiously. These dolls were nearly all the same height, but were cut into various shapes, some being fat and some lean. The girl dolls wore many beautiful costumes of tissue paper, making them quite fluffy; but their heads and hands were no thicker than the paper of which they were made.

Some of the paper people were on the street, walking along or congregated in groups and talking together; but as soon as they saw the strangers they all fluttered into the houses as fast as they could go, so as to be out of danger.

"Excuse me if I go edgewise," remarked the Captain as they came to a slight hill. "I can get along faster that way and not flutter so much."

"That's all right," said Dorothy. "We don't mind how you go, I'm sure."

At one side of the street was a paper pump, and a paper boy was pumping paper water into a paper pail. The Yellow Hen happened to brush against this boy with her wing, and he flew into the air and fell into a paper tree, where he stuck until the Wizard gently pulled him out. At the same time, the pail went into the air, spilling the paper water, while the paper pump bent nearly double.

"Goodness me!" said the Hen. "If I should flop my wings I believe I'd knock over the whole village!"

"Then don't flop them—please don't!" entreated the Captain. "Miss Cuttenclip would be very much distressed if her village was spoiled."

"Oh, I'll be careful," promised Billina.

"Are not all these paper girls and women named Miss Cuttenclips?" inquired Omby Amby.

"No indeed," answered the Captain, who was walking better since he began to move edgewise. "There is but one Miss Cuttenclip, who is our Queen, because she made us all. These girls are Cuttenclips, to be sure, but their names are Emily and Polly and Sue and Betty and such things. Only the Queen is called Miss Cuttenclip."

"I must say that this place beats anything I ever heard of," observed Aunt Em. "I used to play with paper dolls myself, an' cut 'em out; but I never thought I'd ever see such things alive."

"I don't see as it's any more curious than hearing hens talk," returned Uncle Henry.

"You're likely to see many queer things in the Land of Oz, sir," said the Wizard. "But a fairy country is extremely interesting when you get used to being surprised."

"Here we are!" called the Captain, stopping before a cottage.

This house was made of wood, and was remarkably pretty in design. In the Emerald City it would have been considered a tiny dwelling, indeed; but in the midst of this paper village it seemed immense. Real flowers were in the garden and real trees grew beside it. Upon the front door was a sign reading:

MISS CUTTENCLIP.

Just as they reached the porch the front door opened and a little girl stood before them. She appeared to be about the same age as Dorothy, and smiling upon her visitors she said, sweetly:

"You are welcome."

All the party seemed relieved to find that here was a real girl, of flesh and blood. She was very dainty and pretty as she stood there welcoming them. Her hair was a golden blonde and her eyes turquoise blue. She had rosy cheeks and lovely white teeth. Over her simple white lawn dress she wore an apron with pink and white checks, and in one hand she held a pair of scissors.

"May we see Miss Cuttenclip, please?" asked Dorothy.

"I am Miss Cuttenclip," was the reply. "Won't you come in?"

She held the door open while they all entered a pretty sitting-room that was littered with all sorts of paper—some stiff, some thin, and some tissue. The sheets and scraps were of all colors. Upon a table were paints and brushes, while several pair of scissors, of different sizes, were lying about.

"Sit down, please," said Miss Cuttenclip, clearing the paper scraps off some of the chairs. "It is so long since I have had any visitors that I am not properly prepared to receive them. But I'm sure you will pardon my untidy room, for this is my workshop."

"Do you make all the paper dolls?" inquired Dorothy.

"Yes; I cut them out with my scissors, and paint the faces and some of the costumes. It is very pleasant work, and I am happy making my paper village grow."

"But how do the paper dolls happen to be alive?" asked Aunt Em.

"The first dolls I made were not alive," said Miss Cuttenclip. "I used to live near the castle of a great Sorceress named Glinda the Good, and she saw my dolls and said they were very pretty. I told her I thought I would like them better if they were alive, and the next day the Sorceress brought me a lot of magic paper. 'This is live paper,' she said, 'and all the dolls you cut out of it will be alive, and able to think and to talk. When you have used it all up, come to me and I will give you more.'

"Of course I was delighted with this present," continued Miss Cuttenclip, "and at once set to work and made several paper dolls, which, as soon as they were cut out, began to walk around and talk to me. But they were so thin that I found that any breeze would blow them over and scatter them dreadfully; so Glinda found this lonely place for me, where few people ever come. She built the wall to keep any wind from blowing away my people, and told me I could build a paper village here and be its Queen. That is why I came here and settled down to work and started the village you now see. It was many years ago that I built the first houses, and I've kept pretty busy and made my village grow finely; and I need not tell you that I am very happy in my work."

"Many years ago!" exclaimed Aunt Em. "Why, how old are you, child?"

"I never keep track of the years," said Miss Cuttenclip, laughing. "You see, I don't grow up at all, but stay just the same as I was when first I came here. Perhaps I'm older even than you are, madam; but I couldn't say for sure."

They looked at the lovely little girl wonderingly, and the Wizard asked:

"What happens to your paper village when it rains?"

"It does not rain here," replied Miss Cuttenclip. "Glinda keeps all the rain storms away; so I never worry about my dolls getting wet. But now, if you will come with me, it will give me pleasure to show you over my paper kingdom. Of course you must go slowly and carefully, and avoid making any breeze."

They left the cottage and followed their guide through the various streets of the village. It was indeed an amazing place, when one considered that it was all made with scissors, and the visitors were not only greatly interested but full of admiration for the skill of little Miss Cuttenclip.

In one place a large group of especially nice paper dolls assembled to greet their Queen, whom it was easy to see they loved early. These dolls marched and danced before the visitors, and then they all waved their paper handkerchiefs and sang in a sweet chorus a song called "The Flag of Our Native Land."

At the conclusion of the song they ran up a handsome paper flag on a tall flagpole, and all of the people of the village gathered around to cheer as loudly as they could—although, of course, their voices were not especially strong.

Miss Cuttenclip was about to make her subjects a speech in reply to this patriotic song, when the Shaggy Man happened to sneeze.

He was a very loud and powerful sneezer at any time, and he had tried so hard to hold in this sneeze that when it suddenly exploded the result was terrible.

The paper dolls were mowed down by dozens, and flew and fluttered in wild confusion in every direction, tumbling this way and that and getting more or less wrinkled and bent.

A wail of terror and grief came from the scattered throng, and Miss Cuttenclip exclaimed:

"Dear me! dear me!" and hurried at once to the rescue of her overturned people.

"Oh, Shaggy Man! How could you?" asked Dorothy, reproachfully.

"I couldn't help it—really I couldn't," protested the Shaggy Man, looking quite ashamed. "And I had no idea it took so little to upset these paper dolls."

"So little!" said Dorothy. "Why, it was 'most as bad as a Kansas cyclone." And then she helped Miss Cuttenclip rescue the paper folk and stand them on their feet again. Two of the cardboard houses had also tumbled over, and the little Queen said she would have to repair them and paste them together before they could be lived in again.

And now, fearing they might do more damage to the flimsy paper people, they decided to go away. But first they thanked Miss Cuttenclip very warmly for her courtesy and kindness to them.

"Any friend of Princess Ozma is always welcome here—unless he sneezes," said the Queen with a rather severe look at the Shaggy Man, who hung his head. "I like to have visitors admire my wonderful village, and I hope you will call again."

Miss Cuttenclip herself led them to the door in the wall, and as they passed along the street the paper dolls peeped at them half fearfully from the doors and windows. Perhaps they will never forget the Shaggy Man's awful sneeze, and I am sure they were all glad to see the meat people go away.

Chapter 11 - How the General Met the First and Foremost

On leaving the Growleywogs General Guph had to recross the Ripple Lands, and he did not find it a pleasant thing to do. Perhaps having his whiskers pulled out one by one and being used as a pin-cushion for the innocent amusement of a good natured jailer had not improved the quality of Guph's temper, for the old Nome raved and raged at the recollection of the wrongs he had suffered, and vowed to take vengeance upon the Growleywogs after he had used them for his purposes and Oz had been conquered. He went on in this furious way until he was half across the Ripple Land. Then he became seasick, and the rest of the way this naughty Nome was almost as miserable as he deserved to be.

But when he reached the plains again and the ground was firm under his feet he began to feel better, and instead of going back home he turned directly west. A squirrel, perched in a tree, saw him take this road and called to him warningly: "Look out!" But he paid no attention. An eagle paused in its flight through the air to look at him wonderingly and say: "Look out!" But on he went.

No one can say that Guph was not brave, for he had determined to visit those dangerous creatures the Phanfasms, who resided upon the very top of the dread Mountain of Phantastico. The Phanfasms were Erbs, and so dreaded by mortals and immortals alike that no one had been near their mountain home for several thousand years. Yet General Guph hoped to induce them to join in his proposed warfare against the good and happy Oz people.

Guph knew very well that the Phanfasms would be almost as dangerous to the Nomes as they would to the Ozites, but he thought himself so clever that he believed he could manage these strange creatures and make them obey him. And there was no doubt at all that if he could enlist the services of the Phanfasms, their tremendous power, united to the strength of the Growleywogs and the cunning of the Whimsies would doom the Land of Oz to absolute destruction.

So the old Nome climbed the foothills and trudged along the wild mountain paths until he came to a big gully that encircled the Mountain of Phantastico and marked the boundary line of the dominion of the Phanfasms. This gully was about a third of the way up the mountain, and it was filled to the brim with red-hot molten lava in which swam fire-serpents and poisonous salamanders. The heat from this mass and its poisonous smell were both so unbearable that even birds hesitated to fly over the gully, but circled around it. All living things kept away from the mountain.

Now Guph had heard, during his long lifetime, many tales of these dreaded Phanfasms; so he had heard of this barrier of melted lava, and also he had been told that there was a narrow bridge that spanned it in one place. So he walked along the edge until he found the bridge. It was a single arch of gray stone, and lying flat upon the bridge was a scarlet alligator, seemingly fast asleep.

When Guph stumbled over the rocks in approaching the bridge the creature opened its eyes, from which tiny flames shot in all directions, and after looking at the intruder very wickedly the scarlet alligator closed its eyelids again and lay still.

Guph saw there was no room for him to pass the alligator on the narrow bridge, so he called out to it:

"Good morning, friend. I don't wish to hurry you, but please tell me if you are coming down, or going up?"

"Neither," snapped the alligator, clicking its cruel jaws together.

The General hesitated.

"Are you likely to stay there long?" he asked.

"A few hundred years or so," said the alligator.

Guph softly rubbed the end of his nose and tried to think what to do.

"Do you know whether the First and Foremost Phanfasm of Phantastico is at home or not?" he presently inquired.

"I expect he is, seeing he is always at home," replied the alligator.

"Ah; who is that coming down the mountain?" asked the Nome, gazing upward.

The alligator turned to look over its shoulder, and at once Guph ran to the bridge and leaped over the sentinel's back before it could turn back again. The scarlet monster made a snap at the Nome's left foot, but missed it by fully an inch.

"Ah ha!" laughed the General, who was now on the mountain path. "I fooled you that time."

"So you did; and perhaps you fooled yourself," retorted the alligator. "Go up the mountain, if you dare, and find out what the First and Foremost will do to you!"

"I will," declared Guph, boldly; and on he went up the path.

At first the scene was wild enough, but gradually it grew more and more awful in appearance. All the rocks had the shapes of frightful beings and even the tree trunks were gnarled and twisted like serpents.

Suddenly there appeared before the Nome a man with the head of an owl. His body was hairy like that of an ape, and his only clothing was a scarlet scarf twisted around his waist. He bore a huge club in his hand and his round owl eyes blinked fiercely upon the intruder.

"What are you doing here?" he demanded, threatening Guph with his club.

"I've come to see the First and Foremost Phanfasm of Phantastico," replied the General, who did not like the way this creature looked at him, but still was not afraid.

"Ah; you shall see him!" the man said, with a sneering laugh. "The First and Foremost shall decide upon the best way to punish you."

"He will not punish me," returned Guph, calmly, "for I have come here to do him and his people a rare favor. Lead on, fellow, and take me directly to your master."

The owl-man raised his club with a threatening gesture.

"If you try to escape," he said, "beware—"

But here the General interrupted him.

"Spare your threats," said he, "and do not be impertinent, or I will have you severely punished. Lead on, and keep silent!"

This Guph was really a clever rascal, and it seems a pity he was so bad, for in a good cause he might have accomplished much. He realized that he had put himself into a dangerous position by coming to this dreadful mountain, but he also knew that if he showed fear he was lost. So he adopted a bold manner as his best defense. The wisdom of this plan was soon evident, for the Phanfasm with the owl's head turned and led the way up the mountain.

At the very top was a level plain upon which were heaps of rock that at first glance seemed solid. But on looking closer Guph discovered that these rock heaps were dwellings, for each had an opening.

Not a person was to be seen outside the rock huts. All was silent.

The owl-man led the way among the groups of dwellings to one standing in the center. It seemed no better and no worse than any of the others. Outside the entrance to this rock heap the guide gave a low wail that sounded like "Lee-ow-ah!"

Suddenly there bounded from the opening another hairy man. This one wore the head of a bear. In his hand he bore a brass hoop. He glared at the stranger in evident surprise.

"Why have you captured this foolish wanderer and brought him here?" he demanded, addressing the owl-man.

"I did not capture him," was the answer. "He passed the scarlet alligator and came here of his own free will and accord."

The First and Foremost looked at the General.

"Have you tired of life, then?" he asked.

"No indeed," answered Guph. "I am a Nome, and the Chief General of King Roquat the Red's great army of Nomes. I come of a long-lived race, and I may say that I expect to live a long time yet. Sit down, you Phanfasms—if you can find a seat in this wild haunt—and listen to what I have to say."

With all his knowledge and bravery General Guph did not know that the steady glare from the bear eyes was reading his inmost thoughts as surely as if they had been put into words. He did not know that these despised rock heaps of the Phanfasms were merely deceptions to his own eyes, nor could he guess that he was standing in the midst of one of the most splendid and luxurious cities ever built by magic power. All that he saw was a barren waste of rock heaps, a hairy man with an owl's head and another with a bear's head. The sorcery of the Phanfasms permitted him to see no more.

Suddenly the First and Foremost swung his brass hoop and caught Guph around the neck with it. The next instant, before the General could think what had happened to him, he was dragged inside the rock hut. Here, his eyes still blinded to realities, he perceived only a dim light, by which the hut seemed as rough and rude inside as it was outside. Yet he had a strange feeling that many bright eyes were fastened upon him and that he stood in a vast and extensive hall.

The First and Foremost now laughed grimly and released his prisoner.

"If you have anything to say that is interesting," he remarked, "speak out ,before I strangle you."

So Guph spoke out. He tried not to pay any attention to a strange rustling sound that he heard, as of an unseen multitude drawing near to listen to his words. His eyes could see only the fierce bear-man, and to him he addressed his speech. First he told of his plan to conquer the Land of Oz and plunder the country of its riches and enslave its people, who, being fairies, could not be killed. After relating all this, and telling of the tunnel the Nome King was building, he said he had come to ask the First and Foremost to join the Nomes, with his band of terrible warriors, and help them to defeat the Oz people.

The General spoke very earnestly and impressively, but when he had finished the bear-man began to laugh as if much amused, and his laughter seemed to be echoed by a chorus of merriment from an unseen multitude. Then, for the first time, Guph began to feel a trifle worried.

"Who else has promised to help you?" finally asked the First and Foremost.

"The Whimsies," replied the General.

Again the bear-headed Phanfasm laughed.

"Any others?" he inquired.

"Only the Growleywogs," said Guph.

This answer set the First and Foremost laughing anew.

"What share of the spoils am I to have?" was the next question.

"Anything you like, except King Roquat's Magic Belt," replied Guph.

At this the Phanfasm set up a roar of laughter, which had its echo in the unseen chorus, and the bear-man seemed so amused that he actually rolled upon the ground and shouted with merriment.

"Oh, these blind and foolish Nomes!" he said. "How big they seem to themselves and how small they really are!"

Suddenly he arose and seized Guph's neck with one hairy paw, dragging him out of the hut into the open.

Here he gave a curious wailing cry, and, as if in answer, from all the rocky huts on the mountain-top came flocking a horde of Phanfasms, all with hairy bodies, but wearing heads of various animals, birds and reptiles. All were ferocious and repulsive-looking to the deceived eyes of the Nome, and Guph could not repress a shudder of disgust as he looked upon them.

The First and Foremost slowly raised his arms, and in a twinkling his hairy skin fell from him and he appeared before the astonished Nome as a beautiful woman, clothed in a flowing gown of pink gauze. In her dark hair flowers were entwined, and her face was noble and calm.

At the same instant the entire band of Phanfasms was transformed into a pack of howling wolves, running here and there as they snarled and showed their ugly yellow fangs.

The woman now raised her arms, even as the man-bear had done, and in a twinkling the wolves became crawling lizards, while she herself changed into a huge butterfly.

Guph had only time to cry out in fear and take a step backward to avoid the lizards when another transformation occurred, and all returned instantly to the forms they had originally worn.

Then the First and Foremost, who had resumed his hairy body and bear head, turned to the Nome and asked

"Do you still demand our assistance?"

"More than ever," answered the General, firmly.

"Then tell me: what can you offer the Phanfasms that they have not already?" inquired the First and Foremost.

Guph hesitated. He really did not know what to say. The Nome King's vaunted Magic Belt seemed a poor thing compared to the astonishing magical powers of these people. Gold, jewels and slaves they might secure in any quantity without especial effort. He felt that he was dealing with powers greatly beyond him. There was but one argument that might influence the Phanfasms, who were creatures of evil.

"Permit me to call your attention to the exquisite joy of making the happy unhappy," said he at last. "Consider the pleasure of destroying innocent and harmless people."

"Ah! you have answered me," cried the First and Foremost. "For that reason alone we will aid you. Go home, and tell your bandy-legged king that as soon as his tunnel is finished the Phanfasms will be with him and lead his legions to the conquest of Oz. The deadly desert alone has kept us from destroying Oz long ago, and your underground tunnel is a clever thought. Go home, and prepare for our coming!"

Guph was very glad to be permitted to go with this promise. The owl-man led him back down the mountain path and ordered the scarlet alligator to crawl away and allow the Nome to cross the bridge in safety.

After the visitor had gone a brilliant and gorgeous city appeared upon the mountain top, clearly visible to the eyes of the gaily dressed multitude of Phanfasms that lived there. And the First and Foremost, beautifully arrayed, addressed the others in these words:

287

"It is time we went into the world and brought sorrow and dismay to its people. Too long have we remained for ourselves upon this mountain top, for while we are thus secluded many nations have grown happy and prosperous, and the chief joy of the race of Phanfasms is to destroy happiness. So I think it is lucky that this messenger from the Nomes arrived among us just now, to remind us that the opportunity has come for us to make trouble. We will use King Roquat's tunnel to conquer the Land of Oz. Then we will destroy the Whimsies, the Growleywogs and the Nomes, and afterward go out to ravage and annoy and grieve the whole world."

The multitude of evil Phanfasms eagerly applauded this plan, which they fully approved.

I am told that the Erbs are the most powerful and merciless of all the evil spirits, and the Phanfasms of Phantastico belong to the race of Erbs.

Chapter 12 - How they Matched the Fuddles

Dorothy and her fellow travelers rode away from the Cuttenclip village and followed the indistinct path as far as the sign-post. Here they took the main road again and proceeded pleasantly through the pretty farming country. When evening came they stopped at a dwelling and were joyfully welcomed and given plenty to eat and good beds for the night.

Early next morning, however, they were up and eager to start, and after a good breakfast they bade their host good-bye and climbed into the red wagon, to which the Sawhorse had been hitched all night. Being made of wood, this horse never got tired nor cared to lie down. Dorothy was not quite sure whether he ever slept or not, but it was certain that he never did when anybody was around.

The weather is always beautiful in Oz, and this morning the air was cool and refreshing and the sunshine brilliant and delightful.

In about an hour they came to a place where another road branched off. There was a sign-post here which read:

THIS WAY TO FUDDLECUMJIG

"Oh, here is where we turn," said Dorothy, observing the sign.

"What! Are we going to Fuddlecumjig?" asked the Captain General.

"Yes; Ozma thought we might enjoy the Fuddles. They are said to be very interesting," she replied.

"No one would suspect it from their name," said Aunt Em. "Who are they, anyhow? More paper things?"

"I think not," answered Dorothy, laughing; "but I can't say 'zactly, Aunt Em, what they are. We'll find out when we get there."

"Perhaps the Wizard knows," suggested Uncle Henry.

"No; I've never been there before," said the Wizard. "But I've often heard of Fuddlecumjig and the Fuddles, who are said to be the most peculiar people in all the Land of Oz."

"In what way?" asked the Shaggy Man.

"I don't know, I'm sure," said the Wizard.

Just then, as they rode along the pretty green lane toward Fuddlecumjig, they espied a kangaroo sitting by the roadside. The poor animal had its face covered with both its front paws and was crying so bitterly that the tears coursed down its cheeks in two tiny streams and trickled across the road, where they formed a pool in a small hollow.

The Sawhorse stopped short at this pitiful sight, and Dorothy cried out, with ready sympathy:

"What's the matter, Kangaroo?"

"Boo-hoo! Boo-hoo!" wailed the Kangaroo; "I've lost my mi—mi—mi—Oh, boo-hoo! Boo-hoo!"—

"Poor thing," said the Wizard, "she's lost her mister. It's probably her husband, and he's dead."

"No, no, no!" sobbed the kangaroo. "It—it isn't that. I've lost my mi—mi—Oh, boo, boo-hoo!"

"I know," said the Shaggy Man; "she's lost her mirror."

"No; it's my mi—mi—mi—Boo-hoo! My mi—Oh, Boo-hoo!" and the kangaroo cried harder than ever.

"It must be her mince-pie," suggested Aunt Em.

"Or her milk-toast," proposed Uncle Henry.

"I've lost my mi—mi—mittens!" said the kangaroo, getting it out at last.

"Oh!" cried the Yellow Hen, with a cackle of relief. "Why didn't you say so before?"

"Boo-hoo! I—I—couldn't," answered the kangaroo.

"But, see here," said Dorothy, "you don't need mittens in this warm weather."

"Yes, indeed I do," replied the animal, stopping her sobs and removing her paws from her face to look at the little girl reproachfully. "My hands will get all sunburned and tanned without my mittens, and I've worn them so long that I'll probably catch cold without them."

"Nonsense!" said Dorothy. "I never heard of any kangaroo wearing mittens."

"Didn't you?" asked the animal, as if surprised.

"Never!" repeated the girl. "And you'll probably make yourself sick if you don't stop crying. Where do you live?"

"About two miles beyond Fuddlecumjig," was the answer. "Grandmother Gnit made me the mittens, and she's one of the Fuddles."

"Well, you'd better go home now, and perhaps the old lady will make you another pair," suggested Dorothy. "We're on our way to Fuddlecumjig, and you may hop along beside us."

So they rode on, and the kangaroo hopped beside the red wagon and seemed quickly to have forgotten her loss. By and by the Wizard said to the animal:

"Are the Fuddles nice people?"

"Oh, very nice," answered the kangaroo; "that is, when they're properly put together. But they get dreadfully scattered and mixed up, at times, and then you can't do anything with them."

"What do you mean by their getting scattered?" inquired Dorothy.

"Why, they're made in a good many small pieces," explained the kangaroo; "and whenever any stranger comes near them they have a habit of falling apart and scattering themselves around. That's when they get so dreadfully mixed, and it's a hard puzzle to put them together again."

"Who usually puts them together?" asked Omby Amby.

"Any one who is able to match the pieces. I sometimes put Grandmother Gnit together myself, because I know her so well I can tell every piece that belongs to her. Then, when she's all matched, she knits for me, and that's how she made my mittens. But it took a good many days hard knitting, and I had to put Grandmother together a good many times, because every time I came near, she'd scatter herself."

"I should think she would get used to your coming, and not be afraid," said Dorothy.

"It isn't that," replied the kangaroo. "They're not a bit afraid, when they're put together, and usually they're very jolly and pleasant. It's just a habit they have, to scatter themselves, and if they didn't do it they wouldn't be Fuddles."

The travelers thought upon this quite seriously for a time, while the Sawhorse continued to carry them rapidly forward. Then Aunt Em remarked:

"I don't see much use our visitin' these Fuddles. If we find them scattered, all we can do is to sweep 'em up, and then go about our business."

"Oh, I b'lieve we'd better go on," replied Dorothy. "I'm getting hungry, and we must try to get some luncheon at Fuddlecumjig. Perhaps the food won't be scattered as badly as the people."

"You'll find plenty to eat there," declared the kangaroo, hopping along in big bounds because the Sawhorse was going so fast; "and they have a fine cook, too, if you can manage to put him together. There's the town now—just ahead of us!"

They looked ahead and saw a group of very pretty houses standing in a green field a little apart from the main road.

"Some Munchkins came here a few days ago and matched a lot of people together," said the kangaroo. "I think they are together yet, and if you go softly, without making any noise, perhaps they won't scatter."

"Let's try it," suggested the Wizard.

So they stopped the Sawhorse and got out of the wagon, and, after bidding good bye to the kangaroo, who hopped away home, they entered the field and very cautiously approached the group of houses.

So silently did they move that soon they saw through the windows of the houses, people moving around, while others were passing to and fro in the yards between the buildings. They seemed much like other people from a distance, and apparently they did not notice the little party so quietly approaching.

They had almost reached the nearest house when Toto saw a large beetle crossing the path and barked loudly at it. Instantly a wild clatter was heard from the houses and yards. Dorothy thought it sounded like a sudden hailstorm, and the visitors, knowing that caution was no longer necessary, hurried forward to see what had happened.

After the clatter an intense stillness reigned in the town. The strangers entered the first house they came to, which was also the largest, and found the floor strewn with pieces of the people who lived there. They looked much like fragments of wood neatly painted, and were of all sorts of curious and fantastic shapes, no two pieces being in any way alike.

They picked up some of these pieces and looked at them carefully. On one which Dorothy held was an eye, which looked at her pleasantly but with an interested expression, as if it wondered what she was going to do with it. Quite near by she discovered and picked up a nose, and by matching the two pieces together found that they were part of a face.

"If I could find the mouth," she said, "this Fuddle might be able to talk, and tell us what to do next."

"Then let us find it," replied the Wizard, and so all got down on their hands and knees and began examining the scattered pieces.

"I've found it!" cried the Shaggy Man, and ran to Dorothy with a queer-shaped piece that had a mouth on it. But when they tried to fit it to the eye and nose they found the parts wouldn't match together.

"That mouth belongs to some other person," said Dorothy. "You see we need a curve here and a point there, to make it fit the face."

"Well, it must be here some place," declared the Wizard; "so if we search long enough we shall find it."

Dorothy fitted an ear on next, and the ear had a little patch of red hair above it. So while the others were searching for the mouth she hunted for pieces with red hair, and found several of them which, when matched to the other pieces, formed the top of a man's head. She had also found the other eye and the ear by the time Omby Amby in a far corner discovered the mouth. When the face was thus completed, all the parts joined together with a nicety that was astonishing.

"Why, it's like a picture puzzle!" exclaimed the little girl. "Let's find the rest of him, and get him all together."

"What's the rest of him like?" asked the Wizard. "Here are some pieces of blue legs and green arms, but I don't know whether they are his or not."

"Look for a white shirt and a white apron," said the head which had been put together, speaking in a rather faint voice. "I'm the cook."

"Oh, thank you," said Dorothy. "It's lucky we started you first, for I'm hungry, and you can be cooking something for us to eat while we match the other folks together."

It was not so very difficult, now that they had a hint as to how the man was dressed, to find the other pieces belonging to him, and as all of them now worked on the cook, trying piece after piece to see if it would fit, they finally had the cook set up complete.

When he was finished he made them a low bow and said:

"I will go at once to the kitchen to prepare your dinner. You will find it something of a job to get all the Fuddles together, so I advise you to begin on the Lord High Chigglewitz, whose first name is Larry. He's a bald-headed fat man and is dressed in a blue coat with brass buttons, a pink vest and drab breeches. A piece of his left knee is missing, having been lost years ago when he scattered himself too carelessly. That makes him limp a little, but he gets along very well with half a knee. As he is the chief personage in this town of Fuddlecumjig, he will be able to welcome you and assist you with the others. So it will be best to work on him while I'm getting your dinner."

"We will," said the Wizard; "and thank you very much, Cook, for the suggestion."

Aunt Em was the first to discover a piece of the Lord High Chigglewitz.

"It seems to me like a fool business, this matching folks together," she remarked; "but as we haven't anything to do till dinner's ready, we may as well get rid of some of this rubbish. Here, Henry, get busy and look for Larry's bald head. I've got his pink vest, all right."

They worked with eager interest, and Billina proved a great help to them. The Yellow Hen had sharp eyes and could put her head close to the various pieces that lay scattered around. She would examine the Lord High Chigglewitz and see which piece of him was next needed, and then hunt around until she found it. So before an hour had passed old Larry was standing complete before them.

"I congratulate you, my friends," he said, speaking in a cheerful voice. "You are certainly the cleverest people who ever visited us. I was never matched together so quickly in my life. I'm considered a great puzzle, usually."

"Well," said Dorothy, "there used to be a picture puzzle craze in Kansas, and so I've had some 'sperience matching puzzles. But the pictures were flat, while you are round, and that makes you harder to figure out."

"Thank you, my dear," replied old Larry, greatly pleased. "I feel highly complimented. Were I not a really good puzzle, there would be no object in my scattering myself."

"Why do you do it?" asked Aunt Em, severely. "Why don't you behave yourself, and stay put together?"

The Lord High Chigglewitz seemed annoyed by this speech; but he replied, politely:

"Madam, you have perhaps noticed that every person has some peculiarity. Mine is to scatter myself. What your own peculiarity is I will not venture to say; but I shall never find fault with you, whatever you do."

"Now you've got your diploma, Em," said Uncle Henry, with a laugh, "and I'm glad of it. This is a queer country, and we may as well take people as we find them."

"If we did, we'd leave these folks scattered," she returned, and this retort made everybody laugh good-naturedly.

Just then Omby Amby found a hand with a knitting needle in it, and they decided to put Grandmother Gnit together. She proved an easier puzzle than old Larry, and when she was completed they found her a pleasant old lady who welcomed them cordially. Dorothy told her how the kangaroo had lost her mittens, and Grandmother Gnit promised to set to work at once and make the poor animal another pair.

Then the cook came to call them to dinner, and they found an inviting meal prepared for them. The Lord High Chigglewitz sat at the head of the table and Grandmother Gnit at the foot, and the guests had a merry time and thoroughly enjoyed themselves.

After dinner they went out into the yard and matched several other people together, and this work was so interesting that they might have spent the entire day at Fuddlecumjig had not the Wizard suggested that they resume their journey.

"But I don't like to leave all these poor people scattered," said Dorothy, undecided what to do.

"Oh, don't mind us, my dear," returned old Larry. "Every day or so some of the Gillikins, or Munchkins, or Winkies come here to amuse themselves by matching us together, so there will be no harm in leaving these pieces where they are for a time. But I hope you will visit us again, and if you do you will always be welcome, I assure you."

"Don't you ever match each other?" she inquired.

"Never; for we are no puzzles to ourselves, and so there wouldn't be any fun in it."

They now said goodbye to the queer Fuddles and got into their wagon to continue their journey.

"Those are certainly strange people," remarked Aunt Em, thoughtfully, as they drove away from Fuddlecumjig, "but I really can't see what use they are, at all."

"Why, they amused us all for several hours," replied the Wizard. "That is being of use to us, I'm sure."

"I think they're more fun than playing solitaire or mumbletypeg," declared Uncle Henry, soberly. "For my part, I'm glad we visited the Fuddles."

Chapter 13 - How the General Talked to the King

When General Guph returned to the cavern of the Nome King his Majesty asked:

"Well, what luck? Will the Whimsies join us?"

"They will," answered the General. "They will fight for us with all their strength and cunning."

"Good!" exclaimed the King. "What reward did you promise them?"

"Your Majesty is to use the Magic Belt to give each Whimsie a large, fine head, in place of the small one he is now obliged to wear."

"I agree to that," said the King. "This is good news, Guph, and it makes me feel more certain of the conquest of Oz."

"But I have other news for you," announced the General.

"Good or bad?"

"Good, your Majesty."

"Then I will hear it," said the King, with interest.

"The Growleywogs will join us."

"No!" cried the astonished King.

"Yes, indeed," said the General. "I have their promise."

"But what reward do they demand?" inquired the King, suspiciously, for he knew how greedy the Growleywogs were.

"They are to take a few of the Oz people for their slaves," replied Guph. He did not think it necessary to tell Roquat that the Growleywogs demanded twenty thousand slaves. It would be time enough for that when Oz was conquered.

"A very reasonable request, I'm sure," remarked the King. "I must congratulate you, Guph, upon the wonderful success of your journey."

"But that is not all," said the General, proudly.

The King seemed astonished. "Speak out, sir!" he commanded.

"I have seen the First and Foremost Phanfasm of the Mountain of Phantastico, and he will bring his people to assist us."

"What!" cried the King. "The Phanfasms! You don't mean it, Guph!"

"It is true," declared the General, proudly.

The King became thoughtful, and his brows wrinkled.

"I'm afraid, Guph," he said rather anxiously, "that the First and Foremost may prove as dangerous to us as to the Oz people. If he and his terrible band come down from the mountain they may take the notion to conquer the Nomes!"

"Pah! That is a foolish idea," retorted Guph, irritably, but he knew in his heart that the King was right. "The First and Foremost is a particular friend of mine, and will do us no harm. Why, when I was there, he even invited me into his house."

The General neglected to tell the King how he had been jerked into the hut of the First and Foremost by means of the brass hoop. So Roquat the Red looked at his General admiringly and said:

"You are a wonderful Nome, Guph. I'm sorry I did not make you my General before. But what reward did the First and Foremost demand?"

"Nothing at all," answered Guph. "Even the Magic Belt itself could not add to his powers of sorcery. All the Phanfasms wish is to destroy the Oz people, who are good and happy. This pleasure will amply repay them for assisting us."

"When will they come?" asked Roquat, half fearfully.

"When the tunnel is completed," said the General.

"We are nearly halfway under the desert now," announced the King; "and that is fast work, because the tunnel has to be drilled through solid rock. But after we have passed the desert it will not take us long to extend the tunnel to the walls of the Emerald City."

"Well, whenever you are ready, we shall be joined by the Whimsies, the Growleywogs and the Phanfasms," said Guph; "so the conquest of Oz is assured without a doubt."

Again, the King seemed thoughtful.

"I'm almost sorry we did not undertake the conquest alone," said he. "All of these allies are dangerous people, and they may demand more than you have promised them. It might have been better to have conquered Oz without any outside assistance."

"We could not do it," said the General, positively.

"Why not, Guph?"

"You know very well. You have had one experience with the Oz people, and they defeated you."

"That was because they rolled eggs at us," replied the King, with a shudder. "My Nomes cannot stand eggs, any more than I can myself. They are poison to all who live underground."

"That is true enough," agreed Guph.

"But we might have taken the Oz people by surprise, and conquered them before they had a chance to get any eggs. Our former defeat was due to the fact that the girl Dorothy had a Yellow Hen with her. I do not know what ever became of that hen, but I believe there are no hens at all in the Land of Oz, and so there could be no eggs there."

"On the contrary," said Guph, "there are now hundreds of chickens in Oz, and they lay heaps of those dangerous eggs. I met a goshawk on my way home, and the bird informed me that he had lately been to Oz to capture and devour some of the young chickens. But they are protected by magic, so the hawk did not get a single one of them."

"That is a very bad report," said the King, nervously. "Very bad, indeed. My Nomes are willing to fight, but they simply can't face hen's eggs—and I don't blame them."

"They won't need to face them," replied Guph. "I'm afraid of eggs myself, and don't propose to take any chances of being poisoned by them. My plan is to send the Whimsies through the tunnel first, and then the Growleywogs and the Phanfasms. By the time we Nomes get there the eggs will all be used up, and we may then pursue and capture the inhabitants at our leisure."

"Perhaps you are right," returned the King, with a dismal sigh. "But I want it distinctly understood that I claim Ozma and Dorothy as my own prisoners. They are rather nice girls, and I do not intend to let any of those dreadful creatures hurt them, or make them their slaves. When I have captured them I will bring them here and transform them into china ornaments to stand on my mantle. They will look very pretty—Dorothy on one end of the mantle and Ozma on the other—and I shall take great care to see they are not broken when the maids dust them."

"Very well, your Majesty. Do what you will with the girls for all I care. Now that our plans are arranged, and we have the three most powerful bands of evil spirits in the world to assist us, let us make haste to get the tunnel finished as soon as possible."

"It will be ready in three days," promised the King, and hurried away to inspect the work and see that the Nomes kept busy.

Chapter 14 - How the Wizard Practiced Sorcery

"Where next?" asked the Wizard when they had left the town of Fuddlecumjig and the Sawhorse had started back along the road.

"Why, Ozma laid out this trip," replied Dorothy, "and she 'vised us to see the Rigmaroles next, and then visit the Tin Woodman."

"That sounds good," said the Wizard. "But what road do we take to get to the Rigmaroles?"

"I don't know, 'zactly," returned the little girl; "but it must be somewhere just southwest from here."

"Then why need we go way back to the crossroads?" asked the Shaggy Man. "We might save a lot of time by branching off here."

"There isn't any path," asserted Uncle Henry.

"Then we'd better go back to the signposts, and make sure of our way," decided Dorothy.

But after they had gone a short distance farther the Sawhorse, who had overheard their conversation, stopped and said:

"Here is a path."

Sure enough, a dim path seemed to branch off from the road they were on, and it led across pretty green meadows and past leafy groves, straight toward the southwest.

"That looks like a good path," said Omby Amby. "Why not try it?"

"All right," answered Dorothy. "I'm anxious to see what the Rigmaroles are like, and this path ought to take us there the quickest way."

No one made any objection to this plan, so the Sawhorse turned into the path, which proved to be nearly as good as the one they had taken to get to the Fuddles. As first they passed a few retired farm houses, but soon these scattered dwellings were left behind and only the meadows and the trees were before them. But they rode along in cheerful contentment, and Aunt Em got into an argument with Billina about the proper way to raise chickens.

"I do not care to contradict you," said the Yellow Hen, with dignity, "but I have an idea I know more about chickens than human beings do."

"Pshaw!" replied Aunt Em. "I've raised chickens for nearly forty years, Billina, and I know you've got to starve 'em to make 'em lay lots of eggs, and stuff 'em if you want good broilers."

"Broilers!" exclaimed Billina, in horror. "Broil my chickens!"

"Why, that's what they're for, ain't it?" asked Aunt Em, astonished.

"No, Aunt, not in Oz," said Dorothy. "People do not eat chickens here. You see, Billina was the first hen that was ever seen in this country, and I brought her here myself. Everybody liked her an' respected her, so the Oz people wouldn't any more eat her chickens than they would eat Billina."

"Well, I declare," gasped Aunt Em. "How about the eggs?"

"Oh, if we have more eggs than we want to hatch, we allow people to eat them," said Billina. "Indeed, I am very glad the Oz folks like our eggs, for otherwise they would spoil."

"This certainly is a queer country," sighed Aunt Em.

"Excuse me," called the Sawhorse, "the path has ended and I'd like to know which way to go."

They looked around and sure enough there was no path to be seen.

"Well," said Dorothy, "we're going southwest, and it seems just as easy to follow that direction without a path as with one."

"Certainly," answered the Sawhorse. "It is not hard to draw the wagon over the meadow. I only want to know where to go."

"There's a forest over there across the prairie," said the Wizard, "and it lies in the direction we are going. Make straight for the forest, Sawhorse, and you're bound to go right."

So the wooden animal trotted on again and the meadow grass was so soft under the wheels that it made easy riding. But Dorothy was a little uneasy at losing the path, because now there was nothing to guide them.

No houses were to be seen at all, so they could not ask their way of any farmer; and although the Land of Oz was always beautiful, wherever one might go, this part of the country was strange to all the party.

"Perhaps we're lost," suggested Aunt Em, after they had proceeded quite a way in silence.

"Never mind," said the Shaggy Man; "I've been lost many a time—and so has Dorothy—and we've always been found again."

"But we may get hungry," remarked Omby Amby. "That is the worst of getting lost in a place where there are no houses near."

"We had a good dinner at the Fuddle town," said Uncle Henry, "and that will keep us from starving to death for a long time."

"No one ever starved to death in Oz," declared Dorothy, positively; "but people may get pretty hungry sometimes."

The Wizard said nothing, and he did not seem especially anxious. The Sawhorse was trotting along briskly, yet the forest seemed farther away than they had thought when they first saw it. So it was nearly sundown when they finally came to the trees; but now they found themselves in a most beautiful spot, the wide-spreading trees being covered with flowering vines and having soft mosses underneath them. "This will be a good place to camp," said the Wizard, as the Sawhorse stopped for further instructions.

"Camp!" they all echoed.

"Certainly," asserted the Wizard. "It will be dark before very long and we cannot travel through this forest at night. So let us make a camp here, and have some supper, and sleep until daylight comes again."

They all looked at the little man in astonishment, and Aunt Em said, with a sniff:

"A pretty camp we'll have, I must say! I suppose you intend us to sleep under the wagon."

"And chew grass for our supper," added the Shaggy Man, laughing.

But Dorothy seemed to have no doubts and was quite cheerful

"It's lucky we have the wonderful Wizard with us," she said; "because he can do 'most anything he wants to."

"Oh, yes; I forgot we had a Wizard," said Uncle Henry, looking at the little man curiously.

"I didn't," chirped Billina, contentedly.

The Wizard smiled and climbed out of the wagon, and all the others followed him.

"In order to camp," said he, "the first thing we need is tents. Will some one please lend me a handkerchief?"

The Shaggy Man offered him one, and Aunt Em another. He took them both and laid them carefully upon the grass near to the edge of the forest. Then he laid his own handkerchief down, too, and standing a little back from them he waved his left hand toward the handkerchiefs and said:

"Tents of canvas, white as snow, Let me see how fast you grow!"

Then, lo and behold! the handkerchiefs became tiny tents, and as the travelers looked at them the tents grew bigger and bigger until in a few minutes each one was large enough to contain the entire party.

"This," said the Wizard, pointing to the first tent, "is for the accommodation of the ladies. Dorothy, you and your Aunt may step inside and take off your things."

Every one ran to look inside the tent, and they saw two pretty white beds, all ready for Dorothy and Aunt Em, and a silver roost for Billina. Rugs were spread upon the grassy floor and some camp chairs and a table completed the furniture.

"Well, well, well! This beats anything I ever saw or heard of!" exclaimed Aunt Em, and she glanced at the Wizard almost fearfully, as if he might be dangerous because of his great powers.

"Oh, Mr. Wizard! How did you manage to do it?" asked Dorothy.

"It's a trick Glinda the Sorceress taught me, and it is much better magic than I used to practice in Omaha, or when I first came to Oz," he answered. "When the good Glinda found I was to live in the Emerald City always, she promised to help me, because she said the Wizard of Oz ought really to be a clever Wizard, and not a humbug. So we have been much together and I am learning so fast that I expect to be able to accomplish some really wonderful things in time."

"You've done it now!" declared Dorothy. "These tents are just wonderful!"

"But come and see the men's tent," said the Wizard. So they went to the second tent, which had shaggy edges because it has been made from the Shaggy Man's handkerchief, and found that completely furnished also. It contained four neat beds for Uncle Henry, Omby Amby, the Shaggy Man and the Wizard. Also there was a soft rug for Toto to lie upon.

"The third tent," explained the Wizard, "is our dining room and kitchen."

They visited that next, and found a table and dishes in the dining tent, with plenty of those things necessary to use in cooking. The Wizard carried out a big kettle and set it swinging on a crossbar before the tent. While he was doing this Omby Amby and the Shaggy Man brought a supply of twigs from the forest and then they built a fire underneath the kettle.

"Now, Dorothy," said the Wizard, smiling, "I expect you to cook our supper."

"But there is nothing in the kettle," she cried.

"Are you sure?" inquired the Wizard.

"I didn't see anything put in, and I'm almost sure it was empty when you brought it out," she replied.

"Nevertheless," said the little man, winking slyly at Uncle Henry, "you will do well to watch our supper, my dear, and see that it doesn't boil over."

Then the men took some pails and went into the forest to search for a spring of water, and while they were gone Aunt Em said to Dorothy:

"I believe the Wizard is fooling us. I saw the kettle myself, and when he hung it over the fire there wasn't a thing in it but air."

"Don't worry," remarked Billina, confidently, as she nestled in the grass before the fire. "You'll find something in the kettle when it's taken off—and it won't be poor, innocent chickens, either."

"Your hen has very bad manners, Dorothy," said Aunt Em, looking somewhat disdainfully at Billina. "It seems too bad she ever learned how to talk."

There might have been another unpleasant quarrel between Aunt Em and Billina had not the men returned just then with their pails filled with clear, sparkling water. The Wizard told Dorothy that she was a good cook and he believed their supper was ready.

So Uncle Henry lifted the kettle from the fire and poured its contents into a big platter which the Wizard held for him. The platter was fairly heaped with a fine stew, smoking hot, with many kinds of vegetables and dumplings and a rich, delicious gravy.

The Wizard triumphantly placed the platter upon the table in the dining tent and then they all sat down in camp chairs to the feast.

There were several other dishes on the table, all carefully covered, and when the time came to remove these covers they found bread and butter, cakes, cheese, pickles and fruits—including some of the luscious strawberries of Oz.

No one ventured to ask a question as to how these things came there. They contented themselves by eating heartily the good things provided, and Toto and Billina had their full share, you may be sure. After the meal was over, Aunt Em whispered to Dorothy:

"That may have been magic food, my dear, and for that reason perhaps it won't be very nourishing; but I'm willing to say it tasted as good as anything I ever et." Then she added, in a louder voice: "Who's going to do the dishes?"

"No one, madam," answered the Wizard. "The dishes have 'done' themselves."

"La sakes!" ejaculated the good lady, holding up her hands in amazement. For, sure enough, when she looked at the dishes they had a moment before left upon the table, she found them all washed and dried and piled up into neat stacks.

Chapter 15 - How Dorothy Happened to Get Lost

It was a beautiful evening, so they drew their camp chairs in a circle before one of the tents and began to tell stories to amuse themselves and pass away the time before they went to bed.

Pretty soon a zebra was seen coming out of the forest, and he trotted straight up to them and said politely:

"Good evening, people."

The zebra was a sleek little animal and had a slender head, a stubby mane and a paint-brush tail—very like a donkey's. His neatly shaped white body was covered with regular bars of dark brown, and his hoofs were delicate as those of a deer.

"Good evening, friend Zebra," said Omby Amby, in reply to the creature's greeting. "Can we do anything for you?"

"Yes," answered the zebra. "I should like you to settle a dispute that has long been a bother to me, as to whether there is more water or land in the world."

"Who are you disputing with?" asked the Wizard.

"With a soft-shell crab," said the zebra. "He lives in a pool where I go to drink every day, and he is a very impertinent crab, I assure you. I have told him many times that the land is much greater in extent than the water, but he will not be convinced. Even this very evening, when I told him he was an insignificant creature who lived in a small pool, he asserted that the water was greater and more important than the land. So, seeing your camp, I decided to ask you to settle the dispute for once and all, that I may not be further annoyed by this ignorant crab."

When they had listened to this explanation Dorothy inquired:

"Where is the soft-shell crab?"

"Not far away," replied the zebra. "If you will agree to judge between us I will run and get him."

"Run along, then," said the little girl.

So the animal pranced into the forest and soon came trotting back to them. When he drew near they found a soft-shell crab clinging fast to the stiff hair of the zebra's head, where it held on by one claw.

"Now then, Mr. Crab," said the zebra, "here are the people I told you about; and they know more than you do, who lives in a pool, and more than I do, who lives in a forest. For they have been travelers all over the world, and know every part of it."

"There is more of the world than Oz," declared the crab, in a stubborn voice.

"That is true," said Dorothy; "but I used to live in Kansas, in the United States, and I've been to California and to Australia and so has Uncle Henry."

"For my part," added the Shaggy Man, "I've been to Mexico and Boston and many other foreign countries."

"And I," said the Wizard, "have been to Europe and Ireland."

"So you see," continued the zebra, addressing the crab, "here are people of real consequence, who know what they are talking about."

"Then they know there's more water in the world than there is land," asserted the crab, in a shrill, petulant voice.

"They know you are wrong to make such an absurd statement, and they will probably think you are a lobster instead of a crab," retorted the animal.

At this taunt the crab reached out its other claw and seized the zebra's ear, and the creature gave a cry of pain and began prancing up and down, trying to shake off the crab, which clung fast.

"Stop pinching!" cried the zebra. "You promised not to pinch if I would carry you here!"

"And you promised to treat me respectfully," said the crab, letting go the ear.

"Well, haven't I?" demanded the zebra.

"No; you called me a lobster," said the crab.

"Ladies and gentlemen," continued the zebra, "please pardon my poor friend, because he is ignorant and stupid, and does not understand. Also the pinch of his claw is very annoying. So pray tell him that the world contains more land than water, and when he has heard your judgment I will carry him back and dump him into his pool, where I hope he will be more modest in the future."

"But we cannot tell him that," said Dorothy, gravely, "because it would not be true."

"What!" exclaimed the zebra, in astonishment; "do I hear you aright?"

"The soft-shell crab is correct," declared the Wizard. "There is considerably more water than there is land in the world."

"Impossible!" protested the zebra. "Why, I can run for days upon the land, and find but little water."

"Did you ever see an ocean?" asked Dorothy.

"Never," admitted the zebra. "There is no such thing as an ocean in the Land of Oz."

"Well, there are several oceans in the world," said Dorothy, "and people sail in ships upon these oceans for weeks and weeks, and never see a bit of land at all. And the joggerfys will tell you that all the oceans put together are bigger than all the land put together."

At this the crab began laughing in queer chuckles that reminded Dorothy of the way Billina sometimes cackled.

"NOW will you give up, Mr. Zebra?" it cried, jeeringly; "now will you give up?"

The zebra seemed much humbled.

"Of course I cannot read geographys," he said.

"You could take one of the Wizard's School Pills," suggested Billina, "and that would make you learned and wise without studying."

The crab began laughing again, which so provoked the zebra that he tried to shake the little creature off. This resulted in more ear-pinching, and finally Dorothy told them that if they could not behave they must go back to the forest.

"I'm sorry I asked you to decide this question," said the zebra, crossly. "So long as neither of us could prove we were right we quite enjoyed the dispute; but now I can never drink at that pool again without the soft-shell crab laughing at me. So I must find another drinking place."

"Do! Do, you ignoramus!" shouted the crab, as loudly as his little voice would carry. "Rile some other pool with your clumsy hoofs, and let your betters alone after this!"

Then the zebra trotted back to the forest, bearing the crab with him, and disappeared amid the gloom of the trees. And as it was now getting dark the travelers said good night to one another and went to bed.

Dorothy awoke just as the light was beginning to get strong next morning, and not caring to sleep any later she quietly got out of bed, dressed herself, and left the tent where Aunt Em was yet peacefully slumbering.

Outside she noticed Billina busily pecking around to secure bugs or other food for breakfast, but none of the men in the other tent seemed awake. So the little girl decided to take a walk in the woods and try to discover some path or road that they might follow when they again started upon their journey.

She had reached the edge of the forest when the Yellow Hen came fluttering along and asked where she was going.

"Just to take a walk, Billina; and maybe I'll find some path," said Dorothy.

"Then I'll go along," decided Billina, and scarcely had she spoken when Toto ran up and joined them.

Toto and the Yellow Hen had become quite friendly by this time, although at first they did not get along well together. Billina had been rather suspicious of dogs, and Toto had had an idea that it was every dog's duty to chase a hen on sight. But Dorothy had talked to them and scolded them for not being agreeable to one another until they grew better acquainted and became friends.

I won't say they loved each other dearly, but at least they had stopped quarreling and now managed to get on together very well.

The day was growing lighter every minute and driving the black shadows out of the forest; so Dorothy found it very pleasant walking under the trees. She went some distance in one direction, but not finding a path, presently turned in a different direction. There was no path here, either, although she advanced quite a way into the forest, winding here and there among the trees and peering through the bushes in an endeavor to find some beaten track.

"I think we'd better go back," suggested the Yellow Hen, after a time. "The people will all be up by this time and breakfast will be ready."

"Very well," agreed Dorothy. "Let's see—the camp must be over this way."

She had probably made a mistake about that, for after they had gone far enough to have reached the camp they still found themselves in the thick of the woods. So the little girl stopped short and looked around her, and Toto glanced up into her face with his bright little eyes and wagged his tail as if he knew something was wrong. He couldn't tell much about direction himself, because he had spent his time prowling among the bushes and running here and there; nor had Billina paid much attention to where they were going, being interested in picking bugs from the moss as they passed along. The Yellow Hen now turned one eye up toward the little girl and asked:

"Have you forgotten where the camp is, Dorothy?"

"Yes," she admitted; "have you, Billina?"

"I didn't try to remember," returned Billina. "I'd no idea you would get lost, Dorothy."

"It's the thing we don't expect, Billina, that usually happens," observed the girl, thoughtfully. "But it's no use standing here. Let's go in that direction," pointing a finger at random. "It may be we'll get out of the forest over there."

So on they went again, but this way the trees were closer together, and the vines were so tangled that often they tripped Dorothy up.

Suddenly a voice cried sharply:

"Halt!"

At first, Dorothy could see nothing, although she looked around very carefully. But Billina exclaimed:

"Well, I declare!"

"What is it?" asked the little girl: for Toto began barking at something, and following his gaze she discovered what it was.

A row of spoons had surrounded the three, and these spoons stood straight up on their handles and carried swords and muskets. Their faces were outlined in the polished bowls and they looked very stern and severe.

Dorothy laughed at the queer things.

"Who are you?" she asked.

"We're the Spoon Brigade," said one.

"In the service of his Majesty King Kleaver," said another.

"And you are our prisoners," said a third.

Dorothy sat down on an old stump and looked at them, her eyes twinkling with amusement.

"What would happen," she inquired, "if I should set my dog on your Brigade?"

"He would die," replied one of the spoons, sharply. "One shot from our deadly muskets would kill him, big as he is."

"Don't risk it, Dorothy," advised the Yellow Hen. "Remember this is a fairy country, yet none of us three happens to be a fairy."

Dorothy grew sober at this.

"P'raps you're right, Billina," she answered. "But how funny it is, to be captured by a lot of spoons!"

"I do not see anything very funny about it," declared a spoon. "We're the regular military brigade of the kingdom."

"What kingdom?" she asked.

"Utensia," said he.

"I never heard of it before," asserted Dorothy. Then she added thoughtfully, "I don't believe Ozma ever heard of Utensia, either. Tell me, are you not subjects of Ozma of Oz?"

"We have never heard of her," retorted a spoon. "We are subjects of King Kleaver, and obey only his orders, which are to bring all prisoners to him as soon as they are captured. So step lively, my girl, and march with us, or we may be tempted to cut off a few of your toes with our swords."

This threat made Dorothy laugh again. She did not believe she was in any danger; but here was a new and interesting adventure, so she was willing to be taken to Utensia that she might see what King Kleaver's kingdom was like.

Chapter 16 - How Dorothy Visited Utensia

There must have been from six to eight dozen spoons in the Brigade, and they marched away in the shape of a hollow square, with Dorothy, Billina and Toto in the center of the square. Before they had gone very far Toto knocked over one of the spoons by wagging his tail, and then the Captain of the Spoons told the little dog to be more careful, or he would be punished. So Toto was careful, and the Spoon Brigade moved along with astonishing swiftness, while Dorothy really had to walk fast to keep up with it.

By and by they left the woods and entered a big clearing, in which was the Kingdom of Utensia.

Standing all around the clearing were a good many cookstoves, ranges and grills, of all sizes and shapes, and besides these there were several kitchen cabinets and cupboards and a few kitchen tables. These things were crowded with utensils of all sorts: frying pans, sauce pans, kettles, forks, knives, basting and soup spoons, nutmeg graters, sifters, colanders, meat saws, flat irons, rolling pins and many other things of a like nature.

When the Spoon Brigade appeared with the prisoners a wild shout arose and many of the utensils hopped off their stoves or their benches and ran crowding around Dorothy and the hen and the dog.

"Stand back!" cried the Captain, sternly, and he led his captives through the curious throng until they came before a big range that stood in the center of the clearing. Beside this range was a butcher block upon which lay a great cleaver with a keen edge. It rested upon the flat of its back, its legs were crossed and it was smoking a long pipe.

"Wake up, your Majesty," said the Captain. "Here are prisoners."

Hearing this, King Kleaver sat up and looked at Dorothy sharply.

"Gristle and fat!" he cried. "Where did this girl come from?"

"I found her in the forest and brought her here a prisoner," replied the Captain.

"Why did you do that?" inquired the King, puffing his pipe lazily.

"To create some excitement," the Captain answered. "It is so quiet here that we are all getting rusty for want of amusement. For my part, I prefer to see stirring times."

"Naturally," returned the cleaver, with a nod. "I have always said, Captain, without a bit of irony, that you are a sterling officer and a solid citizen, bowled and polished to a degree. But what do you expect me to do with these prisoners?"

"That is for you to decide," declared the Captain. "You are the King."

"To be sure; to be sure," muttered the cleaver, musingly. "As you say, we have had dull times since the steel and grindstone eloped and left us. Command my Counselors and the Royal Courtiers to attend me, as well as the High Priest and the Judge. We'll then decide what can be done."

The Captain saluted and retired and Dorothy sat down on an overturned kettle and asked:

"Have you anything to eat in your kingdom?"

"Here! Get up! Get off from me!" cried a faint voice, at which his Majesty the cleaver said:

"Excuse me, but you're sitting on my friend the Ten-quart Kettle."

Dorothy at once arose, and the kettle turned right side up and looked at her reproachfully.

"I'm a friend of the King, so no one dares sit on me," said he.

"I'd prefer a chair, anyway," she replied.

"Sit on that hearth," commanded the King.

So Dorothy sat on the hearth-shelf of the big range, and the subjects of Utensia began to gather around in a large and inquisitive throng. Toto lay at Dorothy's feet and Billina flew upon the range, which had no fire in it, and perched there as comfortably as she could.

When all the Counselors and Courtiers had assembled—and these seemed to include most of the inhabitants of the kingdom—the King rapped on the block for order and said:

"Friends and Fellow Utensils! Our worthy Commander of the Spoon Brigade, Captain Dipp, has captured the three prisoners you see before you and brought them here for—for—I don't know what for. So I ask your advice how to act in this matter, and what fate I should mete out to these captives. Judge Sifter, stand on my right. It is your business to sift this affair to the bottom. High Priest Colender, stand on my left and see that no one testifies falsely in this matter."

As these two officials took their places, Dorothy asked:

"Why is the colander the High Priest?"

"He's the holiest thing we have in the kingdom," replied King Kleaver.

"Except me," said a sieve. "I'm the whole thing when it comes to holes."

"What we need," remarked the King, rebukingly, "is a wireless sieve. I must speak to Marconi about it. These old-fashioned sieves talk too much. Now, it is the duty of the King's Counselors to counsel the King at all times of emergency, so I beg you to speak out and advise me what to do with these prisoners."

"I demand that they be killed several times, until they are dead!" shouted a pepperbox, hopping around very excitedly.

"Compose yourself, Mr. Paprica," advised the King. "Your remarks are piquant and highly-seasoned, but you need a scattering of commonsense. It is only necessary to kill a person once to make him dead; but I do not see that it is necessary to kill this little girl at all."

"I don't, either," said Dorothy.

"Pardon me, but you are not expected to advise me in this matter," replied King Kleaver.

"Why not?" asked Dorothy.

"You might be prejudiced in your own favor, and so mislead us," he said. "Now then, good subjects, who speaks next?"

"I'd like to smooth this thing over, in some way," said a flatiron, earnestly. "We are supposed to be useful to mankind, you know."

"But the girl isn't mankind! She's womankind!" yelled a corkscrew.

"What do you know about it?" inquired the King.

"I'm a lawyer," said the corkscrew, proudly. "I am accustomed to appear at the bar."

"But you're crooked," retorted the King, "and that debars you. You may be a corking good lawyer, Mr. Popp, but I must ask you to withdraw your remarks."

"Very well," said the corkscrew, sadly; "I see I haven't any pull at this court."

"Permit me," continued the flatiron, "to press my suit, your Majesty. I do not wish to gloss over any fault the prisoner may have committed, if such a fault exists; but we owe her some consideration, and that's flat!"

"I'd like to hear from Prince Karver," said the King.

At this a stately carvingknife stepped forward and bowed.

"The Captain was wrong to bring this girl here, and she was wrong to come," he said. "But now that the foolish deed is done let us all prove our mettle and have a slashing good time."

"That's it! that's it!" screamed a fat choppingknife. "We'll make mincemeat of the girl and hash of the chicken and sausage of the dog!"

There was a shout of approval at this and the King had to rap again for order.

"Gentlemen, gentlemen!" he said, "your remarks are somewhat cutting and rather disjointed, as might be expected from such acute intellects. But you give me no reasons for your demands."

"See here, Kleaver; you make me tired," said a saucepan, strutting before the King very impudently. "You're about the worst King that ever reigned in Utensia, and that's saying a good deal. Why don't you run things yourself, instead of asking everybody's advice, like the big, clumsy idiot you are?"

The King sighed.

"I wish there wasn't a saucepan in my kingdom," he said. "You fellows are always stewing, over something, and every once in a while you slop over and make a mess of it. Go hang yourself, sir—by the handle—and don't let me hear from you again."

Dorothy was much shocked by the dreadful language the utensils employed, and she thought that they must have had very little proper training. So she said, addressing the King, who seemed very unfit to rule his turbulent subjects:

"I wish you'd decide my fate right away. I can't stay here all day, trying to find out what you're going to do with me."

"This thing is becoming a regular broil, and it's time I took part in it," observed a big gridiron, coming forward.

"What I'd like to know," said a can-opener, in a shrill voice, "is why the little girl came to our forest anyhow and why she intruded upon Captain Dipp—who ought to be called Dippy—and who she is, and where she came from, and where she is going, and why and wherefore and therefore and when."

"I'm sorry to see, Sir Jabber," remarked the King to the can-opener, "that you have such a prying disposition. As a matter of fact, all the things you mention are none of our business."

Having said this the King relighted his pipe, which had gone out.

"Tell me, please, what IS our business?" inquired a potato-masher, winking at Dorothy somewhat impertinently. "I'm fond of little girls, myself, and it seems to me she has as much right to wander in the forest as we have."

"Who accuses the little girl, anyway?" inquired a rolling-pin. "What has she done?"

"I don't know," said the King. "What has she done, Captain Dipp?"

"That's the trouble, your Majesty. She hasn't done anything," replied the Captain.

"What do you want me to do?" asked Dorothy.

This question seemed to puzzle them all. Finally, a chafingdish, exclaimed irritably:

"If no one can throw any light on this subject you must excuse me if I go out."

At this, a big kitchen fork pricked up its ears and said in a tiny voice:

"Let's hear from Judge Sifter."

"That's proper," returned the King.

So Judge Sifter turned around slowly several times and then said:

"We have nothing against the girl except the stove-hearth upon which she sits. Therefore I order her instantly discharged."

"Discharged!" cried Dorothy. "Why, I never was discharged in my life, and I don't intend to be. If it's all the same to you, I'll resign."

"It's all the same," declared the King. "You are free—you and your companions—and may go wherever you like."

"Thank you," said the little girl. "But haven't you anything to eat in your kingdom? I'm hungry."

"Go into the woods and pick blackberries," advised the King, lying down upon his back again and preparing to go to sleep. "There isn't a morsel to eat in all Utensia, that I know of."

So Dorothy jumped up and said:

"Come on, Toto and Billina. If we can't find the camp, we may find some blackberries."

The utensils drew back and allowed them to pass without protest, although Captain Dipp marched the Spoon Brigade in close order after them until they had reached the edge of the clearing.

There the spoons halted; but Dorothy and her companions entered the forest again and began searching diligently for a way back to the camp, that they might rejoin their party.

Chapter 17 - How They Came to Bunbury

Wandering through the woods, without knowing where you are going or what adventure you are about to meet next, is not as pleasant as one might think. The woods are always beautiful and impressive, and if you are not worried or hungry you may enjoy them immensely; but Dorothy was worried and hungry that morning, so she paid little attention to the beauties of the forest, and hurried along as fast as she could go. She tried to keep in one direction and not circle around, but she was not at all sure that the direction she had chosen would lead her to the camp.

By and by, to her great joy, she came upon a path. It ran to the right and to the left, being lost in the trees in both directions, and just before her, upon a big oak, were fastened two signs, with arms pointing both ways. One sign read:

TAKE THE OTHER ROAD TO BUNBURY

and the second sign read:

"Well!" exclaimed Billina, eyeing the signs, "this looks as if we were getting back to civilization again."

"I'm not sure about the civil'zation, dear," replied the little girl; "but it looks as if we might get SOMEWHERE, and that's a big relief, anyhow."

"Which path shall we take?" inquired the Yellow Hen.

Dorothy stared at the signs thoughtfully.

"Bunbury sounds like something to eat," she said. "Let's go there."

"It's all the same to me," replied Billina. She had picked up enough bugs and insects from the moss as she went along to satisfy her own hunger, but the hen knew Dorothy could not eat bugs; nor could Toto.

The path to Bunbury seemed little traveled, but it was distinct enough and ran through the trees in a zigzag course until it finally led them to an open space filled with the queerest houses Dorothy had ever seen. They were all made of crackers laid out in tiny squares, and were of many pretty and ornamental shapes, having balconies and porches with posts of bread-sticks and roofs shingled with wafer-crackers.

There were walks of bread-crusts leading from house to house and forming streets, and the place seemed to have many inhabitants.

When Dorothy, followed by Billina and Toto, entered the place, they found people walking the streets or assembled in groups talking together, or sitting upon the porches and balconies.

And what funny people they were!

Men, women and children were all made of buns and bread. Some were thin and others fat; some were white, some light brown and some very dark of complexion. A few of the buns, which seemed to form the more important class of the people, were neatly frosted. Some had raisins for eyes and currant buttons on their clothes; others had eyes of cloves and legs of stick cinnamon, and many wore hats and bonnets frosted pink and green.

There was something of a commotion in Bunbury when the strangers suddenly appeared among them. Women caught up their children and hurried into their houses, shutting the cracker doors carefully behind them. Some men ran so hastily that they tumbled over one another, while others, more brave, assembled in a group and faced the intruders defiantly.

Dorothy at once realized that she must act with caution in order not to frighten these shy people, who were evidently unused to the presence of strangers. There was a delightful fragrant odor of fresh bread in the town, and this made the little girl more hungry than ever. She told Toto and Billina to stay back while she slowly advanced toward the group that stood silently awaiting her.

"You must 'scuse me for coming unexpected," she said, softly, "but I really didn't know I was coming here until I arrived. I was lost in the woods, you know, and I'm as hungry as anything."

"Hungry!" they murmured, in a horrified chorus.

"Yes; I haven't had anything to eat since last night's supper," she exclaimed. "Are there any eatables in Bunbury?"

They looked at one another undecidedly, and then one portly bun man, who seemed a person of consequence, stepped forward and said:

"Little girl, to be frank with you, we are all eatables. Everything in Bunbury is eatable to ravenous human creatures like you. But it is to escape being eaten and destroyed that we have secluded ourselves in this out-of-the-way place, and there is neither right nor justice in your coming here to feed upon us."

Dorothy looked at him longingly.

"You're bread, aren't you?" she asked.

"Yes; bread and butter. The butter is inside me, so it won't melt and run. I do the running myself."

At this joke all the others burst into a chorus of laughter, and Dorothy thought they couldn't be much afraid if they could laugh like that.

"Couldn't I eat something besides people?" she asked. "Couldn't I eat just one house, or a side-walk or something? I wouldn't mind much what it was, you know."

"This is not a public bakery, child," replied the man, sternly. "It's private property."

"I know Mr.—Mr.—"

"My name is C. Bunn, Esquire," said the man. "'C' stands for Cinnamon, and this place is called after my family, which is the most aristocratic in the town."

"Oh, I don't know about that," objected another of the queer people. "The Grahams and the Browns and Whites are all excellent families, and there is none better of their kind. I'm a Boston Brown, myself."

"I admit you are all desirable citizens," said Mr. Bunn rather stiffly; "but the fact remains that our town is called Bunbury."

"'Scuse me," interrupted Dorothy; "but I'm getting hungrier every minute. Now, if you're polite and kind, as I'm sure you ought to be, you'll let me eat SOMETHING. There's so much to eat here that you will never miss it."

Then a big, puffed-up man, of a delicate brown color, stepped forward and said:

"I think it would be a shame to send this child away hungry, especially as she agrees to eat whatever we can spare and not touch our people."

"So do I, Pop," replied a Roll who stood near.

"What, then, do you suggest, Mr. Over?" inquired Mr. Bunn.

"Why, I'll let her eat my back fence, if she wants to. It's made of waffles, and they're very crisp and nice."

"She may also eat my wheelbarrow," added a pleasant looking Muffin. "It's made of nabiscos with a zuzu wheel."

"Very good; very good," remarked Mr. Bunn. "That is certainly very kind of you. Go with Pop Over and Mr. Muffin, little girl, and they will feed you."

"Thank you very much," said Dorothy, gratefully. "May I bring my dog Toto, and the Yellow Hen? They're hungry, too."

"Will you make them behave?" asked the Muffin.

"Of course," promised Dorothy.

"Then come along," said Pop Over.

So Dorothy and Billina and Toto walked up the street and the people seemed no longer to be at all afraid of them. Mr. Muffin's house came first, and as his wheelbarrow stood in the front yard the little girl ate that first. It didn't seem very fresh, but she was so hungry that she was not particular. Toto ate some, too, while Billina picked up the crumbs.

While the strangers were engaged in eating, many of the people came and stood in the street curiously watching them. Dorothy noticed six roguish looking brown children standing all in a row, and she asked:

"Who are you, little ones?"

"We're the Graham Gems," replied one; "and we're all twins."

"I wonder if your mother could spare one or two of you?" asked Billina, who decided that they were fresh baked; but at this dangerous question the six little gems ran away as fast as they could go.

"You musn't say such things, Billina," said Dorothy, reprovingly. "Now let's go into Pop Over's back yard and get the waffles."

"I sort of hate to let that fence go," remarked Mr. Over, nervously, as they walked toward his house. "The neighbors back of us are Soda Biscuits, and I don't care to mix with them."

"But I'm hungry yet," declared the girl. "That wheelbarrow wasn't very big."

"I've got a shortcake piano, but none of my family can play on it," he said, reflectively. "Suppose you eat that."

"All right," said Dorothy; "I don't mind. Anything to be accommodating."

So Mr. Over led her into the house, where she ate the piano, which was of an excellent flavor.

"Is there anything to drink here?" she asked.

"Yes; I've a milk pump and a water pump; which will you have?" he asked.

"I guess I'll try 'em both," said Dorothy.

So Mr. Over called to his wife, who brought into the yard a pail made of some kind of baked dough, and Dorothy pumped the pail full of cool, sweet milk and drank it eagerly.

The wife of Pop Over was several shades darker than her husband.

"Aren't you overdone?" the little girl asked her.

"No indeed," answered the woman. "I'm neither overdone nor done over; I'm just Mrs. Over, and I'm the President of the Bunbury Breakfast Band."

Dorothy thanked them for their hospitality and went away. At the gate Mr. Cinnamon Bunn met her and said he would show her around the town. "We have some very interesting inhabitants," he remarked, walking stiffly beside her on his stick-cinnamon legs; "and all of us who are in good health are well bred. If you are no longer hungry we will call upon a few of the most important citizens."

Toto and Billina followed behind them, behaving very well, and a little way down the street they came to a handsome residence where Aunt Sally Lunn lived. The old lady was glad to meet the little girl and gave her a slice of white bread and butter which had been used as a door-mat. It was almost fresh and tasted better than anything Dorothy had eaten in the town.

"Where do you get the butter?" she inquired.

"We dig it out of the ground, which, as you may have observed, is all flour and meal," replied Mr. Bunn. "There is a butter mine just at the opposite side of the village. The trees which you see here are all doughleanders and doughderas, and in the season we get quite a crop of dough-nuts off them."

"I should think the flour would blow around and get into your eyes," said Dorothy.

"No," said he; "we are bothered with cracker dust sometimes, but never with flour."

Then he took her to see Johnny Cake, a cheerful old gentleman who lived near by.

"I suppose you've heard of me," said old Johnny, with an air of pride. "I'm a great favorite all over the world."

"Aren't you rather yellow?" asked Dorothy, looking at him critically.

"Maybe, child. But don't think I'm bilious, for I was never in better health in my life," replied the old gentleman. "If anything ailed me, I'd willingly acknowledge the corn."

"Johnny's a trifle stale," said Mr. Bunn, as they went away; "but he's a good mixer and never gets cross-grained. I will now take you to call upon some of my own relatives." They visited the Sugar Bunns, the Currant Bunns and the Spanish Bunns, the latter having a decidedly foreign appearance. Then they saw the French Rolls, who were very polite to them, and made a brief call upon the Parker H. Rolls, who seemed a bit proud and overbearing.

"But they're not as stuck up as the Frosted Jumbles," declared Mr. Bunn, "who are people I really can't abide. I don't like to be suspicious or talk scandal, but sometimes I think the Jumbles have too much baking powder in them."

Just then a dreadful scream was heard, and Dorothy turned hastily around to find a scene of great excitement a little way down the street. The people were crowding around Toto and throwing at him everything they could find at hand. They pelted the little dog with hard-tack, crackers, and even articles of furniture which were hard baked and heavy enough for missiles.

Toto howeled a little as the assortment of bake stuff struck him; but he stood still, with head bowed and tail between his legs, until Dorothy ran up and inquired what the matter was.

"Matter!" cried a rye loafer, indignantly, "why the horrid beast has eaten three of our dear Crumpets, and is now devouring a Salt-rising Biscuit!"

"Oh, Toto! How could you?" exclaimed Dorothy, much distressed.

Toto's mouth was full of his salt-rising victim; so he only whined and wagged his tail. But Billina, who had flown to the top of a cracker house to be in a safe place, called out:

"Don't blame him, Dorothy; the Crumpets dared him to do it."

"Yes, and you pecked out the eyes of a Raisin Bunn—one of our best citizens!" shouted a bread pudding, shaking its fist at the Yellow Hen.

"What's that! What's that?" wailed Mr. Cinnamon Bunn, who had now joined them. "Oh, what a misfortune—what a terrible misfortune!"

"See here," said Dorothy, determined to defend her pets, "I think we've treated you all pretty well, seeing you're eatables an' reg'lar food for us. I've been kind to you and eaten your old wheelbarrows and pianos and rubbish, an' not said a word. But Toto and Billina can't be 'spected to go hungry when the town's full of good things they like to eat, 'cause they can't understand your stingy ways as I do."

"You must leave here at once!" said Mr. Bunn, sternly.

"Suppose we won't go?" said Dorothy, who was now much provoked.

"Then," said he, "we will put you into the great ovens where we are made, and bake you."

Dorothy gazed around and saw threatening looks upon the faces of all. She had not noticed any ovens in the town, but they might be there, nevertheless, for some of the inhabitants seemed very fresh. So she decided to go, and calling to Toto and Billina to follow her she marched up the street with as much dignity as possible, considering that she was followed by the hoots and cries of the buns and biscuits and other bake stuff.

Chapter 18 - How Ozma Looked into the Magic Picture

Princess Ozma was a very busy little ruler, for she looked carefully after the comfort and welfare of her people and tried to make them happy. If any quarrels arose she decided them justly; if any one needed counsel or advice she was ready and willing to listen to them.

For a day or two after Dorothy and her companions had started on their trip, Ozma was occupied with the affairs of her kingdom. Then she began to think of some manner of occupation for Uncle Henry and Aunt Em that would be light and easy and yet give the old people something to do.

She soon decided to make Uncle Henry the Keeper of the Jewels, for some one really was needed to count and look after the bins and barrels of emeralds, diamonds, rubies and other precious stones that were in the Royal Storehouses. That would keep Uncle Henry busy enough, but it was harder to find something for Aunt Em to do. The palace was full of servants, so there was no detail of housework that Aunt Em could look after.

While Ozma sat in her pretty room engaged in thought she happened to glance at her Magic Picture.

This was one of the most important treasures in all the Land of Oz. It was a large picture, set in a beautiful gold frame, and it hung in a prominent place upon a wall of Ozma's private room.

Usually this picture seemed merely a country scene, but whenever Ozma looked at it and wished to know what any of her friends or acquaintances were doing, the magic of this wonderful picture was straightway disclosed. For the country scene would gradually fade away and in its place would appear the likeness of the person or persons Ozma might wish to see, surrounded by the actual scenes in which they were then placed. In this way the Princess could view any part of the world she wished, and watch the actions of any one in whom she was interested.

Ozma had often seen Dorothy in her Kansas home by this means, and now, having a little leisure, she expressed a desire to see her little friend again. It was while the travelers were at Fuddlecumjig, and Ozma laughed merrily as she watched in the picture her friends trying to match the pieces of Grandmother Gnit.

"They seem happy and are doubtless having a good time," the girl Ruler said to herself; and then she began to think of the many adventures she herself had encountered with Dorothy.

The image of her friends now faded from the Magic Picture and the old landscape slowly reappeared.

Ozma was thinking of the time when with Dorothy and her army she marched to the Nome King's underground cavern, beyond the Land of Ev, and forced the old monarch to liberate his captives, who belonged to the Royal Family of Ev. That was the time when the Scarecrow nearly frightened the Nome King into fits by throwing one of Billina's eggs at him, and Dorothy had captured King Roquat's Magic Belt and brought it away with her to the Land of Oz.

The pretty Princess smiled at the recollection of this adventure, and then she wondered what had become of the Nome King since then. Merely because she was curious and had nothing better to do, Ozma glanced at the Magic Picture and wished to see in it the King of the Nomes.

Roquat the Red went every day into his tunnel to see how the work was getting along and to hurry his workmen as much as possible. He was there now, and Ozma saw him plainly in the Magic Picture.

She saw the underground tunnel, reaching far underneath the Deadly Desert which separated the Land of Oz from the mountains beneath which the Nome King had his extensive caverns. She saw that the tunnel was being made in the direction of the Emerald City, and knew at once it was being dug so that the army of Nomes could march through it and attack her own beautiful and peaceful country.

"I suppose King Roquat is planning revenge against us," she said, musingly, "and thinks he can surprise us and make us his captives and slaves. How sad it is that any one can have such wicked thoughts! But I must not blame King Roquat too severely, for he is a Nome, and his nature is not so gentle as my own."

Then she dismissed from her mind further thought of the tunnel, for that time, and began to wonder if Aunt Em would not be happy as Royal Mender of the Stockings of the Ruler of Oz. Ozma wore few holes in her stockings; still, they sometimes needed mending. Aunt Em ought to be able to do that very nicely.

Next day, the Princess watched the tunnel again in her Magic Picture, and every day afterward she devoted a few minutes to inspecting the work. It was not especially interesting, but she felt that it was her duty.

Slowly but surely the big, arched hole crept through the rocks underneath the deadly desert, and day by day it drew nearer and nearer to the Emerald City.

Chapter 19 - How Bunnybury Welcomed the Strangers

Dorothy left Bunbury the same way she had entered it and when they were in the forest again she said to Billina:

"I never thought that things good to eat could be so dis'gree'ble."

"Often I've eaten things that tasted good but were disagreeable afterward," returned the Yellow Hen. "I think, Dorothy, if eatables are going to act badly, it's better before than after you eat them."

"P'raps you're right," said the little girl, with a sigh. "But what shall we do now?"

"Let us follow the path back to the signpost," suggested Billina. "That will be better than getting lost again."

"Why, we're lost anyhow," declared Dorothy; "but I guess you're right about going back to that signpost, Billina."

They returned along the path to the place where they had first found it, and at once took "the other road" to Bunnybury. This road was a mere narrow strip, worn hard and smooth but not wide enough for Dorothy's feet to tread. Still, it was a guide, and the walking through the forest was not at all difficult.

Before long they reached a high wall of solid white marble, and the path came to an end at this wall.

At first Dorothy thought there was no opening at all in the marble, but on looking closely she discovered a small square door about on a level with her head, and underneath this closed door was a bell-push. Near the bell-push a sign was painted in neat letters upon the marble, and the sign read:

NO ADMITTANCE
EXCEPT ON BUSINESS

This did not discourage Dorothy, however, and she rang the bell.

Pretty soon a bolt was cautiously withdrawn and the marble door swung slowly open. Then she saw it was not really a door, but a window, for several brass bars were placed across it, being set fast in the marble and so close together that the little girl's fingers might barely go between them. Back of the bars appeared the face of a white rabbit—a very sober and sedate face—with an eye-glass held in his left eye and attached to a cord in his button-hole.

"Well! what is it?" asked the rabbit, sharply.

"I'm Dorothy," said the girl, "and I'm lost, and—"

"State your business, please," interrupted the rabbit.

"My business," she replied, "is to find out where I am, and to—"

"No one is allowed in Bunnybury without an order or a letter of introduction from either Ozma of Oz or Glinda the Good," announced the rabbit; "so that settles the matter," and he started to close the window.

"Wait a minute!" cried Dorothy. "I've got a letter from Ozma."

"From the Ruler of Oz?" asked the rabbit, doubtingly.

"Of course. Ozma's my best friend, you know; and I'm a Princess myself," she announced, earnestly.

"Hum—ha! Let me see your letter," returned the rabbit, as if he still doubted her.

So she hunted in her pocket and found the letter Ozma had given her. Then she handed it through the bars to the rabbit, who took it in his paws and opened it. He read it aloud in a pompous voice, as if to let Dorothy and Billina see that he was educated and could read writing. The letter was as follows:

"It will please me to have my subjects greet Princess Dorothy, the bearer of this royal missive, with the same courtesy and consideration they would extend to me."

"Ha—hum! It is signed 'Ozma of Oz,'" continued the rabbit, "and is sealed with the Great Seal of the Emerald City. Well, well, well! How strange! How remarkable!"

"What are you going to do about it?" inquired Dorothy, impatiently.

"We must obey the royal mandate," replied the rabbit. "We are subjects of Ozma of Oz, and we live in her country. Also we are under the protection of the great Sorceress Glinda the Good, who made us promise to respect Ozma's commands."

"Then may I come in?" she asked.

"I'll open the door," said the rabbit. He shut the window and disappeared, but a moment afterward a big door in the wall opened and admitted Dorothy to a small room, which seemed to be a part of the wall and built into it.

Here stood the rabbit she had been talking with, and now that she could see all of him, she gazed at the creature in surprise. He was a good sized white rabbit with pink eyes, much like all other white rabbits. But the astonishing thing about him was the manner in which he was dressed. He wore a white satin jacket embroidered with gold, and having diamond buttons. His vest was rose-colored satin, with tourmaline buttons. His trousers were white, to correspond with the jacket, and they were baggy at the knees—like those of a zouave—being tied with knots of rose ribbons. His shoes were of white plush with diamond buckles, and his stockings were rose silk.

The richness and even magnificence of the rabbit's clothing made Dorothy stare at the little creature wonderingly. Toto and Billina had followed her into the room and when he saw them the rabbit ran to a table and sprang upon it nimbly. Then he looked at the three through his monocle and said:

"These companions, Princess, cannot enter Bunnybury with you."

"Why not?" asked Dorothy.

"In the first place they would frighten our people, who dislike dogs above all things on earth; and, secondly, the letter of the Royal Ozma does not mention them."

"But they're my friends," persisted Dorothy, "and go wherever I go."

"Not this time," said the rabbit, decidedly. "You, yourself, Princess, are a welcome visitor, since you come so highly recommended; but unless you consent to leave the dog and the hen in this room I cannot permit you to enter the town."

"Never mind us, Dorothy," said Billina. "Go inside and see what the place is like. You can tell us about it afterward, and Toto and I will rest comfortably here until you return."

This seemed the best thing to do, for Dorothy was curious to see how the rabbit people lived and she was aware of the fact that her friends might frighten the timid little creatures. She had not forgotten how Toto and Billina had misbehaved in Bunbury, and perhaps the rabbit was wise to insist on their staying outside the town.

"Very well," she said, "I'll go in alone. I s'pose you're the King of this town, aren't you?"

"No," answered the rabbit, "I'm merely the Keeper of the Wicket, and a person of little importance, although I try to do my duty. I must now inform you, Princess, that before you enter our town you must consent to reduce."

"Reduce what?" asked Dorothy.

"Your size. You must become the size of the rabbits, although you may retain your own form."

"Wouldn't my clothes be too big for me?" she inquired.

"No; they will reduce when your body does."

"Can YOU make me smaller?" asked the girl.

"Easily," returned the rabbit.

"And will you make me big again, when I'm ready to go away?"

"I will," said he.

"All right, then; I'm willing," she announced.

The rabbit jumped from the table and ran—or rather hopped—to the further wall, where he opened a door so tiny that even Toto could scarcely have crawled through it.

"Follow me," he said.

Now, almost any other little girl would have declared that she could not get through so small a door; but Dorothy had already encountered so many fairy adventures that she believed nothing was impossible in the Land of Oz. So she quietly walked toward the door, and at every step she grew smaller and smaller until, by the time the opening was reached, she could pass through it with ease. Indeed, as she stood beside the rabbit, who sat upon his hind legs and used his paws as hands, her head was just about as high as his own.

Then the Keeper of the Wicket passed through and she followed, after which the door swung shut and locked itself with a sharp click.

Dorothy now found herself in a city so strange and beautiful that she gave a gasp of surprise. The high marble wall extended all around the place and shut out all the rest of the world. And here were marble houses of curious forms, most of them resembling overturned kettles but with delicate slender spires and minarets running far up into the sky. The streets were paved with white marble and in front of each house was a lawn of rich green clover. Everything was as neat as wax, the green and white contrasting prettily together.

But the rabbit people were, after all, the most amazing things Dorothy saw. The streets were full of them, and their costumes were so splendid that the rich dress of the Keeper of the Wicket was commonplace when compared with the others. Silks and satins of delicate hues seemed always used for material, and nearly every costume sparkled with exquisite gems.

But the lady rabbits outshone the gentlemen rabbits in splendor, and the cut of their gowns was really wonderful. They wore bonnets, too, with feathers and jewels in them, and some wheeled baby carriages in which the girl could see wee bunnies. Some were lying asleep while others lay sucking their paws and looking around them with big pink eyes.

As Dorothy was no bigger in size than the grown-up rabbits she had a chance to observe them closely before they noticed her presence. Then they did not seem at all alarmed, although the little girl naturally became the center of attraction and regarded her with great curiosity.

"Make way!" cried the Keeper of the Wicket, in a pompous voice; "make way for Princess Dorothy, who comes from Ozma of Oz."

Hearing this announcement, the throng of rabbits gave place to them on the walks, and as Dorothy passed along they all bowed their heads respectfully.

Walking thus through several handsome streets they came to a square in the center of the City. In this square were some pretty trees and a statue in bronze of Glinda the Good, while beyond it were the portals of the Royal Palace—an extensive and imposing building of white marble covered with a filigree of frosted gold.

Chapter 20 - How Dorothy Lunched with a King

A line of rabbit soldiers was drawn up before the palace entrance, and they wore green and gold uniforms with high shakos upon their heads and held tiny spears in their hands. The Captain had a sword and a white plume in his shako.

"Salute!" called the Keeper of the Wicket. "Salute Princess Dorothy, who comes from Ozma of Oz!"

"Salute!" yelled the Captain, and all the soldiers promptly saluted.

They now entered the great hall of the palace, where they met a gaily dressed attendant, from whom the Keeper of the Wicket inquired if the King were at leisure.

"I think so," was the reply. "I heard his Majesty blubbering and wailing as usual only a few minutes ago. If he doesn't stop acting like a cry-baby I'm going to resign my position here and go to work."

"What's the matter with your King?" asked Dorothy, surprised to hear the rabbit attendant speak so disrespectfully of his monarch.

"Oh, he doesn't want to be King, that's all; and he simply HAS to," was the reply.

"Come!" said the Keeper of the Wicket, sternly; "lead us to his Majesty; and do not air our troubles before strangers, I beg of you."

"Why, if this girl is going to see the King, he'll air his own troubles," returned the attendant.

"That is his royal privilege," declared the Keeper.

So the attendant led them into a room all draped with cloth-of-gold and furnished with satin-covered gold furniture. There was a throne in this room, set on a dais and having a big, cushioned seat, and on this seat reclined the Rabbit King. He was lying on his back, with his paws in the air, and whining very like a puppy-dog.

"Your Majesty! your Majesty! Get up. Here's a visitor," called out the attendant.

The King rolled over and looked at Dorothy with one watery pink eye. Then he sat up and wiped his eyes carefully with a silk handkerchief and put on his jeweled crown, which had fallen off.

"Excuse my grief, fair stranger," he said, in a sad voice. "You behold in me the most miserable monarch in all the world. What time is it, Blinkem?"

"One o'clock, your Majesty," replied the attendant to whom the question was addressed.

"Serve luncheon at once!" commanded the King. "Luncheon for two—that's for my visitor and me—and see that the human has some sort of food she's accustomed to."

"Yes, your Majesty," answered the attendant, and went away.

"Tie my shoe, Bristle," said the King to the Keeper of the Wicket. "Ah me! how unhappy I am!"

"What seems to be worrying your Majesty?" asked Dorothy.

"Why, it's this king business, of course," he returned, while the Keeper tied his shoe. "I didn't want to be King of Bunnybury at all, and the rabbits all knew it. So they elected me—to save themselves from such a dreadful fate, I suppose—and here I am, shut up in a palace, when I might be free and happy."

"Seems to me," said Dorothy, "it's a great thing to be a King."

"Were you ever a King?" inquired the monarch.

"No," she answered, laughing.

"Then you know nothing about it," he said. "I haven't inquired who you are, but it doesn't matter. While we're at luncheon, I'll tell you all my troubles. They're a great deal more interesting than anything you can say about yourself."

"Perhaps they are, to you," replied Dorothy.

"Luncheon is served!" cried Blinkem, throwing open the door, and in came a dozen rabbits in livery, all bearing trays which they placed upon the table, where they arranged the dishes in an orderly manner.

"Now clear out—all of you!" exclaimed the King. "Bristle, you may wait outside, in case I want you."

When they had gone and the King was alone with Dorothy he came down from his throne, tossed his crown into a corner and kicked his ermine robe under the table.

"Sit down," he said, "and try to be happy. It's useless for me to try, because I'm always wretched and miserable. But I'm hungry, and I hope you are."

"I am," said Dorothy. "I've only eaten a wheelbarrow and a piano to-day—oh, yes! and a slice of bread and butter that used to be a door-mat."

"That sounds like a square meal," remarked the King, seating himself opposite her; "but perhaps it wasn't a square piano. Eh?"

Dorothy laughed.

"You don't seem so very unhappy now," she said.

"But I am," protested the King, fresh tears gathering in his eyes. "Even my jokes are miserable. I'm wretched, woeful, afflicted, distressed and dismal as an individual can be. Are you not sorry for me?"

"No," answered Dorothy, honestly, "I can't say I am. Seems to me that for a rabbit you're right in clover. This is the prettiest little city I ever saw."

"Oh, the city is good enough," he admitted. "Glinda, the Good Sorceress, made it for us because she was fond of rabbits. I don't mind the City so much, although I wouldn't live here if I had my choice. It is being King that has absolutely ruined my happiness."

"Why wouldn't you live here by choice?" she asked.

"Because it is all unnatural, my dear. Rabbits are out of place in such luxury. When I was young I lived in a burrow in the forest. I was surrounded by enemies and often had to run for my life. It was hard getting enough to eat, at times, and when I found a bunch of clover I had to listen and look for danger while I ate it. Wolves prowled around the hole in which I lived and sometimes I didn't dare stir out for days at a time. Oh, how happy and contented I was then! I was a real rabbit, as nature made me—wild and free!—and I even enjoyed listening to the startled throbbing of my own heart!"

"I've often thought," said Dorothy, who was busily eating, "that it would be fun to be a rabbit."

"It IS fun—when you're the genuine article," agreed his Majesty. "But look at me now! I live in a marble palace instead of a hole in the ground. I have all I want to eat, without the joy of hunting for it. Every day I must dress in fine clothes and wear that horrible crown till it makes my head ache. Rabbits come to me with all sorts of troubles, when my own troubles are the only ones I care about. When I walk out I can't hop and run; I must strut on my rear legs and wear an ermine robe! And the soldiers salute me and the band plays and the other rabbits laugh and clap their paws and cry out: 'Hail to the King!' Now let me ask you, as a friend and a young lady of good judgment: isn't all this pomp and foolishness enough to make a decent rabbit miserable?"

"Once," said Dorothy, reflectively, "men were wild and unclothed and lived in caves and hunted for food as wild beasts do. But they got civ'lized, in time, and now they'd hate to go back to the old days."

"That is an entirely different case," replied the King. "None of you Humans were civilized in one lifetime. It came to you by degrees. But I have known the forest and the free life, and that is why I resent being civilized all at once, against my will, and being made a King with a crown and an ermine robe. Pah!"

"If you don't like it, why don't you resign?" she asked.

"Impossible!" wailed the Rabbit, wiping his eyes again with his handkerchief. "There's a beastly law in this town that forbids it. When one is elected a King, there's no getting out of it."

"Who made the laws?" inquired Dorothy.

"The same Sorceress who made the town—Glinda the Good. She built the wall, and fixed up the City, and gave us several valuable enchantments, and made the laws. Then she invited all the pink-eyed white rabbits of the forest to come here, after which she left us to our fate."

"What made you 'cept the invitation, and come here?" asked the child.

"I didn't know how dreadful city life was, and I'd no idea I would be elected King," said he, sobbing bitterly. "And—and—now I'm It—with a capital I—and can't escape!"

"I know Glinda," remarked Dorothy, eating for dessert a dish of charlotte russe, "and when I see her again, I'll ask her to put another King in your place."

"Will you? Will you, indeed?" asked the King, joyfully.

"I will if you want me to," she replied.

"Hurroo—huray!" shouted the King; and then he jumped up from the table and danced wildly about the room, waving his napkin like a flag and laughing with glee.

After a time he managed to control his delight and returned to the table.

"When are you likely to see Glinda?" he inquired.

"Oh, p'raps in a few days," said Dorothy.

"And you won't forget to ask her?"

"Of course not."

"Princess," said the Rabbit King, earnestly, "you have relieved me of a great unhappiness, and I am very grateful. Therefore I propose to entertain you, since you are my guest and I am the King, as a slight mark of my appreciation. Come with me to my reception hall."

He then summoned Bristle and said to him: "Assemble all the nobility in the great reception hall, and also tell Blinkem that I want him immediately."

The Keeper of the Wicket bowed and hurried away, and his Majesty turned to Dorothy and continued: "We'll have time for a walk in the gardens before the people get here."

The gardens were back of the palace and were filled with beautiful flowers and fragrant shrubs, with many shade and fruit trees and marble-paved walks running in every direction. As they entered this place Blinkem came running to the King, who gave him several orders in a low voice. Then his Majesty rejoined Dorothy and led her through the gardens, which she admired very much.

"What lovely clothes your Majesty wears!" she said, glancing at the rich blue satin costume, embroidered, with pearls in which the King was dressed.

"Yes," he returned, with an air of pride, "this is one of my favorite suits; but I have a good many that are even more elaborate. We have excellent tailors in Bunnybury, and Glinda supplies all the material. By the way, you might ask the Sorceress, when you see her, to permit me to keep my wardrobe."

"But if you go back to the forest you will not need clothes," she said.

"N—o!" he faltered; "that may be so. But I've dressed up so long that I'm used to it, and I don't imagine I'd care to run around naked again. So perhaps the Good Glinda will let me keep the costumes."

"I'll ask her," agreed Dorothy.

Then they left the gardens and went into a fine, big reception hall, where rich rugs were spread upon the tiled floors and the furniture was exquisitely carved and studded with jewels. The King's chair was an especially pretty piece of furniture, being in the shape of a silver lily with one leaf bent over to form the seat. The silver was everywhere thickly encrusted with diamonds and the seat was upholstered in white satin.

"Oh, what a splendid chair!" cried Dorothy, clasping her hands admiringly.

"Isn't it?" answered the King, proudly. "It is my favorite seat, and I think it especially becoming to my complexion. While I think of it, I wish you'd ask Glinda to let me keep this lily chair when I go away."

"It wouldn't look very well in a hole in the ground, would it?" she suggested.

"Maybe not; but I'm used to sitting in it and I'd like to take it with me," he answered. "But here come the ladies and gentlemen of the court; so please sit beside me and be presented."

Chapter 21 - How the King Changed his Mind

Just then a rabbit band of nearly fifty pieces marched in, playing upon golden instruments and dressed in neat uniforms. Following the band came the nobility of Bunnybury, all richly dressed and hopping along on their rear legs. Both the ladies and the gentlemen wore white gloves upon their paws, with their rings on the outside of the gloves, as this seemed to be the fashion here. Some of the lady rabbits carried lorgnettes, while many of the gentlemen rabbits wore monocles in their left eyes.

The courtiers and their ladies paraded past the King, who introduced Princess Dorothy to each couple in a very graceful manner. Then the company seated themselves in chairs and on sofas and looked expectantly at their monarch.

"It is our royal duty, as well as our royal pleasure," he said, "to provide fitting entertainment for our distinguished guest. We will now present the Royal Band of Whiskered Friskers."

As he spoke the musicians, who had arranged themselves in a corner, struck up a dance melody while into the room pranced the Whiskered Friskers. They were eight pretty rabbits dressed only in gauzy purple skirts fastened around their waists with diamond bands. Their whiskers were colored a rich purple, but otherwise they were pure white.

After bowing before the King and Dorothy the Friskers began their pranks, and these were so comical that Dorothy laughed with real enjoyment. They not only danced together, whirling and gyrating around the room, but they leaped over one another, stood upon their heads and hopped and skipped here and there so nimbly that it was hard work to keep track of them. Finally, they all made double somersaults and turned handsprings out of the room.

The nobility enthusiastically applauded, and Dorothy applauded with them.

"They're fine!" she said to the King.

"Yes, the Whiskered Friskers are really very clever," he replied. "I shall hate to part with them when I go away, for they have often amused me when I was very miserable. I wonder if you would ask Glinda—"

"No, it wouldn't do at all," declared Dorothy, positively. "There wouldn't be room in your hole in the ground for so many rabbits, 'spec'ly when you get the lily chair and your clothes there. Don't think of such a thing, your Majesty."

The King sighed. Then he stood up and announced to the company:

"We will now hold a military drill by my picked Bodyguard of Royal Pikemen."

Now the band played a march and a company of rabbit soldiers came in. They wore green and gold uniforms and marched very stiffly but in perfect time. Their spears, or pikes, had slender shafts of polished silver with golden heads, and during the drill they handled these weapons with wonderful dexterity.

"I should think you'd feel pretty safe with such a fine Bodyguard," remarked Dorothy.

"I do," said the King. "They protect me from every harm. I suppose Glinda wouldn't—"

"No," interrupted the girl; "I'm sure she wouldn't. It's the King's own Bodyguard, and when you are no longer King you can't have 'em."

The King did not reply, but he looked rather sorrowful for a time.

When the soldiers had marched out he said to the company:

"The Royal Jugglers will now appear."

Dorothy had seen many jugglers in her lifetime, but never any so interesting as these. There were six of them, dressed in black satin embroidered with queer symbols in silver—a costume which contrasted strongly with their snow-white fur.

First, they pushed in a big red ball and three of the rabbit jugglers stood upon its top and made it roll. Then two of them caught up a third and tossed him into the air, all vanishing, until only the two were left. Then one of these tossed the other upward and remained alone of all his fellows. This last juggler now touched the red ball, which fell apart, being hollow, and the five rabbits who had disappeared in the air scrambled out of the hollow ball.

Next they all clung together and rolled swiftly upon the floor. When they came to a stop only one fat rabbit juggler was seen, the others seeming to be inside him. This one leaped lightly into the air and when he came down he exploded and separated into the original six. Then four of them rolled themselves into round balls and the other two tossed them around and played ball with them.

These were but a few of the tricks the rabbit jugglers performed, and they were so skillful that all the nobility and even the King applauded as loudly as did Dorothy.

"I suppose there are no rabbit jugglers in all the world to compare with these," remarked the King. "And since I may not have the Whiskers Friskers or my Bodyguard, you might ask Glinda to let me take away just two or three of these jugglers. Will you?"

"I'll ask her," replied Dorothy, doubtfully.

"Thank you," said the King; "thank you very much. And now you shall listen to the Winsome Waggish Warblers, who have often cheered me in my moments of anguish."

The Winsome Waggish Warblers proved to be a quartette of rabbit singers, two gentlemen and two lady rabbits. The gentlemen Warblers wore full-dress swallow-tailed suits of white satin, with pearls for buttons, while the lady Warblers were gowned in white satin dresses with long trails.

The first song they sang began in this way:

"When a rabbit gets a habit Of living in a city And wearing clothes and furbelows And jewels rare and pretty, He scorns the Bun who has to run And burrow in the ground And pities those whose watchful foes Are man and gun and hound."

Dorothy looked at the King when she heard this song and noticed that he seemed disturbed and ill at ease.

"I don't like that song," he said to the Warblers. "Give us something jolly and rollicking."

So they sang to a joyous, tinkling melody as follows:

"Bunnies gay Delight to play In their fairy town secure; Ev'ry frisker Flirts his whisker At a pink-eyed girl demure. Ev'ry maid In silk arrayed At her partner shyly glances, Paws are grasped, Waists are clasped As they whirl in giddy dances. Then together Through the heather 'Neath the moonlight soft they stroll; Each is very Blithe and merry, Gamboling with laughter droll. Life is fun To ev'ry one Guarded by our magic charm For to dangers We are strangers, Safe from any thought of harm."

"You see," said Dorothy to the King, when the song ended, "the rabbits all seem to like Bunnybury except you. And I guess you're the only one that ever has cried or was unhappy and wanted to get back to your muddy hole in the ground."

His Majesty seemed thoughtful, and while the servants passed around glasses of nectar and plates of frosted cakes their King was silent and a bit nervous.

When the refreshments had been enjoyed by all and the servants had retired Dorothy said:

"I must go now, for it's getting late and I'm lost. I've got to find the Wizard and Aunt Em and Uncle Henry and all the rest sometime before night comes, if I poss'bly can."

"Won't you stay with us?" asked the King. "You will be very welcome."

"No, thank you," she replied. "I must get back to my friends. And I want to see Glinda just as soon as I can, you know."

So the King dismissed his court and said he would himself walk with Dorothy to the gate. He did not weep nor groan any more, but his long face was quite solemn and his big ears hung dejectedly on each side of it. He still wore his crown and his ermine and walked with a handsome gold-headed cane.

When they arrived at the room in the wall the little girl found Toto and Billina waiting for her very patiently. They had been liberally fed by some of the attendants and were in no hurry to leave such comfortable quarters.

The Keeper of the Wicket was by this time back in his old place, but he kept a safe distance from Toto. Dorothy bade good bye to the King as they stood just inside the wall.

"You've been good to me," she said, "and I thank you ever so much. As soon as poss'ble I'll see Glinda and ask her to put another King in your place and send you back into the wild forest. And I'll ask her to let you keep some of your clothes and the lily chair and one or two jugglers to amuse you. I'm sure she will do it, 'cause she's so kind she doesn't like any one to be unhappy."

"Ahem!" said the King, looking rather downcast. "I don't like to trouble you with my misery; so you needn't see Glinda."

"Oh, yes I will," she replied. "It won't be any trouble at all."

"But, my dear," continued the King, in an embarrassed way, "I've been thinking the subject over carefully, and I find there are a lot of pleasant things here in Bunnybury that I would miss if I went away. So perhaps I'd better stay."

Dorothy laughed. Then she looked grave.

"It won't do for you to be a King and a cry-baby at the same time," she said. "You've been making all the other rabbits unhappy and discontented with your howls about being so miserable. So I guess it's better to have another King."

"Oh, no indeed!" exclaimed the King, earnestly. "If you won't say anything to Glinda I'll promise to be merry and gay all the time, and never cry or wail again."

"Honor bright?" she asked.

"On the royal word of a King I promise it!" he answered.

"All right," said Dorothy. "You'd be a reg'lar lunatic to want to leave Bunnybury for a wild life in the forest, and I'm sure any rabbit outside the city would be glad to take your place."

"Forget it, my dear; forget all my foolishness," pleaded the King, earnestly. "Hereafter I'll try to enjoy myself and do my duty by my subjects."

So then she left him and entered through the little door into the room in the wall, where she grew gradually bigger and bigger until she had resumed her natural size.

The Keeper of the Wicket let them out into the forest and told Dorothy that she had been of great service to Bunnybury because she had brought their dismal King to a realization of the pleasure of ruling so beautiful a city.

"I shall start a petition to have your statue erected beside Glinda's in the public square," said the Keeper. "I hope you will come again, some day, and see it."

"Perhaps I shall," she replied.

Then, followed by Toto and Billina, she walked away from the high marble wall and started back along the narrow path toward the sign-post.

Chapter 22 - How the Wizard Found Dorothy

When they came to the signpost, there, to their joy, were the tents of the Wizard pitched beside the path and the kettle bubbling merrily over the fire. The Shaggy Man and Omby Amby were gathering firewood while Uncle Henry and Aunt Em sat in their camp chairs talking with the Wizard.

They all ran forward to greet Dorothy, as she approached, and Aunt Em exclaimed: "Goodness gracious, child! Where have you been?"

"You've played hookey the whole day," added the Shaggy Man, reproachfully.

"Well, you see, I've been lost," explained the little girl, "and I've tried awful hard to find the way back to you, but just couldn't do it."

"Did you wander in the forest all day?" asked Uncle Henry.

"You must be a'most starved!" said Aunt Em.

"No," said Dorothy, "I'm not hungry. I had a wheelbarrow and a piano for breakfast, and lunched with a King."

"Ah!" exclaimed the Wizard, nodding with a bright smile. "So you've been having adventures again."

"She's stark crazy!" cried Aunt Em. "Whoever heard of eating a wheelbarrow?"

"It wasn't very big," said Dorothy; "and it had a zuzu wheel."

"And I ate the crumbs," said Billina, soberly.

"Sit down and tell us about it," begged the Wizard. "We've hunted for you all day, and at last I noticed your footsteps in this path—and the tracks of Billina. We found the path by accident, and seeing it only led to two places I decided you were at either one or the other of those places. So we made camp and waited for you to return. And now, Dorothy, tell us where you have been—to Bunbury or to Bunnybury?"

"Why, I've been to both," she replied; "but first I went to Utensia, which isn't on any path at all."

She then sat down and related the day's adventures, and you may be sure Aunt Em and Uncle Henry were much astonished at the story.

"But after seeing the Cuttenclips and the Fuddles," remarked her uncle, "we ought not to wonder at anything in this strange country."

"Seems like the only common and ordinary folks here are ourselves," rejoined Aunt Em, diffidently.

"Now that we're together again, and one reunited party," observed the Shaggy Man, "what are we to do next?"

"Have some supper and a night's rest," answered the Wizard promptly, "and then proceed upon our journey."

"Where to?" asked the Captain General.

"We haven't visited the Rigmaroles or the Flutterbudgets yet," said Dorothy. "I'd like to see them—wouldn't you?"

"They don't sound very interesting," objected Aunt Em. "But perhaps they are."

"And then," continued the little Wizard, "we will call upon the Tin Woodman and Jack Pumpkinhead and our old friend the Scarecrow, on our way home."

"That will be nice!" cried Dorothy, eagerly.

"Can't say THEY sound very interesting, either," remarked Aunt Em.

"Why, they're the best friends I have!" asserted the little girl, "and you're sure to like them, Aunt Em, 'cause EVER'body likes them."

By this time twilight was approaching, so they ate the fine supper which the Wizard magically produced from the kettle and then went to bed in the cozy tents.

They were all up bright and early next morning, but Dorothy didn't venture to wander from the camp again for fear of more accidents.

"Do you know where there's a road?" she asked the little man.

"No, my dear," replied the Wizard; "but I'll find one."

After breakfast he waved his hand toward the tents and they became handkerchiefs again, which were at once returned to the pockets of their owners. Then they all climbed into the red wagon and the Sawhorse inquired:

"Which way?"

"Never mind which way," replied the Wizard. "Just go as you please and you're sure to be right. I've enchanted the wheels of the wagon, and they will roll in the right direction, never fear."

As the Sawhorse started away through the trees Dorothy said:

"If we had one of those new-fashioned airships we could float away over the top of the forest, and look down and find just the places we want."

"Airship? Pah!" retorted the little man, scornfully. "I hate those things, Dorothy, although they are nothing new to either you or me. I was a balloonist for many years, and once my balloon carried me to the Land of Oz, and once to the Vegetable Kingdom. And once Ozma had a Gump that flew all over this kingdom and had sense enough to go where it was told to—which airships won't do. The house which the cyclone brought to Oz all the way from Kansas, with you and Toto in it—was a real airship at the time; so you see we've got plenty of experience flying with the birds."

"Airships are not so bad, after all," declared Dorothy. "Some day they'll fly all over the world, and perhaps bring people even to the Land of Oz."

"I must speak to Ozma about that," said the Wizard, with a slight frown. "It wouldn't do at all, you know, for the Emerald City to become a way-station on an airship line."

"No," said Dorothy, "I don't s'pose it would. But what can we do to prevent it?"

"I'm working out a magic recipe to fuddle men's brains, so they'll never make an airship that will go where they want it to go," the Wizard confided to her. "That won't keep the things from flying, now and then, but it'll keep them from flying to the Land of Oz."

Just then the Sawhorse drew the wagon out of the forest and a beautiful landscape lay spread before the travelers' eyes. Moreover, right before them was a good road that wound away through the hills and valleys.

"Now," said the Wizard, with evident delight, "we are on the right track again, and there is nothing more to worry about."

"It's a foolish thing to take chances in a strange country," observed the Shaggy Man. "Had we kept to the roads we never would have been lost. Roads always lead to some place, else they wouldn't be roads."

"This road," added the Wizard, "leads to Rigmarole Town. I'm sure of that because I enchanted the wagon wheels."

Sure enough, after riding along the road for an hour or two they entered a pretty valley where a village was nestled among the hills. The houses were Munchkin shaped, for they were all domes, with windows wider than they were high, and pretty balconies over the front doors.

Aunt Em was greatly relieved to find this town "neither paper nor patch-work," and the only surprising thing about it was that it was so far distant from all other towns.

As the Sawhorse drew the wagon into the main street the travelers noticed that the place was filled with people, standing in groups and seeming to be engaged in earnest conversation. So occupied with themselves were the inhabitants that they scarcely noticed the strangers at all. So the Wizard stopped a boy and asked:

"Is this Rigmarole Town?"

"Sir," replied the boy, "if you have traveled very much you will have noticed that every town differs from every other town in one way or another and so by observing the methods of the people and the way they live as well as the style of their dwelling places it ought not to be a difficult thing to make up your mind without the trouble of asking questions whether the town bears the appearance of the one you intended to visit or whether perhaps having taken a different road from the one you should have taken you have made an error in your way and arrived at some point where—"

"Land sakes!" cried Aunt Em, impatiently; "what's all this rigmarole about?"

"That's it!" said the Wizard, laughing merrily. "It's a rigmarole because the boy is a Rigmarole and we've come to Rigmarole Town."

"Do they all talk like that?" asked Dorothy, wonderingly.

"He might have said 'yes' or 'no' and settled the question," observed Uncle Henry.

"Not here," said Omby Amby. "I don't believe the Rigmaroles know what 'yes' or 'no' means."

While the boy had been talking several other people had approached the wagon and listened intently to his speech. Then they began talking to one another in long, deliberate speeches, where many words were used but little was said. But when the strangers criticized them so frankly one of the women, who had no one else to talk to, began an address to them, saying:

"It is the easiest thing in the world for a person to say 'yes' or 'no' when a question that is asked for the purpose of gaining information or satisfying the curiosity of the one who has given expression to the inquiry has attracted the attention of an individual who may be competent either from personal experience or the experience of others to answer it with more or less correctness or at least an attempt to satisfy the desire for information on the part of the one who has made the inquiry by—"

"Dear me!" exclaimed Dorothy, interrupting the speech. "I've lost all track of what you are saying."

"Don't let her begin over again, for goodness sake!" cried Aunt Em.

But the woman did not begin again. She did not even stop talking, but went right on as she had begun, the words flowing from her mouth in a stream.

"I'm quite sure that if we waited long enough and listened carefully, some of these people might be able to tell us something, in time," said the Wizard.

"Let's don't wait," returned Dorothy. "I've heard of the Rigmaroles, and wondered what they were like; but now I know, and I'm ready to move on."

"So am I," declared Uncle Henry; "we're wasting time here."

"Why, we're all ready to go," said the Shaggy Man, putting his fingers to his ears to shut out the monotonous babble of those around the wagon.

So the Wizard spoke to the Sawhorse, who trotted nimbly through the village and soon gained the open country on the other side of it. Dorothy looked back, as they rode away, and noticed that the woman had not yet finished her speech but was talking as glibly as ever, although no one was near to hear her.

"If those people wrote books," Omby Amby remarked with a smile, "it would take a whole library to say the cow jumped over the moon."

"Perhaps some of 'em do write books," asserted the little Wizard. "I've read a few rigmaroles that might have come from this very town."

"Some of the college lecturers and ministers are certainly related to these people," observed the Shaggy Man; "and it seems to me the Land of Oz is a little ahead of the United States in some of its laws. For here, if one can't talk clearly, and straight to the point, they send him to Rigmarole Town; while Uncle Sam lets him roam around wild and free, to torture innocent people."

Dorothy was thoughtful. The Rigmaroles had made a strong impression upon her. She decided that whenever she spoke, after this, she would use only enough words to express what she wanted to say.

Chapter 23 - How They Encountered the Flutterbudgets

They were soon among the pretty hills and valleys again, and the Sawhorse sped up hill and down at a fast and easy pace, the roads being hard and smooth. Mile after mile was speedily covered, and before the ride had grown at all tiresome they sighted another village. The place seemed even larger than Rigmarole Town, but was not so attractive in appearance.

"This must be Flutterbudget Center," declared the Wizard. "You see, it's no trouble at all to find places if you keep to the right road."

"What are the Flutterbudgets like?" inquired Dorothy.

"I do not know, my dear. But Ozma has given them a town all their own, and I've heard that whenever one of the people becomes a Flutterbudget he is sent to this place to live."

"That is true," Omby Amby added; "Flutterbudget Center and Rigmarole Town are called 'the Defensive Settlements of Oz.'"

The village they now approached was not built in a valley, but on top of a hill, and the road they followed wound around the hill, like a corkscrew, ascending the hill easily until it came to the town.

"Look out!" screamed a voice. "Look out, or you'll run over my child!"

They gazed around and saw a woman standing upon the sidewalk nervously wringing her hands as she gazed at them appealingly.

"Where is your child?" asked the Sawhorse.

"In the house," said the woman, bursting into tears; "but if it should happen to be in the road, and you ran over it, those great wheels would crush my darling to jelly. Oh dear! oh dear! Think of my darling child being crushed into jelly by those great wheels!"

"Gid-dap!" said the Wizard sharply, and the Sawhorse started on.

They had not gone far before a man ran out of a house shouting wildly, "Help! Help!"

The Sawhorse stopped short and the Wizard and Uncle Henry and the Shaggy Man and Omby Amby jumped out of the wagon and ran to the poor man's assistance. Dorothy followed them as quickly as she could.

"What's the matter?" asked the Wizard.

"Help! help!" screamed the man; "my wife has cut her finger off and she's bleeding to death!"

Then he turned and rushed back to the house, and all the party went with him. They found a woman in the front dooryard moaning and groaning as if in great pain.

"Be brave, madam!" said the Wizard, consolingly. "You won't die just because you have cut off a finger, you may be sure."

"But I haven't cut off a finger!" she sobbed.

"Then what HAS happened?" asked Dorothy.

"I—I pricked my finger with a needle while I was sewing, and—and the blood came!" she replied. "And now I'll have blood-poisoning, and the doctors will cut off my finger, and that will give me a fever and I shall die!"

"Pshaw!" said Dorothy; "I've pricked my finger many a time, and nothing happened."

"Really?" asked the woman, brightening and wiping her eyes upon her apron.

"Why, it's nothing at all," declared the girl. "You're more scared than hurt."

"Ah, that's because she's a Flutterbudget," said the Wizard, nodding wisely. "I think I know now what these people are like."

"So do I," announced Dorothy.

"Oh, boo-hoo-hoo!" sobbed the woman, giving way to a fresh burst of grief.

"What's wrong now?" asked the Shaggy Man.

"Oh, suppose I had pricked my foot!" she wailed. "Then the doctors would have cut my foot off, and I'd be lamed for life!"

"Surely, ma'am," replied the Wizard, "and if you'd pricked your nose they might cut your head off. But you see you didn't."

"But I might have!" she exclaimed, and began to cry again. So they left her and drove away in their wagon. And her husband came out and began calling "Help!" as he had before; but no one seemed to pay any attention to him.

As the travelers turned into another street they found a man walking excitedly up and down the pavement. He appeared to be in a very nervous condition and the Wizard stopped him to ask:

"Is anything wrong, sir?"

"Everything is wrong," answered the man, dismally. "I can't sleep."

"Why not?" inquired Omby Amby.

"If I go to sleep I'll have to shut my eyes," he explained; "and if I shut my eyes they may grow together, and then I'd be blind for life!"

"Did you ever hear of any one's eyes growing together?" asked Dorothy.

"No," said the man, "I never did. But it would be a dreadful thing, wouldn't it? And the thought of it makes me so nervous I'm afraid to go to sleep."

"There's no help for this case," declared the Wizard; and they went on.

At the next street corner a woman rushed up to them crying:

"Save my baby! Oh, good, kind people, save my baby!"

"Is it in danger?" asked Dorothy, noticing that the child was clasped in her arms and seemed sleeping peacefully.

"Yes, indeed," said the woman, nervously. "If I should go into the house and throw my child out of the window, it would roll way down to the bottom of the hill; and then if there were a lot of tigers and bears down there, they would tear my darling babe to pieces and eat it up!"

"Are there any tigers and bears in this neighborhood?" the Wizard asked.

"I've never heard of any," admitted the woman, "but if there were—"

"Have you any idea of throwing your baby out of the window?" questioned the little man.

"None at all," she said; "but if—"

"All your troubles are due to those 'ifs'," declared the Wizard. "If you were not a Flutterbudget you wouldn't worry."

"There's another 'if'," replied the woman. "Are you a Flutterbudget, too?"

"I will be, if I stay here long," exclaimed the Wizard, nervously.

"Another 'if'!" cried the woman.

But the Wizard did not stop to argue with her. He made the Sawhorse canter all the way down the hill, and only breathed easily when they were miles away from the village.

After they had ridden in silence for a while Dorothy turned to the little man and asked:

"Do 'ifs' really make Flutterbudgets?"

"I think the 'ifs' help," he answered seriously. "Foolish fears, and worries over nothing, with a mixture of nerves and ifs, will soon make a Flutterbudget of any one."

Then there was another long silence, for all the travelers were thinking over this statement, and nearly all decided it must be true.

The country they were now passing through was everywhere tinted purple, the prevailing color of the Gillikin Country; but as the Sawhorse ascended a hill they found that upon the other side everything was of a rich yellow hue.

"Aha!" cried the Captain General; "here is the Country of the Winkies. We are just crossing the boundary line."

"Then we may be able to lunch with the Tin Woodman," announced the Wizard, joyfully.

"Must we lunch on tin?" asked Aunt Em.

"Oh, no;" replied Dorothy. "Nick Chopper knows how to feed meat people, and he will give us plenty of good things to eat, never fear. I've been to his castle before."

"Is Nick Chopper the Tin Woodman's name?" asked Uncle Henry.

"Yes; that's one of his names," answered the little girl; "and another of his names is 'Emp'ror of the Winkies.' He's the King of this country, you know, but Ozma rules over all the countries of Oz."

"Does the Tin Woodman keep any Flutterbudgets or Rigmaroles at his castle?" inquired Aunt Em, uneasily.

"No indeed," said Dorothy, positively. "He lives in a new tin castle, all full of lovely things."

"I should think it would rust," said Uncle Henry.

"He has thousands of Winkies to keep it polished for him," explained the Wizard. "His people love to do anything in their power for their beloved Emperor, so there isn't a particle of rust on all the big castle."

"I suppose they polish their Emperor, too," said Aunt Em.

"Why, some time ago he had himself nickel-plated," the Wizard answered; "so he only needs rubbing up once in a while. He's the brightest man in all the world, is dear Nick Chopper; and the kindest-hearted."

"I helped find him," said Dorothy, reflectively. "Once the Scarecrow and I found the Tin Woodman in the woods, and he was just rusted still, that time, an' no mistake. But we oiled his joints an' got 'em good and slippery, and after that he went with us to visit the Wizard at the Em'rald City."

"Was that the time the Wizard scared you?" asked Aunt Em.

"He didn't treat us well, at first," acknowledged Dorothy; "for he made us go away and destroy the Wicked Witch. But after we found out he was only a humbug wizard we were not afraid of him."

The Wizard sighed and looked a little ashamed.

"When we try to deceive people we always make mistakes," he said. "But I'm getting to be a real wizard now, and Glinda the Good's magic, that I am trying to practice, can never harm any one."

"You were always a good man," declared Dorothy, "even when you were a bad wizard."

"He's a good wizard now," asserted Aunt Em, looking at the little man admiringly. "The way he made those tents grow out of handkerchiefs was just wonderful! And didn't he enchant the wagon wheels so they'd find the road?"

"All the people of Oz," said the Captain General, "are very proud of their Wizard. He once made some soap-bubbles that astonished the world."

The Wizard blushed at this praise, yet it pleased him. He no longer looked sad, but seemed to have recovered his usual good humor.

The country through which they now rode was thickly dotted with farmhouses, and yellow grain waved in all the fields. Many of the Winkies could be seen working on their farms and the wild and unsettled parts of Oz were by this time left far behind.

These Winkies appeared to be happy, light-hearted folk, and all removed their caps and bowed low when the red wagon with its load of travelers passed by.

It was not long before they saw something glittering in the sunshine far ahead.

"See!" cried Dorothy; "that's the Tin Castle, Aunt Em!"

And the Sawhorse, knowing his passengers were eager to arrive, broke into a swift trot that soon brought them to their destination.

Chapter 24 - How the Tin Woodman Told the Sad News

The Tin Woodman received Princess Dorothy's party with much grace and cordiality, yet the little girl decided that something must be worrying with her old friend, because he was not so merry as usual.

But at first she said nothing about this, for Uncle Henry and Aunt Em were fairly bubbling over with admiration for the beautiful tin castle and its polished tin owner. So her suspicion that something unpleasant had happened was for a time forgotten.

"Where is the Scarecrow?" she asked, when they had all been ushered into the big tin drawing-room of the castle, the Sawhorse being led around to the tin stable in the rear.

"Why, our old friend has just moved into his new mansion," explained the Tin Woodman. "It has been a long time in building, although my Winkies and many other people from all parts of the country have been busily working upon it. At last, however, it is completed, and the Scarecrow took possession of his new home just two days ago."

"I hadn't heard that he wanted a home of his own," said Dorothy. "Why doesn't he live with Ozma in the Emerald City? He used to, you know; and I thought he was happy there."

"It seems," said the Tin Woodman, "that our dear Scarecrow cannot be contented with city life, however beautiful his surroundings might be. Originally he was a farmer, for he passed his early life in a cornfield, where he was supposed to frighten away the crows."

"I know," said Dorothy, nodding. "I found him, and lifted him down from his pole."

"So now, after a long residence in the Emerald City, his tastes have turned to farm life again," continued the Tin Man. "He feels that he cannot be happy without a farm of his own, so Ozma gave him some land and every one helped him build his mansion, and now he is settled there for good."

"Who designed his house?" asked the Shaggy Man.

"I believe it was Jack Pumpkinhead, who is also a farmer," was the reply.

They were now invited to enter the tin dining room, where luncheon was served.

Aunt Em found, to her satisfaction, that Dorothy's promise was more than fulfilled; for, although the Tin Woodman had no appetite of his own, he respected the appetites of his guests and saw that they were bountifully fed.

They passed the afternoon in wandering through the beautiful gardens and grounds of the palace. The walks were all paved with sheets of tin, brightly polished, and there were tin fountains and tin statues here and there among the trees. The flowers were mostly natural flowers and grew in the regular way; but their host showed them one flower bed which was his especial pride.

"You see, all common flowers fade and die in time," he explained, "and so there are seasons when the pretty blooms are scarce. Therefore I decided to make one tin flower bed all of tin flowers, and my workmen have created them with rare skill. Here you see tin camelias, tin marigolds, tin carnations, tin poppies and tin hollyhocks growing as naturally as if they were real."

Indeed, they were a pretty sight, and glistened under the sunlight like spun silver. "Isn't this tin hollyhock going to seed?" asked the Wizard, bending over the flowers.

"Why, I believe it is!" exclaimed the Tin Woodman, as if surprised. "I hadn't noticed that before. But I shall plant the tin seeds and raise another bed of tin hollyhocks."

In one corner of the gardens Nick Chopper had established a fish-pond in which they saw swimming and disporting themselves many pretty tin fishes.

"Would they bite on hooks?" asked Aunt Em, curiously.

The Tin Woodman seemed hurt at this question.

"Madam," said he, "do you suppose I would allow anyone to catch my beautiful fishes, even if they were foolish enough to bite on hooks? No, indeed! Every created thing is safe from harm in my domain, and I would as soon think of killing my little friend Dorothy as killing one of my tin fishes."

"The Emperor is very kind-hearted, ma'am," explained the Wizard. "If a fly happens to light upon his tin body he doesn't rudely brush it off, as some people might do; he asks it politely to find some other resting place."

"What does the fly do then?" enquired Aunt Em.

"Usually it begs his pardon and goes away," said the Wizard, gravely. "Flies like to be treated politely as well as other creatures, and here in Oz they understand what we say to them, and behave very nicely."

"Well," said Aunt Em, "the flies in Kansas, where I came from, don't understand anything but a swat. You have to smash 'em to make 'em behave; and it's the same way with 'skeeters. Do you have 'skeeters in Oz?"

"We have some very large mosquitoes here, which sing as beautifully as song birds," replied the Tin Woodman. "But they never bite or annoy our people, because they are well fed and taken care of. The reason they bite people in your country is because they are hungry—poor things!"

"Yes," agreed Aunt Em; "they're hungry, all right. An' they ain't very particular who they feed on. I'm glad you've got the 'skeeters educated in Oz."

That evening after dinner they were entertained by the Emperor's Tin Cornet Band, which played for them several sweet melodies. Also the Wizard did a few sleight-of-hand tricks to amuse the company; after which they all retired to their cozy tin bedrooms and slept soundly until morning.

After breakfast Dorothy said to the Tin Woodman:

"If you'll tell us which way to go we'll visit the Scarecrow on our way home."

"I will go with you, and show you the way," replied the Emperor; "for I must journey to-day to the Emerald City."

He looked so anxious, as he said this, that the little girl asked:

"There isn't anything wrong with Ozma, is there?"

"Not yet," said he; "but I'm afraid the time has come when I must tell you some very bad news, little friend."

"Oh, what is it?" cried Dorothy.

"Do you remember the Nome King?" asked the Tin Woodman.

"I remember him very well," she replied.

"The Nome King has not a kind heart," said the Emperor, sadly, "and he has been harboring wicked thoughts of revenge, because we once defeated him and liberated his slaves and you took away his Magic Belt. So he has ordered his

Nomes to dig a long tunnel underneath the deadly desert, so that he may march his hosts right into the Emerald City. When he gets there he intends to destroy our beautiful country."

Dorothy was much surprised to hear this.

"How did Ozma find out about the tunnel?" she asked.

"She saw it in her Magic Picture."

"Of course," said Dorothy; "I might have known that. And what is she going to do?"

"I cannot tell," was the reply.

"Pooh!" cried the Yellow Hen. "We're not afraid of the Nomes. If we roll a few of our eggs down the tunnel they'll run away back home as fast as they can go."

"Why, that's true enough!" exclaimed Dorothy. "The Scarecrow once conquered all the Nome King's army with some of Billina's eggs."

"But you do not understand all of the dreadful plot," continued the Tin Woodman. "The Nome King is clever, and he knows his Nomes would run from eggs; so he has bargained with many terrible creatures to help him. These evil spirits are not afraid of eggs or anything else, and they are very powerful. So the Nome King will send them through the tunnel first, to conquer and destroy, and then the Nomes will follow after to get their share of the plunder and slaves."

They were all startled to hear this, and every face wore a troubled look.

"Is the tunnel all ready?" asked Dorothy.

"Ozma sent me word yesterday that the tunnel was all completed except for a thin crust of earth at the end. When our enemies break through this crust, they will be in the gardens of the royal palace, in the heart of the Emerald City. I offered to arm all my Winkies and march to Ozma's assistance; but she said no."

"I wonder why?" asked Dorothy.

"She answered that all the inhabitants of Oz, gathered together, were not powerful enough to fight and overcome the evil forces of the Nome King. Therefore she refuses to fight at all."

"But they will capture and enslave us, and plunder and ruin all our lovely land!" exclaimed the Wizard, greatly disturbed by this statement.

"I fear they will," said the Tin Woodman, sorrowfully. "And I also fear that those who are not fairies, such as the Wizard, and Dorothy, and her uncle and aunt, as well as Toto and Billina, will be speedily put to death by the conquerors."

"What can be done?" asked Dorothy, shuddering a little at the prospect of this awful fate.

"Nothing can be done!" gloomily replied the Emperor of the Winkies. "But since Ozma refuses my army I will go myself to the Emerald City. The least I may do is to perish beside my beloved Ruler."

Chapter 25 - How the Scarecrow Displayed his Wisdom

This amazing news had saddened every heart and all were now anxious to return to the Emerald City and share Ozma's fate. So they started without loss of time, and as the road led past the Scarecrow's new mansion they determined to make a brief halt there and confer with him.

"The Scarecrow is probably the wisest man in all Oz," remarked the Tin Woodman, when they had started upon their journey. "His brains are plentiful and of excellent quality, and often he has told me things I might never have thought of myself. I must say I rely a great deal upon the Scarecrow's brains in this emergency."

The Tin Woodman rode on the front seat of the wagon, where Dorothy sat between him and the Wizard.

"Has the Scarecrow heard of Ozma's trouble?" asked the Captain General.

"I do not know, sir," was the reply.

"When I was a private," said Omby Amby, "I was an excellent army, as I fully proved in our war against the Nomes. But now there is not a single private left in our army, since Ozma made me the Captain General, so there is no one to fight and defend our lovely Ruler."

"True," said the Wizard. "The present army is composed only of officers, and the business of an officer is to order his men to fight. Since there are no men there can be no fighting."

"Poor Ozma!" whispered Dorothy, with tears in her sweet eyes. "It's dreadful to think of all her lovely fairy country being destroyed. I wonder if we couldn't manage to escape and get back to Kansas by means of the Magic Belt? And we might take Ozma with us and all work hard to get money for her, so she wouldn't be so VERY lonely and unhappy about the loss of her fairyland."

"Do you think there would be any work for ME in Kansas?" asked the Tin Woodman.

"If you are hollow, they might use you in a canning factory," suggested Uncle Henry. "But I can't see the use of your working for a living. You never eat or sleep or need a new suit of clothes."

"I was not thinking of myself," replied the Emperor, with dignity. "I merely wondered if I could not help to support Dorothy and Ozma."

As they indulged in these sad plans for the future they journeyed in sight of the Scarecrow's new mansion, and even though filled with care and worry over the impending fate of Oz, Dorothy couldn't help a feeling of wonder at the sight she saw.

The Scarecrow's new house was shaped like an immense ear of corn. The rows of kernels were made of solid gold, and the green upon which the ear stood upright was a mass of sparkling emeralds. Upon the very top of the structure was perched a figure representing the Scarecrow himself, and upon his extended arms, as well as upon his head, were several crows carved out of ebony and having ruby eyes. You may imagine how big this ear of corn was when I tell you that a single gold kernel formed a window, swinging outward upon hinges, while a row of four kernels opened to make the front entrance. Inside there were five stories, each story being a single room.

The gardens around the mansion consisted of cornfields, and Dorothy acknowledged that the place was in all respects a very appropriate home for her good friend the Scarecrow.

"He would have been very happy here, I'm sure," she said, "if only the Nome King had left us alone. But if Oz is destroyed of course this place will be destroyed too."

"Yes," replied the Tin Woodman, "and also my beautiful tin castle, that has been my joy and pride."

"Jack Pumpkinhead's house will go too," remarked the Wizard, "as well as Professor Wogglebug's Athletic College, and Ozma's royal palace, and all our other handsome buildings."

"Yes, Oz will indeed become a desert when the Nome King gets through with it," sighed Omby Amby.

The Scarecrow came out to meet them and gave them all a hearty welcome.

"I hear you have decided always to live in the Land of Oz, after this," he said to Dorothy; "and that will delight my heart, for I have greatly disliked our frequent partings. But why are you all so downcast?"

"Have you heard the news?" asked the Tin Woodman.

"No news to make me sad," replied the Scarecrow.

Then Nick Chopper told his friend of the Nome King's tunnel, and how the evil creatures of the North had allied themselves with the underground monarch for the purpose of conquering and destroying Oz. "Well," said the Scarecrow, "it certainly looks bad for Ozma, and all of us. But I believe it is wrong to worry over anything before it happens. It is surely time enough to be sad when our country is despoiled and our people made slaves. So let us not deprive ourselves of the few happy hours remaining to us."

"Ah! that is real wisdom," declared the Shaggy Man, approvingly. "After we become really unhappy we shall regret these few hours that are left to us, unless we enjoy them to the utmost."

"Nevertheless," said the Scarecrow, "I shall go with you to the Emerald City and offer Ozma my services."

"She says we can do nothing to oppose our enemies," announced the Tin Woodman.

"And doubtless she is right, sir," answered the Scarecrow. "Still, she will appreciate our sympathy, and it is the duty of Ozma's friends to stand by her side when the final disaster occurs."

He then led them into his queer mansion and showed them the beautiful rooms in all the five stories. The lower room was a grand reception hall, with a hand-organ in one corner. This instrument the Scarecrow, when alone, could turn to amuse himself, as he was very fond of music. The walls were hung with white silk, upon which flocks of black crows were embroidered in black diamonds. Some of the chairs were made in the shape of big crows and upholstered with cushions of corn-colored silk.

The second story contained a fine banquet room, where the Scarecrow might entertain his guests, and the three stories above that were bed-chambers exquisitely furnished and decorated.

"From these rooms," said the Scarecrow, proudly, "one may obtain fine views of the surrounding cornfields. The corn I grow is always husky, and I call the ears my regiments, because they have so many kernels. Of course I cannot ride my cobs, but I really don't care shucks about that. Taken altogether, my farm will stack up with any in the neighborhood."

The visitors partook of some light refreshment and then hurried away to resume the road to the Emerald City. The Scarecrow found a seat in the wagon between Omby Amby and the Shaggy Man, and his weight did not add much to the load because he was stuffed with straw.

"You will notice I have one oat-field on my property," he remarked, as they drove away. "Oat-straw is, I have found, the best of all straws to re-stuff myself with when my interior gets musty or out of shape."

"Are you able to re-stuff yourself without help?" asked Aunt Em. "I should think that after the straw was taken out of you there wouldn't be anything left but your clothes."

"You are almost correct, madam," he answered. "My servants do the stuffing, under my direction. For my head, in which are my excellent brains, is a bag tied at the bottom. My face is neatly painted upon one side of the bag, as you may see. My head does not need re-stuffing, as my body does, for all that it requires is to have the face touched up with fresh paint occasionally."

It was not far from the Scarecrow's mansion to the farm of Jack Pumpkinhead, and when they arrived there both Uncle Henry and Aunt Em were much impressed. The farm was one vast pumpkin field, and some of the pumpkins were of enormous size. In one of them, which had been neatly hollowed out, Jack himself lived, and he declared that it was a very comfortable residence. The reason he grew so many pumpkins was in order that he might change his head as often as it became wrinkled or threatened to spoil.

The pumpkin-headed man welcomed his visitors joyfully and offered them several delicious pumpkin pies to eat.

"I don't indulge in pumpkin pies myself, for two reasons," he said. "One reason is that were I to eat pumpkins I would become a cannibal, and the other reason is that I never eat, not being hollow inside."

"Very good reasons," agreed the Scarecrow.

They told Jack Pumpkinhead of the dreadful news about the Nome King, and he decided to go with them to the Emerald City and help comfort Ozma.

"I had expected to live here in ease and comfort for many centuries," said Jack, dolefully; "but of course if the Nome King destroys everything in Oz I shall be destroyed too. Really, it seems too bad, doesn't it?"

They were soon on their journey again, and so swiftly did the Sawhorse draw the wagon over the smooth roads that before twilight fell they had reached the royal palace in the Emerald City, and were at their journey's end.

Chapter 26 - How Ozma Refused to Fight for her Kingdom

Ozma was in her rose garden picking a bouquet when the party arrived, and she greeted all her old and new friends as smilingly and sweetly as ever.

Dorothy's eyes were full of tears as she kissed the lovely Ruler of Oz, and she whispered to her:

"Oh, Ozma, Ozma! I'm SO sorry!"

Ozma seemed surprised.

"Sorry for what, Dorothy?" she asked.

"For all your trouble about the Nome King," was the reply.

Ozma laughed with genuine amusement.

"Why, that has not troubled me a bit, dear Princess," she replied. Then, looking around at the sad faces of her friends, she added: "Have you all been worrying about this tunnel?"

"We have!" they exclaimed in a chorus.

"Well, perhaps it is more serious than I imagined," admitted the fair Ruler; "but I haven't given the matter much thought. After dinner we will all meet together and talk it over."

So they went to their rooms and prepared for dinner, and Dorothy dressed herself in her prettiest gown and put on her coronet, for she thought that this might be the last time she would ever appear as a Princess of Oz.

The Scarecrow, the Tin Woodman and Jack Pumpkinhead all sat at the dinner table, although none of them was made so he could eat. Usually they served to enliven the meal with their merry talk, but to-night all seemed strangely silent and uneasy.

As soon as the dinner was finished Ozma led the company to her own private room in which hung the Magic Picture. When they had seated themselves the Scarecrow was the first to speak.

"Is the Nome King's tunnel finished, Ozma?" he asked.

"It was completed to-day," she replied. "They have built it right under my palace grounds, and it ends in front of the Forbidden Fountain. Nothing but a crust of earth remains to separate our enemies from us, and when they march here, they will easily break through this crust and rush upon us."

"Who will assist the Nome King?" inquired the Scarecrow.

"The Whimsies, the Growleywogs and the Phanfasms," she replied. "I watched to-day in my Magic Picture the messengers whom the Nome King sent to all these people to summon them to assemble in his great caverns."

"Let us see what they are doing now," suggested the Tin Woodman.

So Ozma wished to see the Nome King's cavern, and at once the landscape faded from the Magic Picture and was replaced by the scene then being enacted in the jeweled cavern of King Roquat.

A wild and startling scene it was which the Oz people beheld.

Before the Nome King stood the Chief of the Whimsies and the Grand Gallipoot of the Growleywogs, surrounded by their most skillful generals. Very fierce and powerful they looked, so that even the Nome King and General Guph, who stood beside his master, seemed a bit fearful in the presence of their allies.

Now a still more formidable creature entered the cavern. It was the First and Foremost of the Phanfasms and he proudly sat down in King Roquat's own throne and demanded the right to lead his forces through the tunnel in advance of all the others. The First and Foremost now appeared to all eyes in his hairy skin and the bear's head. What his real form was even Roquat did not know.

Through the arches leading into the vast series of caverns that lay beyond the throne room of King Roquat could be seen ranks upon ranks of the invaders—thousands of Phanfasms, Growleywogs and Whimsies standing in serried lines, while behind them were massed the thousands upon thousands of General Guph's own army of Nomes.

"Listen!" whispered Ozma. "I think we can hear what they are saying."

So they kept still and listened.

"Is all ready?" demanded the First and Foremost, haughtily.

"The tunnel is finally completed," replied General Guph.

"How long will it take us to march to the Emerald City?" asked the Grand Gallipoot of the Growleywogs.

"If we start at midnight," replied the Nome King, "we shall arrive at the Emerald City by daybreak. Then, while all the Oz people are sleeping, we will capture them and make them our slaves. After that we will destroy the city itself and march through the Land of Oz, burning and devastating as we go."

"Good!" cried the First and Foremost. "When we get through with Oz it will be a desert wilderness. Ozma shall be my slave."

"She shall be MY slave!" shouted the Grand Gallipoot, angrily.

"We'll decide that by and by," said King Roquat hastily. "Don't let us quarrel now, friends. First let us conquer Oz, and then we will divide the spoils of war in a satisfactory manner."

The First and Foremost smiled wickedly; but he only said:

"I and my Phanfasms go first, for nothing on earth can oppose our power."

They all agreed to that, knowing the Phanfasms to be the mightiest of the combined forces. King Roquat now invited them to attend a banquet he had prepared, where they might occupy themselves in eating and drinking until midnight arrived.

As they had now seen and heard all of the plot against them that they cared to, Ozma allowed her Magic Picture to fade away. Then she turned to her friends and said:

"Our enemies will be here sooner than I expected. What do you advise me to do?"

"It is now too late to assemble our people," said the Tin Woodman, despondently. "If you had allowed me to arm and drill my Winkies, we might have put up a good fight and destroyed many of our enemies before we were conquered."

"The Munchkins are good fighters, too," said Omby Amby; "and so are the Gillikins."

"But I do not wish to fight," declared Ozma, firmly. "No one has the right to destroy any living creatures, however evil they may be, or to hurt them or make them unhappy. I will not fight, even to save my kingdom." "The Nome King is not so particular," remarked the Scarecrow. "He intends to destroy us all and ruin our beautiful country."

"Because the Nome King intends to do evil is no excuse for my doing the same," replied Ozma.

"Self-preservation is the first law of nature," quoted the Shaggy Man.

"True," she said, readily. "I would like to discover a plan to save ourselves without fighting."

That seemed a hopeless task to them, but realizing that Ozma was determined not to fight, they tried to think of some means that might promise escape.

"Couldn't we bribe our enemies, by giving them a lot of emeralds and gold?" asked Jack Pumpkinhead.

"No, because they believe they are able to take everything we have," replied the Ruler.

"I have thought of something," said Dorothy.

"What is it, dear?" asked Ozma.

"Let us use the Magic Belt to wish all of us in Kansas. We will put some emeralds in our pockets, and can sell them in Topeka for enough to pay off the mortgage on Uncle Henry's farm. Then we can all live together and be happy."

"A clever idea!" exclaimed the Scarecrow.

"Kansas is a very good country. I've been there," said the Shaggy Man.

"That seems to me an excellent plan," approved the Tin Woodman.

"No!" said Ozma, decidedly. "Never will I desert my people and leave them to so cruel a fate. I will use the Magic Belt to send the rest of you to Kansas, if you wish, but if my beloved country must be destroyed and my people enslaved I will remain and share their fate."

"Quite right," asserted the Scarecrow, sighing. "I will remain with you."

"And so will I," declared the Tin Woodman and the Shaggy Man and Jack Pumpkinhead, in turn. Tik-tok, the machine man, also said he intended to stand by Ozma. "For," said he, "I should be of no use at all in Kan-sas."

"For my part," announced Dorothy, gravely, "if the Ruler of Oz must not desert her people, a Princess of Oz has no right to run away, either. I'm willing to become a slave with the rest of you; so all we can do with the Magic Belt is to use it to send Uncle Henry and Aunt Em back to Kansas."

"I've been a slave all my life," Aunt Em replied, with considerable cheerfulness, "and so has Henry. I guess we won't go back to Kansas, anyway. I'd rather take my chances with the rest of you."

Ozma smiled upon them all gratefully.

"There is no need to despair just yet," she said. "I'll get up early to-morrow morning and be at the Forbidden Fountain when the fierce warriors break through the crust of the earth. I will speak to them pleasantly and perhaps they won't be so very bad, after all."

"Why do they call it the Forbidden Fountain?" asked Dorothy, thoughtfully.

"Don't you know, dear?" returned Ozma, surprised.

"No," said Dorothy. "Of course I've seen the fountain in the palace grounds, ever since I first came to Oz; and I've read the sign which says: 'All Persons are Forbidden to Drink at this Fountain.' But I never knew WHY they were forbidden. The water seems clear and sparkling and it bubbles up in a golden basin all the time."

"That water," declared Ozma, gravely, "is the most dangerous thing in all the Land of Oz. It is the Water of Oblivion."

"What does that mean?" asked Dorothy.

"Whoever drinks at the Forbidden Fountain at once forgets everything he has ever known," Ozma asserted.

"It wouldn't be a bad way to forget our troubles," suggested Uncle Henry.

"That is true; but you would forget everything else, and become as ignorant as a baby," returned Ozma.

"Does it make one crazy?" asked Dorothy.

"No; it only makes one forget," replied the girl Ruler. "It is said that once—long, long ago—a wicked King ruled Oz, and made himself and all his people very miserable and unhappy. So Glinda, the Good Sorceress, placed this fountain here, and the King drank of its water and forgot all his wickedness. His mind became innocent and vacant, and when he learned the things of life again they were all good things. But the people remembered how wicked their King had been, and were still afraid of him. Therefore, he made them all drink of the Water of Oblivion and forget everything they had known, so that they became as simple and innocent as their King. After that, they all grew wise together, and their wisdom was good, so that peace and happiness reigned in the land. But for fear some one might drink of the water again, and in an instant forget all he had learned, the King put that sign upon the fountain, where it has remained for many centuries up to this very day."

They had all listened intently to Ozma's story, and when she finished speaking there was a long period of silence while all thought upon the curious magical power of the Water of Oblivion.

Finally the Scarecrow's painted face took on a broad smile that stretched the cloth as far as it would go.

"How thankful I am," he said, "that I have such an excellent assortment of brains!"

"I gave you the best brains I ever mixed," declared the Wizard, with an air of pride.

"You did, indeed!" agreed the Scarecrow, "and they work so splendidly that they have found a way to save Oz—to save us all!"

"I'm glad to hear that," said the Wizard. "We never needed saving more than we do just now."

"Do you mean to say you can save us from those awful Phanfasms, and Growleywogs and Whimsies?" asked Dorothy eagerly.

"I'm sure of it, my dear," asserted the Scarecrow, still smiling genially.

"Tell us how!" cried the Tin Woodman.

"Not now," said the Scarecrow. "You may all go to bed, and I advise you to forget your worries just as completely as if you had drunk of the Water of Oblivion in the Forbidden Fountain. I'm going to stay here and tell my plan to Ozma alone, but if you will all be at the Forbidden Fountain at daybreak, you'll see how easily we will save the kingdom when our enemies break through the crust of earth and come from the tunnel."

So they went away and let the Scarecrow and Ozma alone; but Dorothy could not sleep a wink all night.

"He is only a Scarecrow," she said to herself, "and I'm not sure that his mixed brains are as clever as he thinks they are."

But she knew that if the Scarecrow's plan failed they were all lost; so she tried to have faith in him.

Chapter 27 - How the Fierce Warriors Invaded Oz

The Nome King and his terrible allies sat at the banquet table until midnight. There was much quarreling between the Growleywogs and Phanfasms, and one of the wee-headed Whimsies got angry at General Guph and choked him until he nearly stopped breathing. Yet no one was seriously hurt, and the Nome King felt much relieved when the clock struck twelve and they all sprang up and seized their weapons.

"Aha!" shouted the First and Foremost. "Now to conquer the Land of Oz!"

He marshaled his Phanfasms in battle array and at his word of command they marched into the tunnel and began the long journey through it to the Emerald City. The First and Foremost intended to take all the treasures of Oz for himself; to kill all who could be killed and enslave the rest; to destroy and lay waste the whole country, and afterward to conquer and enslave the Nomes, the Growleywogs and the Whimsies. And he knew his power was sufficient to enable him to do all these things easily.

Next marched into the tunnel the army of gigantic Growleywogs, with their Grand Gal10poot at their head. They were dreadful beings, indeed, and longed to get to Oz that they might begin to pilfer and destroy. The Grand Galipoot was a little afraid of the First and Foremost, but had a cunning plan to murder or destroy that powerful being and secure the wealth of Oz for himself. Mighty little of the plunder would the Nome King get, thought the Grand Galipoot.

The Chief of the Whimsies now marched his false-headed forces into the tunnel. In his wicked little head was a plot to destroy both the First and Foremost and the Grand Galipoot. He intended to let them conquer Oz, since they insisted on going first; but he would afterward treacherously destroy them, as well as King Roquat, and keep all the slaves and treasure of Ozma's kingdom for himself.

After all his dangerous allies had marched into the tunnel the Nome King and General Guph started to follow them, at the head of fifty thousand Nomes, all fully armed.

"Guph," said the King, "those creatures ahead of us mean mischief. They intend to get everything for themselves and leave us nothing."

"I know," replied the General; "but they are not as clever as they think they are. When you get the Magic Belt you must at once wish the Whimsies and Growleywogs and Phanfasms all back into their own countries—and the Belt will surely take them there."

"Good!" cried the King. "An excellent plan, Guph. I'll do it. While they are conquering Oz I'll get the Magic Belt, and then only the Nomes will remain to ravage the country."

So you see there was only one thing that all were agreed upon—that Oz should be destroyed.

On, on, on the vast ranks of invaders marched, filling the tunnel from side to side. With a steady tramp, tramp, they advanced, every step taking them nearer to the beautiful Emerald City.

"Nothing can save the Land of Oz!" thought the First and Foremost, scowling until his bear face was as black as the tunnel.

"The Emerald City is as good as destroyed already!" muttered the Grand Galipoot, shaking his war club fiercely.

"In a few hours Oz will be a desert!" said the Chief of the Whimsies, with an evil laugh.

"My dear Guph," remarked the Nome King to his General, "at last my vengeance upon Ozma of Oz and her people is about to be accomplished."

"You are right!" declared the General. "Ozma is surely lost."

And now the First and Foremost, who was in advance and nearing the Emerald City, began to cough and to sneeze.

"This tunnel is terribly dusty," he growled, angrily. "I'll punish that Nome King for not having it swept clean. My throat and eyes are getting full of dust and I'm as thirsty as a fish!"

The Grand Galipoot was coughing too, and his throat was parched and dry.

"What a dusty place!" he cried. "I'll be glad when we reach Oz, where we can get a drink."

"Who has any water?" asked the Whimsie Chief, gasping and choking. But none of his followers carried a drop of water, so he hastened on to get through the dusty tunnel to the Land of Oz.

"Where did all this dust come from?" demanded General Guph, trying hard to swallow but finding his throat so dry he couldn't.

"I don't know," answered the Nome King. "I've been in the tunnel every day while it was being built, but I never noticed any dust before."

"Let's hurry!" cried the General. "I'd give half the gold in Oz for a drink of water."

The dust grew thicker and thicker, and the throats and eyes and noses of the invaders were filled with it. But not one halted or turned back. They hurried forward more fierce and vengeful than ever.

Chapter 28 - How They Drank at the Forbidden Fountain

The Scarecrow had no need to sleep; neither had the Tin Woodman or Tik-tok or Jack

Pumpkinhead. So they all wandered out into the palace grounds and stood beside the sparkling water of the Forbidden Fountain until daybreak. During this time they indulged in occasional conversation.

"Nothing could make me forget what I know," remarked the Scarecrow, gazing into the fountain, "for I cannot drink the Water of Oblivion or water of any kind. And I am glad that this is so, for I consider my wisdom unexcelled."

"You are cer-tain-ly ve-ry wise," agreed Tik-tok. "For my part, I can on-ly think by ma-chin-er-y, so I do not pretend to know as much as you do."

"My tin brains are very bright, but that is all I claim for them," said Nick Chopper, modestly. "Yet I do not aspire to being very wise, for I have noticed that the happiest people are those who do not let their brains oppress them."

"Mine never worry me," Jack Pumpkinhead acknowledged. "There are many seeds of thought in my head, but they do not sprout easily. I am glad that it is so, for if I occupied my days in thinking I should have no time for anything else."

In this cheery mood they passed the hours until the first golden streaks of dawn appeared in the sky. Then Ozma joined them, as fresh and lovely as ever and robed in one of her prettiest gowns.

"Our enemies have not yet arrived," said the Scarecrow, after greeting affectionately the sweet and girlish Ruler.

"They will soon be here," she said, "for I have just glanced at my Magic Picture, and have seen them coughing and choking with the dust in the tunnel."

"Oh, is there dust in the tunnel?" asked the Tin Woodman.

"Yes; Ozma placed it there by means of the Magic Belt," explained the Scarecrow, with one of his broad smiles.

Then Dorothy came to them, Uncle Henry and Aunt Em following close after her. The little girl's eyes were heavy because she had had a sleepless and anxious night. Toto walked by her side, but the little dog's spirits were very much subdued. Billina, who was always up by daybreak, was not long in joining the group by the fountain.

The Wizard and the Shaggy Man next arrived, and soon after appeared Omby Amby, dressed in his best uniform.

"There lies the tunnel," said Ozma, pointing to a part of the ground just before the Forbidden Fountain, "and in a few moments the dreadful invaders will break through the earth and swarm over the land. Let us all stand on the other side of the Fountain and watch to see what happens."

At once they followed her suggestion and moved around the fountain of the Water of Oblivion. There they stood silent and expectant until the earth beyond gave way with a sudden crash and up leaped the powerful form of the First and Foremost, followed by all his grim warriors.

As the leader sprang forward his gleaming eyes caught the play of the fountain and he rushed toward it and drank eagerly of the sparkling water. Many of the other Phanfasms drank, too, in order to clear their dry and dusty throats. Then they stood around and looked at one another with simple, wondering smiles.

The First and Foremost saw Ozma and her companions beyond the fountain, but instead of making an effort to capture her he merely stared at her in pleased admiration of her beauty—for he had forgotten where he was and why he had come there.

But now the Grand Gallipoot arrived, rushing from the tunnel with a hoarse cry of mingled rage and thirst. He too saw the fountain and hastened to drink of its forbidden waters. The other Growleywogs were not slow to follow suit, and even before they had finished drinking the Chief of the Whimsies and his people came to push them away, while they one and all cast off their false heads that they might slake their thirst at the fountain.

When the Nome King and General Guph arrived they both made a dash to drink, but the General was so mad with thirst that he knocked his King over, and while Roquat lay sprawling upon the ground the General drank heartily of the Water of Oblivion.

This rude act of his General made the Nome King so angry that for a moment he forgot he was thirsty and rose to his feet to glare upon the group of terrible warriors he had brought here to assist him. He saw Ozma and her people, too, and yelled out:

"Why don't you capture them? Why don't you conquer Oz, you idiots? Why do you stand there like a lot of dummies?"

But the great warriors had become like little children. They had forgotten all their enmity against Ozma and against Oz. They had even forgotten who they themselves were, or why they were in this strange and beautiful country. As for the Nome King, they did not recognize him, and wondered who he was.

The sun came up and sent its flood of silver rays to light the faces of the invaders. The frowns and scowls and evil looks were all gone. Even the most monstrous of the creatures there assembled smiled innocently and seemed light-hearted and content merely to be alive.

Not so with Roquat, the Nome King. He had not drunk from the Forbidden Fountain and all his former rage against Ozma and Dorothy now inflamed him as fiercely as ever. The sight of General Guph babbling like a happy child and playing with his hands in the cool waters of the fountain astonished and maddened Red Roquat. Seeing that his terrible allies and his own General refused to act, the Nome King turned to order his great army of Nomes to advance from the tunnel and seize the helpless Oz people.

But the Scarecrow suspected what was in the King's mind and spoke a word to the Tin Woodman. Together they ran at Roquat and grabbing him up tossed him into the great basin of the fountain.

The Nome King's body was round as a ball, and it bobbed up and down in the Water of Oblivion while he spluttered and screamed with fear lest he should drown. And when he cried out, his mouth filled with water, which ran down his throat, so that straightway he forgot all he had formerly known just as completely as had all the other invaders.

Ozma and Dorothy could not refrain from laughing to see their dreaded enemies become as harmless as babies. There was no danger now that Oz would be destroyed. The only question remaining to solve was how to get rid of this horde of intruders.

The Shaggy Man kindly pulled the Nome King out of the fountain and set him upon his thin legs. Roquat was dripping wet, but he chattered and laughed and wanted to drink more of the water. No thought of injuring any person was now in his mind.

Before he left the tunnel he had commanded his fifty thousand Nomes to remain there until he ordered them to advance, as he wished to give his allies time to conquer Oz before he appeared with his own army. Ozma did not wish all these Nomes to overrun her land, so she advanced to King Roquat and taking his hand in her own said gently:

"Who are you? What is your name?"

"I don't know," he replied, smiling at her. "Who are you, my dear?"

"My name is Ozma," she said; "and your name is Roquat."

"Oh, is it?" he replied, seeming pleased.

"Yes; you are King of the Nomes," she said.

"Ah; I wonder what the Nomes are!" returned the King, as if puzzled.

"They are underground elves, and that tunnel over there is full of them," she answered. "You have a beautiful cavern at the other end of the tunnel, so you must go to your Nomes and say: 'March home!' Then follow after them and in time you will reach the pretty cavern where you live."

The Nome King was much pleased to learn this, for he had forgotten he had a cavern. So he went to the tunnel and said to his army: 'March home!' At once the Nomes turned and marched back through the tunnel, and the King followed after them, laughing with delight to find his orders so readily obeyed.

The Wizard went to General Guph, who was trying to count his fingers, and told him to follow the Nome King, who was his master. Guph meekly obeyed, and so all the Nomes quitted the Land of Oz forever.

But there were still the Phanfasms and Whimsies and Growleywogs standing around in groups, and they were so many that they filled the gardens and trampled upon the flowers and grass because they did not know that the tender plants would be injured by their clumsy feet. But in all other respects they were perfectly harmless and played together like children or gazed with pleasure upon the pretty sights of the royal gardens.

After counseling with the Scarecrow Ozma sent Omby Amby to the palace for the Magic Belt, and when the Captain General returned with it the Ruler of Oz at once clasped the precious Belt around her waist.

"I wish all these strange people—the Whimsies and the Growleywogs and the Phanfasms—safe back in their own homes!" she said.

It all happened in a twinkling, for of course the wish was no sooner spoken than it was granted.

All the hosts of the invaders were gone, and only the trampled grass showed that they had ever been in the Land of Oz.

Chapter 29 - How Glinda Worked a Magic Spell

"That was better than fighting," said Ozma, when all our friends were assembled in the palace after the exciting events of the morning; and each and every one agreed with her.

"No one was hurt," said the Wizard, delightedly.

"And no one hurt us," added Aunt Em.

"But, best of all," said Dorothy, "the wicked people have all forgotten their wickedness, and will not wish to hurt any one after this."

"True, Princess," declared the Shaggy Man. "It seems to me that to have reformed all those evil characters is more important than to have saved Oz."

"Nevertheless," remarked the Scarecrow, "I am glad Oz is saved. I can now go back to my new mansion and live happily."

"And I am glad and grateful that my pumpkin farm is saved," said Jack.

"For my part," added the Tin Woodman, "I cannot express my joy that my lovely tin castle is not to be demolished by wicked enemies."

"Still," said Tik-tok, "o-ther en-e-mies may come to Oz some day."

"Why do you allow your clock-work brains to interrupt our joy?" asked Omby Amby, frowning at the machine man.

"I say what I am wound up to say," answered Tik-tok.

"And you are right," declared Ozma. "I myself have been thinking of this very idea, and it seems to me there are entirely too many ways for people to get to the Land of Oz. We used to think the deadly desert that surrounds us was enough protection; but that is no longer the case. The Wizard and Dorothy have both come here through the air, and I am told the earth people have invented airships that can fly anywhere they wish them to go."

"Why, sometimes they do, and sometimes they don't," asserted Dorothy.

"But in time the airships may cause us trouble," continued Ozma, "for if the earth folk learn how to manage them we would be overrun with visitors who would ruin our lovely, secluded fairyland."

"That is true enough," agreed the Wizard.

"Also the desert fails to protect us in other ways," Ozma went on, thoughtfully. "Johnny Dooit once made a sand-boat that sailed across it, and the Nome King made a tunnel under it. So I believe something ought to be done to cut us off from the rest of the world entirely, so that no one in the future will ever be able to intrude upon us."

"How will you do that?" asked the Scarecrow.

"I do not know; but in some way I am sure it can be accomplished. To-morrow I will make a journey to the castle of Glinda the Good, and ask her advice."

"May I go with you?" asked Dorothy, eagerly.

"Of course, my dear Princess; and I also invite any of our friends here who would like to undertake the journey."

They all declared they wished to accompany their girl Ruler, for this was indeed an important mission, since the future of the Land of Oz to a great extent depended upon it. So Ozma gave orders to her servants to prepare for the journey on the morrow.

That day she watched her Magic Picture, and when it showed her that all the Nomes had returned through the tunnel to their underground caverns, Ozma used the Magic Belt to close up the tunnel, so that the earth underneath the desert sands became as solid as it was before the Nomes began to dig.

Early the following morning a gay cavalcade set out to visit the famous Sorceress, Glinda the Good. Ozma and Dorothy rode in a chariot drawn by the Cowardly Lion and the Hungry Tiger, while the Sawhorse drew the red wagon in which rode the rest of the party.

With hearts light and free from care they traveled merrily along through the lovely and fascinating Land of Oz, and in good season reached the stately castle in which resided the Sorceress.

Glinda knew that they were coming.

"I have been reading about you in my Magic Book," she said, as she greeted them in her gracious way.

"What is your Magic Book like?" inquired Aunt Em, curiously.

"It is a record of everything that happens," replied the Sorceress. "As soon as an event takes place, anywhere in the world, it is immediately found printed in my Magic Book. So when I read its pages I am well informed."

"Did it tell you how our enemies drank the Water of 'Blivion?" asked Dorothy.

"Yes, my dear; it told all about it. And also it told me you were all coming to my castle, and why."

"Then," said Ozma, "I suppose you know what is in my mind, and that I am seeking a way to prevent any one in the future from discovering the Land of Oz."

"Yes; I know that. And while you were on your journey I have thought of a way to accomplish your desire. For it seems to me unwise to allow too many outside people to come here. Dorothy, with her uncle and aunt, has now returned to Oz to live always, and there is no reason why we should leave any way open for others to travel uninvited to our fairyland. Let us make it impossible for any one ever to communicate with us in any way, after this. Then we may live peacefully and contentedly."

"Your advice is wise," returned Ozma. "I thank you, Glinda, for your promise to assist me."

"But how can you do it?" asked Dorothy. "How can you keep every one from ever finding Oz?"

"By making our country invisible to all eyes but our own," replied the Sorceress, smiling. "I have a magic charm powerful enough to accomplish that wonderful feat, and now that we have been warned of our danger by the Nome King's invasion, I believe we must not hesitate to separate ourselves forever from all the rest of the world."

"I agree with you," said the Ruler of Oz.

"Won't it make any difference to us?" asked Dorothy, doubtfully.

"No, my dear," Glinda answered, assuringly. "We shall still be able to see each other and everything in the Land of Oz. It won't affect us at all; but those who fly through the air over our country will look down and see nothing at all. Those who come to the edge of the desert, or try to cross it, will catch no glimpse of Oz, or know in what direction it lies. No one will try to tunnel to us again because we cannot be seen and therefore cannot be found. In other words, the Land of Oz will entirely disappear from the knowledge of the rest of the world."

"That's all right," said Dorothy, cheerfully. "You may make Oz invis'ble as soon as you please, for all I care."

"It is already invisible," Glinda stated. "I knew Ozma's wishes, and performed the Magic Spell before you arrived."

Ozma seized the hand of the Sorceress and pressed it gratefully.

"Thank you!" she said.

Chapter 30 - How the Story of Oz Came to an End

The writer of these Oz stories has received a little note from Princess Dorothy of Oz which, for a time, has made him feel rather disconcerted. The note was written on a broad, white feather from a stork's wing, and it said:

"YOU WILL NEVER HEAR ANYTHING MORE ABOUT OZ, BECAUSE WE ARE NOW CUT OFF FOREVER FROM ALL THE REST OF THE WORLD. BUT TOTO AND I WILL ALWAYS LOVE YOU AND ALL THE OTHER CHILDREN WHO LOVE US.
"DOROTHY GALE."

This seemed to me too bad, at first, for Oz is a very interesting fairyland. Still, we have no right to feel grieved, for we have had enough of the history of the Land of Oz to fill six story books, and from its quaint people and their strange adventures we have been able to learn many useful and amusing things.

So good luck to little Dorothy and her companions. May they live long in their invisible country and be very happy!

The End

The Patchwork Girl of Oz

Dedication

Affectionately Dedicated to my young friend Sumner Hamilton Britton of Chicago

Prologue

Through the kindness of Dorothy Gale of Kansas, afterward Princess Dorothy of Oz, an humble writer in the United States of America was once appointed Royal Historian of Oz, with the privilege of writing the chronicle of that wonderful fairyland. But after making six books about the adventures of those interesting but queer people who live in the Land of Oz, the Historian learned with sorrow that by an edict of the Supreme Ruler, Ozma of Oz, her country would thereafter be rendered invisible to all who lived outside its borders and that all communication with Oz would, in the future, be cut off.

The children who had learned to look for the books about Oz and who loved the stories about the gay and happy people inhabiting that favored country, were as sorry as their Historian that there would be no more books of Oz stories. They wrote many letters asking if the Historian did not know of some adventures to write about that had happened before the Land of Oz was shut out from all the rest of the world. But he did not know of any. Finally one of the children inquired why we couldn't hear from Princess Dorothy by wireless telegraph, which would enable her to communicate to the Historian whatever happened in the far-off Land of Oz without his seeing her, or even knowing just where Oz is.

That seemed a good idea; so the Historian rigged up a high tower in his back yard, and took lessons in wireless telegraphy until he understood it, and then began to call "Princess Dorothy of Oz" by sending messages into the air.

Now, it wasn't likely that Dorothy would be looking for wireless messages or would heed the call; but one thing the Historian was sure of, and that was that the powerful Sorceress, Glinda, would know what he was doing and that he desired to communicate with Dorothy. For Glinda has a big book in which is recorded every event that takes place anywhere in the world, just the moment that it happens, and so of course the book would tell her about the wireless message.

And that was the way Dorothy heard that the Historian wanted to speak with her, and there was a Shaggy Man in the Land of Oz who knew how to telegraph a wireless reply. The result was that the Historian begged so hard to be told the latest news of Oz, so that he could write it down for the children to read, that Dorothy asked permission of Ozma and Ozma graciously consented.

That is why, after two long years of waiting, another Oz story is now presented to the children of America. This would not have been possible had not some clever man invented the "wireless" and an equally clever child suggested the idea of reaching the mysterious Land of Oz by its means.

L. Frank Baum.
"OZCOT" at Hollywood in California

LIST OF CHAPTERS

Chapter 1 - Ojo and Unc Nunkie

"Where's the butter, Unc Nunkie?" asked Ojo.

Unc looked out of the window and stroked his long beard. Then he turned to the Munchkin boy and shook his head. "Isn't," said he.

"Isn't any butter? That's too bad, Unc. Where's the jam then?" inquired Ojo, standing on a stool so he could look through all the shelves of the cupboard. But Unc Nunkie shook his head again.

"Gone," he said.

"No jam, either? And no cake—no jelly—no apples—nothing but bread?"

"All," said Unc, again stroking his beard as he gazed from the window.

The little boy brought the stool and sat beside his uncle, munching the dry bread slowly and seeming in deep thought.

"Nothing grows in our yard but the bread tree," he mused, "and there are only two more loaves on that tree; and they're not ripe yet. Tell me, Unc; why are we so poor?"

The old Munchkin turned and looked at Ojo. He had kindly eyes, but he hadn't smiled or laughed in so long that the boy had forgotten that Unc Nunkie could look any other way than solemn. And Unc never spoke any more words than he was obliged to, so his little nephew, who lived alone with him, had learned to understand a great deal from one word.

"Why are we so poor, Unc?" repeated the boy.

"Not," said the old Munchkin.

"I think we are," declared Ojo. "What have we got?"

"House," said Unc Nunkie.

"I know; but everyone in the Land of Oz has a place to live. What else, Unc?"

"Bread."

"I'm eating the last loaf that's ripe. There; I've put aside your share, Unc. It's on the table, so you can eat it when you get hungry. But when that is gone, what shall we eat, Unc?"

The old man shifted in his chair but merely shook his head.

"Of course," said Ojo, who was obliged to talk because his uncle would not, "no one starves in the Land of Oz, either. There is plenty for everyone, you know; only, if it isn't just where you happen to be, you must go where it is."

The aged Munchkin wriggled again and stared at his small nephew as if disturbed by his argument.

"By to-morrow morning," the boy went on, "we must go where there is something to eat, or we shall grow very hungry and become very unhappy."

"Where?" asked Unc.

"Where shall we go? I don't know, I'm sure," replied Ojo. "But you must know, Unc. You must have traveled, in your time, because you're so old. I don't remember it, because ever since I could remember anything we've lived right here in this lonesome, round house, with a little garden back of it and the thick woods all around. All I've ever seen of the great Land of Oz, Unc dear, is the view of that mountain over at the south, where they say the Hammerheads live—who won't let anybody go by them—and that mountain at the north, where they say nobody lives."

"One," declared Unc, correcting him.

"Oh, yes; one family lives there, I've heard. That's the Crooked Magician, who is named Dr. Pipt, and his wife Margolotte. One year you told me about them; I think it took you a whole year, Unc, to say as much as I've just said about the Crooked Magician and his wife. They live high up on the mountain, and the good Munchkin Country, where the fruits and flowers grow, is just the other side. It's funny you and I should live here all alone, in the middle of the forest, isn't it?"

"Yes," said Unc.

"Then let's go away and visit the Munchkin Country and its jolly, good-natured people. I'd love to get a sight of something besides woods, Unc Nunkie."

"Too little," said Unc.

"Why, I'm not so little as I used to be," answered the boy earnestly. "I think I can walk as far and as fast through the woods as you can, Unc. And now that nothing grows in our back yard that is good to eat, we must go where there is food."

Unc Nunkie made no reply for a time. Then he shut down the window and turned his chair to face the room, for the sun was sinking behind the tree-tops and it was growing cool.

By and by Ojo lighted the fire and the logs blazed freely in the broad fireplace. The two sat in the firelight a long time—the old, white-bearded Munchkin and the little boy. Both were thinking. When it grew quite dark outside, Ojo said:

"Eat your bread, Unc, and then we will go to bed."

But Unc Nunkie did not eat the bread; neither did he go directly to bed. Long after his little nephew was sound asleep in the corner of the room the old man sat by the fire, thinking.

Chapter 2 - The Crooked Magician

Just at dawn next morning Unc Nunkie laid his hand tenderly on Ojo's head and awakened him.

"Come," he said.

Ojo dressed. He wore blue silk stockings, blue knee pants with gold buckles, a blue ruffled waist and a jacket of bright blue braided with gold. His shoes were of blue leather and turned up at the toes, which were pointed. His hat had a peaked crown and a flat brim, and around the brim was a row of tiny golden bells that tinkled when he moved. This was the native costume of those who inhabited the Munchkin Country of the Land of Oz, so Unc Nunkie's dress was much like that of his nephew. Instead of shoes, the old man wore boots with turnover tops and his blue coat had wide cuffs of gold braid.

The boy noticed that his uncle had not eaten the bread, and supposed the old man had not been hungry. Ojo was hungry, though; so he divided the piece of bread upon the table and ate his half for breakfast, washing it down with fresh, cool water from the brook. Unc put the other piece of bread in his jacket pocket, after which he again said, as he walked out through the doorway: "Come."

Ojo was well pleased. He was dreadfully tired of living all alone in the woods and wanted to travel and see people. For a long time he had wished to explore the beautiful Land of Oz in which they lived. When they were outside, Unc simply latched the door and started up the path. No one would disturb their little house, even if anyone came so far into the thick forest while they were gone.

At the foot of the mountain that separated the Country of the Munchkins from the Country of the Gillikins, the path divided. One way led to the left and the other to the right—straight up the mountain. Unc Nunkie took this right-hand path and Ojo followed without asking why. He knew it would take them to the house of the Crooked Magician, whom he had never seen but who was their nearest neighbor.

All the morning they trudged up the mountain path and at noon Unc and Ojo sat on a fallen tree-trunk and ate the last of the bread which the old Munchkin had placed in his pocket. Then they started on again and two hours later came in sight of the house of Dr. Pipt.

It was a big house, round, as were all the Munchkin houses, and painted blue, which is the distinctive color of the Munchkin Country of Oz. There was a pretty garden around the house, where blue trees and blue flowers grew in abundance and in one place were beds of blue cabbages, blue carrots and blue lettuce, all of which were delicious to eat. In Dr. Pipt's garden grew bun-trees, cake-trees, cream-puff bushes, blue buttercups which yielded excellent blue butter and a row of chocolate-caramel plants. Paths of blue gravel divided the vegetable and flower beds and a wider path led up to the front door. The place was in a clearing on the mountain, but a little way off was the grim forest, which completely surrounded it.

Unc knocked at the door of the house and a chubby, pleasant-faced woman, dressed all in blue, opened it and greeted the visitors with a smile.

"Ah," said Ojo; "you must be Dame Margolotte, the good wife of Dr. Pipt."

"I am, my dear, and all strangers are welcome to my home."

"May we see the famous Magician, Madam?"

"He is very busy just now," she said, shaking her head doubtfully. "But come in and let me give you something to eat, for you must have traveled far in order to get our lonely place."

"We have," replied Ojo, as he and Unc entered the house. "We have come from a far lonelier place than this."

"A lonelier place! And in the Munchkin Country?" she exclaimed. "Then it must be somewhere in the Blue Forest."

"It is, good Dame Margolotte."

"Dear me!" she said, looking at the man, "you must be Unc Nunkie, known as the Silent One." Then she looked at the boy. "And you must be Ojo the Unlucky," she added.

"Yes," said Unc.

"I never knew I was called the Unlucky," said Ojo, soberly; "but it is really a good name for me."

"Well," remarked the woman, as she bustled around the room and set the table and brought food from the cupboard, "you were unlucky to live all alone in that dismal forest, which is much worse than the forest around here; but perhaps your luck will change, now you are away from it. If, during your travels, you can manage to lose that 'Un' at the beginning of your name 'Unlucky,' you will then become Ojo the Lucky, which will be a great improvement."

"How can I lose that 'Un,' Dame Margolotte?"

"I do not know how, but you must keep the matter in mind and perhaps the chance will come to you," she replied.

Ojo had never eaten such a fine meal in all his life. There was a savory stew, smoking hot, a dish of blue peas, a bowl of sweet milk of a delicate blue tint and a blue pudding with blue plums in it. When the visitors had eaten heartily of this fare the woman said to them:

"Do you wish to see Dr. Pipt on business or for pleasure?"

Unc shook his head.

"We are traveling," replied Ojo, "and we stopped at your house just to rest and refresh ourselves. I do not think Unc Nunkie cares very much to see the famous Crooked Magician; but for my part I am curious to look at such a great man."

The woman seemed thoughtful.

"I remember that Unc Nunkie and my husband used to be friends, many years ago," she said, "so perhaps they will be glad to meet again. The Magician is very busy, as I said, but if you will promise not to disturb him you may come into his workshop and watch him prepare a wonderful charm."

"Thank you," replied the boy, much pleased. "I would like to do that."

She led the way to a great domed hall at the back of the house, which was the Magician's workshop. There was a row of windows extending nearly around the sides of the circular room, which rendered the place very light, and there was a back door in addition to the one leading to the front part of the house. Before the row of windows a broad seat was built and there were some chairs and benches in the room besides. At one end stood a great fireplace, in which a blue log was blazing with a blue flame, and over the fire hung four kettles in a row, all bubbling and steaming at a great rate. The Magician was stirring all four of these kettles at the same time, two with his hands and two with his feet, to the latter, wooden ladles being strapped, for this man was so very crooked that his legs were as handy as his arms.

Unc Nunkie came forward to greet his old friend, but not being able to shake either his hands or his feet, which were all occupied in stirring, he patted the Magician's bald head and asked: "What?"

"Ah, it's the Silent One," remarked Dr. Pipt, without looking up, "and he wants to know what I'm making. Well, when it is quite finished this compound will be the wonderful Powder of Life, which no one knows how to make but myself. Whenever it is sprinkled on anything, that thing will at once come to life, no matter what it is. It takes me several years to make this magic Powder, but at this moment I am pleased to say it is nearly done. You see, I am making it for my good wife Margolotte, who wants to use some of it for a purpose of her own. Sit down and make yourself comfortable, Unc Nunkie, and after I've finished my task I will talk to you."

"You must know," said Margolottte, when they were all seated together on the broad window-seat, "that my husband foolishly gave away all the Powder of Life he first made to old Mombi the Witch, who used to live in the Country of the Gillikins, to the north of here. Mombi gave to Dr. Pipt a Powder of Perpetual Youth in exchange for his Powder of Life, but she cheated him wickedly, for the Powder of Youth was no good and could work no magic at all."

"Perhaps the Powder of Life couldn't either," said Ojo.

"Yes; it is perfection," she declared. "The first lot we tested on our Glass Cat, which not only began to live but has lived ever since. She's somewhere around the house now."

"A Glass Cat!" exclaimed Ojo, astonished.

"Yes; she makes a very pleasant companion, but admires herself a little more than is considered modest, and she positively refuses to catch mice," explained Margolotte. "My husband made the cat some pink brains, but they proved to be too high-bred and particular for a cat, so she thinks it is undignified in her to catch mice. Also she has a pretty blood-red heart, but it is made of stone—a ruby, I think—and so is rather hard and unfeeling. I think the next Glass Cat the Magician makes will have neither brains nor heart, for then it will not object to catching mice and may prove of some use to us."

"What did old Mombi the Witch do with the Powder of Life your husband gave her?" asked the boy.

"She brought Jack Pumpkinhead to life, for one thing," was the reply. "I suppose you've heard of Jack Pumpkinhead. He is now living near the Emerald City and is a great favorite with the Princess Ozma, who rules all the Land of Oz."

"No; I've never heard of him," remarked Ojo. "I'm afraid I don't know much about the Land of Oz. You see, I've lived all my life with Unc Nunkie, the Silent One, and there was no one to tell me anything."

"That is one reason you are Ojo the Unlucky," said the woman, in a sympathetic tone. "The more one knows, the luckier he is, for knowledge is the greatest gift in life."

"But tell me, please, what you intend to do with this new lot of the Powder of Life, which Dr. Pipt is making. He said his wife wanted it for some especial purpose."

"So I do," she answered. "I want it to bring my Patchwork Girl to life."

"Oh! A Patchwork Girl? What is that?" Ojo asked, for this seemed even more strange and unusual than a Glass Cat.

"I think I must show you my Patchwork Girl," said Margolotte, laughing at the boy's astonishment, "for she is rather difficult to explain. But first I will tell you that for many years I have longed for a servant to help me with the housework and to cook the meals and wash the dishes. No servant will come here because the place is so lonely and out-of-the-way, so my clever husband, the Crooked Magician, proposed that I make a girl out of some sort of material and he would make her live by sprinkling over her the Powder of Life. This seemed an excellent suggestion and at once Dr. Pipt set to work to make a new batch of his magic powder. He has been at it a long, long while, and so I have had plenty of time to make the girl. Yet that task was not so easy as you may suppose. At first I couldn't think what to make her of, but finally in searching through a chest I came across an old patchwork quilt, which my grandmother once made when she was young."

"What is a patchwork quilt?" asked Ojo.

"A bed-quilt made of patches of different kinds and colors of cloth, all neatly sewed together. The patches are of all shapes and sizes, so a patchwork quilt is a very pretty and gorgeous thing to look at. Sometimes it is called a 'crazy-quilt,' because the patches and colors are so mixed up. We never have used my grandmother's many-colored patchwork quilt, handsome as it is, for we Munchkins do not care for any color other than blue, so it has been packed away in the chest for about a hundred years. When I found it, I said to myself that it would do nicely for my servant girl, for when she was brought to life she would not be proud nor haughty, as the Glass Cat is, for such a dreadful mixture of colors would discourage her from trying to be as dignified as the blue Munchkins are."

"Is blue the only respectable color, then?" inquired Ojo.

"Yes, for a Munchkin. All our country is blue, you know. But in other parts of Oz the people favor different colors. At the Emerald City, where our Princess Ozma lives, green is the popular color. But all Munchkins prefer blue to anything else and when my housework girl is brought to life she will find herself to be of so many unpopular colors that she'll never dare be rebellious or impudent, as servants are sometimes liable to be when they are made the same way their mistresses are."

Unc Nunkie nodded approval.

"Good i-dea," he said; and that was a long speech for Unc Nunkie because it was two words.

"So I cut up the quilt," continued Margolotte, "and made from it a very well-shaped girl, which I stuffed with cotton-wadding. I will show you what a good job I did," and she went to a tall cupboard and threw open the doors.

Then back she came, lugging in her arms the Patchwork Girl, which she set upon the bench and propped up so that the figure would not tumble over.

Chapter 3 - The Patchwork Girl

Ojo examined this curious contrivance with wonder. The Patchwork Girl was taller than he, when she stood upright, and her body was plump and rounded because it had been so neatly stuffed with cotton. Margolotte had first made the girl's form from the patchwork quilt and then she had dressed it with a patchwork skirt and an apron with pockets in it—using the same gay material throughout. Upon the feet she had sewn a pair of red leather shoes with pointed toes. All the fingers and thumbs of the girl's hands had been carefully formed and stuffed and stitched at the edges, with gold plates at the ends to serve as finger-nails.

"She will have to work, when she comes to life," said Marglotte.

The head of the Patchwork Girl was the most curious part of her. While she waited for her husband to finish making his Powder of Life the woman had found ample time to complete the head as her fancy dictated, and she realized that a good servant's head must be properly constructed. The hair was of brown yarn and hung down on her neck in several neat braids. Her eyes were two silver suspender-buttons cut from a pair of the Magician's old trousers, and they were sewed on with black threads, which formed the pupils of the eyes. Margolotte had puzzled over the ears for some time, for these were important if the servant was to hear distinctly, but finally she had made them out of thin plates of gold and attached them in place by means of stitches through tiny holes bored in the metal. Gold is the most common metal in the Land of Oz and is used for many purposes because it is soft and pliable.

The woman had cut a slit for the Patchwork Girl's mouth and sewn two rows of white pearls in it for teeth, using a strip of scarlet plush for a tongue. This mouth Ojo considered very artistic and lifelike, and Margolotte was pleased when the boy praised it. There were almost too many patches on the face of the girl for her to be considered strictly beautiful, for one cheek was yellow and the other red, her chin blue, her forehead purple and the center, where her nose had been formed and padded, a bright yellow.

"You ought to have had her face all pink," suggested the boy.

"I suppose so; but I had no pink cloth," replied the woman. "Still, I cannot see as it matters much, for I wish my Patchwork Girl to be useful rather than ornamental. If I get tired looking at her patched face I can whitewash it."

"Has she any brains?" asked Ojo.

"No; I forgot all about the brains!" exclaimed the woman. "I am glad you reminded me of them, for it is not too late to supply them, by any means. Until she is brought to life I can do anything I please with this girl. But I must be careful not to give her too much brains, and those she has must be such as are fitted to the station she is to occupy in life. In other words, her brains mustn't be very good."

"Wrong," said Unc Nunkie.

"No; I am sure I am right about that," returned the woman.

"He means," explained Ojo, "that unless your servant has good brains she won't know how to obey you properly, nor do the things you ask her to do."

"Well, that may be true," agreed Margolotte; "but, on the contrary, a servant with too much brains is sure to become independent and high-and-mighty and feel above her work. This is a very delicate task, as I said, and I must take care to give the girl just the right quantity of the right sort of brains. I want her to know just enough, but not too much."

With this she went to another cupboard which was filled with shelves. All the shelves were lined with blue glass bottles, neatly labeled by the Magician to show what they contained. One whole shelf was marked: "Brain Furniture," and the bottles on this shelf were labeled as follows:

"Obedience,"

"Cleverness,"

"Judgment,"

"Courage,"

"Ingenuity,"

"Amiability,"

"Learning,"

"Truth,"

"Poesy,"

"Self Reliance."

"Let me see," said Margolotte; "of those qualities she must have 'Obedience' first of all," and she took down the bottle bearing that label and poured from it upon a dish several grains of the contents. "'Amiability' is also good and 'Truth.'" She poured into the dish a quantity from each of these bottles. "I think that will do," she continued, "for the other qualities are not needed in a servant."

Unc Nunkie, who with Ojo stood beside her, touched the bottle marked "Cleverness."

"Little," said he.

"A little 'Cleverness'? Well, perhaps you are right, sir," said she, and was about to take down the bottle when the Crooked Magician suddenly called to her excitedly from the fireplace.

"Quick, Margolotte! Come and help me."

She ran to her husband's side at once and helped him lift the four kettles from the fire. Their contents had all boiled away, leaving in the bottom of each kettle a few grains of fine white powder. Very carefully the Magician removed this powder, placing it all together in a golden dish, where he mixed it with a golden spoon. When the mixture was complete there was scarcely a handful, all told.

"That," said Dr. Pipt, in a pleased and triumphant tone, "is the wonderful Powder of Life, which I alone in the world know how to make. It has taken me nearly six years to prepare these precious grains of dust, but the little heap on that dish is worth the price of a kingdom and many a king would give all he has to possess it. When it has become cooled I will place it in a small bottle; but meantime I must watch it carefully, lest a gust of wind blow it away or scatter it."

Unc Nunkie, Margolotte and the Magician all stood looking at the marvelous Powder, but Ojo was more interested just then in the Patchwork Girl's brains. Thinking it both unfair and unkind to deprive her of any good qualities that were handy, the boy took down every bottle on the shelf and poured some of the contents in Margolotte's dish. No one saw him do this, for all were looking at the Powder of Life; but soon the woman remembered what she had been doing, and came back to the cupboard.

"Let's see," she remarked; "I was about to give my girl a little 'Cleverness,' which is the Doctor's substitute for 'Intelligence'—a quality he has not yet learned how to manufacture." Taking down the bottle of "Cleverness" she added some of the powder to the heap on the dish. Ojo became a bit uneasy at this, for he had already put quite a lot of the "Cleverness" powder in the dish; but he dared not interfere and so he comforted himself with the thought that one cannot have too much cleverness.

Margolotte now carried the dish of brains to the bench. Ripping the seam of the patch on the girl's forehead, she placed the powder within the head and then sewed up the seam as neatly and securely as before.

"My girl is all ready for your Powder of Life, my dear," she said to her husband. But the Magician replied:

"This powder must not be used before to-morrow morning; but I think it is now cool enough to be bottled."

He selected a small gold bottle with a pepper-box top, so that the powder might be sprinkled on any object through the small holes. Very carefully he placed the Powder of Life in the gold bottle and then locked it up in a drawer of his cabinet.

"At last," said he, rubbing his hands together gleefully, "I have ample leisure for a good talk with my old friend Unc Nunkie. So let us sit down cosily and enjoy ourselves. After stirring those four kettles for six years I am glad to have a little rest."

"You will have to do most of the talking," said Ojo, "for Unc is called the Silent One and uses few words."

"I know; but that renders your uncle a most agreeable companion and gossip," declared Dr. Pipt. "Most people talk too much, so it is a relief to find one who talks too little."

Ojo looked at the Magician with much awe and curiosity.

"Don't you find it very annoying to be so crooked?" he asked.

"No; I am quite proud of my person," was the reply. "I suppose I am the only Crooked Magician in all the world. Some others are accused of being crooked, but I am the only genuine."

He was really very crooked and Ojo wondered how he managed to do so many things with such a twisted body. When he sat down upon a crooked chair that had been made to fit him, one knee was under his chin and the other near the small of his back; but he was a cheerful man and his face bore a pleasant and agreeable expression.

"I am not allowed to perform magic, except for my own amusement," he told his visitors, as he lighted a pipe with a crooked stem and began to smoke. "Too many people were working magic in the Land of Oz, and so our lovely Princess Ozma put a stop to it. I think she was quite right. There were several wicked Witches who caused a lot of trouble; but now they are all out of business and only the great Sorceress, Glinda the Good, is permitted to practice her arts, which never harm anybody. The Wizard of Oz, who used to be a humbug and knew no magic at all, has been taking lessons of Glinda, and I'm told he is getting to be a pretty good Wizard; but he is merely the assistant of the great Sorceress. I've the right to make a servant girl for my wife, you know, or a Glass Cat to catch our mice—which she refuses to do—but I am forbidden to work magic for others, or to use it as a profession."

"Magic must be a very interesting study," said Ojo.

"It truly is," asserted the Magician. "In my time I've performed some magical feats that were worthy of the skill of Glinda the Good. For instance, there's the Powder of Life, and my Liquid of Petrifaction, which is contained in that bottle on the shelf yonder—over the window."

"What does the Liquid of Petrifaction do?" inquired the boy.

"Turns everything it touches to solid marble. It's an invention of my own, and I find it very useful. Once two of those dreadful Kalidahs, with bodies like bears and heads like tigers, came here from the forest to attack us; but I sprinkled some of that Liquid on them and instantly they turned to marble. I now use them as ornamental statuary in my garden. This table looks to you like wood, and once it really was wood; but I sprinkled a few drops of the Liquid of Petrifaction on it and now it is marble. It will never break nor wear out."

"Fine!" said Unc Nunkie, wagging his head and stroking his long gray beard.

"Dear me; what a chatterbox you're getting to be, Unc," remarked the Magician, who was pleased with the compliment. But just then there came a scratching at the back door and a shrill voice cried:

"Let me in! Hurry up, can't you? Let me in!"

Margolotte got up and went to the door.

"Ask like a good cat, then," she said.

"Mee-ee-ow-w-w! There; does that suit your royal highness?" asked the voice, in scornful accents.

"Yes; that's proper cat talk," declared the woman, and opened the door.

At once a cat entered, came to the center of the room and stopped short at the sight of strangers. Ojo and Unc Nunkie both stared at it with wide open eyes, for surely no such curious creature had ever existed before—even in the Land of Oz.

Chapter 4 - The Glass Cat

The cat was made of glass, so clear and transparent that you could see through it as easily as through a window. In the top of its head, however, was a mass of delicate pink balls which looked like jewels, and it had a heart made of a blood-red ruby. The eyes were two large emeralds, but aside from these colors all the rest of the animal was clear glass, and it had a spun-glass tail that was really beautiful.

"Well, Doc Pipt, do you mean to introduce us, or not?" demanded the cat, in a tone of annoyance. "Seems to me you are forgetting your manners."

"Excuse me," returned the Magician. "This is Unc Nunkie, the descendant of the former kings of the Munchkins, before this country became a part of the Land of Oz."

"He needs a haircut," observed the cat, washing its face.

"True," replied Unc, with a low chuckle of amusement.

"But he has lived alone in the heart of the forest for many years," the Magician explained; "and, although that is a barbarous country, there are no barbers there."

"Who is the dwarf?" asked the cat.

"That is not a dwarf, but a boy," answered the Magician. "You have never seen a boy before. He is now small because he is young. With more years he will grow big and become as tall as Unc Nunkie."

"Oh. Is that magic?" the glass animal inquired.

"Yes; but it is Nature's magic, which is more wonderful than any art known to man. For instance, my magic made you, and made you live; and it was a poor job because you are useless and a bother to me; but I can't make you grow. You will always be the same size—and the same saucy, inconsiderate Glass Cat, with pink brains and a hard ruby heart."

"No one can regret more than I the fact that you made me," asserted the cat, crouching upon the floor and slowly swaying its spun-glass tail from side to side. "Your world is a very uninteresting place. I've wandered through your gardens and in the forest until I'm tired of it all, and when I come into the house the conversation of your fat wife and of yourself bores me dreadfully."

"That is because I gave you different brains from those we ourselves possess—and much too good for a cat," returned Dr. Pipt.

"Can't you take 'em out, then, and replace 'em with pebbles, so that I won't feel above my station in life?" asked the cat, pleadingly.

"Perhaps so. I'll try it, after I've brought the Patchwork Girl to life," he said.

The cat walked up to the bench on which the Patchwork Girl reclined and looked at her attentively.

"Are you going to make that dreadful thing live?" she asked.

The Magician nodded.

"It is intended to be my wife's servant maid," he said. "When she is alive she will do all our work and mind the house. But you are not to order her around, Bungle, as you do us. You must treat the Patchwork Girl respectfully."

"I won't. I couldn't respect such a bundle of scraps under any circumstances."

"If you don't, there will be more scraps than you will like," cried Margolotte, angrily.

"Why didn't you make her pretty to look at?" asked the cat. "You made me pretty—very pretty, indeed—and I love to watch my pink brains roll around when they're working, and to see my precious red heart beat." She went to a long mirror, as she said this, and stood before it, looking at herself with an air of much pride. "But that poor patched thing will hate herself, when she's once alive," continued the cat. "If I were you I'd use her for a mop, and make another servant that is prettier."

"You have a perverted taste," snapped Margolotte, much annoyed at this frank criticism. "I think the Patchwork Girl is beautiful, considering what she's made of. Even the rainbow hasn't as many colors, and you must admit that the rainbow is a pretty thing."

The Glass Cat yawned and stretched herself upon the floor.

"Have your own way," she said. "I'm sorry for the Patchwork Girl, that's all."

Ojo and Unc Nunkie slept that night in the Magician's house, and the boy was glad to stay because he was anxious to see the Patchwork Girl brought to life. The Glass Cat was also a wonderful creature to little Ojo, who had never seen or known anything of magic before, although he had lived in the Fairyland of Oz ever since he was born. Back there in the woods nothing unusual ever happened. Unc Nunkie, who might have been King of the Munchkins, had not his people united with all the other countries of Oz in acknowledging Ozma as their sole ruler, had retired into this forgotten forest nook with his baby nephew and they had lived all alone there. Only that the neglected garden had failed to grow food for them, they would always have lived in the solitary Blue Forest; but now they had started out to mingle with other people, and the first place they came to proved so interesting that Ojo could scarcely sleep a wink all night.

Margolotte was an excellent cook and gave them a fine breakfast. While they were all engaged in eating, the good woman said:

"This is the last meal I shall have to cook for some time, for right after breakfast Dr. Pipt has promised to bring my new servant to life. I shall let her wash the breakfast dishes and sweep and dust the house. What a relief it will be!"

"It will, indeed, relieve you of much drudgery," said the Magician. "By the way, Margolotte, I thought I saw you getting some brains from the cupboard, while I was busy with my kettles. What qualities have you given your new servant?"

"Only those that an humble servant requires," she answered. "I do not wish her to feel above her station, as the Glass Cat does. That would make her discontented and unhappy, for of course she must always be a servant."

Ojo was somewhat disturbed as he listened to this, and the boy began to fear he had done wrong in adding all those different qualities of brains to the lot Margolotte had prepared for the servant. But it was too late now for regret, since all the brains were securely sewn up inside the Patchwork Girl's head. He might have confessed what he had done and thus allowed Margolotte and her husband to change the brains; but he was afraid of incurring their anger. He believed that Unc had seen him add to the brains, and Unc had not said a word against it; but then, Unc never did say anything unless it was absolutely necessary.

As soon as breakfast was over they all went into the Magician's big workshop, where the Glass Cat was lying before the mirror and the Patchwork Girl lay limp and lifeless upon the bench.

"Now, then," said Dr. Pipt, in a brisk tone, "we shall perform one of the greatest feats of magic possible to man, even in this marvelous Land of Oz. In no other country could it be done at all. I think we ought to have a little music while the Patchwork Girl comes to life. It is pleasant to reflect that the first sounds her golden ears will hear will be delicious music."

As he spoke he went to a phonograph, which screwed fast to a small table, and wound up the spring of the instrument and adjusted the big gold horn.

"The music my servant will usually hear," remarked Margolotte, "will be my orders to do her work. But I see no harm in allowing her to listen to this unseen band while she wakens to her first realization of life. My orders will beat the band, afterward."

The phonograph was now playing a stirring march tune and the Magician unlocked his cabinet and took out the gold bottle containing the Powder of Life.

They all bent over the bench on which the Patchwork Girl reclined. Unc Nunkie and Margolotte stood behind, near the windows, Ojo at one side and the Magician in front, where he would have freedom to sprinkle the powder. The Glass Cat came near, too, curious to watch the important scene.

"All ready?" asked Dr. Pipt.

"All is ready," answered his wife.

So the Magician leaned over and shook from the bottle some grains of the wonderful Powder, and they fell directly on the Patchwork Girl's head and arms.

Chapter 5 - A Terrible Accident

"It will take a few minutes for this powder to do its work," remarked the Magician, sprinkling the body up and down with much care.

But suddenly the Patchwork Girl threw up one arm, which knocked the bottle of powder from the crooked man's hand and sent it flying across the room. Unc Nunkie and Margolotte were so startled that they both leaped backward and bumped together, and Unc's head joggled the shelf above them and upset the bottle containing the Liquid of Petrifaction.

The Magician uttered such a wild cry that Ojo jumped away and the Patchwork Girl sprang after him and clasped her stuffed arms around him in terror. The Glass Cat snarled and hid under the table, and so it was that when the powerful Liquid of Petrifaction was spilled it fell only upon the wife of the Magician and the uncle of Ojo. With these two the charm worked promptly. They stood motionless and stiff as marble statues, in exactly the positions they were in when the Liquid struck them.

Ojo pushed the Patchwork Girl away and ran to Unc Nunkie, filled with a terrible fear for the only friend and protector he had ever known. When he grasped Unc's hand it was cold and hard. Even the long gray beard was solid marble. The Crooked Magician was dancing around the room in a frenzy of despair, calling upon his wife to forgive him, to speak to him, to come to life again!

The Patchwork Girl, quickly recovering from her fright, now came nearer and looked from one to another of the people with deep interest. Then she looked at herself and laughed. Noticing the mirror, she stood before it and examined her extraordinary features with amazement—her button eyes, pearl bead teeth and puffy nose. Then, addressing her reflection in the glass, she exclaimed:

> "Whee, but there's a gaudy dame!
> Makes a paint-box blush with shame.
> Razzle-dazzle, fizzle-fazzle!
> Howdy-do, Miss What's-your-name?"

She bowed, and the reflection bowed. Then she laughed again, long and merrily, and the Glass Cat crept out from under the table and said:

"I don't blame you for laughing at yourself. Aren't you horrid?"

"Horrid?" she replied. "Why, I'm thoroughly delightful. I'm an Original, if you please, and therefore incomparable. Of all the comic, absurd, rare and amusing creatures the world contains, I must be the supreme freak. Who but poor Margolotte could have managed to invent such an unreasonable being as I? But I'm glad—I'm awfully glad!—that I'm just what I am, and nothing else."

"Be quiet, will you?" cried the frantic Magician; "be quiet and let me think! If I don't think I shall go mad."

"Think ahead," said the Patchwork Girl, seating herself in a chair. "Think all you want to. I don't mind."

"Gee! but I'm tired playing that tune," called the phonograph, speaking through its horn in a brazen, scratchy voice. "If you don't mind, Pipt, old boy, I'll cut it out and take a rest."

The Magician looked gloomily at the music-machine.

"What dreadful luck!" he wailed, despondently. "The Powder of Life must have fallen on the phonograph."

He went up to it and found that the gold bottle that contained the precious powder had dropped upon the stand and scattered its life-giving grains over the machine. The phonograph was very much alive, and began dancing a jig with the legs of the table to which it was attached, and this dance so annoyed Dr. Pipt that he kicked the thing into a corner and pushed a bench against it, to hold it quiet.

"You were bad enough before," said the Magician, resentfully; "but a live phonograph is enough to drive every sane person in the Land of Oz stark crazy."

"No insults, please," answered the phonograph in a surly tone. "You did it, my boy; don't blame me."

"You've bungled everything, Dr. Pipt," added the Glass Cat, contemptuously.

"Except me," said the Patchwork Girl, jumping up to whirl merrily around the room.

"I think," said Ojo, almost ready to cry through grief over Unc Nunkie's sad fate, "it must all be my fault, in some way. I'm called Ojo the Unlucky, you know."

"That's nonsense, kiddie," retorted the Patchwork Girl cheerfully. "No one can be unlucky who has the intelligence to direct his own actions. The unlucky ones are those who beg for a chance to think, like poor Dr. Pipt here. What's the row about, anyway, Mr. Magic-maker?"

"The Liquid of Petrifaction has accidentally fallen upon my dear wife and Unc Nunkie and turned them into marble," he sadly replied.

"Well, why don't you sprinkle some of that powder on them and bring them to life again?" asked the Patchwork Girl.

The Magician gave a jump.

"Why, I hadn't thought of that!" he joyfully cried, and grabbed up the golden bottle, with which he ran to Margolotte.

Said the Patchwork Girl:

"Higgledy, piggledy, dee—
What fools magicians be!
His head's so thick
He can't think quick,
So he takes advice from me."

Standing upon the bench, for he was so crooked he could not reach the top of his wife's head in any other way, Dr. Pipt began shaking the bottle. But not a grain of powder came out. He pulled off the cover, glanced within, and then threw the bottle from him with a wail of despair.

"Gone—gone! Every bit gone," he cried. "Wasted on that miserable phonograph when it might have saved my dear wife!"

Then the Magician bowed his head on his crooked arms and began to cry.

Ojo was sorry for him. He went up to the sorrowful man and said softly:

"You can make more Powder of Life, Dr. Pipt."

"Yes; but it will take me six years—six long, weary years of stirring four kettles with both feet and both hands," was the agonized reply. "Six years! while poor Margolotte stands watching me as a marble image."

"Can't anything else be done?" asked the Patchwork Girl.

The Magician shook his head. Then he seemed to remember something and looked up.

"There is one other compound that would destroy the magic spell of the Liquid of Petrifaction and restore my wife and Unc Nunkie to life," said he. "It may be hard to find the things I need to make this magic compound, but if they were found I could do in an instant what will otherwise take six long, weary years of stirring kettles with both hands and both feet."

"All right; let's find the things, then," suggested the Patchwork Girl. "That seems a lot more sensible than those stirring times with the kettles."

"That's the idea, Scraps," said the Glass Cat, approvingly. "I'm glad to find you have decent brains. Mine are exceptionally good. You can see 'em work; they're pink."

"Scraps?" repeated the girl. "Did you call me 'Scraps'? Is that my name?"

"I—I believe my poor wife had intended to name you 'Angeline,'" said the Magician.

"But I like 'Scraps' best," she replied with a laugh. "It fits me better, for my patchwork is all scraps, and nothing else. Thank you for naming me, Miss Cat. Have you any name of your own?"

"I have a foolish name that Margolotte once gave me, but which is quite undignified for one of my importance," answered the cat. "She called me 'Bungle.'"

"Yes," sighed the Magician; "you were a sad bungle, taken all in all. I was wrong to make you as I did, for a more useless, conceited and brittle thing never before existed."

"I'm not so brittle as you think," retorted the cat. "I've been alive a good many years, for Dr. Pipt experimented on me with the first magic Powder of Life he ever made, and so far I've never broken or cracked or chipped any part of me."

"You seem to have a chip on your shoulder," laughed the Patchwork Girl, and the cat went to the mirror to see.

"Tell me," pleaded Ojo, speaking to the Crooked Magician, "what must we find to make the compound that will save Unc Nunkie?"

"First," was the reply, "I must have a six-leaved clover. That can only be found in the green country around the Emerald City, and six-leaved clovers are very scarce, even there."

339

"I'll find it for you," promised Ojo.

"The next thing," continued the Magician, "is the left wing of a yellow butterfly. That color can only be found in the yellow country of the Winkies, West of the Emerald City."

"I'll find it," declared Ojo. "Is that all?"

"Oh, no; I'll get my Book of Recipes and see what comes next."

Saying this, the Magician unlocked a drawer of his cabinet and drew out a small book covered with blue leather. Looking through the pages he found the recipe he wanted and said: "I must have a gill of water from a dark well."

"What kind of a well is that, sir?" asked the boy.

"One where the light of day never penetrates. The water must be put in a gold bottle and brought to me without any light ever reaching it."

"I'll get the water from the dark well," said Ojo.

"Then I must have three hairs from the tip of a Woozy's tail, and a drop of oil from a live man's body."

Ojo looked grave at this.

"What is a Woozy, please?" he inquired.

"Some sort of an animal. I've never seen one, so I can't describe it," replied the Magician.

"If I can find a Woozy, I'll get the hairs from its tail," said Ojo. "But is there ever any oil in a man's body?"

The Magician looked in the book again, to make sure.

"That's what the recipe calls for," he replied, "and of course we must get everything that is called for, or the charm won't work. The book doesn't say 'blood'; it says 'oil,' and there must be oil somewhere in a live man's body or the book wouldn't ask for it."

"All right," returned Ojo, trying not to feel discouraged; "I'll try to find it."

The Magician looked at the little Munchkin boy in a doubtful way and said:

"All this will mean a long journey for you; perhaps several long journeys; for you must search through several of the different countries of Oz in order to get the things I need."

"I know it, sir; but I must do my best to save Unc Nunkie."

"And also my poor wife Margolotte. If you save one you will save the other, for both stand there together and the same compound will restore them both to life. Do the best you can, Ojo, and while you are gone I shall begin the six years job of making a new batch of the Powder of Life. Then, if you should unluckily fail to secure any one of the things needed, I will have lost no time. But if you succeed you must return here as quickly as you can, and that will save me much tiresome stirring of four kettles with both feet and both hands."

"I will start on my journey at once, sir," said the boy.

"And I will go with you," declared the Patchwork Girl.

"No, no!" exclaimed the Magician. "You have no right to leave this house. You are only a servant and have not been discharged."

Scraps, who had been dancing up and down the room, stopped and looked at him.

"What is a servant?" she asked.

"One who serves. A—a sort of slave," he explained.

"Very well," said the Patchwork Girl, "I'm going to serve you and your wife by helping Ojo find the things you need. You need a lot, you know, such as are not easily found."

"It is true," sighed Dr. Pipt. "I am well aware that Ojo has undertaken a serious task."

Scraps laughed, and resuming her dance she said:

"Here's a job for a boy of brains:
A drop of oil from a live man's veins;
A six-leaved clover; three nice hairs
From a Woozy's tail, the book declares
Are needed for the magic spell,
And water from a pitch-dark well.
The yellow wing of a butterfly
To find must Ojo also try,
And if he gets them without harm,
Doc Pipt will make the magic charm;
But if he doesn't get 'em, Unc

Will always stand a marble chunk."

The Magician looked at her thoughtfully.

"Poor Margolotte must have given you some of the quality of poesy, by mistake," he said. "And, if that is true, I didn't make a very good article when I prepared it, or else you got an overdose or an underdose. However, I believe I shall let you go with Ojo, for my poor wife will not need your services until she is restored to life. Also I think you may be able to help the boy, for your head seems to contain some thoughts I did not expect to find in it. But be very careful of yourself, for you're a souvenir of my dear Margolotte. Try not to get ripped, or your stuffing may fall out. One of your eyes seems loose, and you may have to sew it on tighter. If you talk too much you'll wear out your scarlet plush tongue, which ought to have been hemmed on the edges. And remember you belong to me and must return here as soon as your mission is accomplished."

"I'm going with Scraps and Ojo," announced the Glass Cat.

"You can't," said the Magician.

"Why not?"

"You'd get broken in no time, and you couldn't be a bit of use to the boy and the Patchwork Girl."

"I beg to differ with you," returned the cat, in a haughty tone. "Three heads are better than two, and my pink brains are beautiful. You can see 'em work."

"Well, go along," said the Magician, irritably. "You're only an annoyance, anyhow, and I'm glad to get rid of you."

"Thank you for nothing, then," answered the cat, stiffly.

Dr. Pipt took a small basket from a cupboard and packed several things in it. Then he handed it to Ojo.

"Here is some food and a bundle of charms," he said. "It is all I can give you, but I am sure you will find friends on your journey who will assist you in your search. Take care of the Patchwork Girl and bring her safely back, for she ought to prove useful to my wife. As for the Glass Cat—properly named Bungle—if she bothers you I now give you my permission to break her in two, for she is not respectful and does not obey me. I made a mistake in giving her the pink brains, you see."

Then Ojo went to Unc Nunkie and kissed the old man's marble face very tenderly.

"I'm going to try to save you, Unc," he said, just as if the marble image could hear him; and then he shook the crooked hand of the Crooked Magician, who was already busy hanging the four kettles in the fireplace, and picking up his basket left the house.

The Patchwork Girl followed him, and after them came the Glass Cat.

Chapter 6 - The Journey

Ojo had never traveled before and so he only knew that the path down the mountainside led into the open Munchkin Country, where large numbers of people dwelt. Scraps was quite new and not supposed to know anything of the Land of Oz, while the Glass Cat admitted she had never wandered very far away from the Magician's house. There was only one path before them, at the beginning, so they could not miss their way, and for a time they walked through the thick forest in silent thought, each one impressed with the importance of the adventure they had undertaken.

Suddenly the Patchwork Girl laughed. It was funny to see her laugh, because her cheeks wrinkled up, her nose tipped, her silver button eyes twinkled and her mouth curled at the corners in a comical way.

"Has something pleased you?" asked Ojo, who was feeling solemn and joyless through thinking upon his uncle's sad fate.

"Yes," she answered. "Your world pleases me, for it's a queer world, and life in it is queerer still. Here am I, made from an old bedquilt and intended to be a slave to Margolotte, rendered free as air by an accident that none of you could foresee. I am enjoying life and seeing the world, while the woman who made me is standing helpless as a block of wood. If that isn't funny enough to laugh at, I don't know what is."

"You're not seeing much of the world yet, my poor, innocent Scraps," remarked the Cat. "The world doesn't consist wholly of the trees that are on all sides of us."

"But they're part of it; and aren't they pretty trees?" returned Scraps, bobbing her head until her brown yarn curls fluttered in the breeze. "Growing between them I can see lovely ferns and wild-flowers, and soft green mosses. If the rest of your world is half as beautiful I shall be glad I'm alive."

"I don't know what the rest of the world is like, I'm sure," said the cat; "but I mean to find out."

"I have never been out of the forest," Ojo added; "but to me the trees are gloomy and sad and the wild-flowers seem lonesome. It must be nicer where there are no trees and there is room for lots of people to live together."

"I wonder if any of the people we shall meet will be as splendid as I am," said the Patchwork Girl. "All I have seen, so far, have pale, colorless skins and clothes as blue as the country they live in, while I am of many gorgeous colors—face and body and clothes. That is why I am bright and contented, Ojo, while you are blue and sad."

"I think I made a mistake in giving you so many sorts of brains," observed the boy. "Perhaps, as the Magician said, you have an overdose, and they may not agree with you."

"What had you to do with my brains?" asked Scraps.

"A lot," replied Ojo. "Old Margolotte meant to give you only a few—just enough to keep you going—but when she wasn't looking I added a good many more, of the best kinds I could find in the Magician's cupboard."

"Thanks," said the girl, dancing along the path ahead of Ojo and then dancing back to his side. "If a few brains are good, many brains must be better."

"But they ought to be evenly balanced," said the boy, "and I had no time to be careful. From the way you're acting, I guess the dose was badly mixed."

"Scraps hasn't enough brains to hurt her, so don't worry," remarked the cat, which was trotting along in a very dainty and graceful manner. "The only brains worth considering are mine, which are pink. You can see 'em work."

After walking a long time they came to a little brook that trickled across the path, and here Ojo sat down to rest and eat something from his basket. He found that the Magician had given him part of a loaf of bread and a slice of cheese. He broke off some of the bread and was surprised to find the loaf just as large as it was before. It was the same way with the cheese: however much he broke off from the slice, it remained exactly the same size.

"Ah," said he, nodding wisely; "that's magic. Dr. Pipt has enchanted the bread and the cheese, so it will last me all through my journey, however much I eat."

"Why do you put those things into your mouth?" asked Scraps, gazing at him in astonishment. "Do you need more stuffing? Then why don't you use cotton, such as I am stuffed with?"

"I don't need that kind," said Ojo.

"But a mouth is to talk with, isn't it?"

"It is also to eat with," replied the boy. "If I didn't put food into my mouth, and eat it, I would get hungry and starve.

"Ah, I didn't know that," she said. "Give me some."

Ojo handed her a bit of the bread and she put it in her mouth.

"What next?" she asked, scarcely able to speak.

"Chew it and swallow it," said the boy.

Scraps tried that. Her pearl teeth were unable to chew the bread and beyond her mouth there was no opening. Being unable to swallow she threw away the bread and laughed.

"I must get hungry and starve, for I can't eat," she said.

"Neither can I," announced the cat; "but I'm not fool enough to try. Can't you understand that you and I are superior people and not made like these poor humans?"

"Why should I understand that, or anything else?" asked the girl. "Don't bother my head by asking conundrums, I beg of you. Just let me discover myself in my own way."

With this she began amusing herself by leaping across the brook and back again.

"Be careful, or you'll fall in the water," warned Ojo.

"Never mind."

"You'd better. If you get wet you'll be soggy and can't walk. Your colors might run, too," he said.

"Don't my colors run whenever I run?" she asked.

"Not in the way I mean. If they get wet, the reds and greens and yellows and purples of your patches might run into each other and become just a blur—no color at all, you know."

"Then," said the Patchwork Girl, "I'll be careful, for if I spoiled my splendid colors I would cease to be beautiful."

"Pah!" sneered the Glass Cat, "such colors are not beautiful; they're ugly, and in bad taste. Please notice that my body has no color at all. I'm transparent, except for my exquisite red heart and my lovely pink brains—you can see 'em work."

"Shoo—shoo—shoo!" cried Scraps, dancing around and laughing. "And your horrid green eyes, Miss Bungle! You can't see your eyes, but we can, and I notice you're very proud of what little color you have. Shoo, Miss Bungle, shoo—

shoo—shoo! If you were all colors and many colors, as I am, you'd be too stuck up for anything." She leaped over the cat and back again, and the startled Bungle crept close to a tree to escape her. This made Scraps laugh more heartily than ever, and she said:

"Whoop-te-doodle-doo!
The cat has lost her shoe.
Her tootsie's bare, but she don't care,
So what's the odds to you?"

"Dear me, Ojo," said the cat; "don't you think the creature is a little bit crazy?"

"It may be," he answered, with a puzzled look.

"If she continues her insults I'll scratch off her suspender-button eyes," declared the cat.

"Don't quarrel, please," pleaded the boy, rising to resume the journey. "Let us be good comrades and as happy and cheerful as possible, for we are likely to meet with plenty of trouble on our way."

It was nearly sundown when they came to the edge of the forest and saw spread out before them a delightful landscape. There were broad blue fields stretching for miles over the valley, which was dotted everywhere with pretty, blue domed houses, none of which, however, was very near to the place where they stood. Just at the point where the path left the forest stood a tiny house covered with leaves from the trees, and before this stood a Munchkin man with an axe in his hand. He seemed very much surprised when Ojo and Scraps and the Glass Cat came out of the woods, but as the Patchwork Girl approached nearer he sat down upon a bench and laughed so hard that he could not speak for a long time.

This man was a woodchopper and lived all alone in the little house. He had bushy blue whiskers and merry blue eyes and his blue clothes were quite old and worn.

"Mercy me!" exclaimed the woodchopper, when at last he could stop laughing. "Who would think such a funny harlequin lived in the Land of Oz? Where did you come from, Crazy-quilt?"

"Do you mean me?" asked the Patchwork Girl.

"Of course," he replied.

"You misjudge my ancestry. I'm not a crazy-quilt; I'm patchwork," she said.

"There's no difference," he replied, beginning to laugh again. "When my old grandmother sews such things together she calls it a crazy-quilt; but I never thought such a jumble could come to life."

"It was the Magic Powder that did it," explained Ojo.

"Oh, then you have come from the Crooked Magician on the mountain. I might have known it, for—Well, I declare! here's a glass cat. But the Magician will get in trouble for this; it's against the law for anyone to work magic except Glinda the Good and the royal Wizard of Oz. If you people—or things—or glass spectacles—or crazy-quilts—or whatever you are, go near the Emerald City, you'll be arrested."

"We're going there, anyhow," declared Scraps, sitting upon the bench and swinging her stuffed legs.

"If any of us takes a rest, We'll be arrested sure, And get no restitution 'Cause the rest we must endure."

"I see," said the woodchopper, nodding; "you're as crazy as the crazy-quilt you're made of."

"She really is crazy," remarked the Glass Cat. "But that isn't to be wondered at when you remember how many different things she's made of. For my part, I'm made of pure glass—except my jewel heart and my pretty pink brains. Did you notice my brains, stranger? You can see 'em work."

"So I can," replied the woodchopper; "but I can't see that they accomplish much. A glass cat is a useless sort of thing, but a Patchwork Girl is really useful. She makes me laugh, and laughter is the best thing in life. There was once a woodchopper, a friend of mine, who was made all of tin, and I used to laugh every time I saw him."

"A tin woodchopper?" said Ojo. "That is strange."

"My friend wasn't always tin," said the man, "but he was careless with his axe, and used to chop himself very badly. Whenever he lost an arm or a leg he had it replaced with tin; so after a while he was all tin."

"And could he chop wood then?" asked the boy.

"He could if he didn't rust his tin joints. But one day he met Dorothy in the forest and went with her to the Emerald City, where he made his fortune. He is now one of the favorites of Princess Ozma, and she has made him the Emperor of the Winkies—the Country where all is yellow."

"Who is Dorothy?" inquired the Patchwork Girl.

"A little maid who used to live in Kansas, but is now a Princess of Oz. She's Ozma's best friend, they say, and lives with her in the royal palace."

"Is Dorothy made of tin?" inquired Ojo.

"Is she patchwork, like me?" inquired Scraps.

"No," said the man; "Dorothy is flesh, just as I am. I know of only one tin person, and that is Nick Chopper, the Tin Woodman; and there will never be but one Patchwork Girl, for any magician that sees you will refuse to make another one like you."

"I suppose we shall see the Tin Woodman, for we are going to the Country of the Winkies," said the boy.

"What for?" asked the woodchopper.

"To get the left wing of a yellow butterfly."

"It is a long journey," declared the man, "and you will go through lonely parts of Oz and cross rivers and traverse dark forests before you get there."

"Suits me all right," said Scraps. "I'll get a chance to see the country."

"You're crazy, girl. Better crawl into a rag-bag and hide there; or give yourself to some little girl to play with. Those who travel are likely to meet trouble; that's why I stay at home."

The woodchopper then invited them all to stay the night at his little hut, but they were anxious to get on and so left him and continued along the path, which was broader, now, and more distinct.

They expected to reach some other house before it grew dark, but the twilight was brief and Ojo soon began to fear they had made a mistake in leaving the woodchopper.

"I can scarcely see the path," he said at last. "Can you see it, Scraps?"

"No," replied the Patchwork Girl, who was holding fast to the boy's arm so he could guide her.

"I can see," declared the Glass Cat. "My eyes are better than yours, and my pink brains—"

"Never mind your pink brains, please," said Ojo hastily; "just run ahead and show us the way. Wait a minute and I'll tie a string to you; for then you can lead us."

He got a string from his pocket and tied it around the cat's neck, and after that the creature guided them along the path. They had proceeded in this way for about an hour when a twinkling blue light appeared ahead of them.

"Good! there's a house at last," cried Ojo. "When we reach it the good people will surely welcome us and give us a night's lodging." But however far they walked the light seemed to get no nearer, so by and by the cat stopped short, saying:

"I think the light is traveling, too, and we shall never be able to catch up with it. But here is a house by the roadside, so why go farther?"

"Where is the house, Bungle?"

"Just here beside us, Scraps."

Ojo was now able to see a small house near the pathway. It was dark and silent, but the boy was tired and wanted to rest, so he went up to the door and knocked.

"Who is there?" cried a voice from within.

"I am Ojo the Unlucky, and with me are Miss Scraps Patchwork and the Glass Cat," he replied.

"What do you want?" asked the Voice.

"A place to sleep," said Ojo.

"Come in, then; but don't make any noise, and you must go directly to bed," returned the Voice.

Ojo unlatched the door and entered. It was very dark inside and he could see nothing at all. But the cat exclaimed: "Why, there's no one here!"

"There must be," said the boy. "Some one spoke to me."

"I can see everything in the room," replied the cat, "and no one is present but ourselves. But here are three beds, all made up, so we may as well go to sleep."

"What is sleep?" inquired the Patchwork Girl.

"It's what you do when you go to bed," said Ojo.

"But why do you go to bed?" persisted the Patchwork Girl.

"Here, here! You are making altogether too much noise," cried the Voice they had heard before. "Keep quiet, strangers, and go to bed."

The cat, which could see in the dark, looked sharply around for the owner of the Voice, but could discover no one, although the Voice had seemed close beside them. She arched her back a little and seemed afraid. Then she whispered to Ojo: "Come!" and led him to a bed.

With his hands the boy felt of the bed and found it was big and soft, with feather pillows and plenty of blankets. So he took off his shoes and hat and crept into the bed. Then the cat led Scraps to another bed and the Patchwork Girl was puzzled to know what to do with it.

"Lie down and keep quiet," whispered the cat, warningly.

344

"Can't I sing?" asked Scraps.

"No."

"Can't I whistle?" asked Scraps.

"No."

"Can't I dance till morning, if I want to?" asked Scraps.

"You must keep quiet," said the cat, in a soft voice.

"I don't want to," replied the Patchwork Girl, speaking as loudly as usual. "What right have you to order me around? If I want to talk, or yell, or whistle—"

Before she could say anything more an unseen hand seized her firmly and threw her out of the door, which closed behind her with a sharp slam. She found herself bumping and rolling in the road and when she got up and tried to open the door of the house again she found it locked.

"What has happened to Scraps?" asked Ojo.

"Never mind. Let's go to sleep, or something will happen to us," answered the Glass Cat.

So Ojo snuggled down in his bed and fell asleep, and he was so tired that he never wakened until broad daylight.

Chapter 7 - The Troublesome Phonograph

When the boy opened his eyes next morning he looked carefully around the room. These small Munchkin houses seldom had more than one room in them. That in which Ojo now found himself had three beds, set all in a row on one side of it. The Glass Cat lay asleep on one bed, Ojo was in the second, and the third was neatly made up and smoothed for the day. On the other side of the room was a round table on which breakfast was already placed, smoking hot. Only one chair was drawn up to the table, where a place was set for one person. No one seemed to be in the room except the boy and Bungle.

Ojo got up and put on his shoes. Finding a toilet stand at the head of his bed he washed his face and hands and brushed his hair. Then he went to the table and said:

"I wonder if this is my breakfast?"

"Eat it!" commanded a Voice at his side, so near that Ojo jumped. But no person could he see.

He was hungry, and the breakfast looked good; so he sat down and ate all he wanted. Then, rising, he took his hat and wakened the Glass Cat.

"Come on, Bungle," said he; "we must go."

He cast another glance about the room and, speaking to the air, he said: "Whoever lives here has been kind to me, and I'm much obliged."

There was no answer, so he took his basket and went out the door, the cat following him. In the middle of the path sat the Patchwork Girl, playing with pebbles she had picked up.

"Oh, there you are!" she exclaimed cheerfully. "I thought you were never coming out. It has been daylight a long time."

"What did you do all night?" asked the boy.

"Sat here and watched the stars and the moon," she replied. "They're interesting. I never saw them before, you know."

"Of course not," said Ojo.

"You were crazy to act so badly and get thrown outdoors," remarked Bungle, as they renewed their journey.

"That's all right," said Scraps. "If I hadn't been thrown out I wouldn't have seen the stars, nor the big gray wolf."

"What wolf?" inquired Ojo.

"The one that came to the door of the house three times during the night."

"I don't see why that should be," said the boy, thoughtfully; "there was plenty to eat in that house, for I had a fine breakfast, and I slept in a nice bed."

"Don't you feel tired?" asked the Patchwork Girl, noticing that the boy yawned.

"Why, yes; I'm as tired as I was last night; and yet I slept very well."

"And aren't you hungry?"

"It's strange," replied Ojo. "I had a good breakfast, and yet I think I'll now eat some of my crackers and cheese."

Scraps danced up and down the path. Then she sang:

"Kizzle-kazzle-kore;   The wolf is at the door,   There's nothing to eat but a bone without meat,   And a bill from the grocery store."

"What does that mean?" asked Ojo.

"Don't ask me," replied Scraps. "I say what comes into my head, but of course I know nothing of a grocery store or bones without meat or—very much else."

"No," said the cat; "she's stark, staring, raving crazy, and her brains can't be pink, for they don't work properly."

"Bother the brains!" cried Scraps. "Who cares for 'em, anyhow? Have you noticed how beautiful my patches are in this sunlight?"

Just then they heard a sound as of footsteps pattering along the path behind them and all three turned to see what was coming. To their astonishment they beheld a small round table running as fast as its four spindle legs could carry it, and to the top was screwed fast a phonograph with a big gold horn.

"Hold on!" shouted the phonograph. "Wait for me!"

"Goodness me; it's that music thing which the Crooked Magician scattered the Powder of Life over," said Ojo.

"So it is," returned Bungle, in a grumpy tone of voice; and then, as the phonograph overtook them, the Glass Cat added sternly: "What are you doing here, anyhow?"

"I've run away," said the music thing. "After you left, old Dr. Pipt and I had a dreadful quarrel and he threatened to smash me to pieces if I didn't keep quiet. Of course I wouldn't do that, because a talking-machine is supposed to talk and make a noise—and sometimes music. So I slipped out of the house while the Magician was stirring his four kettles and I've been running after you all night. Now that I've found such pleasant company, I can talk and play tunes all I want to."

Ojo was greatly annoyed by this unwelcome addition to their party. At first he did not know what to say to the newcomer, but a little thought decided him not to make friends.

"We are traveling on important business," he declared, "and you'll excuse me if I say we can't be bothered."

"How very impolite!" exclaimed the phonograph.

"I'm sorry; but it's true," said the boy. "You'll have to go somewhere else."

"This is very unkind treatment, I must say," whined the phonograph, in an injured tone. "Everyone seems to hate me, and yet I was intended to amuse people."

"It isn't you we hate, especially," observed the Glass Cat; "it's your dreadful music. When I lived in the same room with you I was much annoyed by your squeaky horn. It growls and grumbles and clicks and scratches so it spoils the music, and your machinery rumbles so that the racket drowns every tune you attempt."

"That isn't my fault; it's the fault of my records. I must admit that I haven't a clear record," answered the machine.

"Just the same, you'll have to go away," said Ojo.

"Wait a minute," cried Scraps. "This music thing interests me. I remember to have heard music when I first came to life, and I would like to hear it again. What is your name, my poor abused phonograph?"

"Victor Columbia Edison," it answered.

"Well, I shall call you 'Vic' for short," said the Patchwork Girl. "Go ahead and play something."

"It'll drive you crazy," warned the cat.

"I'm crazy now, according to your statement. Loosen up and reel out the music, Vic."

"The only record I have with me," explained the phonograph, "is one the Magician attached just before we had our quarrel. It's a highly classical composition."

"A what?" inquired Scraps.

"It is classical music, and is considered the best and most puzzling ever manufactured. You're supposed to like it, whether you do or not, and if you don't, the proper thing is to look as if you did. Understand?"

"Not in the least," said Scraps.

"Then, listen!"

At once the machine began to play and in a few minutes Ojo put his hands to his ears to shut out the sounds and the cat snarled and Scraps began to laugh.

"Cut it out, Vic," she said. "That's enough."

But the phonograph continued playing the dreary tune, so Ojo seized the crank, jerked it free and threw it into the road. However, the moment the crank struck the ground it bounded back to the machine again and began winding it up. And still the music played.

"Let's run!" cried Scraps, and they all started and ran down the path as fast as they could go. But the phonograph was right behind them and could run and play at the same time. It called out, reproachfully:

"What's the matter? Don't you love classical music?"

"No, Vic," said Scraps, halting. "We will passical the classical and preserve what joy we have left. I haven't any nerves, thank goodness, but your music makes my cotton shrink."

"Then turn over my record. There's a rag-time tune on the other side," said the machine.

"What's rag-time?"

"The opposite of classical."

"All right," said Scraps, and turned over the record.

The phonograph now began to play a jerky jumble of sounds which proved so bewildering that after a moment Scraps stuffed her patchwork apron into the gold horn and cried: "Stop—stop! That's the other extreme. It's extremely bad!"

Muffled as it was, the phonograph played on.

"If you don't shut off that music I'll smash your record," threatened Ojo.

The music stopped, at that, and the machine turned its horn from one to another and said with great indignation: "What's the matter now? Is it possible you can't appreciate rag-time?"

"Scraps ought to, being rags herself," said the cat; "but I simply can't stand it; it makes my whiskers curl."

"It is, indeed, dreadful!" exclaimed Ojo, with a shudder.

"It's enough to drive a crazy lady mad," murmured the Patchwork Girl. "I'll tell you what, Vic," she added as she smoothed out her apron and put it on again, "for some reason or other you've missed your guess. You're not a concert; you're a nuisance."

"Music hath charms to soothe the savage breast," asserted the phonograph sadly.

"Then we're not savages. I advise you to go home and beg the Magician's pardon."

"Never! He'd smash me."

"That's what we shall do, if you stay here," Ojo declared.

"Run along, Vic, and bother some one else," advised Scraps. "Find some one who is real wicked, and stay with him till he repents. In that way you can do some good in the world."

The music thing turned silently away and trotted down a side path, toward a distant Munchkin village.

"Is that the way we go?" asked Bungle anxiously.

"No," said Ojo; "I think we shall keep straight ahead, for this path is the widest and best. When we come to some house we will inquire the way to the Emerald City."

Chapter 8 - The Foolish Owl and the Wise Donkey

On they went, and half an hour's steady walking brought them to a house somewhat better than the two they had already passed. It stood close to the roadside and over the door was a sign that read: "Miss Foolish Owl and Mr. Wise Donkey: Public Advisers."

When Ojo read this sign aloud Scraps said laughingly: "Well, here is a place to get all the advice we want, maybe more than we need. Let's go in."

The boy knocked at the door.

"Come in!" called a deep bass voice.

So they opened the door and entered the house, where a little light-brown donkey, dressed in a blue apron and a blue cap, was engaged in dusting the furniture with a blue cloth. On a shelf over the window sat a great blue owl with a blue sunbonnet on her head, blinking her big round eyes at the visitors.

"Good morning," said the donkey, in his deep voice, which seemed bigger than he was. "Did you come to us for advice?"

"Why, we came, anyhow," replied Scraps, "and now we are here we may as well have some advice. It's free, isn't it?"

"Certainly," said the donkey. "Advice doesn't cost anything—unless you follow it. Permit me to say, by the way, that you are the queerest lot of travelers that ever came to my shop. Judging you merely by appearances, I think you'd better talk to the Foolish Owl yonder."

They turned to look at the bird, which fluttered its wings and stared back at them with its big eyes.

"Hoot-ti-toot-ti-toot!" cried the owl.

"Fiddle-cum-foo,
Howdy-do?
Riddle-cum, tiddle-cum,
Too-ra-la-loo!"

"That beats your poetry, Scraps," said Ojo.

"It's just nonsense!" declared the Glass Cat.

"But it's good advice for the foolish," said the donkey, admiringly. "Listen to my partner, and you can't go wrong."

Said the owl in a grumbling voice:

"Patchwork Girl has come to life;
No one's sweetheart, no one's wife;
Lacking sense and loving fun,
She'll be snubbed by everyone."

"Quite a compliment! Quite a compliment, I declare," exclaimed the donkey, turning to look at Scraps. "You are certainly a wonder, my dear, and I fancy you'd make a splendid pincushion. If you belonged to me, I'd wear smoked glasses when I looked at you."

"Why?" asked the Patchwork Girl.

"Because you are so gay and gaudy."

"It is my beauty that dazzles you," she asserted. "You Munchkin people all strut around in your stupid blue color, while I—"

"You are wrong in calling me a Munchkin," interrupted the donkey, "for I was born in the Land of Mo and came to visit the Land of Oz on the day it was shut off from all the rest of the world. So here I am obliged to stay, and I confess it is a very pleasant country to live in."

"Hoot-ti-toot!" cried the owl;

"Ojo's searching for a charm,
'Cause Unc Nunkie's come to harm.
Charms are scarce; they're hard to get;
Ojo's got a job, you bet!"

"Is the owl so very foolish?" asked the boy.

"Extremely so," replied the donkey. "Notice what vulgar expressions she uses. But I admire the owl for the reason that she is positively foolish. Owls are supposed to be so very wise, generally, that a foolish one is unusual, and you perhaps know that anything or anyone unusual is sure to be interesting to the wise."

The owl flapped its wings again, muttering these words:

"It's hard to be a glassy cat—
No cat can be more hard than that;
She's so transparent, every act
Is clear to us, and that's a fact."

"Have you noticed my pink brains?" inquired Bungle, proudly. "You can see 'em work."

"Not in the daytime," said the donkey. "She can't see very well by day, poor thing. But her advice is excellent. I advise you all to follow it."

"The owl hasn't given us any advice, as yet," the boy declared.

"No? Then what do you call all those sweet poems?"

"Just foolishness," replied Ojo. "Scraps does the same thing."

"Foolishness! Of course! To be sure! The Foolish Owl must be foolish or she wouldn't be the Foolish Owl. You are very complimentary to my partner, indeed," asserted the donkey, rubbing his front hoofs together as if highly pleased.

"The sign says that you are wise," remarked Scraps to the donkey. "I wish you would prove it."

"With great pleasure," returned the beast. "Put me to the test, my dear Patches, and I'll prove my wisdom in the wink of an eye."

"What is the best way to get to the Emerald City?" asked Ojo.

"Walk," said the donkey.

"I know; but what road shall I take?" was the boy's next question.

"The road of yellow bricks, of course. It leads directly to the Emerald City."

"And how shall we find the road of yellow bricks?"

"By keeping along the path you have been following. You'll come to the yellow bricks pretty soon, and you'll know them when you see them because they're the only yellow things in the blue country."

"Thank you," said the boy. "At last you have told me something."

"Is that the extent of your wisdom?" asked Scraps.

"No," replied the donkey; "I know many other things, but they wouldn't interest you. So I'll give you a last word of advice: move on, for the sooner you do that the sooner you'll get to the Emerald City of Oz."

"Hoot-ti-toot-ti-toot-ti-too!" screeched the owl;

"Off you go! fast or slow,
Where you're going you don't know.
Patches, Bungle, Muchkin lad,
Facing fortunes good and bad,
Meeting dangers grave and sad,
Sometimes worried, sometimes glad—
Where you're going you don't know,
Nor do I, but off you go!"

"Sounds like a hint, to me," said the Patchwork Girl.

"Then let's take it and go," replied Ojo.

They said good-bye to the Wise Donkey and the Foolish Owl and at once resumed their journey.

Chapter 9 - They Meet the Woozy

"There seem to be very few houses around here, after all," remarked Ojo, after they had walked for a time in silence.

"Never mind," said Scraps; "we are not looking for houses, but rather the road of yellow bricks. Won't it be funny to run across something yellow in this dismal blue country?"

"There are worse colors than yellow in this country," asserted the Glass Cat, in a spiteful tone.

"Oh; do you mean the pink pebbles you call your brains, and your red heart and green eyes?" asked the Patchwork Girl.

"No; I mean you, if you must know it," growled the cat.

"You're jealous!" laughed Scraps. "You'd give your whiskers for a lovely variegated complexion like mine."

"I wouldn't!" retorted the cat. "I've the clearest complexion in the world, and I don't employ a beauty-doctor, either."

"I see you don't," said Scraps.

"Please don't quarrel," begged Ojo. "This is an important journey, and quarreling makes me discouraged. To be brave, one must be cheerful, so I hope you will be as good-tempered as possible."

They had traveled some distance when suddenly they faced a high fence which barred any further progress straight ahead. It ran directly across the road and enclosed a small forest of tall trees, set close together. When the group of adventurers peered through the bars of the fence they thought this forest looked more gloomy and forbidding than any they had ever seen before.

They soon discovered that the path they had been following now made a bend and passed around the enclosure, but what made Ojo stop and look thoughtful was a sign painted on the fence which read:

"BEWARE OF THE WOOZY!"

"That means," he said, "that there's a Woozy inside that fence, and the Woozy must be a dangerous animal or they wouldn't tell people to beware of it."

"Let's keep out, then," replied Scraps. "That path is outside the fence, and Mr. Woozy may have all his little forest to himself, for all we care."

"But one of our errands is to find a Woozy," Ojo explained. "The Magician wants me to get three hairs from the end of a Woozy's tail."

"Let's go on and find some other Woozy," suggested the cat. "This one is ugly and dangerous, or they wouldn't cage him up. Maybe we shall find another that is tame and gentle."

"Perhaps there isn't any other, at all," answered Ojo. "The sign doesn't say: 'Beware a Woozy'; it says: 'Beware the Woozy,' which may mean there's only one in all the Land of Oz."

"Then," said Scraps, "suppose we go in and find him? Very likely if we ask him politely to let us pull three hairs out of the tip of his tail he won't hurt us."

"It would hurt him, I'm sure, and that would make him cross," said the cat.

"You needn't worry, Bungle," remarked the Patchwork Girl; "for if there is danger you can climb a tree. Ojo and I are not afraid; are we, Ojo?"

"I am, a little," the boy admitted; "but this danger must be faced, if we intend to save poor Unc Nunkie. How shall we get over the fence?"

"Climb," answered Scraps, and at once she began climbing up the rows of bars. Ojo followed and found it more easy than he had expected. When they got to the top of the fence they began to get down on the other side and soon were in the forest. The Glass Cat, being small, crept between the lower bars and joined them.

Here there was no path of any sort, so they entered the woods, the boy leading the way, and wandered through the trees until they were nearly in the center of the forest. They now came upon a clear space in which stood a rocky cave.

So far they had met no living creature, but when Ojo saw the cave he knew it must be the den of the Woozy.

It is hard to face any savage beast without a sinking of the heart, but still more terrifying is it to face an unknown beast, which you have never seen even a picture of. So there is little wonder that the pulses of the Munchkin boy beat fast as he and his companions stood facing the cave. The opening was perfectly square, and about big enough to admit a goat.

"I guess the Woozy is asleep," said Scraps. "Shall I throw in a stone, to waken him?"

"No; please don't," answered Ojo, his voice trembling a little. "I'm in no hurry."

But he had not long to wait, for the Woozy heard the sound of voices and came trotting out of his cave. As this is the only Woozy that has ever lived, either in the Land of Oz or out of it, I must describe it to you.

The creature was all squares and flat surfaces and edges. Its head was an exact square, like one of the building-blocks a child plays with; therefore it had no ears, but heard sounds through two openings in the upper corners. Its nose, being in the center of a square surface, was flat, while the mouth was formed by the opening of the lower edge of the block. The body of the Woozy was much larger than its head, but was likewise block-shaped—being twice as long as it was wide and high. The tail was square and stubby and perfectly straight, and the four legs were made in the same way, each being four-sided. The animal was covered with a thick, smooth skin and had no hair at all except at the extreme end of its tail, where there grew exactly three stiff, stubby hairs. The beast was dark blue in color and his face was not fierce nor ferocious in expression, but rather good-humored and droll.

Seeing the strangers, the Woozy folded his hind legs as if they had been hinged and sat down to look his visitors over.

"Well, well," he exclaimed; "what a queer lot you are! At first I thought some of those miserable Munchkin farmers had come to annoy me, but I am relieved to find you in their stead. It is plain to me that you are a remarkable group—as remarkable in your way as I am in mine—and so you are welcome to my domain. Nice place, isn't it? But lonesome—dreadfully lonesome."

"Why did they shut you up here?" asked Scraps, who was regarding the queer, square creature with much curiosity.

"Because I eat up all the honey-bees which the Munchkin farmers who live around here keep to make them honey."

"Are you fond of eating honey-bees?" inquired the boy.

"Very. They are really delicious. But the farmers did not like to lose their bees and so they tried to destroy me. Of course they couldn't do that."

"Why not?"

"My skin is so thick and tough that nothing can get through it to hurt me. So, finding they could not destroy me, they drove me into this forest and built a fence around me. Unkind, wasn't it?"

"But what do you eat now?" asked Ojo.

"Nothing at all. I've tried the leaves from the trees and the mosses and creeping vines, but they don't seem to suit my taste. So, there being no honey-bees here, I've eaten nothing for years."

"You must be awfully hungry," said the boy. "I've got some bread and cheese in my basket. Would you like that kind of food?"

"Give me a nibble and I will try it; then I can tell you better whether it is grateful to my appetite," returned the Woozy.

So the boy opened his basket and broke a piece off the loaf of bread. He tossed it toward the Woozy, who cleverly caught it in his mouth and ate it in a twinkling.

"That's rather good," declared the animal. "Any more?"

"Try some cheese," said Ojo, and threw down a piece.

The Woozy ate that, too, and smacked its long, thin lips.

"That's mighty good!" it exclaimed. "Any more?"

"Plenty," replied Ojo. So he sat down on a Stump and fed the Woozy bread and cheese for a long time; for, no matter how much the boy broke off, the loaf and the slice remained just as big.

"That'll do," said the Woozy, at last; "I'm quite full. I hope the strange food won't give me indigestion."

"I hope not," said Ojo. "It's what I eat."

"Well, I must say I'm much obliged, and I'm glad you came," announced the beast. "Is there anything I can do in return for your kindness?"

"Yes," said Ojo earnestly, "you have it in your power to do me a great favor, if you will."

"What is it?" asked the Woozy. "Name the favor and I will grant it."

"I—I want three hairs from the tip of your tail," said Ojo, with some hesitation.

"Three hairs! Why, that's all I have—on my tail or anywhere else," exclaimed the beast.

"I know; but I want them very much."

"They are my sole ornaments, my prettiest feature," said the Woozy, uneasily. "If I give up those three hairs I—I'm just a blockhead."

"Yet I must have them," insisted the boy, firmly, and he then told the Woozy all about the accident to Unc Nunkie and Margolotte, and how the three hairs were to be a part of the magic charm that would restore them to life. The beast listened with attention and when Ojo had finished the recital it said, with a sigh:

"I always keep my word, for I pride myself on being square. So you may have the three hairs, and welcome. I think, under such circumstances, it would be selfish in me to refuse you."

"Thank you! Thank you very much," cried the boy, joyfully. "May I pull out the hairs now?"

"Any time you like," answered the Woozy.

So Ojo went up to the queer creature and taking hold of one of the hairs began to pull. He pulled harder. He pulled with all his might; but the hair remained fast.

"What's the trouble?" asked the Woozy, which Ojo had dragged here and there all around the clearing in his endeavor to pull out the hair.

"It won't come," said the boy, panting.

"I was afraid of that," declared the beast. "You'll have to pull harder."

"I'll help you," exclaimed Scraps, coming to the boy's side. "You pull the hair, and I'll pull you, and together we ought to get it out easily."

"Wait a jiffy," called the Woozy, and then it went to a tree and hugged it with its front paws, so that its body couldn't be dragged around by the pull. "All ready, now. Go ahead!"

Ojo grasped the hair with both hands and pulled with all his strength, while Scraps seized the boy around his waist and added her strength to his. But the hair wouldn't budge. Instead, it slipped out of Ojo's hands and he and Scraps both rolled upon the ground in a heap and never stopped until they bumped against the rocky cave.

"Give it up," advised the Glass Cat, as the boy arose and assisted the Patchwork Girl to her feet. "A dozen strong men couldn't pull out those hairs. I believe they're clinched on the under side of the Woozy's thick skin."

"Then what shall I do?" asked the boy, despairingly. "If on our return I fail to take these three hairs to the Crooked Magician, the other things I have come to seek will be of no use at all, and we cannot restore Unc Nunkie and Margolotte to life."

"They're goners, I guess," said the Patchwork Girl.

"Never mind," added the cat. "I can't see that old Unc and Margolotte are worth all this trouble, anyhow."

But Ojo did not feel that way. He was so disheartened that he sat down upon a stump and began to cry.

The Woozy looked at the boy thoughtfully.

"Why don't you take me with you?" asked the beast. "Then, when at last you get to the Magician's house, he can surely find some way to pull out those three hairs."

Ojo was overjoyed at this suggestion.

"That's it!" he cried, wiping away the tears and springing to his feet with a smile. "If I take the three hairs to the Magician, it won't matter if they are still in your body."

"It can't matter in the least," agreed the Woozy.

"Come on, then," said the boy, picking up his basket; "let us start at once. I have several other things to find, you know."

But the Glass Cat gave a little laugh and inquired in her scornful way:

"How do you intend to get the beast out of this forest?"

That puzzled them all for a time.

"Let us go to the fence, and then we may find a way," suggested Scraps. So they walked through the forest to the fence, reaching it at a point exactly opposite that where they had entered the enclosure.

"How did you get in?" asked the Woozy.

"We climbed over," answered Ojo.

"I can't do that," said the beast. "I'm a very swift runner, for I can overtake a honey-bee as it flies; and I can jump very high, which is the reason they made such a tall fence to keep me in. But I can't climb at all, and I'm too big to squeeze between the bars of the fence."

Ojo tried to think what to do.

"Can you dig?" he asked.

"No," answered the Woozy, "for I have no claws. My feet are quite flat on the bottom of them. Nor can I gnaw away the boards, as I have no teeth."

"You're not such a terrible creature, after all," remarked Scraps.

"You haven't heard me growl, or you wouldn't say that," declared the Woozy. "When I growl, the sound echoes like thunder all through the valleys and woodlands, and children tremble with fear, and women cover their heads with their aprons, and big men run and hide. I suppose there is nothing in the world so terrible to listen to as the growl of a Woozy."

"Please don't growl, then," begged Ojo, earnestly.

"There is no danger of my growling, for I am not angry. Only when angry do I utter my fearful, ear-splitting, soul-shuddering growl. Also, when I am angry, my eyes flash fire, whether I growl or not."

"Real fire?" asked Ojo.

"Of course, real fire. Do you suppose they'd flash imitation fire?" inquired the Woozy, in an injured tone.

"In that case, I've solved the riddle," cried Scraps, dancing with glee. "Those fence-boards are made of wood, and if the Woozy stands close to the fence and lets his eyes flash fire, they might set fire to the fence and burn it up. Then he could walk away with us easily, being free."

"Ah, I have never thought of that plan, or I would have been free long ago," said the Woozy. "But I cannot flash fire from my eyes unless I am very angry."

"Can't you get angry 'bout something, please?" asked Ojo.

"I'll try. You just say 'Krizzle-Kroo' to me."

"Will that make you angry?" inquired the boy.

"Terribly angry."

"What does it mean?" asked Scraps.

"I don't know; that's what makes me so angry," replied the Woozy.

He then stood close to the fence, with his head near one of the boards, and Scraps called out "Krizzle-Kroo!" Then Ojo said "Krizzle-Kroo!" and the Glass Cat said "Krizzle-Kroo!" The Woozy began to tremble with anger and small sparks darted from his eyes. Seeing this, they all cried "Krizzle-Kroo!" together, and that made the beast's eyes flash fire so fiercely that the fence-board caught the sparks and began to smoke. Then it burst into flame, and the Woozy stepped back and said triumphantly:

"Aha! That did the business, all right. It was a happy thought for you to yell all together, for that made me as angry as I have ever been. Fine sparks, weren't they?"

"Reg'lar fireworks," replied Scraps, admiringly.

In a few moments the board had burned to a distance of several feet, leaving an opening big enough for them all to pass through. Ojo broke some branches from a tree and with them whipped the fire until it was extinguished.

"We don't want to burn the whole fence down," said he, "for the flames would attract the attention of the Munchkin farmers, who would then come and capture the Woozy again. I guess they'll be rather surprised when they find he's escaped."

"So they will," declared the Woozy, chuckling gleefully. "When they find I'm gone the farmers will be badly scared, for they'll expect me to eat up their honey-bees, as I did before."

"That reminds me," said the boy, "that you must promise not to eat honey-bees while you are in our company."

352

"None at all?"

"Not a bee. You would get us all into trouble, and we can't afford to have any more trouble than is necessary. I'll feed you all the bread and cheese you want, and that must satisfy you."

"All right; I'll promise," said the Woozy, cheerfully. "And when I promise anything you can depend on it, 'cause I'm square."

"I don't see what difference that makes," observed the Patchwork Girl, as they found the path and continued their journey. "The shape doesn't make a thing honest, does it?"

"Of course it does," returned the Woozy, very decidedly. "No one could trust that Crooked Magician, for instance, just because he is crooked; but a square Woozy couldn't do anything crooked if he wanted to."

"I am neither square nor crooked," said Scraps, looking down at her plump body.

"No; you're round, so you're liable to do anything," asserted the Woozy. "Do not blame me, Miss Gorgeous, if I regard you with suspicion. Many a satin ribbon has a cotton back."

Scraps didn't understand this, but she had an uneasy misgiving that she had a cotton back herself. It would settle down, at times, and make her squat and dumpy, and then she had to roll herself in the road until her body stretched out again.

Chapter 10 - Shaggy Man to the Rescue

They had not gone very far before Bungle, *who had run on ahead, came bounding back* to say that the road of yellow bricks was just before them. At once they hurried forward to see what this famous road looked like.

It was a broad road, but not straight, for it wandered over hill and dale and picked out the easiest places to go. All its length and breadth was paved with smooth bricks of a bright yellow color, so it was smooth and level except in a few places where the bricks had crumbled or been removed, leaving holes that might cause the unwary to stumble.

"I wonder," said Ojo, looking up and down the road, "which way to go."

"Where are you bound for?" asked the Woozy.

"The Emerald City," he replied.

"Then go west," said the Woozy. "I know this road pretty well, for I've chased many a honey-bee over it."

"Have you ever been to the Emerald City?" asked Scraps.

"No. I am very shy by nature, as you may have noticed, so I haven't mingled much in society."

"Are you afraid of men?" inquired the Patchwork Girl.

"Me? With my heart-rending growl—my horrible, shudderful growl? I should say not. I am not afraid of anything," declared the Woozy.

"I wish I could say the same," sighed Ojo. "I don't think we need be afraid when we get to the Emerald City, for Unc Nunkie has told me that Ozma, our girl Ruler, is very lovely and kind, and tries to help everyone who is in trouble. But they say there are many dangers lurking on the road to the great Fairy City, and so we must be very careful."

"I hope nothing will break me," said the Glass Cat, in a nervous voice. "I'm a little brittle, you know, and can't stand many hard knocks."

"If anything should fade the colors of my lovely patches it would break my heart," said the Patchwork Girl.

"I'm not sure you have a heart," Ojo reminded her.

"Then it would break my cotton," persisted Scraps. "Do you think they are all fast colors, Ojo?" she asked anxiously.

"They seem fast enough when you run," he replied; and then, looking ahead of them, he exclaimed: "Oh, what lovely trees!"

They were certainly pretty to look upon and the travelers hurried forward to observe them more closely.

"Why, they are not trees at all," said Scraps; "they are just monstrous plants."

That is what they really were: masses of great broad leaves which rose from the ground far into the air, until they towered twice as high as the top of the Patchwork Girl's head, who was a little taller than Ojo. The plants formed rows on both sides of the road and from each plant rose a dozen or more of the big broad leaves, which swayed continually from side to side, although no wind was blowing. But the most curious thing about the swaying leaves was their color. They seemed to have a general groundwork of blue, but here and there other colors glinted at times through the blue— gorgeous yellows, turning to pink, purple, orange and scarlet, mingled with more sober browns and grays—each appearing as a blotch or stripe anywhere on a leaf and then disappearing, to be replaced by some other color of a different shape. The changeful coloring of the great leaves was very beautiful, but it was bewildering, as well, and the novelty of the scene drew our travelers close to the line of plants, where they stood watching them with rapt interest.

Suddenly a leaf bent lower than usual and touched the Patchwork Girl. Swiftly it enveloped her in its embrace, covering her completely in its thick folds, and then it swayed back upon its stem.

"Why, she's gone!" gasped Ojo, in amazement, and listening carefully he thought he could hear the muffled screams of Scraps coming from the center of the folded leaf. But, before he could think what he ought to do to save her, another leaf bent down and captured the Glass Cat, rolling around the little creature until she was completely hidden, and then straightening up again upon its stem.

"Look out," cried the Woozy. "Run! Run fast, or you are lost."

Ojo turned and saw the Woozy running swiftly up the road. But the last leaf of the row of plants seized the beast even as he ran and instantly he disappeared from sight.

The boy had no chance to escape. Half a dozen of the great leaves were bending toward him from different directions and as he stood hesitating one of them clutched him in its embrace. In a flash he was in the dark. Then he felt himself gently lifted until he was swaying in the air, with the folds of the leaf hugging him on all sides.

At first he struggled hard to escape, crying out in anger: "Let me go! Let me go!" But neither struggles nor protests had any effect whatever. The leaf held him firmly and he was a prisoner.

Then Ojo quieted himself and tried to think. Despair fell upon him when he remembered that all his little party had been captured, even as he was, and there was none to save them.

"I might have expected it," he sobbed, miserably. "I'm Ojo the Unlucky, and something dreadful was sure to happen to me."

He pushed against the leaf that held him and found it to be soft, but thick and firm. It was like a great bandage all around him and he found it difficult to move his body or limbs in order to change their position.

The minutes passed and became hours. Ojo wondered how long one could live in such a condition and if the leaf would gradually sap his strength and even his life, in order to feed itself. The little Munchkin boy had never heard of any person dying in the Land of Oz, but he knew one could suffer a great deal of pain. His greatest fear at this time was that he would always remain imprisoned in the beautiful leaf and never see the light of day again.

No sound came to him through the leaf; all around was intense silence. Ojo wondered if Scraps had stopped screaming, or if the folds of the leaf prevented his hearing her. By and by he thought he heard a whistle, as of some one whistling a tune. Yes; it really must be some one whistling, he decided, for he could follow the strains of a pretty Munchkin melody that Unc Nunkie used to sing to him. The sounds were low and sweet and, although they reached Ojo's ears very faintly, they were clear and harmonious.

Could the leaf whistle, Ojo wondered? Nearer and nearer came the sounds and then they seemed to be just the other side of the leaf that was hugging him.

Suddenly the whole leaf toppled and fell, carrying the boy with it, and while he sprawled at full length the folds slowly relaxed and set him free. He scrambled quickly to his feet and found that a strange man was standing before him—a man so curious in appearance that the boy stared with round eyes.

He was a big man, with shaggy whiskers, shaggy eyebrows, shaggy hair—but kindly blue eyes that were gentle as those of a cow. On his head was a green velvet hat with a jeweled band, which was all shaggy around the brim. Rich but shaggy laces were at his throat; a coat with shaggy edges was decorated with diamond buttons; the velvet breeches had jeweled buckles at the knees and shags all around the bottoms. On his breast hung a medallion bearing a picture of Princess Dorothy of Oz, and in his hand, as he stood looking at Ojo, was a sharp knife shaped like a dagger.

"Oh!" exclaimed Ojo, greatly astonished at the sight of this stranger; and then he added: "Who has saved me, sir?"

"Can't you see?" replied the other, with a smile; "I'm the Shaggy Man."

"Yes; I can see that," said the boy, nodding. "Was it you who rescued me from the leaf?"

"None other, you may be sure. But take care, or I shall have to rescue you again."

Ojo gave a jump, for he saw several broad leaves leaning toward him; but the Shaggy Man began to whistle again, and at the sound the leaves all straightened up on their stems and kept still.

The man now took Ojo's arm and led him up the road, past the last of the great plants, and not till he was safely beyond their reach did he cease his whistling.

"You see, the music charms 'em," said he. "Singing or whistling—it doesn't matter which—makes 'em behave, and nothing else will. I always whistle as I go by 'em and so they always let me alone. To-day as I went by, whistling, I saw a leaf curled and knew there must be something inside it. I cut down the leaf with my knife and—out you popped. Lucky I passed by, wasn't it?"

"You were very kind," said Ojo, "and I thank you. Will you please rescue my companions, also?"

"What companions?" asked the Shaggy Man.

"The leaves grabbed them all," said the boy. "There's a Patchwork Girl and—"

"A what?"

"A girl made of patchwork, you know. She's alive and her name is Scraps. And there's a Glass Cat—"

"Glass?" asked the Shaggy Man.

"All glass."

"And alive?"

"Yes," said Ojo; "she has pink brains. And there's a Woozy—"

"What's a Woozy?" inquired the Shaggy Man.

"Why, I—I—can't describe it," answered the boy, greatly perplexed. "But it's a queer animal with three hairs on the tip of its tail that won't come out and—"

"What won't come out?" asked the Shaggy Man; "the tail?"

"The hairs won't come out. But you'll see the Woozy, if you'll please rescue it, and then you'll know just what it is."

"Of course," said the Shaggy Man, nodding his shaggy head. And then he walked back among the plants, still whistling, and found the three leaves which were curled around Ojo's traveling companions. The first leaf he cut down released Scraps, and on seeing her the Shaggy Man threw back his shaggy head, opened wide his mouth and laughed so shaggily and yet so merrily that Scraps liked him at once. Then he took off his hat and made her a low bow, saying:

"My dear, you're a wonder. I must introduce you to my friend the Scarecrow."

When he cut down the second leaf he rescued the Glass Cat, and Bungle was so frightened that she scampered away like a streak and soon had joined Ojo, when she sat beside him panting and trembling. The last plant of all the row had captured the Woozy, and a big bunch in the center of the curled leaf showed plainly where he was. With his sharp knife the Shaggy Man sliced off the stem of the leaf and as it fell and unfolded out trotted the Woozy and escaped beyond the reach of any more of the dangerous plants.

Chapter 11 - A Good Friend

Soon the entire party was gathered on the road of yellow bricks, quite beyond the reach of the beautiful but treacherous plants. The Shaggy Man, staring first at one and then at the other, seemed greatly pleased and interested.

"I've seen queer things since I came to the Land of Oz," said he, "but never anything queerer than this band of adventurers. Let us sit down a while, and have a talk and get acquainted."

"Haven't you always lived in the Land of Oz?" asked the Munchkin boy.

"No; I used to live in the big, outside world. But I came here once with Dorothy, and Ozma let me stay."

"How do you like Oz?" asked Scraps. "Isn't the country and the climate grand?"

"It's the finest country in all the world, even if it is a fairyland. and I'm happy every minute I live in it," said the Shaggy Man. "But tell me something about yourselves."

So Ojo related the story of his visit to the house of the Crooked Magician, and how he met there the Glass Cat, and how the Patchwork Girl was brought to life and of the terrible accident to Unc Nunkie and Margolotte. Then he told how he had set out to find the five different things which the Magician needed to make a charm that would restore the marble figures to life, one requirement being three hairs from a Woozy's tail.

"We found the Woozy," explained the boy, "and he agreed to give us the three hairs; but we couldn't pull them out. So we had to bring the Woozy along with us."

"I see," returned the Shaggy Man, who had listened with interest to the story. "But perhaps I, who am big and strong, can pull those three hairs from the Woozy's tail."

"Try it, if you like," said the Woozy.

So the Shaggy Man tried it, but pull as hard as he could he failed to get the hairs out of the Woozy's tail. So he sat down again and wiped his shaggy face with a shaggy silk handkerchief and said:

"It doesn't matter. If you can keep the Woozy until you get the rest of the things you need, you can take the beast and his three hairs to the Crooked Magician and let him find a way to extract 'em. What are the other things you are to find?"

"One," said Ojo, "is a six-leaved clover."

"You ought to find that in the fields around the Emerald City," said the Shaggy Man. "There is a Law against picking six-leaved clovers, but I think I can get Ozma to let you have one."

"Thank you," replied Ojo. "The next thing is the left wing of a yellow butterfly."

"For that you must go to the Winkie Country," the Shaggy Man declared. "I've never noticed any butterflies there, but that is the yellow country of Oz and it's ruled by a good friend of mine, the Tin Woodman."

"Oh, I've heard of him!" exclaimed Ojo. "He must be a wonderful man."

"So he is, and his heart is wonderfully kind. I'm sure the Tin Woodman will do all in his power to help you to save your Unc Nunkie and poor Margolotte."

"The next thing I must find," said the Munchkin boy, "is a gill of water from a dark well."

"Indeed! Well, that is more difficult," said the Shaggy Man, scratching his left ear in a puzzled way. "I've never heard of a dark well; have you?"

"No," said Ojo.

"Do you know where one may be found?" inquired the Shaggy Man.

"I can't imagine," said Ojo.

"Then we must ask the Scarecrow."

"The Scarecrow! But surely, sir, a scarecrow can't know anything."

"Most scarecrows don't, I admit," answered the Shaggy Man. "But this Scarecrow of whom I speak is very intelligent. He claims to possess the best brains in all Oz."

"Better than mine?" asked Scraps.

"Better than mine?" echoed the Glass Cat. "Mine are pink, and you can see 'em work."

"Well, you can't see the Scarecrow's brains work, but they do a lot of clever thinking," asserted the Shaggy Man. "If anyone knows where a dark well is, it's my friend the Scarecrow."

"Where does he live?" inquired Ojo.

"He has a splendid castle in the Winkie Country, near to the palace of his friend the Tin Woodman, and he is often to be found in the Emerald City, where he visits Dorothy at the royal palace."

"Then we will ask him about the dark well," said Ojo.

"But what else does this Crooked Magician want?" asked the Shaggy Man.

"A drop of oil from a live man's body."

"Oh; but there isn't such a thing."

"That is what I thought," replied Ojo; "but the Crooked Magician said it wouldn't be called for by the recipe if it couldn't be found, and therefore I must search until I find it."

"I wish you good luck," said the Shaggy Man, shaking his head doubtfully; "but I imagine you'll have a hard job getting a drop of oil from a live man's body. There's blood in a body, but no oil."

"There's cotton in mine," said Scraps, dancing a little jig.

"I don't doubt it," returned the Shaggy Man admiringly. "You're a regular comforter and as sweet as patchwork can be. All you lack is dignity."

"I hate dignity," cried Scraps, kicking a pebble high in the air and then trying to catch it as it fell. "Half the fools and all the wise folks are dignified, and I'm neither the one nor the other."

"She's just crazy," explained the Glass Cat.

The Shaggy Man laughed.

"She's delightful, in her way," he said. "I'm sure Dorothy will be pleased with her, and the Scarecrow will dote on her. Did you say you were traveling toward the Emerald City?"

"Yes," replied Ojo. "I thought that the best place to go, at first, because the six-leaved clover may be found there."

"I'll go with you," said the Shaggy Man, "and show you the way."

"Thank you," exclaimed Ojo. "I hope it won't put you out any."

"No," said the other, "I wasn't going anywhere in particular. I've been a rover all my life, and although Ozma has given me a suite of beautiful rooms in her palace I still get the wandering fever once in a while and start out to roam the country over. I've been away from the Emerald City several weeks, this time, and now that I've met you and your friends I'm sure it will interest me to accompany you to the great city of Oz and introduce you to my friends."

"That will be very nice," said the boy, gratefully.

"I hope your friends are not dignified," observed Scraps.

"Some are, and some are not," he answered; "but I never criticise my friends. If they are really true friends, they may be anything they like, for all of me."

"There's some sense in that," said Scraps, nodding her queer head in approval. "Come on, and let's get to the Emerald City as soon as possible." With this she ran up the path, skipping and dancing, and then turned to await them.

"It is quite a distance from here to the Emerald City," remarked the Shaggy Man, "so we shall not get there to-day, nor to-morrow. Therefore let us take the jaunt in an easy manner. I'm an old traveler and have found that I never gain anything by being in a hurry. 'Take it easy' is my motto. If you can't take it easy, take it as easy as you can."

After walking some distance over the road of yellow bricks Ojo said he was hungry and would stop to eat some bread and cheese. He offered a portion of the food to the Shaggy Man, who thanked him but refused it.

"When I start out on my travels," said he, "I carry along enough square meals to last me several weeks. Think I'll indulge in one now, as long as we're stopping anyway."

Saying this, he took a bottle from his pocket and shook from it a tablet about the size of one of Ojo's finger-nails.

"That," announced the Shaggy Man, "is a square meal, in condensed form. Invention of the great Professor Woggle-Bug, of the Royal College of Athletics. It contains soup, fish, roast meat, salad, apple-dumplings, ice cream and chocolate-drops, all boiled down to this small size, so it can be conveniently carried and swallowed when you are hungry and need a square meal."

"I'm square," said the Woozy. "Give me one, please."

So the Shaggy Man gave the Woozy a tablet from his bottle and the beast ate it in a twinkling.

"You have now had a six course dinner," declared the Shaggy Man.

"Pshaw!" said the Woozy, ungratefully, "I want to taste something. There's no fun in that sort of eating."

"One should only eat to sustain life," replied the Shaggy Man, "and that tablet is equal to a peck of other food."

"I don't care for it. I want something I can chew and taste," grumbled the Woozy.

"You are quite wrong, my poor beast," said the Shaggy Man in a tone of pity. "Think how tired your jaws would get chewing a square meal like this, if it were not condensed to the size of a small tablet—which you can swallow in a jiffy."

"Chewing isn't tiresome; it's fun, maintained the Woozy. "I always chew the honey-bees when I catch them. Give me some bread and cheese, Ojo."

"No, no! You've already eaten a big dinner!" protested the Shaggy Man.

"May be," answered the Woozy; "but I guess I'll fool myself by munching some bread and cheese. I may not be hungry, having eaten all those things you gave me, but I consider this eating business a matter of taste, and I like to realize what's going into me."

Ojo gave the beast what he wanted, but the Shaggy Man shook his shaggy head reproachfully and said there was no animal so obstinate or hard to convince as a Woozy.

At this moment a patter of footsteps was heard, and looking up they saw the live phonograph standing before them. It seemed to have passed through many adventures since Ojo and his comrades last saw the machine, for the varnish of its wooden case was all marred and dented and scratched in a way that gave it an aged and disreputable appearance.

"Dear me!" exclaimed Ojo, staring hard. "What has happened to you?"

"Nothing much," replied the phonograph in a sad and depressed voice. "I've had enough things thrown at me, since I left you, to stock a department store and furnish half a dozen bargain-counters."

"Are you so broken up that you can't play?" asked Scraps.

"No; I still am able to grind out delicious music. Just now I've a record on tap that is really superb," said the phonograph, growing more cheerful.

"That is too bad," remarked Ojo. "We've no objection to you as a machine, you know; but as a music-maker we hate you."

"Then why was I ever invented?" demanded the machine, in a tone of indignant protest.

They looked at one another inquiringly, but no one could answer such a puzzling question. Finally the Shaggy Man said:

"I'd like to hear the phonograph play."

Ojo sighed. "We've been very happy since we met you, sir," he said.

"I know. But a little misery, at times, makes one appreciate happiness more. Tell me, Phony, what is this record like, which you say you have on tap?"

"It's a popular song, sir. In all civilized lands the common people have gone wild over it."

"Makes civilized folks wild folks, eh? Then it's dangerous."

"Wild with joy, I mean," explained the phonograph. "Listen. This song will prove a rare treat to you, I know. It made the author rich—for an author. It is called 'My Lulu.'"

Then the phonograph began to play. A strain of odd, jerky sounds was followed by these words, sung by a man through his nose with great vigor of expression:

"Ah wants mah Lulu, mah coal-black Lulu;   Ah wants mah loo-loo, loo-loo, loo-loo, Lu!   Ah loves mah Lulu, mah coal-black Lulu,   There ain't nobody else loves loo-loo, Lu!"

"Here—shut that off!" cried the Shaggy Man, springing to his feet. "What do you mean by such impertinence?"

"It's the latest popular song," declared the phonograph, speaking in a sulky tone of voice.

"A popular song?"

"Yes. One that the feeble-minded can remember the words of and those ignorant of music can whistle or sing. That makes a popular song popular, and the time is coming when it will take the place of all other songs."

"That time won't come to us, just yet," said the Shaggy Man, sternly: "I'm something of a singer myself, and I don't intend to be throttled by any Lulus like your coal-black one. I shall take you all apart, Mr. Phony, and scatter your pieces far and wide over the country, as a matter of kindness to the people you might meet if allowed to run around loose. Having performed this painful duty I shall—"

But before he could say more the phonograph turned and dashed up the road as fast as its four table-legs could carry it, and soon it had entirely disappeared from their view.

The Shaggy Man sat down again and seemed well pleased. "Some one else will save me the trouble of scattering that phonograph," said he; "for it is not possible that such a music-maker can last long in the Land of Oz. When you are rested, friends, let us go on our way."

During the afternoon the travelers found themselves in a lonely and uninhabited part of the country. Even the fields were no longer cultivated and the country began to resemble a wilderness. The road of yellow bricks seemed to have been neglected and became uneven and more difficult to walk upon. Scrubby under-brush grew on either side of the way, while huge rocks were scattered around in abundance.

But this did not deter Ojo and his friends from trudging on, and they beguiled the journey with jokes and cheerful conversation. Toward evening they reached a crystal spring which gushed from a tall rock by the roadside and near this spring stood a deserted cabin. Said the Shaggy Man, halting here:

"We may as well pass the night here, where there is shelter for our heads and good water to drink. Road beyond here is pretty bad; worst we shall have to travel; so let's wait until morning before we tackle it."

They agreed to this and Ojo found some brushwood in the cabin and made a fire on the hearth. The fire delighted Scraps, who danced before it until Ojo warned her she might set fire to herself and burn up. After that the Patchwork Girl kept at a respectful distance from the darting flames, but the Woozy lay down before the fire like a big dog and seemed to enjoy its warmth.

For supper the Shaggy Man ate one of his tablets, but Ojo stuck to his bread and cheese as the most satisfying food. He also gave a portion to the Woozy.

When darkness came on and they sat in a circle on the cabin floor, facing the firelight—there being no furniture of any sort in the place—Ojo said to the Shaggy Man:

"Won't you tell us a story?"

"I'm not good at stories," was the reply; "but I sing like a bird."

"Raven, or crow?" asked the Glass Cat.

"Like a song bird. I'll prove it. I'll sing a song I composed myself. Don't tell anyone I'm a poet; they might want me to write a book. Don't tell 'em I can sing, or they'd want me to make records for that awful phonograph. Haven't time to be a public benefactor, so I'll just sing you this little song for your own amusement."

They were glad enough to be entertained, and listened with interest while the Shaggy Man chanted the following verses to a tune that was not unpleasant:

"I'll sing a song of Ozland,
where wondrous creatures dwell
And fruits and flowers and shady bowers abound in every dell,
Where magic is a science and where no one shows surprise
If some amazing thing takes place before his very eyes.

Our Ruler's a bewitching girl whom fairies love to please;
She's always kept her magic sceptre to enforce decrees
To make her people happy, for her heart is kind and true
And to aid the needy and distressed is what she longs to do.

358

And then there's Princess Dorothy, as sweet as any rose,
A lass from Kansas, where they don't grow fairies, I suppose;
And there's the brainy Scarecrow, with a body stuffed with straw,
Who utters words of wisdom rare that fill us all with awe.

I'll not forget Nick Chopper, the Woodman made of Tin,
Whose tender heart thinks killing time is quite a dreadful sin,
Nor old Professor Woggle-Bug, who's highly magnified
And looks so big to everyone that he is filled with pride.

Jack Pumpkinhead's a dear old chum who might be called a chump,
But won renown by riding round upon a magic Gump;

The Sawhorse is a splendid steed and though he's made of wood
He does as many thrilling stunts as any meat horse could.
And now I'll introduce a beast that ev'ryone adores—

The Cowardly Lion shakes with fear 'most ev'ry time he roars,
And yet he does the bravest things that any lion might,
Because he knows that cowardice is not considered right.

There's Tik-tok—he's a clockwork man and quite a funny sight—
He talks and walks mechanically, when he's wound up tight;

And we've a Hungry Tiger who would babies love to eat
But never does because we feed him other kinds of meat.
It's hard to name all of the freaks this noble Land's acquired;
'Twould make my song so very long that you would soon be tired;
But give attention while I mention one wise Yellow Hen

And Nine fine Tiny Piglets living in a golden pen.
Just search the whole world over—sail the seas from coast to coast—
No other nation in creation queerer folk can boast;

And now our rare museum will include a Cat of Glass,
A Woozy, and—last but not least—a crazy Patchwork Lass."

Ojo was so pleased with this song that he applauded the singer by clapping his hands, and Scraps followed suit by clapping her padded fingers together, although they made no noise. The cat pounded on the floor with her glass paws—gently, so as not to break them—and the Woozy, which had been asleep, woke up to ask what the row was about.

"I seldom sing in public, for fear they might want me to start an opera company," remarked the Shaggy Man, who was pleased to know his effort was appreciated. "Voice, just now, is a little out of training; rusty, perhaps."

"Tell me," said the Patchwork Girl earnestly, "do all those queer people you mention really live in the Land of Oz?"

"Every one of 'em. I even forgot one thing: Dorothy's Pink Kitten."

"For goodness sake!" exclaimed Bungle, sitting up and looking interested. "A Pink Kitten? How absurd! Is it glass?"

"No; just ordinary kitten."

"Then it can't amount to much. I have pink brains, and you can see 'em work."

"Dorothy's kitten is all pink—brains and all—except blue eyes. Name's Eureka. Great favorite at the royal palace," said the Shaggy Man, yawning.

The Glass Cat seemed annoyed.

"Do you think a pink kitten—common meat—is as pretty as I am?" she asked.

"Can't say. Tastes differ, you know," replied the Shaggy Man, yawning again. "But here's a pointer that may be of service to you: make friends with Eureka and you'll be solid at the palace."

"I'm solid now; solid glass."

"You don't understand," rejoined the Shaggy Man, sleepily. "Anyhow, make friends with the Pink Kitten and you'll be all right. If the Pink Kitten despises you, look out for breakers."

"Would anyone at the royal palace break a Glass Cat?"

"Might. You never can tell. Advise you to purr soft and look humble—if you can. And now I'm going to bed."

Bungle considered the Shaggy Man's advice so carefully that her pink brains were busy long after the others of the party were fast asleep.

Chapter 12 - The Giant Porcupine

Next morning they started out bright and early to follow the road of yellow bricks toward the Emerald City. The little Munchkin boy was beginning to feel tired from the long walk, and he had a great many things to think of and consider besides the events of the journey. At the wonderful Emerald City, which he would presently reach, were so many strange and curious people that he was half afraid of meeting them and wondered if they would prove friendly and kind. Above all else, he could not drive from his mind the important errand on which he had come, and he was determined to devote every energy to finding the things that were necessary to prepare the magic recipe. He believed that until dear Unc Nunkie was restored to life he could feel no joy in anything, and often he wished that Unc could be with him, to see all the astonishing things Ojo was seeing. But alas Unc Nunkie was now a marble statue in the house of the Crooked Magician and Ojo must not falter in his efforts to save him.

The country through which they were passing was still rocky and deserted, with here and there a bush or a tree to break the dreary landscape. Ojo noticed one tree, especially, because it had such long, silky leaves and was so beautiful in shape. As he approached it he studied the tree earnestly, wondering if any fruit grew on it or if it bore pretty flowers.

Suddenly he became aware that he had been looking at that tree a long time—at least for five minutes—and it had remained in the same position, although the boy had continued to walk steadily on. So he stopped short. and when he stopped, the tree and all the landscape, as well as his companions, moved on before him and left him far behind.

Ojo uttered such a cry of astonishment that it aroused the Shaggy Man, who also halted. The others then stopped, too, and walked back to the boy.

"What's wrong?" asked the Shaggy Man.

"Why, we're not moving forward a bit, no matter how fast we walk," declared Ojo. "Now that we have stopped, we are moving backward! Can't you see? Just notice that rock."

Scraps looked down at her feet and said: "The yellow bricks are not moving."

"But the whole road is," answered Ojo.

"True; quite true," agreed the Shaggy Man. "I know all about the tricks of this road, but I have been thinking of something else and didn't realize where we were."

"It will carry us back to where we started from," predicted Ojo, beginning to be nervous.

"No," replied the Shaggy Man; "it won't do that, for I know a trick to beat this tricky road. I've traveled this way before, you know. Turn around, all of you, and walk backward."

"What good will that do?" asked the cat.

"You'll find out, if you obey me," said the Shaggy Man.

So they all turned their backs to the direction in which they wished to go and began walking backward. In an instant Ojo noticed they were gaining ground and as they proceeded in this curious way they soon passed the tree which had first attracted his attention to their difficulty.

"How long must we keep this up, Shags?" asked Scraps, who was constantly tripping and tumbling down, only to get up again with a laugh at her mishap.

"Just a little way farther," replied the Shaggy Man.

A few minutes later he called to them to turn about quickly and step forward, and as they obeyed the order they found themselves treading solid ground.

"That task is well over," observed the Shaggy Man. "It's a little tiresome to walk backward, but that is the only way to pass this part of the road, which has a trick of sliding back and carrying with it anyone who is walking upon it."

With new courage and energy they now trudged forward and after a time came to a place where the road cut through a low hill, leaving high banks on either side of it. They were traveling along this cut, talking together, when the Shaggy Man seized Scraps with one arm and Ojo with another and shouted: "Stop!"

"What's wrong now?" asked the Patchwork Girl.

"See there!" answered the Shaggy Man, pointing with his finger.

Directly in the center of the road lay a motionless object that bristled all over with sharp quills, which resembled arrows. The body was as big as a ten-bushel-basket, but the projecting quills made it appear to be four times bigger.

"Well, what of it?" asked Scraps.

"That is Chiss, who causes a lot of trouble along this road," was the reply.

"Chiss! What is Chiss?

"I think it is merely an overgrown porcupine, but here in Oz they consider Chiss an evil spirit. He's different from a reg'lar porcupine, because he can throw his quills in any direction, which an American porcupine cannot do. That's what makes old Chiss so dangerous. If we get too near, he'll fire those quills at us and hurt us badly."

"Then we will be foolish to get too near," said Scraps.

"I'm not afraid," declared the Woozy. "The Chiss is cowardly, I'm sure, and if it ever heard my awful, terrible, frightful growl, it would be scared stiff."

"Oh; can you growl?" asked the Shaggy Man.

"That is the only ferocious thing about me," asserted the Woozy with evident pride. "My growl makes an earthquake blush and the thunder ashamed of itself. If I growled at that creature you call Chiss, it would immediately think the world had cracked in two and bumped against the sun and moon, and that would cause the monster to run as far and as fast as its legs could carry it."

"In that case," said the Shaggy Man, "you are now able to do us all a great favor. Please growl."

"But you forget," returned the Woozy; "my tremendous growl would also frighten you, and if you happen to have heart disease you might expire."

"True; but we must take that risk," decided the Shaggy Man, bravely. "Being warned of what is to occur we must try to bear the terrific noise of your growl; but Chiss won't expect it, and it will scare him away."

The Woozy hesitated.

"I'm fond of you all, and I hate to shock you," it said.

"Never mind," said Ojo.

"You may be made deaf."

"If so, we will forgive you."

"Very well, then," said the Woozy in a determined voice, and advanced a few steps toward the giant porcupine. Pausing to look back, it asked: "All ready?"

"All ready!" they answered.

"Then cover up your ears and brace yourselves firmly. Now, then—look out!"

The Woozy turned toward Chiss, opened wide its mouth and said:

"Quee-ee-ee-eek."

"Go ahead and growl," said Scraps.

"Why, I—I did growl!" retorted the Woozy, who seemed much astonished.

"What, that little squeak?" she cried.

"It is the most awful growl that ever was heard, on land or sea, in caverns or in the sky," protested the Woozy. "I wonder you stood the shock so well. Didn't you feel the ground tremble? I suppose Chiss is now quite dead with fright."

The Shaggy Man laughed merrily.

"Poor Wooz!" said he; "your growl wouldn't scare a fly."

The Woozy seemed to be humiliated and surprised. It hung its head a moment, as if in shame or sorrow, but then it said with renewed confidence: "Anyhow, my eyes can flash fire; and good fire, too; good enough to set fire to a fence!"

"That is true," declared Scraps; "I saw it done myself. But your ferocious growl isn't as loud as the tick of a beetle—or one of Ojo's snores when he's fast asleep."

"Perhaps," said the Woozy, humbly, "I have been mistaken about my growl. It has always sounded very fearful to me, but that may have been because it was so close to my ears."

"Never mind," Ojo said soothingly; "it is a great talent to be able to flash fire from your eyes. No one else can do that."

As they stood hesitating what to do Chiss stirred and suddenly a shower of quills came flying toward them, almost filling the air, they were so many. Scraps realized in an instant that they had gone too near to Chiss for safety, so she sprang in front of Ojo and shielded him from the darts, which stuck their points into her own body until she resembled one of those targets they shoot arrows at in archery games. The Shaggy Man dropped flat on his face to avoid the shower, but one quill struck him in the leg and went far in. As for the Glass Cat, the quills rattled off her body without making even a scratch, and the skin of the Woozy was so thick and tough that he was not hurt at all.

When the attack was over they all ran to the Shaggy Man, who was moaning and groaning, and Scraps promptly pulled the quill out of his leg. Then up he jumped and ran over to Chiss, putting his foot on the monster's neck and holding it a prisoner. The body of the great porcupine was now as smooth as leather, except for the holes where the quills had been, for it had shot every single quill in that one wicked shower.

"Let me go!" it shouted angrily. "How dare you put your foot on Chiss?"

"I'm going to do worse than that, old boy," replied the Shaggy Man. "You have annoyed travelers on this road long enough, and now I shall put an end to you."

"You can't!" returned Chiss. "Nothing can kill me, as you know perfectly well."

"Perhaps that is true," said the Shaggy Man in a tone of disappointment. "Seems to me I've been told before that you can't be killed. But if I let you go, what will you do?"

"Pick up my quills again," said Chiss in a sulky voice.

"And then shoot them at more travelers? No; that won't do. You must promise me to stop throwing quills at people."

"I won't promise anything of the sort," declared Chiss.

"Why not?"

"Because it is my nature to throw quills, and every animal must do what Nature intends it to do. It isn't fair for you to blame me. If it were wrong for me to throw quills, then I wouldn't be made with quills to throw. The proper thing for you to do is to keep out of my way."

"Why, there's some sense in that argument," admitted the Shaggy Man, thoughtfully; "but people who are strangers, and don't know you are here, won't be able to keep out of your way."

"Tell you what," said Scraps, who was trying to pull the quills out of her own body, "let's gather up all the quills and take them away with us; then old Chiss won't have any left to throw at people."

"Ah, that's a clever idea. You and Ojo must gather up the quills while I hold Chiss a prisoner; for, if I let him go, he will get some of his quills and be able to throw them again."

So Scraps and Ojo picked up all the quills and tied them in a bundle so they might easily be carried. After this the Shaggy Man released Chiss and let him go, knowing that he was harmless to injure anyone.

"It's the meanest trick I ever heard of," muttered the porcupine gloomily. "How would you like it, Shaggy Man, if I took all your shags away from you?"

"If I threw my shags and hurt people, you would be welcome to capture them," was the reply.

Then they walked on and left Chiss standing in the road sullen and disconsolate. The Shaggy Man limped as he walked, for his wound still hurt him, and Scraps was much annoyed because the quills had left a number of small holes in her patches.

When they came to a flat stone by the roadside the Shaggy Man sat down to rest, and then Ojo opened his basket and took out the bundle of charms the Crooked Magician had given him.

"I am Ojo the Unlucky," he said, "or we would never have met that dreadful porcupine. But I will see if I can find anything among these charms which will cure your leg."

Soon he discovered that one of the charms was labelled: "For flesh wounds," and this the boy separated from the others. It was only a bit of dried root, taken from some unknown shrub, but the boy rubbed it upon the wound made by the quill and in a few moments the place was healed entirely and the Shaggy Man's leg was as good as ever.

"Rub it on the holes in my patches," suggested Scraps, and Ojo tried it, but without any effect.

"The charm you need is a needle and thread," said the Shaggy Man. "But do not worry, my dear; those holes do not look badly, at all."

"They'll let in the air, and I don't want people to think I'm airy, or that I've been stuck up," said the Patchwork Girl.

"You were certainly stuck up until we pulled out those quills," observed Ojo, with a laugh.

So now they went on again and coming presently to a pond of muddy water they tied a heavy stone to the bundle of quills and sunk it to the bottom of the pond, to avoid carrying it farther.

Chapter 13 - Scraps and the Scarecrow

From here on the country improved and the desert places began to give way to fertile spots; still no houses were yet to be seen near the road. There were some hills, with valleys between them, and on reaching the top of one of these hills the travelers found before them a high wall, running to the right and the left as far as their eyes could reach. Immediately in front of them, where the wall crossed the roadway, stood a gate having stout iron bars that extended from top to bottom. They found, on coming nearer, that this gate was locked with a great padlock, rusty through lack of use.

"Well," said Scraps, "I guess we'll stop here."

"It's a good guess," replied Ojo. "Our way is barred by this great wall and gate. It looks as if no one had passed through in many years."

"Looks are deceiving," declared the Shaggy Man, laughing at their disappointed faces, "and this barrier is the most deceiving thing in all Oz."

"It prevents our going any farther, anyhow," said Scraps. "There is no one to mind the gate and let people through, and we've no key to the padlock."

"True," replied Ojo, going a little nearer to peep through the bars of the gate. "What shall we do, Shaggy Man? If we had wings we might fly over the wall, but we cannot climb it and unless we get to the Emerald City I won't be able to find the things to restore Unc Nunkie to life."

"All very true," answered the Shaggy Man, quietly; "but I know this gate, having passed through it many times."

"How?" they all eagerly inquired.

"I'll show you how," said he. He stood Ojo in the middle of the road and placed Scraps just behind him, with her padded hands on his shoulders. After the Patchwork Girl came the Woozy, who held a part of her skirt in his mouth. Then, last of all, was the Glass Cat, holding fast to the Woozy's tail with her glass jaws.

"Now," said the Shaggy Man, "you must all shut your eyes tight, and keep them shut until I tell you to open them."

"I can't," objected Scraps. "My eyes are buttons, and they won't shut."

So the Shaggy Man tied his red handkerchief over the Patchwork Girl's eyes and examined all the others to make sure they had their eyes fast shut and could see nothing.

"What's the game, anyhow—blind-man's-buff?" asked Scraps.

"Keep quiet!" commanded the Shaggy Man, sternly. "All ready? Then follow me."

He took Ojo's hand and led him forward over the road of yellow bricks, toward the gate. Holding fast to one another they all followed in a row, expecting every minute to bump against the iron bars. The Shaggy Man also had his eyes closed, but marched straight ahead, nevertheless, and after he had taken one hundred steps, by actual count, he stopped and said:

"Now you may open your eyes."

They did so, and to their astonishment found the wall and the gateway far behind them, while in front the former Blue Country of the Munchkins had given way to green fields, with pretty farm-houses scattered among them.

"That wall," explained the Shaggy Man, "is what is called an optical illusion. It is quite real while you have your eyes open, but if you are not looking at it the barrier doesn't exist at all. It's the same way with many other evils in life; they seem to exist, and yet it's all seeming and not true. You will notice that the wall—or what we thought was a wall—separates the Munchkin Country from the green country that surrounds the Emerald City, which lies exactly in the center of Oz. There are two roads of yellow bricks through the Munchkin Country, but the one we followed is the best of the two. Dorothy once traveled the other way, and met with more dangers than we did. But all our troubles are over for the present, as another day's journey will bring us to the great Emerald City."

They were delighted to know this, and proceeded with new courage. In a couple of hours they stopped at a farmhouse, where the people were very hospitable and invited them to dinner. The farm folk regarded Scraps with much curiosity but no great astonishment, for they were accustomed to seeing extraordinary people in the Land of Oz.

The woman of this house got her needle and thread and sewed up the holes made by the porcupine quills in the Patchwork Girl's body, after which Scraps was assured she looked as beautiful as ever.

"You ought to have a hat to wear," remarked the woman, "for that would keep the sun from fading the colors of your face. I have some patches and scraps put away, and if you will wait two or three days I'll make you a lovely hat that will match the rest of you."

"Never mind the hat," said Scraps, shaking her yarn braids; "it's a kind offer, but we can't stop. I can't see that my colors have faded a particle, as yet; can you?"

"Not much," replied the woman. "You are still very gorgeous, in spite of your long journey."

The children of the house wanted to keep the Glass Cat to play with, so Bungle was offered a good home if she would remain; but the cat was too much interested in Ojo's adventures and refused to stop.

"Children are rough playmates," she remarked to the Shaggy Man, "and although this home is more pleasant than that of the Crooked Magician I fear I would soon be smashed to pieces by the boys and girls."

After they had rested themselves they renewed their journey, finding the road now smooth and pleasant to walk upon and the country growing more beautiful the nearer they drew to the Emerald City.

By and by Ojo began to walk on the green grass, looking carefully around him.

"What are you trying to find?" asked Scraps.

"A six-leaved clover," said he.

"Don't do that!" exclaimed the Shaggy Man, earnestly. "It's against the Law to pick a six-leaved clover. You must wait until you get Ozma's consent."

"She wouldn't know it," declared the boy.

"Ozma knows many things," said the Shaggy Man. "In her room is a Magic Picture that shows any scene in the Land of Oz where strangers or travelers happen to be. She may be watching the picture of us even now, and noticing everything that we do."

"Does she always watch the Magic Picture?" asked Ojo.

"Not always, for she has many other things to do; but, as I said, she may be watching us this very minute."

"I don't care," said Ojo, in an obstinate tone of voice; "Ozma's only a girl."

The Shaggy Man looked at him in surprise.

"You ought to care for Ozma," said he, "if you expect to save your uncle. For, if you displease our powerful Ruler, your journey will surely prove a failure; whereas, if you make a friend of Ozma, she will gladly assist you. As for her being a girl, that is another reason why you should obey her laws, if you are courteous and polite. Everyone in Oz loves Ozma and hates her enemies, for she is as just as she is powerful."

Ojo sulked a while, but finally returned to the road and kept away from the green clover. The boy was moody and bad tempered for an hour or two afterward, because he could really see no harm in picking a six-leaved clover, if he found one, and in spite of what the Shaggy Man had said he considered Ozma's law to be unjust.

They presently came to a beautiful grove of tall and stately trees, through which the road wound in sharp curves—first one way and then another. As they were walking through this grove they heard some one in the distance singing, and the sounds grew nearer and nearer until they could distinguish the words, although the bend in the road still hid the singer. The song was something like this:

"Here's to the hale old bale of straw
That's cut from the waving grain,
The sweetest sight man ever saw
In forest, dell or plain.

It fills me with a crunkling joy
A straw-stack to behold,
For then I pad this lucky boy
With strands of yellow gold."

"Ah!" exclaimed the Shaggy Man; "here comes my friend the Scarecrow."

"What, a live Scarecrow?" asked Ojo.

"Yes; the one I told you of. He's a splendid fellow, and very intelligent. You'll like him, I'm sure."

Just then the famous Scarecrow of Oz came around the bend in the road, riding astride a wooden Sawhorse which was so small that its rider's legs nearly touched the ground.

The Scarecrow wore the blue dress of the Munchkins, in which country he was made, and on his head was set a peaked hat with a flat brim trimmed with tinkling bells. A rope was tied around his waist to hold him in shape, for he was stuffed with straw in every part of him except the top of his head, where at one time the Wizard of Oz had placed sawdust, mixed with needles and pins, to sharpen his wits. The head itself was merely a bag of cloth, fastened to the body at the neck, and on the front of this bag was painted the face—ears, eyes, nose and mouth.

The Scarecrow's face was very interesting, for it bore a comical and yet winning expression, although one eye was a bit larger than the other and ears were not mates. The Munchkin farmer who had made the Scarecrow had neglected to sew him together with close stitches and therefore some of the straw with which he was stuffed was inclined to stick out between the seams. His hands consisted of padded white gloves, with the fingers long and rather limp, and on his feet he wore Munchkin boots of blue leather with broad turns at the tops of them.

The Sawhorse was almost as curious as its rider. It had been rudely made, in the beginning, to saw logs upon, so that its body was a short length of a log, and its legs were stout branches fitted into four holes made in the body. The tail was formed by a small branch that had been left on the log, while the head was a gnarled bump on one end of the body. Two knots of wood formed the eyes, and the mouth was a gash chopped in the log. When the Sawhorse first came to life it had no ears at all, and so could not hear; but the boy who then owned him had whittled two ears out of bark and stuck them in the head, after which the Sawhorse heard very distinctly.

This queer wooden horse was a great favorite with Princess Ozma, who had caused the bottoms of its legs to be shod with plates of gold, so the wood would not wear away. Its saddle was made of cloth-of-gold richly encrusted with precious gems. It had never worn a bridle.

As the Scarecrow came in sight of the party of travelers, he reined in his wooden steed and dismounted, greeting the Shaggy Man with a smiling nod. Then he turned to stare at the Patchwork Girl in wonder, while she in turn stared at him.

"Shags," he whispered, drawing the Shaggy Man aside, "pat me into shape, there's a good fellow!"

While his friend punched and patted the Scarecrow's body, to smooth out the humps, Scraps turned to Ojo and whispered: "Roll me out, please; I've sagged down dreadfully from walking so much and men like to see a stately figure."

She then fell upon the ground and the boy rolled her back and forth like a rolling-pin, until the cotton had filled all the spaces in her patchwork covering and the body had lengthened to its fullest extent. Scraps and the Scarecrow both finished their hasty toilets at the same time, and again they faced each other.

"Allow me, Miss Patchwork," said the Shaggy Man, "to present my friend, the Right Royal Scarecrow of Oz. Scarecrow, this is Miss Scraps Patches; Scraps, this is the Scarecrow. Scarecrow—Scraps; Scraps—Scarecrow."

They both bowed with much dignity.

"Forgive me for staring so rudely," said the Scarecrow, "but you are the most beautiful sight my eyes have ever beheld."

"That is a high compliment from one who is himself so beautiful," murmured Scraps, casting down her suspender-button eyes by lowering her head. "But, tell me, good sir, are you not a trifle lumpy?"

"Yes, of course; that's my straw, you know. It bunches up, sometimes, in spite of all my efforts to keep it even. Doesn't your straw ever bunch?"

"Oh, I'm stuffed with cotton," said Scraps. "It never bunches, but it's inclined to pack down and make me sag."

"But cotton is a high-grade stuffing. I may say it is even more stylish, not to say aristocratic, than straw," said the Scarecrow politely. "Still, it is but proper that one so entrancingly lovely should have the best stuffing there is going. I—er—I'm so glad I've met you, Miss Scraps! Introduce us again, Shaggy."

"Once is enough," replied the Shaggy Man, laughing at his friend's enthusiasm.

"Then tell me where you found her, and—Dear me, what a queer cat! What are you made of—gelatine?"

"Pure glass," answered the cat, proud to have attracted the Scarecrow's attention. "I am much more beautiful than the Patchwork Girl. I'm transparent, and Scraps isn't; I've pink brains—you can see 'em work; and I've a ruby heart, finely polished, while Scraps hasn't any heart at all."

"No more have I," said the Scarecrow, shaking hands with Scraps, as if to congratulate her on the fact. "I've a friend, the Tin Woodman, who has a heart, but I find I get along pretty well without one. And so—Well, well! here's a little Munchkin boy, too. Shake hands, my little man. How are you?"

Ojo placed his hand in the flabby stuffed glove that served the Scarecrow for a hand, and the Scarecrow pressed it so cordially that the straw in his glove crackled.

Meantime, the Woozy had approached the Sawhorse and begun to sniff at it. The Sawhorse resented this familiarity and with a sudden kick pounded the Woozy squarely on its head with one gold-shod foot.

"Take that, you monster!" it cried angrily.

The Woozy never even winked.

"To be sure," he said; "I'll take anything I have to. But don't make me angry, you wooden beast, or my eyes will flash fire and burn you up."

The Sawhorse rolled its knot eyes wickedly and kicked again, but the Woozy trotted away and said to the Scarecrow:

"What a sweet disposition that creature has! I advise you to chop it up for kindling-wood and use me to ride upon. My back is flat and you can't fall off."

"I think the trouble is that you haven't been properly introduced," said the Scarecrow, regarding the Woozy with much wonder, for he had never seen such a queer animal before.

"The Sawhorse is the favorite steed of Princess Ozma, the Ruler of the Land of Oz, and he lives in a stable decorated with pearls and emeralds, at the rear of the royal palace. He is swift as the wind, untiring, and is kind to his friends. All the people of Oz respect the Sawhorse highly, and when I visit Ozma she sometimes allows me to ride him—as I am doing to-day. Now you know what an important personage the Sawhorse is, and if some one—perhaps yourself—will tell me your name, your rank and station, and your history, it will give me pleasure to relate them to the Sawhorse. This will lead to mutual respect and friendship."

The Woozy was somewhat abashed by this speech and did not know how to reply. But Ojo said:

"This square beast is called the Woozy, and he isn't of much importance except that he has three hairs growing on the tip of his tail."

The Scarecrow looked and saw that this was true.

"But," said he, in a puzzled way, "what makes those three hairs important? The Shaggy Man has thousands of hairs, but no one has ever accused him of being important."

So Ojo related the sad story of Unc Nunkie's transformation into a marble statue, and told how he had set out to find the things the Crooked Magician wanted, in order to make a charm that would restore his uncle to life. One of the requirements was three hairs from a Woozy's tail, but not being able to pull out the hairs they had been obliged to take the Woozy with them.

The Scarecrow looked grave as he listened and he shook his head several times, as if in disapproval.

"We must see Ozma about this matter," he said. "That Crooked Magician is breaking the Law by practicing magic without a license, and I'm not sure Ozma will allow him to restore your uncle to life."

"Already I have warned the boy of that," declared the Shaggy Man.

At this Ojo began to cry. "I want my Unc Nunkie!" he exclaimed. "I know how he can be restored to life, and I'm going to do it—Ozma or no Ozma! What right has this girl Ruler to keep my Unc Nunkie a statue forever?"

"Don't worry about that just now," advised the Scarecrow. "Go on to the Emerald City, and when you reach it have the Shaggy Man take you to see Dorothy. Tell her your story and I'm sure she will help you. Dorothy is Ozma's best friend, and if you can win her to your side your uncle is pretty safe to live again." Then he turned to the Woozy and said: "I'm afraid you are not important enough to be introduced to the Sawhorse, after all."

"I'm a better beast than he is," retorted the Woozy, indignantly. "My eyes can flash fire, and his can't."

"Is this true?" inquired the Scarecrow, turning to the Munchkin boy.

"Yes," said Ojo, and told how the Woozy had set fire to the fence.

"Have you any other accomplishments?" asked the Scarecrow.

"I have a most terrible growl—that is, sometimes," said the Woozy, as Scraps laughed merrily and the Shaggy Man smiled. But the Patchwork Girl's laugh made the Scarecrow forget all about the Woozy. He said to her:

"What an admirable young lady you are, and what jolly good company! We must be better acquainted, for never before have I met a girl with such exquisite coloring or such natural, artless manners."

"No wonder they call you the Wise Scarecrow," replied Scraps.

"When you arrive at the Emerald City I will see you again," continued the Scarecrow. "Just now I am going to call upon an old friend—an ordinary young lady named Jinjur—who has promised to repaint my left ear for me. You may have noticed that the paint on my left ear has peeled off and faded, which affects my hearing on that side. Jinjur always fixes me up when I get weather-worn."

"When do you expect to return to the Emerald City?" asked the Shaggy Man.

"I'll be there this evening, for I'm anxious to have a long talk with Miss Scraps. How is it, Sawhorse; are you equal to a swift run?"

"Anything that suits you suits me," returned the wooden horse.

So the Scarecrow mounted to the jeweled saddle and waved his hat, when the Sawhorse darted away so swiftly that they were out of sight in an instant.

Chapter 14 - Ojo Breaks the Law

"What a queer man," remarked the Munchkin boy, when the party had resumed its journey.

"And so nice and polite," added Scraps, bobbing her head. "I think he is the handsomest man I've seen since I came to life."

"Handsome is as handsome does," quoted the Shaggy Man; "but we must admit that no living scarecrow is handsomer. The chief merit of my friend is that he is a great thinker, and in Oz it is considered good policy to follow his advice."

"I didn't notice any brains in his head," observed the Glass Cat.

"You can't see 'em work, but they're there, all right," declared the Shaggy Man. "I hadn't much confidence in his brains myself, when first I came to Oz, for a humbug Wizard gave them to him; but I was soon convinced that the Scarecrow is really wise; and, unless his brains make him so, such wisdom is unaccountable."

"Is the Wizard of Oz a humbug?" asked Ojo.

"Not now. He was once, but he has reformed and now assists Glinda the Good, who is the Royal Sorceress of Oz and the only one licensed to practice magic or sorcery. Glinda has taught our old Wizard a good many clever things, so he is no longer a humbug."

They walked a little while in silence and then Ojo said:

"If Ozma forbids the Crooked Magician to restore Unc Nunkie to life, what shall I do?"

The Shaggy Man shook his head.

"In that case you can't do anything," he said. "But don't be discouraged yet. We will go to Princess Dorothy and tell her your troubles, and then we will let her talk to Ozma. Dorothy has the kindest little heart in the world, and she has been through so many troubles herself that she is sure to sympathize with you."

"Is Dorothy the little girl who came here from Kansas?" asked the boy.

"Yes. In Kansas she was Dorothy Gale. I used to know her there, and she brought me to the Land of Oz. But now Ozma has made her a Princess, and Dorothy's Aunt Em and Uncle Henry are here, too." Here the Shaggy Man uttered a long sigh, and then he continued: "It's a queer country, this Land of Oz; but I like it, nevertheless."

"What is queer about it?" asked Scraps.

"You, for instance," said he.

"Did you see no girls as beautiful as I am in your own country?" she inquired.

"None with the same gorgeous, variegated beauty," he confessed. "In America a girl stuffed with cotton wouldn't be alive, nor would anyone think of making a girl out of a patchwork quilt."

"What a queer country America must be!" she exclaimed in great surprise. "The Scarecrow, whom you say is wise, told me I am the most beautiful creature he has ever seen."

"I know; and perhaps you are—from a scarecrow point of view," replied the Shaggy Man; but why he smiled as he said it Scraps could not imagine.

As they drew nearer to the Emerald City the travelers were filled with admiration for the splendid scenery they beheld. Handsome houses stood on both sides of the road and each had a green lawn before it as well as a pretty flower garden.

"In another hour," said the Shaggy Man, "we shall come in sight of the walls of the Royal City."

He was walking ahead, with Scraps, and behind them came the Woozy and the Glass Cat. Ojo had lagged behind, for in spite of the warnings he had received the boy's eyes were fastened on the clover that bordered the road of yellow bricks and he was eager to discover if such a thing as a six-leaved clover really existed.

Suddenly he stopped short and bent over to examine the ground more closely. Yes; here at last was a clover with six spreading leaves. He counted them carefully, to make sure. In an instant his heart leaped with joy, for this was one of the important things he had come for—one of the things that would restore dear Unc Nunkie to life.

He glanced ahead and saw that none of his companions was looking back. Neither were any other people about, for it was midway between two houses. The temptation was too strong to be resisted.

"I might search for weeks and weeks, and never find another six-leaved clover," he told himself, and quickly plucking the stem from the plant he placed the prized clover in his basket, covering it with the other things he carried there. Then, trying to look as if nothing had happened, he hurried forward and overtook his comrades.

The Emerald City, which is the most splendid as well as the most beautiful city in any fairyland, is surrounded by a high, thick wall of green marble, polished smooth and set with glistening emeralds. There are four gates, one facing the Munchkin Country, one facing the Country of the Winkies, one facing the Country of the Quadlings and one facing the Country of the Gillikins. The Emerald City lies directly in the center of these four important countries of Oz. The gates had bars of pure gold, and on either side of each gateway were built high towers, from which floated gay banners. Other towers were set at distances along the walls, which were broad enough for four people to walk abreast upon.

This enclosure, all green and gold and glittering with precious gems, was indeed a wonderful sight to greet our travelers, who first observed it from the top of a little hill; but beyond the wall was the vast city it surrounded, and hundreds of jeweled spires, domes and minarets, flaunting flags and banners, reared their crests far above the towers of the gateways. In the center of the city our friends could see the tops of many magnificent trees, some nearly as tall as the spires of the buildings, and the Shaggy Man told them that these trees were in the royal gardens of Princess Ozma.

They stood a long time on the hilltop, feasting their eyes on the splendor of the Emerald City.

"Whee!" exclaimed Scraps, clasping her padded hands in ecstacy, "that'll do for me to live in, all right. No more of the Munchkin Country for these patches—and no more of the Crooked Magician!"

"Why, you belong to Dr. Pipt," replied Ojo, looking at her in amazement. "You were made for a servant, Scraps, so you are personal property and not your own mistress."

"Bother Dr. Pipt! If he wants me, let him come here and get me. I'll not go back to his den of my own accord; that's certain. Only one place in the Land of Oz is fit to live in, and that's the Emerald City. It's lovely! It's almost as beautiful as I am, Ojo."

"In this country," remarked the Shaggy Man, "people live wherever our Ruler tells them to. It wouldn't do to have everyone live in the Emerald City, you know, for some must plow the land and raise grains and fruits and vegetables, while others chop wood in the forests, or fish in the rivers, or herd the sheep and the cattle."

"Poor things!" said Scraps.

"I'm not sure they are not happier than the city people," replied the Shaggy Man. "There's a freedom and independence in country life that not even the Emerald City can give one. I know that lots of the city people would like to get back to the land. The Scarecrow lives in the country, and so do the Tin Woodman and Jack Pumpkinhead; yet all three would be welcome to live in Ozma's palace if they cared to. Too much splendor becomes tiresome, you know. But, if we're to reach the Emerald City before sundown, we must hurry, for it is yet a long way off."

The entrancing sight of the city had put new energy into them all and they hurried forward with lighter steps than before. There was much to interest them along the roadway, for the houses were now set more closely together and they met a good many people who were coming or going from one place or another. All these seemed happy-faced, pleasant people, who nodded graciously to the strangers as they passed, and exchanged words of greeting.

At last they reached the great gateway, just as the sun was setting and adding its red glow to the glitter of the emeralds on the green walls and spires. Somewhere inside the city a band could be heard playing sweet music; a soft, subdued hum, as of many voices, reached their ears; from the neighboring yards came the low mooing of cows waiting to be milked.

They were almost at the gate when the golden bars slid back and a tall soldier stepped out and faced them. Ojo thought he had never seen so tall a man before. The soldier wore a handsome green and gold uniform, with a tall hat in which was a waving plume, and he had a belt thickly encrusted with jewels. But the most peculiar thing about him was his long green beard, which fell far below his waist and perhaps made him seem taller than he really was.

"Halt!" said the Soldier with the Green Whiskers, not in a stern voice but rather in a friendly tone.

They halted before he spoke and stood looking at him.

"Good evening, Colonel," said the Shaggy Man. "What's the news since I left? Anything important?"

"Billina has hatched out thirteen new chickens," replied the Soldier with the Green Whiskers, "and they're the cutest little fluffy yellow balls you ever saw. The Yellow Hen is mighty proud of those children, I can tell you."

"She has a right to be," agreed the Shaggy Man. "Let me see; that's about seven thousand chicks she has hatched out; isn't it, General?"

"That, at least," was the reply. "You will have to visit Billina and congratulate her."

"It will give me pleasure to do that," said the Shaggy Man. "But you will observe that I have brought some strangers home with me. I am going to take them to see Dorothy."

"One moment, please," said the soldier, barring their way as they started to enter the gate. "I am on duty, and I have orders to execute. Is anyone in your party named Ojo the Unlucky?"

"Why, that's me!" cried Ojo, astonished at hearing his name on the lips of a stranger.

The Soldier with the Green Whiskers nodded. "I thought so," said he, "and I am sorry to announce that it is my painful duty to arrest you."

"Arrest me!" exclaimed the boy. "What for?"

"I haven't looked to see," answered the soldier. Then he drew a paper from his breast pocket and glanced at it. "Oh, yes; you are to be arrested for willfully breaking one of the Laws of Oz."

"Breaking a law!" said Scraps. "Nonsense, Soldier; you're joking."

"Not this time," returned the soldier, with a sigh. "My dear child—what are you, a rummage sale or a guess-me-quick?—in me you behold the Body-Guard of our gracious Ruler, Princess Ozma, as well as the Royal Army of Oz and the Police Force of the Emerald City."

"And only one man!" exclaimed the Patchwork Girl.

"Only one, and plenty enough. In my official positions I've had nothing to do for a good many years—so long that I began to fear I was absolutely useless—until to-day. An hour ago I was called to the presence of her Highness, Ozma of Oz, and told to arrest a boy named Ojo the Unlucky, who was journeying from the Munchkin Country to the Emerald City and would arrive in a short time. This command so astonished me that I nearly fainted, for it is the first time anyone has merited arrest since I can remember. You are rightly named Ojo the Unlucky, my poor boy, since you have broken a Law of Oz.

"But you are wrong," said Scraps. "Ozma is wrong—you are all wrong—for Ojo has broken no Law."

"Then he will soon be free again," replied the Soldier with the Green Whiskers. "Anyone accused of crime is given a fair trial by our Ruler and has every chance to prove his innocence. But just now Ozma's orders must be obeyed."

With this he took from his pocket a pair of handcuffs made of gold and set with rubies and diamonds, and these he snapped over Ojo's wrists.

Chapter 15 - Ozma's Prisoner

The boy was so bewildered by this calamity that he made no resistance at all. He knew very well he was guilty, but it surprised him that Ozma also knew it. He wondered how she had found out so soon that he had picked the six-leaved clover. He handed his basket to Scraps and said:

"Keep that, until I get out of prison. If I never get out, take it to the Crooked Magician, to whom it belongs."

The Shaggy Man had been gazing earnestly in the boy's face, uncertain whether to defend him or not; but something he read in Ojo's expression made him draw back and refuse to interfere to save him. The Shaggy Man was greatly surprised and grieved, but he knew that Ozma never made mistakes and so Ojo must really have broken the Law of Oz.

The Soldier with the Green Whiskers now led them all through the gate and into a little room built in the wall. Here sat a jolly little man, richly dressed in green and having around his neck a heavy gold chain to which a number of great golden keys were attached. This was the Guardian of the Gate and at the moment they entered his room he was playing a tune upon a mouth-organ.

"Listen!" he said, holding up his hand for silence. "I've just composed a tune called 'The Speckled Alligator.' It's in patch-time, which is much superior to rag-time, and I've composed it in honor of the Patchwork Girl, who has just arrived."

"How did you know I had arrived?" asked Scraps, much interested.

"It's my business to know who's coming, for I'm the Guardian of the Gate. Keep quiet while I play you 'The Speckled Alligator.'"

It wasn't a very bad tune, nor a very good one, but all listened respectfully while he shut his eyes and swayed his head from side to side and blew the notes from the little instrument. When it was all over the Soldier with the Green Whiskers said:

"Guardian, I have here a prisoner."

"Good gracious! A prisoner?" cried the little man, jumping up from his chair. "Which one? Not the Shaggy Man?"

"No; this boy."

"Ah; I hope his fault is as small as himself," said the Guardian of the Gate. "But what can he have done, and what made him do it?"

"Can't say," replied the soldier. "All I know is that he has broken the Law."

"But no one ever does that!"

"Then he must be innocent, and soon will be released. I hope you are right, Guardian. Just now I am ordered to take him to prison. Get me a prisoner's robe from your Official Wardrobe."

The Guardian unlocked a closet and took from it a white robe, which the soldier threw over Ojo. It covered him from head to foot, but had two holes just in front of his eyes, so he could see where to go. In this attire the boy presented a very quaint appearance.

As the Guardian unlocked a gate leading from his room into the streets of the Emerald City, the Shaggy Man said to Scraps:

"I think I shall take you directly to Dorothy, as the Scarecrow advised, and the Glass Cat and the Woozy may come with us. Ojo must go to prison with the Soldier with the Green Whiskers, but he will be well treated and you need not worry about him."

"What will they do with him?" asked Scraps.

"That I cannot tell. Since I came to the Land of Oz no one has ever been arrested or imprisoned—until Ojo broke the Law."

"Seems to me that girl Ruler of yours is making a big fuss over nothing," remarked Scraps, tossing her yarn hair out of her eyes with a jerk of her patched head. "I don't know what Ojo has done, but it couldn't be anything very bad, for you and I were with him all the time."

The Shaggy Man made no reply to this speech and presently the Patchwork Girl forgot all about Ojo in her admiration of the wonderful city she had entered.

They soon separated from the Munchkin boy, who was led by the Soldier with the Green Whiskers down a side street toward the prison. Ojo felt very miserable and greatly ashamed of himself, but he was beginning to grow angry because he was treated in such a disgraceful manner. Instead of entering the splendid Emerald City as a respectable traveler who was entitled to a welcome and to hospitality, he was being brought in as a criminal, handcuffed and in a robe that told all he met of his deep disgrace.

Ojo was by nature gentle and affectionate and if he had disobeyed the Law of Oz it was to restore his dear Unc Nunkie to life. His fault was more thoughtless than wicked, but that did not alter the fact that he had committed a fault. At first he had felt sorrow and remorse, but the more he thought about the unjust treatment he had received—unjust merely because he considered it so—the more he resented his arrest, blaming Ozma for making foolish laws and then punishing folks who broke them. Only a six-leaved clover! A tiny green plant growing neglected and trampled under foot. What harm could there be in picking it? Ojo began to think Ozma must be a very bad and oppressive Ruler for such a lovely fairyland as Oz. The Shaggy Man said the people loved her; but how could they?

The little Munchkin boy was so busy thinking these things—which many guilty prisoners have thought before him—that he scarcely noticed all the splendor of the city streets through which they passed. Whenever they met any of the happy, smiling people, the boy turned his head away in shame, although none knew who was beneath the robe.

By and by they reached a house built just beside the great city wall, but in a quiet, retired place. It was a pretty house, neatly painted and with many windows. Before it was a garden filled with blooming flowers. The Soldier with the Green Whiskers led Ojo up the gravel path to the front door, on which he knocked.

A woman opened the door and, seeing Ojo in his white robe, exclaimed:

"Goodness me! A prisoner at last. But what a small one, Soldier."

"The size doesn't matter, Tollydiggle, my dear. The fact remains that he is a prisoner," said the soldier. "And, this being the prison, and you the jailer, it is my duty to place the prisoner in your charge."

"True. Come in, then, and I'll give you a receipt for him."

They entered the house and passed through a hall to a large circular room, where the woman pulled the robe off from Ojo and looked at him with kindly interest. The boy, on his part, was gazing around him in amazement, for never had he dreamed of such a magnificent apartment as this in which he stood. The roof of the dome was of colored glass, worked into beautiful designs. The walls were paneled with plates of gold decorated with gems of great size and many colors, and upon the tiled floor were soft rugs delightful to walk upon. The furniture was framed in gold and upholstered in satin brocade and it consisted of easy chairs, divans and stools in great variety. Also there were several tables with mirror tops and cabinets filled with rare and curious things. In one place a case filled with books stood against the wall, and elsewhere Ojo saw a cupboard containing all sorts of games.

"May I stay here a little while before I go to prison?" asked the boy, pleadingly.

"Why, this is your prison," replied Tollydiggle, "and in me behold your jailor. Take off those handcuffs, Soldier, for it is impossible for anyone to escape from this house."

"I know that very well," replied the soldier and at once unlocked the handcuffs and released the prisoner.

The woman touched a button on the wall and lighted a big chandelier that hung suspended from the ceiling, for it was growing dark outside. Then she seated herself at a desk and asked:

"What name?"

"Ojo the Unlucky," answered the Soldier with the Green Whiskers.

"Unlucky? Ah, that accounts for it," said she. "What crime?"

"Breaking a Law of Oz."

"All right. There's your receipt, Soldier; and now I'm responsible for the prisoner. I'm glad of it, for this is the first time I've ever had anything to do, in my official capacity," remarked the jailer, in a pleased tone.

"It's the same with me, Tollydiggle," laughed the soldier. "But my task is finished and I must go and report to Ozma that I've done my duty like a faithful Police Force, a loyal Army and an honest Body-Guard—as I hope I am."

Saying this, he nodded farewell to Tollydiggle and Ojo and went away.

"Now, then," said the woman briskly, "I must get you some supper, for you are doubtless hungry. What would you prefer: planked whitefish, omelet with jelly or mutton-chops with gravy?"

Ojo thought about it. Then he said: "I'll take the chops, if you please."

"Very well; amuse yourself while I'm gone; I won't be long," and then she went out by a door and left the prisoner alone.

Ojo was much astonished, for not only was this unlike any prison he had ever heard of, but he was being treated more as a guest than a criminal. There were many windows and they had no locks. There were three doors to the room and none were bolted. He cautiously opened one of the doors and found it led into a hallway. But he had no intention of trying to escape. If his jailor was willing to trust him in this way he would not betray her trust, and moreover a hot supper was being prepared for him and his prison was very pleasant and comfortable. So he took a book from the case and sat down in a big chair to look at the pictures.

This amused him until the woman came in with a large tray and spread a cloth on one of the tables. Then she arranged his supper, which proved the most varied and delicious meal Ojo had ever eaten in his life.

Tollydiggle sat near him while he ate, sewing on some fancy work she held in her lap. When he had finished she cleared the table and then read to him a story from one of the books.

"Is this really a prison?" he asked, when she had finished reading.

"Indeed it is," she replied. "It is the only prison in the Land of Oz."

"And am I a prisoner?"

"Bless the child! Of course."

"Then why is the prison so fine, and why are you so kind to me?" he earnestly asked.

Tollydiggle seemed surprised by the question, but she presently answered:

"We consider a prisoner unfortunate. He is unfortunate in two ways—because he has done something wrong and because he is deprived of his liberty. Therefore we should treat him kindly, because of his misfortune, for otherwise he would become hard and bitter and would not be sorry he had done wrong. Ozma thinks that one who has committed a fault did so because he was not strong and brave; therefore she puts him in prison to make him strong and brave. When that is accomplished he is no longer a prisoner, but a good and loyal citizen and everyone is glad that he is now strong enough to resist doing wrong. You see, it is kindness that makes one strong and brave; and so we are kind to our prisoners."

Ojo thought this over very carefully. "I had an idea," said he, "that prisoners were always treated harshly, to punish them."

"That would be dreadful!" cried Tollydiggle. "Isn't one punished enough in knowing he has done wrong? Don't you wish, Ojo, with all your heart, that you had not been disobedient and broken a Law of Oz?"

"I—I hate to be different from other people," he admitted.

"Yes; one likes to be respected as highly as his neighbors are," said the woman. "When you are tried and found guilty, you will be obliged to make amends, in some way. I don't know just what Ozma will do to you, because this is the first time one of us has broken a Law; but you may be sure she will be just and merciful. Here in the Emerald City people are too happy and contented ever to do wrong; but perhaps you came from some faraway corner of our land, and having no love for Ozma carelessly broke one of her Laws."

"Yes," said Ojo, "I've lived all my life in the heart of a lonely forest, where I saw no one but dear Unc Nunkie."

"I thought so," said Tollydiggle. "But now we have talked enough, so let us play a game until bedtime."

Chapter 16 - Princess Dorothy

Dorothy Gale was sitting in one of her rooms in the royal palace, while curled up at her feet was a little black dog with a shaggy coat and very bright eyes. She wore a plain white frock, without any jewels or other ornaments except an emerald-green hair-ribbon, for Dorothy was a simple little girl and had not been in the least spoiled by the magnificence surrounding her. Once the child had lived on the Kansas prairies, but she seemed marked for adventure, for she had made several trips to the Land of Oz before she came to live there for good. Her very best friend was the beautiful Ozma of Oz, who loved Dorothy so well that she kept her in her own palace, so as to be near her. The girl's Uncle Henry and Aunt Em—the only relatives she had in the world—had also been brought here by Ozma and given a pleasant home. Dorothy knew almost everybody in Oz, and it was she who had discovered the Scarecrow, the Tin Woodman and the Cowardly Lion, as well as Tik-tok the Clockwork Man. Her life was very pleasant now, and although she had been made a Princess of Oz by her friend Ozma she did not care much to be a Princess and remained as sweet as when she had been plain Dorothy Gale of Kansas.

Dorothy was reading in a book this evening when Jellia Jamb, the favorite servant-maid of the palace, came to say that the Shaggy Man wanted to see her.

"All right," said Dorothy; "tell him to come right up."

"But he has some queer creatures with him—some of the queerest I've ever laid eyes on," reported Jellia.

"Never mind; let 'em all come up," replied Dorothy.

But when the door opened to admit not only the Shaggy Man, but Scraps, the Woozy and the Glass Cat, Dorothy jumped up and looked at her strange visitors in amazement. The Patchwork Girl was the most curious of all and Dorothy was uncertain at first whether Scraps was really alive or only a dream or a nightmare. Toto, her dog, slowly uncurled himself and going to the Patchwork Girl sniffed at her inquiringly; but soon he lay down again, as if to say he had no interest in such an irregular creation.

"You're a new one to me," Dorothy said reflectively, addressing the Patchwork Girl. "I can't imagine where you've come from."

"Who, me?" asked Scraps, looking around the pretty room instead of at the girl. "Oh, I came from a bed-quilt, I guess. That's what they say, anyhow. Some call it a crazy-quilt and some a patchwork quilt. But my name is Scraps—and now you know all about me."

"Not quite all," returned Dorothy with a smile. "I wish you'd tell me how you came to be alive."

"That's an easy job," said Scraps, sitting upon a big upholstered chair and making the springs bounce her up and down. "Margolotte wanted a slave, so she made me out of an old bed-quilt she didn't use. Cotton stuffing, suspender-button eyes, red velvet tongue, pearl beads for teeth. The Crooked Magician made a Powder of Life, sprinkled me with it and—here I am. Perhaps you've noticed my different colors. A very refined and educated gentleman named the Scarecrow, whom I met, told me I am the most beautiful creature in all Oz, and I believe it."

"Oh! Have you met our Scarecrow, then?" asked Dorothy, a little puzzled to understand the brief history related.

"Yes; isn't he jolly?"

"The Scarecrow has many good qualities," replied Dorothy. "But I'm sorry to hear all this 'bout the Crooked Magician. Ozma'll be mad as hops when she hears he's been doing magic again. She told him not to."

"He only practices magic for the benefit of his own family," explained Bungle, who was keeping at a respectful distance from the little black dog.

"Dear me," said Dorothy; "I hadn't noticed you before. Are you glass, or what?"

"I'm glass, and transparent, too, which is more than can be said of some folks," answered the cat. "Also I have some lovely pink brains; you can see 'em work."

"Oh; is that so? Come over here and let me see."

The Glass Cat hesitated, eyeing the dog.

"Send that beast away and I will," she said.

"Beast! Why, that's my dog Toto, an' he's the kindest dog in all the world. Toto knows a good many things, too; 'most as much as I do, I guess."

"Why doesn't he say anything?" asked Bungle.

"He can't talk, not being a fairy dog," explained Dorothy. "He's just a common United States dog; but that's a good deal; and I understand him, and he understands me, just as well as if he could talk."

Toto, at this, got up and rubbed his head softly against Dorothy's hand, which she held out to him, and he looked up into her face as if he had understood every word she had said.

"This cat, Toto," she said to him, "is made of glass, so you mustn't bother it, or chase it, any more than you do my Pink Kitten. It's prob'ly brittle and might break if it bumped against anything."

"Woof!" said Toto, and that meant he understood.

The Glass Cat was so proud of her pink brains that she ventured to come close to Dorothy, in order that the girl might "see 'em work." This was really interesting, but when Dorothy patted the cat she found the glass cold and hard and unresponsive, so she decided at once that Bungle would never do for a pet.

"What do you know about the Crooked Magician who lives on the mountain?" asked Dorothy.

"He made me," replied the cat; "so I know all about him. The Patchwork Girl is new—three or four days old—but I've lived with Dr. Pipt for years; and, though I don't much care for him, I will say that he has always refused to work magic for any of the people who come to his house. He thinks there's no harm in doing magic things for his own family, and he made me out of glass because the meat cats drink too much milk. He also made Scraps come to life so she could do the housework for his wife Margolotte."

"Then why did you both leave him?" asked Dorothy.

"I think you'd better let me explain that," interrupted the Shaggy Man, and then he told Dorothy all of Ojo's story and how Unc Nunkie and Margolotte had accidentally been turned to marble by the Liquid of Petrifaction. Then he related how the boy had started out in search of the things needed to make the magic charm, which would restore the unfortunates to life, and how he had found the Woozy and taken him along because he could not pull the three hairs out of its tail. Dorothy listened to all this with much interest, and thought that so far Ojo had acted very well. But when the Shaggy Man told her of the Munchkin boy's arrest by the Soldier with the Green Whiskers, because he was accused of wilfully breaking a Law of Oz, the little girl was greatly shocked.

"What do you s'pose he's done?" she asked.

"I fear he has picked a six-leaved clover," answered the Shaggy Man, sadly. "I did not see him do it, and I warned him that to do so was against the Law; but perhaps that is what he did, nevertheless."

"I'm sorry 'bout that," said Dorothy gravely, "for now there will be no one to help his poor uncle and Margolotte 'cept this Patchwork Girl, the Woozy and the Glass Cat."

"Don't mention it," said Scraps. "That's no affair of mine. Margolotte and Unc Nunkie are perfect strangers to me, for the moment I came to life they came to marble."

"I see," remarked Dorothy with a sigh of regret; "the woman forgot to give you a heart."

"I'm glad she did," retorted the Patchwork Girl. "A heart must be a great annoyance to one. It makes a person feel sad or sorry or devoted or sympathetic—all of which sensations interfere with one's happiness."

"I have a heart," murmured the Glass Cat. "It's made of a ruby; but I don't imagine I shall let it bother me about helping Unc Nunkie and Margolotte."

"That's a pretty hard heart of yours," said Dorothy. "And the Woozy, of course—"

"Why, as for me," observed the Woozy, who was reclining on the floor with his legs doubled under him, so that he looked much like a square box, "I have never seen those unfortunate people you are speaking of, and yet I am sorry for them, having at times been unfortunate myself. When I was shut up in that forest I longed for some one to help me, and by and by Ojo came and did help me. So I'm willing to help his uncle. I'm only a stupid beast, Dorothy, but I can't help that, and if you'll tell me what to do to help Ojo and his uncle, I'll gladly do it."

Dorothy walked over and patted the Woozy on his square head.

"You're not pretty," she said, "but I like you. What are you able to do; anything 'special?"

"I can make my eyes flash fire—real fire—when I'm angry. When anyone says: 'Krizzle-Kroo' to me I get angry, and then my eyes flash fire."

"I don't see as fireworks could help Ojo's uncle," remarked Dorothy. "Can you do anything else?"

"I—I thought I had a very terrifying growl," said the Woozy, with hesitation; "but perhaps I was mistaken."

"Yes," said the Shaggy Man, "you were certainly wrong about that." Then he turned to Dorothy and added: "What will become of the Munchkin boy?"

"I don't know," she said, shaking her head thoughtfully. "Ozma will see him 'bout it, of course, and then she'll punish him. But how, I don't know, 'cause no one ever has been punished in Oz since I knew anything about the place. Too bad, Shaggy Man, isn't it?"

While they were talking Scraps had been roaming around the room and looking at all the pretty things it contained. She had carried Ojo's basket in her hand, until now, when she decided to see what was inside it. She found the bread and cheese, which she had no use for, and the bundle of charms, which were curious but quite a mystery to her. Then, turning these over, she came upon the six-leaved clover which the boy had plucked.

Scraps was quick-witted, and although she had no heart she recognized the fact that Ojo was her first friend. She knew at once that because the boy had taken the clover he had been imprisoned, and she understood that Ojo had given her the basket so they would not find the clover in his possession and have proof of his crime. So, turning her head to see that no one noticed her, she took the clover from the basket and dropped it into a golden vase that stood on Dorothy's table. Then she came forward and said to Dorothy:

"I wouldn't care to help Ojo's uncle, but I will help Ojo. He did not break the Law—no one can prove he did—and that green-whiskered soldier had no right to arrest him."

"Ozma ordered the boy's arrest," said Dorothy, "and of course she knew what she was doing. But if you can prove Ojo is innocent they will set him free at once."

"They'll have to prove him guilty, won't they?" asked Scraps.

"I s'pose so."

"Well, they can't do that," declared the Patchwork Girl.

As it was nearly time for Dorothy to dine with Ozma, which she did every evening, she rang for a servant and ordered the Woozy taken to a nice room and given plenty of such food as he liked best.

"That's honey-bees," said the Woozy.

"You can't eat honey-bees, but you'll be given something just as nice," Dorothy told him. Then she had the Glass Cat taken to another room for the night and the Patchwork Girl she kept in one of her own rooms, for she was much interested in the strange creature and wanted to talk with her again and try to understand her better.

Chapter 17 - Ozma and Her Friends

The Shaggy Man had a room of his own in the royal palace, so there he went to change his shaggy suit of clothes for another just as shaggy but not so dusty from travel. He selected a costume of pea-green and pink satin and velvet, with embroidered shags on all the edges and iridescent pearls for ornaments. Then he bathed in an alabaster pool and brushed his shaggy hair and whiskers the wrong way to make them still more shaggy. This accomplished, and arrayed in his splendid shaggy garments, he went to Ozma's banquet hall and found the Scarecrow, the Wizard and Dorothy already assembled there. The Scarecrow had made a quick trip and returned to the Emerald City with his left ear freshly painted.

A moment later, while they all stood in waiting, a servant threw open a door, the orchestra struck up a tune and Ozma of Oz entered.

Much has been told and written concerning the beauty of person and character of this sweet girl Ruler of the Land of Oz—the richest, the happiest and most delightful fairyland of which we have any knowledge. Yet with all her queenly qualities Ozma was a real girl and enjoyed the things in life that other real girls enjoy. When she sat on her splendid emerald throne in the great Throne Room of her palace and made laws and settled disputes and tried to keep all her subjects happy and contented, she was as dignified and demure as any queen might be; but when she had thrown aside her jeweled robe of state and her sceptre, and had retired to her private apartments, the girl—joyous, light-hearted and free—replaced the sedate Ruler.

In the banquet hall to-night were gathered only old and trusted friends, so here Ozma was herself—a mere girl. She greeted Dorothy with a kiss, the Shaggy Man with a smile, the little old Wizard with a friendly handshake and then she pressed the Scarecrow's stuffed arm and cried merrily:

"What a lovely left ear! Why, it's a hundred times better than the old one."

"I'm glad you like it," replied the Scarecrow, well pleased. "Jinjur did a neat job, didn't she? And my hearing is now perfect. Isn't it wonderful what a little paint will do, if it's properly applied?"

"It really is wonderful," she agreed, as they all took their seats; "but the Sawhorse must have made his legs twinkle to have carried you so far in one day. I didn't expect you back before to-morrow, at the earliest."

"Well," said the Scarecrow, "I met a charming girl on the road and wanted to see more of her, so I hurried back." Ozma laughed.

"I know," she returned; "it's the Patchwork Girl. She is certainly bewildering, if not strictly beautiful."

"Have you seen her, then?" the straw man eagerly asked.

"Only in my Magic Picture, which shows me all scenes of interest in the Land of Oz."

"I fear the picture didn't do her justice," said the Scarecrow.

"It seemed to me that nothing could be more gorgeous," declared Ozma. "Whoever made that patchwork quilt, from which Scraps was formed, must have selected the gayest and brightest bits of cloth that ever were woven."

"I am glad you like her," said the Scarecrow in a satisfied tone. Although the straw man did not eat, not being made so he could, he often dined with Ozma and her companions, merely for the pleasure of talking with them. He sat at the table and had a napkin and plate, but the servants knew better than to offer him food. After a little while he asked: "Where is the Patchwork Girl now?"

"In my room," replied Dorothy. "I've taken a fancy to her; she's so queer and—and—uncommon."

"She's half crazy, I think," added the Shaggy Man.

"But she is so beautiful!" exclaimed the Scarecrow, as if that fact disarmed all criticism. They all laughed at his enthusiasm, but the Scarecrow was quite serious. Seeing that he was interested in Scraps they forbore to say anything against her. The little band of friends Ozma had gathered around her was so quaintly assorted that much care must be exercised to avoid hurting their feelings or making any one of them unhappy. It was this considerate kindness that held them close friends and enabled them to enjoy one another's society.

Another thing they avoided was conversing on unpleasant subjects, and for that reason Ojo and his troubles were not mentioned during the dinner. The Shaggy Man, however, related his adventures with the monstrous plants which had seized and enfolded the travelers, and told how he had robbed Chiss, the giant porcupine, of the quills which it was accustomed to throw at people. Both Dorothy and Ozma were pleased with this exploit and thought it served Chiss right.

Then they talked of the Woozy, which was the most remarkable animal any of them had ever before seen—except, perhaps, the live Sawhorse. Ozma had never known that her dominions contained such a thing as a Woozy, there being but one in existence and this being confined in his forest for many years. Dorothy said she believed the Woozy was a good beast, honest and faithful; but she added that she did not care much for the Glass Cat.

"Still," said the Shaggy Man, "the Glass Cat is very pretty and if she were not so conceited over her pink brains no one would object to her as a companion."

The Wizard had been eating silently until now, when he looked up and remarked:

"That Powder of Life which is made by the Crooked Magician is really a wonderful thing. But Dr. Pipt does not know its true value and he uses it in the most foolish ways."

"I must see about that," said Ozma, gravely. Then she smiled again and continued in a lighter tone: "It was Dr. Pipt's famous Powder of Life that enabled me to become the Ruler of Oz."

"I've never heard that story," said the Shaggy Man, looking at Ozma questioningly.

"Well, when I was a baby girl I was stolen by an old Witch named Mombi and transformed into a boy," began the girl Ruler. "I did not know who I was and when I grew big enough to work, the Witch made me wait upon her and carry wood for the fire and hoe in the garden. One day she came back from a journey bringing some of the Powder of Life, which Dr. Pipt had given her. I had made a pumpkin-headed man and set it up in her path to frighten her, for I was fond of fun and hated the Witch. But she knew what the figure was and to test her Powder of Life she sprinkled some of it on the man I had made. It came to life and is now our dear friend Jack Pumpkinhead. That night I ran away with Jack to escape punishment, and I took old Mombi's Powder of Life with me. During our journey we came upon a wooden Sawhorse standing by the road and I used the magic powder to bring it to life. The Sawhorse has been with me ever since. When I got to the Emerald City the good Sorceress, Glinda, knew who I was and restored me to my proper person, when I became the rightful Ruler of this land. So you see had not old Mombi brought home the Powder of Life I might never have run away from her and become Ozma of Oz, nor would we have had Jack Pumpkinhead and the Sawhorse to comfort and amuse us."

That story interested the Shaggy Man very much, as well as the others, who had often heard it before. The dinner being now concluded, they all went to Ozma's drawing-room, where they passed a pleasant evening before it came time to retire.

Chapter 18 - Ojo is Forgiven

The next morning the Soldier with the Green Whiskers went to the prison and took Ojo away to the royal palace, where he was summoned to appear before the girl Ruler for judgment. Again the soldier put upon the boy the jeweled handcuffs and white prisoner's robe with the peaked top and holes for the eyes. Ojo was so ashamed, both of his disgrace and the fault he had committed, that he was glad to be covered up in this way, so that people could not see him or know who he was. He followed the Soldier with the Green Whiskers very willingly, anxious that his fate might be decided as soon as possible.

The inhabitants of the Emerald City were polite people and never jeered at the unfortunate; but it was so long since they had seen a prisoner that they cast many curious looks toward the boy and many of them hurried away to the royal palace to be present during the trial.

When Ojo was escorted into the great Throne Room of the palace he found hundreds of people assembled there. In the magnificent emerald throne, which sparkled with countless jewels, sat Ozma of Oz in her Robe of State, which was embroidered with emeralds and pearls. On her right, but a little lower, was Dorothy, and on her left the Scarecrow. Still lower, but nearly in front of Ozma, sat the wonderful Wizard of Oz and on a small table beside him was the golden vase from Dorothy's room, into which Scraps had dropped the stolen clover.

At Ozma's feet crouched two enormous beasts, each the largest and most powerful of its kind. Although these beasts were quite free, no one present was alarmed by them; for the Cowardly Lion and the Hungry Tiger were well known and respected in the Emerald City and they always guarded the Ruler when she held high court in the Throne Room. There was still another beast present, but this one Dorothy held in her arms, for it was her constant companion, the little dog Toto. Toto knew the Cowardly Lion and the Hungry Tiger and often played and romped with them, for they were good friends.

Seated on ivory chairs before Ozma, with a clear space between them and the throne, were many of the nobility of the Emerald City, lords and ladies in beautiful costumes, and officials of the kingdom in the royal uniforms of Oz. Behind these courtiers were others of less importance, filling the great hall to the very doors.

At the same moment that the Soldier with the Green Whiskers arrived with Ojo, the Shaggy Man entered from a side door, escorting the Patchwork Girl, the Woozy and the Glass Cat. All these came to the vacant space before the throne and stood facing the Ruler.

"Hullo, Ojo," said Scraps; "how are you?"

"All right," he replied; but the scene awed the boy and his voice trembled a little with fear. Nothing could awe the Patchwork Girl, and although the Woozy was somewhat uneasy in these splendid surroundings the Glass Cat was delighted with the sumptuousness of the court and the impressiveness of the occasion—pretty big words but quite expressive.

At a sign from Ozma the soldier removed Ojo's white robe and the boy stood face to face with the girl who was to decide his punishment. He saw at a glance how lovely and sweet she was, and his heart gave a bound of joy, for he hoped she would be merciful.

Ozma sat looking at the prisoner a long time. Then she said gently:

"One of the Laws of Oz forbids anyone to pick a six-leaved clover. You are accused of having broken this Law, even after you had been warned not to do so."

Ojo hung his head and while he hesitated how to reply the Patchwork Girl stepped forward and spoke for him.

"All this fuss is about nothing at all," she said, facing Ozma unabashed. "You can't prove he picked the six-leaved clover, so you've no right to accuse him of it. Search him, if you like, but you won't find the clover; look in his basket and you'll find it's not there. He hasn't got it, so I demand that you set this poor Munchkin boy free."

The people of Oz listened to this defiance in amazement and wondered at the queer Patchwork Girl who dared talk so boldly to their Ruler. But Ozma sat silent and motionless and it was the little Wizard who answered Scraps.

"So the clover hasn't been picked, eh?" he said. "I think it has. I think the boy hid it in his basket, and then gave the basket to you. I also think you dropped the clover into this vase, which stood in Princess Dorothy's room, hoping to get rid of it so it would not prove the boy guilty. You're a stranger here, Miss Patches, and so you don't know that nothing can be hidden from our powerful Ruler's Magic Picture—nor from the watchful eyes of the humble Wizard of Oz. Look, all of you!" With these words he waved his hands toward the vase on the table, which Scraps now noticed for the first time.

From the mouth of the vase a plant sprouted, slowly growing before their eyes until it became a beautiful bush, and on the topmost branch appeared the six-leaved clover which Ojo had unfortunately picked.

The Patchwork Girl looked at the clover and said: "Oh, so you've found it. Very well; prove he picked it, if you can."

Ozma turned to Ojo.

"Did you pick the six-leaved clover?" she asked.

"Yes," he replied. "I knew it was against the Law, but I wanted to save Unc Nunkie and I was afraid if I asked your consent to pick it you would refuse me."

"What caused you to think that?" asked the Ruler.

"Why, it seemed to me a foolish law, unjust and unreasonable. Even now I can see no harm in picking a six-leaved clover. And I—I had not seen the Emerald City, then, nor you, and I thought a girl who would make such a silly Law would not be likely to help anyone in trouble."

Ozma regarded him musingly, her chin resting upon her hand; but she was not angry. On the contrary she smiled a little at her thoughts and then grew sober again.

"I suppose a good many laws seem foolish to those people who do not understand them," she said; "but no law is ever made without some purpose, and that purpose is usually to protect all the people and guard their welfare. As you are a stranger, I will explain this Law which to you seems so foolish. Years ago there were many Witches and Magicians in the Land of Oz, and one of the things they often used in making their magic charms and transformations was a six-leaved clover. These Witches and Magicians caused so much trouble among my people, often using their powers for evil rather than good, that I decided to forbid anyone to practice magic or sorcery except Glinda the Good and her assistant, the Wizard of Oz, both of whom I can trust to use their arts only to benefit my people and to make them happier. Since I issued that Law the Land of Oz has been far more peaceful and quiet; but I learned that some of the Witches and Magicians were still practicing magic on the sly and using the six-leaved clovers to make their potions and charms. Therefore I made another Law forbidding anyone from plucking a six-leaved clover or from gathering other plants and herbs which the Witches boil in their kettles to work magic with. That has almost put an end to wicked sorcery in our land, so you see the Law was not a foolish one, but wise and just; and, in any event, it is wrong to disobey a Law."

Ojo knew she was right and felt greatly mortified to realize he had acted and spoken so ridiculously. But he raised his head and looked Ozma in the face, saying:

"I am sorry I have acted wrongly and broken your Law. I did it to save Unc Nunkie, and thought I would not be found out. But I am guilty of this act and whatever punishment you think I deserve I will suffer willingly."

Ozma smiled more brightly, then, and nodded graciously.

"You are forgiven," she said. "For, although you have committed a serious fault, you are now penitent and I think you have been punished enough. Soldier, release Ojo the Lucky and—"

"I beg your pardon; I'm Ojo the Unlucky," said the boy.

"At this moment you are lucky," said she. "Release him, Soldier, and let him go free."

The people were glad to hear Ozma's decree and murmured their approval. As the royal audience was now over, they began to leave the Throne Room and soon there were none remaining except Ojo and his friends and Ozma and her favorites.

The girl Ruler now asked Ojo to sit down and tell her all his story, which he did, beginning at the time he had left his home in the forest and ending with his arrival at the Emerald City and his arrest. Ozma listened attentively and was thoughtful for some moments after the boy had finished speaking. Then she said:

"The Crooked Magician was wrong to make the Glass Cat and the Patchwork Girl, for it was against the Law. And if he had not unlawfully kept the bottle of Liquid of Petrifaction standing on his shelf, the accident to his wife Margolotte and to Unc Nunkie could not have occurred. I can understand, however, that Ojo, who loves his uncle, will be unhappy unless he can save him. Also I feel it is wrong to leave those two victims standing as marble statues, when they ought to be alive. So I propose we allow Dr. Pipt to make the magic charm which will save them, and that we assist Ojo to find the things he is seeking. What do you think, Wizard?"

"That is perhaps the best thing to do," replied the Wizard. "But after the Crooked Magician has restored those poor people to life you must take away his magic powers."

"I will," promised Ozma.

"Now tell me, please, what magic things must you find?" continued the Wizard, addressing Ojo.

"The three hairs from the Woozy's tail I have," said the boy. "That is, I have the Woozy, and the hairs are in his tail. The six-leaved clover I—I—"

"You may take it and keep it," said Ozma. "That will not be breaking the Law, for it is already picked, and the crime of picking it is forgiven."

"Thank you!" cried Ojo gratefully. Then he continued: "The next thing I must find is a gill of water from a dark well."

The Wizard shook his head. "That," said he, "will be a hard task, but if you travel far enough you may discover it."

"I am willing to travel for years, if it will save Unc Nunkie," declared Ojo, earnestly.

"Then you'd better begin your journey at once," advised the Wizard.

Dorothy had been listening with interest to this conversation. Now she turned to Ozma and asked: "May I go with Ojo, to help him?"

"Would you like to?" returned Ozma.

"Yes. I know Oz pretty well, but Ojo doesn't know it at all. I'm sorry for his uncle and poor Margolotte and I'd like to help save them. May I go?"

"If you wish to," replied Ozma.

"If Dorothy goes, then I must go to take care of her," said the Scarecrow, decidedly. "A dark well can only be discovered in some out-of-the-way place, and there may be dangers there."

"You have my permission to accompany Dorothy," said Ozma. "And while you are gone I will take care of the Patchwork Girl."

"I'll take care of myself," announced Scraps, "for I'm going with the Scarecrow and Dorothy. I promised Ojo to help him find the things he wants and I'll stick to my promise."

"Very well," replied Ozma. "But I see no need for Ojo to take the Glass Cat and the Woozy."

"I prefer to remain here," said the cat. "I've nearly been nicked half a dozen times, already, and if they're going into dangers it's best for me to keep away from them."

"Let Jellia Jamb keep her till Ojo returns," suggested Dorothy. "We won't need to take the Woozy, either, but he ought to be saved because of the three hairs in his tail."

"Better take me along," said the Woozy. "My eyes can flash fire, you know, and I can growl—a little."

"I'm sure you'll be safer here," Ozma decided, and the Woozy made no further objection to the plan.

After consulting together they decided that Ojo and his party should leave the very next day to search for the gill of water from a dark well, so they now separated to make preparations for the journey.

Ozma gave the Munchkin boy a room in the palace for that night and the afternoon he passed with Dorothy—getting acquainted, as she said—and receiving advice from the Shaggy Man as to where they must go. The Shaggy Man had wandered in many parts of Oz, and so had Dorothy, for that matter, yet neither of them knew where a dark well was to be found.

"If such a thing is anywhere in the settled parts of Oz," said Dorothy, "we'd prob'ly have heard of it long ago. If it's in the wild parts of the country, no one there would need a dark well. P'raps there isn't such a thing."

"Oh, there must be!" returned Ojo, positively; "or else the recipe of Dr. Pipt wouldn't call for it."

"That's true," agreed Dorothy; "and, if it's anywhere in the Land of Oz, we're bound to find it."

"Well, we're bound to search for it, anyhow," said the Scarecrow. "As for finding it, we must trust to luck."

"Don't do that," begged Ojo, earnestly. "I'm called Ojo the Unlucky, you know."

Chapter 19 - Trouble with the Tottenhots

A day's journey from the Emerald City brought the little band of adventurers to the home of Jack Pumpkinhead, which was a house formed from the shell of an immense pumpkin. Jack had made it himself and was very proud of it. There was a door, and several windows, and through the top was stuck a stovepipe that led from a small stove inside. The door was reached by a flight of three steps and there was a good floor on which was arranged some furniture that was quite comfortable.

It is certain that Jack Pumpkinhead might have had a much finer house to live in had he wanted it, for Ozma loved the stupid fellow, who had been her earliest companion; but Jack preferred his pumpkin house, as it matched himself very well, and in this he was not so stupid, after all.

The body of this remarkable person was made of wood, branches of trees of various sizes having been used for the purpose. This wooden framework was covered by a red shirt—with white spots in it—blue trousers, a yellow vest, a jacket of green-and-gold and stout leather shoes. The neck was a sharpened stick on which the pumpkin head was set, and the eyes, ears, nose and mouth were carved on the skin of the pumpkin, very like a child's jack-o'-lantern.

The house of this interesting creation stood in the center of a vast pumpkin-field, where the vines grew in profusion and bore pumpkins of extraordinary size as well as those which were smaller. Some of the pumpkins now ripening on the vines were almost as large as Jack's house, and he told Dorothy he intended to add another pumpkin to his mansion.

The travelers were cordially welcomed to this quaint domicile and invited to pass the night there, which they had planned to do. The Patchwork Girl was greatly interested in Jack and examined him admiringly.

"You are quite handsome," she said; "but not as really beautiful as the Scarecrow."

Jack turned, at this, to examine the Scarecrow critically, and his old friend slyly winked one painted eye at him.

"There is no accounting for tastes," remarked the Pumpkinhead, with a sigh. "An old crow once told me I was very fascinating, but of course the bird might have been mistaken. Yet I have noticed that the crows usually avoid the Scarecrow, who is a very honest fellow, in his way, but stuffed. I am not stuffed, you will observe; my body is good solid hickory."

"I adore stuffing," said the Patchwork Girl.

"Well, as for that, my head is stuffed with pumpkin-seeds," declared Jack. "I use them for brains, and when they are fresh I am intellectual. Just now, I regret to say, my seeds are rattling a bit, so I must soon get another head."

"Oh; do you change your head?" asked Ojo.

"To be sure. Pumpkins are not permanent, more's the pity, and in time they spoil. That is why I grow such a great field of pumpkins—that I may select a new head whenever necessary."

"Who carves the faces on them?" inquired the boy.

"I do that myself. I lift off my old head, place it on a table before me, and use the face for a pattern to go by. Sometimes the faces I carve are better than others—more expressive and cheerful, you know—but I think they average very well."

Before she had started on the journey Dorothy had packed a knapsack with the things she might need, and this knapsack the Scarecrow carried strapped to his back. The little girl wore a plain gingham dress and a checked sunbonnet, as she knew they were best fitted for travel. Ojo also had brought along his basket, to which Ozma had added a bottle of "Square Meal Tablets" and some fruit. But Jack Pumpkinhead grew a lot of things in his garden besides pumpkins, so he cooked for them a fine vegetable soup and gave Dorothy, Ojo and Toto, the only ones who found it necessary to eat, a pumpkin pie and some green cheese. For beds they must use the sweet dried grasses which Jack had strewn along one side of the room, but that satisfied Dorothy and Ojo very well. Toto, of course, slept beside his little mistress.

The Scarecrow, Scraps and the Pumpkinhead were tireless and had no need to sleep, so they sat up and talked together all night; but they stayed outside the house, under the bright stars, and talked in low tones so as not to disturb the sleepers. During the conversation the Scarecrow explained their quest for a dark well, and asked Jack's advice where to find it.

The Pumpkinhead considered the matter gravely.

"That is going to be a difficult task," said he, "and if I were you I'd take any ordinary well and enclose it, so as to make it dark."

"I fear that wouldn't do," replied the Scarecrow. "The well must be naturally dark, and the water must never have seen the light of day, for otherwise the magic charm might not work at all."

"How much of the water do you need?" asked Jack.

"A gill."

"How much is a gill?"

"Why—a gill is a gill, of course," answered the Scarecrow, who did not wish to display his ignorance.

"I know!" cried Scraps. "Jack and Jill went up the hill to fetch—"

"No, no; that's wrong," interrupted the Scarecrow. "There are two kinds of gills, I think; one is a girl, and the other is—"

"A gillyflower," said Jack.

"No; a measure."

"How big a measure?"

"Well, I'll ask Dorothy."

So next morning they asked Dorothy, and she said:

"I don't just know how much a gill is, but I've brought along a gold flask that holds a pint. That's more than a gill, I'm sure, and the Crooked Magician may measure it to suit himself. But the thing that's bothering us most, Jack, is to find the well."

Jack gazed around the landscape, for he was standing in the doorway of his house.

"This is a flat country, so you won't find any dark wells here," said he. "You must go into the mountains, where rocks and caverns are."

"And where is that?" asked Ojo.

"In the Quadling Country, which lies south of here," replied the Scarecrow. "I've known all along that we must go to the mountains."

"So have I," said Dorothy.

"But—goodness me!—the Quadling Country is full of dangers," declared Jack. "I've never been there myself, but—"

"I have," said the Scarecrow. "I've faced the dreadful Hammerheads, which have no arms and butt you like a goat; and I've faced the Fighting Trees, which bend down their branches to pound and whip you, and had many other adventures there."

"It's a wild country," remarked Dorothy, soberly, "and if we go there we're sure to have troubles of our own. But I guess we'll have to go, if we want that gill of water from the dark well."

So they said good-bye to the Pumpkinhead and resumed their travels, heading now directly toward the South Country, where mountains and rocks and caverns and forests of great trees abounded. This part of the Land of Oz, while it belonged to Ozma and owed her allegiance, was so wild and secluded that many queer peoples hid in its jungles and lived in their own way, without even a knowledge that they had a Ruler in the Emerald City. If they were left alone, these creatures never troubled the inhabitants of the rest of Oz, but those who invaded their domains encountered many dangers from them.

It was a two days journey from Jack Pumkinhead's house to the edge of the Quadling Country, for neither Dorothy nor Ojo could walk very fast and they often stopped by the wayside to rest. The first night they slept on the broad fields, among the buttercups and daisies, and the Scarecrow covered the children with a gauze blanket taken from his knapsack, so they would not be chilled by the night air. Toward evening of the second day they reached a sandy plain where walking was difficult; but some distance before them they saw a group of palm trees, with many curious black dots under them; so they trudged bravely on to reach that place by dark and spend the night under the shelter of the trees.

The black dots grew larger as they advanced and although the light was dim Dorothy thought they looked like big kettles turned upside down. Just beyond this place a jumble of huge, jagged rocks lay scattered, rising to the mountains behind them.

Our travelers preferred to attempt to climb these rocks by daylight, and they realized that for a time this would be their last night on the plains.

Twilight had fallen by the time they came to the trees, beneath which were the black, circular objects they had marked from a distance. Dozens of them were scattered around and Dorothy bent near to one, which was about as tall as she was, to examine it more closely. As she did so the top flew open and out popped a dusky creature, rising its length into the air and then plumping down upon the ground just beside the little girl. Another and another popped out of the circular, pot-like dwelling, while from all the other black objects came popping more creatures—very like jumping-jacks when their boxes are unhooked—until fully a hundred stood gathered around our little group of travelers.

By this time Dorothy had discovered they were people, tiny and curiously formed, but still people. Their skins were dusky and their hair stood straight up, like wires, and was brilliant scarlet in color. Their bodies were bare except for skins fastened around their waists and they wore bracelets on their ankles and wrists, and necklaces, and great pendant earrings.

Toto crouched beside his mistress and wailed as if he did not like these strange creatures a bit. Scraps began to mutter something about "hoppity, poppity, jumpity, dump!" but no one paid any attention to her. Ojo kept close to the Scarecrow and the Scarecrow kept close to Dorothy; but the little girl turned to the queer creatures and asked:

"Who are you?"

They answered this question all together, in a sort of chanting chorus, the words being as follows:

"We're the jolly Tottenhots;
We do not like the day,
But in the night 'tis our delight
To gambol, skip and play.

"We hate the sun and from it run,
The moon is cool and clear,
So on this spot each Tottenhot
Waits for it to appear.

"We're ev'ry one chock full of fun,
And full of mischief, too;
But if you're gay and with us play
We'll do no harm to you.

"Glad to meet you, Tottenhots," said the Scarecrow solemnly. "But you mustn't expect us to play with you all night, for we've traveled all day and some of us are tired."

"And we never gamble," added the Patchwork Girl. "It's against the Law."

These remarks were greeted with shouts of laughter by the impish creatures and one seized the Scarecrow's arm and was astonished to find the straw man whirl around so easily. So the Tottenhot raised the Scarecrow high in the air and tossed him over the heads of the crowd. Some one caught him and tossed him back, and so with shouts of glee they continued throwing the Scarecrow here and there, as if he had been a basket-ball.

Presently another imp seized Scraps and began to throw her about, in the same way. They found her a little heavier than the Scarecrow but still light enough to be tossed like a sofa-cushion, and they were enjoying the sport immensely when Dorothy, angry and indignant at the treatment her friends were receiving, rushed among the Tottenhots and began slapping and pushing them until she had rescued the Scarecrow and the Patchwork Girl and held them close on either side of her. Perhaps she would not have accomplished this victory so easily had not Toto helped her, barking and snapping at the bare legs of the imps until they were glad to flee from his attack. As for Ojo, some of the creatures had attempted to toss him, also, but finding his body too heavy they threw him to the ground and a row of the imps sat on him and held him from assisting Dorothy in her battle.

The little brown folks were much surprised at being attacked by the girl and the dog, and one or two who had been slapped hardest began to cry. Then suddenly they gave a shout, all together, and disappeared in a flash into their various houses, the tops of which closed with a series of pops that sounded like a bunch of firecrackers being exploded.

The adventurers now found themselves alone, and Dorothy asked anxiously:

"Is anybody hurt?"

"Not me," answered the Scarecrow. "They have given my straw a good shaking up and taken all the lumps out of it. I am now in splendid condition and am really obliged to the Tottenhots for their kind treatment."

"I feel much the same way," said Scraps. "My cotton stuffing had sagged a good deal with the day's walking and they've loosened it up until I feel as plump as a sausage. But the play was a little rough and I'd had quite enough of it when you interfered."

"Six of them sat on me," said Ojo, "but as they are so little they didn't hurt me much."

Just then the roof of the house in front of them opened and a Tottenhot stuck his head out, very cautiously, and looked at the strangers.

"Can't you take a joke?" he asked, reproachfully; "haven't you any fun in you at all?"

"If I had such a quality," replied the Scarecrow, "your people would have knocked it out of me. But I don't bear grudges. I forgive you."

"So do I," added Scraps. "That is, if you behave yourselves after this."

"It was just a little rough-house, that's all," said the Tottenhot. "But the question is not if we will behave, but if you will behave? We can't be shut up here all night, because this is our time to play; nor do we care to come out and be chewed up by a savage beast or slapped by an angry girl. That slapping hurts like sixty; some of my folks are crying about it. So here's the proposition: you let us alone and we'll let you alone."

"You began it," declared Dorothy.

"Well, you ended it, so we won't argue the matter. May we come out again? Or are you still cruel and slappy?"

"Tell you what we'll do," said Dorothy. "We're all tired and want to sleep until morning. If you'll let us get into your house, and stay there until daylight, you can play outside all you want to."

"That's a bargain!" cried the Tottenhot eagerly, and he gave a queer whistle that brought his people popping out of their houses on all sides. When the house before them was vacant, Dorothy and Ojo leaned over the hole and looked in, but could see nothing because it was so dark. But if the Tottenhots slept there all day the children thought they could sleep there at night, so Ojo lowered himself down and found it was not very deep.

"There's a soft cushion all over," said he. "Come on in."

Dorothy handed Toto to the boy and then climbed in herself. After her came Scraps and the Scarecrow, who did not wish to sleep but preferred to keep out of the way of the mischievous Tottenhots.

There seemed no furniture in the round den, but soft cushions were strewn about the floor and these they found made very comfortable beds. They did not close the hole in the roof but left it open to admit air. It also admitted the shouts and ceaseless laughter of the impish Tottenhots as they played outside, but Dorothy and Ojo, being weary from their journey, were soon fast asleep.

Toto kept an eye open, however, and uttered low, threatening growls whenever the racket made by the creatures outside became too boisterous; and the Scarecrow and the Patchwork Girl sat leaning against the wall and talked in whispers all night long. No one disturbed the travelers until daylight, when in popped the Tottenhot who owned the place and invited them to vacate his premises.

Chapter 20 - The Captive Yoop

As they were preparing to leave, Dorothy asked: "Can you tell us where there is a dark well?"

"Never heard of such a thing," said the Tottenhot. "We live our lives in the dark, mostly, and sleep in the daytime; but we've never seen a dark well, or anything like one."

"Does anyone live on those mountains beyond here?" asked the Scarecrow.

"Lots of people. But you'd better not visit them. We never go there," was the reply.

"What are the people like?" Dorothy inquired.

"Can't say. We've been told to keep away from the mountain paths, and so we obey. This sandy desert is good enough for us, and we're not disturbed here," declared the Tottenhot.

So they left the man snuggling down to sleep in his dusky dwelling, and went out into the sunshine, taking the path that led toward the rocky places. They soon found it hard climbing, for the rocks were uneven and full of sharp points and edges, and now there was no path at all. Clambering here and there among the boulders they kept steadily on, gradually rising higher and higher until finally they came to a great rift in a part of the mountain, where the rock seemed to have split in two and left high walls on either side.

"S'pose we go this way," suggested Dorothy; "it's much easier walking than to climb over the hills."

"How about that sign?" asked Ojo.

"What sign?" she inquired.

The Munchkin boy pointed to some words painted on the wall of rock beside them, which Dorothy had not noticed. The words read:

"LOOK OUT FOR YOOP."

 The girl eyed this sign a moment and turned to the Scarecrow, asking:

"Who is Yoop; or what is Yoop?"

The straw man shook his head. Then looked at Toto and the dog said "Woof!"

"Only way to find out is to go on," said Scraps.

This being quite true, they went on. As they proceeded, the walls of rock on either side grew higher and higher. Presently they came upon another sign which read:

"BEWARE THE CAPTIVE YOOP."

"Why, as for that," remarked Dorothy, "if Yoop is a captive there's no need to beware of him. Whatever Yoop happens to be, I'd much rather have him a captive than running around loose."

"So had I," agreed the Scarecrow, with a nod of his painted head.

"Still," said Scraps, reflectively:

"Yoop-te-hoop-te-loop-te-goop!   Who put noodles in the soup?   We may beware but we don't care,   And dare go where we scare the Yoop."

"Dear me! Aren't you feeling a little queer, just now?" Dorothy asked the Patchwork Girl.

"Not queer, but crazy," said Ojo. "When she says those things I'm sure her brains get mixed somehow and work the wrong way.

"I don't see why we are told to beware the Yoop unless he is dangerous," observed the Scarecrow in a puzzled tone.

"Never mind; we'll find out all about him when we get to where he is," replied the little girl.

The narrow canyon turned and twisted this way and that, and the rift was so small that they were able to touch both walls at the same time by stretching out their arms. Toto had run on ahead, frisking playfully, when suddenly he uttered a sharp bark of fear and came running back to them with his tail between his legs, as dogs do when they are frightened.

"Ah," said the Scarecrow, who was leading the way, "we must be near Yoop."

Just then, as he rounded a sharp turn, the Straw man stopped so suddenly that all the others bumped against him.

"What is it?" asked Dorothy, standing on tip-toes to look over his shoulder. But then she saw what it was and cried "Oh!" in a tone of astonishment.

In one of the rock walls—that at their left—was hollowed a great cavern, in front of which was a row of thick iron bars, the tops and bottoms being firmly fixed in the solid rock. Over this cavern was a big sign, which Dorothy read with much curiosity, speaking the words aloud that all might know what they said:

"MISTER YOOP—HIS CAVE

The Largest Untamed Giant in Captivity.

Height, 21 Feet.—(And yet he has but 2 feet.)

Weight, 1640 Pounds.—(But he waits all the time.)

Age, 400 Years 'and Up' (as they say in the Department Store advertisements).

Temper, Fierce and Ferocious.—(Except when asleep.)

Appetite, Ravenous.—(Prefers Meat People and Orange Marmalade.)

STRANGERS APPROACHING THIS CAVE DO SO AT THEIR OWN PERIL!

P.S.—Don't feed the Giant yourself."

"Very well," said Ojo, with a sigh; "let's go back."

"It's a long way back," declared Dorothy.

"So it is," remarked the Scarecrow, "and it means a tedious climb over those sharp rocks if we can't use this passage. I think it will be best to run by the Giant's cave as fast as we can go. Mister Yoop seems to be asleep just now."

But the Giant wasn't asleep. He suddenly appeared at the front of his cavern, seized the iron bars in his great hairy hands and shook them until they rattled in their sockets. Yoop was so tall that our friends had to tip their heads way back to look into his face, and they noticed he was dressed all in pink velvet, with silver buttons and braid. The Giant's boots were of pink leather and had tassels on them and his hat was decorated with an enormous pink ostrich feather, carefully curled.

"Yo-ho!" he said in a deep bass voice; "I smell dinner."

"I think you are mistaken," replied the Scarecrow. "There is no orange marmalade around here."

"Ah, but I eat other things," asserted Mister Yoop. "That is, I eat them when I can get them. But this is a lonely place, and no good meat has passed by my cave for many years; so I'm hungry."

"Haven't you eaten anything in many years?" asked Dorothy.

"Nothing except six ants and a monkey. I thought the monkey would taste like meat people, but the flavor was different. I hope you will taste better, for you seem plump and tender."

"Oh, I'm not going to be eaten," said Dorothy.

"Why not?"

"I shall keep out of your way," she answered.

"How heartless!" wailed the Giant, shaking the bars again. "Consider how many years it is since I've eaten a single plump little girl! They tell me meat is going up, but if I can manage to catch you I'm sure it will soon be going down. And I'll catch you if I can."

With this the Giant pushed his big arms, which looked like tree-trunks (except that tree-trunks don't wear pink velvet) between the iron bars, and the arms were so long that they touched the opposite wall of the rock passage. Then he extended them as far as he could reach toward our travelers and found he could almost touch the Scarecrow—but not quite.

"Come a little nearer, please," begged the Giant.

"I'm a Scarecrow."

"A Scarecrow? Ugh! I don't care a straw for a scarecrow. Who is that bright-colored delicacy behind you?"

"Me?" asked Scraps. "I'm a Patchwork Girl, and I'm stuffed with cotton."

"Dear me," sighed the Giant in a disapointed tone; "that reduces my dinner from four to two—and the dog. I'll save the dog for dessert."

Toto growled, keeping a good distance away.

"Back up," said the Scarecrow to those behind him. "Let us go back a little way and talk this over."

So they turned and went around the bend in the passage, where they were out of sight of the cave and Mister Yoop could not hear them.

"My idea," began the Scarecrow, when they had halted, "is to make a dash past the cave, going on a run."

"He'd grab us," said Dorothy.

"Well, he can't grab but one at a time, and I'll go first. As soon as he grabs me the rest of you can slip past him, out of his reach, and he will soon let me go because I am not fit to eat."

They decided to try this plan and Dorothy took Toto in her arms, so as to protect him. She followed just after the Scarecrow. Then came Ojo, with Scraps the last of the four. Their hearts beat a little faster than usual as they again approached the Giant's cave, this time moving swiftly forward.

It turned out about the way the Scarecrow had planned. Mister Yoop was quite astonished to see them come flying toward him, and thrusting his arms between the bars he seized the Scarecrow in a firm grip. In the next instant he realized, from the way the straw crunched between his fingers, that he had captured the non-eatable man, but during that instant of delay Dorothy and Ojo had slipped by the Giant and were out of reach. Uttering a howl of rage the monster threw the Scarecrow after them with one hand and grabbed Scraps with the other.

The poor Scarecrow went whirling through the air and so cleverly was he aimed that he struck Ojo's back and sent the boy tumbling head over heels, and he tripped Dorothy and sent her, also, sprawling upon the ground. Toto flew out of the little girl's arms and landed some distance ahead, and all were so dazed that it was a moment before they could scramble to their feet again. When they did so they turned to look toward the Giant's cave, and at that moment the ferocious Mister Yoop threw the Patchwork Girl at them.

Down went all three again, in a heap, with Scraps on top. The Giant roared so terribly that for a time they were afraid he had broken loose; but he hadn't. So they sat in the road and looked at one another in a rather bewildered way, and then began to feel glad.

"We did it!" exclaimed the Scarecrow, with satisfaction. "And now we are free to go on our way."

"Mister Yoop is very impolite," declared Scraps. "He jarred me terribly. It's lucky my stitches are so fine and strong, for otherwise such harsh treatment might rip me up the back."

"Allow me to apologize for the Giant," said the Scarecrow, raising the Patchwork Girl to her feet and dusting her skirt with his stuffed hands. "Mister Yoop is a perfect stranger to me, but I fear, from the rude manner in which he has acted, that he is no gentleman."

Dorothy and Ojo laughed at this statement and Toto barked as if he understood the joke, after which they all felt better and resumed the journey in high spirits.

"Of course," said the little girl, when they had walked a way along the passage, "it was lucky for us the Giant was caged; for, if he had happened to be loose, he—he—"

"Perhaps, in that case, he wouldn't be hungry any more," said Ojo gravely.

Chapter 21 - Hip Hopper the Champion

They must have had good courage to climb all those rocks, for after getting out of the canyon they encountered more rock hills to be surmounted. Toto could jump from one rock to another quite easily, but the others had to creep and climb with care, so that after a whole day of such work Dorothy and Ojo found themselves very tired.

As they gazed upward at the great mass of tumbled rocks that covered the steep incline, Dorothy gave a little groan and said:

"That's going to be a ter'ble hard climb, Scarecrow. I wish we could find the dark well without so much trouble."

"Suppose," said Ojo, "you wait here and let me do the climbing, for it's on my account we're searching for the dark well. Then, if I don't find anything, I'll come back and join you."

"No," replied the little girl, shaking her head positively, "we'll all go together, for that way we can help each other. If you went alone, something might happen to you, Ojo."

So they began the climb and found it indeed difficult, for a way. But presently, in creeping over the big crags, they found a path at their feet which wound in and out among the masses of rock and was quite smooth and easy to walk upon. As the path gradually ascended the mountain, although in a roundabout way, they decided to follow it.

"This must be the road to the Country of the Hoppers," said the Scarecrow.

"Who are the Hoppers?" asked Dorothy.

"Some people Jack Pumpkinhead told me about," he replied.

"I didn't hear him," replied the girl.

"No; you were asleep," explained the Scarecrow. "But he told Scraps and me that the Hoppers and the Horners live on this mountain."

"He said in the mountain," declared Scraps; "but of course he meant on it."

384

"Didn't he say what the Hoppers and Horners were like?" inquired Dorothy.

"No; he only said they were two separate nations, and that the Horners were the most important."

"Well, if we go to their country we'll find out all about 'em," said the girl. "But I've never heard Ozma mention those people, so they can't be very important."

"Is this mountain in the Land of Oz?" asked Scraps.

"Course it is," answered Dorothy. "It's in the South Country of the Quadlings. When one comes to the edge of Oz, in any direction, there is nothing more to be seen at all. Once you could see sandy desert all around Oz; but now it's diff'rent, and no other people can see us, any more than we can see them."

"If the mountain is under Ozma's rule, why doesn't she know about the Hoppers and the Horners?" Ojo asked.

"Why, it's a fairyland," explained Dorothy, "and lots of queer people live in places so tucked away that those in the Emerald City never even hear of 'em. In the middle of the country it's diff'rent, but when you get around the edges you're sure to run into strange little corners that surprise you. I know, for I've traveled in Oz a good deal, and so has the Scarecrow."

"Yes," admitted the straw man, "I've been considerable of a traveler, in my time, and I like to explore strange places. I find I learn much more by traveling than by staying at home."

During this conversation they had been walking up the steep pathway and now found themselves well up on the mountain. They could see nothing around them, for the rocks beside their path were higher than their heads. Nor could they see far in front of them, because the path was so crooked. But suddenly they stopped, because the path ended and there was no place to go. Ahead was a big rock lying against the side of the mountain, and this blocked the way completely.

"There wouldn't be a path, though, if it didn't go somewhere," said the Scarecrow, wrinkling his forehead in deep thought.

"This is somewhere, isn't it?" asked the Patchwork Girl, laughing at the bewildered looks of the others.

"The path is locked, the way is blocked,

Yet here we've innocently flocked;

And now we're here it's rather queer

There's no front door that can be knocked."

"Please don't, Scraps," said Ojo. "You make me nervous."

"Well," said Dorothy, "I'm glad of a little rest, for that's a drea'ful steep path."

As she spoke she leaned against the edge of the big rock that stood in their way. To her surprise it slowly swung backward and showed behind it a dark hole that looked like the mouth of a tunnel.

"Why, here's where the path goes to!" she exclaimed.

"So it is," answered the Scarecrow. "But the question is, do we want to go where the path does?"

"It's underground; right inside the mountain," said Ojo, peering into the dark hole. "Perhaps there's a well there; and, if there is, it's sure to be a dark one."

"Why, that's true enough!" cried Dorothy with eagerness. "Let's go in, Scarecrow; 'cause, if others have gone, we're pretty safe to go, too."

Toto looked in and barked, but he did not venture to enter until the Scarecrow had bravely gone first. Scraps followed closely after the straw man and then Ojo and Dorothy timidly stepped inside the tunnel. As soon as all of them had passed the big rock, it slowly turned and filled up the opening again; but now they were no longer in the dark, for a soft, rosy light enabled them to see around them quite distinctly.

It was only a passage, wide enough for two of them to walk abreast—with Toto in between them—and it had a high, arched roof. They could not see where the light which flooded the place so pleasantly came from, for there were no lamps anywhere visible. The passage ran straight for a little way and then made a bend to the right and another sharp turn to the left, after which it went straight again. But there were no side passages, so they could not lose their way.

After proceeding some distance, Toto, who had gone on ahead, began to bark loudly. They ran around a bend to see what was the matter and found a man sitting on the floor of the passage and leaning his back against the wall. He had probably been asleep before Toto's barks aroused him, for he was now rubbing his eyes and staring at the little dog with all his might.

There was something about this man that Toto objected to, and when he slowly rose to his foot they saw what it was. He had but one leg, set just below the middle of his round, fat body; but it was a stout leg and had a broad, flat foot at the bottom of it, on which the man seemed to stand very well. He had never had but this one leg, which looked something like a pedestal, and when Toto ran up and made a grab at the man's ankle he hopped first one way and then another in a very active manner, looking so frightened that Scraps laughed aloud.

385

Toto was usually a well behaved dog, but this time he was angry and snapped at the man's leg again and again. This filled the poor fellow with fear, and in hopping out of Toto's reach he suddenly lost his balance and tumbled heel over head upon the floor. When he sat up he kicked Toto on the nose and made the dog howl angrily, but Dorothy now ran forward and caught Toto's collar, holding him back.

"Do you surrender?" she asked the man.

"Who? Me?" asked the Hopper.

"Yes; you," said the little girl.

"Am I captured?" he inquired.

"Of course. My dog has captured you," she said.

"Well," replied the man, "if I'm captured I must surrender, for it's the proper thing to do. I like to do everything proper, for it saves one a lot of trouble."

"It does, indeed," said Dorothy. "Please tell us who you are."

"I'm Hip Hopper—Hip Hopper, the Champion."

"Champion what?" she asked in surprise.

"Champion wrestler. I'm a very strong man, and that ferocious animal which you are so kindly holding is the first living thing that has ever conquered me."

"And you are a Hopper?" she continued.

"Yes. My people live in a great city not far from here. Would you like to visit it?"

"I'm not sure," she said with hesitation. "Have you any dark wells in your city?"

"I think not. We have wells, you know, but they're all well lighted, and a well lighted well cannot well be a dark well. But there may be such a thing as a very dark well in the Horner Country, which is a black spot on the face of the earth."

"Where is the Horner Country?" Ojo inquired.

"The other side of the mountain. There's a fence between the Hopper Country and the Horner Country, and a gate in the fence; but you can't pass through just now, because we are at war with the Horners."

"That's too bad," said the Scarecrow. "What seems to be the trouble?"

"Why, one of them made a very insulting remark about my people. He said we were lacking in understanding, because we had only one leg to a person. I can't see that legs have anything to do with understanding things. The Horners each have two legs, just as you have. That's one leg too many, it seems to me."

"No," declared Dorothy, "it's just the right number."

"You don't need them," argued the Hopper, obstinately. "You've only one head, and one body, and one nose and mouth. Two legs are quite unnecessary, and they spoil one's shape."

"But how can you walk, with only one leg?" asked Ojo.

"Walk! Who wants to walk?" exclaimed the man. "Walking is a terribly awkward way to travel. I hop, and so do all my people. It's so much more graceful and agreeable than walking."

"I don't agree with you," said the Scarecrow. "But tell me, is there any way to get to the Horner Country without going through the city of the Hoppers?"

"Yes; there is another path from the rocky lowlands, outside the mountain, that leads straight to the entrance of the Horner Country. But it's a long way around, so you'd better come with me. Perhaps they will allow you to go through the gate; but we expect to conquer them this afternoon, if we get time, and then you may go and come as you please."

They thought it best to take the Hopper's advice, and asked him to lead the way. This he did in a series of hops, and he moved so swiftly in this strange manner that those with two legs had to run to keep up with him.

Chapter 22 - The Joking Horners

It was not long before they left the passage and came to a great cave, so high that it must have reached nearly to the top of the mountain within which it lay. It was a magnificent cave, illumined by the soft, invisible light, so that everything in it could be plainly seen. The walls were of polished marble, white with veins of delicate colors running through it, and the roof was arched and fantastic and beautiful.

Built beneath this vast dome was a pretty village—not very large, for there seemed not more than fifty houses altogether—and the dwellings were of marble and artistically designed. No grass nor flowers nor trees grew in this cave, so the yards surrounding the houses carved in designs both were smooth and bare and had low walls around them to mark their boundaries.

In the streets and the yards of the houses were many people all having one leg growing below their bodies and all hopping here and there whenever they moved. Even the children stood firmly upon their single legs and never lost their balance.

"All hail, Champion!" cried a man in the first group of Hoppers they met; "whom have you captured?"

"No one," replied the Champion in a gloomy voice; "these strangers have captured me."

"Then," said another, "we will rescue you, and capture them, for we are greater in number."

"No," answered the Champion, "I can't allow it. I've surrendered, and it isn't polite to capture those you've surrendered to."

"Never mind that," said Dorothy. "We will give you your liberty and set you free."

"Really?" asked the Champion in joyous tones.

"Yes," said the little girl; "your people may need you to help conquer the Horners."

At this all the Hoppers looked downcast and sad. Several more had joined the group by this time and quite a crowd of curious men, women and children surrounded the strangers.

"This war with our neighbors is a terrible thing," remarked one of the women. "Some one is almost sure to get hurt."

"Why do you say that, madam?" inquired the Scarecrow.

"Because the horns of our enemies are sharp, and in battle they will try to stick those horns into our warriors," she replied.

"How many horns do the Horners have?" asked Dorothy.

"Each has one horn in the center of his forehead," was the answer.

"Oh, then they're unicorns," declared the Scarecrow.

"No; they're Horners. We never go to war with them if we can help it, on account of their dangerous horns; but this insult was so great and so unprovoked that our brave men decided to fight, in order to be revenged," said the woman.

"What weapons do you fight with?" the Scarecrow asked.

"We have no weapons," explained the Champion. "Whenever we fight the Horners, our plan is to push them back, for our arms are longer than theirs."

"Then you are better armed," said Scraps.

"Yes; but they have those terrible horns, and unless we are careful they prick us with the points," returned the Champion with a shudder. "That makes a war with them dangerous, and a dangerous war cannot be a pleasant one."

"I see very clearly," remarked the Scarecrow, "that you are going to have trouble in conquering those Horners— unless we help you."

"Oh!" cried the Hoppers in a chorus; "can you help us? Please do! We will be greatly obliged! It would please us very much!" and by these exclamations the Scarecrow knew that his speech had met with favor.

"How far is it to the Horner Country?" he asked.

"Why, it's just the other side of the fence," they answered, and the Champion added:

"Come with me, please, and I'll show you the Horners."

So they followed the Champion and several others through the streets and just beyond the village came to a very high picket fence, built all of marble, which seemed to divide the great cave into two equal parts.

But the part inhabited by the Horners was in no way as grand in appearance as that of the Hoppers. Instead of being marble, the walls and roof were of dull gray rock and the square houses were plainly made of the same material. But in extent the city was much larger than that of the Hoppers and the streets were thronged with numerous people who busied themselves in various ways.

Looking through the open pickets of the fence our friends watched the Horners, who did not know they were being watched by strangers, and found them very unusual in appearance. They were little folks in size and had bodies round as balls and short legs and arms. Their heads were round, too, and they had long, pointed ears and a horn set in the center of the forehead. The horns did not seem very terrible, for they were not more than six inches long; but they were ivory white and sharp pointed, and no wonder the Hoppers feared them.

The skins of the Horners were light brown, but they wore snow-white robes and were bare-footed. Dorothy thought the most striking thing about them was their hair, which grew in three distinct colors on each and every head—red, yellow and green. The red was at the bottom and sometimes hung over their eyes; then came a broad circle of yellow and the green was at the top and formed a brush-shaped top-knot.

None of the Horners was yet aware of the presence of strangers, who watched the little brown people for a time and then went to the big gate in the center of the dividing fence. It was locked on both sides and over the latch was a sign reading:

"WAR IS DECLARED"

"Can't we go through?" asked Dorothy.

"Not now," answered the Champion.

"I think," said the Scarecrow, "that if I could talk with those Horners they would apologize to you, and then there would be no need to fight."

"Can't you talk from this side?" asked the Champion.

"Not so well," replied the Scarecrow. "Do you suppose you could throw me over that fence? It is high, but I am very light."

"We can try it," said the Hopper. "I am perhaps the strongest man in my country, so I'll undertake to do the throwing. But I won't promise you will land on your feet."

"No matter about that," returned the Scarecrow. "Just toss me over and I'll be satisfied."

So the Champion picked up the Scarecrow and balanced him a moment, to see how much he weighed, and then with all his strength tossed him high into the air.

Perhaps if the Scarecrow had been a trifle heavier he would have been easier to throw and would have gone a greater distance; but, as it was, instead of going over the fence he landed just on top of it, and one of the sharp pickets caught him in the middle of his back and held him fast prisoner. Had he been face downward the Scarecrow might have managed to free himself, but lying on his back on the picket his hands waved in the air of the Horner Country while his feet kicked the air of the Hopper Country; so there he was.

"Are you hurt?" called the Patchwork Girl anxiously.

"Course not," said Dorothy. "But if he wiggles that way he may tear his clothes. How can we get him down, Mr. Champion?"

The Champion shook his head.

"I don't know," he confessed. "If he could scare Horners as well as he does crows, it might be a good idea to leave him there."

"This is terrible," said Ojo, almost ready to cry. "I s'pose it's because I am Ojo the Unlucky that everyone who tries to help me gets into trouble."

"You are lucky to have anyone to help you," declared Dorothy. "But don't worry. We'll rescue the Scarecrow somehow."

"I know how," announced Scraps. "Here, Mr. Champion; just throw me up to the Scarecrow. I'm nearly as light as he is, and when I'm on top the fence I'll pull our friend off the picket and toss him down to you."

"All right," said the Champion, and he picked up the Patchwork Girl and threw her in the same manner he had the Scarecrow. He must have used more strength this time, however, for Scraps sailed far over the top of the fence and, without being able to grab the Scarecrow at all, tumbled to the ground in the Horner Country, where her stuffed body knocked over two men and a woman and made a crowd that had collected there run like rabbits to get away from her.

Seeing the next moment that she was harmless, the people slowly returned and gathered around the Patchwork Girl, regarding her with astonishment. One of them wore a jeweled star in his hair, just above his horn, and this seemed a person of importance. He spoke for the rest of his people, who treated him with great respect.

"Who are you, Unknown Being?" he asked.

"Scraps," she said, rising to her feet and patting her cotton wadding smooth where it had bunched up.

"And where did you come from?" he continued.

"Over the fence. Don't be silly. There's no other place I could have come from," she replied.

He looked at her thoughtfully.

"You are not a Hopper," said he, "for you have two legs. They're not very well shaped, but they are two in number. And that strange creature on top the fence—why doesn't he stop kicking?—must be your brother, or father, or son, for he also has two legs."

"You must have been to visit the Wise Donkey," said Scraps, laughing so merrily that the crowd smiled with her, in sympathy. "But that reminds me, Captain—or King—"

"I am Chief of the Horners, and my name is Jak."

"Of course; Little Jack Horner; I might have known it. But the reason I volplaned over the fence was so I could have a talk with you about the Hoppers."

"What about the Hoppers?" asked the Chief, frowning.

"You've insulted them, and you'd better beg their pardon," said Scraps. "If you don't, they'll probably hop over here and conquer you."

"We're not afraid—as long as the gate is locked," declared the Chief. "And we didn't insult them at all. One of us made a joke that the stupid Hoppers couldn't see."

The Chief smiled as he said this and the smile made his face look quite jolly.

"What was the joke?" asked Scraps.

"A Horner said they have less understanding than we, because they've only one leg. Ha, ha! You see the point, don't you? If you stand on your legs, and your legs are under you, then—ha, ha, ha!—then your legs are your under-standing. Hee, hee, hee! Ho, ho! My, but that's a fine joke. And the stupid Hoppers couldn't see it! They couldn't see that with only one leg they must have less under-standing than we who have two legs. Ha, ha, ha! Hee, hee! Ho, ho!" The Chief wiped the tears of laughter from his eyes with the bottom hem of his white robe, and all the other Horners wiped their eyes on their robes, for they had laughed just as heartily as their Chief at the absurd joke.

"Then," said Scraps, "their understanding of the understanding you meant led to the misunderstanding."

"Exactly; and so there's no need for us to apologize," returned the Chief.

"No need for an apology, perhaps, but much need for an explanation," said Scraps decidedly. "You don't want war, do you?"

"Not if we can help it," admitted Jak Horner. "The question is, who's going to explain the joke to the Horners? You know it spoils any joke to be obliged to explain it, and this is the best joke I ever heard."

"Who made the joke?" asked Scraps.

"Diksey Horner. He is working in the mines, just now, but he'll be home before long. Suppose we wait and talk with him about it? Maybe he'll be willing to explain his joke to the Hoppers."

"All right," said Scraps. "I'll wait, if Diksey isn't too long."

"No, he's short; he's shorter than I am. Ha, ha, ha! Say! that's a better joke than Diksey's. He won't be too long, because he's short. Hee, hee, ho!"

The other Horners who were standing by roared with laughter and seemed to like their Chief's joke as much as he did. Scraps thought it was odd that they could be so easily amused, but decided there could be little harm in people who laughed so merrily.

Chapter 23 - Peace Is Declared

"Come with me to my dwelling and I'll introduce you to my daughters," said the Chief.
"We're bringing them up according to a book of rules that was written by one of our leading old bachelors, and everyone says they're a remarkable lot of girls."

So Scraps accompanied him along the street to a house that seemed on the outside exceptionally grimy and dingy. The streets of this city were not paved nor had any attempt been made to beautify the houses or their surroundings, and having noticed this condition Scraps was astonished when the Chief ushered her into his home.

Here was nothing grimy or faded, indeed. On the contrary, the room was of dazzling brilliance and beauty, for it was lined throughout with an exquisite metal that resembled translucent frosted silver. The surface of this metal was highly ornamented in raised designs representing men, animals, flowers and trees, and from the metal itself was radiated the soft light which flooded the room. All the furniture was made of the same glorious metal, and Scraps asked what it was.

"That's radium," answered the Chief. "We Horners spend all our time digging radium from the mines under this mountain, and we use it to decorate our homes and make them pretty and cosy. It is a medicine, too, and no one can ever be sick who lives near radium."

"Have you plenty of it?" asked the Patchwork Girl.

"More than we can use. All the houses in this city are decorated with it, just the same as mine is."

"Why don't you use it on your streets, then, and the outside of your houses, to make them as pretty as they are within?" she inquired.

"Outside? Who cares for the outside of anything?" asked the Chief. "We Horners don't live on the outside of our homes; we live inside. Many people are like those stupid Hoppers, who love to make an outside show. I suppose you strangers thought their city more beautiful than ours, because you judged from appearances and they have handsome marble houses and marble streets; but if you entered one of their stiff dwellings you would find it bare and uncomfortable, as all their show is on the outside. They have an idea that what is not seen by others is not important, but with us the rooms we live in are our chief delight and care, and we pay no attention to outside show."

"Seems to me," said Scraps, musingly, "it would be better to make it all pretty—inside and out."

"Seems? Why, you're all seams, my girl!" said the Chief; and then he laughed heartily at his latest joke and a chorus of small voices echoed the chorus with "tee-hee-hee! ha, ha!"

Scraps turned around and found a row of girls seated in radium chairs ranged along one wall of the room. There were nineteen of them, by actual count, and they were of all sizes from a tiny child to one almost a grown woman. All were neatly dressed in spotless white robes and had brown skins, horns on their foreheads and three-colored hair.

"These," said the Chief, "are my sweet daughters. My dears, I introduce to you Miss Scraps Patchwork, a lady who is traveling in foreign parts to increase her store of wisdom."

The nineteen Horner girls all arose and made a polite curtsey, after which they resumed their seats and rearranged their robes properly.

"Why do they sit so still, and all in a row?" asked Scraps.

"Because it is ladylike and proper," replied the Chief.

"But some are just children, poor things! Don't they ever run around and play and laugh, and have a good time?"

"No, indeed," said the Chief. "That would he improper in young ladies, as well as in those who will sometime become young ladies. My daughters are being brought up according to the rules and regulations laid down by a leading bachelor who has given the subject much study and is himself a man of taste and culture. Politeness is his great hobby, and he claims that if a child is allowed to do an impolite thing one cannot expect the grown person to do anything better."

"Is it impolite to romp and shout and be jolly?" asked Scraps.

"Well, sometimes it is, and sometimes it isn't," replied the Horner, after considering the question. "By curbing such inclinations in my daughters we keep on the safe side. Once in a while I make a good joke, as you have heard, and then I permit my daughters to laugh decorously; but they are never allowed to make a joke themselves."

"That old bachelor who made the rules ought to be skinned alive!" declared Scraps, and would have said more on the subject had not the door opened to admit a little Horner man whom the Chief introduced as Diksey.

"What's up, Chief?" asked Diksey, winking nineteen times at the nineteen girls, who demurely cast down their eyes because their father was looking.

The Chief told the man that his joke had not been understood by the dull Hoppers, who had become so angry that they had declared war. So the only way to avoid a terrible battle was to explain the joke so they could understand it.

"All right," replied Diksey, who seemed a good-natured man; "I'll go at once to the fence and explain. I don't want any war with the Hoppers, for wars between nations always cause hard feelings."

So the Chief and Diksey and Scraps left the house and went back to the marble picket fence. The Scarecrow was still stuck on the top of his picket but had now ceased to struggle. On the other side of the fence were Dorothy and Ojo, looking between the pickets; and there, also, were the Champion and many other Hoppers.

Diksey went close to the fence and said:

"My good Hoppers, I wish to explain that what I said about you was a joke. You have but one leg each, and we have two legs each. Our legs are under us, whether one or two, and we stand on them. So, when I said you had less understanding than we, I did not mean that you had less understanding, you understand, but that you had less standundering, so to speak. Do you understand that?"

The Hoppers thought it over carefully. Then one said:

"That is clear enough; but where does the joke come in?'"

Dorothy laughed, for she couldn't help it, although all the others were solemn enough.

"I'll tell you where the joke comes in," she said, and took the Hoppers away to a distance, where the Horners could not hear them. "You know," she then explained, "those neighbors of yours are not very bright, poor things, and what they think is a joke isn't a joke at all—it's true, don't you see?"

"True that we have less understanding?" asked the Champion.

"Yes; it's true because you don't understand such a poor joke; if you did, you'd be no wiser than they are."

"Ah, yes; of course," they answered, looking very wise.

"So I'll tell you what to do," continued Dorothy. "Laugh at their poor joke and tell 'em it's pretty good for a Horner. Then they won't dare say you have less understanding, because you understand as much as they do."

The Hoppers looked at one another questioningly and blinked their eyes and tried to think what it all meant; but they couldn't figure it out.

"What do you think, Champion?" asked one of them.

"I think it is dangerous to think of this thing any more than we can help," he replied. "Let us do as this girl says and laugh with the Horners, so as to make them believe we see the joke. Then there will be peace again and no need to fight."

They readily agreed to this and returned to the fence laughing as loud and as hard as they could, although they didn't feel like laughing a bit. The Horners were much surprised.

"That's a fine joke—for a Horner—and we are much pleased with it," said the Champion, speaking between the pickets. "But please don't do it again."

"I won't," promised Diksey. "If I think of another such joke I'll try to forget it."

"Good!" cried the Chief Horner. "The war is over and peace is declared."

There was much joyful shouting on both sides of the fence and the gate was unlocked and thrown wide open, so that Scraps was able to rejoin her friends.

"What about the Scarecrow?" she asked Dorothy.

"We must get him down, somehow or other," was the reply.

"Perhaps the Horners can find a way," suggested Ojo. So they all went through the gate and Dorothy asked the Chief Horner how they could get the Scarecrow off the fence. The Chief didn't know how, but Diksey said:

"A ladder's the thing."

"Have you one?" asked Dorothy.

"To be sure. We use ladders in our mines," said he. Then he ran away to get the ladder, and while he was gone the Horners gathered around and welcomed the strangers to their country, for through them a great war had been avoided.

In a little while Diksey came back with a tall ladder which he placed against the fence. Ojo at once climbed to the top of the ladder and Dorothy went about halfway up and Scraps stood at the foot of it. Toto ran around it and barked. Then Ojo pulled the Scarecrow away from the picket and passed him down to Dorothy, who in turn lowered him to the Patchwork Girl.

As soon as he was on his feet and standing on solid ground the Scarecrow said:

"Much obliged. I feel much better. I'm not stuck on that picket any more."

The Horners began to laugh, thinking this was a joke, but the Scarecrow shook himself and patted his straw a little and said to Dorothy: "Is there much of a hole in my back?"

The little girl examined him carefully.

"There's quite a hole," she said. "But I've got a needle and thread in the knapsack and I'll sew you up again."

"Do so," he begged earnestly, and again the Hoppers laughed, to the Scarecrow's great annoyance.

While Dorothy was sewing up the hole in the straw man's back Scraps examined the other parts of him.

"One of his legs is ripped, too!" she exclaimed.

"Oho!" cried little Diksey; "that's bad. Give him the needle and thread and let him mend his ways."

"Ha, ha, ha!" laughed the Chief, and the other Horners at once roared with laughter.

"What's funny?" inquired the Scarecrow sternly.

"Don't you see?" asked Diksey, who had laughed even harder than the others. "That's a joke. It's by odds the best joke I ever made. You walk with your legs, and so that's the way you walk, and your legs are the ways. See? So, when you mend your legs, you mend your ways. Ho, ho, ho! hee, hee! I'd no idea I could make such a fine joke!"

"Just wonderful!" echoed the Chief. "How do you manage to do it, Diksey?"

"I don't know," said Diksey modestly. "Perhaps it's the radium, but I rather think it's my splendid intellect."

"If you don't quit it," the Scarecrow told him, "there'll be a worse war than the one you've escaped from."

Ojo had been deep in thought, and now he asked the Chief: "Is there a dark well in any part of your country?"

"A dark well? None that ever I heard of," was the answer.

"Oh, yes," said Diksey, who overheard the boy's question. "There's a very dark well down in my radium mine."

"Is there any water in it?" Ojo eagerly asked.

"Can't say; I've never looked to see. But we can find out."

So, as soon as the Scarecrow was mended, they decided to go with Diksey to the mine. When Dorothy had patted the straw man into shape again he declared he felt as good as new and equal to further adventures.

"Still," said he, "I prefer not to do picket duty again. High life doesn't seem to agree with my constitution." And then they hurried away to escape the laughter of the Horners, who thought this was another joke.

Chapter 24 - Ojo Finds the Dark Well

They now followed Diksey to the farther end of the great cave, beyond the Horner city, where there were several round, dark holes leading into the ground in a slanting direction. Diksey went to one of these holes and said:

"Here is the mine in which lies the dark well you are seeking. Follow me and step carefully and I'll lead you to the place."

He went in first and after him came Ojo, and then Dorothy, with the Scarecrow behind her. The Patchwork Girl entered last of all, for Toto kept close beside his little mistress.

A few steps beyond the mouth of the opening it was pitch dark. "You won't lose your way, though," said the Horner, "for there's only one way to go. The mine's mine and I know every step of the way. How's that for a joke, eh? The mine's mine." Then he chuckled gleefully as they followed him silently down the steep slant. The hole was just big enough to permit them to walk upright, although the Scarecrow, being much the taller of the party, often had to bend his head to keep from hitting the top.

The floor of the tunnel was difficult to walk upon because it had been worn smooth as glass, and pretty soon Scraps, who was some distance behind the others, slipped and fell head foremost. At once she began to slide downward, so swiftly that when she came to the Scarecrow she knocked him off his feet and sent him tumbling against Dorothy, who tripped up Ojo. The boy fell against the Horner, so that all went tumbling down the slide in a regular mix-up, unable to see where they were going because of the darkness.

Fortunately, when they reached the bottom the Scarecrow and Scraps were in front, and the others bumped against them, so that no one was hurt. They found themselves in a vast cave which was dimly lighted by the tiny grains of radium that lay scattered among the loose rocks.

"Now," said Diksey, when they had all regained their feet, "I will show you where the dark well is. This is a big place, but if we hold fast to each other we won't get lost."

They took hold of hands and the Horner led them into a dark corner, where he halted.

"Be careful," said he warningly. "The well is at your feet."

"All right," replied Ojo, and kneeling down he felt in the well with his hand and found that it contained a quantity of water. "Where's the gold flask, Dorothy?" he asked, and the little girl handed him the flask, which she had brought with her.

Ojo knelt again and by feeling carefully in the dark managed to fill the flask with the unseen water that was in the well. Then he screwed the top of the flask firmly in place and put the precious water in his pocket.

"All right!" he said again, in a glad voice; "now we can go back."

They returned to the mouth of the tunnel and began to creep cautiously up the incline. This time they made Scraps stay behind, for fear she would slip again; but they all managed to get up in safety and the Munchkin boy was very happy when he stood in the Horner city and realized that the water from the dark well, which he and his friends had traveled so far to secure, was safe in his jacket pocket.

Chapter 25 - They Bribe the Lazy Quadling

"Now," said Dorothy, as they stood on the mountain path, having left behind them the cave in which dwelt the Hoppers and the Horners, "I think we must find a road into the Country of the Winkies, for there is where Ojo wants to go next."

"Is there such a road?" asked the Scarecrow.

"I don't know," she replied. "I s'pose we can go back the way we came, to Jack Pumpkinhead's house, and then turn into the Winkie Country; but that seems like running 'round a haystack, doesn't it?"

"Yes," said the Scarecrow. "What is the next thing Ojo must get?"

"A yellow butterfly," answered the boy.

"That means the Winkie Country, all right, for it's the yellow country of Oz," remarked Dorothy. "I think, Scarecrow, we ought to take him to the Tin Woodman, for he's the Emp'ror of the Winkies and will help us to find what Ojo wants."

"Of course," replied the Scarecrow, brightening at the suggestion. "The Tin Woodman will do anything we ask him, for he's one of my dearest friends. I believe we can take a crosscut into his country and so get to his castle a day sooner than if we travel back the way we came."

"I think so, too," said the girl; "and that means we must keep to the left."

They were obliged to go down the mountain before they found any path that led in the direction they wanted to go, but among the tumbled rocks at the foot of the mountain was a faint trail which they decided to follow. Two or three hours walk along this trail brought them to a clear, level country, where there were a few farms and some scattered houses. But they knew they were still in the Country of the Quadlings, because everything had a bright red color. Not that the trees and grasses were red, but the fences and houses were painted that color and all the wild-flowers that bloomed by the wayside had red blossoms. This part of the Quadling Country seemed peaceful and prosperous, if rather lonely, and the road was more distinct and easier to follow.

But just as they were congratulating themselves upon the progress they had made they came upon a broad river which swept along between high banks, and here the road ended and there was no bridge of any sort to allow them to cross.

"This is queer," mused Dorothy, looking at the water reflectively. "Why should there be any road, if the river stops everyone walking along it?"

"Wow!" said Toto, gazing earnestly into her face.

"That's the best answer you'll get," declared the Scarecrow, with his comical smile, "for no one knows any more than Toto about this road."

Said Scraps:
"Ev'ry time I see a river,
I have chills that make me shiver,
For I never can forget
All the water's very wet.
If my patches get a soak
It will be a sorry joke;
So to swim I'll never try
Till I find the water dry."

"Try to control yourself, Scraps," said Ojo; "you're getting crazy again. No one intends to swim that river."

"No," decided Dorothy, "we couldn't swim it if we tried. It's too big a river, and the water moves awful fast."

"There ought to be a ferryman with a boat," said the Scarecrow; "but I don't see any."

"Couldn't we make a raft?" suggested Ojo.

"There's nothing to make one of," answered Dorothy.

"Wow!" said Toto again, and Dorothy saw he was looking along the bank of the river.

"Why, he sees a house over there!" cried the little girl. "I wonder we didn't notice it ourselves. Let's go and ask the people how to get 'cross the river."

A quarter of a mile along the bank stood a small, round house, painted bright red, and as it was on their side of the river they hurried toward it. A chubby little man, dressed all in red, came out to greet them, and with him were two children, also in red costumes. The man's eyes were big and staring as he examined the Scarecrow and the Patchwork Girl, and the children shyly hid behind him and peeked timidly at Toto.

"Do you live here, my good man?" asked the Scarecrow.

"I think I do, Most Mighty Magician," replied the Quadling, bowing low; "but whether I'm awake or dreaming I can't be positive, so I'm not sure where I live. If you'll kindly pinch me I'll find out all about it!"

"You're awake," said Dorothy, "and this is no magician, but just the Scarecrow."

"But he's alive," protested the man, "and he oughtn't to be, you know. And that other dreadful person—the girl who is all patches—seems to be alive, too."

"Very much so," declared Scraps, making a face at him. "But that isn't your affair, you know."

"I've a right to be surprised, haven't I?" asked the man meekly.

"I'm not sure; but anyhow you've no right to say I'm dreadful. The Scarecrow, who is a gentleman of great wisdom, thinks I'm beautiful," retorted Scraps.

"Never mind all that," said Dorothy. "Tell us, good Quadling, how we can get across the river."

"I don't know," replied the Quadling.

"Don't you ever cross it?" asked the girl.

"Never."

"Don't travelers cross it?"

"Not to my knowledge," said he.

They were much surprised to hear this, and the man added: "It's a pretty big river, and the current is strong. I know a man who lives on the opposite bank, for I've seen him there a good many years; but we've never spoken because neither of us has ever crossed over."

"That's queer," said the Scarecrow. "Don't you own a boat?"

The man shook his head.

"Nor a raft?"

"Where does this river go to?" asked Dorothy.

"That way," answered the man, pointing with one hand, "it goes into the Country of the Winkies, which is ruled by the Tin Emperor, who must be a mighty magician because he's all made of tin, and yet he's alive. And that way," pointing with the other hand, "the river runs between two mountains where dangerous people dwell."

The Scarecrow looked at the water before them.

"The current flows toward the Winkie Country," said he; "and so, if we had a boat, or a raft, the river would float us there more quickly and more easily than we could walk."

"That is true," agreed Dorothy; and then they all looked thoughtful and wondered what could be done.

"Why can't the man make us a raft?" asked Ojo.

"Will you?" inquired Dorothy, turning to the Quadling.

The chubby man shook his head.

"I'm too lazy," he said. "My wife says I'm the laziest man in all Oz, and she is a truthful woman. I hate work of any kind, and making a raft is hard work."

"I'll give you my em'rald ring," promised the girl.

"No; I don't care for emeralds. If it were a ruby, which is the color I like best, I might work a little while."

"I've got some Square Meal Tablets," said the Scarecrow. "Each one is the same as a dish of soup, a fried fish, a mutton pot-pie, lobster salad, charlotte russe and lemon jelly—all made into one little tablet that you can swallow without trouble."

"Without trouble!" exclaimed the Quadling, much interested; "then those tablets would be fine for a lazy man. It's such hard work to chew when you eat."

"I'll give you six of those tablets if you'll help us make a raft," promised the Scarecrow. "They're a combination of food which people who eat are very fond of. I never eat, you know, being straw; but some of my friends eat regularly. What do you say to my offer, Quadling?"

"I'll do it," decided the man. "I'll help, and you can do most of the work. But my wife has gone fishing for red eels to-day, so some of you will have to mind the children."

Scraps promised to do that, and the children were not so shy when the Patchwork Girl sat down to play with them. They grew to like Toto, too, and the little dog allowed them to pat him on his head, which gave the little ones much joy.

There were a number of fallen trees near the house and the Quadling got his axe and chopped them into logs of equal length. He took his wife's clothesline to bind these logs together, so that they would form a raft, and Ojo found some strips of wood and nailed them along the tops of the logs, to render them more firm. The Scarecrow and Dorothy helped roll the logs together and carry the strips of wood, but it took so long to make the raft that evening came just as it was finished, and with evening the Quadling's wife returned from her fishing.

The woman proved to be cross and bad-tempered, perhaps because she had only caught one red eel during all the day. When she found that her husband had used her clothesline, and the logs she had wanted for firewood, and the boards she had intended to mend the shed with, and a lot of gold nails, she became very angry. Scraps wanted to shake the woman, to make her behave, but Dorothy talked to her in a gentle tone and told the Quadling's wife she was a Princess of Oz and a friend of Ozma and that when she got back to the Emerald City she would send them a lot of things to repay them for the raft, including a new clothesline. This promise pleased the woman and she soon became more pleasant, saying they could stay the night at her house and begin their voyage on the river next morning.

This they did, spending a pleasant evening with the Quadling family and being entertained with such hospitality as the poor people were able to offer them. The man groaned a good deal and said he had overworked himself by chopping the logs, but the Scarecrow gave him two more tablets than he had promised, which seemed to comfort the lazy fellow.

Chapter 26 - The Trick River

Next morning they pushed the raft into the water and all got aboard. The Quadling man had to hold the log craft fast while they took their places, and the flow of the river was so powerful that it nearly tore the raft from his hands. As soon as they were all seated upon the logs he let go and away it floated and the adventurers had begun their voyage toward the Winkie Country.

The little house of the Quadlings was out of sight almost before they had cried their good-byes, and the Scarecrow said in a pleased voice: "It won't take us long to get to the Winkie Country, at this rate."

They had floated several miles down the stream and were enjoying the ride when suddenly the raft slowed up, stopped short, and then began to float back the way it had come.

"Why, what's wrong?" asked Dorothy, in astonishment; but they were all just as bewildered as she was and at first no one could answer the question. Soon, however, they realized the truth: that the current of the river had reversed and the water was now flowing in the opposite direction—toward the mountains.

They began to recognize the scenes they had passed, and by and by they came in sight of the little house of the Quadlings again. The man was standing on the river bank and he called to them:

"How do you do? Glad to see you again. I forgot to tell you that the river changes its direction every little while. Sometimes it flows one way, and sometimes the other."

They had no time to answer him, for the raft was swept past the house and a long distance on the other side of it.

"We're going just the way we don't want to go," said Dorothy, "and I guess the best thing we can do is to get to land before we're carried any farther."

But they could not get to land. They had no oars, nor even a pole to guide the raft with. The logs which bore them floated in the middle of the stream and were held fast in that position by the strong current.

So they sat still and waited and, even while they were wondering what could be done, the raft slowed down, stopped, and began drifting the other way—in the direction it had first followed. After a time they repassed the Quadling house and the man was still standing on the bank. He cried out to them:

"Good day! Glad to see you again. I expect I shall see you a good many times, as you go by, unless you happen to swim ashore."

By that time they had left him behind and were headed once more straight toward the Winkie Country.

"This is pretty hard luck," said Ojo in a discouraged voice. "The Trick River keeps changing, it seems, and here we must float back and forward forever, unless we manage in some way to get ashore."

"Can you swim?" asked Dorothy.

"No; I'm Ojo the Unlucky."

"Neither can I. Toto can swim a little, but that won't help us to get to shore."

"I don't know whether I could swim, or not," remarked Scraps; "but if I tried it I'd surely ruin my lovely patches."

"My straw would get soggy in the water and I would sink," said the Scarecrow.

So there seemed no way out of their dilemma and being helpless they simply sat still. Ojo, who was on the front of the raft, looked over into the water and thought he saw some large fishes swimming about. He found a loose end of the clothesline which fastened the logs together, and taking a gold nail from his pocket he bent it nearly double, to form a hook, and tied it to the end of the line. Having baited the hook with some bread which he broke from his loaf, he dropped the line into the water and almost instantly it was seized by a great fish.

They knew it was a great fish, because it pulled so hard on the line that it dragged the raft forward even faster than the current of the river had carried it. The fish was frightened, and it was a strong swimmer. As the other end of the clothesline was bound around the logs he could not get it away, and as he had greedily swallowed the gold hook at the first bite he could not get rid of that, either.

When they reached the place where the current had before changed, the fish was still swimming ahead in its wild attempt to escape. The raft slowed down, yet it did not stop, because the fish would not let it. It continued to move in the same direction it had been going. As the current reversed and rushed backward on its course it failed to drag the raft with it. Slowly, inch by inch, they floated on, and the fish tugged and tugged and kept them going.

"I hope he won't give up," said Ojo anxiously. "If the fish can hold out until the current changes again, we'll be all right."

The fish did not give up, but held the raft bravely on its course, till at last the water in the river shifted again and floated them the way they wanted to go. But now the captive fish found its strength failing. Seeking a refuge, it began to drag the raft toward the shore. As they did not wish to land in this place the boy cut the rope with his pocket-knife and set the fish free, just in time to prevent the raft from grounding.

The next time the river backed up the Scarecrow managed to seize the branch of a tree that overhung the water and they all assisted him to hold fast and prevent the raft from being carried backward. While they waited here, Ojo spied a long broken branch lying upon the bank, so he leaped ashore and got it. When he had stripped off the side shoots he believed he could use the branch as a pole, to guide the raft in case of emergency.

They clung to the tree until they found the water flowing the right way, when they let go and permitted the raft to resume its voyage. In spite of these pauses they were really making good progress toward the Winkie Country and having found a way to conquer the adverse current their spirits rose considerably. They could see little of the country through which they were passing, because of the high banks, and they met with no boats or other craft upon the surface of the river.

Once more the trick river reversed its current, but this time the Scarecrow was on guard and used the pole to push the raft toward a big rock which lay in the water. He believed the rock would prevent their floating backward with the current, and so it did. They clung to this anchorage until the water resumed its proper direction, when they allowed the raft to drift on.

Floating around a bend they saw ahead a high bank of water, extending across the entire river, and toward this they were being irresistibly carried. There being no way to arrest the progress of the raft they clung fast to the logs and let the river sweep them on. Swiftly the raft climbed the bank of water and slid down on the other side, plunging its edge deep into the water and drenching them all with spray.

As again the raft righted and drifted on, Dorothy and Ojo laughed at the ducking they had received; but Scraps was much dismayed and the Scarecrow took out his handkerchief and wiped the water off the Patchwork Girl's patches as well as he was able to. The sun soon dried her and the colors of her patches proved good, for they did not run together nor did they fade.

After passing the wall of water the current did not change or flow backward any more but continued to sweep them steadily forward. The banks of the river grew lower, too, permitting them to see more of the country, and presently they discovered yellow buttercups and dandelions growing amongst the grass, from which evidence they knew they had reached the Winkie Country.

"Don't you think we ought to land?" Dorothy asked the Scarecrow.

"Pretty soon," he replied. "The Tin Woodman's castle is in the southern part of the Winkie Country, and so it can't be a great way from here."

Fearing they might drift too far, Dorothy and Ojo now stood up and raised the Scarecrow in their arms, as high as they could, thus allowing him a good view of the country. For a time he saw nothing he recognized, but finally he cried:

"There it is! There it is!"

"What?" asked Dorothy.

"The Tin Woodman's tin castle. I can see its turrets glittering in the sun. It's quite a way off, but we'd better land as quickly as we can."

They let him down and began to urge the raft toward the shore by means of the pole. It obeyed very well, for the current was more sluggish now, and soon they had reached the bank and landed safely.

The Winkie Country was really beautiful, and across the fields they could see afar the silvery sheen of the tin castle. With light hearts they hurried toward it, being fully rested by their long ride on the river.

By and by they began to cross an immense field of splendid yellow lilies, the delicate fragrance of which was very delightful.

"How beautiful they are!" cried Dorothy, stopping to admire the perfection of these exquisite flowers.

"Yes," said the Scarecrow, reflectively, "but we must be careful not to crush or injure any of these lilies."

"Why not?" asked Ojo.

"The Tin Woodman is very kind-hearted," was the reply, "and he hates to see any living thing hurt in any way."

"Are flowers alive?" asked Scraps.

"Yes, of course. And these flowers belong to the Tin Woodman. So, in order not to offend him, we must not tread on a single blossom."

"Once," said Dorothy, "the Tin Woodman stepped on a beetle and killed the little creature. That made him very unhappy and he cried until his tears rusted his joints, so he couldn't move 'em."

"What did he do then?" asked Ojo.

"Put oil on them, until the joints worked smooth again."

"Oh!" exclaimed the boy, as if a great discovery had flashed across his mind. But he did not tell anybody what the discovery was and kept the idea to himself.

It was a long walk, but a pleasant one, and they did not mind it a bit. Late in the afternoon they drew near to the wonderful tin castle of the Emperor of the Winkies, and Ojo and Scraps, who had never seen it before, were filled with amazement.

Tin abounded in the Winkie Country and the Winkies were said to be the most skillful tinsmiths in all the world. So the Tin Woodman had employed them in building his magnificent castle, which was all of tin, from the ground to the tallest turret, and so brightly polished that it glittered in the sun's rays more gorgeously than silver. Around the grounds of the castle ran a tin wall, with tin gates; but the gates stood wide open because the Emperor had no enemies to disturb him.

When they entered the spacious grounds our travelers found more to admire. Tin fountains sent sprays of clear water far into the air and there were many beds of tin flowers, all as perfectly formed as any natural flowers might be. There were tin trees, too, and here and there shady bowers of tin, with tin benches and chairs to sit upon. Also, on the sides of the pathway leading up to the front door of the castle, were rows of tin statuary, very cleverly executed. Among these Ojo recognized statues of Dorothy, Toto, the Scarecrow, the Wizard, the Shaggy Man, Jack Pumpkinhead and Ozma, all standing upon neat pedestals of tin.

Toto was well acquainted with the residence of the Tin Woodman and, being assured a joyful welcome, he ran ahead and barked so loudly at the front door that the Tin Woodman heard him and came out in person to see if it were really his old friend Toto. Next moment the tin man had clasped the Scarecrow in a warm embrace and then turned to hug Dorothy. But now his eye was arrested by the strange sight of the Patchwork Girl, and he gazed upon her in mingled wonder and admiration.

Chapter 27 - The Tin Woodman Objects

The Tin Woodman was one of the most important personages in all Oz. Though Emperor of the Winkies, he owed allegiance to Ozma, who ruled all the land, and the girl and the tin man were warm personal friends. He was something of a dandy and kept his tin body brilliantly polished and his tin joints well oiled. Also he was very courteous in manner and so kind and gentle that everyone loved him. The Emperor greeted Ojo and Scraps with cordial hospitality and ushered the entire party into his handsome tin parlor, where all the furniture and pictures were made of tin. The walls were paneled with tin and from the tin ceiling hung tin chandeliers.

The Tin Woodman wanted to know, first of all, where Dorothy had found the Patchwork Girl, so between them the visitors told the story of how Scraps was made, as well as the accident to Margolotte and Unc Nunkie and how Ojo had set out upon a journey to procure the things needed for the Crooked Magician's magic charm. Then Dorothy told of their adventures in the Quadling Country and how at last they succeeded in getting the water from a dark well.

While the little girl was relating these adventures the Tin Woodman sat in an easy chair listening with intense interest, while the others sat grouped around him. Ojo, however, had kept his eyes fixed upon the body of the tin Emperor, and now he noticed that under the joint of his left knee a tiny drop of oil was forming. He watched this drop of oil with a fast-beating heart, and feeling in his pocket brought out a tiny vial of crystal, which he held secreted in his hand.

Presently the Tin Woodman changed his position, and at once Ojo, to the astonishment of all, dropped to the floor and held his crystal vial under the Emperor's knee joint. Just then the drop of oil fell, and the boy caught it in his bottle and immediately corked it tight. Then, with a red face and embarrassed manner, he rose to confront the others.

"What in the world were you doing?" asked the Tin Woodman.

"I caught a drop of oil that fell from your knee-joint," confessed Ojo.

"A drop of oil!" exclaimed the Tin Woodman. "Dear me, how careless my valet must have been in oiling me this morning. I'm afraid I shall have to scold the fellow, for I can't be dropping oil wherever I go."

"Never mind," said Dorothy. "Ojo seems glad to have the oil, for some reason."

"Yes," declared the Munchkin boy, "I am glad. For one of the things the Crooked Magician sent me to get was a drop of oil from a live man's body. I had no idea, at first, that there was such a thing; but it's now safe in the little crystal vial."

"You are very welcome to it, indeed," said the Tin Woodman. "Have you now secured all the things you were in search of?"

"Not quite all," answered Ojo. "There were five things I had to get, and I have found four of them. I have the three hairs in the tip of a Woozy's tail, a six-leaved clover, a gill of water from a dark well and a drop of oil from a live man's body. The last thing is the easiest of all to get, and I'm sure that my dear Unc Nunkie—and good Margolotte, as well—will soon be restored to life."

The Munchkin boy said this with much pride and pleasure.

"Good!" exclaimed the Tin Woodman; "I congratulate you. But what is the fifth and last thing you need, in order to complete the magic charm?"

"The left wing of a yellow butterfly," said Ojo. "In this yellow country, and with your kind assistance, that ought to be very easy to find."

The Tin Woodman stared at him in amazement.

"Surely you are joking!" he said.

"No," replied Ojo, much surprised; "I am in earnest."

"But do you think for a moment that I would permit you, or anyone else, to pull the left wing from a yellow butterfly?" demanded the Tin Woodman sternly.

"Why not, sir?"

"Why not? You ask me why not? It would be cruel—one of the most cruel and heartless deeds I ever heard of," asserted the Tin Woodman. "The butterflies are among the prettiest of all created things, and they are very sensitive to pain. To tear a wing from one would cause it exquisite torture and it would soon die in great agony. I would not permit such a wicked deed under any circumstances!"

Ojo was astounded at hearing this. Dorothy, too, looked grave and disconcerted, but she knew in her heart that the Tin Woodman was right. The Scarecrow nodded his head in approval of his friend's speech, so it was evident that he agreed with the Emperor's decision. Scraps looked from one to another in perplexity.

"Who cares for a butterfly?" she asked.

"Don't you?" inquired the Tin Woodman.

"Not the snap of a finger, for I have no heart," said the Patchwork Girl. "But I want to help Ojo, who is my friend, to rescue the uncle whom he loves, and I'd kill a dozen useless butterflies to enable him to do that."

The Tin Woodman sighed regretfully.

"You have kind instincts," he said, "and with a heart you would indeed be a fine creature. I cannot blame you for your heartless remark, as you cannot understand the feelings of those who possess hearts. I, for instance, have a very neat and responsive heart which the wonderful Wizard of Oz once gave me, and so I shall never—never—never permit a poor yellow butterfly to be tortured by anyone."

"The yellow country of the Winkies," said Ojo sadly, "is the only place in Oz where a yellow butterfly can be found."

"I'm glad of that," said the Tin Woodman. "As I rule the Winkie Country, I can protect my butterflies."

"Unless I get the wing—just one left wing—" said Ojo miserably, "I can't save Unc Nunkie."

"Then he must remain a marble statue forever," declared the Tin Emperor, firmly.

Ojo wiped his eyes, for he could not hold back the tears.

"I'll tell you what to do," said Scraps. "We'll take a whole yellow butterfly, alive and well, to the Crooked Magician, and let him pull the left wing off."

"No, you won't," said the Tin Woodman. "You can't have one of my dear little butterflies to treat in that way."

"Then what in the world shall we do?" asked Dorothy.

They all became silent and thoughtful. No one spoke for a long time. Then the Tin Woodman suddenly roused himself and said:

"We must all go back to the Emerald City and ask Ozma's advice. She's a wise little girl, our Ruler, and she may find a way to help Ojo save his Unc Nunkie."

So the following morning the party started on the journey to the Emerald City, which they reached in due time without any important adventure. It was a sad journey for Ojo, for without the wing of the yellow butterfly he saw no way to save Unc Nunkie—unless he waited six years for the Crooked Magician to make a new lot of the Powder of Life. The boy was utterly discouraged, and as he walked along he groaned aloud.

"Is anything hurting you?" inquired the Tin Woodman in a kindly tone, for the Emperor was with the party.

"I'm Ojo the Unlucky," replied the boy. "I might have known I would fail in anything I tried to do."

"Why are you Ojo the Unlucky?" asked the tin man.

"Because I was born on a Friday."

"Friday is not unlucky," declared the Emperor. "It's just one of seven days. Do you suppose all the world becomes unlucky one-seventh of the time?"

"It was the thirteenth day of the month," said Ojo.

"Thirteen! Ah, that is indeed a lucky number," replied the Tin Woodman. "All my good luck seems to happen on the thirteenth. I suppose most people never notice the good luck that comes to them with the number 13, and yet if the least bit of bad luck falls on that day, they blame it to the number, and not to the proper cause."

"Thirteen's my lucky number, too," remarked the Scarecrow.

"And mine," said Scraps. "I've just thirteen patches on my head."

"But," continued Ojo, "I'm left-handed."

"Many of our greatest men are that way," asserted the Emperor. "To be left-handed is usually to be two-handed; the right-handed people are usually one-handed."

"And I've a wart under my right arm," said Ojo.

"How lucky!" cried the Tin Woodman. "If it were on the end of your nose it might be unlucky, but under your arm it is luckily out of the way."

"For all those reasons," said the Munchkin boy, "I have been called Ojo the Unlucky."

"Then we must turn over a new leaf and call you henceforth Ojo the Lucky," declared the tin man. "Every reason you have given is absurd. But I have noticed that those who continually dread ill luck and fear it will overtake them, have no time to take advantage of any good fortune that comes their way. Make up your mind to be Ojo the Lucky."

"How can I?" asked the boy, "when all my attempts to save my dear uncle have failed?"

"Never give up, Ojo," advised Dorothy. "No one ever knows what's going to happen next."

Ojo did not reply, but he was so dejected that even their arrival at the Emerald City failed to interest him.

The people joyfully cheered the appearance of the Tin Woodman, the Scarecrow and Dorothy, who were all three general favorites, and on entering the royal palace word came to them from Ozma that she would at once grant them an audience.

Dorothy told the girl Ruler how successful they had been in their quest until they came to the item of the yellow butterfly, which the Tin Woodman positively refused to sacrifice to the magic potion.

"He is quite right," said Ozma, who did not seem a bit surprised. "Had Ojo told me that one of the things he sought was the wing of a yellow butterfly I would have informed him, before he started out, that he could never secure it. Then you would have been saved the troubles and annoyances of your long journey."

"I didn't mind the journey at all," said Dorothy; "it was fun."

"As it has turned out," remarked Ojo, "I can never get the things the Crooked Magician sent me for; and so, unless I wait the six years for him to make the Powder of Life, Unc Nunkie cannot be saved."

Ozma smiled.

"Dr. Pipt will make no more Powder of Life, I promise you," said she. "I have sent for him and had him brought to this palace, where he now is, and his four kettles have been destroyed and his book of recipes burned up. I have also had brought here the marble statues of your uncle and of Margolotte, which are standing in the next room."

They were all greatly astonished at this announcement.

"Oh, let me see Unc Nunkie! Let me see him at once, please!" cried Ojo eagerly.

"Wait a moment," replied Ozma, "for I have something more to say. Nothing that happens in the Land of Oz escapes the notice of our wise Sorceress, Glinda the Good. She knew all about the magic-making of Dr. Pipt, and how he had brought the Glass Cat and the Patchwork Girl to life, and the accident to Unc Nunkie and Margolotte, and of Ojo's quest and his journey with Dorothy. Glinda also knew that Ojo would fail to find all the things he sought, so she sent for our Wizard and instructed him what to do. Something is going to happen in this palace, presently, and that 'something' will, I am sure, please you all. And now," continued the girl Ruler, rising from her chair, "you may follow me into the next room."

Chapter 28 - The Wonderful Wizard of Oz

When Ojo entered the room he ran quickly to the statue of Unc Nunkie and kissed the marble face affectionately.

"I did my best, Unc," he said, with a sob, "but it was no use!"

Then he drew back and looked around the room, and the sight of the assembled company quite amazed him.

Aside from the marble statues of Unc Nunkie and Margolotte, the Glass Cat was there, curled up on a rug; and the Woozy was there, sitting on its square hind legs and looking on the scene with solemn interest; and there was the Shaggy Man, in a suit of shaggy pea-green satin, and at a table sat the little Wizard, looking quite important and as if he knew much more than he cared to tell.

Last of all, Dr. Pipt was there, and the Crooked Magician sat humped up in a chair, seeming very dejected but keeping his eyes fixed on the lifeless form of his wife Margolotte, whom he fondly loved but whom he now feared was lost to him forever.

Ozma took a chair which Jellia Jamb wheeled forward for the Ruler, and back of her stood the Scarecrow, the Tin Woodman and Dorothy, as well as the Cowardly Lion and the Hungry Tiger. The Wizard now arose and made a low bow to Ozma and another less deferent bow to the assembled company.

"Ladies and gentlemen and beasts," he said, "I beg to announce that our Gracious Ruler has permitted me to obey the commands of the great Sorceress, Glinda the Good, whose humble Assistant I am proud to be. We have discovered that the Crooked Magician has been indulging in his magical arts contrary to Law, and therefore, by Royal Edict, I hereby deprive him of all power to work magic in the future. He is no longer a crooked magician, but a simple Munchkin; he is no longer even crooked, but a man like other men."

As he pronounced these words the Wizard waved his hand toward Dr. Pipt and instantly every crooked limb straightened out and became perfect. The former magician, with a cry of joy, sprang to his feet, looked at himself in wonder, and then fell back in his chair and watched the Wizard with fascinated interest.

"The Glass Cat, which Dr. Pipt lawlessly made," continued the Wizard, "is a pretty cat, but its pink brains made it so conceited that it was a disagreeable companion to everyone. So the other day I took away the pink brains and replaced them with transparent ones, and now the Glass Cat is so modest and well behaved that Ozma has decided to keep her in the palace as a pet."

"I thank you," said the cat, in a soft voice.

"The Woozy has proved himself a good Woozy and a faithful friend," the Wizard went on, "so we will send him to the Royal Menagerie, where he will have good care and plenty to eat all his life."

"Much obliged," said the Woozy. "That beats being fenced up in a lonely forest and starved."

"As for the Patchwork Girl," resumed the Wizard, "she is so remarkable in appearance, and so clever and good tempered, that our Gracious Ruler intends to preserve her carefully, as one of the curiosities of the curious Land of Oz. Scraps may live in the palace, or wherever she pleases, and be nobody's servant but her own."

"That's all right," said Scraps.

"We have all been interested in Ojo," the little Wizard continued, "because his love for his unfortunate uncle has led him bravely to face all sorts of dangers, in order that he might rescue him. The Munchkin boy has a loyal and generous heart and has done his best to restore Unc Nunkie to life. He has failed, but there are others more powerful than the Crooked Magician, and there are more ways than Dr. Pipt knew of to destroy the charm of the Liquid of Petrifaction. Glinda the Good has told me of one way, and you shall now learn how great is the knowledge and power of our peerless Sorceress."

As he said this the Wizard advanced to the statue of Margolotte and made a magic pass, at the same time muttering a magic word that none could hear distinctly. At once the woman moved, turned her head wonderingly this way and that, to note all who stood before her, and seeing Dr. Pipt, ran forward and threw herself into her husband's outstretched arms.

Then the Wizard made the magic pass and spoke the magic word before the statue of Unc Nunkie. The old Munchkin immediately came to life and with a low bow to the Wizard said: "Thanks."

But now Ojo rushed up and threw his arms joyfully about his uncle, and the old man hugged his little nephew tenderly and stroked his hair and wiped away the boy's tears with a handkerchief, for Ojo was crying from pure happiness.

Ozma came forward to congratulate them.

"I have given to you, my dear Ojo and Unc Nunkie, a nice house just outside the walls of the Emerald City," she said, "and there you shall make your future home and be under my protection."

"Didn't I say you were Ojo the Lucky?" asked the Tin Woodman, as everyone crowded around to shake Ojo's hand.

"Yes; and it is true!" replied Ojo, gratefully.

The End

Made in the USA
Lexington, KY
15 January 2011